Human Perception

The International Library of Psychology

Series Editor: David Canter

Titles in the Series:

Human Perception
Marco Bertamini and Michael Kubovy

Environmental Psychology
David Canter, Terry Hartig and
Mirilia Bonnes

Hypnosis
Michael Heap and Irving Kirsch

Counseling Psychology
Frederick Leong

Psychology and Law:
Criminal and Civil Perspectives
Ronald Roesch

Psychology and Law:
Clinical Forensic Perspectives
Ronald Roesch

Psychology and Law:
Criminal and Civil Perspectives
Ronald Roesch

Parapsychology
Richard Wiseman and Caroline Watt

History of Psychology Revisited
William Woodward and Sandy Lovie

Human Perception

Edited by

Marco Bertamini

University of Liverpool

Michael Kubovy

University of Virginia, USA

Routledge
Taylor & Francis Group

LONDON AND NEW YORK

First published 2006 Ashgate Publishing

Reissued 2018 by Routledge
2 Park Square, Milton Park, Abingdon, Oxon OX14 4RN
605 Third Avenue, New York, NY 10017

First issued in paperback 2021

Routledge is an imprint of the Taylor & Francis Group, an informa business

A Library of Congress record exists under LC control number: 2006929149

Notice:
Product or corporate names may be trademarks or registered trademarks, and are used only for identification and explanation without intent to infringe.

Publisher's Note
The publisher has gone to great lengths to ensure the quality of this reprint but points out that some imperfections in the original copies may be apparent.

Disclaimer
The publisher has made every effort to trace copyright holders and welcomes correspondence from those they have been unable to contact.

ISBN 13: 978-0-815-38954-5 (hbk)
ISBN 13: 978-1-351-15628-8 (ebk)
ISBN 13: 978-1-138-35597-2 (pbk)

DOI: 10.4324/9781351156288

Contents

Acknowledgements   vii
Series Preface   ix
Introduction   xi

PART I   ATTENTION

1   Anne M. Treisman and Garry Gelade (1980), 'A Feature-Integration Theory of
    Attention', *Cognitive Psychology*, **12**, pp. 97–136.   3
2   Michael I. Posner, Charles R.R. Snyder and Brian J. Davidson (1980), 'Attention
    and the Detection of Signals', *Journal of Experimental Psychology: General*, **109**,
    pp. 160–74.   43
3   Steven Yantis and John Jonides (1990), 'Abrupt Visual Onsets and Selective
    Attention: Voluntary Versus Automatic Allocation', *Journal of Experimental
    Psychology: Human Perception and Performance*, **16**, pp. 121–34.   59
4   Jeremy M. Wolfe and Todd S. Horowitz (2004), 'What Attributes Guide the
    Deployment of Visual Attention and How do they do it?', *Nature Reviews:
    Neuroscience*, **5**, pp. 1–7.   73

PART II   BRAIN SYSTEMS

5   Bruno G. Breitmeyer and Leo Ganz (1976), 'Implications of Sustained
    and Transient Channels for Theories of Visual Pattern Masking, Saccadic
    Suppression, and Information Processing', *Psychological Review*, **83**, pp. 1–36.   83
6   Nikos K. Logothetis and Jeffrey D. Schall (1989), 'Neuronal Correlates of
    Subjective Visual-Perception', *Science*, **245**, pp. 761–63.   119
7   Melvyn A. Goodale and A. David Milner (1992), 'Separate Visual Pathways for
    Perception and Action', *Trends in Neurosciences*, **15**, pp. 20–25.   123

PART III OBJECT INTERPOLATION AND COMPLETION

8   Gaetano Kanizsa (1976), 'Subjective Contours', *Scientific American*, **234**,
    pp. 48–52.   131
9   Philip J. Kellman and Thomas F. Shipley (1992), 'Perceiving Objects Across
    Gaps in Space and Time', *Current Directions in Psychological Science*, **1**,
    pp. 193–99.   137

10   Renée Baillargeon (2004), 'Infants' Physical World', *Current Directions in Psychological Science*, **13**, pp. 89–94.   145

PART IV   OBJECT RECOGNITION AND CLASSIFICATION

11   Barbara Tversky and Kathleen Hemenway (1984), 'Objects, Parts, and Categories', *Journal of Experimental Psychology: General*, **113**, pp. 169–93.   153

12   D.D. Hoffman and W.A. Richards (1984), 'Parts of Recognition', *Cognition*, **18**, pp. 65–96.   179

13   Irving Biederman (1987), 'Recognition-by-Components: A Theory of Human Image Understanding', *Psychological Review*, **94**, pp. 115–47.   211

PART V   DIFFERENT TYPES OF OBJECTS

14   Martha J. Farah, Kevin D. Wilson, Maxwell Drain and James N. Tanaka (1998), 'What is "Special" about Face Perception?', *Psychological Review*, **105**, pp. 482–98.   247

15   Daniel Kahneman, Anne Treisman and Brian J. Gibbs (1992), 'The Reviewing of Object Files: Object-Specific Integration of Information', *Cognitive Psychology*, **24**, pp. 175–219.   265

16   Michael Kubovy and David Van Valkenburg (2001), 'Auditory and Visual Objects', *Cognition*, **80**, pp. 97–126.   311

17   Marco Bertamini and Camilla J. Croucher (2003), 'The Shape of Holes', *Cognition*, **87**, pp. 33–54.   341

PART VI   INFORMATION PROCESSING AND MODELS

18   Saul Sternberg (1969), 'The Discovery of Processing Stages: Extensions of Donders' Method', *Acta Psychologica*, **30**, pp. 276–315.   365

19   Roger N. Shepard (1984), 'Ecological Constraints on Internal Representation: Resonant Kinematics of Perceiving, Imagining, Thinking, and Dreaming', *Psychological Review*, **91**, pp. 417–47.   405

20   Stephen Grossberg and Ennio Mingolla (1985), 'Neural Dynamics of Perceptual Grouping: Textures, Boundaries, and Emergent Segmentations', *Perception and Psychophysics*, **38**, pp. 141–71.   437

21   Steven P. Tipper (1985), 'The Negative Priming Effect: Inhibitory Priming by Ignored Objects', *Quarterly Journal of Experimental Psychology*, **37**, pp. 571–90.   469

Name Index   489

Acknowledgements

The editors and publishers wish to thank the following for permission to use copyright material.

American Associaton for the Advancement of Science for the essay: Nikos K. Logothetis and Jeffrey D. Schall (1989), 'Neuronal Correlates of Subjective Visual-Perception', *Science*, **245**, pp. 761–63. Copyright © 1989 AAAS.

American Psychological Association for the essays: Michael I. Posner, Charles R.R. Snyder and Brian J. Davidson (1980), 'Attention and the Detection of Signals', *Journal of Experimental Psychology: General*, **109**, pp. 160–74. Copyright © 1980 by the American Psychological Association. Reprinted with permission; Steven Yantis and John Jonides (1990), 'Abrupt Visual Onsets and Selective Attention: Voluntary Versus Automatic Allocation', *Journal of Experimental Psychology: Human Perception and Performance*, **16**, pp. 121–34. Copyright © 1990 by the American Psychological Association. Reprinted with permission; Bruno G. Breitmeyer and Leo Ganz (1976), 'Implications of Sustained and Transient Channels for Theories of Visual Pattern Masking, Saccadic Suppression, and Information Processing', *Psychological Review*, **83**, pp. 1–36. Copyright © 1976 by the American Psychological Association. Reprinted with permission; Barbara Tversky and Kathleen Hemenway (1984), 'Objects, Parts, and Categories', *Journal of Experimental Psychology: General*, **113**, pp. 169–93. Copyright © 1984 by the American Psychological Association. Reprinted with permission; Martha J. Farah, Kevin D. Wilson, Maxwell Drain and James N. Tanaka (1998), 'What is "Special" about Face Perception?', *Psychological Review*, **105**, pp. 482–98. Copyright © 1998 by the American Psychological Association. Reprinted with permission; Daniel Kahneman, Anne Treisman and Brian J. Gibbs (1992), 'The Reviewing of Object Files: Object-Specific Integration of Information', *Cognitive Psychology*, **24**, pp. 175–219. Copyright © 1992 by the American Psychological Association. Reprinted with permission; Roger N. Shepard (1984), 'Ecological Constraints on Internal Representation: Resonant Kinematics of Perceiving, Imagining, Thinking, and Dreaming', *Psychological Review*, **91**, pp. 417–47. Copyright © 1984 by the American Psychological Association. Reprinted with permission.

Blackwell Publishing for the essays: Philip J. Kellman and Thomas F. Shipley (1992), 'Perceiving Objects Across Gaps in Space and Time', *Current Directions in Psychological Science*, **1**, pp. 193–99; Renée Baillargeon (2004), 'Infants' Physical World', *Current Directions in Psychological Science*, **13**, pp. 89–94; Saul Sternberg (1969), 'The Discovery of Processing Stages: Extensions of Donders' Method', *Acta Psychologica*, **30**, pp. 276–315.

Copyright Clearance Center for the essay: Jeremy M. Wolfe and Todd S. Horowitz (2004), 'What Attributes Guide the Deployment of Visual Attention and How do they do it?', *Nature Reviews: Neuroscience*, **5**, pp. 1–7.

Series Preface

Psychology now touches every corner of our lives. No serious consideration of any newsworthy topic, from eating disorders to crime, from terrorism to new age beliefs, from trauma to happiness, is complete without some examination of what systematic, scientific psychology has to say on these matters. This means that psychology now runs the gamut from neuroscience to sociology, by way of medicine and anthropology, geography and molecular biology, connecting to virtually every area of scientific and professional life. This diversity produces a vibrant and rich discipline in which every area of activity finds outlets across a broad spectrum of publications.

Those who wish to gain an understanding of any area of psychology therefore either have to rely on secondary sources or, if they want to connect with the original contributions that define any domain of the discipline, must hunt through many areas of the library, often under diverse headings.

The volumes in this series obviate those difficulties by bringing together under one set of covers, carefully selected existing publications that are the definitive papers that characterize a specific topic in psychology.

The editors for each volume have been chosen because they are internationally recognized authorities. Therefore the selection of each editor, and the way in which it is organized into discrete sections, is an important statement about the field.

Each volume of the International Library of Psychology thus collects in one place the seminal and definitive journal articles that are creating current understanding of a specific aspect of present-day psychology. As a resource for study and research the volumes ensure that scholars and other professionals can gain ready access to original source material. As a statement of the essence of the topic covered they provide a benchmark for understanding and evaluating that aspect of psychology.

As this International Library emerges over the coming years it will help to specify what the nature of 21st century psychology is and what its contribution is to the future of humanity.

DAVID CANTER
Series Editor
Professor of Psychology
University of Liverpool, UK

Introduction

If we think about it, we have no difficulty in appreciating that our senses provide a great amount of information about the world around us. But our senses are not something we can control the way we control a camera. With a camera in our hands we can decide if and when to take a snapshot. Our experience of the world on the other hand is constantly based on the activity of our senses, both at a conscious and a subconscious level. On the one hand, to see, hear, taste, smell and feel is to be alive. On the other hand, it is probably because perception is a constant aspect of our life that we can take it for granted. It is effortless for us to gather information by means of our senses but it would be a mistake to take this lack of effort as a sign that perception is simple.

One consequence of the fact that we take perception for granted is that its study did not progress at a fast pace during the history of science. For instance, the idea that we see thanks to the extramission of rays from our eyes was held by Empedocles, Plato and even Euclid, and was not clearly rejected until Alahzen (965–1040). We have to wait for the middle of the 19th century for the oldest quantitative law in perception (and also in psychology). This is known as Fechner's law, and it describes the relationship between the intensity of a physical stimulus and its perceptual effect.

It was only in the 20th century, and after the establishment of psychology as a scientific discipline, that the study of perception flourished. But it would be a mistake to think that perception as a subject is the reserve of psychologists. In this book we offer a selection of contributions that cover some of the most interesting discoveries and theories. More importantly, the book tries to give a flavour of the different approaches and ideas.

It is a challenge to collect important contributions to human perception. The main reason is that the study of perception is shared by many disciplines. Because we are cognitive psychologists, we have confined our selection to publications by cognitive psychologists. The cognitive approach is dominant in psychology today and has been very successful in its study of perception, attention and human information processing. Even so, the body of work is huge. To ease our task, we started with a list of the most frequently cited essays in the major journals of our discipline. The ISI Web of Science® is a bibliographic search tool that accesses the ISI citation databases. It allowed us to access information gathered from thousands of scholarly journals (for more information, see <http://www.isinet.com/>).

We selected the following psychology journals: *Behavioral and Brain Sciences*, *Psychological Bulletin*, *Psychological Review*, *Journal of Experimental Psychology: General*, *Cognition*, *Cognitive Psychology*, *Psychological Science*, *Journal of Experimental Psychology: Human Perception and Performance*, *Perception and Psychophysics*, *Acta Psychologica*, *Perception*, *Visual Cognition* and *Quarterly Journal of Experimental Psychology: Human Experimental Psychology*. To these, we added essays on human perception published in *Science* and *Nature*.

Citation indices and the associated impact factors are helpful but they must be used with care. There is a debate about the use and abuse of the ISI impact factor as a measure of the quality of a journal, its research essays, and the researchers who wrote those essays. Because comparing average numbers of citations across different subject areas is fraught with problems, one would like to make such comparisons within subject areas. Yet, it is not always easy to determine where an area ends and another begins. Furthermore, a scholar who wishes to index influence by citation frequency may overestimate the scientific importance of an essay because of a snowball effect that makes some essays on a popular topic take off and multiply their citations. On the other hand, some seminal contributions to the field may have been absorbed without generating a great amount of data or debate, and therefore do not appear at the top of a most cited list.

We began by compiling a database of the most cited essays in human perception. We ranked them by average number of citations per year. In keeping with our skepticism, we used the resulting list only as a guide and not prescriptively. The selection was compiled in October 2004; it is a snapshot at that particular time because any citation ranking changes slowly but continuously (for more information, see <http://www.liv.ac.uk/vp/marco.html>).

For those interested in the most influential publications in cognitive science (many of them relevant to human perception), we recommend consulting the Millennium Project by the University of Minnesota. It is a list of the 100 most influential works in cognitive science from the 20th century, starting from nominations on their website. The final list of publications includes comments about what makes them important (for more information, see <http://www.cogsci.umn.edu/OLD/calendar/past_events/millennium/home.html>).

Our citation analysis was only the first step in the selection process. Some of the essays we have chosen are drawn from our list of highly cited essays, some from more recent publications for which no clear pattern of citations is yet available, and some from review essays. To maintain the book's balance we decided to organize the book into six parts covering the six topics:

I   Attention
II   Brain Systems
III Object Interpolation and Completion
IV Object Recognition and Classification
V   Different Types of Objects
VI Information Processing and Models.

Part I 'Attention', opens with a classic essay by Anne Treisman and Garry Gelade (Chapter 1), which is at the top of the most cited list. Treisman and Gelade's essay has been cited on average 87.5 times every year since it was published. The problem of searching for an item in a crowded scene had been studied before, but Treisman provided an elegant explanation for why an item sometimes *pops out* and at other times we need to scan every item in turn. Some so-called *basic features* are processed in parallel pre-attentively, but attention is required to bind features together. The idea is that attention operates serially; meaning that if a basic feature does not define a target, the task will require a serial, self-terminating search. One might say that this idea of a detailed inspection of one item at a time made the concept of attention more concrete. Although the feature integration theory has since been criticized and updated, this has been an evolution from a solid start and its continuous development is one reason why so many essays still cite Treisman's work. For instance, another highly cited essay,

(Wolfe, Cave and Franzel, 1989) provides an alternative (albeit a closely related alternative) to feature integration theory. Instead of including this and other essays from this literature, we chose to include a more recent essay by Jeremy Wolfe and Todd Horowitz (Chapter 4) to provide an up-to-date review.

Part I includes two other essays, both on attention cueing. The essay by Michael Posner, Charles Snyder and Brian Davidson (Chapter 2) is a classic study of how attention can be deployed. It has been cited 35.1 times per year since publication. In their essay, Steven Yantis and John Jonides (Chapter 3) have suggested that new perceptual objects have high priority for visually guided behaviour. This essay is also among the most cited papers in our list, with an average of 23.0 citations per year.

Part II 'Brain Systems', is slightly different from the other parts. We thought it useful to include essays that show how behaviour is best understood by linking the behavioural findings to our knowledge of the brain. In particular, it is important to know that the visual system contains distinct parallel channels. Starting as early as the ganglion cells of the retina we find classes of cells with important physiological and functional differences. Bruno Breitmeyer and Leo Ganz (Chapter 5) argue that the interactions between transient and sustained pathways provide a basis for better understanding visual masking, iconic memory, motion and pattern perception. Of the many essays written by Mel Goodale and David Milner, we chose a short review one (Chapter 7). Their work on the two separate pathways (the *what* and the *how* pathways) is an elegant synthesis of clinical, physiological and behavioural data. For those interested in this area we also recommend other books by the same authors (Milner and Goodale, 1995; and Goodale and Milner, 2003). We include an essay by Nikos Logothetis and Jeff Schall (Chapter 6) illustrating an important neural correlate of perception.

Our experience of the visual world is much richer than the metaphor of a camera would suggest. For instance, subjective contours and amodal completion testify to that. This is the topic of Part III 'Object Interpolation and Completion'. Gaetano Kanizsa (Chapter 8) was a pioneer in the study of both. Amodal completion refers to the fact that objects partly occluded retain (at one level) their perceived completeness. Subjective contours refer to perceived contours in the absence of local visual stimulation. In both cases the visual system seems to go beyond the information available in the image. Kanizsa is also the author of several books (for the most influential of these see Kanizsa, 1979). The essay by Phillip Kellman and Thomas Shipley (Chapter 9) reviews their work on boundary interpolation. Surprisingly, the visual world of infants, less than one year old, has been shown to be rich in assumptions about the physical world such as the fact that objects are solid and they do not go out of existence when occluded. Since we could only fit one developmental essay into the book, we chose a recent review essay by Renée Baillargeon (Chapter 10) to provide an up-to-date summary.

A key question in perception is, 'How do people recognize and classify objects?' In Part IV 'Object Recognition and Classification', we include an essay by Barbara Tversky and Kathy Hemenway (Chapter 11), in which they observe how, at the basic level, one kind of feature in particular proliferates, namely, parts. However, what parts are exactly is a critical issue, and how the visual system finds parts from visual information is challenging. One hypothesis is that the visual system uses a set of volume primitives. (For probably the most influential essay on volume primitives see David Marr and Keith Nishihara, 1978). We did not include it in this book because the key idea is also summarized in the essay by Irving Biederman (Chapter 13).

In our list based on number of citations, Irv Biederman's essay was the next most cited after that of Treisman and Gelade. It has been cited on average 64.3 times every year since it was published. As already mentioned, the idea that the representation of shapes is based on their structure, and in particular their part-structure, has a long history. Yet, Biederman's essay was an important turning point because not only did it provide a clear description of what the nature of parts are, but also why they are important. There is an analogy between object recognition and speech perception in that a small number of phonemes (geons) are combined using organizational rules to produce an unbounded set of different words (objects). The importance of parts comes from the fact that they are derived from contrasts of five edge cues in a two-dimensional image: curvature, collinearity, symmetry, parallelism and co-termination. What is important here is that this information is present in the image and invariant over viewing position. The debate in this literature has been robust, especially on the issue of how much view independent object recognition really is. We wish we could have included some of the highly cited papers that present a different view from Biederman's (Michael Tarr and Steven Pinker, 1989; Tarr and Heinrich Bülthoff, 1995).

Volume primitives are one attractive solution to how human observers parse an object into parts. However, other authors have developed a more bottom-up approach to part parsing. On the grounds of differential geometry, Donald Hoffman and Whitman Richards (Chapter 12) have suggested that there is information along the contour which is useful in segmenting a shape into subparts. This work builds on earlier suggestions, (eg Fred Attneave, 1954), that curvature, and in particular locations of high curvature along a contour, are critically important in describing the perceived three-dimensional shape. Hoffman and Richards' essay combined an elegant mathematical analysis with a specific proposal, known as the minima rule that says that minima of curvature (concave extrema) are likely to signal the boundary between parts. Jan Koenderink published an essay in the same year that also deals with how contour information is related to solid shape (Koenderink, 1984). Much empirical work was inspired by these theories.

Part V 'Different Types of Objects', is probably more heterogeneous than the other parts. Here we deal with some important issues, like what is special about visual information of faces in an essay by Martha Farah and collaborators (Chapter 14). The authors propose that faces are unlike other objects because of relatively less part-based shape representation for faces. In other words, faces are always recognized holistically. Daniel Kahneman, Anne Treisman and Brian Gibbs (Chapter 15) deal with the question of how information about visual objects is stored and used. Using a priming paradigm, they found an object-specific advantage: naming is facilitated by a preview of the target if the two appearances are linked to the same object. An object file is a temporary episodic representation, within which successive states of an object are linked and integrated. This essay has inspired much empirical investigation and helped frame our view of what a perceptual object is.

Michael Kubovy and David Van Valkenburg (Chapter 16) propose a cross-modal concept of objecthood that focuses on the similarities between modalities. They also propose that the auditory system might consist of two parallel streams of processing (the *what* and *where* subsystems). These are analogous to the visual subsystems that were mentioned earlier (see Goodale and Milner, Chapter 7).

The final essay in Part V, by Marco Bertamini and Camillla Croucher (Chapter 17), is closely linked to the topic of perceived part structure, and in particular, the work by Hoffman and Richards discussed earlier. To study perceived parts Bertamini and Croucher have chosen a type of stimulus that turns out to be uniquely useful: visual holes. Even though an object and a hole can have an identical contour, the fact that the contour is always assigned to only one side (it describes the figure but not the ground) means that they are perceived as having a different shape. The authors have confirmed a qualitative difference in how human observers perceive objects and holes.

Part VI 'Information Processing and Models', includes some essays of great theoretical impact. The oldest is by Saul Sternberg (Chapter 18). Since publication it has been cited an average of 38.26 times per year. Complex tasks can be broken down into a series of distinct stages. If one believes that these stages are sequential, early stages must begin before later stages. This is a useful assumption; from it, it is possible to derive discrete processing models in which information is passed from one stage to the next when processing at the earlier stage is completed.

We could have included in this book several essays by Roger Shepard. We did not include Shepard (1962), only because it combines issues of learning with issues of perception. The essay we did include (Chapter 19) also crosses boundaries. It concerns the concept of internal representation, bringing cognitive science, ecology, evolutionary theory and measurement theory together. Shepard's argument is that mental representations have internalized relations of the physical world that have proven useful to the human species through evolution. Those interested in the legacy of Shepard's ideas should also consider finding the 2001 special issue of the journal *Behavioral and Brain Sciences*, entirely dedicated to this topic.

We decided to include an essay by Stephen Grossberg and Ennio Mingolla (Chapter 20) because it is an example of a model that combines behavioural data with a detailed model of information processing in the brain. This model may not be perfect but is one of the most sophisticated and detailed available, and it builds on a large number of empirical findings.

The final essay, by Steven Tipper (Chapter 21), takes us back full circle to the topic of Part I, that of attention. The paradigm of negative priming it describes is original: things that have been ignored previously are more difficult to identify than those that were not.

With this selection, we make no claim of exhaustiveness (exhaustion comes closer to describe the criterion used). Human perception is a vast ocean that scientists are still exploring. Some technological advances in recent years have allowed us to get deeper, for instance the advent of new imaging techniques. Different disciplines are coming together more and more in new and exciting ways. At the same time, there is still plenty of uncharted territory. This book combines a selection of classic essays with some more recent review essays on key topics. Because of this, we hope it will suit both experienced researchers and those new to the area.

References

Attneave, Fred (1954), 'Some Informational Aspects of Visual Perception', *Psychological Review*, **61**, pp. 183–93.

Baillargeon, Renée (2004), 'Infants' Physical World', *Current Directions in Psychological Science*, **13**, pp. 89–94.

Bertamini, Marco and Croucher, Camilla (2003), 'The Shape of Holes', *Cognition*, **87**, pp. 33–54.

Biederman, Irving (1987), 'Recognition by Components – A Theory of Human Image Understanding', *Psychological Review*, **94**, pp. 115–47.

Breitmeyer, Bruno and Ganz, Leo (1976), 'Implications of Sustained and Transient Channels for Theories of Visual-Pattern Masking, Saccadic Suppression, and Information-Processing', *Psychological Review*, **83**, pp. 1–36.

Farah, Martha, Wilson, Kevin D., Drain, Maxwell and Tanaka, James N. (1998), 'What is "Special" About Face Perception?', *Psychological Review*, **105**, pp. 3; 482–98.

Goodale, Mel and Milner, David (1992), 'Separate Visual Pathways for Perception and Action', *Trends in Neuroscience*, **1**, pp. 20–25.

Goodale, Mel and Milner, David (2003), *Sight Unseen*, Oxford: Oxford University Press.

Grossberg, Stephen and Mingolla, Ennio (1985), 'Neural Dynamics of Perceptual Grouping – Textures, Boundaries, and Emergent Segmentations', *Perception and Psychophysics*, **38**, pp. 141–71.

Hoffman, Donald and Richards, Whitman (1984), 'Parts of Recognition', *Cognition*, **18**, pp. 1–3; 65–96.

Kahneman, Daniel, Treisman, Anne and Gibbs, Brian (1992), 'The Reviewing of Object Files – Object-Specific Integration of Information', *Cognitive Psychology*, **24**, 175–219.

Kanizsa, Gaetano (1976), 'Subjective Contours', *Scientific American*, **234**, pp. 48–52.

Kanizsa, Gaetano (1979), *Organization in Vision: Essays on Gestalt Perception*, New York: Praeger.

Kellman, Phillip and Shipley, Thomas (1992), 'Perceiving Objects Across Gaps in Space and Time', *Current Directions in Psychological Science*, **1**, pp. 193–99.

Koenderink, Jan (1984), 'What Does the Occluding Contour Tell Us About Solid Shape', *Perception*, **13**, pp. 321–30.

Kubovy, Michael and Van Vankenbury, David (2001), 'Auditory and Visual Objects', *Cognition*, **80**, pp. 97–126.

Logothetis, Nikos and Schall, Jeff (1989), 'Neuronal Correlates of Subjective Visual-Perception', *Science*, **245**, pp. 761–63.

Marr, David and Nishihara, Keith (1978), 'Representation and Recognition of the Spatial Organization of Three Dimensional Structure', *Proceedings of the Royal Society, London, Series B*, **200**, pp. 269–94.

Milner, David and Goodale, Mel (1995), *The Visual Brain in Action*, Oxford: Oxford University Press.

Posner, Michael, Snyder, Charles and Davidson, Brian (1980), 'Attention and the Detection of Signals', *Journal of Experimental Psychology: General*, **109**, pp. 160–74.

Shepard, Roger (1962), 'The Analysis of Proximities: Multidimensional Scaling with an Unknown Distance Function', *Psychometrika*, **27**, pp. 125–34.

Shepard, Roger (1984), 'Ecological Constraints on Internal Representation – Resonant Kinematics of Perceiving, Imagining, Thinking, and Dreaming', *Psychological Review*, **91**, pp. 417–47.

Sternbert, Saul (1969), 'Discovery of Processing Stages – Extensions of Donders' Method', *Acta Psychologica*, **30**, pp. 286–315.

Tarr, Michael and Bütlhoff, Heinrich (1995), 'Is Human Object Recognition Better Described by Geon Structural Descriptions or by Multiple Views?', *Journal of Experimental Psychology: Human Perception and Performance*, **21**, pp. 1494–505.

Tarr, Michael and Pinker, Steven (1989), 'Mental Rotation and Orientation-Dependence in Shape-Recognition'. *Cognitive Psychology*, **21**, pp. 233–82.

Tipper, Steven (1985), 'The Negative Priming Effect – Inhibitory Priming by Ignored Objects', *Quarterly Journal of Experimental Psychology: Human Experimental Psychology*, **37**, pp. 571–90.

Treisman, Anne M. and Gelade, Garry (1980), 'A Feature-Integration Theory of Attention', *Cognitive Psychology*, **12**, pp.97–136.

Tversky, Barbara and Hemenway, Kathy (1984), 'Objects, Parts, and Categories', *Journal of Experimental Psychology: General*, **113**, pp. 169–93.

Wolfe, Jeremy and Horowitz, Todd (2004), 'What Attributes Guide the Deployment of Visual Attention and How Do They Do It?', *Nature Reviews Neuroscience*, **5**, pp. 1–7.

Wolfe, Jeremy, Cave, K.R. and Franzel, S.L. (1989), 'Guided Search – An Alternative to the Feature Integration Model for Visual Search', *Journal of Experimental Psychology: Human Perception and Performance*, **15**, pp. 419–33.

Yantis, Steven and Jonides, John (1990), 'Abrupt Visual Onsets and Selective Attention – Voluntary versus Automatic Allocation', *Journal of Experimental Psychology: Human Perception and Performance*, **16**, pp. 121–34.

Part I
Attention

[1]

A Feature-Integration Theory of Attention

ANNE M. TREISMAN
University of British Columbia

AND

GARRY GELADE
Oxford University

A new hypothesis about the role of focused attention is proposed. The feature-integration theory of attention suggests that attention must be directed serially to each stimulus in a display whenever conjunctions of more than one separable feature are needed to characterize or distinguish the possible objects presented. A number of predictions were tested in a variety of paradigms including visual search, texture segregation, identification and localization, and using both separable dimensions (shape and color) and local elements or parts of figures (lines, curves, etc. in letters) as the features to be integrated into complex wholes. The results were in general consistent with the hypothesis. They offer a new set of criteria for distinguishing separable from integral features and a new rationale for predicting which tasks will show attention limits and which will not.

When we open our eyes on a familiar scene, we form an immediate impression of recognizable objects, organized coherently in a spatial framework. Analysis of our experience into more elementary sensations is difficult, and appears subjectively to require an unusual type of perceptual activity. In contrast, the physiological evidence suggests that the visual scene is analyzed at an early stage by specialized populations of receptors that respond selectively to such properties as orientation, color, spatial frequency, or movement, and map these properties in different areas of the brain (Zeki, 1976). The controversy between analytic and synthetic theories of perception goes back many years: the Associationists asserted that the experience of complex wholes is built by combining more elementary sensations, while the Gestalt psychologists claimed that the whole precedes its parts, that we initially register unitary objects and relationships, and only later, if necessary, analyze these objects into their component parts or properties. This view is still active now (e.g., Monahan & Lockhead, 1977; Neisser, 1976).

The Gestalt belief surely conforms to the normal subjective experience

Address reprint requests to Anne Treisman, Department of Psychology, University of British Columbia, 2075 Wesbrook Mall, Vancouver, B.C. V6T 1W5, Canada. We are grateful to the British Medical Research Council, the Canadian Natural Sciences and Engineering Research Council, the Center for Advanced Study in the Behavioral Sciences, Stanford, California, and the Spencer Foundation for financial support, to Melanie Meyer, Martha Nagle, and Wendy Kellogg of the University of Santa Cruz for running four of the subjects in Experiment V, and to Daniel Kahneman for many helpful comments and suggestions.

of perception. However the immediacy and directness of an impression are no guarantee that it reflects an early stage of information processing in the nervous system. It is logically possible that we become aware only of the final outcome of a complicated sequence of prior operations. "Top-down" processing may describe what we consciously experience; as a theory about perceptual coding it needs more objective support (Treisman, 1979).

We have recently proposed a new account of attention which assumes that features come first in perception (Treisman, Sykes, & Gelade, 1977). In our model, which we call the feature-integration theory of attention, features are registered early, automatically, and in parallel across the visual field, while objects are identified separately and only at a later stage, which requires focused attention. We assume that the visual scene is initially coded along a number of separable dimensions, such as color, orientation, spatial frequency, brightness, direction of movement. In order to recombine these separate representations and to ensure the correct synthesis of features for each object in a complex display, stimulus locations are processed serially with focal attention. Any features which are present in the same central "fixation" of attention are combined to form a single object. Thus focal attention provides the "glue" which integrates the initially separable features into unitary objects. Once they have been correctly registered, the compound objects continue to be perceived and stored as such. However with memory decay or interference, the features may disintegrate and "float free" once more, or perhaps recombine to form "illusory conjunctions" (Treisman, 1977).

We claim that, without focused attention, features cannot be related to each other. This poses a problem in explaining phenomenal experience. There seems to be no way we can consciously "perceive" an unattached shape without also giving it a color, size, brightness, and location. Yet unattended areas are not perceived as empty space. The integration theory therefore needs some clarification. Our claim is that attention is necessary for the *correct* perception of conjunctions, although unattended features are also conjoined prior to conscious perception. The top-down processing of unattended features is capable of utilizing past experience and contextual information. Even when attention is directed elsewhere, we are unlikely to see a blue sun in a yellow sky. However, in the absence of focused attention and of effective constraints on top-down processing, conjunctions of features could be formed on a random basis. These unattended couplings will give rise to "illusory conjunctions."

There is both behavioral and physiological evidence for the idea that stimuli are initially analyzed along functionally separable dimensions, although not necessarily by physically distinct channels (Shepard, 1964; Garner, 1974; De Valois & De Valois, 1975). We will use the term "dimension" to refer to the complete range of variation which is separately analyzed by some functionally independent perceptual subsystem, and "feature" to refer to a particular value on a dimension. Thus color and orientation are dimensions; red and vertical are features on those dimensions. Perceptual dimensions do not correspond uniquely to distinct physical dimensions. Some relational aspects of physical attributes may be registered as basic features; for example we code intensity contrast rather than absolute intensity, and we may even directly sense such higher-order properties as symmetry or homogeneity. We cannot predict a priori what the elementary words of the perceptual language may be.

The existence of particular perceptual dimensions should be inferred from empirical criteria, such as those proposed by Shepard and by Garner. This paper will suggest several new diagnostics for the separability of dimensions, which derive from the feature-integration theory of attention. In this theory, we assume that integral features are conjoined automatically, while separable features require attention for their integration. Consequently, we can infer separability from a particular pattern of results in the preattentive and divided attention tasks to be described in this paper.

We have stated the feature-integration hypothesis in an extreme form, which seemed to us initially quite implausible. It was important, therefore, to vary the paradigms and the predictions as widely as possible, in order to maximize the gain from converging operations. We developed a number of different paradigms testing different predictions from the theory. Each experiment on its own might allow other interpretations, but the fact that all were derived as independent predictions from the same theory should allow them, if confirmed, to strengthen it more than any could individually.

(1) Visual search. The visual search paradigm allows us to define a target either by its separate features or by their conjunction. If, as we assume, simple features can be detected in parallel with no attention limits, the search for targets defined by such features (e.g., red, or vertical) should be little affected by variations in the number of distractors in the display. Lateral interference and acuity limits should be the only factors tending to increase search times as display size is increased, perhaps by forcing serial eye fixations. In contrast, we assume that focal attention is necessary for the detection of targets that are defined by a conjunction of properties (e.g., a vertical red line in a background of horizontal red and vertical green lines). Such targets should therefore be found only after a serial scan of varying numbers of distractors.

(2) Texture segregation. It seems likely that texture segregation and figure-ground grouping are preattentive, parallel processes. If so, they should be determined only by spatial discontinuities between groups of stimuli differing in separable features and not by discontinuities defined by conjunctions of features.

(3) *Illusory conjunctions.* If focused attention to particular objects is prevented, either because time is too short or because attention is directed to other objects, the features of the unattended objects are "free floating" with respect to one another. This allows the possibility of incorrect combinations of features when more than one unattended object is presented. Such "illusory conjunctions" have been reported. For example, the pitch and the loudness of dichotic tones are sometimes heard in the wrong combinations (Efron & Yund, 1974), and so are the distinctive features of dichotic syllables (Cutting, 1976). In vision, subjects sometimes wrongly recombine the case and the content of visual words presented successively in the same location (Lawrence, 1971). Treisman (1977) obtained a large number of false-positive errors in a successive same−different matching task when the shapes and colors of two target items were interchanged in the two test stimuli. Each such interchange also added a constant to the correct response times, suggesting that the conjunction of features was checked separately from the presence of those features.

(4) *Identity and location.* Again, if focused attention is prevented, the features of unattended objects may be free floating spatially, as well as unrelated to one another. Thus we may detect the presence of critical features without knowing exactly where they are located, although we can certainly home in on them rapidly. Locating a feature would, on this hypothesis, be a separate operation from identifying it, and could logically follow instead of preceding identification. However, the theory predicts that this could not occur with conjunctions of features. If we have correctly detected or identified a particular conjunction, we must first have located it in order to focus attention on it and integrate its features. Thus location must precede identification for conjunctions, but the two could be independent for features.

(5) *Interference from unattended stimuli.* Unattended stimuli should be registered only at the feature level. The amount of interference or facilitation with an attended task that such stimuli can generate should therefore depend only on the features they comprise and should not be affected by the particular conjunctions in which those features occur.

There is considerable evidence in speech perception that the meaning of unattended words can sometimes be registered without reaching conscious awareness (e.g., Corteen & Wood, 1972; Lewis, 1970; MacKay, 1973; Treisman, Squire, & Green, 1974). Since words are surely defined by conjunctions, the evidence of word-recognition without attention appears to contradict our hypothesis. However, the data of these studies indicate that responses to primed and relevant words on the unattended channel occurred only on 5−30% of trials. It may be possible for a response occasionally to be triggered by one or more features of an expected word, without requiring exact specification of how these features are combined. One study has looked at false-positive responses to relevant words on un unattended channel (Forster & Govier, 1978). They found far more GSRs to words which sounded similar to the shock-associated word when these were presented on the unattended than on the attended channel. This suggests either incomplete analysis of unattended items or incomplete sensory data.

These predictions identify two clusters of results, corresponding to the perception of separable features and of conjunctions. Separable features should be detectable by parallel search; they are expected to give rise to illusory conjunctions in the absence of attention; they can be identified without necessarily being located, and should mediate easy texture segregation; they can have behavioral effects even when unattended. Conjunctions, on the other hand, are expected to require serial search; they should have no effect on performance unless focally attended; they should yield highly correlated performance in the tasks of identification and location; they should prove quite ineffective in mediating texture segregation. Our aim was to test these predictions using two dimensions, form and color, which are likely, both on physiological and on behavioral grounds, to be separable. If the predictions are confirmed, we may be able to add our tests to Garner's criteria, to form a more complete behavioral syndrome diagnostic of separable or integral dimensions. Thus, if two physical properties are integral, they should function as a single feature in our paradigms, allowing parallel search, texture segregation, and detection without localization. If on the other hand, they are separable, their conjunctions will require focused attention for accurate perception, and its absence should result in illusory conjunctions. We may then use these paradigms to diagnose less clear-cut candidates for separability, such as the components of letters or schematic faces.

The first three experiments are concerned with visual search; they compare color–shape conjunctions with disjunctive color and shape features as targets; they investigate the effects of practice and the role of feature discriminability in conjunction search, and test an alternative account in terms of similarity relations. Experiment IV explores the possibility that local elements of compound shapes (e.g., letters) also function as separable features, requiring serial search when incorrect conjunctions could be formed. Experiments V, VI, and VII are concerned with texture segregation, using colored shapes and letters as texture elements. Experiments VIII and IX explore the relation between identification and spatial localization, for targets defined by a single feature or by a conjunction.

EXPERIMENT I

In an experiment reported earlier, Treisman et al. (1977) compared search for targets specified by a single feature ("pink" in "brown" and "purple" distractors in one condition, "O" in "N" and "T" distractors in another) and for targets specified by a conjunction of features, a "pink O" (O_{pink}, in distractors O_{green} and N_{pink}). The function relating search times to display size was flat or nonmonotonic when a single feature was sufficient to define the target, but increased linearly when a conjunction of features was required. Experiment I replicates this study with some changes in the design, to confirm and generalize the conclusions. The most important change was in the feature search condition: subjects were now asked to search concurrently for two targets, each defined by a different single feature: a color (blue) and a shape (S). Thus they were forced to attend to both dimensions in the feature condition as well as in the conjunction condition, although they had to check how the features were combined only when the target was a conjunction (T_{green}). The distractors were identical in the two conditions (X_{green} and T_{brown}), to ensure that differences between feature and conjunction search could not result from greater heterogeneity of the distractors in the conjunction condition. (This had been a possibility in the previous experiment.)

Another question which has become important in evaluating information-processing hypotheses is how stably they apply across different stages of practice. Neisser, Novick, and Lazar (1963), Rabbitt (1967), and Shiffrin and Schneider (1977) have all shown qualitative changes in performance as subjects repeatedly perform a particular task. Search appears to change from conscious, limited capacity, serial decision making to automatic, fast, and parallel detection. LaBerge (1973) studied the effects of practice on priming in a visual successive matching task. He found that familiarity with the stimuli eventually made matching independent of expectancy, and suggested that this was due to unitization of the features of highly familiar stimuli. We propose that feature unitization may account also for the change with practice from serial to parallel processing in a display, in conditions in which such a change occurs. Thus the development of new unitary detectors for what were previously conjunctions of features would free us from the constraints of focal attention to these features both in memory and in a physically present display. Experiment I explored the possibility that extended practice on a particular shape–color conjunction (T_{green}) could lead to a change from serial to parallel detection, which would suggest the possible emergence of a unitary "green T" detector.

Method

    Stimuli. The stimulus displays were made by hand, using letter stencils and colored inks on white cards. The distractors were scattered over the card in positions which appeared random, although no systematic randomization procedure was used. Four different display sizes, consisting of 1, 5, 15, and 30 items were used in each condition. An area subtending 14 × 8° was used for all display sizes, so that the displays with fewer items were less densely packed, but the average distance from the fovea was kept approximately constant. Each letter subtended $0.8 \times 0.6°$. To ensure that the target locations did not vary systematically across conditions, the area of each card was divided into eight sections. This was done by superimposing a tracing of the two diagonals and an inner elliptical boundary, which subtended $8.5° \times 5.5°$. For each condition and each display size, eight cards were made, one with a target randomly placed in each of the resulting eight areas (top outer, top inner, left outer, left inner, right outer, etc.). Another eight cards in each condition and display size contained no target.

The distractors in both conditions were T_{brown} and X_{green} in as near equal numbers on each card as possible. The target in the conjunction condition was T_{green}; in the feature condition, it was either a blue letter or an S. The blue letter (T_{blue} or X_{blue}) matched half the distractors in shape, and the S (S_{brown} or S_{green}) matched half the distractors in color. The fact that there were four possible disjunctive targets in the feature condition (although the definition specified only "blue or S"), should, if anything, impair performance relative to the conjunction condition.

Procedure. The stimulus cards were presented in an Electronics Development three-field tachistoscope and RT was recorded as described below.

At the beginning of each trial, subjects viewed a plain white card in the tachistoscope, and each of their index fingers rested on a response key. The experimenter gave a verbal "Ready" signal and pressed a button to display a second white card bearing a central fixation spot, which remained in view for 1 sec and was then immediately replaced in the field of view by a card bearing a search array. Subjects were instructed to make a key press with the dominant hand if they detected a target and with the nondominant hand otherwise, and to respond as quickly as possible without making any errors. RT was recorded to the nearest millisecond on a digital timer [Advance Electronics, TC11], which was triggered by the onset of the search array and stopped when a response key was pressed. Trials on which an error was made were repeated later in the testing session, and following each error a dummy trial was given, the results of which were not recorded. Subjects were told their RT and whether or not they were correct after each trial; they were not however informed of the dummy trials procedure, the purpose of which was to exclude slow posterror responses from the data.

Each subject was tested both on conjunctions and on features in separate sessions following an ABBAAB order. Half the subjects began with the feature targets and half with the conjunction targets. Six subjects did 3 blocks of 128 trials each in each condition, then two of these subjects volunteered to continue for another 4 blocks in the conjunction condition and two for another 10 blocks, making 13 altogether (a total of 1664 trials). The mean RTs for these two subjects on the first 3 blocks closely approximated the group means.

Within each block the presentation order of positive and negative trials and of different display sizes was randomized; thus in each block the subject knew what the target or the two alternative targets were, but did not know what the array size would be on any given trial. Each block contained 16 positive and 16 negative trials for each display size.

Subjects. The six subjects, four men and two women, were members of the Oxford Subject Panel, ages between 24 and 29. Three of them had previously taken part in the search experiment described in Treisman et al. (1977).

Results

Figure 1 shows the mean search times for the six subjects over the second and third blocks in each condition; the first block was treated as practice. Table 1 gives the details of linear regression analyses on these data. The results show that search time increased linearly with display

SEARCH FOR COLORED SHAPES

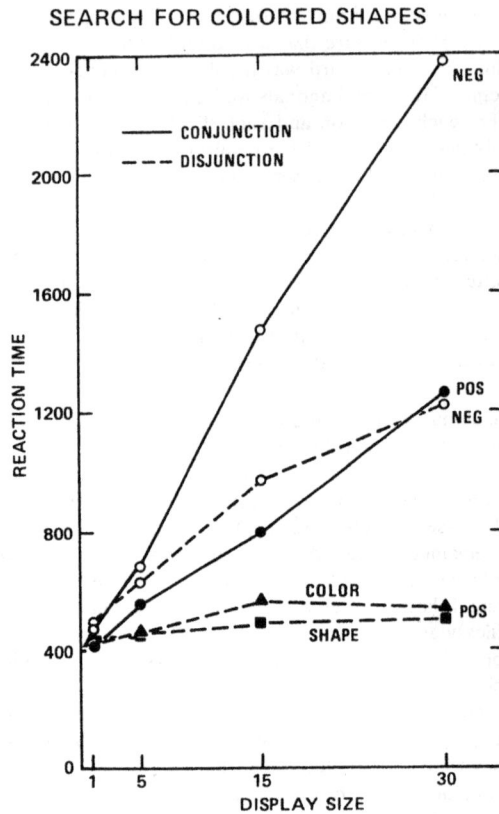

FIG. 1. Search times in Experiment I.

size in the conjunction condition, the linear component accounting for more than 99% of the variance due to display size. The ratio of the positive to the negative slopes in the conjunction condition was 0.43, which is quite close to half. These results suggest that search is serial and self-terminating with a scanning rate of about 60 msec per item. The variances increased more steeply for positive than for negative trials, and for positives the root mean square of the RTs increased linearly with display size as predicted for serial self-terminating search.

With the feature targets, the results were very different. For the positive displays, search times were hardly affected by the number of distractors, the slopes averaging only 3.1 msec. Deviations from linearity were significant, and the linear component accounted for only 68% of the variance due to display size. For the negatives, the linear component accounted for 96% of the variance due to display size, and departures from linearity did not reach significance. The slope was, however, less than

TABLE 1

Linear Regressions of Reaction Times on Display Size in Experiment I

		Slope	Intercept	Percentage variance with display size which is due to linearity
Conjunction	Positives	28.7	398	99.7
	Negatives	67.1	397	99.6
Feature mean	Positives	3.1	448	67.9[a]
	Negatives	25.1	514	96.6
Feature color	Positive	3.8	455	61.0[a]
Feature shape	Positive	2.5	441	78.5

[a] Cases where deviations from linearity are significant at $p < .01$. The positive shape feature also deviates considerably from linearity, but the significance level here is only .08.

half the slope for conjunction negatives. The ratio of positive to negative slopes with feature targets was only 0.12. In both conditions, all subjects showed the same pattern of results, with individuals varying mainly in the absolute values of slopes and intercepts.

Errors in the feature condition averaged 2.2% false positives and 2.1% false negatives; for the conjunction condition there were 0.8% false positives and 4.9% false negatives. There were no systematic effects of display size on errors, except that false negatives in the conjunction condition were higher for display size 30 than for 15, 5, or 1 (8.2% compared to 3.8%). The highest mean error rate for an individual subject was 5.5% in the conjunction condition and 3.5% in the feature condition.

It is important to the theory that the difference between conjunction and feature conditions is present only when more than one stimulus is presented. The mean positive RT for display size 1 was 422 msec for the conjunction targets, compared to 426 msec for shape and 446 msec for color in the feature condition. The negatives with display size 1 were also faster in the conjunction than in the feature conditions, 473 msec compared to 500 msec. Thus the difficulty of search for conjunctions arises only when more than one stimulus is presented.

The effects of practice on conjunction search are shown in Fig. 2. The positive slopes and intercepts decrease over the first 7 blocks and change little for the remaining 6 blocks. The negative slopes fluctuate across the first 9 blocks and stabilize at block 10. Both positive and negative slopes remained linear throughout: the proportion of the variance with display

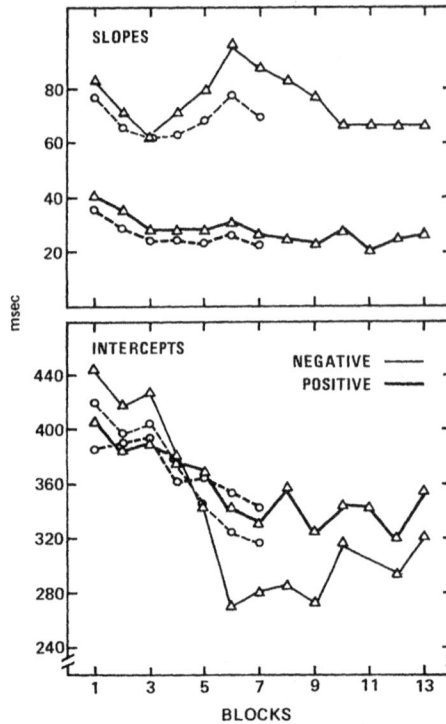

Fig. 2. The effects of practice on the slope and intercept of the function relating search time to display size. (The dotted lines are the data for the four subjects who did 7 sessions and the solid lines for the two subjects who continued for 13 sessions.)

size that was due to linearity was above 0.99 in every block except positive blocks 3 and 12, when it was 0.98 and 0.97, respectively. Thus there is little indication of any change in the pattern of results and no sign of a switch from serial to parallel search over the 13 blocks of practice. The mean results for the two subjects who volunteered for this extensive practice were typical of the group as a whole on blocks 2 and 3 (negative and positive slopes of 67 and 31, respectively, compared to the group means of 67 and 29; intercepts 423 and 389 compared to 397 and 398).

Discussion

We suggested that focal attention, scanning successive locations serially, is the means by which the correct integration of features into multidimensional percepts is ensured. When this integration is not required by the task, parallel detection of features should be possible. The results, especially on positive trials, fit these predictions well. Despite the major changes in the feature search condition between this experiment and the earlier one (Treisman et al., 1977), the results are almost identical. The requirement to search for values on two different dimensions instead of one on each trial produced no qualitative and almost no quantitative change in performance; neither did the greater heterogeneity of the distractors. In both experiments the display was apparently searched spatially in parallel whenever targets could be detected on the basis of a single feature, either color or shape. Another important difference between the conjunction and the feature conditions is the difference in the relation between positive and negative displays. The slope for conjunction positives is about half the slope for the negatives, suggesting a serial self-terminating search. In the feature condition, however, the slope ratio is only 1/8, and the function is linear only for the negatives. This suggests that with single feature targets, a qualitatively different process may mediate the responses to positive and to negative displays. If the target is present, it is detected automatically; if it is not, subjects tend to scan the display, although they may not check item by item in the strictly serial way they do in conjunction search.

Practice for up to 13 sessions on the same target and distractors produced no qualitative changes in performance in conjunction search, no decrease in linearity, and no systematic decrease in either slope or intercept after about the seventh session. We had been interested in seeing whether practice could lead to unitization, in the sense of developing a special detector for the conjunction of green and "T," which could allow a change to parallel search. It is of course possible that longer practice, different stimuli, or a different training method could result in a change to parallel search. The present experiment, however suggests that unitization of color and shape is difficult and may be impossible to achieve. There may be built-in neural constraints on which dimensions can be unitized in this way.

EXPERIMENT II

The next experiment explores the relation between the discriminability of the features which define a conjunction and the speed of detecting that conjunction as a target in a display. If each item must be scanned serially in order to determine how its features are conjoined, it should be possible to change the slope relating search time to display size, by slowing the decision about the features composing each item. Thus by making the two shapes and the two colors in a conjunction search easier or harder to distinguish, we should be able to change the rate of scanning while retaining the characteristic serial search pattern of linear slopes and the 2/1 ratio of negative to positive slopes. We compared search for a conjunction target in distractors which were similar to each other (T_{green} in X_{green} and T_{blue}) and in distractors which differed maximally from each other (O_{red} in

O_{green} and N_{red}). The decisions whether each item had the target color and the target shape should be easier for O versus N and red versus green than for T versus X and green versus blue. (We chose green and blue inks which were very similar to each other.)

A second question we investigated in this experiment was whether the previous results depended on the haphazard spatial arrangement of the items in the display. In this experiment, the letters were arranged in regular matrices of 2 × 2, 4 × 4, and 6 × 6. The mean distance of the letters from the fixation point was equated, so that density again covaried with display size, but acuity was again approximately matched for each condition.

Method

Subjects. Six subjects (three females and three males) volunteered for the experiment which involved a test and re-test session. They were students and employees of the University of British Columbia ages between 16 and 45. They were paid $3.00 a session for their participation.

Apparatus. A two-field Cambridge tachistoscope connected to a millisecond timer was used. The stimuli consisted, as before, of white cards with colored letters. Displays contained 1, 4, 16, or 36 items. The letters were arranged in matrices of 2 × 2, 4 × 4, or 6 × 6 positions. For the displays of 1 item each of the positions in the 2 × 2 matrix was used equally often. The 6 × 6 display subtended 12.3 × 9.7°; the 4 × 4 matrix subtended 9.7 × 9.7° and the 2 × 2 matrix subtended 7 × 7°. The mean distance of items from the fixation point was about 4.3° for all displays. Sixteen different cards, of which 8 contained a target, were made for each display size in each condition. In the easy condition, the distractors were O_{green} and N_{red} and the target was O_{red}. In the difficult condition, the distractors were T_{blue} and X_{green} and the target was T_{green}. The target was presented twice in each display position for the displays of 1 and 4, in half the display positions for displays of 16 (twice in each row and twice in each column), and twice in each 3 × 3 quadrant for the displays of 36.

Results

Figure 3 shows the mean RTs in each condition. The details of the linear regressions are given in Table 2. None of the slopes deviates significantly from linearity, which accounts for more than 99.8% of the variance due to display size in every case. The ratio of positive to negative slopes is 0.52 for the easy stimuli and 0.60 for the difficult ones. The slopes in the difficult discrimination are nearly three times larger than those in the easy discrimination, but the linearity and the 2/1 slope ratio is preserved across these large differences. The intercepts do not differ significantly across conditions.

Error rates were higher in the difficult discrimination condition. Two subjects were dropped from the experiment because they were unable to keep their false-negative errors in the large positive displays in this condition below 30%. For the remaining subjects, errors averaged 5.3% for the difficult discrimination and 2.5% for the easy discrimination. They were not systematically related to display size except that the difficult positive

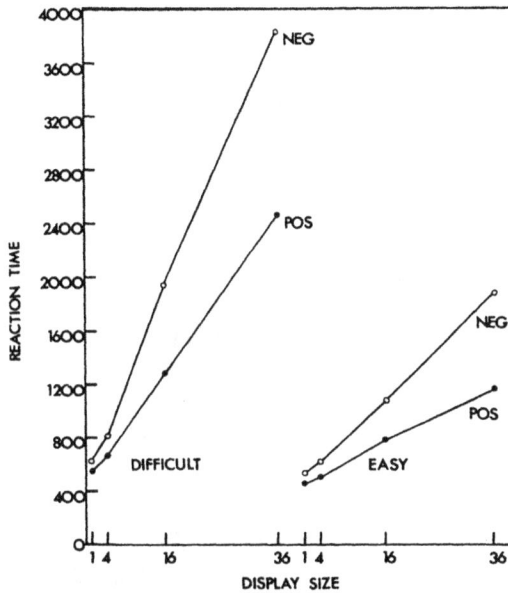

Fig. 3. Search times in Experiment II.

displays of 16 and 36 averaged 5.9 and 20.7% false-negative errors, respectively, compared to a mean of 2.2% errors for all other displays.

Discussion

In both conditions we have evidence supporting serial, self-terminating search through the display for the conjunction targets. The slopes are linear and the positives give approximately half the slope of the negatives. However, the rates vary dramatically: The more distinctive colors and

TABLE 2

Linear Regressions of Search Times against Display Size in Experiment II

		Slope	Intercept	Percentage variance with display size which is due to linearity
Difficult discrimination	Positives	55.1	453	99.8
	Negatives	92.4	472	99.9
Easy discrimination	Positives	20.5	437	99.8
	Negatives	39.5	489	99.9

shapes allow search to proceed nearly three times as fast as the less distinctive. The mean scanning rate of 62 msec per item obtained in the conjunction condition of Experiment I lies between the rates obtained here with the confusable stimuli and with the highly discriminable stimuli. This wide variation in slopes, combined with maintained linearity and 2/1 slope ratios, is consistent with the theory, and puts constraints on alternative explanations. For example, we can no longer suppose that search becomes serial only when it is difficult. The need for focused attention to each item in turn must be induced by something other than overall load. The fact that the intercepts were the same for the easy and the difficult conditions is also consistent with the theory.

Experiment I used pseudo-random locations for the targets and distractors. The present experiment extends the conclusions to displays in which the stimuli are arranged in a regular matrix. The serial scan is therefore not induced by any artifact of the locations selected or by their haphazard arrangement.

EXPERIMENT III

Experiment III explores an alternative explanation for the difference between conjunction and feature targets. This attributes the difficulty of the conjunction condition to the centrality of the target in the set of distractors: a conjunction target shares one or another feature with every distractor in the display, while each disjunctive feature target shares a feature with only half the distractors (see Fig. 4). In this sense, the conjunction targets are more similar to the set of distractors than the feature targets.

We replicated this aspect of the similarity structure, but using unidimensional stimuli in which checking for conjunctions would not be necessary. We compared search times for a single unidimensional target, which was intermediate between two types of distractors on the single relevant dimension, with search times for either of two disjunctive

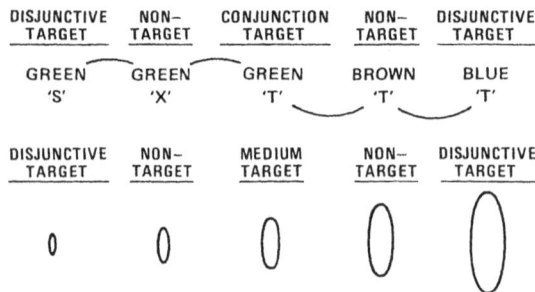

FIG. 4. Similarity relations between the stimuli in Experiments I and III.

targets, each of which was similar only to one of the distractors. We used ellipses varying in size in steps that were subjectively approximately equal, as shown in Fig. 4. If similarity to both types of distractors instead of only one type is the critical variable, the ellipses should show the same pattern of results as the colored shapes: serial for the intermediate target and parallel for the disjunctive large or small targets. The results should also be of some general interest for the theoretical analysis of search and the effects of different similarity relationships between target(s) and distractors.

Method

Stimuli. These were the same as in Experiment I except for the following substitutions: black ellipses of sizes 1.0×0.3 and $2.0 \times 0.6°$ replaced the distractors; ellipses of sizes 0.6×0.18 and $2.5 \times 0.8°$ replaced the disjunctive targets and an ellipse of size $1.4 \times 0.4°$ replaced the conjunction target. These sizes were selected after a pilot experiment on three subjects, sampling a wider range of sizes, had determined that the mean RT in a same–different matching task was approximately the same for discriminating the medium-sized target from each of the two distractors as it was for discriminating the large and small targets from the nearest distractor (a mean difference of only 15 msec).

Procedure. This was also the same as in Experiment I except that each subject did only three blocks in each condition; we did not investigate the effects of extended practice.

Subjects. The six subjects were drawn from the same panel as those in Experiment I, and three of them had actually taken part in Experiment I.

Results and Discussion

The mean search times are shown in Fig. 5. All the functions relating latency to display size are negatively accelerated. Deviations from linearity were significant for the large and small negatives ($p < .05$) and for the intermediate positives ($p < .01$) and approached significance for the large positives and intermediate negatives ($p = .12$ and .10, respectively). The pattern of results is quite different from that obtained with the color–shape conjunctions and disjunctive features. With ellipses the intermediate target, which is most "central" in terms of similarity, gives the least linear detection function, and its detection times lie between those for the large and small targets. With negative displays the intermediate targets did produce a steeper function than the large and small targets. A different process may again be mediating positive and negative search times. When subjects are least confident in deciding that the target is absent, they may be most inclined to check the distractors serially before responding "No." The important point for the present theory is that when the intermediate target is *present,* its detection does not depend on a serial check of the distractors, whereas detection of the color–shape conjunction did. This rules out an explanation of the conjunction effect in terms of the "centrality" of the target to the set of distractors.

The results also reinforce the important conclusion that the difference

SEARCH FOR ELLIPSES

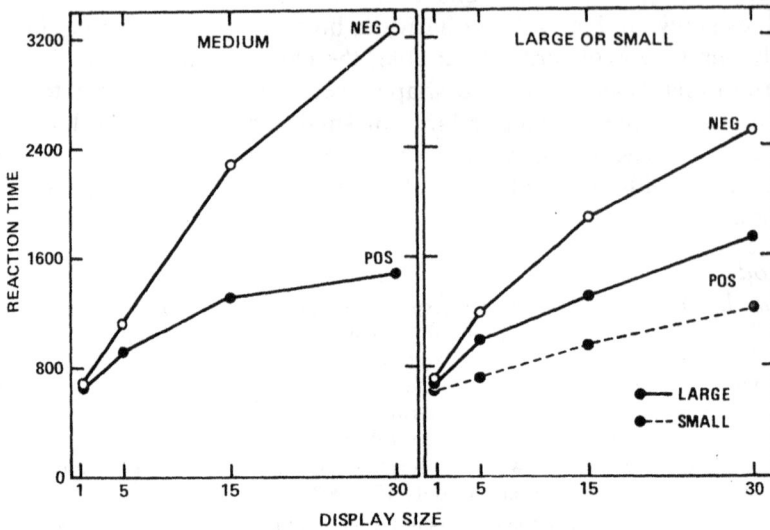

FIG. 5. Search times in Experiment III.

between conjunctions and disjunctions cannot be attributed simply to their relative difficulty. Search for the intermediate ellipses was considerably slower on average than for the color–shape conjunctions, yet the relation of latency to display size was linear for the conjunctions, and not for the ellipses. When a single feature (size) defines the target, search can be slow but need not be serial in the sense of checking each item in turn.

Clearly, with search times which were sometimes as long as 3 sec for the ellipses, some aspects of processing are likely to be serial. Subjects certainly changed fixation and scanned the display with their eyes, so that different areas of the display received foveal processing successively. In this sense processing was serial. However, serial eye fixations do not imply serial decisions about each item, one at a time, and we believe the two patterns have different theoretical implications which are worth distinguishing. Serial fixations will be made when the discriminations require foveal acuity, either because they are below threshold with peripheral vision or because there is some form of lateral interference which increases towards the periphery. However, within each successive fixation it is at least logically possible that the whole display receives parallel processing, the foveal areas receiving the most detailed sensory information, but all or many stimuli being checked simultaneously. Since density increased with number of items in the present experiment, more stimuli would on average have been within foveal vision for each fixation with the larger display sizes, allowing the number that could be accurately processed in parallel to increase with display size. This would result in the negatively accelerated functions that we obtained.

These findings suggest that there are at least two ways in which a search task can be difficult, and in which its difficulty can interact with display size: (1) The difficulty can arise, as with the ellipses, because the targets and distractors are difficult to discriminate and therefore require serial fixations with foveal vision. This can occur either with unidimensional variation or with conjunctions. (2) A search task that requires the identification of conjunctions depends on a more central scan with focused attention, which deals serially with each item rather than with each spatial area foveally fixated. In this case the difficulty should be restricted to conditions in which more than one item is presented, allowing the possibility of feature interchanges or "illusory conjunctions." Retinal area should have no effect, within the limits set by acuity. Only the number of items should affect search times, and not their density or spatial distribution.

EXPERIMENT IV

The next experiment explores the possibility that local elements or parts of shapes function as separable features which must be integrated by focused attention whenever their conjunctions are relevant to the task. In particular we were interested to discover whether integrative attention is required even with highly familiar stimuli, such as letters of the alphabet, or whether letters function as integral perceptual units, which can be registered by unitary "detectors." Treisman et al. (1977) obtained evidence that schematic faces are treated as conjunctions of local features (e.g., eyes and mouth). These apparently required a serial check both in the display and in memory whenever a conjunction error could occur. Moreover conjunction errors actually occurred on about 20% of trials when the response was made too quickly. Faces had seemed good candidates for Gestalt or wholistic recognition. However, the schematic faces we used were unfamiliar as units, and the varied permutation of a fixed limited set of features may have increased the likelihood that features would be processed separably. Letters are both simpler and more familiar.

Letters have long been controversial units in perceptual theory. There have been arguments (1) over whether they are decomposed into features and (2) over whether the letters themselves are processed serially or in parallel. LaBerge (1973), for example, suggests that our great familiarity with letters has "unitized" them, so that they no longer require "attention," but can be automatically registered as wholes. Gibson (1971) on the other hand argues from confusion errors that letter features do have psychological reality as perceptual elements. Gardner (1973) showed that parallel detection of letters is possible when target and background letters are easily discriminable; he attributes any effects of display size to an increased risk of confusions at the decision level. Estes (1972) however, argues that there are inhibitory effects at the feature level which reduce perceptual efficiency as the number of items increases.

Integration theory should tie the two questions together, and predict that letters will be processed serially only if (a) they are analyzed into separate features and (b) these are interchangeable to form conjunction errors in the particular task the subject is given. Moreover, we would distinguish two senses of confusability. In one sense, letters would be difficult to search when they are similar in a wholistic way. They might then require successive foveal fixations and produce results analogous to those we obtained with the ellipses in Experiment III. Search for "R" in a background of "P"s and "B"s might be a task which reflects confusability in this sense. In another sense, *sets* of letters would be confusable if their features were interchangeable and could potentially give rise to illusory conjunctions. In this case each letter should be checked serially, giving linear rather than negatively accelerated search functions. For example, "P" and "Q" could form an illusory "R" if the diagonal of the "Q" is registered as a separable feature. Search for "R" in a background of "P"s and "Q"s should therefore be serial, if (a) our hypothesis about the role of focal attention is correct, and (b) these component features are in fact registered as separable elements.

Wolford (1975) has proposed a perturbation model of letter identification which shares some assumptions with our hypothesis. He suggests that features of shapes are registered by parallel independent channels and are then grouped and serially identified as letters. The features have some probability of interchange depending on both distance and time. These perturbations can give rise to identification errors if they alter the set of features in a particular location sufficiently to change which letter is best predicted from those features. The integration model differs from that of Wolford in several ways: (1) It is more general in that it applies to dimensions like shape and color as well as to the local elements of letters. (2) We claim that serial processing is necessary only when feature sets must be spatially conjoined; some sets of letters could therefore be identified in parallel. (3) The relative locations of different features with respect to each other are initially indeterminate, even with the display physically present, and remain so if focused attention to them is prevented. For Wolford, on the other hand, the features are initially localized and their locations are gradually lost by a random walk process in memory when the display is no longer present. (4) Spatial uncertainty in our model depends on the distribution of attention rather than on retinal distance and time, so that feature interchanges can occur either within or outside the momentary focus of attention but not across its boundary. (5) Finally, we make further related predictions about the role of attention, suggesting, for example, that preattentive processing (in texture segregation) and nonattentive processing (in focused attention tasks) will reflect distinctions only at the feature and not at the conjunction level.

The next experiment contrasts the effects of conjunction difficulties with those of interitem similarity on visual search for letters. We used two sets of letters which could result in conjunction errors if their features were interchanged. Subjects were to search for a target "R" in a background of Ps and Qs (R/PQ), and for a target T in a background of "Z"'s and "I"'s (T/ZI). To simplify exposition, we will refer only to the R/PQ set, but equivalent procedures were also applied for the T/ZI set. We contrasted the conjunction condition with a control condition in which the similarity of target and distractors was greater. For this similarity control, we replaced one of the distractors (Q) with a letter ("B") which, on its own, is more confusable with the target, but whose features could not recombine with the other distractor (P) to form an illusory target. We also ran a control condition with a single type of distractor to check that similarity effects were in the predicted direction: Thus we compared the speed of search for R in Qs alone with search for R in Bs alone. Finally we ran a control for distractor heterogeneity. A possible artifact in the main experiment was the greater difference between the two distractors in the conjunction condition (PQ) than in the similarity condition (PB). This heterogeneity might make them harder to "filter out" or to reject as irrelevant. We therefore ran a condition using the same distractors as we used in the conjunction condition (P and Q) but with a target (T) which could be distinguished by a single feature (horizontal line).

In addition, we collected pilot data on several other sets of letters, to check on the generality of the results with the two sets used in the main experiment. We compared search for conjunction targets N/VH, E/FL, and Q/OK with search for more similar targets which did not require conjunction checks, N/VW, E/FT, and Q/OG.

It is not clear what Wolford's model would predict for our tasks: Since the displays were physically present until the subject made his response, feature interchanges should probably not occur. If they did, they would lead to errors with the conjunction displays (R/PQ and T/IZ). However there should also be errors arising from the greater number of shared features between distractors and targets in the similarity sets (R/PB and T/IY). It is not clear either how these predicted error rates should differ, or more important, how the relative accuracy would translate into different search latencies given unlimited exposure times. Wolford assumes that the time it takes to process a letter depends on the amount of information required. If search for R in Qs alone is faster than for R in Bs alone, it is difficult to see how this would reverse when the Qs are presented together with Ps.

Method

Stimuli. Sets of cards were prepared for tachistoscopic display in the same way as for Experiment I, with only the following changes. The letters were all drawn in black ink. There were four main conditions: target R in mixed distractors Ps and Qs (R/PQ); target R in Ps and Bs (R/PB); target T in Is and Zs (T/IZ); target T in Is and Ys (T/IY). We selected these letters after considering the matrices of letter confusion errors collected by Townsend (1971), Fisher, Monty, and Glucksberg (1967), Hodge (1962), and Pew and Gardner (1965). Pooling all these tables, we found that R was confused with Q 6 times and with B 61 times, and T was confused with Z 20 times and with Y 107 times. The other two distractors, P and I, were the same in the conjunction and the similarity conditions.

Eight further single letter control cards were made for each condition, containing either 15 identical distractors (Qs, Bs, Zs or Ys) or 14 distractors and one target (R or T, respectively). Finally, a set of cards with target T in distractors P and Q was also made, to be used in the heterogeneity control condition.

Subjects. The subjects were members of the Oxford subject panel, ages between 24 and 29. Six took part in the main experiment with conjunction and similarity conditions; four of them had previously taken part in one of the "search" experiments for colored letters. Two of these and four new subjects were subsequently tested in the heterogeneity control condition.

Procedure. For the main experiment, the sequence of events within each trial was the same as in Experiment I. Each session, lasting about 1 hr, tested only one of the two target letters, but included, in separate blocks, all the conditions for that target letter—the conjunction condition (C), the similarity condition (S), and the two controls with a single type of distractor (labeled by lower case c and s). The different display sizes in any one condition were presented in random order within each block. The order in which the conditions were given was counterbalanced across subjects, but the two control conditions each preceded or succeeded the appropriate experimental condition. Thus there were four possible orders within a session: CcSs, cCsS, SsCc, and sScC. Each subject did at least six sessions, three with target R and three with target T in the order RTTRRT reversing the order of conditions within sessions on the third and fifth sessions. Two subjects did a further two sessions, one with each target letter in the order TR, because the early results on these subjects suggested that they had not developed a consistent strategy in the similarity condition. We were interested in comparing search which could use a single feature with search that required conjunction detection, so we decided after the first four sessions on these two subjects to instruct them and future subjects to use a consistent strategy of searching for a distinctive feature when this was possible.

The heterogeneity control experiment consisted of 4 blocks of search for T/PQ and for T in 15 Ps alone and T in 15 Qs alone, following the same within-block orders as in the main experiment.

Results

Figure 6 shows the mean search times in the last two sessions for each condition of the main experiment, averaged over the R and T replications. Linear regressions were carried out on the search times for each letter set; the results are given in Table 3. Deviations from linearity were significant ($p < .01$ and $p < .05$) for the similarity positives, R/PB and T/IY, respec-

LETTER SEARCH

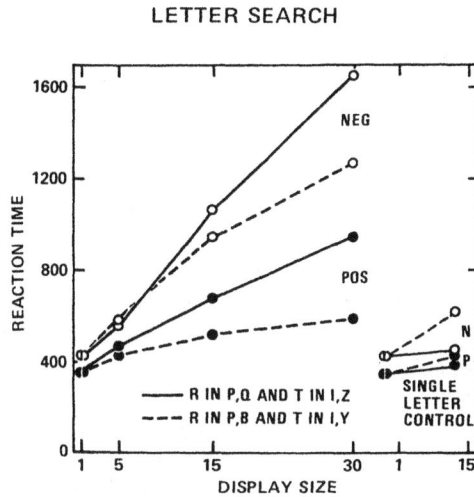

FIG. 6. Search times in Experiment IV.

tively. Errors averaged 3.5% and were less than 7% in every condition except the positives in the conjunction condition with display size 30, where they increased to 15.5% false negatives. These errors were on average 539 msec slower than the correct detections in the same blocks and conditions. Thus if subjects had continued to search until they found the target, the mean search time in this condition would have been 84 msec longer (0.155×539), improving the linearity of the function.

The ratio of positive to negative slopes differed for the conjunction and the similarity conditions: for the conjunctions it was 0.45, which is close to half and suggests a serial self-terminating search. For the similarity condition it was much lower (0.26), as it was with the single feature color

TABLE 3

Linear Regressions of Search Times against Display Size in Experiment IV

		Positives		Negatives	
		Slope	Intercept	Slope	Intercept
Conjunction	T/IZ	12.2	363	34.7	349
	R/PQ	27.2	362	52.1	388
Similarity	T/IY	5.3	363	18.1	417
	R/PB	9.7	403	40.5	446
Heterogeneity control	T/PQ	4.9	340	20.5	386

or shape targets in Experiment I, suggesting again that different processes determined the positive and negative decisions.

The control conditions, in which subjects searched for the same target letters in a background containing only one type of distractor, reversed the relative difficulty of the two conditions. The conjunction controls, R/Q and T/Z, were faster than the similarity controls, R/B and T/Y ($t(7) =$ 3.69, $p < .02$). The effects of similarity were therefore in the predicted direction, when they were not competing with the conjunction effect.

The heterogeneity control condition, T/PQ, gave results very like those obtained in the similarity condition, T/YI. We can therefore reject the alternative explanation of the conjunction results, which attributed them ʼ,ʼ greater heterogeneity of the distractors.

Finally, the pilot data on three additional sets of conjunction letters (N/VH, E/FL, Q/OK) and similarity letters (N/VW, E/FT and Q/OG) gave results that were clearly in the same direction. With display size 30 (the only one tested), we obtained the following mean times: conjunction positives 1330; conjunction negatives 1754; similarity positives 674; similarity negatives 974.

Discussion

We suggested that letter search would be serial and self-terminating if the particular sets of distractor and target letters were composed of perceptually separable features which could be wrongly recombined to yield conjunction errors. Otherwise search could be parallel (although not necessarily with unlimited capacity and no interference). The predicted pattern was therefore a linear increase with display size in search times for the R/PQ and T/ZI sets, with positive slopes equaling half the negative slopes, and either a flat function or a nonlinearly increasing function for the R/PB and T/YI sets. The results on positive trials were consistent with these predictions. On negative trials, no departures from linearity reached significance, although the functions relating search time to display size were less steep and less linear for the similarity than for the conjunction letter sets. Most interesting is the interaction between the single distractor controls (P/Q, P/B, T/Z, T/Y) and the two-distractor experimental conditions (P/QR, P/BR, T/ZI, T/YI): with the single distractor controls, search times were clearly slower and more affected by display size in the similarity conditions (P/B and T/Y), while with the two-distractor displays the conjunction conditions (P/QR and T/ZI) were much slower. Thus the situation was crucially changed in the absence of a unique identifying feature for the target and when, according to our theory, the possibility of conjunction errors was introduced.

There was a large overall difference in the rate of search between the R and the T sets. This makes the replication of the pattern of results across the two sets all the more striking. The change from linear functions with conjunctions to nonlinear functions with the similarity controls again appears to be independent of the level of difficulty, over a wide range; the search rate is approximately doubled for T compared to R and is about as fast for the T conjunctions as for the R similarity set. We cannot therefore attribute the difference between conjunctions and similarity controls to the overall level of difficulty or to a general demand for capacity.

It is interesting that our hypothesis about the role of focal attention in integrating separable features appears to hold not only with arbitrary pairings of colors and shapes, or with unfamiliar schematic faces (Treisman et al., 1977), but also with highly familiar, potentially "unitized" stimuli like letters. These results suggest that it may be crucial in experiments using letters or digits to distinguish sets which could form illusory conjunctions from sets which could not.

The finding that the similarity or confusability of individual items is not the only, or even the most powerful variable controlling search throws doubt on the adequacy of models such as those of Gardner (1973) and Estes (1972). The effects that have been attributed to similarity or confusability could in some cases have been due to a greater risk of conjunction errors; "similar" letters are more likely to share separable features, which could be interchanged to form different letters. These effects need to be tested separately before appropriate explanations can be developed.

Wolford's perturbation model (1975), like ours, specifically allows the possibility of conjunction errors. It could therefore predict lower accuracy for the conjunction condition, if displays were brief and response times unlimited. It is less easy, however, to derive from Wolford's model the prediction that search times should be linearly related to display size only for conjunction targets, in a task in which the displays remained physically present until the subject responded, or to see why they should contrast with the negatively accelerated functions for similar letters, even across very different levels of overall difficulty.

Although long-term familiarity with letters seems not to eliminate the conjunction effect, specific practice in particular search tasks may do so. Shiffrin and Schneider (1977) found that subjects could learn to search in parallel for a particular set of letters, provided that targets and distractors never interchanged their roles. In terms of our model, two explanations could be offered: Either subjects within the particular experimental context eventually set up unitary detectors for each of the targets, eliminating the need to check conjunctions; or they eventually learned a set of disjunctive features which distinguished the targets from the distractors (e.g., even for the very similar sets of letters GMFP and CNHD the tail of the G, the right-sloping diagonal of the M, the parallel horizontals of the F, and the small closed curve of the P are a possible set of disjunctive features which could function as the disjunctive "blue" or "curved" features did in our Experiment I). This account could be tested by seeing whether, after extended practice, the targets function as unitary features in the other paradigms we have studied, for example texture segregation (Experiment V) and target localization (Experiment VIII).

An apparent difficulty for the integration model arises from the flat functions of search time against display size obtained when subjects search for letters in digits or digits in letters (Jonides & Gleitman, 1972; Shiffrin & Schneider, 1977). It should be stressed that our model predicts serial search only when targets must be identified by specifying conjunctions of features, and when no disjunctive set of features can be found that discriminate targets from distractors. There may be disjunctive features which distinguish most digits from most letters: for example digits tend to be narrower, asymmetrical, open to the left, and to have shorter contours than letters. However, Jonides and Gleitman obtained the category effect using a single physical target O and calling it either "zero" or "oh". The objective features of the target must have been the same here, whether search was within or between categories; but, as Gleitman and Jonides (1976) point out, subjects could have adopted different strategies in the two conditions. The present analysis suggests that subjects may have used a single feature for the between-category condition (e.g., symmetry for oh in digits), and a conjunction of features (e.g., closed and curved) for the within-category conditions. White (1977) has shown that the category effect disappears when digits and letters are typed in a number of different type-faces, so that their physical features are less consistent and offer less reliable cues to discriminate the categories.

EXPERIMENT V

The next experiment investigates the "preattentive" segregation of groups and textures, which could guide the subsequent direction of attention. Early detection of boundaries is a primary requirement in perception (Neisser, 1967). Before we can identify an object, we must separate it from its background. If texture segregation does depend on the early parallel registration of homogeneities, integration theory predicts easy segregation when areas differ in one or more simple, separable features, and not when they differ only in conjunctions of features. We tested this prediction using different arrangements of color and shape (chosen again as clear exemplars of separable dimensions). We used the same elements in each condition (O_{red}, V_{red}, O_{blue}, and V_{blue}), but grouped them differently in the three conditions. In the feature conditions the boundary divided red items from blue ones or Os from Vs, while in the conjunction condition, it divided O_{red} and V_{blue} from V_{red} and O_{blue}.

Method

Stimuli. These were 3 by 5-in cards with stenciled red and blue letters arranged in a square matrix of five rows by five columns. The items were red and blue Os and Vs, about

0.7 cm high and wide, their centers spaced 1.0 cm apart both vertically and horizontally. The task used was card sorting; the visual angle subtended by the letters was therefore variable but averaged about 1.3°. The matrix was divided into two groups of letters by an imaginary horizontal or vertical boundary which divided two rows or columns from the other three. The boundary was placed equally often on the left and right sides of the middle column and immediately above or below the middle row. In the color condition, all the items to one side of the boundary were O_{red} and V_{red} (randomly mixed but in as near equal numbers as possible) and all the items to the other side were O_{blue} and V_{blue}. In the shape condition, the division was between O_{red} and O_{blue} on one side and V_{red} and V_{blue} on the other. In the conjunction condition, it was between O_{red} and V_{blue} on one side and O_{blue} and V_{red} on the other. Twenty-four cards were made for each condition, three different randomly chosen exemplars for each of the eight combinations of four possible boundary positions and two possible allocations of items to one or other side of the boundary.

In addition 24 control cards were made, containing an outline square the same size as the letter matrix with one horizontal or vertical line drawn across the square, equally often in each of the four positions of the boundary in the letter matrices.

Procedure. The task was to sort the packs of cards as rapidly and accurately as possible into two piles, one containing cards with a horizontal and one with a vertical boundary. Each subject sorted the line pack as often as was necessary to reach an asymptote (defined as a mean decrease of less than 1 sec over four consecutive pairs of trials). The times taken for these last five trials were used as the data for analysis. The line pack was designed to ensure prelearning of the response allocation and of the physical responses, and to provide a baseline sorting time, for a task which presumably matched the experimental task in all respects except the requirement to segregate elements.

Each subject then sorted the three experimental packs to the same criterion, completing one pack before moving on to the next. The data to be analyzed were again the mean times taken on the last five trials in each condition. The packs were held so that the Vs were horizontal and half the time pointed left and half the time right (to reduce the chance that individual cards would be learned and recognized). The order in which the three experimental packs were sorted was counterbalanced across subjects. After completing the experimental packs, subjects sorted the line pack again five times, to control for any further learning of nonperceptual task components. Subjects were encouraged to make as few errors as possible, and to correct any that they did make. This occurred rarely, once or twice in every five trials.

Subjects. The eight subjects were high school and University students and two faculty members, ages 14 to 44. Four subjects sorted the cards with the pack face up and four sorted them with the pack face down, turning each card over in turn. The change to face down presentation for the last four subjects was made to ensure that differences in sorting time for the first four subjects were not concealed by a floor effect, produced by subjects processing one card at the same time as manually placing its predecessor.

Results and Discussion

The difference between the two feature packs and the conjunction pack was qualitative and immediately obvious. The division between the two areas was highly salient with the feature packs and not at all with the conjunction pack. This difference was reflected in the mean times taken to sort the packs, which were as follows: line 14.5 sec, color 15.9 sec, shape 16.2 sec; and conjunctions 24.4 sec for the subjects who sorted face-up, and line 24.6 sec, color 25.1 sec, shape 25.6 sec, and conjunction 35.2 sec for the subjects who sorted face-down. The mean of the five asymptotic trials at the beginning and the five at the end of the experiment were used for the line pack in analyzing the results. The change to face-down presentation had no effect on the sorting time differences between the packs. An ANOVA was therefore carried out on the differences between the experimental packs and the line pack for all eight subjects. It showed a significant difference between packs ($F(2,14) = 42.2, p < .001$). A Newman–Keuls test showed that the conjunction condition differed significantly from the color and shape conditions, but these did not differ from each other. The color and shape conditions did not differ (by t tests) from the line control. With more subjects, the differences between color, shape, and line conditions might have proved significant. Certainly their relative difficulty could be manipulated by varying the discriminability of the single feature colors and shapes used. However, this issue is irrelevant to our present concern, which was to show differences between conjunction and single feature tasks when the discriminability of the individual features was identical for the conjunction and for the feature cards.

If the time taken to sort the line pack represents the shared nonperceptual components of the task plus some nominal or baseline perceptual time, any increments with the other packs should represent the time taken to discover the texture boundary with each type of stimulus set. The increment in the single feature sets was very small and not statistically significant. On the conjunction set it averaged 430 msec per card. This is a large difference, suggesting that the boundary cannot be directly perceived in the conjunction condition and has to be inferred from attentive scanning of several individual items. Most subjects spontaneously developed the same strategy for the conjunction condition; they looked for all the instances of one of the four conjunctions (e.g., O_{red}) and located the boundary which segregated those from the rest. The scanning rate of 39 msec/item found for the easy conjunctions in Experiment II would allow up to 11 items per card to be checked before the boundary was located, i.e., nearly half the display of 25 items. The results are therefore consistent with a complete failure of preattentive texture segregation with the conjunction displays.

EXPERIMENT VI

Experiment V showed that two spatially grouped sets of items can be perceptually segregated on the basis of a simple, consistent, feature difference, despite variation within each group on another feature. Thus texture segregation can be mediated by a consistent difference in color despite irrelevant variation in shape, or by a consistent difference in shape despite irrelevant variation in color.

The advantage of the feature packs could, however, derive from the fact that only one dimension was relevant and items on the same side of the boundary were homogeneous on that dimension; the conjunction pack, on the other hand, required attention to both dimensions. The next experiment was designed to discover whether this could fully or partly explain the difference in the ease of perceptual segregation. Can texture segregation still be mediated by feature differences when the criterion is a disjunctive one, i.e., half the items on either side of the boundary differ in shape and share color and half differ in color and share shape? The feature displays again contained four different types of items: those on one side of the boundary were O_{red} and Π_{green} and those on the other were O_{blue} and V_{green}. The difference across the boundary was therefore no longer consistent and unidimensional.

Method

Stimuli. These were identical to those in Experiment V, except that the shape and the color packs were replaced by one disjunctive feature pack in which the items were O_{red} and Π_{green} on one side of the boundary and O_{blue} and V_{green} on the other.

Procedure. This new disjunctive feature pack, the previous conjunction pack, and the previous line pack were sorted as in Experiment V by eight new subjects. They held the pack face down. The order was counterbalanced across subjects and again each subject both started and finished with the line pack. The criterion for asymptotic performance was again a mean decrease of less than 1 sec across four successive pairs of trials, but in addition a minimum of eight trials per condition was required. The data analyzed were the means for the last five trials in each condition.

Subjects. The eight subjects were students, research assistants, and one faculty member at the University of British Columbia, ages between 16 and 44.

Results

The mean sorting times on the last five trials in each condition were 24.2 sec for the line pack, 26.9 sec for the disjunctive feature pack, and 32.9 sec for the conjunction pack. Analysis of variance showed a significant effect of conditions ($F(2,14) = 42.3, p < .001$), and a Newman–Keuls test showed that each of the three conditions differed significantly from the others ($p < .05$ for line and feature, $p < 0.01$ for conjunctions compared to line and to feature). We also did an ANOVA on both Experiments V and VI, taking the differences between the line condition and the feature and conjunction conditions. For the feature condition in Experiment V we used the mean of the shape and color packs. The analysis showed a significant effect of conditions ($F(1,14) = 102.8, p < .001$) and an interaction between conditions and experiments, just bordering on significance ($F(1,14) = 4.48, p = .0527$). This interaction reflects the greater difference between feature and conjunction packs when the features were defined uniquely (by either a shape or a color difference) than when they were disjunctively defined.

Discussion

Disjunctive features appear slightly less effective than single features in defining a texture boundary. In Experiment VI, the disjunctive feature pack was slightly but significantly slower than the line control (a within-subjects comparison), while there was no difference between single features and line control in Experiment V. However, the mean difference between the two single feature conditions and the disjunctive feature condition is small, only 1.5 sec a pack or 61 msec a card. In both experiments, conjunctions are very much less effective than features in defining a texture boundary. Experiment VI shows that the greater heterogeneity of items in the conjunction condition, and the relevance of two dimensions rather than a single dimension can explain only a small fraction of the difference between features and conjunctions in Experiment V. The ease of feature segregation certainly varies to some extent, both with the number and with the discriminability of the relevant features. However, the important conclusion from our data is that, regardless of the discriminability of their component features, conjunctions alone do not give rise to perceptual grouping.

EXPERIMENT VII

The next experiment investigates texture segregation with letters, to see whether the distinction between features and conjunctions is equally crucial when the features are local components of more complex shapes rather than values on different dimensions.

Method

Stimuli. The displays were 5 × 5 matrices containing four different letters, grouped by pairs on either side of a vertical or horizontal boundary, as in Experiments V and VI. The letters were all black rather than colored. When presented tachistoscopically, each letter subtended 0.8 × 0.6° and the complete matrix subtended 5.0 × 5.0°.

We chose pairs of similar letters (PR, EF, OQ, and XK) and varied the combinations in which they were presented. In two single feature conditions there were letters containing short diagonal lines (Q and/or R) on one side of the boundary and not on the other (PO/RQ and EO/FQ). In two conjunction conditions, on the other hand, there were no simple features distinguishing the letters on one side of the boundary from those on the other (PQ/RO and FK/EX). Comparing the feature and the conjunction conditions, the similarity of letters across the boundary is approximately matched according to confusion matrices. There were 24 cards in each set, 3 for each position of the boundary and each allocation of the particular letters to one side or the other of the boundary.

If subjects focus on groups of items rather than single items and process groups in parallel, we predict feature interchanges both within the focus of attention and outside it. This should make the PQ and RO sets indistinguishable and the FK and EX sets highly similar. The PO and RQ sets and the FQ and EO sets, however, remain distinguishable at the feature level as well as at the letter level. Texture segregation should therefore be easier with these displays than with the others.

Procedure. The cards were shown in a tachistoscope. Subjects were shown a fixation point for a 1-sec warning interval, followed by the array, which terminated when the response was made. The task was to press one key if the boundary was horizontal and the other if it was vertical, as rapidly as possible without making many errors. Each subject was run for two sessions in each condition with the order of conditions reversed in the second session. The order of conditions was also counterbalanced across subjects, as far as possible with four conditions and six subjects. Subjects were given a few practice trials in each condition before each set of experimental trials began.

Subjects. The six subjects (five men and one woman) were from the Oxford subject panel and had previously taken part in Experiments I or IV, or in both.

Results and Discussion

One subject gave very anomalous results on the two "single feature" sets (PO/QR and FQ/EO); his mean times on these two sets were 5.7 and 7.4 *SD* deviations above the mean of the other five subjects and did not differ from his mean times on the conjunction sets (PQ/OR and FK/EX). For these sets his mean was within the range of the other subjects (about 1.3 *SD* above their mean). He appears to have used a different strategy from the other five subjects on the feature sets and his results will be discussed separately.

The mean times and error rates for the other five subjects were as follows: for the feature sets, PO/RQ 779 msec (7.9%) and FQ/EO 799 msec (5.4%); for the conjunction sets, PQ/RO 978 msec (9.2%), FK/EX 1114 msec (7.9%). The conditions differed significantly in mean response times ($F(3,12) = 3.71$, $p < .05$) but not in error rates. Condition PQ/RO was significantly slower than both PO/RQ ($t(4) = 6.8, p < .01$) and FQ/EO ($t(4) = 5.08$, $p < .01$), but did not differ significantly from the other conjunction condition FK/EX. (These conclusions also held when the sixth subject was included, but only at $p < .05$.)

It seems that the critical variable determining texture segregation with these letter sets was, again, whether the boundary divided areas differing in a single feature or only in a conjunction of features. The fact that one subject failed to show any feature advantage suggests, however, that a choice of strategy may be possible. Subjects may respond to the feature representation or only to the fully identified letters. The one very slow subject showed no difference in latency to the feature and to the conjunction sets. He appears to have treated all displays in the same way using only the conjunction level. Thus the feature level may not be automatically accessed by all subjects.

Julesz (1975) proposed that texture segregation is determined only by first- or second-order regularities, those that can be registered by the frequencies of points and of dipoles, and that higher-order dependencies can be seen only with careful scrutiny, if at all. His dipole model, like the integration model, would predict that different conjunctions of features should fail to segregate one area from another. The approach to the problem is different, however: Julesz offers an objective, physical specification of the properties which, he believes, allow texture segregation; we, on the other hand, try to define them by relating them to inferred properties of the perceptual system. Thus we predict texture segregation from the presence of separable feature analyzers, inferred from the converging results of other psychological, and perhaps physiological, experiments. If the hypothesis is correct, any feature which meets other criteria for separability should also produce texture segregation, however simple or complex that feature might objectively appear, and however it has been acquired (innately or through experience). Julesz (Note 1) has very recently discovered evidence for three specific higher-order patterns of dependency which also mediate texture segregation. The particular patterns involved are quasi-colinear dots, angles, and closed versus open shapes, all of which seem strong candidates for "separable featurehood." It will be interesting to see whether these three patterns also allow parallel search, form illusory conjunctions, control selective attention, and show independence of identity and location judgements.

EXPERIMENT VIII

The last two experiments test a hypothesis which goes further than the theory requires, although it follows naturally from the central assertions we have made. The hypothesis is that precise information about spatial location may not be available at the feature level which registers the whole display in parallel. Perceptual tasks in which subjects must locate as well as detect or identify an item may require focal attention. When attention is prevented, we suggest features are free floating with respect to one another; they may also be free floating spatially, in the sense that their individual locations are not directly accessible. We can of course rapidly find the location of a detected target, perhaps by "homing in" on it with focal attention. But the hypothesis is that this requires an additional operation. On the other hand, since we claim that focal attention is a prerequisite for the identification of conjunctions, these could not be spatially free floating in the same sense. Locating a conjunction is a necessary condition for its detection and further analysis.

Experiment VIII tests this possibility by looking at the dependency between reports of identity and reports of location on each trial. For conjunctions we predict that the dependency should be high, that if the subject correctly identifies a conjunction he must have located it, in order to focus attention on it and integrate its features. On the other hand, it should be possible to detect or identify a feature without necessarily knowing where it is.

Method

Stimuli. The displays consisted of two rows of six colored letters, subtending approximately 0.8° each, with the whole array taking a rectangular area of 7.1° (horizontal) × 2.3° (vertical). Each display contained one target item in any of eight inner positions, i.e., excluding the two positions at each end of each row. The distractors were O_{pink} and X_{blue} in approximately equal numbers and distributed pseudo-randomly within the available array positions. In the disjunctive feature condition, the possible targets were H (in pink or blue) and the color orange (in the shape of an X or an O). In the conjunction condition the possible targets were X_{pink} and O_{blue}. Each of the two targets appeared equally often in each of the eight positions. There were 32 different arrays in each condition; each could be inverted to give effectively 64 different arrays per condition.

Subjects. The six male subjects were drawn from the same Oxford pool as those in the other experiments. Four of them had taken part in one or more of the earlier experiments.

Procedure. The dependent variable in this experiment was accuracy with brief exposures, rather than response time. The stimuli were presented tachistoscopically and each trial was initiated by the subject pressing a key. At the beginning of each trial, subjects viewed a masking field, which consisted of colored segments of the target and distractor letters scattered at random over a rectangular area slightly larger than that of the letter array (8.0° horizontal × 3.6° vertical). When the subject pressed a key, the mask was replaced by a central black fixation dot which was displayed for 1 sec and was itself then replaced by the array. The array was in view for a time determined by the experimenter (see below) and was then replaced by the original masking field.

Subjects recorded their own responses; in the feature condition they used the codes H and O for the H and orange targets, respectively, and in the conjunction condition the codes X and 'O' for the X_{pink} and O_{blue} targets. Each response was recorded in one cell of a 4 × 2 matrix, whose eight cells corresponded to the eight possible target positions. After each trial subjects told the experimenter what they had written, so that the experimenter could keep account of the error rate and give error feedback.

The presentation times of the arrays were chosen so that in each condition the target was correctly identified on 80% of the trials. A preliminary testing session, prior to the main experiment, served to obtain an initial estimate of this value for each subject in each condition. After every 16 trials the error rate for identifications was checked, and the presentation time adjusted if necessary to keep the number of correct responses close to 80%.

The conjunction and feature conditions were presented in separate blocks of 64 trials each, and on each of 2 days subjects were given one block of trials for each condition. Half of the subjects started with the conjunction and half with the feature condition. For each subject the order of conditions on the second day was the reverse of that on the first.

Results

The mean exposure durations needed to maintain the proportion of correct identity judgments at about 0.8 were 414 msec for the conjunctions and 65 msec for the features. This very large difference is consistent with the hypothesis of serial search for conjunctions and parallel search for features.

The main point of interest concerns the conditional probability of reporting the target's identity correctly given that the location was wrong and the conditional probability of reporting the location correctly given that the identity was wrong. We analyzed separately the cases where the location was correct, where an adjacent location error was made (displaced by one place horizontally or vertically from the correct position), and where a distant location error was made (all other location errors). Initially we also separately classified diagonal errors (displaced by one place diagonally), but these proved to be very similar to the distant errors and were therefore grouped with them. We carried out the analysis separately for the four inner and the four outer locations in the 2 × 8 matrix, since the chance probabilities of guessing adjacent and distant locations are different for inner and outer locations. The conditional probabilities were slightly higher for inner than for outer locations, but the pattern of results and the conclusions were essentially the same; we therefore report only the pooled data. The upper half of Table 4 gives the conditional probabilities that the target was correct given each of the three categories of location response. Chance performance would be .5. For conjunction trials on which a distant location error occurred, target identification was random, as predicted by our model. For feature targets, it was well above chance, again as predicted ($t(5) = 7.0$, $p < .001$).

The chance level of performance is less clear for report of location, since neither the distribution of errors nor the distribution of missed targets was random for every subject. In order to control for bias on inner versus outer locations and top versus bottom rows, we compared the probability of reporting the correct location with the probability of reporting its mirror image location. The median probability of correctly locating a target that was wrongly identified was at chance for conjunctions (.16 compared to .15). For the feature targets, subjects were a little more likely to place the incorrectly identified target in the correct than in the mirror image location (.16 compared to .06). The data for each subject were few, however, and the difference seems due to an unusually low conditional probability for the mirror image location. The results will be further discussed together with those of Experiment IX.

EXPERIMENT IX

There is a problem in interpreting the findings of Experiment VIII: the duration required for 80% correct target identification was much greater for the conjunctions than for the feature targets. It is possible that this large difference in exposure duration affected performance in some qualitative way. We therefore replicated the experiment using equal presentation times for features and conjunctions. The times were chosen separately for each subject in each block, in order to ensure performance that

TABLE 4

Median Probabilities of Reporting the Target Identity Correctly Given Different Categories of Location Responses

		Location response			
		Correct	Adjacent	Distant	Overall
Experiment VIII	Conjunction	0.930	0.723	0.500	0.793
	Feature	0.897	0.821	0.678	0.786
Experiment IX	Conjunction	0.840	0.582	0.453	0.587
	Feature	0.979	0.925	0.748	0.916

was above chance in the conjunction condition, but included sufficient errors in the feature condition for analysis to be possible.

Method

Stimuli. The same stimulus cards were used as in Experiment VIII. They were presented this time in a Cambridge two-field tachistoscope and were preceded as well as succeeded by the mask. There was no warning interval and the exposure was triggered by the subject pressing a button.

Procedure. The same procedure was followed as in Experiment VIII, except for the following changes. Subjects completed three blocks of 32 trials each in the conjunction condition and three in the feature condition in the first of two sessions, and then either three of four blocks in each condition in the second session. Half the subjects started with three feature blocks and half with three conjunction blocks; the order was reversed in the second session. The first block in the first session used an exposure duration of 150 msec. At the end of the first block, the following rules were followed: if there were fewer than 19 trials with correct responses of either target or location, the duration was increased to 200 msec for the next block; if there were fewer than 19 trials with errors on either target or location, the exposure duration was reduced to 100 msec. After the second and third blocks the same rules were followed except that the second reduction (if two were needed) was to 60 msec. No increase beyond 200 msec was made. One reduction to 40 msec was made for one subject. Within each session, the three blocks in the second condition were exactly matched for exposure durations to the three blocks in the first condition. The same procedure for selecting exposure durations was followed in the second session, with the order of conditions reversed; thus exposure durations were calibrated for the feature condition in one session and for the conjunction condition in the other. The mean exposure duration across all subjects and blocks was 117 msec.

Subjects. The six subjects were high school students, University students, and research assistants at the University of British Columbia, ages between 16 and 23. They were paid $3 for each 1-hr session.

Results and Discussion

The conditional probabilities of identifying the target given different types of location response were calculated in the same way as those of Experiment VIII; the results are given in the lower half of Table 4. While the absolute frequencies of correct identification and localization were very different from those in Experiment VIII—lower, as expected, for conjunctions and higher for features—the conditional probabilities follow a very similar pattern. As before, we also analyzed the conditional probability of locating a wrongly identified target in the correct compared to the mirror image location. This time the difference was significant neither for conjunctions (.11 compared to .13) nor for features (.14 compared to .09).

The predictions are in fact even better borne out with matched exposure durations than with matched target identification rates. The results rule out the possibility that the large difference in exposure durations in Experiment VIII induced the different strategies for locating and identifying conjunctions and features. The difference seem to be inherent in the tasks, as integration theory predicts. We can therefore discuss the results of both experiments together.

Feature-integration theory claims that conjunction targets cannot be identified without focal attention. It seems likely that in order to focus attention on an item, we must spatially localize it and direct attention to its location. If this hypothesis is correct, it follows that when the subject failed to locate the target, the conditional probability of identifying a conjunction should be at chance (.5). The results of both experiments are consistent with this prediction for trials on which distant location errors were made. Thus, at least approximate perception of location appears to be a necessary condition for the identification of conjunction targets. Adjacent location errors were, however, associated with better than chance identification of targets. Some of these errors most likely reflect failures of memory. However, the integration model is consistent with some degree of perceptual uncertainty between adjacent locations, even when a conjunction target is correctly detected. We claim that focused attention is necessary for accurate identification of conjunctions; but it may not be necessary on all trials to narrow the focus down to a single item. If the focused area includes adjacent items which share one feature and differ on the other, it follows in our task that one of the two must be a target. Thus a proportion of conjunction trials could result in correct identification despite a location error of one position. With nonadjacent location errors, identification would have to be at chance, as in fact it proved to be. Similarly, the results of both experiments indicate that location reports are at chance when conjunction targets are not correctly identified. Thus, when chance successes are removed, a correct or approximately correct localization response is both necessary and sufficient for correct identification of the conjunction target.

The feature condition shows a different pattern, which is also consistent with integration theory. In both experiments, target identification was well above chance, even when major location errors were made. Corrected for guessing, the data suggest that the identity of the target was correctly perceived on perhaps 40% of trials on which the location was completely misjudged. Thus the identity of features can be registered not only without attention but also without any spatial information about their location. The results suggest also that focused attention may be necessary not only to ensure correct identification of conjunctions, but also to localize single features accurately. Feature localization is in fact a special kind of conjunction task—a conjunction of feature and spatial location— and our findings suggest that feature-location conjunctions may require the same conditions for accurate perception as seem necessary for conjunctions of other features.

Location errors for feature targets were not randomly distributed. On a large number of trials, subjects had partial information about the location of correctly identified features. The theoretical account would be as follows: On trials when attention happened to be focused on or around the target, or when the subject had time to move his attention toward the detected target, we should expect him also to localize it, either accurately or partially. On trials when his attention was distributed rather than focused or when it was focused on the wrong items, the target could still be correctly identified, but its location would be guessed.

With a minor exception for feature targets in Experiment VIII, location responses were generally at chance when the target was wrongly identified. It appears that we cannot normally locate an item which differs from a field of distractors without also knowing at least on which dimension (color or shape) that difference exists. This is consistent with the idea that we form separate, parallel representations for the colors and shapes present in a display, and that detection of an odd item must be specific to one such representation. According to the theory, the registration of unlocalized features in separate maps permits illusory conjunctions to be formed from incorrectly integrated features. The serial focusing of attention on items in the display, which is required to ensure the correct identification of conjunction targets, induces a dependence of identity information on location.

Our finding that feature targets can be identified without being even approximately localized seems inconsistent with a new account of visual attention by Posner (1978). Posner suggests that the orientation of attention to the location of a target is a necessary prior condition for conscious detection in the visual domain. The main support for this proposal is the observation of large benefits of spatial precuing in vision and the absence of such effects in audition and touch. However, a demonstration of an advantage of appropriate orienting does not imply that orienting invariably occurs prior to detection. In another experiment using both visual and tactile stimuli, Posner found a greater benefit from precuing the modality of the stimulus than from precuing its location. This is consistent with the hypothesis that stimuli are initially processed by separate specific feature detectors rather than registered as global objects in a general cross-modal representation of space. Posner concludes from his data, as we do from ours, that "the phenomenological unity of objects in space is imposed relatively late in the nervous system."

GENERAL CONCLUSIONS

The experiments have tested most of the predictions we made and their results offer converging evidence for the feature-integration theory of attention. While any one set of data, taken alone, could no doubt be explained in other ways, the fact that all were derived from one theory and tested in a number of different paradigms should lend them more weight when taken together than any individual finding would have on its own.

To summarize the conclusions: it seems that we can detect and identify separable features in parallel across a display (within the limits set by acuity, discriminability, and lateral interference); that this early, parallel, process of feature registration mediates texture segregation and figure-ground grouping; that locating any individual feature requires an additional operation; that if attention is diverted or overloaded, illusory conjunctions may occur (Treisman et al., 1977). Conjunctions, on the other hand, require focal attention to be directed serially to each relevant location; they do not mediate texture segregation, and they cannot be identified without also being spatially localized. The results offer a new set of criteria for determining which features are perceptually "separable," which may be added to the criteria listed by Garner. It will be important to see whether they converge on the same candidates for unitary features, the basic elements of the perceptual language.

The findings also suggest a convergence between two perceptual phenomena—parallel detection of visual targets and perceptual grouping or segregation. Both appear to depend on a distinction at the level of separable features. Neither requires focal attention, so both may precede its operation. This means that both could be involved in the control of attention. The number of items receiving focal attention at any moment of time can vary. Visual attention, like a spotlight or zoom lens, can be used over a small area with high resolution or spread over a wider area with some loss of detail (Eriksen & Hoffman, 1972). We can extend the analogy in the present context to suggest that attention can either be narrowed to focus on a single feature, when we need to see what other features are present and form an object, or distributed over a whole group of items which share a relevant feature. Our hypothesis is that illusory conjunctions occur either outside the spotlight of focal attention, or within it, if the spotlight happens to contain interchangeable features (e.g., more than one color and more than one shape), but they will not occur across its boundary. It follows that search for a conjunction target could be mediated by a serial scan of *groups* of items rather than individual items, whenever the display contains groups of items among which no illusory conjunctions can form. In a display divided into 15 red Os on the left and 15 blue Xs on the right, we are very unlikely to scan serially through each of the 30 items to find a blue O, even though it is a conjunction target. We may need to focus attention only twice in order to exclude the risk of illusory conjunctions. By treating each half of the display separately, we can convert the task into two successive feature search tasks, for blue on the left and for O on the right. The time taken should therefore be no longer than the time taken to search through just two items.

This discussion, however, raises a further question, since in a sense the conjunction results are paradoxical. The problem they pose is that any conjunction search could, in principle, be achieved by two parallel feature checks, one selecting, for example, all the green items and the second checking these for the presence of a T. Results with the disjunctive feature targets suggest that either of these operations should be possible without serial processing or focal attention. We have to explain, therefore, why the two operations cannot be applied to all relevant items in parallel when combined. Presumably the reason is that attention cannot be focused simultaneously on a number of different locations, when these are interleaved with other locations to be excluded. Kahneman and Henik (1977) showed that subjects were much worse at reporting the red letters in a mixed display of red and blue letters when these were alternated in a checkerboard arrangement then when they were spatially separated into homogeneous groups. This suggests that selective attention to particular sets of items (e.g., all red items) must be mediated by attention to their spatial locations and cannot be directly controlled by their color. Moreover, there must be limits to the number and perhaps the complexity of the spatial areas on which the "spotlight" of attention can be simultaneously focused. The nature of these limits needs clarification; they could be set by simple parameters such as a requirement that the area be bounded by convex or straight edges, or by more complex Gestalt properties, such as symmetry or good continuation.

What problems does the integration model raise for our everyday perception of objects, complex scenes, words, and sentences in reading? Can we reconcile our theory with the apparent speed and richness of information processing that we constantly experience? Perhaps this richness at the level of objects or scenes is largely an informed hallucination. We can certainly register a rich array of features in parallel, and probably do this along a number of dimensions at once. But if we apply more stringent tests to see how accurate and detailed we are in putting features together without prior knowledge or redundancy in the scene, the results are much less impressive (e.g. Biederman, Glass, & Stacy, 1973; Rock, Halper, & Clayton, 1972).

It is of interest to note that some patients with visual agnosia appear to have difficulties specifically in assembling the different components or properties of objects. For example, one patient (Critchley, 1964) described his difficulty as follows: "At first I saw the front part—it looked like a fountain pen. Then it looked like a knife because it was so sharp, but I thought it could not be a knife because it was green. Then I saw the spokes . . ." etc. Another patient commented "Previously I'd have said 'well, of course that's a carnation—no doubt about it—it's quite evident. Now I recognize it in a more scientific fashion. To get it right I've got to assemble it.'" Gardner (1975) proposes an account of one type of agnosia, which seems closely related to the feature integration hypothesis: he says "if we assume that the ability to recognize configurations such as faces and objects requires the integration over a brief interval of a number of visual elements, then an impairment in simultaneous synthesis—in the capacity to pull the relevant elements together into a coherent unity— would be suffcient to explain the disorder." The suggestion in fact goes back to Liepmann's "disjunctive agnosia" (1908), which he believed resulted from the "fractionation of representations into primary elements" (Hecaen & Albert, 1978). Finally, Luria's account (1972) of "the man with the shattered mind" suggests a defect in retaining conjunctions in memory as well as in perception. His patient says "I'm in a kind of fog all the time, like a heavy half-sleep. Whatever I do remember is scattered, broken down into disconnected bits and pieces."

To conclude: the feature-integration theory suggests that we become aware of unitary objects, in two different ways—through focal attention, or through top-down processing. We may not know on any particular occasion which has occurred, or which has contributed most to what we see. In normal conditions, the two routes operate together, but in extreme conditions we may be able to show either of the two operating almost independently of the other. The first route to object identification depends on focal attention, directed serially to different locations, to integrate the features registered within the same spatio-temporal "spotlight" into a unitary percept. This statement is of course highly oversimplified; it begs many questions, such as how we deal with spatially overlapping objects and how we register the relationships between features which distinguish many otherwise identical objects. These problems belong to a theory of object recognition and are beyond the scope of this paper.

The second way in which we may "identify" objects, when focused attention is prevented by brief exposure or overloading, is through top-down processing. In a familiar context, likely objects can be predicted. Their presence can then be checked by matching their disjunctive features to those in the display, without also checking how they are spatially conjoined. If the context is misleading, this route to object recognition should give rise to errors; but in the highly redundant and familiar environments in which we normally operate, it should seldom lead us astray. When the environment is less predictable or the task requires conjunctions to be specified, we are in fact typically much less efficient. Searching for a face, even as familiar as one's own child, is a school photograph, can be a painstakingly serial process and focused attention is certainly recommended in proof reading and instrument monitoring.

REFERENCES

Biederman, I., Glass, A. L., & Stacy, E. W. Searching for objects in real-world scenes. *Journal of Experimental Psychology*, 1973, **97**, 22–27.

Corteen, R. S., & Wood, B. Autonomic responses to shock-associated words in an unattended channel. *Journal of Experimental Psychology*, 1972, **94**, 308–313.

Critchley, M. The problem of visual agnosia. *Journal of Neurological Sciences,* 1964, **1,** 274−290.

Cutting, J. E. Auditory and linguistic processes in speech perception: Inferences from six fusions in dichotic listening. *Psychological Review,* 1976, **83,** 114−140.

De Valois, R. L., & De Valois, K. K. Neural coding of color. In E. C. Carterette & M. P. Friedman (Eds.), *Handbook of perception.* New York: Academic Press, 1975. Vol. V, pp. 117−166.

Efron, R., & Yund, E. W. Dichotic competition of simultaneous tone bursts of different frequency. I. Dissociation of pitch from lateralization and loudness. *Neuropsychologia,* 1974, **12,** 149−156.

Eriksen, C. W. W., & Hoffman, J. E. Temporal and spatial characteristics of selective encoding from visual displays. *Perception and Psychophysics,* 1972, **12,** 201−204.

Estes, W. K. Interactions of signal and background variables in visual processing. *Perception and Psychophysics,* 1972, **12,** 278−286.

Fisher, D. F., Monty, R. A. & Glucksberg, S. Visual confusion matrices: fact or artifact. *Journal of Psychology,* 1969, **71,** 111−125.

Forster, P. M., & Govier, E. Discrimination without awareness. *Quarterly Journal of Experimental Psychology,* 1978, **30,** 289−296.

Gardner, G. T. Evidence for independent parallel channels in tachistoscopic perception. *Cognitive Psychology,* 1973, **4,** 130−155.

Gardner, H. *The shattered mind.* New York: Alfred A. Knopf, 1975. P. 166.

Garner, W. R. *The processing of information and structure.* Potomac, MD: Lawrence Erlbaum, 1974.

Gibson, E. J. Perceptual learning and the theory of word perception. *Cognitive Psychology,* 1971, **2,** 351−368.

Hecaen, H., & Albert, M. L. *Human neuropsychology.* New York: Wiley, 1978.

Hodge, D. C. Legibility of a uniform stroke width alphabet: I. Relative legibility of upper and lower case letters. *Journal of Engineering Psychology,* 1962, **1,** 34−46.

Jonides, J., & Gleitman, H. A conceptual category effect in visual search: O as letter or as digit. *Perception and Psychophysics,* 1972, **12,** 457−460.

Julesz, B. Experiments in the visual perception of texture. *Scientific American,* 1975, **232,** 34−43.

Kahneman, D., & Henik, A. Effects of visual grouping on immediate recall and selective attention. In S. Dornic (Ed.), *Attention and performance VI,* Hillsdale, NJ: Lawrence Erlbaum, 1977. Pp. 307−332.

LaBerge, D. Attention and the measurement of perceptual learning. *Memory and Cognition,* 1973, **1,** 268−276.

Lawrence, D. H. Two studies of visual search for word targets with controlled rates of presentation. *Perception and Psychophysics,* 1971, **10,** 85−89.

Lewis, J. L. Semantic processing of unattended messages using dichotic listening. *Journal of Experimental Psychology,* 1970, **85,** 225−228.

Liepmann, H. Uber die agnostischen Storungen. *Neurologisches Zentralblatt,* 1908, **27,** 609−617.

Luria, A. R. *The man with a shattered world.* New York: Basic Books, 1972.

MacKay, D. G. Aspects of the theory of comprehension, memory and attention. *Quarterly Journal of Experimental Psychology,* 1973, **25,** 22−40.

Monahan, J. S., & Lockhead, G. R. Identification of integral stimuli. *Journal of Experimental Psychology: General,* 1977, **106,** 94−110.

Neisser, U. *Cognitive psychology.* New York: Appleton−Century−Crofts, 1967.

Neisser, U. *Cognition and reality.* San Francisco: Freeman, 1977.

Neisser, U., Novick, R. & Lazar, R. Searching for ten targets simultaneously. *Perceptual and Motor Skills,* 1963, **17,** 955−961.

Pew, R. W. & Gardner, G. T. Unpublished data, University of Michigan, summarized in Fisher, Monty and Glucksberg, 1969.

Posner, M. I. *Chronometric explorations of mind.* Hillsdale, NJ: Lawrence Erlbaum, 1978.

Rabbitt, P. M. A. Learning to ignore irrelevant information. *British Journal of Psychology,* 1967, 55, 403–414.

Rock, I., Halper, F., & Clayton, R. The perception and recognition of complex figures. *Cognitive Psychology,* 1972, 3, 655–673.

Shepard, R. N. Attention and the metric structure of the stimulus space. *Journal of Mathematical Psychology,* 1964, 1, 54–87.

Shiffrin, R. M., & Schneider, W. Controlled and automatic human information processing. II. Perceptual learning, automatic attending and a general theory. *Psychological Review,* 1977, 84, 127–190.

Townsend, J. T. Theoretical analysis of an alphabetic confusion matrix, *Perception and Psychophysics,* 9, 40–50.

Treisman, A. Focused attention in the perception and retrieval of multidimensional stimuli. *Perception and Psychophysics,* 1977, 22, 1–11.

Treisman, A. The psychological reality of levels of processing. In L. S. Cermak & F. I. M. Craik (Eds.), *Levels of processing and human memory.* Hillsdale, NJ: Lawrence Erlbaum, 1979.

Treisman, A., Squire, R., & Green, J. Semantic processing in dichotic listening? A replication. *Memory and Cognition,* 1974, 2, 641–646.

Treisman, A., Sykes, M., & Gelade, G. Selective attention and stimulus integration. In S. Dornic (Ed.), *Attention and performance VI.* Hillsdale, NJ: Lawrence Erlbaum, 1977. Pp. 333–361.

White, M. J. Identification and categorization in visual search. *Memory and Cognition,* 1977, 5, 648–657.

Wolford, G. Perturbation model for letter identification. *Psychological Review,* 1975, 82, 184–199.

Zeki, S. M. The functional organization of projections from striate to prestriate visual cortex in the rhesus monkey. *Cold Spring Harbor Symposia on Quantitative Biology,* 1976, 15, 591–600.

REFERENCE NOTE

1. Julesz, B. Colloquium given at Stanford University, 1978.

(Accepted July 4, 1979)

[2]

Attention and the Detection of Signals

Michael I. Posner, Charles R. R. Snyder, and Brian J. Davidson
University of Oregon

SUMMARY

Detection of a visual signal requires information to reach a system capable of eliciting arbitrary responses required by the experimenter. Detection latencies are reduced when subjects receive a cue that indicates where in the visual field the signal will occur. This shift in efficiency appears to be due to an alignment (orienting) of the central attentional system with the pathways to be activated by the visual input.

It would also be possible to describe these results as being due to a reduced criterion at the expected target position. However, this description ignores important constraints about the way in which expectancy improves performance. First, when subjects are cued on each trial, they show stronger expectancy effects than when a probable position is held constant for a block, indicating the active nature of the expectancy. Second, while information on spatial position improves performance, information on the form of the stimulus does not. Third, expectancy may lead to improvements in latency without a reduction in accuracy. Fourth, there appears to be little ability to lower the criterion at two positions that are not spatially contiguous.

A framework involving the employment of a limited-capacity attentional mechanism seems to capture these constraints better than the more general language of criterion setting. Using this framework, we find that attention shifts are not closely related to the saccadic eye movement system. For luminance detection the retina appears to be equipotential with respect to attention shifts, since costs to unexpected stimuli are similar whether foveal or peripheral. These results appear to provide an important model system for the study of the relationship between attention and the structure of the visual system.

Detecting the presence of a clear signal in an otherwise noise-free environment is probably the simplest perceptual act of which the human is capable. For this reason it may serve as an ideal model task for investigating the role of sensory and attentional factors in controlling our awareness of environmental events. Although there are a number of empirical approaches to the study of detection, most have not clearly separated between attentional factors and sensory factors and are thus incapable of providing an analysis of the relationship between the two.

The classical psychophysical approach to detection has generally involved the use of near-threshold signals (e.g., Hecht, Schlaer, & Pirenne, 1942). This approach has been concerned with such stimulus factors as intensity, duration, wavelength, and sensory organismic factors such as the degree of dark adaptation, retinal position of the stimulus, and so on. Evidence that a signal has been

These studies were supported by National Science Foundation Grant BNS 76-18907A01 to the University of Oregon. Portions of the data were adapted from *Chronometric Explorations of Mind* (Posner, 1978). Parts of these experiments were presented to the Psychonomic Society, November 1976 and 1977.

Requests for reprints should be sent to Michael I. Posner, Psychology Department, University of Oregon, Eugene, Oregon 97403.

detected usually involves verbal reports by the subjects as an indication that they are aware of the event. An effort is made to optimize the state of attention, and it is assumed that the organism has its attention aligned to the input channel over which the event occurs.

A different approach to signal detection is represented by a body of research using the components of the orienting reflex rather than verbal reports as an indicant of detection. Research on the orienting reflex is concerned with both stimulus and contextual factors controlling its elicitation. Sokolov (1963) has suggested that subjects build up a neural model (i.e., an expectancy) of the repeated signal that blocks elicitation of the reflex by stimuli resembling the model. Little is known about whether the reflex is prior to or only follows our awareness of the signal. Indeed, the relatively slow times of some components of the orienting reflex, such as vasodilation and galvanic skin response (GSR), may prevent precise specification of the temporal relation of the orienting reflex to awareness of the signal. Some components of the orienting reflex, such as alignment of the eyes, may well precede our awareness of the signal, whereas other components of the orienting reflex, such as changes in GSR and vasoconstriction, almost surely must follow it.

The theory of signal detection (Green & Swets, 1974) has greatly influenced studies of detecting stimuli. One needs to distinguish between the mathematical theory and its psychological application. The mathematical theory of signal detection is a powerful tool for the analysis of many problems. It is a normative theory that may be used to describe a large number of psychological situations. However, like many tools it often produces in its users some implicit assumptions.

The use of detection has involved situations all the way from separating a pure tone in white noise (Green & Swets, 1974) to the task of a radiologist locating a tumor (Green & Birdsall, 1978). It seems unlikely that the same processes are involved in these situations. Often, in addition to detecting the presence of a stimulus, a person must identify it in order to discriminate it from complex backgrounds. Accordingly, sometimes it has been concluded that attention aids detection more than would be expected from an ideal observer (Sekuler & Ball, 1977), and sometimes no effects of attention are found (Lappin & Uttal, 1976). The one task in which signal detection theory is not applied is where there is a clear above-threshold signal in uncluttered background. Since the signal would be detected 100% of the time, the method does not apply. Yet in many ways this is the perfect task for understanding the roles of orienting and detecting in their simplest forms.

Users of signal detection theory often assume a two-stage model of information processing in which sensory systems are coupled in series to a central statistical decision process. This view runs counter to studies that have forced the distinction between physical, phonetic, and semantic codes of letters and words (LaBerge & Samuels, 1974; Posner, 1978). In systems involving multiple codes, changes induced in the criterion within one code can affect the inflow of evidence to other systems.

Another approach to the detection of signals has been developing in the last several years. It applies the methods of mental chronometry (Posner, 1978) through the use of evoked potentials, poststimulus latency histograms of single cells, or reaction time to try to determine when and where central attentional states influence the input message produced by a signal. It has been shown, for example, that independent of eye position, the instruction to attend to a particular position in visual space affects occipital recording for that event in comparison to a control stimulus arising at another position within the first 150 msec after input (Eason, Harter, & White, 1969; Von Voorhis & Hillyard, 1977). Similarly, enhancement of single cells whose receptive field is the target of an eye movement occurs well within 100 msec after input (Goldberg & Wurtz, 1972; Wurtz & Mohler, 1976). These enhancements are not necessarily coupled to the eye movement but are unique to the stimulus toward which the eye will be moved. All these studies show evidence of interaction of central systems with input processing. They suggest that central control modifies the stimulus evidence rather than merely providing a criterion for choices among fixed states of evidence. These chronometric studies suggest that it may be possible to study the detailed processes involved in the detection of a suprathreshold signal even in an empty visual field.

By *detection*, we will mean the entry of information concerning the presence of a signal into a system that allows the subject to report the existence of the signal by an arbitrary response indicated by the experimenter. We mean to distinguish detection in this sense from more limited automatic responses that may occur to the event. *Orienting*, as we will use the term, involves the more limited process of aligning sensory (e.g., eyes) or central systems with the input channel over which the signal is to occur. Thus it is possible to entertain the hypothesis that subjects may orient toward a signal without having first detected it. This would mean simply that the signal was capable of eliciting certain kinds of responses (e.g., eye movements or shifts of attention) but has not yet reached systems capable of generating responses not habitual for that type of signal.

The purpose of this article is to examine the relationship of the two component processes, orienting and detecting, in the task of reporting the presence of a visual signal.

In the course of the article, we will try to show that central processes can seriously affect the efficiency with which we detect stimuli in even the most simple of detection tasks and that the nature of these changes in efficiency is such that it implies a separate attentional system in close interaction with the visual system. The article is structured in terms of four propositions. First, knowledge of the location of a clear visual signal can be shown to affect the efficiency of processing signals that arise from that location. Second, this improved efficiency is not due to a general tendency for any kind of information to improve performance nor to an improvement in speed at the expense of accuracy, but implies a centrally controlled attentional system. Third, the attentional system cannot be allocated freely but can be directed only over contiguous portions of the visual field. Finally, this attentional mechanism appears not to be closely coupled to the structure of the saccadic eye movement system nor to differ between fovea and periphery.

Knowledge of Spatial Position Affects Performance

Evoked potential and single-cell results show that when a signal occurs at a position for which the subject is prepared, electrical activity is enhanced in the first 100 msec following input. This result suggests that it should be possible to observe this enhancement in terms of changes in detection. There is much evidence that knowledge of where a stimulus will occur affects processing efficiency in a complex visual field (Engle, 1971); Sperling & Melchner, 1978). However, there has been a great deal of dispute about this fact when above-threshold signals have been used in an empty field. Posner, Nissen, and Ogden (1978) provided subjects with a precue as to whether a given event would occur to the left or right of fixation. One second following the cue, a .5° square was plotted on the cathode ray tube. As shown in Figure 1, when the stimulus occurred at the expected position (.8 probability), subjects' detection (simple reaction time) responses were faster than following the neutral cue (.5 probability each side) and when the stimulus occurred at an unexpected position (.2 probability), they were slower. Careful monitoring of eye position and the use of a single response key insure that neither changes in eye position nor differential preparation of responses could be responsible for such a result.[1]

In addition to the data reported above,

---

[1] After having found that movements of the eyes of more than one degree occurred on less than 4% of the trials (Posner et al., 1978) and that these trials did not in any way change the cost-benefit results of the study, we did not maintain careful monitoring of eye position in all subsequent studies, although we used the same instructions and training to suppress movements. When monitoring was instituted in some of the later studies, results were not substantially altered by the eye movements that were detected.

some other performance experiments have also shown improvement in performance at expected spatial positions. These experiments include the use of signal detection measures (d'; Smith & Blaha, Note 1), vocal reaction time (Eriksen & Hoffman, 1973), and percent correct identifications (Shaw & Shaw, 1977).

Nonetheless, it has been difficult in many experiments to obtain significant benefits from knowledge of spatial position (Grindley & Townsend, 1968; Mertens, 1956; Mowrer, 1941; Shiffrin & Gardner, 1972). There may be many reasons why some studies have been successful in showing improved performance from expected spatial positions and others not. One of the reasons that seemed most likely to us was that most experiments, other than ours, examined only the benefits involved when subjects knew something about the location of a visual object when compared to a condition where no such knowledge was present. Our design showed about equal costs and benefits. However, in our design, subjects received a cue on each trial indicating the most likely position of the target, whereas in most studies subjects prepared for an expected position for a block of trials. We found that it was difficult for subjects to maintain a differential preparation for a particular location and suspected that many of the studies examining benefits due to knowledge of visual location did not find them because the subjects did not continue to set themselves for the position in space at which the signal was most expected. To test this view, we compared our standard cuing condition with a method in which noncued blocks were used.

Experiment 1

Method

Subjects. Six volunteers were recruited through the subject pool of the Center for Cognitive and Perceptual Research at the University of Oregon. All were college age and possessed normal hearing and vision. The subjects were run individually in two 1-hour sessions on consecutive days and were paid $2 for each session.

Apparatus. All testing was conducted in an acoustical chamber. Subjects were seated approximately 1.3 m in front of a cathode-ray tube (CRT) on which fixation markers, warning signals, and

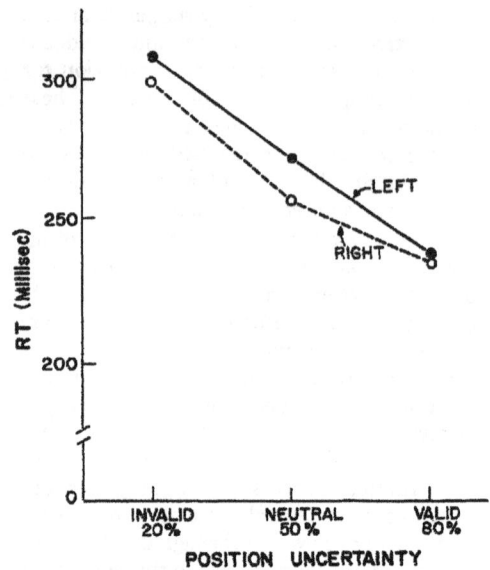

Figure 1. Reaction time (RT) to expected, unexpected, and neutral signals that occur 7° to the left or right of fixation. (Benefits are calculated by subtracting expected RTs from neutral, and costs by subtracting neutral from unexpected.)

feedback occurred. The displays were viewed binocularly. Four red light-emitting diodes (LEDs) were arrayed horizontally immediately below the CRT. Two LEDs were positioned 24° left and right of fixation (far stimuli). The other two stimuli were 8° to either side of fixation (near stimuli). The LEDs were driven by 15 V through either a 560Ω or a 1.5Ω resistor, producing two suprathreshold intensities. Subjects indicated their responses by pressing a key-operated microswitch with the right index finger. A PDP-9 computer controlled the timing, stimulus presentation, and collection.

Procedure. The experimental task was a simple reaction time (RT) to the onset of an LED. Trial blocks consisted of 120 trials, including 20 catch trials. Stimulus trials consisted of a visual warning signal, a stimulus (LED), subject's response, feedback, and an intertrial interval (ITI). Subjects were asked to fixate the center of the CRT where a 1° square was displayed. Warning signals, either a plus sign (+) or a digit from 1 to 4, indicating one of the stimulus locations from left to right, were presented in the square. Following a warning interval of 1 sec, the stimulus was presented. Subjects were encouraged to respond quickly, but not so quickly that they anticipated the stimulus. The response terminated the warning signal and stimulus display. Feedback was the RT in milliseconds unless an anticipation had occurred, in which case the word ERROR was presented. To re-

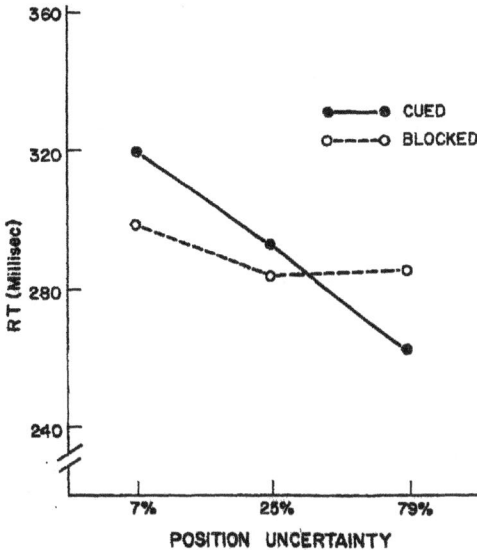

Figure 2. Reaction times (RT) for events of varying probability. (79% = expected, 25% = neutral, and 7% = unexpected for blocked presentation and presentation where cues are presented on each trial.)

duce anticipatory responses, no stimulus occurred on approximately 20 trials per block. These catch trials consisted of only a warning signal and an ITI. The proportion of catch trials was constant across experimental conditions.

The central objective was to compare detection latencies when the stimulus location was cued on each trial (mixed blocks) to a noncued situation in which subjects prepared for one location for a block of trials (pure blocks). Two conditions were used in the pure blocks. In the equal condition, the warning signal was always a plus sign, and each of the four locations was equally probable. In the unequal condition the warning signal was also a plus sign, but during each trial block one location was presented 79% of the time, and the other three locations occurred 7% of the time each. At the beginning of each unequal block, subjects were informed of the most likely stimulus location. In the mixed blocks (i.e., the cued condition), 20% of the warning signals were plus signs, indicating that the four locations were equally probable for that trial. On the remaining 80% of the trials, the warning signal was a digit (*1, 2, 3,* or *4*), indicating the most probable location (79%) for that trial. Each of the non-cued locations was equally probable (7%). In both the unequal and cued conditions subjects were encouraged to set themselves for the expected stimulus but not to move their eyes from the warning cue. No actual monitoring of eye position was used, since previous work had shown

that costs and benefits were not dependent on changes in eye position (Posner et al., 1978).

Design. Each subject was tested in the three conditions (equal, unequal, and cued) on 2 days in an ABC-CBA order, with order balanced across subjects. There were two blocks in the equal condition, four blocks in the unequal condition (one for each position most likely), and two blocks in the cued condition on each day. Each session for each subject contained a different random order of the four blocks within the unequal condition.

Results and Discussion

The results of these mixed and pure blocks are shown in Figure 2. Note that once again when the cuing technique was used, we obtained very significant costs and benefits over a neutral condition. However, in the pure block technique, only the costs were significantly different from the neutral condition. There was no evidence of benefit.[2]

We attribute this failure to find benefit in the expected position over the neutral condition to the tendency of subjects to avoid the task of placing their attention at the expected position when they were not cued to do so on each trial. It is not clear why benefits are more labile than costs. However, since both costs and benefits are aspects of our knowledge of the position of an expected signal, it is clear that the difference between the benefit trials and the cost trials is a legitimate way of asking whether expectancy changes the efficiency of performance of signals arriving from expected versus unexpected conditions. The failure of most other paradigms to examine the cost of unexpected positions in space makes them far less sensitive than the techniques we have outlined. This, together with the general use of blocking rather than cuing, helps to reconcile several of the conflicts in the literature.

Experiment 2: Attention Is Involved

Investigators using the signal detection theory to guide work on detecting signals often argue that any information provided to

---

[2] This experiment was subsequently replicated with 12 additional subjects in the same design, except that the LEDs were 2° and 8° from fixation. The results were identical.

the subject about a signal will be useful in disentangling the signal from background noise. For this reason, evidence that some particular type of information, for example, about the location of a signal, improves performance is not taken to mean that there is any special mechanism associated with the utilization of that information. Lappin and Uttal (1976) have argued that knowledge of any orthogonal stimulus parameter ought to improve detection of that stimulus (p. 368). In their experiments they use a high level of background noise and ask the subjects to detect a line within the noise. Detection involves a difficult discrimination between background and signal. They find that the subject's information about the location of the line does improve performance, but not more than would be expected from a model in which no attentional assumptions are used. From this they conclude that the demonstrations of costs and benefits of the type indicated above are not evidence in favor of specific attentional mechanisms.

According to our view, evidence that only some types of information serve to improve performance would indicate that our effects are not due to general knowledge serving to allow separation of signal from noise. For example, consider a comparison of providing subjects with information about the shape of a stimulus with providing information about the location of the stimulus. It seems clear that in the Lappin and Uttal experiment, knowledge of the target shape would affect performance. This fits with the notion that information about the target's shape serves to disentangle the signal from noise. On the other hand, in our experiment it seems somewhat unlikely that information about shape would improve detection of signals.

Method

Subjects. Twelve volunteers were recruited in the same manner as in Experiment 1. The subjects were paid $2 for each of three 1-hour sessions run on consecutive days. Each session consisted of eight blocks of 130 trials.

Stimuli. Warning signals, stimuli, and feedback were presented on the CRT. Warning signals occurred at the center of the CRT. The stimulus, one of 10 capital letters selected at random, was

presented 7° to the left or right of the warning signal.

Procedure. The experimental task was a simple RT to the occurrence of a letter. Each trial began with a warning signal indicating either the form or location of the stimulus. The stimulus was presented after a variable warning interval that ranged between 800 and 1200 msec. Subjects were encouraged to respond quickly but not to anticipate the stimulus. About 25% of the trials were catch trials in which no letter was presented. As in Experiment 1, catch trial rates were constant across conditions. Feedback consisted of the RT in milliseconds, or the word ERROR if an anticipation had occurred.

The primary objective was to compare the effectiveness of location and form cues on simple detection. Location cues were left or right arrows. Following a location cue, the stimulus occurred on the indicated side on 80% of the trials. The neutral location cue was a plus sign. Following this cue, each location was equally probable. The form cue was one of the letters that were used as stimuli. On 80% of the trials following this cue, the stimulus was the indicated letter. The form cue always occurred with either a neutral or an informative location cue. Half of the form cues were presented slightly below a plus sign. This warning signal indicated that the cued letter was the most probable stimulus but did not indicate its location (i.e., each location was equally probable). On the remaining trials the form cue occurred below the left or right arrow, informing subjects of both the form and location of the stimulus. Since the location and form cues were each valid on 80% of the trials, the combined form and location cue was valid on 64% of the trials. On 16% of the trials, the cued letter occurred in the unexpected location. On 16% of the trials, an unexpected letter occurred in the cued location. Finally, on 4% of the trials, an unexpected letter occurred in the unexpected location. Each type of warning signal (plus sign alone, arrow alone, letter with plus sign, letter with arrow) occurred equally often. Subjects were encouraged to use the warning signals to prepare for the stimulus but not to move their eyes from the warning cue.

Results and Discussion

The results of this experiment are shown in Table 1. Clearly, information about the location of the letter improves performance, but information about the form does not.[3]

---

[3] It should be noted that the prime reduced the letter uncertainty from 10 alternatives, whereas the spatial uncertainty had only 2 alternatives. It seems unlikely that a different result would have obtained had only 2 letters been used, however.

Table 1
*Mean Reaction Time for Expected,
Unexpected, and Neutral Form and
Location Cues*

Form	Location			
	Expected	Neutral	Unexpected	M
Expected	247	263	292	267
Neutral	252	271	299	274
Unexpected	248	263	299	270
M	249	266	297	

Note. Time is measured in milliseconds.

Another form of objection to our studies is to suppose that changes in the latency of processing the stimulus arising at the expected location are a result of changes in the amount of information that the subjects sampled from the expected location. Consider a comparison of the neutral trials with the trials cued by an arrow. In the latter, subjects may decide to reduce their criterion for pressing the key at the risk of making an increased number of anticipations. Indeed, we generally find that conditions involving the arrow do show an increased number of anticipatory responses over those times when the plus sign is used. This is evidence of a shift in amount of evidence that the subjects require to respond. However, this kind of shift cannot account for differences in cost plus benefit, since both of these RTs are from the arrow conditions, and subjects cannot differentially prepare prior to making the response. One might suppose that in some way the subjects are able to reduce their criterion when the stimulus arises from the particular position in space that was cued. It is possible to test whether improvement in reaction time obtained from knowledge of the location of the stimulus is accompanied by an increase in error. To do this we used a choice reaction time task.

Experiment 3

We modified our standard simple reaction time method (Posner et al., 1978) by providing the subjects with a toggle switch that moved up or down. The cues were left or right arrows or a plus sign. The imperative

stimulus was a .5° square of light that occurred 7° from fixation and either below or above the line on the scope indicated by the cue stimulus. If it occurred above, the subject was required to move the toggle switch up, and if below, the toggle switch was to be moved down. This was a highly compatible stimulus–response combination that did not require a great deal of learning by the subject. Eight subjects were run for five blocks of 96 trials on each of the 2 days.

The results for Day 2 are shown in Figure 3. It is clear that we did find costs and benefits in reaction time in the same direction but not in as great a magnitude as had been found in the simple reaction time detection experiments. Analysis of variance indicated that both costs and benefits are significant.[4] There clearly is no significant difference in the error rates. Error rates on cost trials are somewhat larger than error rates in neutral or benefit trials. There is no evidence that the reaction time results are produced by an opposite effect on errors. A speed–accuracy tradeoff is not a necessary factor in producing the costs and benefits found in our experiment.

Experiment 4

It seemed important to determine the relationship of our results using luminance detection to those obtained when subjects are required to identify a target. In Experiment 2 it was shown that a subject's knowledge about the form of the target did not influence luminance detection. These findings suggest that luminance detection may be a simpler domain in which to examine the effects of set on performance than the more frequently studied tasks in which it is important to identify or match forms.

---

[4] There is also an interaction apparent in the graph between the target location (up vs. down) and position uncertainty. This probably results from a tendency to associate an unexpected position with a downward response. Presumably there is also a tendency to associate an expected position with an upward response. Despite this complication, the main result of the experiment is to show highly significant effects of knowledge of spatial position for both choice responses.

To examine this question we displayed four boxes arrayed around a central fixation point. The maximum visual angle of the display was about 1.5° so that all stimuli were foveal. Subjects saw either a neutral warning cue or an arrow pointing to one of the four positions. Following the neutral cue, a stimulus was equally likely to appear at any of the four positions and following an arrow the target appeared at the cued position 79% of the time and at the other positions 7% of the time. The stimulus could be the digits 4 or 7 or the letters D or Q. The subjects' task was to respond to designated target stimuli.

In pilot research we provided subjects with only a single key that they were to press whenever a digit was presented. If a letter was presented, they were to refrain from pressing a key. In this paradigm RTs to the expected position were very fast, but error rates were always much higher than in unexpected or neutral trials. Subjects found it very difficult to withhold responding when a nontarget occurred in the expected position. This result indicates that there is a strong tendency to react with a false alarm to a visual event occurring in an expected position. Subjectively, it felt as if one were all set to respond when an event ocurred in the indicated position, and it was very frustrating to inhibit the response while waiting to determine if it was a digit (target). When an event occurred in an unexpected position, it felt as though the answer was already present by the time one was ready to make a response. These subjective impressions fit very well with the idea that the attentional system is responsible for releasing the response rather than for the accrual of information relevant to the decision that a target was present.

It was relatively easy to show that costs and benefits were not due entirely to rapid but inaccurate responses. We simply provided subjects with a second key so that on each trial they were required to decide whether the target was a letter or digit. Figure 4 indicates the results from 14 subjects run in such a study for 2 days. Half the subjects were presented with a brief target

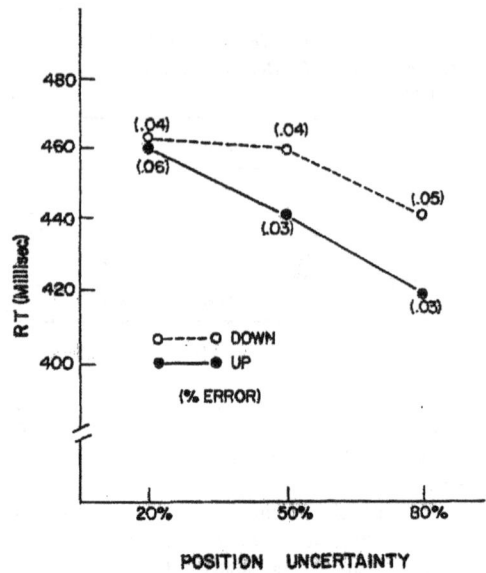

Figure 3. Reaction times (RT) for expected (80%), neutral (50%), and unexpected (20%) stimulus locations. (The task is to determine if the stimulus is above [up response] or below [down response] the center line. Error rates are in parentheses.)

masked after 40 msec (short duration) and half with a target remaining present until the response. For reaction time there are clear costs when the stimulus occurs in the unexpected position and benefits when it occurs in the expected position in comparison with the neutral control. On the other hand, error rates are constant over the various positions. These results argue clearly that subjects did not simply sacrifice accuracy for speed when the stimulus occurred in the expected location. This finding is incompatible with the view that central decision processes are responsible for setting a criterion for the response, since that implies that more rapid responding will be associated with increased error.

The results of the pilot study and of Experiment 4 also indicate to us that there are quite different processes present when subjects are required merely to detect a luminance change from those present when they must identify the stimulus. The false alarms found in the pilot study were far greater than were found in any study involving the detec-

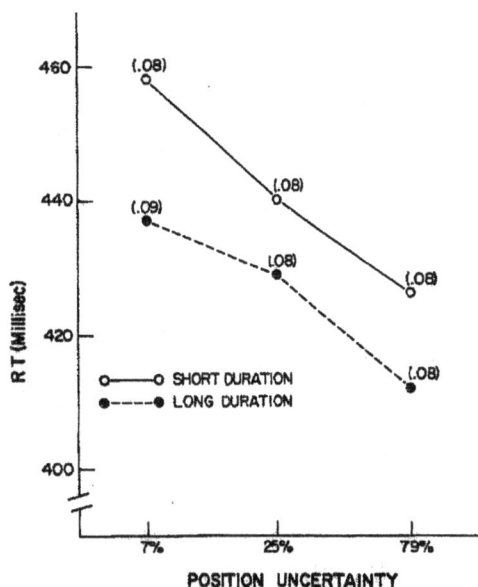

Figure 4. Reaction times (RT) for expected (79%), neutral (25%), and unexpected (7%) positions. (The task requires separate responses for letters and digits. Short duration = 40 msec masked presentation. Long duration = stimulus present until response is made. Error rates are in parentheses.)

tion of a stimulus. It is as though the occurrence of a luminance change at the expected position gives rise to detection of an event. It is the speed of this detection that we have been measuring in our previous work. If the subject is given only one key, there is a very strong bias to use the act of detecting the event as the basis for pressing the key. If the key press is to be made to only one class of stimuli, it is difficult to withhold the response. On the other hand, if subjects have to make a choice between keys, they are able to inhibit rapid responses and still obtain benefits from the cue.

These results all suggest that luminance detection is facilitated when subjects know where in space a stimulus will occur. They also indicate that such facilitation is not due to a bias introduced by the tendency to respond quickly and inaccurately to stimuli occurring at the expected position. On the other hand, they also suggest that the results of luminance detection cannot necessarily be generalized to studies in which subjects are

required to identify the form present at a particular position. Although attention is quickly available at the expected position, this may result either in quick but error-prone reactions or in improved speed without increases in error, depending upon how the task is structured.

Although we have not done any formal comparisons, it seems obvious that the size of the effects in the choice RT tasks are much smaller than we have typically obtained in simple RT. This may seem counterintuitive, since the actual RTs are much greater in the choice tasks. We believe that this is due to the necessity of the subject's switching attention from the spatial location indicated by the cue to the internal lookup processes that identify (e.g., digit) or determine (e.g., above) the discriminative responses. Spatial cues are very effective for simple RT to luminance increments because this task does not require determining what the event is before responding, since subjects are required to respond to any event. Whether a spatial cue is effective in a more complex task will depend upon the details of the task and the competing stimuli. Spatial cues will be of great help in complex cluttered fields because they tell the subjects which stimuli are to be dealt with; in an empty field they may or may not help, depending upon the difficulty of reorienting from the location to the internal lookup of item identity.

Another perspective on our results from the point of view of signal detection theory is to suppose that they depend upon the reciprocal nature of the stimulus conditions that we impose upon the subjects (Duncan, 1980). If subjects follow the correlations in the experiment, they may seek to raise their criterion at the unexpected position and lower it at the expected position. This might have nothing to do with capacity or attentional limitations but would simply be an adaptation to the experimental contingencies. This view is more difficult to deal with. It is possible to design a study without introducing a contingency by, for example, presenting a stimulus that occurs with equal likelihood to the left, right, or both positions. However, such an experiment is probably not sufficient to dispose of the more general idea that performance in these tasks is mediated by independent shifts in criterion at different positions in space and not by the allocation of any central mechanism. It is to this question that the next section of the article is addressed.

Attention Cannot Be Allocated at Will

Recently, Shaw and Shaw (1977) have proposed that subjects can allocate their attention pretty much at will over the visual field. Shaw and Shaw presented letters at one of eight positions in a circular array. In one condition, the positions varied in the probability with which a target would occur. Performance was compared with a condition in which targets occurred at all eight positions with equal likelihood. Subjects showed significant costs and benefits in detection according to the assigned probabilities. From this, Shaw and Shaw argued for a model in which subjects were able to allocate a limited-capacity attentional resource to different areas of the visual field. While their results are consistent with allocation of a limited-capacity mechanism, they would also be consistent with the sort of view discussed in the last paragraph. It could be that subjects are able to set criteria for different positions in the visual field according to the probability that those positions will be sampled. However, there is a serious problem with this interpretation. The results of Shaw and Shaw could also be obtained if subjects sometimes attend to one position in space and sometimes to another, and these probabilities match those assigned to target presentation.

Our goal was to determine whether subjects were able to allocate their attention to different positions on a given trial. To do this we gave subjects both a most frequent position and a second most frequent position on each trial. We examined their RTs to the second most likely position in comparison to lower frequency positions to see if they could allocate attention simultaneously both to the most frequent and the second most frequent events.

Experiment 5

Method

Subjects. Twelve subjects participated in two 1-hour sessions on consecutive days. Experiment 5A involved 12 additional subjects and Experiment 5B 7 subjects. All were paid for their participation.

Apparatus. The apparatus from Experiment 1, including the LED displays, was used in this study. The LEDs were positioned either 2° (foveal stimuli) or 8° (peripheral stimuli) from fixation, with two LEDs on either side of fixation.

Procedure. The experimental task was a simple RT to the onset of an LED. Trial blocks consisted of 100 trials, including catch trials. Subjects fixated a 1° square in the center of the cathode-ray tube. Warning signals, either a plus sign or a digit from *1* to *4* indicating one of the stimulus locations from left to right, were presented in the square. After a variable warning interval, the stimulus occurred. Approximately 25% of the trials were catch trials in which no LED was presented. The feedback consisted of the RT in milliseconds or, in the event of an anticipation, the word ERROR.

On Day 1 subjects were seated in the test chamber and allowed to adapt to the dark for about 5 minutes before testing was begun. Prior to each block a most likely (65%) and next most likely (25%) stimulus location were indicated on the cathode-ray tube. Subjects were asked to remember these positions throughout the block and to try to prepare for stimuli at these locations on those trials (80%) when a digit appeared as the warning signal. The digit indicated the most likely position during that block, with the stimulus positions numbered from 1 to 4 from left to right. On trials preceded by a plus sign as a warning signal (20%), subjects were told that all four stimuli would be equally likely to occur and were asked to prepare themselves accordingly. Subjects were also informed that the first four blocks would be practice, and the final three blocks on Day 1, plus nine blocks on Day 2, would be test blocks.

On Day 2, subjects were again shown the apparatus, task instructions were reviewed, and about 5 min. were allowed for dark adaptation. Following testing, subjects were asked for their impressions of the helpfulness of advance information concerning stimulus location and whether they had felt they could prepare for stimuli at two locations.

Experiment 5A was an exact replication of Experiment 5 except that blocks of trials in which one signal had a probability of .64 and the other three had probabilities of .12 were also included. In addition, Experiment 5A was run under light-adapted conditions. Experiment 5B was identical to 5A but run under conditions of dark adaptation as in Experiment 5.

Design. Each subject received the same set of four practice blocks, which sampled the four positions as most likely and as next most likely. Each

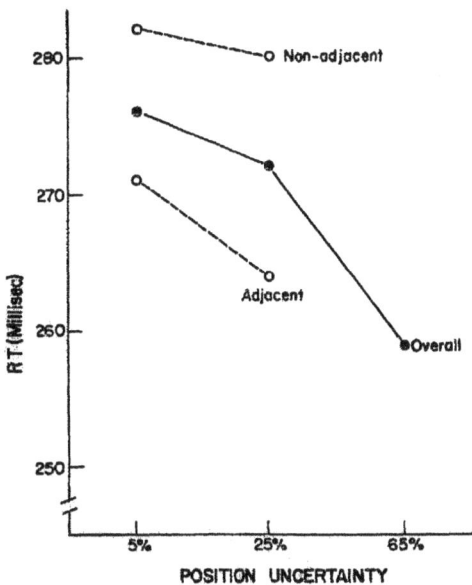

Figure 5. Reaction times (RT) to unexpected (5%), second most likely (25%), and most likely (65%) events as a function of the adjacency of the less probable events to the most probable (65%) event.

subject was then tested at all twelve combinations of most likely and next most likely stimulus locations.

The most likely position was cued on each trial by the central digit while the next most likely position remained constant for three consecutive blocks, with order of the four positions counterbalanced across subjects. Within each three-block set, order of the most likely positions was also counterbalanced.[5]

Results and Discussion

The data of all three experiments are given in Table 2. The statistical analysis of Experiment 5 showed that both the most likely and the second most likely target position were significantly faster in reaction time than the two least likely positions. In addition, foveal events showed some advantage over peripheral events, and intense stimuli showed some advantage over weak stimuli.

However, the important result is a comparison of the reaction times to the second most likely position (25%) and least likely position (5%) when the former was either adjacent to or remote from the 65% position. This is shown in Figure 5. The results are really quite clear-cut. When the second most likely target position was adjacent to the most likely target position, its RT resembled the most likely targets. There was a slight (5 msec) nonsignificant advantage to the most likely over the second most likely position in this condition. However, when the second most likely was separated by a position from the most likely, its reaction time resembled the least likely (5%) position. This constellation of results was independent of whether the two most likely events occurred at the central position or whether one of them occurred at the periphery. These results suggest that for detection, it is not possible for subjects to split their attentional mechanism so that it is allocated to two separated positions in space.

Experiment 5 did not contain a condition in which there was only one likely event. Thus we were unable to tell whether subjects were reducing their efficiency in detecting the most likely event. This condition was present in both Experiment 5A and 5B. From Table 2 it is clear that the requirement to give attention to a second most likely event had no effect on RT to the most likely event. In both experiments the blocks in which there was and was not a secondary focus had the same detection RTs for the most likely event.

In other ways Experiments 5A and 5B are a replication of Experiment 5 except the interaction between adjacency and probability (5% vs. 25%) was not statistically significant. Overall, the 25% event is only 5 msec faster than the 5% event when they are both remote from the most likely event. There is no evidence of an ability to divide attention. When the events are adjacent to the 65% event, the 25% event has a 16-msec advantage. This advantage is statistically significant in each study.

---

[5] The use of a blocking rather than a cuing technique for the second most likely event was made necessary by the difficulty we found in getting subjects to process two target position cues on each trial. Since the 25% target position (second most likely) is compared in RT to the 5% target position, differences should reflect a sum of costs and benefits that do show up in the blocking method as shown in Experiment 1.

Table 2
Splitting Attention: Reaction Time as a Function of Stimulus Event and Expectancy Condition.

Experiment	One only	Most likely	25% adj.	5% adj.	25% non-adj.	5% non-adj.
			Expectancy			
		Stimulus central (Positions 2–3)				
5		252	257	270	272	276
5A	256	253	273	281	284	294
5B	270	269	275	280	296	295
M	263	258	268	277	284	288
		Stimulus peripheral (Positions 1–4)				
5		266	272	272	288	288
5A	255	256	272	284	293	303
5B	301	289	312	328	328	337
M	278	274	285	295	303	309
			Overall			
M	270	266	276	286	294	299

Note. Time is measured in milliseconds. Adj. = adjacent.

Overall our results suggest severe limits in the ability of subjects to assign attention to a secondary focus in addition to a primary focus. Clear evidence for such an ability occurs only when the secondary focus is adjacent to the primary focus.

This finding favors the view of a unified attentional mechanism under the conditions of this experiment. These conditions include the use of a luminance detection task and the blocking of the second most likely target position.

Attention and Visual System Structure

The results summarized so far argue that subjects' knowledge about where in space the signal will occur does affect processing efficiency both in facilitating latencies at the expected position and retarding them at the unexpected positions. Our results suggest an attentional mechanism that cannot be allocated freely to positions in space but appears to have a central focus that may vary in size according to the requirements of the experiment. These findings are consonant with the idea of attention as an internal eye or spotlight. The metaphor of attention as a kind of spotlight has been used by Norman (1968), among others.

It seems useful to summarize the relation-ship between the attentional spotlight and features of vision such as saccadic movements and foveal versus peripheral acuity. Our results have shown that orienting is not dependent upon actually moving the eye. Moreover, the extent of benefit to a signal is not affected by its distance from the fovea (Posner, 1978, Figure 7.9) from .5°–25° of visual angle. This finding for detection differs markedly from one obtained by Engle (1971) for a task demanding a high level of acuity. Engle required subjects to find a single form embedded in a complex visual field. He provided both a fixation point and a point away from fixation where attention was to be concentrated. He found that the field of high acuity (conspicuity) for the ability to identify the target stimulus included the fovea but was elongated in the direction of the subject's attention. This result contrasts sharply with our results. In our detection experiments when subjects are told to attend away from the fovea, the point of maximum speed of reaction shifts to surround the area of attention and does not include any special ability at the fovea itself. Costs of unexpected foveal stimuli are quite comparable to those with unexpected peripheral stimuli (Posner, 1978, Figure 7.9).

This equipotentiality of attention with respect to visual detection shows that the at-

M. POSNER, C. SNYDER, AND B. DAVIDSON

tentional spotlight is not related to the field of clear foveal vision. Moreover, taken with Engle's study it shows that attention cannot compensate for structural deficiencies in acuity. Attending away from the fovea does not compensate for the lack of acute vision in that part of the retina, though it does produce a complete shift in the speed of detection of luminance changes in that area of the visual field.

Our results may seem paradoxical because of the strong belief that attention is tied closely to the fovea. In the real world, we are always moving our eyes to stimuli that interest us, and thus we are habitually paying attention to the stimuli to which we are looking. We found that this belief affected the strategies our subjects employed when events could be either foveal or peripheral in mixed blocks (Posner, 1978, Figures 7.10 and 7.11). When subjects were cued as to which side of the field was most likely, they uniformly prepared for the peripheral (7°) stimulus and not the foveal (.5°) stimulus. The costs and benefits for peripheral stimulus in such mixed blocks were the same as when only peripheral stimuli could occur (pure blocks). The benefits for foveal events were greatly reduced in blocks when they were mixed with peripheral events. This shows that subjects behave as though peripheral events benefit from attention, whereas foveal events do not require attention. This strategy is quite wrong in our task, since both foveal and peripheral events show equal costs and benefits in pure blocks. Nonetheless, it is a reasonable strategy to carry over from the real world in which attention is closely associated with the fovea.

Conclusions

The conclusions from this series of experiments are of two kinds. The first kind is somewhat general and concerns the theoretical framework most appropriate for the study of detection. In the introduction we outlined four alternative approaches based upon whether a distinction is made between central decision and sensory processes and, if it is, whether the two are thought to be indepen-dent and serial or interactive. Our experiments have shown clearly that the subject's knowledge about where in space a stimulus will occur affects the efficiency of detection. Moreover, the kind of effect one finds (costs alone or costs and benefits) depends upon whether a general set is maintained over many trials or is precued on each trial. These two results indicate that central factors influence the efficiency of detection. By themselves these results merely reinforce a point made at the advent of signal detection theory concerning the importance of taking central factors into explicit consideration as a part of understanding sensory processes.

How shall these central factors or cognitive factors be viewed? The idea of separate sensory and decision stages suggests an essentially noninteractive mode. Cognitive effects are seen to establish logical criteria for the selection of sensory evidence. These selection criteria modify our reports about the evidence but not the evidence itself. Our data suggest an interactive framework, because they show serious constraints upon the way knowledge of a signal can aid detection. It helps us to know where a signal will occur but not the form in which it occurs. It helps to know that a stimulus will occur in adjacent regions of space, but we cannot prepare efficiently for two separated regions. Knowledge of where a stimulus will occur produces benefits when it is used actively (cued) but not when it is used to maintain a general set (blocked). None of these results disprove the signal detection language but all suggest constraints upon how our knowledge affects processing that go beyond a general improvement to be found by a logical selection criterion. Thus, our data seem to lead one to view detection as an interaction between the structure of the visual system and the structure of the attentional system.

The second set of conclusions deals with the structure of the attentional system implied by our experimental results. It is here that our findings are more specific. Attention can be likened to a spotlight that enhances the efficiency of detection of events within its beam. Unlike when acuity is involved, the effect of the beam is not related to the fovea. When the fovea is unilluminated by attention, its ability to lead to detection is diminished, as would be the case with any other area of the visual system. Subjects' assumption that the fovea is closely coupled to attentional systems is a correlation they carry over from everyday life. It is usually appropriate, because we move our eyes to those things in which we are interested, but when this correlation is broken, the fovea has no special connection to attention. Nor are we good at dividing the attentional beam so as to simultaneously illuminate different corners of our visual space. This failure to find an ability to divide attention contrasts sharply with views arising from more complex tasks (Moray, 1967; Shaw & Shaw, 1977) that stress attentional allocation. Perhaps the difference lies in the complex pathway-activation processes involved when linguistic stimuli are to be identified before responding and in their use of more than one stimulus event.

How is this attentional system brought to bear upon stimulus input? We distinguish between two different aspects of the attentional system. The first we call *orienting*. Orienting involves the direction in which attention is pointed. Since the visual cortex is organized by spatial position, orienting can be viewed as the selection of a position in space. However, orienting may also involve the selection of a modality, and within modalities it may differ based upon the nature of the organization of information in that sensory system (Posner, 1978). When input involves more than one modality, it is possible to compare orienting by modality with orienting by position in real space. When this is done (Posner et al., 1978), modality information dominates over spatial position, supporting the view that the sensory pathways matter more than a reconstructed internal model of space. Orienting, as we have described it, may be an entirely central phenomenon without any overt change in eye position. Usually the eyes do follow the direction of our attention, however. Orienting, as we have described it, cannot be identified with the orienting reflex. The orienting reflex doubtless includes orienting in the sense

we have used it, but it also involves the operation that we call *detecting*. By detection we mean the contact between the attentional system and the input signal, such that arbitrary response to it can be made.

In our experiments we provide the subjects with cues that allow them to perform the act of orienting. When this is done, detection proceeds more quickly. In the real world it is usual for a signal to produce both orienting (covert and often overt) and detection. Since the efficiency of detection is affected by orienting, orienting must either be in parallel or precede detecting. It might seem paradoxical that orienting toward a signal could precede or occur at the same time as detecting the signal. This paradox is similar to the problem of subception. How can we orient to something that is as yet undetected? The answer to both paradoxes lies in the specific nature of the attentive system that underlies detection. Much of our information processing does not depend upon this system. It is now well documented that complex semantic analysis can go on outside this system (Posner, 1978). Attention is important for nonhabitual responses such as are implied by detection responses. Habitual responses such as orienting the eyes to an event or aligning attention to the stimulated pathway do not appear to require support from this system.

Our experiments also suggest several directions for the analysis of detection. If the movement of attention can be time-locked to an input event, it should be possible to determine (a) the latency with which attention can be switched, (b) whether the time to reach the target is a function of distance, and (c) how such attention switches relate to the articulation of visual space and to the movement of the eyes.[6] It is clear that the general framework for viewing detection experiments outlined in this article is quite con-

---

[6] While this article has been in press much of the work outlined here has been accomplished. For a discussion of movements of covert attention see Shulman, Remington, and McLean (1979). A broader treatment of the relationship between overt and covert attention movements may be found in Posner (1980).

174 M. POSNER, C. SNYDER, AND B. DAVIDSON

sistent with the ideas developing from evoked potential and single-cell work. A more detailed integration of the two approaches may eventually enhance our knowledge of the nature of attention.

Reference Note

1. Smith, S. W., & Blaha, J. *Preliminary report summarizing the results of location uncertainty: Experiments I–VII*. Unpublished experiments, Ohio State University, 1969.

References

Duncan, J. The demonstration of capacity limitation. *Cognitive Psychology*, 1980, *12*, 75–96.

Eason, R. G., Harter, R., & White, C. T. Effects of attention and arousal on visually evoked cortical potentials and reaction time in man. *Physiology and Behavior*, 1969, *4*, 283–289.

Engle, F. L. Visual conspicuity, direction attention and retinal locus. *Vision Research*, 1971, *11*, 563–576.

Eriksen, C. W., & Hoffman, J. E. The extent of processing of noise elements during selective encoding from visual displays. *Perception & Psychophysics*, 1973, *14*, 155–160.

Goldberg, M. E., & Wurtz, R. H. Activity of superior colliculus in behaving monkeys: II. Effects of attention on neuronal response. *Journal of Neurophysiology*, 1972, *35*, 560–574.

Green, D. M., & Birdsall, R. G. Detection and recognition. *Psychological Review*, 1978, *85*, 192–206.

Green, D. M., & Swets, J. A. *Signal detection theory and psychophysics*. Huntington, N.Y.: Krieger, 1974.

Grindley, C. G., & Townsend, V. Voluntary attention in peripheral vision and its effects on acuity and differential thresholds. *Quarterly Journal of Experimental Psychology*, 1968, *20*, 11–19.

Hecht, S., Schlaer, S., & Pirenne, M. H. Energy, quanta and vision. *Journal of General Psychology*, 1942, *25*, 819–840.

LaBerge, D. S., & Samuels, J. Toward a theory of automatic information processing in reading. *Cognitive Psychology*, 1974, *6*, 293–323.

Lappin, J. S., & Uttal, W. R. Does prior knowledge facilitate the detection of visual targets in random noise? *Perception & Psychophysics*, 1976, *20*, 367–374.

Mertens, J. J. Influence of knowledge of target location upon the probability of observation of peripherally observable test flashes. *Journal of the Optical Society of America*, 1956, *46*, 1069–1070.

Moray, N. Where is attention limited? A survey and a model. *Acta Psychologica*, 1967, *27*, 84–92.

Mowrer, O. H. Preparatory set (expectancy)—Further evidence of its central locus. *Journal of Experimental Psychology*, 1941, *28*, 116–133.

Norman, D. A. Toward a theory of memory and attention. *Psychological Review*, 1968, *75*, 522–536.

Posner, M. I. *Chronometric explorations of mind*. Hillsdale, N.J.: Erlbaum 1978.

Posner, M. I. Orienting of attention. *Quarterly Journal of Experimental Psychology*, 1980, *32*, 3–25.

Posner, M. I., Nissen, M. J., & Ogden, W. C. Attended and unattended processing modes: The role of set for spatial location. In H. L. Pick & I. J. Saltzman (Eds.), *Modes of perceiving and processing information*. Hillsdale, N.J.: Erlbaum, 1978.

Sekuler, R., & Ball, K. Mental set alters visibility of moving targets. *Science*, 1977, *198*, 60–62.

Shaw, M., & Shaw, P. Optimal allocation of cognitive resources to spatial location. *Journal of Experimental Psychology: Human Perception and Performance*, 1977, *3*, 201–211.

Shiffrin, R. M., & Gardner, G. T. Visual processing capacity and attentional control. *Journal of Experimental Psychology*, 1972, *93*, 72–82.

Shulman, G. L., Remington, R. W., & McLean, J. P. Moving attention through space. *Journal of Experimental Psychology: Human Perception and Performance*, 1979, *5*, 522–526.

Sokolov, E. N. *Perception and the conditioned reflex*. New York: Macmillan, 1963.

Sperling, G., & Melchner, M. J. Visual search, visual attention and the attention operating characteristic. In J. Requin (Ed.), *Attention and performance VII*. New York: Academic Press, 1978.

Von Voorhis, S., & Hillyard, S. A. Visual evoked potentials and selective attention to points in space. *Perception & Psychophysics*, 1977, *22*, 54–62.

Wurtz, R. H., & Mohler, C. W. Organization of monkey superior colliculus: Enhanced visual response of superficial layer cells. *Journal of Neurophysiology*, 1976, *39*, 745–765.

Received October 30, 1978 ∎

[3]

Abrupt Visual Onsets and Selective Attention: Voluntary Versus Automatic Allocation

Steven Yantis
Johns Hopkins University

John Jonides
University of Michigan

The hypothesis that abrupt visual onsets capture attention automatically, as suggested by Yantis and Jonides (1984) was tested in four experiments. A centrally located cue directed attention to one of several stimulus positions in preparation for the identification of a target letter embedded in an array of distractor letters. In all experiments, one stimulus (either the target or one of the distractors) had an abrupt onset; the remaining letters did not. The effectiveness of the cue was manipulated (varying either its duration or its predictive validity) to test whether abrupt onsets capture attention even when subjects are in a highly focused attentional state. Results showed that onsets do not necessarily capture attention in violation of an observer's intentions. A mechanism for partially automatic attentional capture by abrupt onset is proposed, and the diagnosticity of the intentionality criterion for automaticity is discussed.

Introspective and empirical evidence both suggest that the abrupt appearance of an object in the visual field "draws attention." A plausible account of this phenomenon is that there exists a mechanism that is tuned to abrupt onsets and that one of its functions is to direct visual attention to the locus of an abrupt onset. This in turn could result in the efficient identification of information at that location. Another way of stating the hypothesis is that abrupt onsets may capture visual attention *automatically* and cause the observer to process abrupt visual events with high priority.

This hypothesis has two components. The first is that there is a mechanism that detects abrupt onsets and signals the visual attention system to allocate attentional resources to events exhibiting abrupt onsets. The second is that the allocation of attention resulting from such a signal is automatic. We examine each of these components in turn. The central thesis of this article is that although attention may be efficiently allocated to abrupt onset under some circumstances, this may not happen in a truly automatic fashion, as defined by widely held criteria. The implication of this thesis is either that attentional capture by abrupt onset is not automatic or that one of the commonly cited criteria for automaticity is not really diagnostic of automaticity.

This research was supported in part by funds from National Institute of Mental Health Grant RO1-MH43924 and from BRSG Grant SO7-RR07041 awarded by the Biomedical Research Support Grant Program, National Institutes of Health, to Steven Yantis and in part by Grant 82-0297 from the Air Force Office of Scientific Research to John Jonides.

We are grateful to Seema Chaudhari, Alyson Holoubek, and Scott Tebo for technical assistance. We thank Doug Johnson and James C. Johnston for valuable comments concerning the research, and James Cutting, John Duncan, Jeff Miller, Roger Remington, and an anonymous reviewer for suggestions and comments on an earlier version of this article.

Correspondence concerning this article should be addressed to Steven Yantis, Department of Psychology, Johns Hopkins University, Baltimore, Maryland 21218.

Attentional Capture by Abrupt Onset

The existence of a mechanism that may subserve attentional capture by abrupt onset is supported by evidence from several sources (see Yantis & Jonides, 1984, for a more complete review). Electrophysiological (e.g., Cleland, Levick, & Sanderson, 1973; Lennie, 1980) and psychophysical (e.g., Breitmeyer & Ganz, 1976; Tolhurst, 1975) results have revealed visual mechanisms that are selectively sensitive to the abrupt onset and offset of visual stimuli, relative to their sustained presence. However, although some investigators (e.g., Breitmeyer & Ganz, 1976) have speculated that channels sensitive to abrupt onset may subserve the allocation of visual attention, additional evidence is required to establish the functional relationship between these mechanisms and attention allocation.

Several kinds of evidence may be brought to bear on this functionality question. First, Todd and Van Gelder (1979) compared responses to stimuli that had abrupt onsets with responses to stimuli that did not. Rather than using gradual onsets as a control condition, as some other investigators had done, Todd and Van Gelder developed what they called the *no-onset* procedure. No-onset stimuli are presented by illuminating the stimuli in advance of the target display but camouflaging them with irrelevant line segments; the camouflaging segments are then removed, which reveals the no-onset stimuli. Thus, the stimulus contours themselves are present before the stimulus is presented, and no localized abrupt onset accompanies their appearance (see Figures 1 and 3 for examples). The no-onset procedure is preferable to the use of gradual onset in reaction time experiments, because it permits one to anchor the appearance of stimuli precisely in time, as required for meaningful reaction time measurements. This is not possible with gradual-onset stimuli, or at least it is not possible without additional, complicating assumptions about detection and identification processes.

Todd and Van Gelder (1979) found that onset stimuli were detected more rapidly than were no-onset stimuli in tasks requiring rapid eye movement responses. The magnitude of the advantage for onset stimuli increased with the complexity of the decision that was required (from detection to categorization). Krumhansl (1982) reported data that confirmed and extended this result.

One account of these findings, advanced by Yantis and Jonides (1984), holds that abrupt onset captures attention automatically, which results in more favorable performance for onset versus no-onset stimuli. This hypothesis was supported by the results of a visual search experiment in which a prespecified target letter was to be detected in an array of two or four items. (Jonides and Yantis, 1988, replicated the results with display sizes of three, five, and seven stimuli, verifying the linearity of the display-size functions.) Every search display contained one onset stimulus and one or more no-onset stimuli. When the target was present (as it was on half of all trials), it was either an onset or a no-onset stimulus.

The critical measurements in this experiment concerned the effect of display size on reaction time as a function of whether the target was an onset or a no-onset stimulus. Standard visual search experiments yield linearly increasing reaction time functions of display size. When target-present functions have slopes that are roughly half those of target-absent functions, the increase is usually interpreted as reflecting a serial, self-terminating search of the display.[1] Flat display-size functions obtained under other conditions (e.g., Egeth, Jonides, & Wall, 1972; Schneider & Shiffrin, 1977; Treisman & Gelade, 1980) typically are thought to reflect parallel visual search. Yantis and Jonides (1984) reasoned that if onsets capture attention automatically, this should be reflected in the slopes of the display-size functions: Reaction time should not increase with display size for onset targets, but it should increase in the usual serial, self-terminating fashion when the target is not an onset item.

The results were consistent with this hypothesis. Onset targets were evidently processed first regardless of their identity or position, and the data were quite well fit by a model in which the remaining stimuli were then scanned in a serial, self-terminating search. That attentional capture was automatic in this task was supported by the finding that reaction time did not increase with display size when the target had an abrupt onset while there was a significant slope when the target was of the no-onset type. As predicted by the self-terminating search model, the slope of the display-size function when the target was a no-onset stimulus was about half that of the function when the target was absent. The capture model provided a superior quantitative fit to the data than did several competing models.

Although Yantis and Jonides (1984) attributed capture by abrupt onset to properties of the visual system that are differentially sensitive to abrupt onset, it was nevertheless possible that the mere presence of a unique stimulus feature was the cause of attentional capture. According to this argument, any sufficiently salient and unique stimulus feature could yield the same result. Recently, Jonides and Yantis (1988) tested this idea by comparing the attention-capturing ability of abrupt onset with two other salient stimulus properties: color and intensity. In these experiments, the ability of an odd item (unique in either color or intensity) to capture attention was compared with the corresponding ability of an onset item. Only abrupt stimulus onset yielded the pattern of results characteristic of attentional capture. The results were inconsistent with the uniqueness account. Instead, it appears that abrupt onset has a privileged status in capturing attention.

The evidence reviewed in this section suggests that abrupt onsets draw attention and result in rapid identification of onset stimuli compared with no-onset stimuli. That attentional capture by abrupt onset may be automatic is supported by satisfaction of a load criterion for automaticity. In the next section, we examine more closely some of the criteria commonly applied to diagnose automaticity in visual search processes.

Criteria for Automaticity

Treatments of automatic information processing typically identify two properties that consistently accompany what are thought to be automatic processes (e.g., Hasher & Zacks, 1979; Logan, 1978; Posner & Snyder, 1975; Regan, 1981; Schneider & Fisk, 1982; Schneider & Shiffrin, 1977). Only if both of these criteria are satisfied is a process said to exhibit strong automaticity. The first criterion is insensitivity to concurrent perceptual or cognitive load: An automatic process is not hindered when concurrent information load is increased (we refer to this as the *load-insensitivity criterion*). The second criterion is that an automatic process is not subject to voluntary control: Attempts by a subject to prevent an automatic process from proceeding are not successful. We refer to this as the *intentionality criterion* (see Jonides, Naveh-Benjamin, & Palmer, 1985; Palmer & Jonides, 1988, for further discussion of these criteria).

Kahneman and Treisman (1984) defined three levels of automaticity in perception. A process is strongly automatic if it is not facilitated by focusing attention on a stimulus and not inhibited by focusing attention away from it. Thus a strongly automatic process satisfies both the load insensitivity criterion and the intentionality criterion. If either of these criteria is at least sometimes violated, a process is said to be partially or occasionally automatic (or, of course, not automatic at all). The Stroop effect is an example of a process (word recognition) that is normally completed even when attention is diverted from the stimulus but can be facilitated by allocating attention to it; word recognition is therefore a partially automatic process, according to Kahneman and Treisman. As discussed later, because the load-insensitivity and intentionality criteria are not inseparable, these shades of meaning influence the conclusions that are justified by our data.

As we stated above, in our previous work we speculated that abrupt onset may capture attention automatically. However, although we have found supporting evidence for the

---

[1] There are exceptions and complications associated with the interpretation of linear display-size functions in visual search (see, e.g., Townsend & Ashby, 1983). These complications do not materially affect our argument and are therefore beyond the scope of the present discussion. We refer to linearly increasing display-size functions with 2:1 (negative:positive) slope ratios as reflecting serial, self-terminating search, with the understanding that such an interpretation is not the only one possible.

load-insensitivity criterion, converging evidence for strong automaticity has not yet been obtained for the intentionality criterion. In the experiments reported below, we tested the intentionality criterion to determine whether attentional capture by abrupt onset may be characterized as strongly automatic.

A related effort was reported by Jonides (1981), who examined the extent to which a peripheral visual cue elicits an automatic shift of attention to the spatial location it indicates. He tested three criteria for automaticity and compared peripheral and central cues under each criterion. He found that cues appearing in the peripheral visual field capture attention automatically according to all three tested criteria. In particular, Jonides (1981) found in his Experiment 1 that peripheral cues produced attentional benefits regardless of whether a concurrent memory load was imposed on the subject whereas the effectiveness of a central cue was severaly attenuated under a concurrent memory load. This satisfied the load-insensitivity criterion. In his Experiment 2, Jonides discovered that even when peripheral cues were randomly associated with a visual search target and subjects were told to ignore the cues, reaction time was significantly faster when the cue was valid than when it Was not. In contrast, subjects were able to ignore central cues that were only randomly related to the target position. A third experiment verified this resistance to subjects' intentions and expectancies evidenced by peripheral cues. Experiments 2 and 3 together provided evidence satisfying the intentionality criterion for automaticity. In summary, the results reported by Jonides (1981) are consistent with the hypothesis that peripheral visual events capture attention automatically.

Posner and Cohen (1984) subsequently showed that with short intervals between the cue and target events, attention appears to be summoned to the cue, but that at longer intervals there is a relative inhibition in detecting events at the cued location. Posner and Cohen argued that neither of these effects is under voluntary control, on the basis, in part, that the capture of attention at short intervals occurred even when the cue was not predictive of the target location.

Lambert, Spencer, and Mohindra (1987) examined this question further by providing explicit instructions to subjects to avoid attending to the cued location. They found that even under these instructions, subjects evidently could not completely avoid a tendency to attend to an abrupt peripheral cue. However, instructions did significantly reduce the tendency to attend to such cues, compared with a no-instruction condition. These results undermine the notion that attention is unavoidably and inevitably summoned by a peripheral cue.

In a recent study by Müller and Rabbitt (1989), subjects were to attend to a location cued by a central arrow; at various moments after the arrow appeared and before the target stimulus appeared, a box surrounding one of the four possible target positions brightened briefly. The box brightening was not predictive of target location and was to be ignored. Müller and Rabbitt found that performance was impaired when a box brightened at an uncued location, even when the cue correctly and predictably indicated the location of the target. They concluded that attention was involuntarily captured to some extent even when attention was directed to the cued

location, although the extent of the performance impairment was modulated by voluntary allocation. It is worth noting that Müller and Rabbit used long cue-to-target stimulus onset asynchronies (SOAs; 600–1200 ms) and cues of moderate validity (50%). Both of these factors might have prevented optimal attentional focusing, thus permitting some degree of attentional capture by the irrelevant box brightenings. In fact, in the experiments we report below, this is exactly what appears to happen.

In all of the studies we have reviewed in the preceding paragraphs, the effects of cues on capturing attention were examined. There was in all cases some period of time between the onset of the summoning event (the cue) and the imperative event (the target). In the experiments reported here, attention was allocated in advance, and the imperative event itself either did or did not have an abrupt onset. So the present approach may allow more direct assessment of the influence of abrupt peripheral onset on the capture of attention.

Another experiment that speaks to the intentionality criterion in a somewhat different domain was reported by Shiffrin and Schneider (1977, Experiment 4d). In this experiment subjects first underwent extensive training in a consistently mapped (CM) visual search task. CM training leads to automatic detection of target stimuli, as reflected in flat memory- and display-size functions. In order to demonstrate that CM targets also satisfy the intentionality criterion, Shiffrin and Schneider transferred these highly trained subjects to a new varied mapping (VM) visual search task in which none of the stimuli from the training task participated with the exception of occasional "CM foils" (i.e., letters that had been targets in the previous CM task). Subjects were to attend to one diagonal of a four-element display and to ignore the other diagonal. CM foils sometimes appeared in the to-be-ignored diagonal. The data revealed significant visual search interference on trials in which a CM foil was present compared with trials in which one was not, a result suggesting that subjects could not suppress an automatic attention response to the foil. Of course, attentional capture by a CM target is fundamentally different from attentional capture by an abrupt onset. The former is learned, whereas the latter may or may not be learned (e.g., it could be "hard-wired"). Nevertheless, this experiment provides further evidence that there may be conditions under which certain stimuli capture attention in violation of an individual's intentions.

In the experiments reported below, we pursued this question by testing the intentionality criterion for the automaticity of capture by abrupt-onset stimuli. According to this criterion, attention is said to be captured automatically only if capture cannot be prevented at will. In our earlier experiments (Yantis & Jonides, 1984), subjects were not attempting to attend to any particular location; instead, they were prepared for the target in any position (in what Eriksen & Yeh, 1985, called a *diffuse attention mode*). In the present experiments, in contrast, we provided subjects with advance information about the likely position of an upcoming target, to induce focused attention at a cued spatial location. We then examined the effects of an abruptly onset stimulus appearing in the cued or in an uncued location. If attention is captured automatically by an abrupt onset, reaction time to a target item should reflect capture whether attention was focused on it or not. On the other hand, if subjects are able to focus attention and prevent an abrupt onset from disrupting performance, the automaticity hypothesis must be reexamined.

Experiment 1

The purpose of Experiment 1 was to determine whether there is any reason to believe that abrupt onsets do not satisfy the intentionality criterion for automaticity. According to this criterion, the mere presence of an abrupt onset in a display should capture attention regardless of the subject's voluntary allocation of attention induced by an attentional precue. Consequently, whether the cue is valid or not should have little or no impact on performance in the presence of abrupt stimulus onset; in all cases the onset stimulus should exhibit priority.

On each trial of the task, a central cue appeared, indicating a position to the left or right of fixation. After 200 ms, a letter appeared in each position. Subjects were to determine whether an E or an H appeared in the display (exactly one of these letters appearing in each display, with an irrelevant letter appearing in the opposite position). The cue was valid (i.e., indicated the position occupied by the target E or H) on 80% of the trials. In this experiment we monitored eye position to ensure that covert movements of attention, and not overt movements of the eyes, were responsible for performance.

Method

Subjects. Seventeen University of Michigan undergraduates were paid to participate in two 50-min sessions. All had uncorrected normal vision.

Equipment and stimuli. Stimulus events were controlled and responses were collected by a PDP-11/60 computer. Stimuli appeared on a DEC VT-11 graphics scope. Subjects responded by pressing keys on an HP-2621A terminal keyboard. Subjects sat in a sound-attenuating booth under comfortable illumination.

Eye position was monitored by a Gulf + Western Model 200 scleral reflectance device. Eye movement data were collected via an analog-to-digital converter on the computer sampling at 1 kHz. Head position was maintained by a chin rest. The monitor was calibrated at the start of each block of trials and again whenever departures from fixation were detected on three trials since the last calibration run. A position criterion of ±1.5° horizontally was established for defining eye movements. Trials on which an eye movement was detected were marked for identification in subsequent analyses; these trials were not rerun.

The stimulus letters were constructed by illuminating five of the seven segments of a box figure eight. The letters so constructed were E, H, P, S, and U. Each letter subtended a visual angle of 1.9° in height and 1° in width from a viewing distance of 45 cm. The letters appeared 5.8° to the left and to the right of fixation. The vertical separation of the nearest contours of the stimuli was 0.5°.

Two letter-presentation modes were used. *Onset* letters were presented by illuminating a five-segment letter in a location that had previously contained no segments. *No-onset* letters were presented by removing two segments from a seven-segment box figure eight to reveal a previously camouflaged five-segment letter. In the former case, the letter segments appeared abruptly; in the latter, the camouflaged letter segments were present for 1,200 ms before display onset and did not themselves change during the course of presentation.[2]

In order to equate the two presentation modes as much as possible, we began each trial with two placeholders on each side of the display. One of these was the required box figure eight, which would serve as camouflage for a no-onset letter (if one were to appear on that side of the display). The other placeholder consisted of six dots arranged at the vertices of a box figure eight. The two placeholders appeared one directly above the other, 0.5° apart at their nearest contours, two on the left and two on the right of the display. They were illuminated 1,200 ms before the onset of the display. The relative positions (top or bottom) of the dot and figure eight placeholders were chosen randomly and independently for the two sides on each trial. At trial onset, one of the two placeholders on each side disappeared, and the other changed into a letter. On trials on which an onset letter appeared on a given side of the display, the figure eight placeholder disappeared, and the six dots changed into a letter. On trials on which a no-onset letter appeared on a given side of the display, the six-dot placeholder disappeared, and two segments of the figure eight were removed to reveal a letter. These events are illustrated in Figure 1.

Design. A 2 × 2 × 2 design was used, the factors of which were target type (onset/no-onset), distractor type (onset/no-onset), and cue validity (valid/invalid). Target type and distractor type were completely crossed factors, so that half of all trials involved onset targets and half no-onset targets; within each of these conditions, half of the distractors were onset and half no-onset. Thus 25% of the trials fell under each of the four combinations of target and distractor type.

On 80% of the trials, the cue arrow indicated the side that the target (E or H) would occupy, and on the remaining 20% of the trials, the cue indicated the opposite side. The target appeared on each side about equally often. The target was E on half of the trials and H on the other half. Target location, target identity, distractor identity (the distractors came from among P, S, and U), and the relative positions of the letters (top or bottom) within a side were chosen randomly on each trial. The ordering of trial types determined by the three main factors was also random. Each session was divided into 10 blocks of 40 trials each, for a total of 400 trials per session. Session 1 was considered practice.

Procedure. Trial events are depicted in Figure 1. A fixation cross, along with the four placeholders, was first illuminated. After 1,000 ms a single arrow appeared at fixation for 200 ms, pointing either to the left or the right. Subjects were told to maintain fixation on the center of the screen throughout the trial (the penalty for repeated failure being recalibration of the eye movement monitor, a mildly annoying event). Finally, the placeholders were replaced by two letters, one on the left and one on the right, as described above. One of the two letters was the target to be discriminated (E or H), and the other was an irrelevant distractor (P, S, or U). Subjects determined which of the two targets was present and responded by pressing the period key (.) with their right index finger if the H appeared and the slash key (/) with their right middle finger if the E appeared. The display was then erased, and the next trial started 500 ms later. Error feedback was provided via an auditory beep. The duration of the cuing arrow was chosen so as to generate the maximum attentional facilitation typically observed in experiments of this type (e.g., Remington & Pierce, 1984).

At the end of each block of trials, a performance summary giving mean reaction time and total number of errors was displayed. Subjects were encouraged to respond quickly while maintaining a low error rate (i.e., no more than one or two errors in each block of 40 trials).

---

[2] Abrupt offset of the camouflaging contours was shown by Yantis and Jonides (1984, Experiment 3) to have no significant disruptive effect on attentional capture by abrupt onset; however, see Miller (1989).

Subjects were told that the target would be E half of the time and H half of the time and that it would appear on the left and the right sides equally often. They were further told that the cuing arrow would provide important preparatory information: The target would appear on the side indicated by the arrow 80% of the time. It was made clear that it would be to their advantage to attend to the indicated side while maintaining fixation, so as to increase their speed and accuracy. Subjects readily understood and indicated compliance with these instructions.

Results

The results of Experiment 1 revealed that abrupt onset alone did not determine the focus of attention. Instead, whether the target was cued or not modulated the effect of abrupt onset. This conclusion is reflected in the results of a three-way analysis of variance (ANOVA), with target type (onset/no-onset), distractor type (onset/no-onset), and cue validity (valid/invalid) as factors. There was a significant main effect of validity, $F(1, 16) = 55.2, p < .001$, and target type, $F(1, 16) = 20.6, p < .001$; the effect of distractor type was not significant, $F(1, 16) < 1$. Most important, there was a significant interaction between cue validity and target type, $F(1, 16) = 9.5, p < .01$; the effect of target type was larger when the cue was invalid (25 ± 12 ms) than when it was valid (8 ± 9 ms).[3] This suggests that when subjects attended to the target position before its appearance, it mattered little whether the target had an abrupt onset but when subjects were misled by the cue, a target with an abrupt onset was more rapidly identified than one without an abrupt onset.

The comparison afforded by the factorial analysis above is not completely illuminating, however, because it includes the relatively uninformative conditions in which the target and distractor were either both onset or both no-onset stimuli. It is more revealing to analyze separately the subset of the data in which the target was an onset and the distractor a no-onset, or vice versa (i.e., those trials on which exactly one onset and one no-onset stimulus appeared). An analysis of variance was therefore conducted with this subset of the data (shown in Figure 2).

There was a significant main effect of cue validity, $F(1, 16) = 79.3, p < .001$: Reaction time was much faster with a valid than an invalid cue. There was also a significant effect of

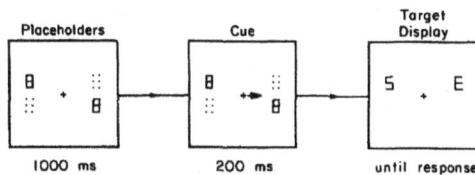

Figure 1. Trial events in Experiment 1. (In this example, the target is an E and the cue is valid; the target is an onset stimulus, and the distractor [S] is a no-onset stimulus. The relative positions of the figure eight and dot placeholders were varied from trial to trial with the constraint that there was always one of each on each side of fixation. Letters could appear in either the upper or the lower position on each side. The target could be either an E or an H.)

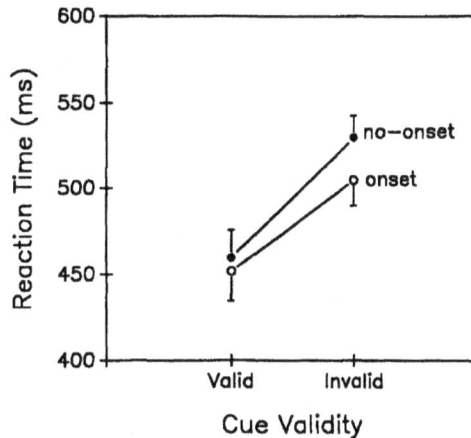

Figure 2. Mean reaction time for the conditions of Experiment 1 that involved one onset and one no-onset stimulus. (Curve parameter is target type. Error bars extend to ±1 *SE*.)

target type, $F(1, 16) = 32.5, p < .001$: When the target was an onset and the distractor was not, reaction time was faster than when the distractor was an onset and the target was not. Finally, the interaction between these two factors was significant, $F(1, 16) = 8.2, p < .05$. The effect of target type was larger when the cue was invalid than when it was valid. This interaction is what calls into question the hypothesis that abrupt onset always captures attention involuntarily.

Error rate in this experiment was 5.3% overall. There was a strong positive correlation between error rate and mean reaction time (.64), which indicates that there was no strong speed/accuracy trade-off.

Discussion

The results of Experiment 1 provide preliminary evidence that abrupt onsets may not satisfy the intentionality criterion for strong automaticity. This conclusion would undermine our earlier speculation (Yantis & Jonides, 1984) that abrupt onsets capture attention automatically.

To clarify this point, we considered what the very strongest version of the intentionality hypothesis would state. If abrupt onset captured attention regardless of the volitional state of the subject (e.g., whether or not the subject was focusing attention on a specific location in space), then reaction time to identify a target with an abrupt onset should not vary at

[3] Effect sizes are given throughout this article in terms of the mean ± *SE*, rounded to the nearest millisecond. Because all within-subjects comparisons in Experiments 2 and 3 involved groups of 10 subjects, there are 9 degrees of freedom for *t* tests using these values. Thus, whenever $M/SE > 2.262$, the effect is significant at the .05 level. Reported *t* values may vary from the ratios of the values given in the text because of rounding.

all with cue validity, and reaction time to onset targets should be faster everywhere than reaction time to no-onset targets. In other words, according to this account, the two functions in Figure 2 should be horizontal and parallel to one another, with the onset function below the no-onset function. It is clear that this pattern did not emerge.

A slightly weaker version of the hypothesis would state that there might be a small delay associated with drawing attention from an attended location to an unattended onset stimulus, which would yield an effect of cue validity, but that subjects would always take the time to process the onset stimulus. According to this account, reaction time in the valid-cue condition should have been influenced a great deal by whether the target was an onset or not: On trials when the target was an onset, reaction time should have been fast; on trials when the distractor was an onset, subjects' attention should have been captured by the distractor in the uncued position, which would result in a substantial delay in responding.

Indeed, the effect of target type in the valid-cue condition should have been at least as large as in the invalid-cue condition; in the invalid-cue condition, subjects would either be captured by the (uncued) onset target, which would yield a fast reaction time, or be required to process the (cued) onset distractor and then shift attention to the (uncued) target position. In other words, the effect of target type on the valid-cue trials should have been to add two shifts of attention and an analysis of a distractor to reaction time; the corresponding effect on the invalid-cue trials should have involved only one shift of attention and an analysis of the distractor. However, the data reveal that the effect of target type was significantly smaller on the valid- than on the invalid-cue trials.

Together, these detailed predictions of various versions of the intentionality criterion are clearly violated by the results from Experiment 1 and lead us to question whether abrupt onsets satisfy that criterion for automaticity.

The next task was to explore the boundaries of this violation of the intentionality criterion. In Experiments 2 and 3, respectively, we manipulated two factors that are thought to influence the allocation of attention: cue–target SOA and cue validity. This permitted us to determine whether the voluntary allocation of attention dominates capture by abrupt onset and, if so, to what extent.

In Experiments 2 and 3, we also removed the six-dot placeholders that were used in Experiment 1. The six-dot placeholders were used to address a confounding in previous experiments: Onset stimuli always appeared in blank locations, whereas no-onset stimuli appeared in nonblank locations. The purpose of the placeholders was to show that the unavoidable attentional capture induced by abrupt onsets could not be attributed to the absence of some kind of object in the location subsequently occupied by the onset stimuli. If there is some small effect of this manipulation, it would serve to diminish the influence of abrupt onset in Experiment 1. We found in Experiment 1 that abrupt onsets did not capture attention regardless of intention; this shifted our a priori null hypothesis to one stating that abrupt onsets do not capture attention involuntarily. Consequently, in Experiments 2 and 3 we did not use the six-dot placeholders in order to maximize the opportunity for attentional capture by abrupt onset.

Experiment 2

In Experiment 2, subjects were required to determine which of two letters (E or H) was present in a display of four letters arranged at a subset of the vertices of an imaginary hexagon centered at fixation. On each trial a central arrowhead cue reliably indicated the location of the critical letter. The cue appeared 200 ms before, simultaneously with, or 200 ms after the onset of the display. Subjects are known to be capable of aligning attention with a spatial location that is likely to contain task-relevant information within 200 ms of receiving that information (e.g., Eriksen & St. James, 1986; Murphy & Eriksen, 1987; Posner, 1980; Posner, Cohen, & Rafal, 1982; Remington & Pierce, 1984). Thus the leading cue placed subjects in a state of maximal attentional readiness for the appearance of the critical item, and the trailing cue did not permit subjects to align attention with the cued location before the display appears. The three cuing conditions were run with three separate groups of subjects. Crossed with the cuing factor was an onset factor. In each display, exactly one item had an abrupt onset, and the remaining three items did not have an abrupt onset.

The automaticity hypothesis asserts that regardless of the subject's state of attentional readiness, an abrupt onset appearing in an uncued location should capture attention and slow responding to cued items that do not have abrupt onsets, because, by hypothesis, attention is involuntarily drawn to the onset location and can be applied only subsequently to the cued item. On the other hand, if the preliminary allocation of attention dominates performance, then whether or not the target has an abrupt onset should not influence performance.

Method

Subjects. Thirty undergraduates at the Johns Hopkins University served in one 50-min session for class credit. All subjects had normal or corrected-to-normal vision. Ten subjects were randomly assigned to each of the three SOA conditions.

Stimuli and equipment. Stimuli were presented on a NEC Multisync monitor driven by a Color-400 EGA card controlled by an IBM PC/AT microcomputer. Letters were high-contrast yellow against a black background. The letters E, H, P, S, and U served as stimuli. The letters were formed by illuminating the appropriate segments of a seven-segment box figure eight. From a viewing distance of about 40 cm, each letter subtended 0.9° of visual angle in height and 0.5° in width. The letters appeared at a subset of the vertices of an imaginary hexagon centered at fixation with radius 4.2°, and they were 4.2° apart, center to center. The cue was a triangular arrowhead, appearing directly at fixation, pointing at one of the six potential stimulus locations. The arrowhead subtended about 0.6° in length and 0.3° in width at its base (see Figure 3 for an example of the display).

Responses were made by pressing with the right or left index finger one of two buttons mounted in an angled response box placed on the table in front of the subject.

Design. Each subject participated in eight 72-trial blocks. A 2 × 2 factorial design was used within subjects. The two within-subjects factors were target identity (E or H) and trial type (onset or no-onset). The target was an E on half of the trials in each block and an H on the other half. Within each of these factors, the target had an abrupt onset on half of the trials, and the three nontargets were of the no-onset type; on the other half of the trials, one of the nontargets had

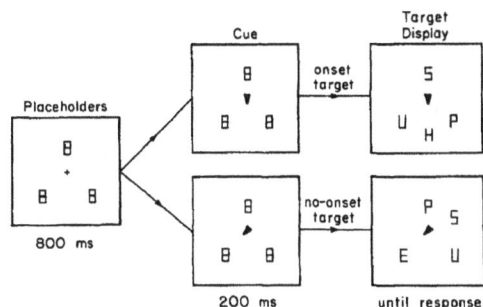

Figure 3. Trial events in the −200-ms stimulus onset asynchrony (SOA) condition of Experiment 2. (In the top row, right, the target [H] is an onset letter. In the bottom row, right, the target [E] is a no-onset letter, and one of the distractors [S] is an onset. The cue in both examples precedes the target display by 200 ms; in two other conditions, not shown, the cue appears simultaneous with or 200 ms after the start of the target display. The initial positions of the three figure-eight placeholders alternated between the upward-pointing triangle, shown, and an inverted triangle.)

an abrupt onset, and the target and two of the distractors were of the no-onset type.

There was one between-subjects factor, SOA. The asynchrony between the onsets of the letter display and the cue was −200 ms (i.e., the cue preceded the onset of the display by 200 ms), 0 ms (i.e., the cue and the display appeared simultaneously), or 200 ms (i.e., the cue followed the display by 200 ms). The cue pointed at the critical letter (E or H) on every trial and thus represented a 100% valid attention cue.

The target appeared in each display location equally often. On no-onset trials, the location of the onset nontarget was chosen from each of the nontarget locations equally often.

A number of precautions were taken to avoid transient practice effects. The session began with a block of 20 practice trials; each block began with 3 warm-up trials, and every error was followed by a randomly chosen recovery trial. Responses from the practice, warm-up, and recovery trials were not recorded and did not enter into any analyses.

Procedure. On each trial (see Figure 3) a fixation point was displayed for 500 ms as a warning that the trial was about to begin. Three box figure-eight placeholders were then displayed (along with the fixation point) at three of the stimulus positions, forming either an upward-pointing or a downward-pointing triangle (randomly and equally often within each block). The placeholders were always present for 1,000 ms before the onset of the test display regardless of SOA. The test display consisted of four letters. Three of these (the no-onset letters) appeared in the locations previously occupied by the placeholders; they were revealed by removing the appropriate segments of the figure eight, thereby avoiding abrupt onset of the contours of the letter itself. The fourth letter (the onset stimulus) appeared abruptly in a previously blank location at the same time that the no-onset letters were revealed.

The cue appeared at fixation and always indicated the location of the critical letter (E or H). The cue appeared at one of three possible SOAs with respect to the start of the letter display: −200, 0, or 200 ms. Because the placeholders were always present for 1,000 ms before the onset of the letters, the cue appeared 800, 1,000, or 1,200 ms after the onset of the placeholders.

Subjects were instructed to determine whether an E or an H was present in each test display and to press the right button with their right index finger if the E was present and the left button with their left index finger if the H was present. They were told to use the cue to direct their attention to the critical location, if possible. To reiterate, the cue was 100% valid: It always indicated the location of the critical letter. A 100-ms, 800-Hz tone was presented as feedback if an incorrect response was made. No tone was provided after correct responses.

Subjects were instructed not to move their eyes at any time during the experiment, as this would make their task more difficult and slow their responses. None of the subjects expressed any difficulty in maintaining steady fixation. Previous work in similar paradigms has shown that subjects can and do reliably maintain fixation when this is required; task replications under eye movement monitoring have repeatedly failed to detect any effect on performance. The results of Experiment 1, in which we did monitor eye position, support our contention that eye position remained constant in this experiment.

Results

Mean reaction times from correct responses for the various conditions of Experiment 2 are shown in Figure 4. The results are straightforward: Under an effective attentional cue (i.e., in the −200-ms SOA condition), there was no reliable difference in reaction time between trials on which the critical item had an abrupt onset and trials on which one of the distractors had an abrupt onset. In contrast, when the cue was relatively ineffective (i.e., in the 0-ms and 200-ms SOA conditions), whether the target or a distractor had an abrupt onset had a large and significant effect.

To verify these trends, we carried out a two-way repeated measures ANOVA, with the between-subjects factor of SOA (−200, 0, and 200 ms) and the within-subjects factor of trial type (onset and no-onset). This analysis revealed a significant main effect of both factors, $F(2, 18) = 4.57$, $p < .05$ for SOA and $F(1, 9) = 39.60$, $p < .001$ for trial type. The interaction between SOA and trial type was also highly significant, $F(2, 18) = 30.69$, $p < .001$. The effect of trial type was 8 ± 5, 52 ± 10, and 117 ± 18 ms for the −200-, 0-, and 200-ms SOA groups, respectively (see Footnote 3). Planned comparisons of these values revealed that the difference between the onset

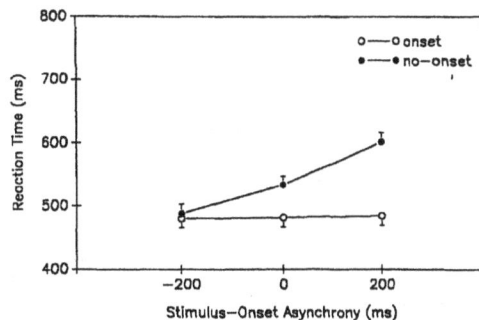

Figure 4. Mean reaction time for each condition of Experiment 2. (The bars extend to ±1 *SE.*)

and the no-onset trials in the −200-ms group was not significantly greater than zero, $t(9) = 1.71$, $p > .1$ and that the corresponding differences in the 0- and 200-ms groups were significantly greater than zero, $t(9) = 4.98$ and 6.45 for the two groups, respectively, both $ps < .001$.

The overall error rate was 2.4%. Analysis of the error rate differences in the three SOA conditions revealed a pattern similar to that for the reaction times. The differences in error rate between the onset and the no-onset trials were 0.6 ± 0.2, 1.4 ± 0.5, and 2.6 ± 0.9% for the −200-, 0-, and 200-ms SOAs, respectively. There was a positive correlation of .93 between mean reaction time and mean error rate in the six experimental conditions. No suggestion of a speed/accuracy trade-off is present.

Discussion

A straightforward characterization of these data is that focusing attention in response to a valid and temporally useful cue (in the −200-ms SOA condition) virtually eliminated any effect of abrupt onset in the discrimination task. This can be seen by noting that the results for onset and no-onset targets are virtually identical in this condition. It should be recalled that when the target is of the no-onset type, there is an onset elsewhere in the display. If this distractor onset had captured attention, it should have disrupted performance on these trials compared with onset-target trials. It did not. Evidently, then, abrupt onset did not overcome the volitional allocation of attention in this experiment, and the intentionality criterion for automaticity was violated.

When the attentional cue was not available in advance of the onset of the test display in the 0-ms and 200-ms SOA conditions, attentional resources could not be focused in anticipation of the critical item. Under these circumstances, abrupt onset had a substantial influence on reaction time: When the target had an abrupt onset, responses were much more rapid than when one of the distractors had an abrupt onset. It is important to establish this result, because it demonstrates that abrupt onset can capture attention in the discrimination task used here, thereby providing validation of the task.

One might wonder why the effect of abrupt onset was greater in the 200-ms condition than in the 0-ms condition. After all, in both of these conditions, subjects were presumably unable to focus attention on the relevant position before the onset of the display. We suggest that attention was drawn to the onset position rapidly in both of these conditions (because in neither of them was attention focused in advance). Indeed, the data from the onset conditions suggest that attentional capture by abrupt onset was nearly as efficient in these conditions as when attention was allocated in advance. Now consider the no-onset conditions. Here, attention is assumed to be drawn to a distractor with an abrupt onset. In the 0-ms condition, the information from the cue might still have been used to shift attention from the distractor position to the cued target position. In the 200-ms condition, however, information provided by the cue about the position of the target was not available until later, and so subjects may have had to engage in a search for the target until it was found or until

the cue appeared. Because some search time may have been required in the 200-ms no-onset condition, reaction time was slower than in the 0-ms no-onset condition.

The finding that abrupt onsets capture attention when attention is unfocused is consistent with the results of Yantis and Jonides (1984). In that study, subjects were in a state of diffuse attention (there were no additional cues), and therefore they had not allocated attention to specific locations in preparation for the display. As in the present experiment, onsets did capture attention in that case.

The present experiment also verifies a conclusion drawn from Experiment 2 of Yantis and Jonides (1984). That experiment was conducted to determine whether the superior performance for onset stimuli over no-onset stimuli might be attributed not to attentional capture but to some perceptual difficulty in processing no-onset stimuli compared with onset stimuli. In the experiment subjects were provided with an advance cue indicating the position of a target that was to be identified. We found that reaction time to discriminate the target was the same for onset and no-onset stimuli, as long as attention was suitably allocated in advance. This demonstrated that when differential attentional effects were removed, there was no residual difference in the time required to process onset and no-onset letters. The present experiment verifies and extends that result: When attention is effectively allocated in advance, reaction time to discriminate a letter does not depend on whether it is an abrupt onset. The present experiment goes further in demonstrating that this holds even when a to-be-ignored onset stimulus appears elsewhere in the visual field.

Experiment 3

Experiment 2 established that an effective attentional cue could subvert the attention-capturing power of an abrupt onset. In that experiment we manipulated the effectiveness of the attentional cue by varying its temporal position. Less effective cues (i.e., those that could not be used to focus attention in advance of the display) yielded performance that was most susceptible to capture by abrupt onset. To provide converging evidence for this conclusion, we conducted another experiment in which we again manipulated cue effectiveness, this time by varying the predictive validity of the cue while keeping its temporal position fixed at −200-ms SOA (which has been shown to be effective in focusing attention, as verified by Experiment 2; see also Eriksen & St. James, 1986; Remington & Pierce, 1984). The cues had validities of 100%, 75%, or 25% (with four stimulus positions, 25% provides only random predictive validity).

The results of Experiments 1 and 2 already undermine a strong version of the automatic-capture hypothesis. On the basis of those results, we hypothesized that functional (i.e., high-validity) cues would tend to rivet attention to the cued position and thus prevent the disruption of performance by an onset occurring elsewhere in the field. It should be noted that we obtained just this result in the −200-ms SOA condition of Experiment 2. In contrast, when the cue was not as functional (i.e., in low-validity conditions), subjects would be likely to spread their attention over the entire display area, and the appearance of an onset should capture attention and dominate performance. This hypothesis, then, predicts an interaction between cue validity and trial type.

Method

Subjects. Thirty undergraduate students at the Johns Hopkins University served as subjects for course credit. None of the subjects had served in Experiments 1 or 2, and all had normal or corrected-to-normal vision. Ten subjects were randomly assigned to each of three validity groups.

Stimuli and equipment. The stimuli and equipment were the same as in Experiment 2.

Design. Each subject participated in eight blocks of 72 trials. The two within-subjects factors in the 2 × 2 design were target identity (E or H) and trial type (onset or no-onset). As before, the target was an E on half of the trials in each block and an H on the other half; within each of these factors, the target had an abrupt onset on half of the trials (and the three nontargets were of the no-onset type), and on the other half of the trials one of the nontargets had an abrupt onset (and the target was of the no-onset type).

The between-subjects factor was cue validity. One group of subjects experienced a cue validity of 100%, one group 75%, and one group 25%. For the 75% group, the cue indicated the location of the target on 75% of the trials and a randomly chosen nontarget location on the remaining trials. For the 25% group, the cue indicated the target on just 25% of the trials and a randomly chosen nontarget on the remaining 75% of the trials. This yields five conditions, which we denote as follows: 100V, 75V, 75I, 25V, and 25I. The number corresponds to the validity condition (100%, 75%, or 25% validity), and the letter corresponds to whether the cue was valid or invalid (V or I). Thus, Condition 75I consisted of those 25% of the trials for the 75% validity group on which the cue was not valid. Similarly, Condition 25I consisted of those 75% of the trials for the 25% validity group on which the cue was not valid. Of course, there were no invalid trials for the 100% validity group.

Each condition can be categorized according to whether the target had an abrupt onset. The target appeared in each location equally often. On no-onset trials the location of the onset nontarget was chosen from each of the nontarget locations equally often.

The 100%-valid group underwent exactly the same stimulus conditions as the −200-ms SOA group in Experiment 2 (all SOAs in the present experiment were −200 ms, and all cue validities in Experiment 2 were 100%). This condition therefore represents an exact replication of the corresponding condition of Experiment 2.

As in Experiment 2, we included practice, warm-up, and recovery trials in the design, the responses to which were not recorded and did not enter into any analyses.

Procedure. The procedure was just as in Experiment 2 with the exception that the cue always appeared 200 ms before the onset of the test display and that the cue sometimes indicated a nontarget location (for the 75% and the 25% groups). Figure 3 shows the sequence of stimulus events.

Subjects in all three groups were informed of the effective cue validity. Subjects in the 100% and in the 75% conditions were encouraged to attend to the cued location, because that location was certain (for the 100% group) or likely (for the 75% group) to contain the target item on each trial. Subjects in the 25% condition were told that the target was equally likely to appear in any of the display locations (including the cued one) regardless of where the cue pointed. They were told to ignore the cue and to be prepared to make a perceptual judgment about stimuli in any of the display locations. We thus attempted to encourage subjects in the 25% group to remain in a diffuse attention mode.

Results

Mean reaction times from correct responses for the various conditions of Experiment 3 are shown in Figure 5. There was no effect of target type in the 100V condition. This finding, which verifies the result obtained from the −200-ms SOA condition of Experiment 2, demonstrates that highly focused attention can overcome attentional capture by abrupt onset. In the 75% and 25% conditions, in contrast, there was a larger effect of abrupt onset even on valid trials and a very large effect of abrupt onset on invalid trials.

A two-way ANOVA, with the between-subjects factor of cue validity (100V, 75V, 75I, 25V, and 25I) and the within-subjects factor of trial type (onset or no-onset), revealed a significant main effect of both factors, $F(4,36) = 27.01$ for validity and $F(1,9) = 85.23$ for trial type, both $ps < .001$. The interaction between validity and trial type was also significant, $F(4,36) = 13.46$, $p < .001$. A clearer picture of the data is obtained by examining the individual effects of abrupt onset for each validity condition.

The effect of trial type was 17 ± 10, 48 ± 6, and 46 ± 11 ms for the 100V, 75V, and 25V conditions, respectively (see Footnote 3). The effect of trial type for the 75I and 25I conditions was 121 ± 9 and 69 ± 19, respectively. Individual t tests of these effects revealed that the difference between the onset and the no-onset trials in the 100V condition was not significantly greater than zero, $t(9) = 1.8$, $p > .1$, and that the corresponding differences in the 75V and 25V groups were significantly greater than zero, $t(9) = 8.4$ and 4.3 for the two groups, respectively, both $ps < .01$. The effects in the two invalid conditions were also reliable, $t(9) = 13.9$ and 3.6 for the 75I and 25I conditions, respectively.

The overall error rate was 3.0%. There was a positive correlation of .90 between mean reaction time and mean error rate in the 10 experimental conditions, a result suggesting that there was not a speed/accuracy trade-off.

Discussion

We consider first the 100V condition. As in the corresponding condition of Experiment 2 (−200-SOA), there was vir-

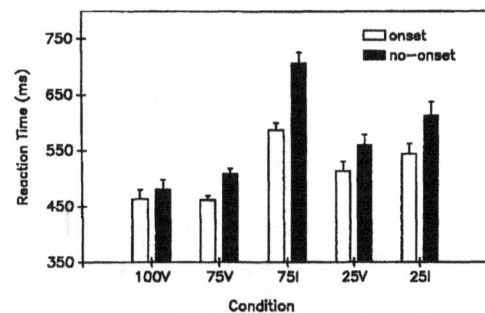

Figure 5. Mean reaction time for each condition of Experiment 3. (The error bars represent 1 *SE*.)

tually no effect of target type. This replicates our finding that when attention is effectively focused on a spatial location, abrupt onset does not capture attention.

Next we look at the 25% condition (25V and 25I in Figure 5). If subjects had completely ignored the cue (as they should have, given its low validity and our instructions), we would expect the bars representing the 25V and the 25I conditions to be the same height, to reflect the irrelevance of the cue. The bars are clearly not the same height. However, neither are they very different (compared, e.g., with the corresponding bars in the 75% validity conditions). To the extent that subjects were in something like a diffuse attention mode here, we would expect to see a noticeable effect of trial type (onset vs. no-onset), according to our hypothesis. This prediction was satisfied: Onset targets were identified more rapidly than no-onset targets were (an average difference of 57 ms).

We now discuss the 75% condition (75V and 75I in Figure 5). There are several possible strategies that a subject could adopt when the cue is highly, but not completely, valid. We consider three of the most plausible here. The first (Strategy 1) is always to attend maximally to the cued location, even though this is known to be harmful on some trials. This strategy is disconfirmed by the data, however, because it predicts that in the 75V condition, the effect of target type should be as small as it is in the 100V condition, and this is clearly not the case. The mean differences between the onset and the no-onset conditions were 17 ± 10 ms for the 100V condition and 48 ± 6 ms for the 75V condition, a significant difference, $t(18) = 2.3$, $p < .05$. Evidently, then, Strategy 1 was not used by subjects in this task.

The second strategy for the 75% condition (Strategy 2) is to probability match over trials (Jonides, 1980), attending to the cued location on a randomly selected 75% of the trials and either selecting a random uncued position to attend to on the remaining trials (Substrategy 2A) or remaining in the diffuse attention state on those trials (Substrategy 2B; Eriksen & Yeh, 1985).

These strategies predict a probability mixture of two different attentional states on valid trials: those on which attention is highly focused (as in the 100V condition) and those on which attention is either focused incorrectly (Substrategy 2A) or unfocused (Substrategy 2B). In other words, Strategy 2 predicts that the distribution of reaction times in the 75V onset and no-onset conditions should be a 75/25 mixture of the corresponding distributions in the 100V and the 75I (Substrategy 2A) or the 100V and 25V (Substrategy 2B) conditions.[4] The power required for formal statistical tests of this prediction is not sufficient for these data (see Meyer, Yantis, Osman, & Smith; 1985; Smith, Yantis, & Meyer, 1990, for details). Qualitatively, however, the data do not strongly violate the predictions of Strategy 2.

The third strategy (Strategy 3) is to devote on each trial 75% of one's attentional resources to the cued location and 25% to the uncued locations (Shaw, 1978). This strategy predicts that in Condition 75V there should be an effect of target type (onset vs. no-onset) that is larger than when attention is completely focused (Condition 100V) but less than when attention is diffuse (Condition 25V). This derives from the idea that attention is not completely focused in the

75V condition and so may be subject to partial capture, but it is not completely diffuse and so should be resistant to complete capture.[5] An idea like this one was also proposed by Müller and Rabbitt (1989). The results confirm one aspect of this model: The effect of onset versus no onset is larger in the 75V than in the 100V condition. However, the effect of onset in the 75V condition is not smaller than in the 25V condition (48 ± 6 vs. 46 ± 11, respectively).

A further prediction of Strategy 3 is that both overall reaction time and the effect of target type should be much larger in the 75I condition than in the 75V condition. This prediction is supported by the significant main effect of validity (75V vs. 75I), $t(9) = 13.6$, $p < .001$, and the significant interaction between target type (onset vs. no-onset) and validity (75V vs. 75I), $t(9) = 11.7$, $p < .001$.

We conclude that the data are consistent with the predictions of Strategy 2 or Strategy 3. They are not consistent, however, with the hypothesis that abrupt visual onset captures attention automatically regardless of attentional state. Experiment 3 has demonstrated that the specific attentional strategy adopted by a subject given partially valid cues significantly influences the extent to which abrupt onset captures attention and verifies the conclusion from Experiments 1 and 2 that abrupt visual onset does not satisfy the intentionality criterion of strong automaticity.

The results of Experiment 3 also help to reconcile the present findings and those of Müller and Rabbit (1989). In their study, a to-be-ignored peripheral flash interrupted the detection of a target in a cued location. However, because the cue was only moderately valid (50%), it cannot be said to have placed subjects into a state of highly focused attention. In the present experiment, even validities of as high as 75% yielded significant effects of to-be-ignored abrupt onsets. It is only when attention is highly focused in advance (as in the 100V condition) that irrelevant abrupt onsets can be overridden by voluntary attentional focussing.

Experiment 4

We have ruled out versions of automatic attentional capture by abrupt onset in which attention is always immediately drawn to an abrupt onset regardless of subjects' intention. This is a strong version of automaticity that specifies a complete lack of control. However, there are less stringent (and perhaps more plausible) versions of automaticity that should

---

[4] The data suggest that subjects were not completely unfocused in the 25V condition; instead, there is evidence that subjects used the cue to direct attention, even when it was randomly associated with the target location. To the extent that subjects were indeed using the cue in Condition 25V, it would not be appropriate to use data from that condition as one basis distribution in a test of the mixture prediction of Substrategy 2B.

[5] The idea implicit in this prediction is that because one can flexibly allocate portions of attention to different spatial locations, it follows that portions of attention can be captured by an abrupt onset; the more attention is allocated to a position, the less attention will be drawn away by an abrupt onset.

still be entertained. It could be the case that an abrupt onset is always registered as an important, high-priority event by the visual system, but when attention is focused elsewhere, the "interrupt" generated by the onset is placed in a queue to be serviced only after attention is freed from its current task. In Experiment 4, we tested such a version of automaticity.[6]

In the experiment we used an interference paradigm (e.g., Eriksen & Schultz, 1979; Yantis & Johnston, 1990). On each trial of the task, a different letter was assigned to each of two responses. One position in the display was cued in advance, and the task was to respond according to the letter in the cued location. Uncued locations were usually occupied by neutral letters. On some trials, however, the letter assigned to the incorrect response for the trial appeared in one of the uncued positions. As before, the cued stimulus or one of the uncued stimuli could have an abrupt onset; the remaining letters were always no-onset letters.

With this paradigm, we can assess the extent to which interference from to-be-ignored items (if any) depends on whether those items have an abrupt onset. To perform this test, we must first establish that onsets per se do not interfere with the identification of the cued stimuli, in replication of our earlier results. Then we must determine whether there is any interference from to-be-ignored positions at all (indeed, it is possible to maximize the degree of interference through the careful choice of task parameters) and, if so, whether that interference is modulated by whether the interfering stimulus has an abrupt onset.

If interference is greater when the interfering letter is an onset rather than a no-onset item, the idea that the onset stimuli are registered as high priority by the visual system is supported. This would be consistent with the weaker view of automaticity described above. On the other hand, if the effect of the interfering item does not depend on whether it has an abrupt onset, the notion that onsets automatically capture attention, even in a weak sense, is undermined.

In this experiment we enhanced the potential for interference from to-be-ignored stimuli by varying the stimulus-to-response mapping on each trial. This kind of procedure causes the mappings to be highly primed and may permit them to penetrate the filter established when attention is focused.

Method

Subjects. Sixteen undergraduates from the Johns Hopkins University (9 female) served in one 50-min session to satisfy a requirement for an introductory psychology course. All subjects had normal or corrected-to-normal vision, and none had participated in Experiments 1–3.

Equipment and stimuli. The equipment and stimuli were the same as in Experiment 2.

Procedure. At the start of each trial, two target letters appeared on the screen for 500 ms, one above the right response key and one above the left response key. This was followed by a display consisting of three placeholders and a fixation cross for 1,000 ms. A cue as in Experiment 3 then appeared for 200 ms. Of course, this cue was always 100% valid, because the task was *defined* such that the cued letter was the one to be reported. Finally, the display of four letters appeared; one of these had an abrupt onset, and the other three were no-onset letters. One of the two target letters always appeared in the

cued location, and subjects were to press the key corresponding to the cued target letter. The display disappeared when the response was made, and a beep was emitted if the response was in error. The next trial started after 1,000 ms.

Design. The left and right responses were each required on half of the trials. The cued target letter was an onset letter on half of the trials, and one of the uncued letters was the onset on the remaining trials. On half of the trials of each of these types, there was an interfering letter (i.e., the target letter mapped onto the incorrect response) present in an uncued position, and on the remaining trials all the uncued positions were occupied by neutral letters. When the cued letter was a no-onset one and an interfering letter was present, the interfering letter was an onset on half of the trials and a no-onset on the other half.

There were eight blocks of 64 trials each. In each block, then, the cued target was an onset on 32 trials; an interfering target was present on 16 and absent on 16 of these trials. When the cued target was a no-onset (32 trials), the interfering target was again present on 16 trials and absent on 16 trials. Of the trials in which the target was a no-onset and the interfering target was present (16 trials), the interfering target was an onset on 8 trials and a no-onset on 8 trials. It is the results from this last pair of conditions that are the focus of this experiment.

Results

Mean reaction times for the main conditions of Experiment 4 are shown in Table 1. These data were subjected to a two-way analysis of variance, with cued target type (onset vs. no-onset) and distractor type (interfering target present vs. absent) as factors. The 3-ms main effect of cued target type was not significant, $F(1, 15) = 1.2$, $p > .2$. The 33-ms main effect of the interfering target was highly significant, $F(1, 15) = 143.1$, $p < .001$. The interaction between these factors was not significant, $F(1, 15) < 1$. This analysis establishes that when subjects attended to the cued position, it mattered not at all whether the cued target was an abrupt onset or the onset was elsewhere in the display. This replicates the observed pattern of Experiments 1–3: abrupt onsets do not capture attention if attention is directed effectively in advance. The analysis also revealed that the identity of the to-be-ignored items *did* matter to some extent; that is to say, on those trials in which an interfering target appeared in an uncued location, reaction time was slowed compared with that on trials in which the interfering target did not appear. This result was obtained by design, of course: We selected task parameters that would maximize the possibility of interference from to-be-ignored letters.

What remains to be determined is whether the interference was modulated by whether the interfering target had an abrupt onset. For this analysis, we looked at the subset of trials on which the onset stimulus was one of the uncued letters and an interfering target was present. Reaction time when the interfering target was an onset was 525 ms, and when it was a no-onset (and one of the other uncued letters was an onset), reaction time was 513 ms. This effect of 12 ± 4 ms was

---

[6] We thank Roger Remington for encouraging us to pursue this possibility. Preliminary evidence from a different paradigm used in our laboratory suggests that something like this model may be correct (Yantis & Johnson, 1990).

Table 1

Mean Reaction Time (in ms) of Each Condition of Experiment 4

Interfering target	Cued target		
	Onset	No onset	*M*
Present	514	519	516
Absent	483	484	483
M	498	501	

significantly greater than zero, $t(15) = 2.7$, $p < .02$. This effect demonstrates that even though attention was not immediately captured by the uncued abrupt onset, the interfering effect of a to-be-ignored stimulus was modulated by whether it had an abrupt onset. Thus the attentional effect of an abrupt onset evidently persists for some time beyond its immediate occurrence.

Discussion

According to the weaker version of automaticity we are testing, interfering targets that are themselves onsets should have a larger effect than those that are not onsets, even given that attention was not immediately drawn by the onset stimulus. The results of Experiment 4 are consistent with this model. Evidently, abrupt onsets may maintain the ability to summon attention, even if they are prevented from doing so immediately because attention is focused elsewhere.

The results we have described require that the effects of interfering stimuli in a task such as the one used in this experiment must be mediated by a series of overlapping processes. According to this account, attention is first allocated to the cued location, and information is extracted from that location; then attention goes on to the next-highest priority location, which in this case would be the onset location (if any). Information extracted from that location influences responses to the letter in the cued location—presumably via a response-competition mechanism.

General Discussion

Four experiments were conducted to test the hypothesis that abrupt visual onset captures attention automatically. In Experiment 1, we showed that subjects' state of attentional readiness does modulate the extent to which abrupt onsets draw attention; this was essentially an existence proof. In Experiment 2, the effectiveness of a completely valid spatial cue was manipulated by presenting it before, simultaneous with, or after the appearance of a test display. Precues, which can, with the proper spatiotemporal properties, promote highly focused attention (e.g., Yantis & Johnston, 1990), virtually eliminated the effect of abrupt onset on performance. In contrast, cues presented simultaneously with or after the onset of the display yielded strong effects of abrupt onset. We concluded that highly focused attention is resistant to attentional capture by abrupt onset.

In Experiment 3, we pursued this finding by manipulating the predictive validity of the cue. As in Experiment 2, with

highly focused attention induced by completely valid cues, there was little effect of abrupt onset. However, with cues of lower validity, which evidently resulted in more diffuse attention allocation, abrupt onsets had a strong effect on performance.

In Experiment 4, we tested a somewhat weaker form of automaticity that might still be satisfied by abrupt onsets. We found that although abrupt onsets have no immediate effect on performance, they may still have a delayed or secondary effect in that they potentiate the interference caused by a response-incompatible letter in a to-be-ignored location. The picture emerging from this finding is that onsets may produce a "priority signal" that enters a queue. The signals in the queue are serviced in order of priority. When subjects are in a diffuse attention mode, an onset will have the highest priority, and attention will be captured. When attention is focused because of task demands, the focused location will have the highest priority and will be serviced before the next-highest priority location, which might be the location containing an onset. Other preliminary evidence from our laboratory suggests that if there are multiple onsets present among a number of no-onsets, up to four of the onset stimuli may be serviced before any of the no-onsets are (Yantis & Johnson, 1990). This is also consistent with the queuing notion.

One possible challenge to our conclusions is presented by our use of cues that themselves exhibit abrupt onsets. One might think that onset cues would interrupt the attentional capture produced by abrupt-onset stimuli and thereby compromise the effect of attentional capture by abrupt-onset letters with unwanted attentional capture by abrupt-onset cues. Upon closure scrutiny, however, it will be seen that the use of abrupt-onset cues is not problematic. First, the cues in these experiments are central ones. Jonides (1981) showed that central cues do not effectively capture attention (as peripheral cues, for example, do).

Second, one should consider the results of Experiment 3. In that experiment the cues always appeared 200 ms before the onset of the display. By the time the display itself appeared, attention was already effectively focused on the cued position, as indicated by the negligible effect of target type in the 100% validity condition. Consequently, we conclude that any possible attentional capture by the abrupt-onset cues had already dissipated by the time the display appeared 200 ms later.

Finally, we consider the results of Experiment 2. The condition that is most likely to present problems for our analysis is the 200-ms SOA condition in which the cue appeared 200 ms after the onset of the display. These abrupt-onset targets were identified just as rapidly as in the −200-ms condition, a result suggesting that the abrupt-onset targets did effectively capture attention; if the 200-ms cue had disrupted target processing, we would have expected reaction time in the 200-ms onset condition to be slower than the −200-ms onset condition. That it was not bolsters our claim that the abrupt-onset cue did not compromise the experiment. A similar argument applies to the 0-ms condition of Experiment 2.

Another feature of the data that merits comment is the effect of onset type in the −200 SOA, 100% valid conditions of Experiments 2, 3, and 4. Although in any given experiment this effect was not significantly greater than zero, it was consistently positive in all experiments. One might wonder if a real effect of onset was present but was too small to be statistically detected. We would argue that a more plausible explanation for this small but consistent effect is that on some small proportion of the trials, subjects may not have focused their attention with maximal efficiency (e.g., they were momentarily distracted or they lost concentration for a trial). On those trials we would expect that their attention would be drawn to the abrupt-onset stimulus. Indeed, it would be surprising if there were not at least *some* trials of this sort. This mixture of trials on which subjects focused well and onsets had no effect (most trials) and trials on which subjects did not focus well and onsets had a strong effect (a few trials) would be reflected in a small effect of onsets overall. However, because the effect of onsets was so small, the power of any formal statistical tests of this mixture hypothesis would not be sufficient to draw meaningful conclusions (Smith et al., 1990).

Conclusion

The overall conclusion to which we are led is that attentional capture by abrupt stimulus onset is not strongly automatic because, although it satisfies the load-insensitivity criterion, it does not strictly satisfy the intentionality criterion. The visual attention system is evidently prepared to give high priority to abrupt onsets when in diffuse attention mode. This is adaptively sensible, because onsets usually signal novel stimulus information, and this information may often be perceptually important. At the same time, the system delays the potentially distractive influence of abrupt onset when other task demands have led to highly focused attention—also adaptively sensible. The mechanism for delaying the servicing of an abrupt onset may involve the setting of priorities that mandate the place where attentional resources must be committed.

The notion that priority signals are generated and queued to be serviced by the system as resources become available accounts for the results of Experiment 4 in which a to-be-ignored onset stimulus evidently had a higher priority than a to-be-ignored no-onset stimulus did. In addition, this account provides an explanation for the advantage of onsets over no-onsets in the invalid conditions of Experiments 1 and 3.[7] In those conditions attention was focused on a position not containing a target letter; the effect of onset versus no-onset on target identification could have been mediated by a persisting code specifying higher priority for the onset than the no-onset items.

One possible computational mechanism that could support this kind of scheme was proposed by Koch and Ullman (1985). According to their model, visual information occupying the position in the visual field of highest salience or conspicuity is marked and passed on to a central representation that is responsible for further stimulus analysis. The priority code generated by an onset detector could easily be incorporated into this scheme and serve to activate nodes in Koch and Ullman's "saliency map" at the position of an abrupt onset. The even higher priority associated with a cued location could be represented on the saliency map as well.

The conclusion we have advanced is that attentional capture by abrupt visual onset does not satisfy all the common criteria for strong automaticity (Kahneman & Treisman, 1984); therefore it should not, perhaps, be termed strongly automatic. A quite different conclusion is available, however. It is possible that the intentionality criterion for automaticity is not adequately diagnostic and should be abandoned or reformed (see Jonides et al., 1985). Of course, this issue has no objective answer. Definitions are not subject to empirical scrutiny. The criteria we choose to apply in ascribing automaticity to a cognitive or perceptual process are valid precisely to the extent that they are theoretically useful. If there are few processes that can satisfy the intentionality criterion, or if there are processes that appear prima facie to be good examples of automatic processes and yet do not satisfy the intentionality criterion, then the criterion itself may be suspect. The present data concerning abrupt onset represent one example of this type, which, if corroborated by other converging sources of evidence, may undermine the utility of the intentionality criterion.

———
[7] We thank Jeff Miller for pointing this out.

References

Breitmeyer, B. G., & Ganz, L. (1976). Implications of sustained and transient channels for theories of visual pattern masking, saccadic suppression, and information processing. *Psychological Review, 83*, 1–36.

Cleland, B. G., Levick, W. R., & Sanderson, K. J. (1973). Properties of sustained and transient cells in the cat retina. *Journal of Physiology, 228*, 649–680.

Egeth, H., Jonides, J., & Wall, S. (1972). Parallel processing of multielement displays. *Cognitive Psychology, 3*, 674–698.

Eriksen, C. W., & St. James, J. D. (1986). Visual attention within and around the field of focal attention: A zoom lens model. *Perception & Psychophysics, 40*, 225–240.

Eriksen, C. W., & Schultz, D. W. (1979). Information processing in visual search: A continuous flow conception and experimental results. *Perception & Psychophysics, 25*, 249–263.

Eriksen, C. W., & Yeh, Y. Y. (1985). Allocation of attention in the visual field. *Journal of Experimental Psychology: Human Perception and Performance, 11*, 583–597.

Hasher, L., & Zacks, R. T. (1979). Automatic and effortful processes in memory. *Journal of Experimental Psychology: General, 108*, 356–388.

Jonides, J. (1980). Towards a model of the mind's eye's movement. *Canadian Journal of Psychology, 34*, 103–112.

Jonides, J. (1981). Voluntary vs. automatic control over the mind's eye's movement. In J. B. Long & A. D. Baddeley (Eds.), *Attention and performance IX* (pp. 187–203). Hillsdale, NJ: Erlbaum.

Jonides, J., Naveh-Benjamin, M., & Palmer, J. (1985). Assessing automaticity. *Acta Psychologica, 60*, 157–171.

Jonides, J., & Yantis, S. (1988). Uniqueness of abrupt visual onset as an attention-capturing property. *Perception & Psychophysics, 43*, 346–354.

Kahneman, D., & Treisman, A. (1984). Changing views of attention and automaticity. In R. Parasuraman, R. Davies, & J. Beatty (Eds.), *Varieties of attention* (pp. 29–61). New York: Academic Press.

Koch, C., & Ullman, S. (1985). Shifts in selective visual attention: Toward the underlying neural circuitry. *Human Neurobiology, 4*, 219–227.

Krumhansl, C. L. (1982). Abrupt changes in visual stimulation enhance processing of form and location information. *Perception & Psychophysics, 32,* 511–523.

Lambert, A., Spencer, E., & Mohindra, N. (1987). Automaticity and the capture of attention by a peripheral display change. *Current Psychological Research & Reviews, 6,* 136–147.

Lennie, P. (1980). Parallel visual pathways: A review. *Vision Research, 20,* 561–594.

Logan, G. D. (1978). Attention in character-classification tasks: Evidence for the automaticity of component stages. *Journal of Experimental Psychology: General, 107,* 32–63.

Meyer, D. E., Yantis, S., Osman, A. M., & Smith, J. E. K. (1985). Temporal properties of human information processing: Tests of discrete versus continuous models. *Cognitive Psychology, 17,* 445–518.

Miller, J. (1989). The control of attention by abrupt visual onsets and offsets. *Perception & Psychophysics, 45,* 567–571.

Müller, H. J., & Rabbitt, P. M. A. (1989). Reflexive and voluntary orienting of visual attention: Time course of activation and resistance to interruption. *Journal of Experimental Psychology: Human Perception and Performance, 15,* 315–330.

Murphy, T. D., & Eriksen, C. W. (1987). Temporal changes in the distribution of attention in the visual field in response to precues. *Perception & Psychophysics, 42,* 576–586.

Palmer, J., & Jonides, J. (1988). Automatic memory search and the effects of information load and irrelevant information. *Journal of Experimental Psychology: Learning, Memory, and Cognition, 14,* 136–144.

Posner, M. I. (1980). Orienting of attention. *Quarterly Journal of Experimental Psychology, 32,* 3–25.

Posner, M. I., & Cohen, Y. (1984). Components of visual orienting. In D. Bouma & D. Bonwhuis (Eds.), *Attention and Performance X* (pp. 531–556). Hillsdale, NJ: Erlbaum.

Posner, M. I., Cohen, Y., & Rafal, R. D. (1982). Neural systems control of spatial orienting. *Philosophical Transactions of the Royal Society of London, Series B, 298,* 187–198.

Posner, M. I., & Snyder, C. R. R. (1975). Attention and cognitive control. In R. L. Solso (Ed.), *Information processing and cognition* (pp. 55–85). Hillsdale, NJ: Erlbaum.

Regan, J. E. (1981). Automaticity and learning: Effects of familiarity on naming letters. *Journal of Experimental Psychology: Human Perception and Performance, 7,* 180–195.

Remington, R., & Pierce, L. (1984). Moving attention: Evidence for

time-invariant shifts of visual selective attention. *Perception & Psychophysics, 35,* 393–399.

Schneider, W., & Fisk, A. D. (1982). Concurrent automatic and controlled visual search: Can processing occur without resource cost? *Journal of Experimental Psychology: Learning, Memory, and Cognition, 8,* 261–278.

Schneider, W., & Shiffrin, R. M. (1977). Controlled and automatic human information processing: I. Detection, search, and attention. *Psychological Review, 84,* 1–66.

Shaw, M. L. (1978). A capacity allocation model for reaction time. *Journal of Experimental Psychology: Human Perception and Performance, 4,* 586–598.

Shiffrin, R. M., & Schneider, W. (1977). Controlled and automatic human information processing: II. Perceptual learning, automatic attending, and a general theory. *Psychological Review, 84,* 127–190.

Smith, J. E. K., Yantis, S., & Meyer, D. E. (1990). Analyses of multinomial mixture distributions: New tests for stochastic models of cognition and action. Submitted for publication.

Todd, J. T., & Van Gelder, P. (1979). Implications of a transient-sustained dichotomy for the measurement of human performance. *Journal of Experimental Psychology: Human Perception and Performance, 5,* 625–638.

Tolhurst, D. J. (1975). Sustained and transient channels in human vision. *Vision Research, 15,* 1151–1155.

Townsend, J. T., & Ashby, F. G. (1983). *Stochastic modeling of elementary psychological processes.* Cambridge: Cambridge University Press.

Treisman, A. M., & Gelade, G. (1980). A feature-integration theory of attention. *Cognitive Psychology, 12,* 97–136.

Yantis, S., & Johnson, D. N. (in press). Mechanisms of attentional priority. *Journal of Experimental Psychology: Human Perception and Performance.*

Yantis, S., & Johnston, J. C. (1990). On the locus of visual selection: Evidence from focused attention tasks. *Journal of Experimental Psychology: Human Perception and Performance, 16,* 135–149.

Yantis, S., & Jonides, J. (1984). Abrupt visual onsets and selective attention: Evidence from visual search. *Journal of Experimental Psychology: Human Perception and Performance, 10,* 601–621.

Received May 24, 1988
Revision received January 9, 1989
Accepted January 10, 1989 ∎

[4]

What attributes guide the deployment of visual attention and how do they do it?

Jeremy M. Wolfe and Todd S. Horowitz

As you drive into the centre of town, cars and trucks approach from several directions, and pedestrians swarm into the intersection. The wind blows a newspaper into the gutter and a pigeon does something unexpected on your windshield. This would be a demanding and stressful situation, but you would probably make it to the other side of town without mishap. Why is this situation taxing, and how do you cope?

The world presents the visual system with an embarrassment of riches. Given a brain of any reasonable size, it is impossible to process everything everywhere at one time[1]. The human visual system copes with this problem in a number of ways. Rather than having high-resolution processing at all locations, the best resolution is confined to the fovea, with massive losses in acuity occurring only a few degrees into the periphery. There are restrictions in the wavelengths of light that are processed, the spatial and temporal frequencies that can be detected, and so forth. All of these 'front-end' reductions in the amount of information fail to solve the problem. To deal with the still-overwhelming excess of input, the visual system has attentional mechanisms for selecting a small subset of possible stimuli for more extensive processing while relegating the rest to only limited analysis.

Even though William James famously declared that "Everyone knows what attention is"[2], there is no single, satisfying definition of attention. The term covers a diverse set of selective processes in the nervous system. We can attend to a specific task, attend to tactile stimuli in preference to auditory, attend to a specific visible stimulus that is 2° to the left of fixation, and so on. This article is restricted to consideration of visual attention. Even within vision, there is good evidence that attention has its effects in diverse ways. Attention to a stimulus might enhance the signal produced by that stimulus[3,4]. It might more precisely tune the visual system to a stimulus attribute, excluding other input as noise[3]. Attention might restrict processing to one part of the visual field[5] or to an object[6], or it might restrict processing to a window in time[7].

Faced with this welter of possibilities, we will use an operational definition of one aspect of attention in this paper. We are concerned with the deployment of attention in visual search tasks. It is possible to discuss the role of attention in these tasks while remaining agnostic about distinctions between noise reduction, stimulus enhancement and so forth. In a typical visual search task, an observer looks for a target item among distracting items. In the laboratory, this might be a search for a big red vertical line in a display containing lines of other colours, sizes and orientations. However, visual search is no mere laboratory curiosity. From the search for socks in the laundry to the search for weapons in carry-on luggage, our environment abounds with search tasks. Indeed, these processes of attentional selection, revealed by visual search experiments, are presumably the processes that are used whenever anything in the world becomes the current object of visual attention.

The starting point for any understanding of the deployment of attention in visual search is the observation that some search tasks are easy and efficient while others are not. Consider FIG. 1a. If you are asked to find the red target or the tilted target or the big target, it is intuitively clear that the number of distracting items does not make much difference. The colour, orientation or size attributes that define the targets can efficiently guide attention to the target. On the other hand, among these '5's there is a '2' target. Once it has been found, there is no difficulty in discriminating a 2 from a 5. However, attention cannot be guided by the spatial position information that differentiates those characters. The more 5s that are present, the more difficult the search task will be[8].

The purpose of this article is to review the status of these guiding attributes. What properties can guide attention and what cannot? For about 25 years, the answer to that question has been framed in terms of Treisman's highly influential feature integration theory[9]. Treisman followed Neisser[10] in proposing a two-stage architecture for human vision (FIG. 2a) in which a set of basic features was generated in an initial, parallel, 'preattentive' stage. Other processes, like those that bound features to objects and permitted object recognition, were restricted to one or at most a few objects at a time. Consequently, attention was required to select a subset of the input for this more advanced processing. Later models, such as guided search[11,12], kept the two-stage architecture but noted that the preattentive stage could guide the deployment of attention to select appropriate objects for the second stage. Therefore, a preattentive stage that could process colour and orientation could efficiently guide attention to a target that was defined by the combination of colour and orientation (for example, a red vertical item) even if preattentive stages could not bind colour to orientation in parallel at all locations.

PERSPECTIVES

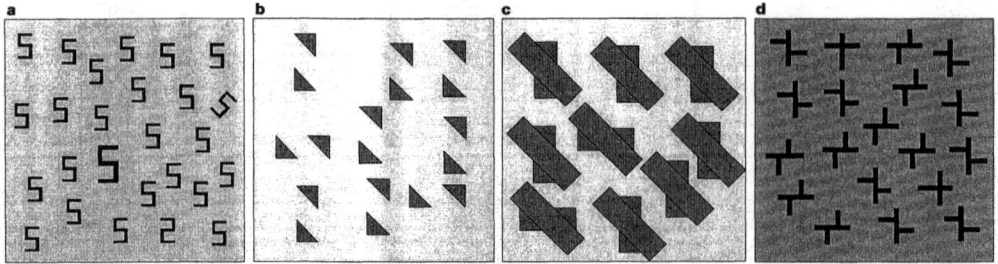

Figure 1 | **Easy and difficult examples of visual search. a** | It is easy to find the red, tilted or big '5'. It is not easy to find the '2' among the '5's. **b,c** | It is difficult to find the horizontal pairs of triangles in **b**, but in **c** it is easy because the early visual system can use intersection information to infer that the blue items occlude pink rectangles. **d** | In this panel, search for the 'plus' is inefficient because the intersection information here does not guide attention.

The original account was appealing. Simple features such as size and motion were extracted preattentively. More complex properties required attention. However, the accumulation of information about guiding attributes over the past 20 years makes it clear that this two-stage, linear approach will not work. Several lines of objection have been raised[13,14], but the core problem for us is that there are multiple examples of 'features' that are available early in visual processing and also in attentive vision, but that are not available to guide the deployment of attention. At the same time, there are properties of guiding attributes that are not reflected in attentive vision. This makes it difficult to envision the guiding representation as a stage in a linear sequence of visual processes, like a filter — even a tunable filter — between early vision and the attentional bottleneck.

As an example, consider intersections. In FIG. 1b, it is not easy to find the two horizontal pairs of triangles. In FIG. 1c, it is quite easy because early visual processes can handle occlusion information[15]. Interpreting occlusion requires that the early visual system successfully interprets intersections. Clearly, later object recognition processes can use intersection information. However, as shown in FIG. 1d, intersection does not serve as a source of guidance[8]. The linear model would have to explain how intersection information could be present, then absent, then present again.

It might be better to think of a 'guiding representation' as a control device, sitting to one side of the main pathway from early vision to object recognition (FIG. 2b). Its contents are abstracted from the main pathway and it, in turn, controls access to the attentional bottleneck. However, it would not, itself, be part of the pathway.

Departure from the linear model has been a feature of several recent theoretical approaches to the guidance of attention. Hochstein and Ahissar[16] offer a 'reverse hierarchy' model

in which properties that are abstracted late in visual processing feed back onto early stages. In an approach that more closely resembles the architecture of FIG. 2b, DiLollo and colleagues[13] propose that "Initial processing is performed by a set of input filters whose functional characteristics are programmable under the control of prefrontal cortex." For our purposes, there are two important points to be made about a guidance control module — wherever it is located in the brain. First, as the intersection example illustrates, it does not have access to all of the information that is available in the visual pathway that runs from early vision through the bottleneck to object recognition. Second, as DiLollo et al. note, when the control module exerts its control over access to the bottleneck, it is not acting as a filter in the simple physical sense of that term.

The problem with filters is that they remove information. Consider the following: as we discuss below, guidance by attributes such as colour and orientation seems to be coarse and categorical. Attention is guided to 'red' and 'steep', not to 640 nm or 23° left of vertical. Suppose that a target is known to be categorically 'red'. Filtering for 'red' would pass what was red and reject what was not. However, imagine a task in which observers must determine whether a red object has a green spot on it, and not a black or a blue one. Introspection will tell you that this is a straightforward task, but a filter that eliminated the 'not-red' would make it impossible. Rather than altering the stimulus, as a filter might, the hypothetical control module guides selection like a security screener at an airport. Based on a rather abstract representation of the notion of 'threat', the screener selects some individuals for more attention than others. Although attending to an object or location might have perceptual consequences[17], guidance itself should not.

Conceiving of guidance as a control module also avoids a potential pitfall in models of the reverse hierarchy[16] variety. It is reasonable to assume that attention can be guided by some 'late' information (see, for example, Torralba's theoretical work on guidance by scene properties[18]). If that information fed back onto early visual processes and acted as a filter, one could imagine odd recursive problems where feedback about a scene reduced the ability to see the scene. Torralba's model, for example, generates images where only the ground plane is visible during a search for people, but we are not meant to suppose that this is what is seen. As with the search for 'red', it seems more plausible that late information could inform the guidance of attention by altering the representation in a guiding module placed outside the main pathway to object recognition.

In the remainder of this article, we discuss the attributes that are abstracted from early vision that can guide attention. In keeping with the hypothesis that guidance is separate from the main pathway to object recognition, we avoid the use of the term 'preattentive' and its associated theoretical implications. Attributes will be discussed in terms of their ability to guide the deployment of attention.

Identifying 'guiding' attributes

One of the most productive ways to study the differences between visual search tasks is to measure reaction time (RT) — the time that is required to say that a target is present or absent — as a function of the set size (the number of items in the display). The slope of the RT × set size function indexes the cost of adding an item to the search display. So, varying the set size in the colour search task in FIG. 1 will produce little or no change in RT. The slope will be near zero and we can label such a search as efficient. By contrast, in the search for a 2 among 5s, the slope will increase at a rate of about 20–40 ms per item for trials when a target is present. The slope will be a bit more than twice that steep when the target is absent. We can label such tasks as inefficient. Note that this assumes that the stimuli are large enough and sparse enough that it is not necessary to fixate each one. If search is limited by the rate of eye movements, slopes are in the range of 150–300 ms per item.

If the world were simple, search tasks would fall into two dichotomous groups, as originally proposed by Treisman[9]. There would be parallel tasks, where a guiding feature defined the target, and serial tasks, where no adequate guiding feature was present. We could then use some objective slope criterion (such as 10 ms per item, which has often been proposed in the search literature) as the marker for the presence of a guiding feature. However, when we pool data from many different subjects in many different tasks (as in FIG. 3), the resulting histogram makes it clear that there is no obvious division that splits search tasks into different categories based on slope[19]. Note that this does not mean that the distribution in FIG. 3 could not be the sum of two or more distinct, underlying distributions[20]. But it does mean that no simple slope criterion defines the presence of a guiding feature.

If a simple slope value is not definitive, what can define a guiding attribute? There are several measures, none of which is completely definitive by itself. An accumulation of converging evidence makes the most convincing case. Note, for the remainder of this paper, that a 'feature' will generally refer to a specific value (such as red) on a specific 'dimension' (such as colour).

Simple feature searches are generally very efficient. Although features cannot be defined by applying a simple criterion slope value, the closer the slope is to 0 ms per item, the more likely it is that the target is defined by a guiding feature. A shallow slope is not perfectly definitive because combinations of features can produce shallow slopes. For example, as shown in FIG. 4a, it is easy to find a black 'X' defined by a conjunction of shape and luminance polarity[21]. In this case, luminance or colour processes can guide attention to the black items and some shape process can guide attention to the item with line terminators[22]. These guiding signals are strong enough that attention can be swiftly guided to the intersection of the two sets of items[11,12].

Other criteria. Efficient search is, therefore, a necessary but not sufficient property for showing the presence of a guiding feature. There are at least four other indicators that can provide converging evidence.

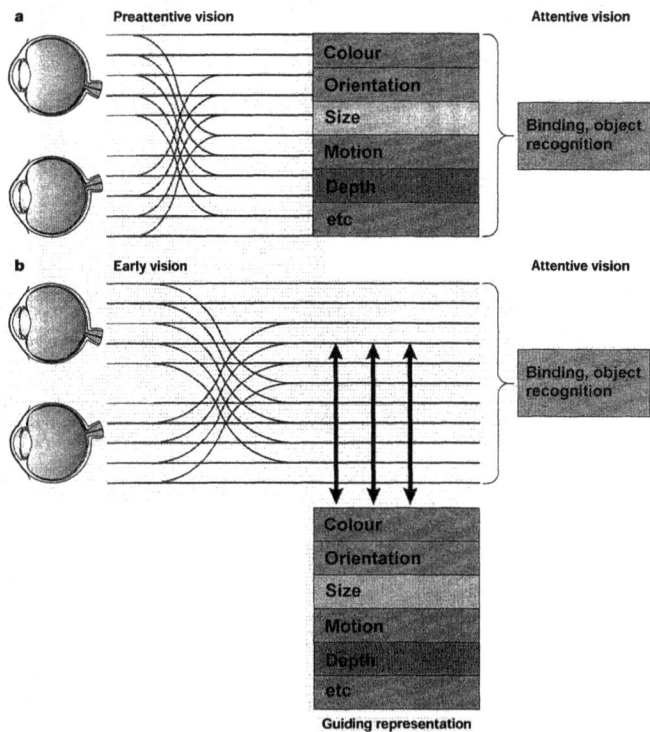

Figure 2 | **Models of visual processing. a** | A standard two-stage model with a parallel front end followed by an attentional bottleneck leading to processes such as object recognition. **b** | We suggest that it is useful to think of a 'guiding representation' that is derived from the main visual pathway and that guides access to the attentional bottleneck in the pathway but that is not, itself, part of the pathway.

First, in many cases, a texture region that possesses a unique basic feature segments 'effortlessly' from a background texture that does not[23,24]. This is illustrated in FIG. 4b for colour and orientation. This is not a perfect diagnostic because there are instances of segmentation without efficient search, and efficient search without segmentation[25]. Still, a property that produces both efficient search and effortless texture segmentation is a good candidate for guiding attribute status.

Second, for many attributes, the presence of a property is more readily detected than its absence. This leads to so-called 'search asymmetries'[26–28]. So, for example, it is easier to find a moving item among stationary distractors than vice versa[29]. This is useful only if the easy search is efficient. For example, it is easier to find a mirror-reversed letter among regular letters than vice versa, but both searches are inefficient and the mirrored target is easier to

find only because the regular letter distractors can be rejected more rapidly. Rosenholtz[30] describes other important cautions about the interpretation of search asymmetries.

Third, Treisman[31] suggests that the ability to participate in 'illusory conjunctions' is evidence for feature status. For example, if red vertical and green horizontal items are briefly presented, then observers will often report seeing the occasional red horizontal or green vertical item. The interpretation of this information is complicated by existence of higher-order illusory conjunctions, for example in word formation[32].

Finally, detection of a target that is defined by a candidate feature should be able to tolerate some distractor heterogeneity (FIG. 4c,d). On the basis of FIG. 4c, one might be tempted to conclude that junction type (T versus L) or perhaps even letter identity has featural status. However, what should be irrelevant variation

PERSPECTIVES

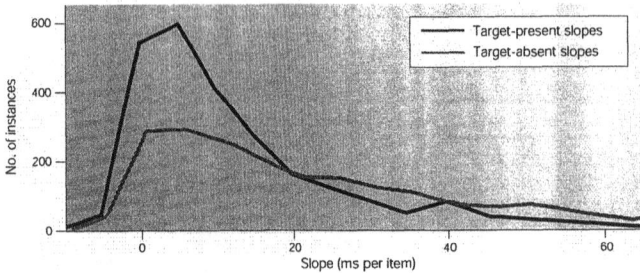

Figure 3 | **Distribution of slopes from individual sessions in a wide range of search tasks.** Sessions are generally 300–400 trials. The distribution is clearly not biomodal. Modified, with permission, from REF. 19 © (1998) American Psychological Society.

in orientation destroys the efficiency of that search (FIG. 4d). On the other hand, efficient colour search for the red L survives orientation variation with ease. Disruption by distractor heterogeneity can indicate that the wrong feature has been identified as the source of guidance. In FIG. 4c, the T might be found by the orientation of the triangle that would enclose it (its convex hull). This would be disrupted by orientation variation, whereas the identity of a T-junction would not be. This test is most important for 'higher order' features, where it is often possible that other simpler, more basic features are driving the efficient search.

To summarize, no single diagnostic assures the presence of a guiding feature. Converging evidence from several of the tests described here makes it possible to identify guiding attributes with some assurance.

Signal and noise in feature search. When a unique feature defines a target in visual search, efficient visual search is not guaranteed. The difference between the target and the distractors can be considered to be a signal that must be found amidst the noise of the

surrounding distractors. The qualitative nature of this signal detection problem is neatly captured by Duncan and Humphreys'[33] formulation of their 'attentional engagement theory'. Search efficiency increases as a function of target–distractor (TD) difference (signal) and decreases as a function of distractor–distractor (DD) difference (noise). More formal signal detection approaches (generally involving relatively simple stimuli) can be found elsewhere[34–36].

Research on visual search for colour illustrates these ideas and reveals certain limitations. FIGURE 5a–d shows a set of stimuli with varying TD differences. FIGURE 5e shows, schematically, the data that might be expected from such an experiment[37]. For a range of relatively large TD differences (as in FIG. 5c,d), RTs will be fast, slopes of the RT × set size function will be near zero, and error rates, even for briefly presented displays, will be low. Once the TD difference drops below some critical value, RTs, slopes and/or errors will begin to increase. The first important point is that any type of search for a target defined by a unique basic feature can be made arbitrarily difficult if the TD difference can be made

arbitrarily small, whereas search for targets not defined by a unique basic feature cannot be made arbitrarily easy by increasing the TD difference.

The second important point is that the bend in the function in FIG. 5e is not located at the resolution limit for that feature. Staying with the example of colour, for a given point in colour space, one can define an elliptical set of other points that represent 'just noticeable differences' in colour known as a MacAdam ellipse[38]. To have an efficient search for one colour among homogeneous distractors, the difference needs to be much greater than the just noticeable difference. Moreover, the shape of the efficient search contour around a specific location in colour space does not look like a scaled version of a MacAdam ellipse[37]. The metrics of colour difference for foveal colour discrimination are quite unlike those that govern deployment of attention in visual search.

FIGURE 5f–h illustrates the effects of DD differences. It is easy to find the orange target among red or yellow homogeneous distractors (FIG. 5f or h). However, when the distractors are heterogeneous, the task becomes more difficult. The nature of the heterogeneity is important. Specifically, search is inefficient if distractors flank the target in the feature space. If a line can be drawn in a two-dimensional colour space, with the target colour on one side and the distractors on another, then search will be easy. Assuming that the TD differences are large enough, these targets and distractors are 'linearly separable'[39,40]. If such a line cannot be drawn, search will be inefficient.

These are general principles — not curiosities of colour processing. In the search for oriented targets, large TD differences in orientation will support efficient search[9]. Smaller differences will not[41]. Foster's data show that the critical TD difference for efficient orientation search is much larger (~15°) than the minimum difference needed

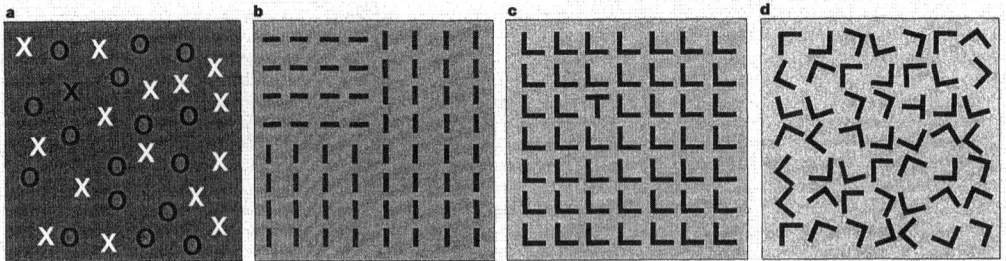

Figure 4 | **Clues to guidance. a** | Some conjunctions are very easy to find. In this case, the target is the black X — a shape–luminance polarity conjunction[21]. **b** | Segmentation of texture regions on the basis of the colour or orientation of their local elements. **c** | Both the 'T' and the red 'L' appear to 'pop out', but pop-out of the T does not survive irrelevant variation in orientation (**d**). This indicates that the distinction between T- and L-junctions is not a guiding feature.

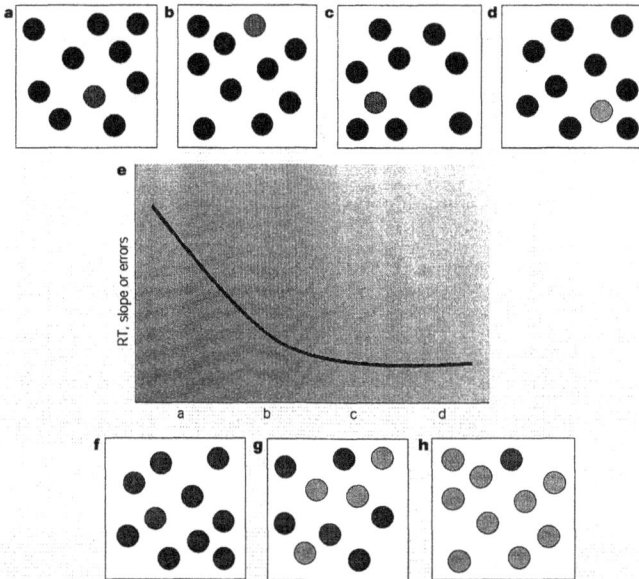

Figure 5 | **Target–distractor and distractor–distractor differences. a–d** | Search is easier when the target–distractor (TD) difference is larger. A simple feature search can produce steep slopes and/or long reaction times (RTs) if the TD difference is small (**e**). **f–h** | Distractor heterogeneity makes search harder (compare **g** with **f** or **h**). Part **e** modified, with permission, from REF. 37 © (1990) Optical Society of America.

to discriminate oriented lines (~1–2°). His data also show that variation in these critical values is not the same as the variation in discriminability with orientation. Search is inefficient when distractor orientations flank target orientations. So, it is easy to find a vertical target among homogeneous distractors tilted 20° to the left or 20° to the right. It is quite difficult to find the same vertical target among heterogeneous distractors tilted 20° left and right[42]. The effects of distractor heterogeneity again reinforce the differences between determinants of search performance and determinants of discriminability. In search, the categorical status of the target is important. So, search is more efficient if the target is uniquely steep, shallow, or tilted left or right[42].

What attributes guide visual search?
One goal of this review is to provide the best current list of the attributes that guide the deployment of attention. Most of the candidates for this list have not been put through all the tests described above. Nevertheless, TABLE 1 is an effort to make such a list. Note that the references are representative, not exhaustive. They are intended to provide the interested reader with pointers to the main evidence for

and, in some cases, against the featural status of various attributes. Further discussion can be found in various review chapters[43–45].

The list is organized into five groups of candidate sources of guidance. The first category of 'undoubted' attributes are those for which there is so much evidence that it is almost beyond question that these are dimensions whose features can guide search. This certainty fades as we go along the categories until we reach the final category of proposed attributes where the best evidence indicates that these are not guiding attributes. In the remainder of this paper, we briefly consider some of the issues raised by this list.

The undoubted guiding attributes. Colour, motion, orientation and size are all supported as guiding attributes by large amounts of convincing data. However, in the case of size, it is possible that properties such as size and spatial frequency might be disentangled into two or more separate dimensions[46].

Probable guiding attributes. These are attributes where more data would help to clear up ambiguities. For example, in the case of luminance onset, under some circumstances,

luminance offsets might also work[47]. The only reason to question luminance polarity as a guiding attribute is that it might be a subset of colour (that is, it might be the black–white or luminance axis of a three-dimensional colour space). Motion might be a single dimension, or speed and direction might be separate dimensions[48].

Vernier offset — a small lateral break in a line — is a less than assured guiding property, because it might be reducible to a form of an orientation cue[49]. In the case of stereopsis, there might be a broader dimension of something like three-dimensional layout that would capture various depth cues including stereopsis, the various pictorial depth cues, and shading. The cues would merely serve to create three-dimensional surfaces in the way that wavelength (not a guiding dimension) creates colour.

Shape is, perhaps, the most vexed of the guiding attributes, and several other attributes on this list have the same problems. It is clear that some aspects of shape are available to guide attention. It is not clear exactly what those aspects are. Evidence can be mustered for closure (for example, O versus C) or the topological property of having a 'hole', but closure could also be the state of not having clear line terminators. The various claims for the featural status of letters (see below) are endlessly complicated by our inability to settle on a set of shape features. For the present, it is clear that a feature such as line termination can distinguish between 'O' and 'Q', but it is not clear that such features can account for all of the search effects that are seen with letter stimuli.

Observers are sensitive to the direction of curvature (for example, left versus right)[27]. If the curves are part of the bounding contour of an object, this becomes concavity and convexity, with a possible preference for concavities[50]. So, concavity and convexity could be features of a curvature dimension. Taken into three dimensions, the concavity and convexity of surfaces might be the 'real' features in studies that argue for shading as a feature.

Possible guiding attributes. Shading or lighting direction is also an interesting case for other reasons. Early evidence such as Ramachandran's 'eggs' study[51] looked persuasive, but recent work (Ostrovsky, Y., Cavanagh, P. & Sinha, P., unpublished observations) suggests that we are not very sensitive to the actual properties of shadows. It might be that shading information is available in early vision. Like other depth cues, it might merely create other guiding attributes (such as surface orientation, convexity and concavity) while not guiding attention itself.

PERSPECTIVES

Table1 | Attributes that might guide the deployment of attention

Undoubted attributes*	Probable attributes†	Possible attributes‡	Doubtful cases§	Probable non-attributes¶
-Colour[26 27,37,39,40] -Motion[30,56,57] -Orientation[41,42,58–61] -Size (including length and spatial frequency)[27,62,63]	-Luminance onset (flicker)[64,65] -Luminance polarity[21 66] -Vernier offset[67] -Stereoscopic depth and tilt[68–70] -Pictorial depth cues[71–73] -Shape[27,58,74–80] -Line termination[22,81,82] -Closure[26,77,83–85] -Topological status[77 86,87] -Curvature[27,67,88]	-Lighting direction (shading)[51,89] -Glossiness (luster)[52] -Expansion[90,91] -Number[27,81] -Aspect ratio[27]	-Novelty[28,53,92] -Letter identity (over-learned sets, in general)[93–95] -Alphanumeric category[96–99]	-Intersection[8 58] -Optic flow[29,91] -Colour change[64] -Three-dimensional volumes (such as geons)[100,101] -Faces (familiar, upright, angry and so on)[102–108] -Your name[109] -Semantic category (for example, 'animal','scary')[10]

Attributes are grouped by the likelihood that they are, in fact, sources of guidance of attention. References are representative but not exhaustive. *'Undoubted' meaning that they are supported by many studies with converging methods. †Less confidence owing to limited data, dissenting opinions or the possibility of alternative explanations. ‡Still less confidence §Unconvincing, but still possible. ¶Suggested guiding features where the balance of evidence argues against inclusion on the list.

The evidence for shininess or gloss as a guiding attribute comes from a single experiment on binocular luster[52]. Current work in our laboratory casts doubt on the generality of the finding.

Expansion is problematic because of limited data and because it could be a version of a depth cue, a size cue, a motion cue or some combination of these. Its independent status has not been verified. Candidate dimensions such as number (is this clump made of one item or two?) and aspect ratio (for example, ovals among circles) could be on the list, but the evidence is scant and these should be revisited.

Doubtful cases. The central issue in the case of novelty is whether a novelty feature can survive any degree of distractor heterogeneity. For example, a mirror-reversed 'N' will pop-out among Ns and a mirror-reversed 'Z' will pop-out among Zs[53], but it is unclear whether novel mirror Ns and Zs will pop-out from a mixture of boring Ns and Zs. They should, if 'novel letter' had the status of a guiding feature.

Nobody believes that nature has equipped us with parallel processors for the Roman alphabet. The crucial question in letter search (and some related tasks) is whether over-learned sets acquire the ability to guide attention[54,55]. In the case of alphanumeric stimuli, it is exceedingly difficult to sort out possible visual confounds. It is worth noting that letter search tasks (like novelty tasks, above) seem to be vulnerable to distractor heterogeneity. The alphanumeric category refers to the specific claim that a letter might pop-out among numbers and vice versa. These effects (such as the 'zero–oh' effect) have been difficult to replicate.

Probably not guiding attributes. Intersection, once a plausible guiding attribute, has fallen off the list of guiding attributes[8]. Earlier

experiments used stimuli that confounded intersection with other features such as line termination. Optic flow, colour change and three-dimensional volume are reasonable candidates that might have guided the deployment of attention. However, the data indicate that they do not. Faces are also natural candidates for guiding features. However, the preponderance of evidence indicates that, although faces are 'special' stimuli, they are processed one at a time. Evidence for guidance by faces tends to be followed by a study that shows that another visual feature is at work. This point is debatable and, certainly, there are others who would place faces higher on this list. The substantial and growing literature on search for semantically or affectively meaningful stimuli has a similar feel to it. An ability to find threatening snakes and spiders efficiently seems to have more to do with their visual status as distinctive shapes than their affective status as scary objects.

Conclusion

Some properties of visual stimuli can be used to control the deployment of attention. These are not simply the properties of early stages of visual processing. Instead, they seem to be a specific abstraction from the visual input. We can call this abstraction the guiding representation. On the basis of several decades of research, a list of guiding attributes can be proposed. Some dimensions, such as colour, size and orientation, are assured places on that list. Others, such as line termination, are probably guiding attributes, whereas others, such as threat, are probably not. For each of these dimensions, the specific rules of guidance must be worked out by experimentation. It is useful to think of the guiding representation as a control device that sits to one side of the pathway from early vision to object recognition. Whether this psychophysical structure has a neuroanatomical manifestation remains to be seen.

Jeremy M. Wolfe and Todd S. Horowitz are at the Visual Attention Laboratory, Brigham and Women's Hospital and Harvard Medical School, 64 Sidney Street, Cambridge, Massachusetts 02139, USA. Correspondence to J.M.W. e-mail wolfe@search.bwh.harvard.edu.

doi:10.1038/nrn1411

1. Tsotsos, J. K. Analyzing vision at the complexity level. *Brain Behav. Sci.* **13**, 423–469 (1990).
2. James, W. *The Principles of Psychology* (Henry Holt and Co., New York, 1890).
3. Lu, Z.-L. & Dosher, B. A. External noise distinguishes attention mechanisms. *Vision Res.* **38**, 1183–1198 (1998).
4. Treue, S. & Maunsell, J. H. R. Attentional modulation of visual motion processing in cortical areas MT and MST. *Nature* **382**, 539–541 (1996).
5. Moran, J. & Desimone, R. Selective attention gates visual processing in the extrastriate cortex. *Science* **229**, 782–784 (1985).
6. Goldsmith, M. What's in a location? Comparing object-based and space-based models of feature integration in visual search. *J. Exp. Psychol. Gen.* **127**, 189–219 (1998).
7. Chun, M. M. & Potter, M. C. A two-stage model for multiple target detection in RSVP. *J. Exp. Psychol. Hum. Percept. Perform.* **21**, 109–127 (1995).
8. Wolfe, J. M. & DiMase, J. S. Do intersections serve as basic features in visual search? *Perception* **32**, 645–656 (2003).
9. Treisman, A. & Gelade, G. A feature-integration theory of attention. *Cognit. Psychol.* **12**, 97–136 (1980).
10. Neisser, U. *Cognitive Psychology* (Appleton, Century, Crofts, New York, 1967).
11. Wolfe, J. M., Cave, K. R. & Franzel, S. L. Guided search: an alternative to the feature integration model for visual search. *J. Exp. Psychol. Hum. Percept. Perform.* **15**, 419–433 (1989).
12. Wolfe, J. M. Guided search 2 0: a revised model of visual search *Psychon. Bull.* **1**, 202–238 (1994).
13. DiLollo, V., Kawahara, J., Zuvic, S. M. & Visser, T. A. W. The preattentive emperor has no clothes: a dynamic redressing. *J. Exp. Psychol. Gen.* **130**, 479–492 (2001).
14. Nakayama, K. & Joseph, J. S. In *The Attentive Brain* (ed. Parasuraman, R.) 279–298 (MIT Press, Cambridge, 1998).
15. Rensink, R. A. & Enns, J. T. Pre-emption effects in visual search: evidence for low-level grouping. *Psychol. Rev.* **102**, 101–130 (1995).
16. Hochstein, S. & Ahissar, M. View from the top: hierarchies and reverse hierarchies in the visual system. *Neuron* **36**, 791–804 (2002).
17. Carrasco, M., Penpeci-Talgar, C. & Eckstein, M. Spatial covert attention increases contrast sensitivity across the CSF. support for signal enhancement. *Vision Res.* **40**, 1203–1215 (2000).
18. Torralba, A. Modeling global scene factors in attention. *J. Opt. Soc. Am. A* **20**, (2003).
19. Wolfe, J. M. What do 1,000,000 trials tell us about visual search? *Psychol. Sci.* **9**, 33–39 (1998).
20. Haslam, N., Porter, M. & Rothschild, L. Visual search: efficiency continuum or distinct processes? *Psychon. Bull. Rev* **8**, 742–746 (2001).
21. Theeuwes, J. & Kooi, J. L. Parallel search for a conjunction of shape and contrast polarity. *Vision Res.* **34**, 3013–3016 (1994).

22. Julesz, B & Bergen, J. R. Textons, the fundamental elements in preattentive vision and perceptions of textures. *Bell Sys. Tech. J.* **62**, 1619–1646 (1983).
23. Beck, J. Perceptual grouping produced by changes in orientation and shape. *Science* **154**, 538–540 (1966).
24. Julesz, B. A brief outline of the texton theory of human vision. *Trends Neurosci.* **7**, 41–45 (1984).
25. Wolfe, J. M. 'Effortless' texture segmentation and 'parallel' visual search are not the same thing. *Vision Res.* **32**, 757–763 (1992).
26. Treisman, A. & Souther, J. Search asymmetry: a diagnostic for preattentive processing of seperable features. *J. Exp. Psychol. Gen.* **114**, 285–310 (1985).
27. Treisman, A. & Gormican, S. Feature analysis in early vision. evidence from search asymmetries *Psychol. Rev.* **95**, 15–48 (1988)
28. Wolfe, J. M. Asymmetries in visual search: an introduction. *Percept. Psychophys.* **63**, 381–389 (2001).
29. Royden, C. S., Wolfe, J. & Klempen, N. Visual search asymmetries in motion and optic flow fields. *Percept. Psychophys.* **63**, 436–444 (2001).
30. Rosenholtz, R. Search asymmetries? What search asymmetries? *Percept. Psychophys.* **63**, 476–489 (2001).
31. Treisman, A. M. & Schmidt, H. Illusory conjunctions in the perception of objects. *Cognit. Psychol.* **14**, 107–141 (1982).
32. Treisman, A. & Souther, J. Illusory words: the roles of attention and of top-down constraints in conjoining letters to form words. *J. Exp. Psychol. Hum. Percept. Perform.* **12**, 3–17 (1986).
33. Duncan, J. & Humphreys, G. W. Visual search and stimulus similarity. *Psychol. Rev.* **96**, 433–458 (1989).
34. Verghese, P. Visual search and attention: a signal detection approach. *Neuron* **31**, 523–535 (2001).
35. Eckstein, M. P. The lower visual search efficiency for conjunctions is due to noise and not serial attentional processing. *Psychol. Sci.* **9**, 111–118 (1998).
36. Palmer, J., Verghese, P. & Pavel, M. The psychophysics of visual search. *Vision Res.* **40**, 1227–1268 (2000).
37. Nagy, A. L. & Sanchez, R. R. Critical color differences determined with a visual search task. *J. Opt. Soc. Am. A* **7**, 1209–1217 (1990).
38. MacAdam, D. L. Visual sensitivities to color differences in daylight. *J. Opt. Soc. Am.* **32**, 247–274 (1942).
39. D'Zmura, M. Color in visual search. *Vision Res.* **31**, 951–966 (1991).
40. Bauer, B., Jolicœur, P. & Cowan, W. B. Visual search for colour targets that are or are not linearly-separable from distractors. *Vision Res.* **36**, 1439–1466 (1996).
41. Foster, D. H. & Ward, P. A. Asymmetries in oriented-line detection indicate two orthogonal filters in early vision. *Proc. R Soc. Lond. B* **243**, 75–81 (1991).
42. Wolfe, J. M., Friedman-Hill, S. R., Stewart, M. I. & O'Connell, K. M. The role of categorization in visual search for orientation. *J. Exp. Psychol. Hum. Percept. Perform.* **18**, 34–49 (1992).
43. Treisman, A. in *Handbook of Human Perception and Performance* (eds Boff, K. R., Kaufmann, L. & Thomas, J. P.) 35.1–35.70 (John Wiley and Sons, New York, 1986).
44. Wolfe, J. M. in *Attention* (ed. Pashler, H.) 13–74 (Psychology Press Ltd., Hove, East Sussex, UK, 1998).
45. Chun, M. M. & Wolfe, J. M. in *Blackwell's Handbook of Perception* (ed. Goldstein, E. B.) 272–310 (Blackwell, Oxford, UK, 2001).
46. Bilsky, A. A. & Wolfe, J. M. Part-whole information is useful in size X size but not in orientation X orientation conjunction searches. *Percept. Psychophys.* **57**, 749–760 (1995).
47. Chastain, G. & Cheal, M. Attentional capture with various distractor and target types. *Percept. Psychophys.* **63**, 979–990 (2001).
48. Driver, J., McLeod, P. & Dienes, Z. Are direction and speed coded independently by the visual system? Evidence from visual search. *Spat. Vis.* **6**, 133–147 (1992).
49. Findlay, J. M. Feature detectors and vernier acuity. *Nature* **241**, 135–137 (1973).
50. Barenholtz, E., Cohen, E. H., Feldman, J. & Singh, M. Detection of change in shape: an advantage for concavities. *Cognition* **89**, 1–9 (2003).
51. Ramachandran, V. S. Perception of shape from shading. *Nature* **331**, 163–165 (1988).
52 Wolfe, J. M. & Franzel, S. L. Binocularity and visual search. *Percept. Psychophys.* **44**, 81–93 (1988).
53. Wang, Q., Cavanagh, P. & Green, M. Familiarity and pop-out in visual search. *Percept. Psychophys.* **56**, 495–500 (1994).
54. Malinowski, P. & Hübner, R. The effect of familiarity on visual-search performance: evidence for learned basic features. *Percept. Psychophys.* **63**, 458–463 (2001).
55. Caerwinski, M., Lightfoot, N & Shiffrin, R. Automatization and training in visual search *Am J Psychol.* **105**, 271–315 (1992).
56. Dick, M., Ullman, S. & Sagi, D. Parallel and serial processes in motion detection. *Science* **237**, 400–402 (1987)
57. McLeod, P., Driver, J. & Crisp, J. Visual search for conjunctions of movement and form is parallel *Nature* **332**, 154–155 (1988).
58. Bergen, J. R. & Julesz, B. Rapid discrimination of visual patterns. *IEEE Trans Syst. Man Cybern.* **SMC-13**, 857–863 (1983).
59. Moraglia, G. Display organization and the detection of horizontal lines segments. *Percept. Psychophys.* **45**, 265–272 (1989).
60 Cavanagh, P., Arguin, M & Treisman, A Effect of surface medium on visual search for orientation and size features. *J. Exp. Psychol. Hum. Percept. Perform.* **16**, 479–492 (1990)
61 Wolfe, J. M., Klempen, N. L. & Shulman, E. P. Which end is up? Two representations of orientation in visual search. *Vision Res.* **39**, 2075–2086 (1999).
62 Sagi, D The combination of spatial frequency and orientation is effortlessly perceived. *Percept Psychophys.* **43**, 601–603 (1988).
63. Moraglia, G. Visual search: spatial frequency and orientation. *Percept. Mot. Skills* **69**, 675–689 (1989).
64. Theeuwes, J. Abrupt luminance change pops out; abrupt color change does not. *Percept. Psychophys.* **57**, 637–644 (1995).
65. Yantis, S. & Jonides, J. Abrupt visual onsets and selective attention voluntary versus automatic allocation. *J. Exp. Psychol. Hum. Percept. Perform* **16**, 121–134 (1990).
66. Gilchrist, I D., Humphreys, G. W. & Riddoch, M. J Grouping and extinction. evidence for low-level modulation of visual selection. *Cognit. Neuropsychol* **13**, 1223–1249 (1996).
67. Fahle, M. Parallel perception of vernier offests, curvature, and chevrons in humans. *Vision Res.* **31**, 2149–2184 (1991).
68. Nakayama, K. & Silverman, G. H. Serial and parallel processing of visual feature conjunctions. *Nature* **320**, 264–265 (1986).
69. O'Toole, A. J. & Walker, C. L. On the preattentive accessibility of stereoscopic disparity: evidence from visual search. *Percept. Psychophys.* **59**, 202–218 (1997).
70. He, Z. J & Nakayama, K. Surfaces versus features in visual search. *Nature* **359**, 231–233 (1992).
71. Enns, J. T., Rensink, R. A. & Douglas, R. The influence of line relations on visual search. *Invest. Ophthalmol. Vis Sci.* (Suppl.) **31(4)**, 105 (1990).
72. Enns, J. T. & Rensink, R. A. in *Visual Search 2* (eds Brogan, D., Gale, A. & Carr, K.) 73–89 (Taylor & Francis, London, UK, 1993).
73. Sun, J. & Perona, P. Preattentive perception of elementary three dimensional shapes. *Vision Res.* **36**, 2515–2529 (1996).
74. Tsal, Y., Meiran, N. & Lamy, D. Towards a resolution theory of visual attention. *Vis. Cognit.* **2**, 313–330 (1995).
75. Wolfe, J. M. & Bennett, S. C. Preattentive object files: shapeless bundles of basic features *Vision Res.* **37**, 25–43 (1997).
76. Kristjansson, A. & Tse, P. U. Curvature discontinuities are cues for rapid shape analysis. *Percept. Psychophys.* **63**, 390–403 (2001).
77. Chen, L. Toplogical structure in visual perception. *Science* **218**, 699–700 (1982).
78. Chen, L. Holes and wholes: a reply to Rubin and Kanwisher. *Percept. Psychophys.* **47**, 47–53 (1990).
79. Cheal, M. & Lyon, D. Attention in visual search: multiple search classes. *Percept. Psychophys.* **52**, 113–138 (1992).
80. Pomerantz, J. R. & Pristach, E. A. Emergent features, attention, and perceptual glue in visual form perception. *J. Exp. Psychol. Hum. Percept. Perform.* **15**, 635–649 (1989).
81. Taylor, S. & Badcock, D. Processing feature density in preattentive perception. *Percept. Psychophys.* **44**, 551–562 (1988).
82. Donnelly, N., Humphreys, G. W. & Riddoch, M. J. Parallel computation of primitive shape descriptions. *J. Exp Psychol. Hum. Percept. Perform.* **17**, 561–570 (1991).
83. Elder, J. & Zucker, S. A measure of closure. *Vision Res.* **34**, 3361–3369 (1994).
84. Kovacs, I. & Julesz, B. A closed curve is much more than an incomplete one. effect of closure in figure-ground segmentation. *Proc. Natl Acad. Sci. USA* **90**, 7495–7497 (1993).
85. Williams, D. & Julesz, B. Perceptual asymmetry in texture perception *Proc. Natl Acad. Sci USA* **89**, 6531–6534 (1992).
86. Chen, L. The topological approach to perceptual organization *Vis. Cognit.* (in the press).
87. Rubin, J. M. & Kanwisher, N. Topological perception. holes in an experiment. *Percept. Psychophys.* **37**, 179–180 (1985).
88. Wolfe, J M, Yee, A. & Friedman-Hill, S R Curvature is a basic feature for visual search. *Perception* **21**, 465–480 (1992).
89. Kleffner, D. A. & Ramachandran, V S On the perception of shape from shading. *Percept. Psychophys* **52**, 18–36 (1992).
90. Takeuchi, T. Visual search of expansion and contraction. *Vision Res.* **37**, 2083–2090 (1997).
91. Braddick, O. J. & Holliday, I. E. Serial search for targets defined by divergence or deformation of optic flow. *Perception* **20**, 345–354 (1991).
92. Frith, U. A curious effect with reversed letters explained by a theory of schema. *Percept. Psychophys.* **16**, 113–116 (1974).
93. Kinchla, R. A & Collyer, C. E. Detecting a target letter in briefly presented arrays. a confidence rating analysis in terms of a weighted additive effects model. *Percept. Psychophys* **16**, 117–122 (1974).
94. Shiffrin, R. M. & Gardner, G. T. Visual processing capacity and attentional control. *J. Exp. Psychol.* **93**, 72–82 (1972)
95. Grice, G. R. & Canham, L. Redundancy phenomena are affected by response requirments. *Percept. Psychophys.* **48**, 209–213 (1990).
96. Brand, J. Classification without identification in visual search. *Quart. J. Exp. Psychol.* **23**, 178–186 (1971).
97. Jonides, J. & Gleitman, H. A conceptual category effect in visual search: O as letter or digit. *Percept Psychophys.* **12**, 457–460 (1972).
98. Duncan, J. Category effects in visual search: a failure to replicate the 'oh–zero' phenomenon. *Percept. Psychophys.* **34**, 221–232 (1983).
99. Krueger, L. E. The category effect in visual search depends on physical rather than conceptual differences. *Percept. Psychophys.* **35**, 558–564 (1984).
100. Brown, J. M., Weisstein, N. & May, J. G. Visual search for simple volumetric shapes. *Percept. Psychophys.* **51**, 40–48 (1992).
101. Pilon, D. & Friedman, A. Grouping and detecting vertices in 2-D, 3-D, and quasi-3-D objects. *Can. J. Exp. Psychol.* **52**, 114–127 (1998).
102. Nothdurft, H. C. Faces and facial expression do not pop-out. *Perception* **22**, 1287–1298 (1993).
103. Suzuki, S. & Cavanagh, P. Facial organization blocks access to low-level features an object inferiority effect *J. Exp. Psychol. Hum. Percept. Perform.* **21**, 901–913 (1995).
104. Purcell, D. G., Stewart, A. L. & Skov, R. B. It takes a confounded face to pop out of a crowd. *Perception* **25**, 1091–1108 (1996).
105. Hansen, C. H. & Hansen, R. D. Finding the face in the crowd: An anger superiority effect. *J. Pers. Soc. Psychol* **54**, 917–924 (1988).
106. von Grunau, M. & Anston, C. The detection of gaze direction: a stare-in-the-crowd effect. *Perception* **24**, 1297–1313 (1995).
107. Tong, F. & Nakayama, K. Robust representations for faces: evidence from visual search. *J. Exp. Psychol. Hum. Percept. Perform.* **25**, 1016–1035 (1999).
108. Eastwood, J. D., Smilek, D. & Merikle, P. M. Differential attentional guidance by unattended faces expressing positive and negative emotion. *Percept. Psychophys.* **63**, 1004–1013 (2001).
109. Bundesen, C., Kyllingsbaek, S., Houmann, K. J. & Jensen, R. M. Is visual attention automatically attracted by one's own name? *Percept. Psychophys.* **59**, 714–720 (1997).
110. Tipples, J., Young, A., Quinlan, P., Broks, P. & Ellis, A. Searching for threat. *Quart J. Exp Psychol* **55**, 1007–1026 (2002).

Competing interests statement

The authors declare that they have no competing financial interests.

Online links

FURTHER INFORMATION

Visual attention lab: http://search.bwh.harvard.edu

Access to this interactive links box is free online.

Part II
Brain Systems

[5]

Implications of Sustained and Transient Channels for Theories of Visual Pattern Masking, Saccadic Suppression, and Information Processing

Bruno G. Breitmeyer
University of Houston

Leo Ganz
Stanford University

A review of the visual masking literature in the context of known neurophysiological and psychophysical properties of the visual system's spatiotemporal response reveals that three consistent and typical pattern masking effects—(a) Type B forward or paracontrast, (b) Type B backward or metacontrast, and (c) Type A forward and backward—can be explained in terms of three simple sensory processes. It is hypothesized that sustained channels are involved in the processing of structural or figural information, whereas transient channels are involved in signaling the spatial location or change in spatial location (motion) of a stimulus. In the proposed model, Type B forward masking or paracontrast is mediated via lateral inhibition realized in the center-surround antagonism of the receptive fields of the sustained cells. In apposition to this mechanism of *intra*channel inhibition, Type B backward masking or metacontrast is produced by a mechanism of *inter*channel inhibition, that is, transient cells laterally inhibit the activity of sustained cells. Both mechanisms are assumed to be operating at or prior to the contour-forming levels of visual processing. Type A masking effects are explained in terms of sensory integration of sustained channel information at preiconic and iconic levels of visual processing. The implications of this multichannel model for saccadic-suppression and information-processing approaches to pattern recognition are discussed.

The visibility of a briefly displayed target pattern can be reduced in several ways by another briefly displayed masking pattern. Perhaps the most effective way is to display concurrently with the target a spatially overlapping pattern mask of sufficiently high contrast, which partially or totally obscures the target. However, besides this rather obvious type of masking procedure, methods of visual pattern masking have been employed in which the target and mask displays do not overlap in time and/or space. Such methods are especially interesting because they can be employed to probe the spatiotemporal properties of information processing and, in particular, pattern-forming operations in the visual system.

This study was supported in part by National Eye Institute Grant EY01241-02 to the second author.

Much of the scholarly and experimental research that contributed to this paper was done while the first author was on leave of absence from the University of Houston, between July 1973 and August 1974, at the Bell Laboratories, Murray Hill, New Jersey. He thanks Bela Julesz of the Bell Laboratories for sponsoring and encouraging his research efforts. We also thank Naomi Weisstein for helpful criticisms and suggestions.

Requests for reprints should be sent to Bruno G. Breitmeyer, Department of Psychology, University of Houston, Houston, Texas 77004.

2   BRUNO G. BREITMEYER AND LEO GANZ

MASK   O   [checkerboard pattern]   [maze-like pattern]

TARGET   ●   A   T

         a   b   c

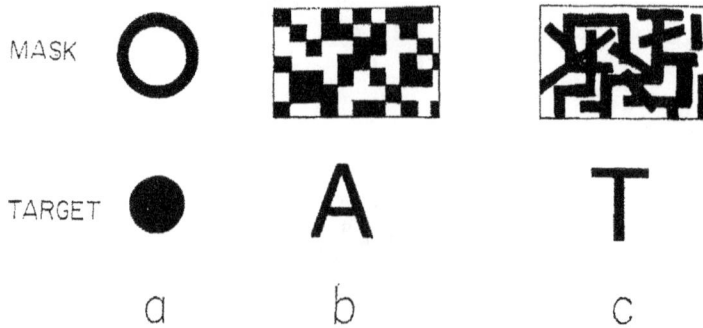

FIGURE 1. Mask and target stimuli typically used in (a) metacontrast and paracontrast masking,
(b) masking by noise, and (c) masking by structure.

The methods, data, and theories of various types of visual pattern masking have been reviewed extensively elsewhere (Kahneman, 1968; Lefton, 1973; Scheerer, 1973; Weisstein, 1972). It is the aim of this paper to briefly review the major types of masking effects obtained with various methods and the major theories or models that have been proposed to account for these effects, and to outline a three-mechanism model of visual pattern masking based on psychophysical and neurophysiological properties of the visual system.

To this end it is important to introduce the standard terminology that will be used repeatedly in the following discussions. The temporal interval separating the onsets of the target and mask is the *stimulus onset asynchrony* (SOA). By convention, positive SOA values indicate that the mask follows the target in time, a procedure known as *backward masking*. Negative SOA values indicate that the mask precedes the target in time; this procedure is known as *forward masking*. Masking in which the contours of the mask do not overlap but are contiguous with or proximate to contours of the target (see Figure 1a) are called *paracontrast* and *metacontrast* when forward and backward masking procedures, respectively, are employed (Stigler, 1910). When the contours of the mask overlap the contours of the target, and the mask consists of a random array of black and white areas that bear little or no structural relation to the target pattern (see Figure 1b), the masking procedure is called

masking by noise (Kinsbourne & Warrington, 1962). When the spatially overlapping mask is structurally related to the target pattern (see Figure 1c)—that is, when it shares the contour orientation, curvature, and other figural features of the target—it is called *masking by structure.*

For both forward and backward masking, two types of effects, as illustrated in Figure 2, can be obtained (Kahneman, 1968). Using Kolers' (1962) nomenclature, when masking magnitude decreases monotonically as the absolute SOA value increases, a "Type A" masking effect prevails; when the masking magnitude varies in a nonmonotonic, U-shaped fashion, a "Type B" masking effect prevails.

CONDITIONS PRODUCING AND AFFECTING TYPE A AND TYPE B MASKING FUNCTIONS

Any comprehensive theory of masking eventually should be able to satisfactorily explain the masking effects alluded to above. The masking functions and the stimulus conditions that play a major influence in determining their magnitude and shape are listed below.

Paracontrast

Paracontrast is a Type B forward masking effect in which the brightness or spatial contrast of a target is reduced by a preceding mask with adjacent but nonoverlapping contours (as in Figure 1a). The magnitude of the effect increases as the mask energy increases relative to the target energy (Weis-

THEORIES OF VISUAL MASKING 3

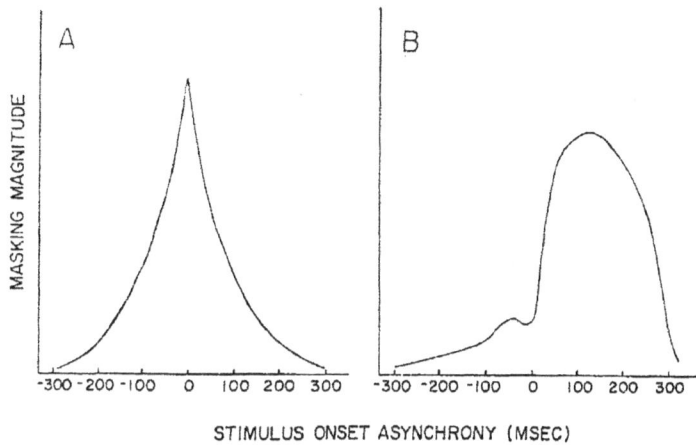

FIGURE 2. Functions typically obtained in visual masking. (A) Type A monotonic forward and backward functions; (B) Type B nonmonotonic forward and backward functions.

stein, 1972) and can be obtained dichoptically (Kolers & Rosner, 1960), that is, when the target is presented to one eye and the surrounding mask to the other eye.

Metacontrast

Metacontrast is a Type B backward masking effect in which target information is suppressed by a spatially adjacent mask (as in Figure 1a) following the target in time. In metacontrast one can obtain suppression of brightness or spatial contrast (Alpern, 1953; Growney & Weisstein, 1972; Weisstein, 1972), of contour and contour detail (Breitmeyer, Love, & Wepman, 1974; Burchard & Lawson, 1973; Sukale-Wolf, 1971) and of form identity (Averbach & Coriell, 1961; Mayzner et al., 1965; Weisstein & Haber, 1965).

These metacontrast effects can be obtained monoptically (target and mask presented to same eye) and dichoptically (Kolers & Rosner, 1960; McFadden & Gummerman, 1973; Schiller & Smith, 1968; Werner, 1940). Moreover, metacontrast is sensitive to the degree of contour separation between target and mask. As the intercontour distance increases, the magnitude of metacontrast masking decreases (Alpern, 1953; Kolers & Rosner, 1960; Weisstein & Growney, 1969), and the SOA value at which peak masking occurs also may become smaller (Alpern, 1953).

Another parameter that affects the overall magnitude of the metacontrast masking effect is the retinal location of the target and mask relative to the fovea. Metacontrast effects are either absent or relatively weak when the target and the mask are confined to the fovea (Alpern, 1953; Kolers & Rosner, 1960; Toch, 1956); however, the overall effects progressively increase as both target and mask are displayed parafoveally at progressively greater eccentricities (Kolers & Rosner, 1960; Stewart & Purcell, 1970). Moreover, Kolers and Rosner (1960) note that when confined to the fovea, very small contour separations between the target and mask drastically reduce or eliminate the already weak masking effects, whereas at parafoveal locations the effects are sufficiently robust to withstand total elimination until fairly large contour separations (about 2° visual angle—Alpern, 1953) are employed.

Although Type B metacontrast effects are obtained when brightness rating, contour discrimination, or form identification are used as indicator responses, they are not obtained if a forced-choice detection criterion or simple reaction time (RT) measures are used (Fehrer & Biederman, 1962; Fehrer & Raab, 1962; Schiller & Smith, 1966). For instance, Fehrer and Raab (1962) and Fehrer and Biederman (1962) show that simple RT to the target does not change as a function of

4   BRUNO G. BREITMEYER AND LEO GANZ

SOA; that is, no Type B effect is obtained. Moreover, Schiller and Smith (1966) showed that choice RT to a disk displayed at one of two possible locations and followed by two simultaneously presented masking rings—one of which surrounded the disk when displayed at one location and the other at the other disk location—did not change as a function of SOA. That is, in this study as in the two studies above, the subjects were able to detect the *presence* and *location* of a target despite the suppression of its brightness, contour detail, or form. This implies that some target information is immune to the masking effect.

Biederman (Note 1) observed that even at SOAs that are optimal for brightness suppression, the target presence was readily detectable as an apparent expanding motion of the target into the surrounding ring. In this connection, Kolers (1963) showed that although the shape or form of the first of two spatially separated disks can be masked by a metacontrast ring, it nonetheless contributes to the perception of stroboscopic motion obtained when the second disk follows the first at optimal SOAs. This implies again that some information in the first disk is immune to the masking effect of the ring and contributes to the stroboscopic motion effect.

Type B Functions During Stroboscopic Motion

In fact, one can obtain masking effects in a stroboscopic motion situation. Wertheimer (1912) noted that at temporal intervals yielding optimal stroboscopic (beta) motion, some brightness suppression was observable in the first of the two sequentially presented stimuli. Moreover, in regard to contour masking, Breitmeyer et al. (1974) and Breitmeyer, Battaglia, and Weber (in press) showed that the degree of contour suppression is directly related to the degree of perceived stroboscopic motion, which is a Type B or U-shaped function of SOA. The fact that stroboscopic motion can be obtained with dichoptic presentation of the two stimuli (Anstis & Moulden, 1970; Shipley, Kenney, & King, 1945; Verhoeff, 1940; Wertheimer, 1912) indicates that brightness and contour suppression attending stroboscopic motion may also be a dichoptically obtained effect.

Masking of Pattern by Noise and Structure Masks

Both noise and structure masks yield strong Type A forward masking effects when the target and mask are presented to the same eye (Kinsbourne & Warrington, 1962; Scharf & Lefton, 1970; Schiller, 1966; Schiller & Smith, 1965). However, when the target and mask are presented dichoptically, the Type A forward masking effect is relatively weak and extends over a smaller temporal range (Greenspoon & Eriksen, 1968; Smith & Schiller, 1966; Turvey, 1973).

In backward masking by noise or structure, strong Type A masking effects can be obtained monoptically (Scharf & Lefton, 1970; Schiller, 1966; Schiller & Smith, 1965) and dichoptically (Greenspoon & Eriksen, 1968; Smith & Schiller, 1966). Moreover, with masking by structure, it is also possible to obtain Type B backward masking effects monoptically (Michaels & Turvey, 1973; Purcell & Stewart, 1970; Spencer & Shuntich, 1970; Turvey, 1973; Weisstein, 1971) and dichoptically (Weisstein, 1971), if the energy or contrast of the structure mask is equal to or lower than that of the target. When the mask energy is higher than that of the target, a strong Type A backward masking effect, which obscures the Type B effect, prevails (Spencer & Shuntich, 1970; Turvey, 1973; Weisstein, 1971). Because under certain stimulus conditions the Type A effect obscures the Type B effect, experiments failing to find Type B effects cannot be used as evidence for the nonexistence of Type B mechanisms (Eriksen, Becker, & Hoffman, 1970).[1]

---

[1] An asymmetry is involved here. When the mask is made stronger relative to the target, the Type A effect (monotonic masking) becomes progressively stronger and thus eventually obscures a relatively fixed Type B effect (see paragraph number 8 in the discussion of the scope of the present model). However, if the mask is weakened relative to the target, Type B masking (U-shaped function) does not necessarily become stronger and obscure a Type A effect. Rather, the Type A effect weakens. Eventually, as the target becomes much more powerful than the mask, all masking effects are weakened or absent. Hence the A effect can obscure the B effect, but not vice versa (for a good illustration of this relationship see Weisstein, 1971, Figure 1).

THEORIES OF PATTERN MASKING

Two major theoretical approaches seem to be taken currently to explain forward and backward pattern masking. One approach relies heavily on the modeling of interactions between the neurosensory representations of the target and mask stimuli (Bridgeman, 1971; Purcell, Stewart, & Dember, 1968; Weisstein, 1968); the other relies more on concepts derived from studies of cognition and information processing (Coltheart, 1975; Haber, 1969a, 1969b; Scheerer, 1973; Spencer & Shuntich, 1970; Sperling, 1963, 1967; Turvey, 1973; Uttal, 1970, 1971), such as the notion of iconic storage (Neisser, 1967).

Theories of Metacontrast

Two neurosensory models of metacontrast, both based on quantitatively defined interactions between excitatory and lateral inhibitory neural processes, have been particularly prominent in the last few years. Weisstein (1968, 1972) has proposed a Rashevsky-Landahl neural net model composed of five two-factor neurons, that is, neurons in which excitation and inhibition combine. Two of the neurons are peripheral and convey information about the target and mask, respectively. Each of these peripheral neurons makes contact with one of two respective, second-order central neurons. The second-order target neuron transmits an excitatory signal to a more central third-order decision neuron, which also receives inhibitory input via collateral fibres of the second-order mask neuron. As noted in Lefton's (1973) review of metacontrast, this model rests on several critical assumptions, the most crucial of which is that the collateral inhibition generated by the second-order mask neuron develops about 50–100 msec sooner than the excitation generated by the second-order target neuron. This assumption, although correct in principle, has found little if any support in the neurophysiological literature until quite recently. This recent evidence is reviewed in a following section of the present paper, and Weisstein, Ozog, and Szoc (1975) have incorporated these findings in a revision of her original model of metacontrast (Weisstein, 1968).

The other major neural model proposed by Bridgeman (1971) is based on a Hartline-Ratliff neural net of *Limulus* eye. It assumes a given time constant characterizing a recurrent lateral inhibitory network, and while correctly predicting a Type B masking effect over a fixed range of SOAs (determined by the time constant), beyond this range the model predicts pronounced oscillatory functions not observed in studies of metacontrast (Weisstein et al., 1975). However, it does have the advantage of predicting paracontrast (forward masking) effects when the target is spatially surrounded by the mask.

Besides the neural model approach to metacontrast, several other theoretical approaches relying on higher order cognitive or perceptual processes have also been proposed. Kahneman (1967) proposed that metacontrast is simply an anomalous or impossible type of stroboscopic motion. For instance, visibility of a disklike target stimulus followed at optimal SOAs by an annular mask is suppressed by the perceptual system, because it cannot simultaneously accommodate the perception of an expanding disk and a subsequent nonexistent disk as marked by the "hole" of the annulus.

This account can be challenged on several grounds. Weisstein and Growney (1969) have demonstrated that stroboscopic motion is clearly obtainable when the two sequentially presented stimuli are separated spatially by two or more degrees; however, metacontrast brightness suppression, as previously shown by Alpern (1953), is substantially or entirely attenuated when the test and mask stimuli have similar, large spatial separations. Moreover, Breitmeyer et al. (1974, in press) have shown that contour suppression can occur under highly perceivable and possible stroboscopic motion. Anomalous or impossible stroboscopic motion thus need not be invoked as a mechanism for metacontrast. However, the two phenomena may share mechanisms in common (Breitmeyer et al., 1974; Kahneman, 1967).

Several other investigators, notably Uttal (1970, 1971) and Turvey (1973), have argued that metacontrast effects are not simply due to interactions between target and mask contour-forming processes but rather are due to fairly late and central decision processes that are involved in the *identification* of form. According to this view, the metacontrast

6   BRUNO G. BREITMEYER AND LEO GANZ

effects occur at processing levels beyond a precategorical, iconic representation or storage (Coltheart, 1975; Neisser, 1967) of the visual input. This explanation seems unlikely for the following reasons. It is known that in the flow of visual information processing, retinotopic organization is progressively lost at stages beyond primary visual cortex (Gross, 1973b; Zeki, 1971). The fact that metacontrast effects are highly sensitive to contour separation argues for its occurring at an early stage of visual processing in which retinotopic information is still present, not at later stages such as those in which visual stimuli have been categorized, and retinotopic information is presumably lost (Gross, Bender, & Roch-Miranda, 1974; Weiskrantz, 1974). Moreover, in unpublished observations, one of the present authors has shown that when the target and spatially flanking mask stimuli (sharing the same figural properties as the target) are presented through the use of static or dyanmic random-dot stereograms (Julesz, 1971), the rather slight backward masking effects are Type A. Type B effects (i.e., metacontrast) are not obtained. The random-dot stereogram displays of the target and masks were of equal luminous energy. Under such conditions Type B effects are obtained when standard stimuli are employed. The fact that Type B effects are not obtained with equal-energy random-dot stereograms but are obtained with equal-energy standard stimuli leads to the following argument.

It is unlikely that stereopsis in man occurs prior to Brodmann's Area 18 (Hubel & Wiesel, 1970). Therefore, the stereogram experiment suggests that metacontrast interactions do not occur at Area 18 or beyond. In addition, Simon (Note 2) has reported that Type B metacontrast effects show a high degree of chromatic specificity. That is to say, without changing the spatial properties of the target and surrounding mask, Type B metacontrast effects were obtained only when the wavelengths of the target and mask were the same. All these experiments suggest that metacontrast effects are highly sensory-specific, which would be unlikely at a posticonic stage. That figural similarity between target and mask is an important modulator of metacontrast is not disputed. What is disputed is the assertion that metacontrast effects are due

to posticonic rather than iconic or more peripheral levels of visual information processing.

Definitions of the iconic storage differ. However, a recent characterization of iconic store (Coltheart, 1975) ascribes to it the following important properties: It is a visual the assertion that metacontrast effects are due representation of the stimulus, which is literal, precategorical or unidentified, wholistic, of high capacity, and of fairly rapid decay. The decay period has been estimated to be on the order of 200–300 msec. We define a *central, contour-specific iconic store*, henceforth ISc, as that neural level at which figural information—in particular, contour orientation and size of a stimulus—is processed in retinotopic fashion. We define more peripheral retinotopic sensory representations as *peripheral iconic stores* (Barlow & Sparrock, 1964; Sakitt, Note 3), henceforth ISp. This latter iconic representation is not orientation-specific. Finally we define as *posticonic store*, henceforth PS, representations more central than ISc, whose retinotopic information is highly degraded. Presumably, PS representations are more associative and categorical (rather than purely visuosensory) in character and therefore are not amenable to visual masking (Gross, 1973b). A suitable candidate for a PS could be inferotemporal cortex (Gross, 1973a, 1973b; Gross et al., 1974; Weiskrantz, 1974).

Theories of Type B Backward Structure Masking

As noted previously, Type B backward masking functions can be obtained when a structure mask is used, particularly if the energy of the mask is less than that of the target (Michaels & Turvey, 1973; Purcell & Stewart, 1970; Spencer & Shuntich, 1970; Turvey, 1973; Weisstein, 1971). Several investigators (Averbach & Coriell, 1961; Coltheart, 1975; Haber, 1969a, 1969b; Spencer & Shuntich, 1970; Sperling, 1963) argue that in backward structure masking the target stimulus establishes a clear ISc. The structure mask erases the target and replaces it with its own ISc representation. The erasure of the target ISc occurs prior to PS.

A somewhat different viewpoint of Type B masking has been proposed recently by Turvey (1973, pp. 40, 47). According to this view, information in the target ISc is transferred to PS; the subsequent structure mask is also transferred to PS, thus overloading its processing capacity. Masking at the PS stage, as conceptualized by Turvey, is a function of both structural and semantic properties of the stimulus (Mayzner & Tresselt, 1970; Uttal, 1970, 1971).

Theories of Type A Forward and Backward Pattern Masking

Type A forward and backward pattern masking effects have usually been explained in terms of an integration hypothesis similar to Eriksen's (1966) luminance-summation contrast-reduction hypothesis. According to this hypothesis, due to limits in the temporal resolution of the visual system, or in other words, due to persistence of the sensory response to a brief stimulus display (Efron, 1970; Haber, 1969b), sensory representations of target and mask stimuli can combine—not necessarily in a linear or additive manner (Boynton, 1961)—to form a representation in which the mask camouflages or obscures the target. In regard to backward masking, several investigators have shown that as in forward masking, the Type A integration effect is most dominant at target–mask synchrony and decreases over a short SOA range. Type B effects, which some theorists have attributed not to integration but to processing "interruption" (Coltheart, 1975; Haber, 1969a), are minimal at short SOAs and become dominant at larger SOA values (Averbach & Coriell, 1961; Spencer & Shuntich, 1970; Turvey, 1973; Weisstein, 1971). The current consensus seems to be that both integration and interruption mechanisms are involved in backward structure masking, whereas only integration mechanisms are involved in forward Type A pattern masking (Scheerer, 1973; Turvey, 1973). Moreover, from the above discussion it is evident that the interruption mechanism is thought to involve only ISc or PS processes, whereas integration can occur at ISp levels.

The two-channel model to be proposed in this paper will retain the integration mechanism to explain Type A forward and backward masking effects. However, to explain Type B forward and backward masking, two other mechanisms are involved. One involves lateral inhibitory activity within a given class of visual cells, which we call intrachannel lateral inhibition; the other involves lateral inhibitory activity between two classes of visual cells, which we call interchannel lateral inhibition. To lay the groundwork for a description of the model, the visual psychophysics and physiology relevant to pattern perception is outlined below.

PSYCHOPHYSIOLOGY OF PATTERN PERCEPTION

Organization of the Visual Pathways

There are two organizational features of the visual system that play a prominent role in its functioning. One is the existence of antagonistic excitatory and inhibitory processes; the other is the hierarchical organization of the visual pathway. Both give rise, among other things, to the spatial and structural specificity or neuronal receptive fields (Benevento, Creutzfeldt, & Kuhnt, 1972; Hubel & Wiesel, 1962, 1968).

At the retinal level of organization the receptive fields of ganglion cells are characterized by circularly symmetric, antagonistically organized regions (Kuffler, 1953). "On-center" cells have circular receptive field centers, which at light onset yield an increase in firing rate. The annular surround region yields an antagonistic effect, that is, a decrease in firing rate at light onset. "Off-center" cells are similarly organized, except in each antagonistic region the polarity of the response is reversed relative to on-center cells. The center-surround antagonism reflects the interaction between excitatory and lateral inhibitory activity.

At the next level of processing, the lateral geniculate nucleus (LGN), the neuronal receptive fields are still circularly symmetric; however, the organization of their antagonistic regions is spatially more complex and specific (Freund, 1973). In the past few years, increasing electrophysiological evidence suggests that LGN receptive fields do not have the simple center-surround organization found in retinal cells. In particular, the surround inhibition is stronger at the LGN level and does not disappear with dark adaptation as it does at the retinal level (Barlow, Fitzhugh, & Kuffler, 1957; Hubel & Wiesel, 1961; Maffei & Fiorentini, 1972b;

8   BRUNO G. BREITMEYER AND LEO GANZ

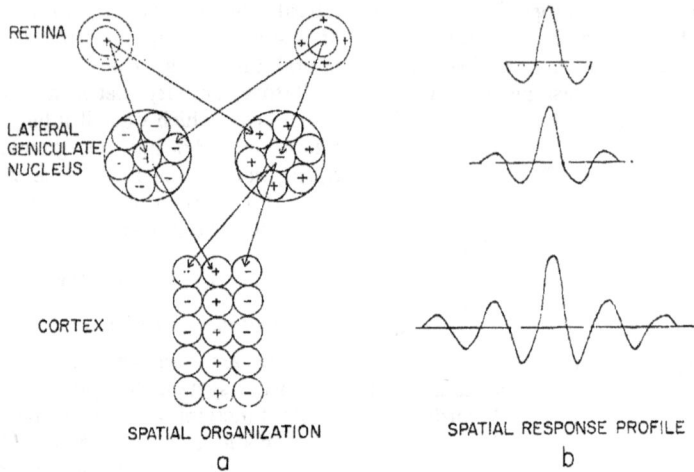

FIGURE 3. (a) Hypothetical hierarchical spatial organization of visual receptive fields along retino-geniculo-cortical pathway. (b) Corresponding spatial response profiles (after Hammond, 1973).

Singer, Pöppel, & Creutzfeldt, 1972). Several studies have shown that this is most likely due to the fact that the center of LGN receptive fields receives inputs from one or more spatially overlapping retinal receptive fields, whereas the antagonistic surrounds receive their inputs from retinal receptive fields of opposite polarity, as shown in Figure 3a (Cleland, Dubin, & Levick, 1971a; Hammond, 1973; Maffei & Fiorentini, 1972b; Michael, 1973; Singer & Creutzfeldt, 1970). This hierarchical receptive field organization implies not only the existence of a center and a powerful antagonistic surround but also the existence of another synergistic outer surround (Hammond, 1973), which gives a response of the same polarity as, but weaker than, the center (see Figure 3b).

LGN receptive fields, through another similar stage of hierarchical organization, in turn presumably determine the spatial characteristics of cortical simple-cell receptive fields. The latter are characterized by two important features, which differentiate them from subcortical receptive fields. Their antagonistic center-surround regions lie along a common axis of orientation. In the cat, for the most part, they receive input from both eyes, although some of the cortical simple receptive fields are innervated only monocu-

larly (Hubel & Wiesel, 1962). In the monkey there is a monocular stage converging on a binocular one at a subsequent level in the hierarchy (Hubel & Wiesel, 1968).

The orientation of simple cells at striate cortex could derive from a set of LGN receptive fields whose centers, falling along a given axis, form the center of the simple-cell receptive field (Benevento et al., 1972), and a set of oppositely signed LGN receptive fields whose centers make up the antagonistic surround regions as shown in the bottom of Figure 3a (Hammond, 1971). As a consequence of this hierarchical organization, the simple-cell receptive fields would be characterized not only by a specific axis of orientation but also by a damped, oscillating spatial-response profile as shown in the bottom of Figure 3b (Pollen & Ronner, 1975).

Fourier Approach to Visual Pattern Perception

Thus far we have described the neurophysiology of the visual system in the spatial domain. Mathematically, an alternative approach is to describe it in the Fourier or spatial-frequency domain. The following is descriptive and is not meant to imply or deny the existence of any concrete Fourier-transformational processes in the visual system.

It can be shown via Fourier transformation of the spatial-response profile of such cortical cells that they are maximally sensitive to a fairly narrow range of spatial frequencies of periodic gratings oriented along the preferred axis (Pollen & Ronner, 1975). Indeed, Maffei and Fiorentini's (1973) and Pollen and Ronner's (1975) electrophysiological results indicate that cortical cells are characterized by narrow spatial-frequency tuning. In fact, a host of psychophysical studies are consistent with this approach (Blakemore & Campbell, 1969; Campbell & Robson, 1968; Carpenter & Ganz, 1972; Graham, in press; Maffei & Fiorentini, 1972a; Julesz & Miller, Note 4). Pollen, Lee, and Taylor (1971) have argued that cortical cells, each of which represents a particular spatial frequency and orientation specificity, but a large set of which represents a sufficiently wide range of spatial frequencies and orientations, can provide the neural basis for computing a two-dimensional Fourier transform (spectral analysis) of a stimulus pattern.

According to Fourier theory, any two-dimensional spatial pattern can be analyzed in terms of its spatial-frequency components. The above psychophysical and electrophysiological studies suggest that the visual system performs a rough analogue to such an analysis. For pattern perception, however, a subsequent synthesis of these spatial-frequency components needs to be performed. Synthesis is required because a subject can attach a perceptual response to the conjunction of two or more spatial-frequency components, which differs from the response to the components presented in isolation (Maffei & Fiorentini, 1972a). That is to say, the varying spatial-frequency analyzers must integrate their information at a later stage to construct a representation of the input pattern. Psychophysical studies by Maffei and Fiorentini (1972a) indicate that the synthesis occurs with dichoptic presentations of the separate spatial-frequency components. Thus an analogue of Fourier synthesis may well occur cortically and at a processing level beyond the analytic stage which, as indicated, presumably occurs as early as the simple cell level of Area 17 of visual cortex.

The implication is that figural synthesis and consequently form perception occur at a level later than the monocular stage of Area 17, a view that certainly is neither without precedent (Hebb, 1949) nor without psychophysical evidence in support of it (Blake & Fox, 1974).

The consequences of the Fourier approach for pattern perception can be more explicitly outlined by considering how different spatial-frequency components contribute to the entire pattern percept. It can be shown that sharp edge or contour information in a spatial pattern is contained in its high spatial-frequency components, and insofar as the brightness or spatial contrast of a pattern depends to a substantial extent on sharp edges or contours (Campbell, Howell, & Robson, 1971; Cornsweet, 1970; Hood, 1973), high as well as intermediate spatial-frequency components are important in spatial brightness perception.

However, very high spatial harmonics (those at or near the limits of spatial resolution) are not necessary for pattern formation and recognition (Ginsburg, 1973; Harmon & Julesz, 1973). Intermediate to high spatial frequencies can provide sufficient information for pattern perception. Indeed, using the Fourier approach, Ginsburg (1973) has shown that certain Gestalt factors of closure, proximity, similarity, etc., as well as certain spatial illusions, can be predicted by assuming that the visual system relies largely on the output of spatial-frequency channels that do not extend into the extreme high frequency range. According to this model, the visual system need not extract and synthesize all the possible spatial-frequency information to form a percept, but, depending on the nature of the perceptual task, it only needs to extract and synthesize spatial-frequency components up to a given value (Carpenter & Ganz, 1972).

That the presence of very high spatial-frequency information is not a requisite for pattern perception is even more clearly illustrated in a recent study by Bodis-Wollner (1972). He found that, prior to recovery, neurological patients with presumed damage in striate cortex who show little if any loss in acuity—that is, who have the ability to perceive very high spatial-frequency information—but do show a substantial loss of contrast sensitivity in the intermediate to high spatial-frequency range, also show impairments in pattern recognition tasks such as reading. It thus seems that the activation of intermediate to high spatial-frequency channels is more important to pattern perception than the activation of very high spatial-frequency channels. The presence of very high spatial-frequency information may accentuate the contour and thus the spatial contrast and clarity of the visual image, but lack of that information, while resulting in blurring of contours and a reduction of contrast, does not substantially impair the identifiability of a stimulus.

Transient and Sustained Visual Channels

In order to understand the nature of masking in terms of interactions between spatial-frequency channels, the spatiotemporal response properties of these channels need to be explored. Recent psychophysical studies have shown that low spatial-frequency channels are particularly sensitive to transient stimulation produced by rapid motion (Breitmeyer, 1973; Pantle, 1970; Tolhurst, 1973), flicker (Keesey, 1972; Kulikowski & Tolhurst, 1973), and abrupt stimulus onset (Breitmeyer & Julesz, 1975). High spatial-frequency channels seem to prefer slowly moving or stationary stimuli (Breitmeyer, 1973; Keesey, 1972; Kulikowski & Tolhurst, 1973; Pantle, 1970).

A result reported by Kulikowski and Tolhurst (1973) is particularly illustrative. These investigators found that when a grating of intermediate (10 cycles/degree) spatial frequency was flickered in counterphase at variable temporal frequencies, the ability to detect the spatial properties of the grating, that is, its spatial periodicity, was lost at temporal frequencies at and above which flicker was still detectable. Kulikowski and Tolhurst concluded that form analyzers have a lower temporal resolution than do flicker detectors. They suggest further that the flicker-detecting channels would yield transient responses to the onset of a prolonged stimulus presentation, whereas form-detecting channels would yield sustained responses that last for the duration of the stimulus presentation. Moreover, whereas the flicker-detecting channels preferred low to intermediate spatial frequencies, the sustained channels preferred intermediate to high spatial frequencies—results consistent with those reported by Breitmeyer and Julesz (1975).

Another way of interpreting these data is that the lower critical flicker frequency or fusion frequency of form-detecting channels reflects a longer response persistence or integration time. This longer persistence or integration time is probably also reflected in other response indicators, such as the time—intensity reciprocity expressed by Bloch's law. For instance, Kahneman (1964) and Kahneman and Norman (1964) found that the critical duration for brightness discrimination in which Bloch's law holds is on the order of 100 msec, whereas for form identification or acuity the critical duration can range from 200–350 msec. Schober and Hilz (1965) also have shown that detectability of square wave gratings of high spatial frequencies benefits more from long exposure durations than the detectability of low spatial-frequency, square wave gratings. The use of square wave gratings renders interpretations of these results equivocal because square wave gratings are composed of a set of spatial harmonics. Recently, Breitmeyer and Ganz (in press) have demonstrated that the critical duration—the longest duration at which perfect Contrast × Time reciprocity determines detection threshold—increases from approximately 50 msec to 200 msec, as the spatial frequency of a *sinusoidal* test grating increases from .5 to 16 cycles/degree.

Besides having a longer response persistence or integration time (see Figure 4), sustained channels are also characterized by a longer response latency to brief stimulation. In a psychophysical study, Breitmeyer (in press) showed that the simple RT to sinusoidal gratings increased by 40–80 msec over spatial frequencies ranging from .5 to 11.0 cycles/degree, even when the gratings were matched for subjective contrast. This suggests that low spatial-frequency, transient channels indeed respond faster by several tens

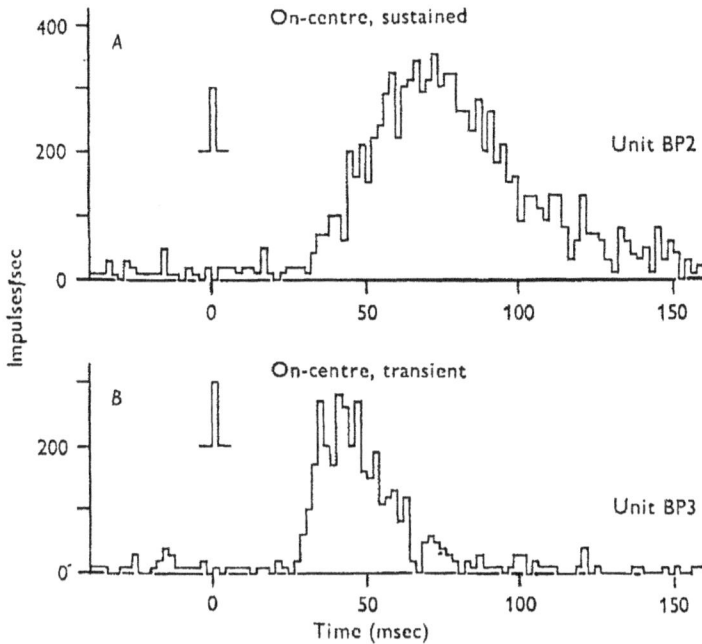

FIGURE 4. Impulse responses obtained from two retinal ganglion cells. (A) Impulse response of on-center sustained cell; (B) impulse response of on-center transient cell. Each graph is the poststimulus time-histogram of the summed responses to 50 presentations of a 2 msec flash. (From "Properties of Sustained and Transient Cells in the Cat Retina" by B. G. Cleland, W. R. Levick, and K. J. Sanderson, *Journal of Physiology*, 1973, *228*, 649–680. Copyright 1973 by the Cambridge University Press. Reprinted by permission.)

of milliseconds than high spatial-frequency, sustained channels.

All of these psychophysical results have their electrophysiological correlate findings revealed in single-cell studies of the mammalian visual system. Enroth-Cugell and Robson (1966) originally showed that a class of cat retinal ganglion cells, which they called Y cells (transient cells), signal only the abrupt onsets and/or offsets of a sinusoidal grating presentation (see Figure 5).

These two cell types differ in several ways when their spatial and temporal response properties are compared. Transient cells show selectivity for large or low spatial-frequency patterns (Cleland, Dubin, & Levick, 1971b; Cleland, Levick, & Sanderson, 1973; Ikeda & Wright, 1974) and are not sensitive to refractive error or image blur (Ikeda & Wright, 1972a). However, they show selectivity for intermittent stimulation, such as high-frequency flicker (Fukuda & Saito,

1971) or rapid motion (Cleland et al., 1971b, 1973; Hoffman, Stone, & Sherman, 1972). Sustained cells, on the other hand, generally show opposite spatiotemporal response selectivities. They respond selectively to small or high spatial-frequency patterns that are presented for prolonged periods or at low temporal rates (Cleland et al., 1971b, 1973; Fukuda & Saito, 1971; Ikeda & Wright, 1974) and to sharply focused images (Ikeda & Wright, 1972a).

Both cell types are found in the retina (Cleland et al., 1973; Ikeda & Wright, 1972b), LGN (Cleland et al., 1971b; Hoffman et al., 1972), and visual cortex (Dow, 1974; Ikeda & Wright, 1974, 1975a, 1975b; Stone & Dreher, 1973). Moreover, it has been shown that sustained retinal ganglion cells project onto sustained LGN neurons, which in turn project onto sustained striate neurons, and similarly for transient cells (Hoffman & Stone, 1971; Hoffman et al.,

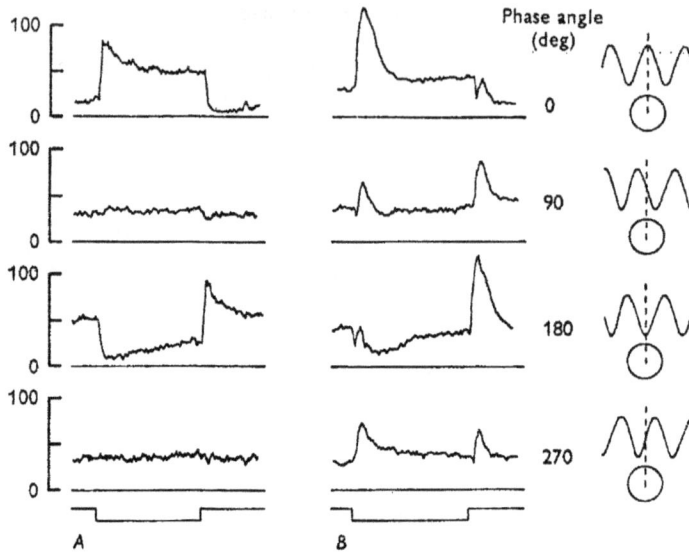

FIGURE 5. Response histograms of two retinal ganglion cells: (A) an off-center sustained cell and (B) an off-center transient cell. Column on the right shows the location of a sinusoidal grating relative to the receptive field centers prior to offset. Duration of each offset was 2 sec. Note that the transient cell (B) gives on and off responses at phase angles of 90°, whereas the sustained cell (A) does not. (From "The Contrast Sensitivity of Retinal Ganglion Cells of the Cat" by C. Enroth-Cugell and J. G. Robson, *Journal of Physiology*, 1966, *187*, 517–552. Copyright 1966 by the Cambridge University Press. Reprinted by permission.)

1972; Stone & Hoffman, 1971). Therefore, the sustained–transient response dichotomy is relayed in parallel channels from the retina, through LGN, to the visual cortex.

These differences are particularly well illustrated in studies conducted by Dow (1974) on cells found in striate cortex of the monkey. One class of cells, namely, simple cells, responded in a sustained manner to preferably stationary stimuli of proper orientation and dimension. Another class of cells, namely, transient cells, reported only the onsets and offsets of the stimulus. These transient cells were sensitive to rapid motion and showed direction and orientation selectivity, although not as precisely as that of simple cells. Moreover, the response latencies of transient cells were on the order of 50 msec, whereas those of sustained simple cells were on the order of 100 msec or more; a latency difference consistent with the psychophysical results reported by Breitmeyer (in press). This latter result is also consistent with other electrophysiological evidence, which shows

that transient (relative to sustained) channels have a shorter response latency to photic and electric stimulation of the optic nerve (Fukuda, 1973; Fukuda, Sugitani, & Iwama, 1973; Ikeda & Wright, 1975a) and a faster impulse propagation velocity (Cleland et al., 1973; Fukuda, 1971; Hoffman, 1973; Hoffman & Stone, 1971).

Other important properties that differentiate sustained cells from transient cells are their respective receptive field sizes and distributions over the retina. Hoffman et al. (1972) report that at a fixed retinal location transient-cell receptive fields are generally larger than receptive fields of sustained cells. They also report that the sizes of both types of receptive fields increase as receptive field location shifts from the fovea to the periphery. Moreover, Fukuda and Stone (1974) found that the number of sustained-cell receptive fields is highest in the fovea and drops off sharply with increases in retinal eccentricity. Transient cells were found only sparsely in the fovea and are more heavily

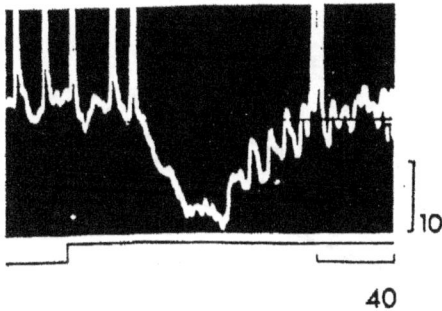

]10

40

FIGURE 6. Demonstration of inhibition of a sustained LGN neuron by transient neurons. Recording is intracellular of a sustained on-center neuron. The five spikes on the left are due to spontaneous activity. Thirty-five msec after onset of the light stimulus, a hyperpolarizing (i.e., inhibitory) potential starts and terminates about 100 msec later. Excitatory potentials begin 80 msec after light onset. Light-evoked spike activity begins only 110 msec after light onset. Thus inhibition precedes excitations by 40–50 msec. Horizontal calibration line equals 40 msec. Vertical calibration line equals 10 mV. (From "Inhibitory Interaction Between X and Y Units in the Cat Lateral Geniculate Nucleus" by W. Singer and N. Bedworth, *Brain Research*, 1973, *49*, 291–307. Copyright 1973 by the ASP Biological and Medical Press. Reprinted by permission.)

concentrated in parafoveal and peripheral regions of the retina. Thus the ratio of transient to sustained cells increases as one moves from the fovea to the periphery of the retina (Hoffman et al., 1972).

It is of prime significance to theories of visual backward pattern masking that *transient cells inhibit the activity of sustained cells* (see Figure 6). This has been demonstrated conclusively at LGN (Singer & Bedworth, 1973) and seems likely also at visual cortex (Stone & Dreher, 1973).[2]

THREE MECHANISMS FOR VISUAL PATTERN MASKING

Intrachannel Inhibition: A Mechanism for Paracontrast

What we call intrachannel inhibition is realized in the antagonistic center-surround organization of sustained-type visual receptive fields (see Figures 3a and 3b). The effect of the surround on the center response is in the form of lateral inhibition. One

aspect of the antagonistic center–surround interaction is that the response of the excitatory center is faster than the response of the antagonistic surround. For instance, Maffei, Cervetto, and Fiorentini (1970) found that the response of the antagonistic surround of cat retinal ganglion cells lags by about 20 msec over the response of the center. This is part of a more general property, namely, the poorer temporal resolution of the antagonistic surround relative to the center. At the LGN, Poggio, Baker, Lamarre, and Sanseverino (1969) found that in a majority of LGN cells the surround inhibition attains its maximal effectiveness when the center excitatory stimulus is delivered 10–30 msec after the onset of the surround inhibitory stimulus (see Figure 7). This is consistent with Singer and Creutzfeldt's (1970) findings, showing that the center response latencies of LGN cells were about 20–30 msec shorter than the antagonistic-surround response latencies. Psychophysical evidence independent of paracontrast studies is consistent with these findings. Fiorentini and Maffei (1970) found that when the luminance of a disk and annulus are modulated sinusoidally in time at frequencies of 1 to 6 cycles/sec, the masking properties of the annulus are optimal at phase lags of 45°. This corresponds to an optimal forward masking effect—annulus preceding the center disk—reaching its maximum at center-surround asynchronies of 20 to 120 msec. This suggests a mechanism for obtaining paracontrast monoptically (Weisstein, 1972).

Paracontrast is also obtained dichoptically (Kolers & Rosner, 1960). If it is assumed that this asynchrony in response latencies to center and surround stimulation also characterizes the largely binocularly activated striate cortex cells (Hubel & Wiesel, 1962, 1968), dichoptic paracontrast effects are readily explainable.

---

[2] While the neurophysiology of the transient–sustained cell dichotomy has been worked out in considerable detail in the cat, for primates (including man) the electrophysiological evidence is sparse (Dow, 1974; Kulikowski, 1974). However, in man the psychophysical evidence points to the existence of a similar dichotomy.

14   BRUNO G. BREITMEYER AND LEO GANZ

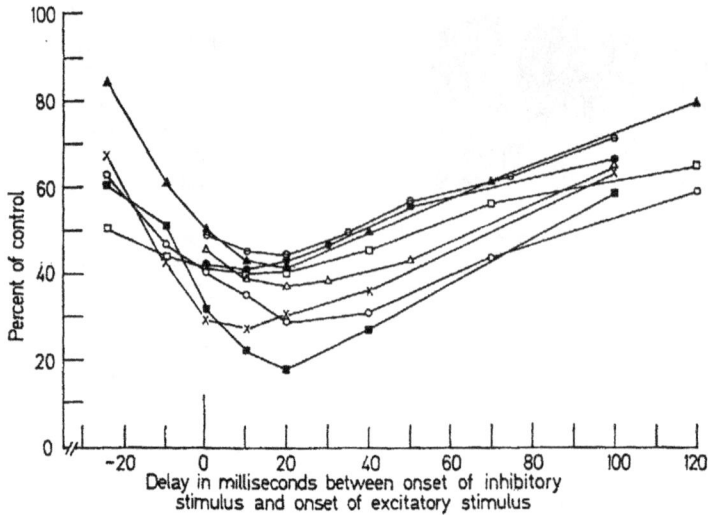

FIGURE 7. Response of 8 on-center LGN neurons to a disk-annulus display sequence, where the disk falls on the receptive field center and the annulus falls on the antagonistic surround. Ordinate values below 100% indicate an inhibitory effect. Note that paracontrast inhibition can extend to 120 msec. Positive delay values indicate that the onset of the annulus precedes the onset of the disk; negative delay values indicate a reversed onset sequence. Just the opposite terminology is used in the present paper to conform to the psychophysical literature. (From "Afferent Inhibition at Input to Visual Cortex of the Cat" by G. B. Poggio, F. H. Baker, Y. Lamarre, and E. R. Sanseverino, *Journal of Neurophysiology*, 1969, *32*, 916–929. Copyright 1969 by the American Physiological Society. Reprinted by permission.)

The model described here specifies paracontrast as resulting from the asynchrony in the operation of center and surround of sustained-type neurons in the visual system. We exclude transient-type neurons from involvement in paracontrast on the basis of the following argument. Fiorentini and Maffei (1970) found, as noted, that the forward masking effect of the annulus on a disk-shaped target was optimal at 45° positive phase lag (annulus leads disk), as shown in Figure 8. But this was only true for temporal frequencies up to 6 cycles/sec and below. At faster alternations, 8 cycles/sec and above, optimal masking was obtained at a negative phase angle (disk leads annulus). For instance, at 8 cycles/sec, optimal masking was obtained at a negative phase angle of 90°. This corresponds to the annulus reaching its peak intensity 30 msec *after* the disk, that is, metacontrast prevails. At low temporal frequencies—for example, less than 6 cycles/sec—where the target and mask *both* activate predominantly sustained-response channels

(Ikeda & Wright, 1975b; Keesey, 1972; Kulikowsky & Tolhurst, 1973) paracontrast effects are obtained. At intermediate to high temporal frequencies—approximately 7 cycles/sec or above—where the target and mask activate *both* transient and sustained channels (Ikeda & Wright, 1975b; Kulikowsky & Tolhurst, 1973), with transient channels probably predominating, metacontrast effects are obtained.

Our explanation of paracontrast differs from that offered by Weisstein et al. (1975) in the following way. They attribute paracontrast to the inhibition of transient channels by sustained channels. However, since transient channels are not activated at low temporal frequencies and since Fiorentini and Maffei (1970) report strong paracontrast effects when *both* disk and annulus are modulated at *low* temporal frequencies, it is apparent that paracontrast effects can be obtained without involvement of transient channels. In our explanation, paracontrast effects arise from the center–surround antagonism within sustained channels.

Interchannel Inhibition: Backward Type B Masking Mechanism

Some of the essential aspects of the operation of the backward Type B masking mechanism, as illustrated in Figure 9, involve differences in response latency and persistence among the various transient and sustained channels in the visual system. After a brief stimulus presentation, transient channels are first to respond with a brief burst of activity. This response is followed at variable intervals by sustained-channel responses. The response latency, persistence, and amplitude of sustained channels depends on their spatial-frequency specificity. It is assumed that progressively higher spatial-frequency channels have a longer response latency, a lower response amplitude (Cornsweet, 1970; Davidson, 1968), and a longer response persistence. These spatial-frequency dependent response properties of sustained units are assumed to hold also at subcortical levels of visual processing, except that response latencies are shorter overall at subcortical levels than at cortical levels.

The mechanism of interchannel inhibition consists of transient cells inhibiting the activity of sustained cells. Sustained neurons show a high degree of spatial (orientation and frequency or size) specificity (Dow, 1974; Maffei & Fiorentini, 1973). Cortical transient units also show orientation- and direction-specific responses (Dow, 1974; Ikeda & Wright, 1975b); however, their orientation specificity is sometimes not as precise as that of sustained units (Dow, 1974). This specificity, though limited, nonetheless is an important feature in explaining Type B backward masking effects.

Two basic assumptions characterize the process of interchannel inhibition:

1. It is assumed that interchannel inhibition is strongest when the preferred orientations of transient and sustained channels activated by target and mask, respectively, are the same and decreases with increasingly divergent orientation preferences. Such orientation-specific inhibition at the visual cortex is shown in Figure 10 (Blakemore & Tobin, 1972).

2. The interchannel inhibition is most effective when the inhibitory activity generated by transient channels is temporally superimposed on the excitatory activity generated

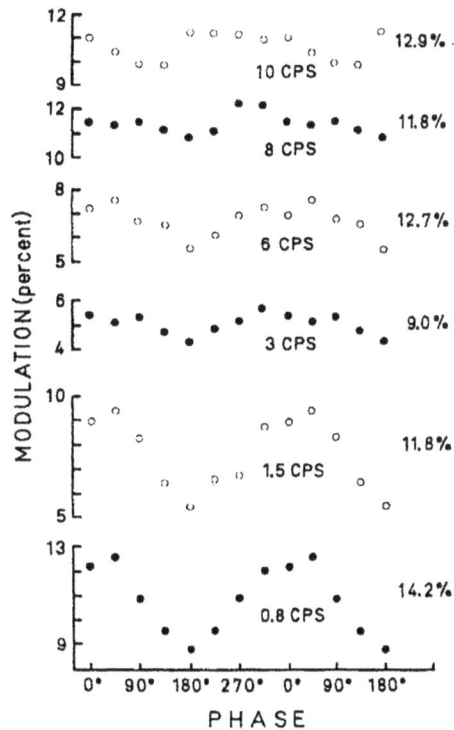

FIGURE 8. Psychophysical temporal modulation threshold to a small light spot as a function of the temporal phase angle of a surrounding annulus. Both spot and annulus intensities are modulated sinusoidally in time at temporal frequencies (CPS = cycles per second) as indicated. The ordinate gives the percent modulation at threshold. Horizontal axis depicts the phase differences between the spot and annulus modulations. For example, at a phase angle of 0°, both spot and annulus are modulated in phase; at +90°, the annulus reaches its peak intensity before the spot; at −90° degrees (or 270°), the annulus reaches its peak intensity after the spot. The fixed amplitudes of modulation of the annulus at each temporal frequency are given in the right column. (From "Transfer Characteristics of Excitation and Inhibition in the Human Visual System" by A. Fiorentini and L. Maffei, *Journal of Neurophysiology*, 1970, *33*, 285–292. Copyright 1970 by the American Physiological Society. Reprinted by permission.)

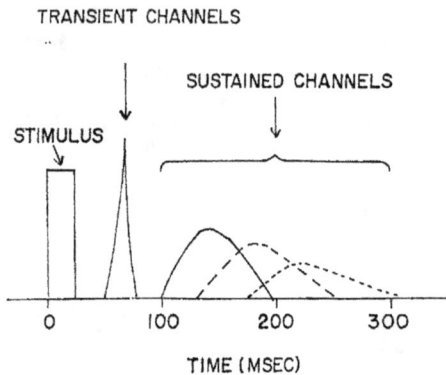

FIGURE 9. The hypothesized time course of activation of transient and sustained channels after a brief presentation of a stimulus. Among the sustained channels, the solid line indicates activity of intermediate spatial-frequency channels; the dashed line, high spatial-frequency channels; the dotted line, very high spatial-frequency channels.

by sustained channels (as shown in Figure 11c and 11d). Since cortical transient activity precedes sustained activity by 50–100 msec or more (Dow, 1974), optimal interchannel inhibition should be obtained when the mask pattern onset is delayed by 50–100 msec relative to the onset of the target pattern. It is easy to see how this would give rise to a Type B backward pattern masking effect.

Assumption 1 finds support from the functional architecture of the striate cortex, which consists of a columnar organization of cells that are functionally related in terms of, say, their orientation selectivity and the region of retinal space they represent (Brooks & Jung, 1973; Hubel & Wiesel, 1962, 1968, 1974).

Transient as well as sustained cells are found in the same cortical columns in monkey cortex; transient cells are predominantly in the lower layers; sustained cells are in lower, middle, and upper layers (Dow, 1974). Moreover, neural inhibition among different columns also exists (Benevento et al., 1972; Hess, Negishi, & Creutzfeldt, 1975). Under such conditions, the inhibition of sustained cells by transient cells in the same column or in neighboring columns that show similar orientation specificity would result in the high degree of spatial and structural specificity found in Type B metacontrast effects (Ut-

tal, 1970, 1971; Weisstein, 1972; Werner, 1935) *and* masking by structure (Michaels & Turvey, 1973; Turvey, 1973). The fact that target and mask overlap spatially in masking by structure, whereas they do not in metacontrast, is not critical, Scheerer (1973) and Turvey (1973) notwithstanding; what is relevant is the structural similarity

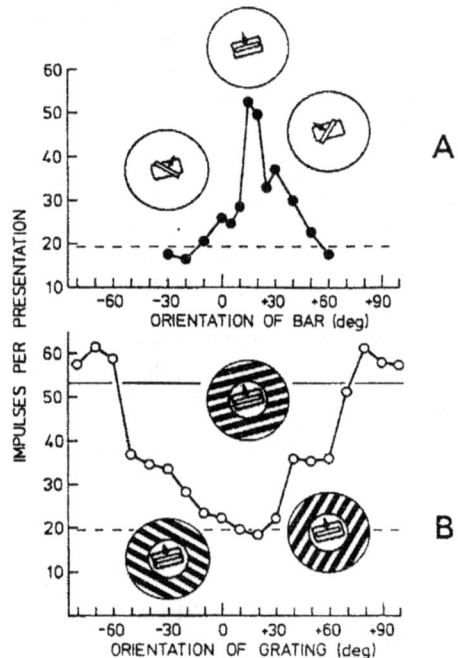

FIGURE 10. Demonstration of orientation-specific inhibition of an orientation-selective cell in cat visual cortex. (A) The cell's response to varying orientations moving through its receptive field. Optimal orientation is +20°. (B) In the center of the receptive field the bar is maintained at an optimal orientation but in motion. A grating of variable orientation was present in the surround. The solid horizontal line shows the level of response (about 53 impulses/presentation) that the cell produced in the absence of a grating. Points below this line indicate an inhibitory effect of the grating. The graph shows that inhibition of the bar response with the grating is orientation-specific. Note that maximal inhibition is obtained when the grating orientation is at the neurons' preferred bar orientation, that is, about +20°. (From "Lateral Inhibition Between Orientation Detectors in the Cat's Visual Cortex" by C. Blakemore and E. A. Tobin, *Experimental Brain Research*, 1972, *15*, 439–440. Copyright 1972 by J. F. Bergmann Verlag. Reprinted by permission.)

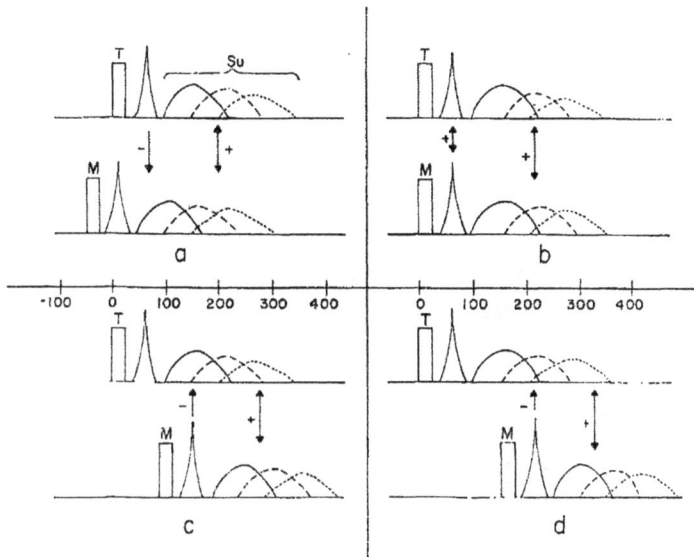

FIGURE 11. This figure illustrates how the time course of the transient and sustained channels activated by a target and mask interact at various target–mask asynchronies. The figure shows in a schematic way the interaction of mask (M) and target (T) neural activity when (a) mask precedes the target, (b) mask is presented concurrently with the target, (c) mask follows target at a short onset asynchrony, and (d) mask follows target at a long onset asynchrony. (Transient channels are indicated by short-latency spike-like responses. Su = sustained channels. Arrows indicate the direction of target–mask interaction. A minus sign indicates that the interaction is inhibitory, a plus sign indicates that the interaction is one of sensory integration.)

(e.g., contour orientation) between target and mask in both situations.

Figure 11 shows a very simple model of the possible interactions between transient and sustained channels under forward, simultaneous, and backward masking. The simple version of the model involves direct inhibition of the sustained channels by the transient channels. When the mask onset precedes the target onset (Figure 11a), the transient activity generated by the mask obviously precedes the sustained activity generated by the target, and no interchannel inhibition of mask on target is predicted by the model. The same argument holds when target and mask onsets are synchronized (Figure 11b).

When the mask onset follows the target onest by 70 msec (Figure 11c), Type B masking effects can occur. Most relevant to the present discussion is the fact that the cortical transient channels activated by the mask inhibit the activity of intermediate to high spatial-frequency channels activated by

the target and thus eliminate that range of spatial frequencies from the ISc synthetic process.

At still longer SOA values (Figure 11d) the transient channels activated by the mask would optimally inhibit the activity of high to very high spatial-frequency channels. While the consequent failure to transfer this spatial-frequency information into the iconic process may not appreciably affect the identifiability of a target, it would nonetheless be expected to reduce the clarity or spatial contrast of the target as well as make discrimination of its contour detail more difficult.

The above arguments imply the existence of a family of Type B backward masking curves, as shown in Figure 12a. Strongest Type B masking effects are obtained at progressively longer SOAs as cortical sustained channels selective to progressively higher spatial frequencies are utilized. Thus, the Type B backward masking effect one obtains is a function of the spatial-frequency composi-

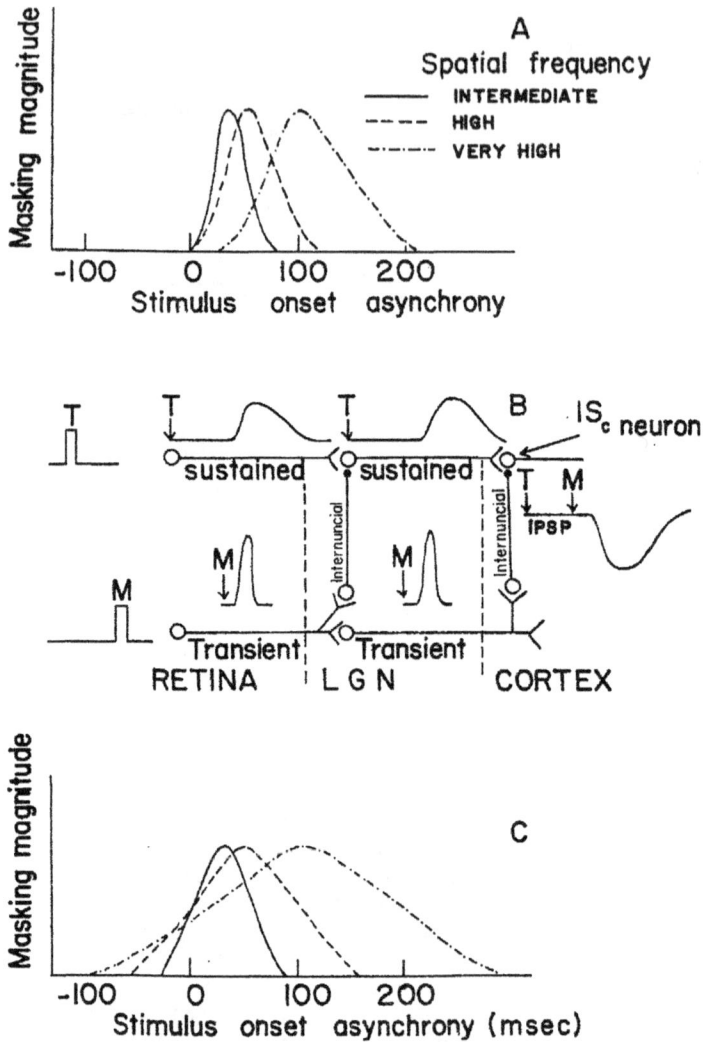

FIGURE 12. (A) Predictions of metacontrast effects obtained as a function of spatial frequency under the simple assumption that transient channels directly inhibit sustained channels. Note the absence of masking at negative SOA values. (B) Hypothetical time course of responses of a sustained and transient neural network activated by a target (T) and mask (M), respectively. In the sustained neurons, note the longer latency and longer persistence of the excitatory impulse responses. In transient neurons the impulse response is of shorter latency and duration. It is postulated that transient neurons inhibit sustained ones via internuncial neurons at the LGN and cortex. In this illustration the impulse response of the internuncial neurons is inhibitory (inhibitory postsynaptic potential or IPSP) as shown by a downward deflection, and integrates with the excitatory impulse response of sustained neurons at the ISc level. Excitatory axonal terminations are indicated by Y-shaped terminals, and inhibitory axonal terminations are indicated by filled circles. Although not shown, the network is symmetric in that the target and mask also activate transient and sustained neural networks, respectively. (C) Changes in predicted metacontrast effects as a function of spatial frequency when internuncials as shown in (B) are assumed to mediate the inhibition of sustained cells by transient cells. Note that metacontrast functions at each spatial frequency are broader and also are obtained at negative SOAs.

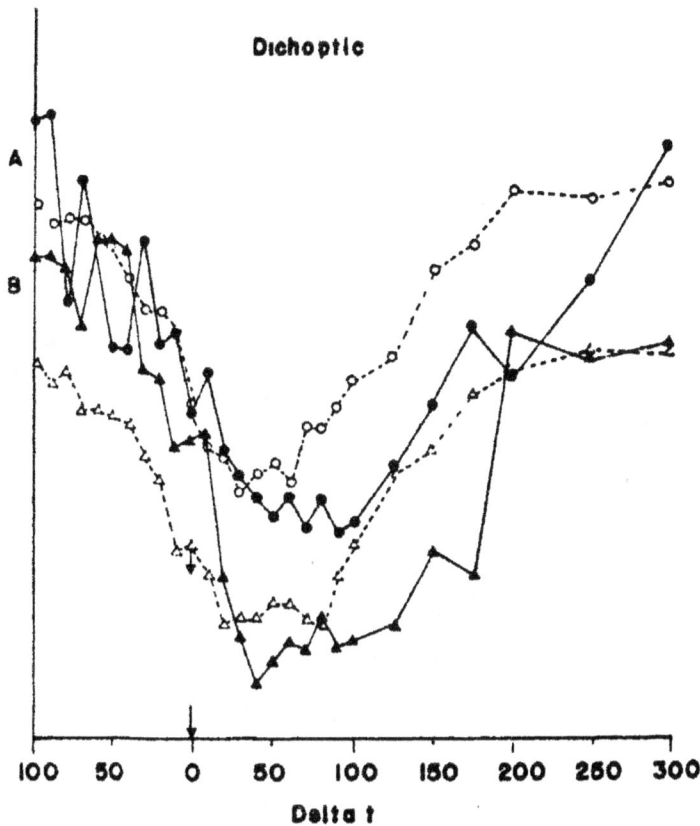

FIGURE 13. Empirical dichoptic metacontrast functions obtained when a disk masks another disk (solid lines) or when an annulus masks a disk (dashed lines). Ordinate depicts direct magnitude estimations of the completeness of the target disk. Horizontal axis depicts stimulus onset asynchrony (SOA). Note that whereas optimal metacontrast is obtained at positive SOAs of 50–100 msec, metacontrast effects manifest themselves even when the mask onset precedes the target onset by 100 msec. (From "W-shaped and U-Shaped Functions Obtained for Monoptic and Dichoptic Disk-Disk Masking" by N. Weisstein, *Perception and Psychophysics,* 1971, *9,* 275–278. Copyright 1971 by the Psychonomic Society. Reprinted by permission.)

tion of the target and the nature of the perceptual task, which determines what and how much of the spatial-frequency information is relevant.

This simple model, however, is probably incorrect for the following reasons. The burst of activity within the transient channels is brief. Therefore, the inhibition of the sustained channels should be correspondingly brief. Since the sustained channels respond in a prolonged manner, a brief inhibition should not exert much masking. Moreover, as stated, the model predicts no interchannel

forward inhibition, that is, when the mask precedes the test target. Figure 13 shows that masking effects can be strong and that forward inhibition is present with the mask preceding the target by as much as 100 msec. This suggests that the transient channels generate tonic inhibition (see Figure 6).

Neurophysiologically, it is very likely that afferents to LGN (Singer & Bedworth, 1973) and to striate cortex (Toyama, Matsunami, Ohno, & Tokashiki, 1974; Wanatabe, Konishi, & Creutzfeldt, 1966) are always excitatory and at least at the cortex always exert their inhibition via an internuncial neuron. Furthermore, intracellular recording at LGN (Singer & Bedworth, 1973) and at striate cortex (Creutzfeldt, Kuhnt, & Benevento, 1974) indicates the inhibition is prolonged. Thus, our model is modified as shown in Figure 12 to include an internuncial, which generates sustained inhibition. Formally, this changes the model so as to spread in time the effects of interchannel inhibition. Figure 12b shows how these prolonged interchannel inhibition effects may occur. Figure 12c shows the masking functions, which the model incorporating an inhibitory interneuron predicts, and which accord more closely (see Figure 13) with obtained results (Weisstein, 1971).

Intrachannel Integration: Backward and Forward Type A Masking Mechanism

Due to the response persistence of sustained channels, integration of target and mask information can occur over time (see Figure 11a–d, + symbols) at both the ISp and ISc levels. The iconic integration of spatial frequency information is assumed to occur over a period of time—on the order of 200 msec—with progressively higher spatial-frequency information being transferred into the iconic process at progressively later times.

Sensory integration in the context of visual pattern masking can occur at ISp and ISc levels of processing. ISp levels include the retina and LGN; ISc levels involve striate and poststriate stages of visual processing. To the extent that masking by integration occurs at ISp as well as ISc, one should obtain stronger forward and backward masking by noise or structure when the target and mask are presented monoptically than when they are presented dichoptically, since monoptic masking involves more stages of interaction—a result obtained by Smith and Schiller (1966).

Two response properties of sustained spatial-frequency analyzers are crucial in determining masking by integration:

1. The spatial-frequency specificity of masking (Stromeyer & Julesz, 1972). Stromeyer and Julesz have shown that under relatively prolonged (i.e., sustained) stimulus presentations of a target grating of fixed spatial frequency against a background consisting of a band-limited noise mask, masking is most effective if the target frequency is centered on the band of frequencies composing the noise mask. Moreover, the effectiveness of the noise mask increases as its band width increases to about two octaves, but not beyond. That is, masking was specific to spatial-frequency components within that band.

2. Response persistence increases as spatial-frequency selectivity increases (see Figure 9; also Breitmeyer & Ganz, in press). The increase in response persistence with increases in spatial-frequency specificity of sustained channels in turn determines the temporal limits of masking by integration in both forward and backward masking.

The *peripheral* (ISp) masking by integration can be thought of as being produced by the target and mask *competing* for common peripheral spatial-frequency analyzing channels, the degree of masking being determined by the spatial-frequency composition of the target and mask and the temporal delay between them. The conception of *central* (ISc) masking by *composite integration* is different in that masking is not due to adding noise to a spatial-frequency analytic channel, but rather due to adding noise to a spatial-frequency synthetic process, that is, the contour-forming process. It was mentioned previously that the perceptual synthesis of spatial-frequency components can occur dichoptically (Maffei & Fiorentini, 1972a) and that this synthesis most likely occurs beyond the monocular stage of Area 17 of the cortex (Blake & Fox, 1974; Hebb, 1949), that is, at the ISc level. If this is true, then ISc masking by composite integration can be thought of more specifically as the finite duration process in which spatial-frequency components of the target and the mask are synthesized to form a composite iconic representation of target and mask patterns. The degree to which the target and mask share this synthetic process again is inversely related to the temporal interval or SOA separating them (see Figure 11a–d) and also depends on the sharing of spatial-frequency components by the target and mask. For instance, the iconic synthesis of intermediate to high spatial-frequency information from both

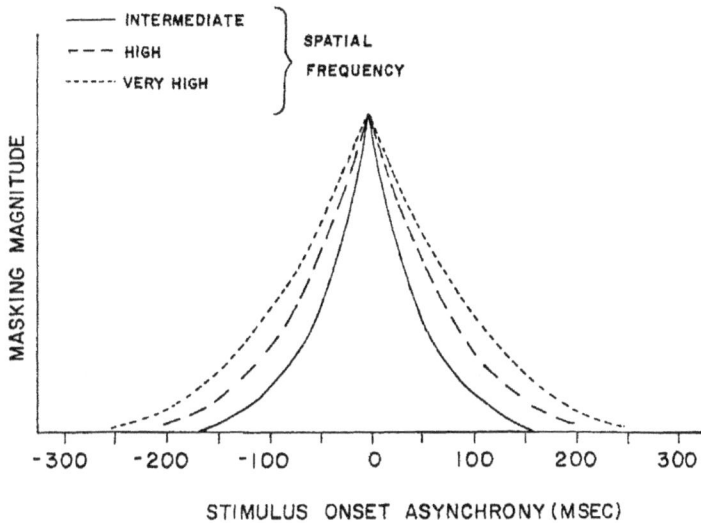

FIGURE 14. Hypothesized Type A masking effects obtained as a function of the spatial frequency content of the target as indicated and the onset asynchrony between target and mask stimuli.

target and mask should have a greater masking effect on the identifiability of a pattern than the iconic synthesis of intermediate to high spatial-frequency information from the target and, say, high spatial-frequency information from the mask.[3]

For integration masking at both ISc and ISp levels, given that a target and mask have similar spatial-frequency compositions, the above considerations suggest that the overall Type A forward and backward masking effects, as would be obtained in masking situations diagramed in Figure 11a–d, are a combination of a family of spatial-frequency-specific and temporal-range-specific Type A forward and backward masking effects, as shown in Figure 14. Figure 14 shows three Type A forward and backward masking curves, corresponding to the masking of intermediate, high, and very high spatial-frequency components. For all components the masking effect is strongest at target–mask synchrony (see Figure 11b), when maximal response integration of spatial frequency components shared by the target and mask occurs. The effect is an increase in the noise and hence a reduction in the signal-to-noise ratio at ISp and ISc levels. As the temporal

interval between target and mask increases, the degree of competition at ISp, composite integration at ISc, and hence masking should all decrease, but over a temporal range dependent on the target's spatial-frequency components. For progressively higher components the temporal range is progressively longer, as shown in Figure 14. This implies that the temporal range over which Type A forward and backward masking mechanisms are effective is a function of the nature of the perceptual task. For pattern identification, when only intermediate to high spatial-frequency information is required, the temporal range should be shorter than for tasks involving detailed contour discrimination or resolution, which requires still higher spatial-frequency information.

The above considerations, as indicated in Figure 14, suggest that Type A forward and backward masking by integration—whether at ISp, ISc, or both levels—are symmetrical,

[3] The ineffectiveness of two-dimensional, high-spatial-frequency noise in masking the recognition of faces composed of low to intermediate spatial frequencies has been elegantly demonstrated by Harmon and Julesz (1973).

22   BRUNO G. BREITMEYER AND LEO GANZ

TABLE 1

Masking Mechanisms Operative Under Forward and Backward Conditions
and Monoptic and Dichoptic Viewing

Viewing condition	Masking condition	
	Forward	Backward
Monoptic	1. Paracontrast (weak with equal energy stimuli)	1. Integration at ISp (weak due to absence of "on-effect")
	2. Integration at ISp (accentuated by strong peripheral "on-effect")	2. Inhibition of "target" contour by "mask" transient
	3. Integration at ISc (attenuated by inhibition of "mask" contour by "target" transient)	3. Integration at ISc
Dichoptic	1. Paracontrast (weak with equal energy stimuli)	1. Inhibition of "target" contour by "mask" transient
	2. Integration at ISc (attenuated by inhibition of "mask" contour by "target" transient)	2. Integration at ISc

that is, for the same absolute SOA values, forward and backward masking magnitudes are the same. That this is not so has been shown by Smith and Schiller (1966). Under monoptic viewing conditions, forward pattern masking extends over a much longer temporal range than does backward masking. However, under dichoptic viewing conditions, the reverse asymmetry holds. These asymmetries are discussed in the next section.

EXPLANATORY SCOPE OF INTEGRATION AND INHIBITION MECHANISMS

The exposition of the model of visual mechanisms mediating pattern masking is now relatively complete. It has already been used to explain some of the available results on pattern masking. Its explanatory scope can be further expanded and tested against existing findings mentioned previously. Below are enumerated major observed masking effects and the properties of the model and the visual system that are relevant to their explanation.

1. Type A and B masking effects are obtained dichoptically as well as monoptically (Kinsbourne & Warrington, 1962; Kolers & Rosner, 1960; Michaels & Turvey, 1973; Turvey, 1973; Weisstein, 1972; Werner, 1940). This is readily explainable in terms of the predominantly binocular innervation of visual cells in striate cortex (Hubel & Wiesel, 1962, 1968). For instance, Table 1 shows the masking mechanisms that are active in both forward and backward directions

and in both monoptic and dichoptic conditions.

2. Forward monoptic pattern masking is more powerful and extends over a larger range of SOAs than backward masking (Kinsbourne & Warrington, 1962; Smith & Schiller, 1966; Turvey, 1973). This is probably attributable to powerful peripheral on-effects produced by the mask (Boynton & Siegfried, 1962; Crawford, 1947; Sperling, 1965). Note in Figure 15 that the loss in sensitivity is greater and more prolonged following an extremely brief masking flash than preceding it. We know these on-effects are peripheral because they are not obtained dichoptically (Battersby, Oesterreich, & Sturr, 1964).

However, in dichoptic pattern masking, backward is more pronounced than forward (Greenspoon & Erickson, 1968; Smith & Schiller, 1966; see Kinsbourne & Warrington, 1962, for discrepant results, however). For dichoptic presentations, the mask's peripherally generated on-effects do not interact with the target (Battersby et al., 1964). Consequently, the only effective mechanisms are composite integration at ISc and interchannel inhibition. As Table 1 shows, in dichoptic forward masking, interchannel inhibition is weaker (because of latency difference between sustained and transient channels; see Figure 11a). For the very same reasons, the transient activity generated by the target can locally inhibit the sustained activity generated by the mask (see Figure

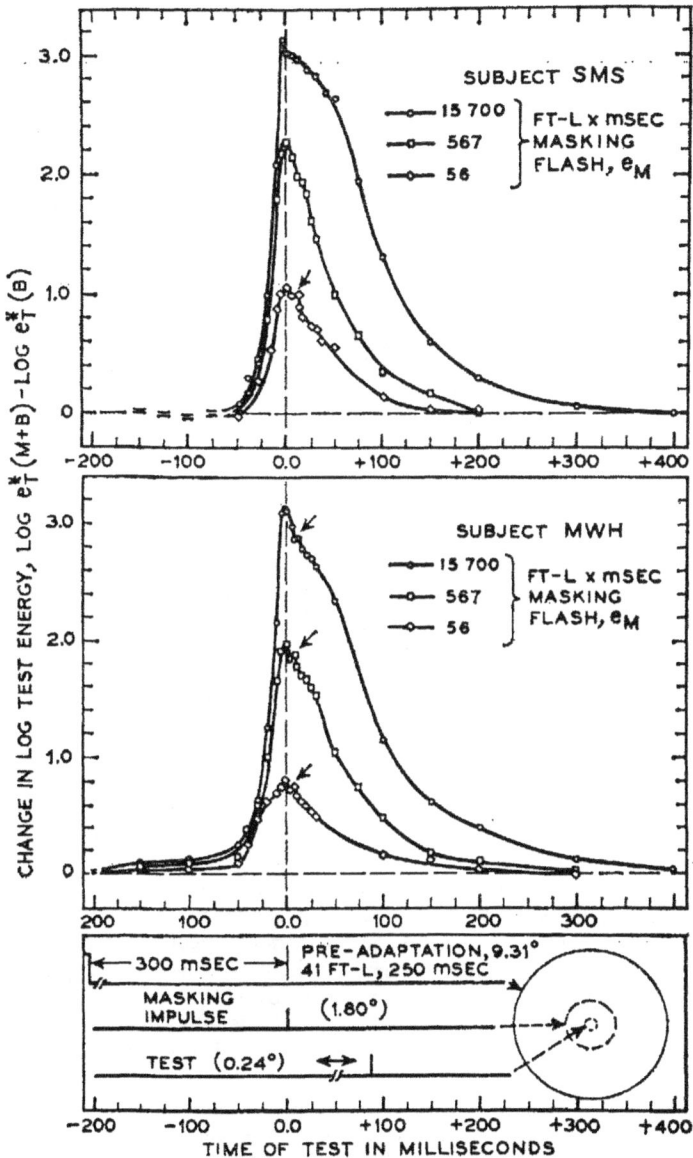

FIGURE 15. Illustration of a briefly presented test spot masked by a larger concentric homogeneous disk of light. The two are presented on a still larger pre-adaptation field. The ordinate represents the change in log test energy; the abscissa depicts the asynchrony between mask and test. Negative values indicate that the test precedes the mask; positive value indicates the reverse sequence. The three families of curves represent masking effects obtained at three different energies of the masking disk. Note that at all mask energies the forward masking is more persistent than is backward masking. (From "Temporal and Spatial Visual Masking: I. Masking by Impulse Flashes" by G. Sperling, *Journal of the Optical Society of America*, 1965, *55*, 541–559. Copyright 1965 by the American Institute of Physics. Reprinted by permission.)

at ISc. Consequently, in dichoptic viewing, 11a) and thus reduce masking by integration forward pattern masking should be generally weaker than backward masking, given that the target and mask are of approximately equal energy.

3. Metacontrast Type B effects decrease as the spatial separation between the target and mask increases (Alpern, 1953; Weisstein & Growney, 1969). Presumably interchannel inhibition is strongest within a cortical column and decreases as the physical separation of columns in cortical space increases. Since each column subserves a fixed region of retinal space, and since the striate cortex is retinotopically organized (Brooks & Jung, 1973), separation of pattern in retinal space would result in a decrease of interaction (excitatory as well as inhibitory) among correspondingly separated points in cortical space.

4. In the fovea, metacontrast is weak (Alpern, 1953; Kolers & Rosner, 1960) and the slightest target–mask spatial separation eliminates the already weak effect (Kolers & Rosner, 1960). At progressively greater retinal (parafoveal) eccentricities, the metacontrast effect becomes progressively more robust (Kolers & Rosner, 1960; Stewart & Purcell, 1970) and can be obtained with target–mask contour separations exceeding 1° visual angle (Alpern, 1953; Weisstein & Growney, 1969).

The weakness of the effect in the fovea and its increase with retinal eccentricity is consistent with and explained by (a) the very high concentration of sustained channels in the fovea relative to a very low concentration of foveal transient channels and (b) the precipitous decrease in the number of sustained channels with retinal eccentricity accompanied by an increase in transient channels, giving rise to an increase in the transient cell-to-sustained-cell ratio (Fukuda & Stone, 1974; Hoffman et al., 1972). This trend for transient neurons to increase and sustained to decrease with retinal eccentricity is maintained at the striate cortex (Ikeda & Wright, 1975a). Moreover, the fact that transient-cell (as well as sustained-cell) receptive fields increase in size with retinal eccentricity (Hoffman et al., 1972) may provide a means of extending their inhibitory

target and mask are presented in the parainfluence over larger retinal regions when the fovea rather than in the fovea.[4]

5. Type B contour masking effects are obtained during stroboscopic motion (Breitmeyer et al., in press, 1974). Specifically, the first of two stroboscopic stimuli is masked in accordance with a U-shaped function. Since low-spatial-frequency transient channels are most likely involved in the detection of rapid motion (Breitmeyer, 1973; Cleland et al., 1973; Dow, 1974; Pantle, 1970; Tolhurst, 1973), and since transient neurons inhibit sustained neurons, a Type B suppression of high-spatial-frequency contour information carried in sustained channels would be expected during stroboscopic motion, just as in metacontrast.

6. Simple RT to the target (Fehrer & Biederman, 1962; Fehrer & Raab, 1962) and forced-choice detection of the target location (Schiller & Smith, 1966) in a metacontrast situation does not produce a Type B masking effect. Under conditions producing optimal contour recognition masking, simple RT and forced-choice detection of target location are unaffected. Our model states that transient activity generated by the target is immune from the subsequent inhibitory effects of the transient activity generated by the surrounding mask (see Figure 11b–d). The transient activity generated by the onset of the target could be detected by transient channels in the cortex or by transient channels in the superior colliculus, activated via direct retinocollicular projections (Hoffman, 1973) or indirectly via projections from transient cells in the ipsilateral striate cortex (Dow, 1974; Palmer & Rosenquist, 1974).

7. Kolers (1963) reports that when the shape or contour of the first of two spatially separated disk stimuli is masked by a metacontrast ring, it nevertheless contributes to the perception of stroboscopic motion obtained when the second disk follows the first at optimal SOAs. In paragraph 6, just above, we

---

[4] It has been noted by Matin (1974) that transient cells, having large receptive fields, are particularly good candidates for exerting lateral masking evident in saccadic suppression.

noted that transient activity generated by the first disk would be immune from the masking effects of the following ring. Furthermore, since transient-type neurons are most likely involved in producing the perception of stroboscopic motion (Ganz & Felder, in press), Kolers' results are readily explained.

8. In backward masking by structure (see Figure 1c) Type A effects prevail at high mask-to-target energy ratios and Type B effects prevail at low mask-to-target ratios (Michaels & Turvey, 1973; Purcell & Stewart, 1970; Spencer & Shuntich, 1970; Turvey, 1973; Weisstein, 1971). Ikeda reports (Note 5) that the contrast range over which transient neurons at the retina respond dynamically (i.e., give an increase in response to an increase in stimulation) is smaller than the corresponding contrast range of sustained neurons. In other words, as intensity of stimulation is increased, the transient neurons saturate sooner than the sustained neurons. Psychophysical evidence supporting this physiological finding, derives from observations on the motion aftereffect, in which it is reported that the strength of the motion aftereffect reaches an asymptote for low values of the contrast of the motion-aftereffect-inducing pattern (Keck, Pallela, & Pantle, in press; Sekuler, Pantle, & Levinson, in press). These observations imply that as the energy of the mask increases relative to the target, one expects an increase in the output of sustained channels activated by the mask and little if any increase in the output of transient channels activated by the mask. Thus there is a shift in the *relative* activity of the two types of channels. Since the sustained channels are involved in Type A backward masking and transient in Type B, we predict a shift from Type B to Type A *effects* as the mask energy is increased relative to that of the target. Conversely, low mask energies predispose to Type B effects.

9. Our model predicts that an increase in the activity of sustained channels relative to transient channels as stimulus energy increases should produce a change in the metacontrast effects. Our model attributes backward U-shaped functions to transient versus sustained latency differences. With progres-

sively higher mask energies, larger intrachannel inhibition, namely sustained channels inhibiting sustained channels, should prevail. Hence, the model predicts a shift of the peak metacontrast effect toward lower SOAs as the mask–target energy ratio increases, with Type A masking effects eventually prevailing (Weisstein, 1971, 1972).

10. Both retinal on-center and off-center neurons are found distributed similarly in transient and sustained neurons (Enroth-Cugell & Robson, 1966). However, Figure 5 shows that the placement of a stimulus on the sustained cell's receptive field is quite critical. In contrast, many different placements on the transient cell's receptive field will evoke *both* on and off responses. The sustained–transient model of masking specifies inhibition of sustained channels by transient channels as the basis of U-shaped metacontrast effects. Since transient channels characteristically respond to stimulus onset as well as offset, the spatial contrast of the mask relative to that of the target is predicted to be noncritical. Sherrick, Keating, and Dember (1974) show (see their Experiment 2) that a black target is masked almost equally by a white ring as by a black ring. Moreover, Turvey, Michaels, and Kewley-Port (1974) report that the *offset* of a pattern-mask field can produce U-shaped backward masking.

Such findings are particularly difficult to explain by integration theories (Coltheart & Arthur, 1972; Eriksen & Collins, 1964; Kinsbourne & Warrington, 1962). For instance, the detectability of a black disk surrounded by a following white ring should be enhanced according to the luminance-summation hypothesis (Eriksen, 1966). In contrast, the detectability of a black disk surrounded by a following black ring should decrease. What is found, in fact, is that both annuli mask equally strongly. These findings and those of Turvey, Michaels, and Kewley-Port are readily explained by the sustained–transient theory of metacontrast.

11. A further prediction of the sustained–transient theory of metacontrast concerns the spatial-frequency characteristics of target and mask. To obtain a U-shaped backward masking function, the theory specifies that the

mask must activate transient channels and the target must activate sustained channels. Transient channels, relative to sustained channels, are insensitive to high spatial frequencies. If a stimulus were blurred, it is predominantly the high spatial frequencies that would be deleted. Hence, transient channels should be activated without much attenuation when a stimulus is blurred. Ikeda and Wright (1972a) have shown in fact that transient cells at the retina are not sensitive to image blurring; such blurring substantially reduces the response of sustained retinal cells. Therefore, the prediction follows that blurring of the mask should not substantially reduce metacontrast of a nonblurred target, but not vice versa. In fact, Growney (in press) has shown that blurring of the mask does not substantially reduce metacontrast; blurring of the target does reduce it.

IMPLICATIONS OF THE SUSTAINED–TRANSIENT DICHOTOMY FOR SACCADIC SUPPRESSION

Inspection of the visual world is characterized by, roughly, 250-msec periods of fixation alternating with saccades of 20–50 msec (depending on the length of the traverse). Saccadic suppression refers to the fact that sensitivity to visual stimulation is reduced by a saccade. The loss in sensitivity actually begins 50 msec or more *before* the saccade, continues through the traverse, and terminates some 50 or so msec after the eyes have reached their destination (e.g., Volkmann, 1962; Volkmann, Schick, & Riggs, 1968; for a review, see Matin, 1974). Matin (1974) distinguishes several causal components, among which the more important are (a) blurring of the retinal image during the rapid movement, (b) an afferent component, attributed to backward masking, and (c) an efferent component, central inhibition, which is related to corollary discharges originating from the motor command (Holst & Mittelstadt, 1950).

Some recent psychophysical evidence for the afferent component derives from studies by MacKay (1970a, 1970b). He showed that when a subject is fixating a target, thus eliminating saccades (and thus eliminating corollary discharges from eye movement commands), fast movement of a contoured field

causes a loss in sensitivity to a test flash. The suppression begins about 50 msec before the movement and lasts about 100 msec after the displacement. Jeannerod and Chouvet (1973) have obtained similar suppression effects in cat LGN, using macroelectrode techniques. The neurophysiological suppression also begins some 50 msec before the displacement and extends some 100 msec after the movement is terminated. We, like Matin (1974), attribute this component specifically to metacontrast by the stimulation of transient channels at the beginning, middle, and end of the saccade. It is likely that the test flash at threshold requires the presence of sharp contours (or high spatial-frequency components) for optimal sensitivity (Hood, 1973) and consequently, activation of sustained channels. In light of our model, it is easy to see how the transient stimulation produced by the saccade generates inhibition of sustained channels, which, as in metacontrast, starts several tens of msec prior to the saccade and lasts some 100 msec or more (see Figures 12b and 12c).

Recent psychophysical evidence for an efferent component in saccadic suppression derives from Riggs, Merton, and Morton (1974). They showed that, in complete darkness, electrically induced visual phosphenes were suppressed during saccades. The degree of suppression was only about .15 log units. This contrasts with estimates of .5 log units or more obtained during saccades in a lighted, structured environment (Volkmann, 1962) when, presumably, both afferent and efferent components summate. Recent neurophysiological recordings (Duffy & Burchfiel, 1975) from single neurons in monkey striate cortex have shown suppressive effects during saccades performed in total darkness. These efferent suppressive effects began about 20–30 msec *after* the onset of eye movements and lasted an average of about 200 msec. It should be noted that this latency corresponds, approximately, to the latency of cortical transient responses *after* stimulation of the retina (Dow, 1974). Thus if, as argued here, it is specifically the activation of transient channels that produces metacontrast suppression, and hence the afferent component of saccadic suppression, it would initiate its inhibitory effect at the cortex just as the efferent component (from corollary discharge) would initiate its own inhibition. This would explain why saccadic suppression is generally larger under lighted viewing conditions, such as used by Volkmann (1962), than under darkness conditions, such as employed by Riggs et al. (1974).

In this context, it seems appropriate to discuss the functional role of metacontrast (see also Matin, 1974). One way of conceptualizing saccadic suppression is that it plays a role in eliminating blur during a saccade (Matin, Clymer, & Matin, 1972). But a more important function, also discussed by Matin (1974), is the suppression of sustained channel activity generated in the 100-msec interval prior to the saccade. We recall the long integration time of sustained channels (see Figures 4 and 9), and more particularly, the increase in integration time with selectivity for higher spatial frequencies (Breitmeyer & Ganz, in press). It is easy to see how the last 100 msec or more of fixation in a prior fixation interval could interfere, via masking by integration, with the first 100 msec of the following fixation interval. *This problem would increase in severity as the spatial resolution of the task increased* (since higher spatial frequencies comprise fine contour detail). This *forward masking by integration,* we claim, *is prevented or attenuated both by metacontrast suppression and by efferent inhibition.*

The benefit of metacontrast on the preceding interval, however, may be mitigated if the preceding fixation interval is too short. Tinker (1958) notes that under luminance conditions in which a 100-msec stimulus presentation results in a clear percept, 200-msec intersaccade fixation intervals are required to attain a clear percept of equivalent stimuli. Within the framework of our model, it becomes clear why an additional 100 msec of stimulus presentation during a fixation interval is required. To wit, the last 100 msec provide a temporal buffer to reduce metacontrast suppression of the pattern processing in sustained channels activated during the initial 100 msec. Thus *metacontrast sets*

a lower limit on intersaccade interval. We suggest furthermore that *this lower limit is dependent on the spatial resolution requirements of the task.* Recalling Figure 12c, in which higher spatial frequencies are masked over a wider SOA range, we predict that the lower limit for intersaccade fixation intervals increases as finer discriminations are required.

IMPLICATIONS OF THE SUSTAINED–TRANSIENT DICHOTOMY FOR INFORMATION PROCESSING APPROACHES TO VISION

Sustained–Transient Dichotomy and Attention

Following a discussion on mechanisms of pattern recognition, Neisser, in his *Cognitive Psychology* (1967), states:

None of the theories can do justice to human or even mechanical pattern recognition, unless they are supplemented by some notion of "attention." There must be a way *to concentrate the processes of analysis on a selected portion of the field* [italics ours]. This implies that there are also "pre-attentive processes": wholistic operations to which attention may then be directed, and which can directly control simple motor behavior. (p. 86)

Neisser is emphasizing, in this passage, two sequentially organized stages of perception. At the early phase, the location of a stimulus is registered, so that focal attention can be directed to that region of space. Within our framework, we take this to mean that there must be a mechanism which directs readout from ISc into PS (e.g., categorical STM). For example, in a typical partial report experiment, visuospatial cues such as bar markers or arrows (Averbach & Coriell, 1961; Spencer, 1969; Sperling, 1960; Weisstein, 1966) can be employed to indicate which of several items represented at the iconic level a subject is required to read out and identify. The fact that the presence and location of a briefly presented target can be detected in a metacontrast situation (Fehrer & Biederman, 1962; Fehrer & Raab, 1962; Schiller & Smith, 1966) when its figural properties are masked (Breitmeyer et al., 1974; Sukale-Wolf, 1971; Weisstein & Haber, 1965) suggests that *figural* and *location* information enters the iconic level of processing through parallel and quasi-independent channels.

Sustained channels are concerned with transmission of figural information; transient channels, it is hypothesized here, transmit information about location or rapid changes in location (e.g., see Ikeda & Wright, 1972b).

Further evidence of a selective attention process, which can be directed to different regions of visual space, derives from experiments on the *functional fovea*. Using stabilized retinal images of complex patterns such as Japanese characters, geometric shapes, and tables of numbers, Zinchenko and Vergiles (1972) found that subjects could selectively scan such patterns without the usually accompanying scanning of the anatomical fovea over the visual display. That is,

Under stabilization conditions, during the solution of difficult visual tasks a mechanism compensating for image stabilization relative to the [anatomical] fovea comes into operation, and it can be likened to a functional fovea moving over the field of perception. (Zinchenko & Vergiles, 1972, p. 17)

It is assumed here that the iconic representation of a briefly presented target display is essentialy a spatially localized but temporally decaying image. However, this image localization does not occur so much in retinal space as it does in cortical space. It is further assumed that this internal image can be scanned by the *functional* fovea, that is, the functional locus of attention, in order to read out or abstract information from it. Moreover, target items falling within the spatial limits of the functional fovea are assumed to be read out of the iconic store in parallel. If the visual display size exceeds the spatial limits of the functional fovea, a sequential scanning superimposed on the parallel readout is required. A demonstration of spatially directed selective attention derives from the study of Eriksen and Hoffman (1974). Subjects were shown single letters tachistoscopically, which could appear at one of four possible locations along an imaginary circle concentric with the fixation point. A visual marker preceded this display at intervals up to 150 msec. The longer the marker preceded the display, the shorter the subject's recognition RT. This suggests that the subjects could read out information from ISc to PS more quickly when

their selective attention was first directed to the appropriate location, before the target stimulus was presented. The facilitative effects of selective attention, directed to circumscribed regions of visual space, implies that the mechanism controlling selective attention is retinotopically organized. The following is known about the anatomy of retinotopic organization.

Sustained channels are retinotopically organized, that is, they preserve spatial-location information, through striate cortex and Areas 18 and 19 in circumstriate cortex (Zeki, 1971). After Zeki, these are referred to as areas V1, V2, and V3, respectively. However, in circumstriate areas V4, V4A, and V5 (which receive input from V2 and V3) as well as in inferotemporal cortex, retinotopic information is not preserved within single cortical columns of neurons (Gross et al., 1974; Zeki, 1971). Therefore the latter is probably not the *origin* of this type of selective mechanism. However, the colliculus-pulvinar complex is retinotopically organized, and hence it could provide the information for *initiating selective orientation or attention responses* to locations in visual space that contain potentially significant figural information (Gross et al., 1974). It is known that superior colliculus ablation results in severe losses in attending selectively to objects in visual space (Schneider, 1967; Sprague, Berlucchi, & Rizzolatti, 1973; Trevarthen, 1968).

We believe that specifically it is transient neurons, bifurcating as they do to LGN and superior colliculus, which direct the selective-attention mechanisms. What is the evidence that transient channels are involved? The evidence derives primarily from metacontrast literature (Fehrer & Biederman, 1962; Fehrer & Raab, 1962; Schiller & Smith, 1966) showing that the presence and location of a target can be detected while its shape is suppressed. The subjects can report on its location quickly, as quickly as when no suppression is present (Fehrer & Raab, 1962). This suggests that location information is handled by rapid-responding channels, that is, the transient neurons, rather than the long-latency sustained channels.

One prediction that this model generates is that pattern recognition should be most efficient when the selective-attention mechanism operates in its most concentrated manner on a single spatial location. Several experiments (Averbach & Coriell, 1961; Spencer, 1969; Weisstein, 1966) have shown that backward masking of a single-pattern display is noticeably weaker than masking of the same pattern embedded in a multi-element display. When a single target is presented and followed by a mask, the transient channels activated by the target give unequivocal information to the visual system regarding the location to which attention or the functional fovea should be directed for readout of information from the ISc representation. Since transient activity at the cortex precedes sustained activity by 50–100 msec (Dow, 1974), the visual system is given that much time to direct its functional fovea to the relevant location in visual space where activation of sustained channels has taken place. This time interval corresponds to the time required to switch attention as determined psychophysically (LaBerge, 1973). Thus via the "early warning signal" carried by the transient channels, the visual system can immediately direct and focus attention to an ISc of the single target item.

In the multi-element display, unequivocal deployment of the selective-attention mechanism is delayed until presentation of the mask. Therefore, the selective-attention mechanism operates on information in sustained channels at the ISc level, which has already decayed in intensity (Sperling, 1960). Accuracy of report in the multi-element display condition is relatively impaired, because a weaker ISc representation is transferred to PS (i.e., to a categorical STM stage).

A further implication for attentional mechanisms of the transient–sustained dichotomy derives from observations reported by Kinsbourne (Note 6). Attention to a flashed display first concentrates on the peripheral contents and progressively shifts toward the center of the display. This correlates closely with the relatively high concentration of transient neurons and low concentration of sustained neurons in the periphery, whereas in the center the opposite asymmetry holds.

Sustained–Transient Dichotomy and the Interruption Theory of Visual Backward Masking

There have been two broad classes of theories of visual masking (Kahneman, 1968): integration theories (e.g., Ericksen's 1966 theory of contrast reduction by luminance-summation) and interruption theories (Averbach & Coriell, 1961; Haber, 1969a; Scheerer, 1973; Sperling, 1963). The former states that due to the limited temporal resolution of the visual system, successive target and mask stimuli interact in such a way as to lower the signal-to-noise ratio within the visual system. The degree of interaction is assumed to decrease with SOA (Type A masking). Two types of interactions can occur: (a) An excitatory one in which target and mask combine their excitatory effects, forming a composite at the ISp as well as ISc stages; here the reduction of signal-to-noise ratio is produced primarily by an increase of noise, and (b) an inhibitory one in which opponent processes—excitation and inhibition—integrate, one cancelling the other (see also Kahneman, 1968); here the reduction of signal-to-noise ratio is produced primarily by a diminution of the signal. In either case neural integrative mechanisms result in a *degradation* of the target ISc.

Interruption theories state that a *clear* target ISc is established. Subsequently, the masks interrupt the transfer of information from ISc to posticonic storage (PS). Therefore, one of the central differences between the two positions concerns the stage of visual information processing at which masking is postulated to occur.

Within the backward masking paradigm, four classes of evidence have been used to support interruption theory:

1. The U-shaped backward masking functions (Averbach & Coriell, 1961; Coltheart, 1975; Haber, 1969a; Turvey, 1973). The fact that under certain conditions strongest masking is obtained not at SOA = 0, but several tens of msec later, has been interpreted as *crucial* evidence that the mask must be delayed so as to synchronize with the initiation of the transfer from ISc to PS. For example, Haber (1969a) claims that "only at

the time when active transfer is under way can the masking interfere with that transfer" (p. 11).

2. The SOA Law. Turvey (1973) has shown that for a fairly large range of target energies, obtained by varying target duration, the effects of a subsequent mask can be just evaded by a target only if a fixed amount of time (called the critical SOA) is allowed to elapse from target to mask onsets. That is to say, for a range of energy values, critical SOA = target duration + ISI = constant. This has been interpreted to mean that a constant central processing time is required before transfer to a posticonic stage can occur.

3. Icon clarity (Haber & Standing, 1969; Liss, 1968). One of the findings that has been used to support the interruption theory of backward masking is the observation that while subjects report seeing a clear test stimulus, they nevertheless cannot identify it. For example, Haber and Standing (1969) had subjects make clarity judgments and recognition judgments of letters, either under conditions of short exposure (without a mask) or under conditions in which a mask followed a letter. They found that at a particular level of reported clarity, perceptual recognition was significantly lowered in the mask condition. This result was used to support interruption theory, since it was felt that the iconic representations were equally clear under both mask and nonmask conditions but that processing time was cut short under visual backward masking.

4. Direct estimates of icon duration (Haber & Standing, 1970; Sperling, 1967). The procedure originated by Sperling (1967) involves the following: In a target-then-mask paradigm, subjects are asked to synchronize the onsets of two tones to the perceived onset and, at a later time, to the perceived termination of the target icon (Haber & Standing, 1970). The asynchrony between the two tone onsets presumably provides an estimate of icon duration. These estimates were interpreted to be consistent with the view that a clear icon is established and then terminated by the mask.

These four classes of observations garnered from backward masking studies have been difficult, if not impossible, to explain within integration theory. The sustained–transient channel model proposed here can incorporate these observations without assuming that transfer from ISc to PS is interrupted.

The first and second classes of observations (1 and 2 above) are explained by the sustained–transient channel model in terms of the difference between response latency in transient channels activated by the mask and response latency in sustained channels activated by the target (see Figure 11b–d): Strongest masking occurs at SOAs where the transient channels activated by the mask *synchronize* their inhibitory effects with the excitatory activity of the sustained channels activated by the target. Thus U-shaped backward masking functions are generated by the *integration* of excitatory processes activated by the target and inhibitory processes activated by the mask.

The sustained–transient channel model also can explain the clarity-recognition observations (described in 3 above). It is evident from the model that the target stimulus establishes a fast and short-duration icon within transient channels. The short-duration icon is presumably sufficient to elicit *reports* of clarity but not sufficient to activate form-recognition mechanisms, which, according to the present view, require activation of sustained channels. The latter, having progressively longer response latencies with increases in spatial-frequency specificity, are more prone to interference by the after-coming mask, interference by both excitatory and inhibitory integration. As a consequence, under equal "clarity" conditions letter recognition should be poorer with the mask than without.

With regard to direct estimates of icon duration (Haber & Standing, 1970; Sperling, 1967), it is highly likely that the subject makes his duration judgments in these direct duration-estimate experiments simply on the basis of the interval between the onsets of the transient channels activated first by the target stimulus and second by the mask stimulus. This is doubly plausible, since in order to make a high-resolution temporal judgment, such as is required in this task, a subject would want to use channels in the CNS, which, in fact, are characterized by high temporal resolution. In the visual system, both psychophysical (Keesey, 1972; Kulikowsky & Tolhurst, 1973) and neurophysiological (Fukuda & Saito, 1971) evidence indicates that only transient channels are capable of high temporal resolution. Therefore, icon-duration estimates so acquired probably indicate more about the activity of transient channels than of sustained channels. The activity of the latter, low temporal resolution channels, is required to form an ISc necessary for letter recognition. *Judgments based on transient channel activity cannot be used to estimate temporal processes in sustained channels.*

An important methodological point that emerges from these considerations is that the four observations above cannot justifiably be used to measure processing time at the ISc level. A better estimate of processing time of the target stimulus at this processing level would be determined by the combined knowledge of (a) the spatial-frequency composition of the target and (b) the increased latencies and durations of the impulse responses (the temporal wave shapes elicited by a brief stimulus pulse) of sustained channels activated by progressively higher spatial-frequency components (see Figure 9).

CONCLUSIONS

The sustained–transient model presented here conceptualizes the visual system as comprised of two parallel and semi-independent channels, which are in a complementary relationship. The transient system is functionally characterized by high temporal resolution, short latency, and relatively low spatial resolution and comprises part of an "early warning system" that orients an organism and directs its attention to locations in visual space that potentially contain novel pattern information. This pattern information is subsequently analyzed by the sustained system, which is characterized by high spatial resolution, long latency, and long integration time. High-acuity tasks, such as the recognition of small forms and high-resolution stereoacuity, would accordingly require a longer perception time than low-acuity tasks.

One of the design problems inherent in the sustained system is that its long integration time permits strong proactive or forward masking by integration between successive fixations of the visual world. This could be solved simply by increasing the duration of the fixation or intersaccade interval. The price, however, would be a reduction in the rate of visual information processing.

This design problem is to some extent overcome by the existence of inhibitory actions of the transient system on the sustained system. The interaction between the transient and sustained systems is illustrated by the following sequence of events. An organism is fixating and analyzing a given spatial pattern. The sustained channels are slowly accumulating the pattern information. Suddenly a novel object appears in the periphery of the visual field (e.g., by moving). The novel object stimulates transient neurons, presumably in the superior colliculus, which command a reorientation of head and eyes so as to foveate the novel object. The command to move the eyes is realized in a saccade. Concomitantly, transient channels in the retino-geniculo-cortical pathway inhibit sustained channels at various levels of the visual system and thus help to terminate the long integration within sustained channels, which would otherwise persist into the next fixation period.

In this context, Type A masking mechanisms and metacontrast mechanisms, respectively, are laboratory demonstrations of (a) the long integration time characterizing sustained channels and (b) the inhibition of these sustained channels by transient channels found in normal, nonlaboratory settings. The purpose of delaying the onset of the mask in a metacontrast situation is to compensate for the greater speed of the transient system.

The visual system is characterized by a complementarity of spatial and temporal resolution. For any neuron, the better its capacity to resolve details in space, the poorer its capacity to resolve details in time. This implies that any stimulus gives rise to a family of impulse responses varying in latency, strength, and persistence, which depend on the spatial-frequency composition of the stimulus. Quantitative formalization of the mechanisms of masking presented here, in terms of both Type A and Type B masking effects, awaits elucidation of the spatio-temporal properties of these diverse visual channels.

REFERENCE NOTES

1. Biederman, I. Personal communication, March, 1974.
2. Simon, L. G. *Color specific effects in metacontrast masking.* Paper presented at the annual meeting of the Association for Research in Vision and Ophthalmology, Sarasota, Fla., April 1974.
3. Sakitt, B. *The locus of short-term visual storage.* Manuscript in preparation, 1975.
4. Julesz, B., & Miller, J. E. *Independent spatial-frequency-tuned channels in binocular fusion and rivalry.* Unpublished Bell Laboratories technical memorandum, March 1974.
5. Ikeda, H. Personal communication, August, 1975.
6. Kinsbourne, M. Personal communication, April, 1975.

REFERENCES

Alpern, M. Metacontrast. *Journal of the Optical Society of America,* 1953, *43,* 648–657.

Anstis, S. M., & Moulden, B. P. After effects of seen movement: Evidence for peripheral and central components. *Quarterly Journal of Experimental Psychology,* 1970, *22,* 222–229.

Averbach, E., & Coriell, A. S. Short-term memory in vision. *Bell System Technical Journal,* 1961, *40,* 309–328.

Barlow, H. B., Fitzhugh, R., & Kuffler, S. W. Change of organization in the receptive fields of the cat's retina during dark adaptation. *Journal of Physiology,* 1957, *137,* 338–354.

Barlow, H. B., & Sparrock, J. M. B. The role of afterimages in dark adaptation. *Science,* 1964, *144,* 1309–1314.

Battersby, W. S., Oesterreich, R. E., & Sturr, G. F. Neural limitations of visual excitability. VII. Non-homogeneous retrochiasmal interaction. *American Journal of Physiology,* 1964, *206,* 1181–1188.

Benevento, L. A., Creutzfeldt, O. D., & Kuhnt, U. Significance of intracortical inhibition in the visual cortex. *Nature* (London), 1972, *238,* 124–126.

Blake, R., & Fox, R. Adaptation to invisible gratings and the site of binocular rivalry suppression. *Nature* (London), 1974, *249,* 488–490.

Blakemore, C., & Campbell, F. W. On the existence of neurons in the human visual system selectively sensitive to the orientation and size of retinal images. *Journal of Physiology,* 1969, *203,* 237–260.

Blakemore, C., & Tobin, E. A. Lateral inhibition between orientation detectors in the cat's visual cortex. *Experimental Brain Research,* 1972, *15,* 439–440.

Bodis-Wollner, I. Visual acuity and contrast sensitivity in patients with cerebral lesions. *Science,* 1972, *178,* 769–771.

Boynton, R. Some temporal factors in vision. In W. A. Rosenblith (Ed.), *Sensory communication.* New York: Wiley, 1961.

Boynton, R. M., & Siegfried, J. B. Psychophysical estimates of on-responses to brief light flashes. *Journal of the Optical Society of America,* 1962, *52,* 720–721.

Breitmeyer, B. G. A relationship between the detection of size, rate, orientation and direction in the human visual system. *Vision Research,* 1973, *13,* 41–58.

Breitmeyer, B. G. Simple reaction time as a measure of the temporal response properties of transient and sustained channels. *Vision Research,* in press.

Breitmeyer, B., Battaglia, F., & Weber, C. U-shaped backward contour masking during stroboscopic motion. *Journal of Experimental Psychology: Human Perception and Performance,* in press.

Breitmeyer, B. G., & Ganz, L. Temporal integration as a function of spatial frequency. *Vision Research,* in press.

Breitmeyer, B., & Julesz, B. The role of on and off transients in determining the psychophysical spatial frequency response. *Vision Research,* 1975, *15,* 411–415.

Breitmeyer, B., Love, R., & Wepman, B. Contour suppression during stroboscopic motion and metacontrast. *Vision Research,* 1974, *14,* 1451–1456.

Bridgeman, B. Metacontrast and lateral inhibition. *Psychological Review,* 1971, *78,* 528–539.

Brooks, B., & Jung, R. Neuronal physiology of the visual cortex. In R. Jung (Ed.), *Handbook of sensory physiology* (Vol. 7, part 3, *Central processing of visual information*). New York: Springer-Verlag, 1973.

Burchard, S., & Lawson, R. B. A U-shaped detection function for backward masking of similar contours. *Journal of Experimental Psychology,* 1973, *99,* 35–41.

Campbell, F. W., Howell, E. R., & Robson, J. G. The appearance of gratings with and without the fundamental Fourier component. *Journal of Physiology,* 1971, *217,* 17–18.

Campbell, F. W., & Robson, J. G. Application of Fourier analysis to the visibility of gratings. *Journal of Physiology,* 1968, *197,* 551–566.

Carpenter, P., & Ganz, L. An attentional mechanism in the analysis of spatial frequency. *Perception & Psychophysics,* 1972, *12,* 57–60.

Cleland, B. G., Dubin, M. W., & Levick, W. R. Simultaneous recording of input and output of lateral geniculate nucleus. *Nature* (London), 1971, *231,* 191–192. (a)

Cleland, B. G., Dubin, M. W., & Levick, W. R. Sustained and transient neurones in the cat's retina and lateral geniculate nucleus. *Journal of Physiology,* 1971, *217,* 473–496. (b)

Cleland, B. G., Levick, W. R., & Sanderson, K. J. Properties of sustained and transient cells in the cat retina. *Journal of Physiology,* 1973, *228,* 649–680.

Coltheart, M. Iconic memory: A reply to Professor Holding. *Memory and Cognition,* 1975, *3,* 42–48.

Coltheart, M., & Arthur, B. Evidence for an integration theory of visual masking. *Quarterly Journal of Experimental Psychology,* 1972, *24,* 262–269.

Cornsweet, T. *Visual perception.* New York: Academic Press, 1970.

Crawford, B. H. Visual adaptation in relation to brief conditioning stimuli. *Proceedings of the Royal Society of London,* 1947, *134B,* 283–302.

Creutzfeldt, O., Kuhnt, U., & Benevento, L. An intracellular analysis of visual cortical neurons to moving stimuli: Responses in cooperative neural networks. *Experimental Brain Research*, 1974, *21*, 251–274.

Davidson, M. L. Perturbation approach to spatial brightness interaction in human vision. *Journal of the Optical Society of America*, 1968, *58*, 1300–1309.

Dow, B. M. Functional classes of cells and their laminar distribution in monkey visual cortex. *Journal of Neurophysiology*, 1974, *37*, 927–946.

Duffy, F. H., & Burchfiel, J. L. Eye movement-related inhibition of primate visual neurons. *Brain Research*, 1975, *89*, 121–132.

Efron, R. The relationship between the duration of a stimulus and the duration of perception. *Neuropsychologia*, 1970, *8*, 37–55.

Enroth-Cugell, C., & Robson, J. G. The contrast sensitivity of retinal ganglion cells of the cat. *Journal of Physiology*, 1966, *187*, 517–552.

Eriksen, C. W. Temporal luminance summation effects in backward and forward masking. *Perception & Psychophysics*, 1966, *1*, 87–92.

Eriksen, C. W., Becker, B. B., & Hoffman, J. E. Safari to masking land: A hunt for the elusive U. *Perception & Psychophysics*, 1970, *8*, 245–250.

Eriksen, C. W., & Collins, J. F. Backward masking in vision. *Psychonomic Science*, 1964, *1*, 101–102.

Eriksen, C. W., & Hoffman, J. E. Selective attention: Noise suppression or signal enhancement. *Bulletin of the Psychonomic Society*, 1974, *4*, 587–589.

Fehrer, E., & Biederman, I. A comparison of reaction and verbal report in the detection of masked stimuli. *Journal of Experimental Psychology*, 1962, *64*, 126–130.

Fehrer, E., & Raab, D. Reaction time to stimuli masked by metacontrast. *Journal of Experimental Psychology*, 1962, *63*, 143–147.

Fiorentini, A., & Maffei, L. Transfer characteristics of excitation and inhibition in the human visual system. *Journal of Neurophysiology*, 1970, *33*, 285–292.

Freund, H.-J. Neuronal mechanisms in the lateral geniculate body. In R. Jung (Ed.), *Handbook of sensory physiology* (Vol. 7, part 3, *Central processing of visual information*). New York: Springer-Verlag, 1973.

Fukuda, Y. Receptive field organization of cat optic nerve fibers with special reference to conduction velocity. *Vision Research*, 1971, *11*, 209–226.

Fukuda, Y. Differentiation of principal cells of the rat lateral geniculate body into two groups; fast and slow cells. *Experimental Brain Research*, 1973, *17*, 242–260.

Fukuda, Y., & Saito, H.-I. The relationship between response characteristics to flicker stimulation and receptive field organization in the cat's optic nerve fibers. *Vision Research*, 1971, *11*, 227–240.

Fukuda, Y., & Stone, J. Retinal distribution and central projections of Y-, X-, and W-cells of the cat's retina. *Journal of Neurophysiology*, 1974, *37*, 749–772.

Fukuda, Y., Sugitani, M., & Iwama, K. Flash-evoked response of two types of principal cells of the rat lateral geniculate body. *Brain Research*, 1973, *57*, 208–212.

Ganz, L., & Felder, R. C. Quantitative analysis of motion selectivity in complex neurons of cat visual cortex: I. Receptive field analysis. *Vision Research*, in press.

Ginsburg, A. P. Pattern recognition techniques suggested from psychological correlates of a model of the human visual system. *IEEE Transactions on Aerospace and Electronics*, 1973, *9*, 625.

Graham, N. Spatial frequency channels in human vision: Detecting edges without edge detectors. In C. S. Harris (Ed.), *Visual coding and adaptability*. Hillsdale, N. J.: Erlbaum, in press.

Greenspoon, T. S., & Eriksen, C. W. Interocular non-independence. *Perception & Psychophysics*, 1968, *3*, 93–96.

Gross, C. G. Inferotemporal cortex and vision. In E. Stellar & J. M. Sprague (Eds.), *Progress in physiological psychology* (Vol. 5). New York: Academic Press, 1973. (a)

Gross, C. G. Visual functions of the inferotemporal cortex. In R. Jung (Ed.), *Handbook of sensory physiology* (Vol. 7, part 3, *Central processing of visual information*). New York: Springer-Verlag, 1973. (b)

Gross, C. G., Bender, D. B., & Roch-Miranda, C. E. Inferotemporal cortex: A single unit analysis. In F. O. Schmitt & F. G. Worden (Eds.), *The neurosciences third study program*. Cambridge, Mass.: MIT Press, 1974.

Growney, R. L. The function of contour in metacontrast. *Vision Research*, in press.

Growney, R., & Weisstein, N. Spatial characteristics of metacontrast. *Journal of the Optical Society of America*, 1972, *62*, 690–696.

Haber, R. N. *Information-processing approaches to visual perception*. New York: Holt, Rinehart & Winston, 1969. (a)

Haber, R. N. Repetition, visual persistence, visual noise and information processing. In K. N. Leibovic (Ed.), *Information processing in the nervous system*. New York: Springer, 1969. (b)

Haber, R. N., & Standing, L. Clarity and recognition of masked and degraded stimuli. *Psychonomic Science*, 1969, *13*, 83–84.

Haber, R. N., & Standing, L. Direct estimates of apparent duration of a flash followed by visual noise. *Canadian Journal of Psychology*, 1970, *24*, 216–229.

Hammond, P. Chromatic sensitivity and spatial organization of cat visual cortical cells: Cone–rod interaction. *Journal of Physiology*, 1971, *213*, 475–494.

Hammond, P. Contrasts in spatial organization of receptive fields at geniculate and retinal levels: Centre, surround and outer surround. *Journal of Physiology*, 1973, *228*, 115–137.

Harmon, L. D., & Julesz, B. Masking in visual recognition: Effects of two-dimensional filtered noise. *Science*, 1973, *180*, 1194–1197.

Hebb, D. O. *Organization of behavior*. New York: Wiley, 1949.

Hess, R., Negishi, K., & Creutzfeldt, O. The horizontal spread of intracortical inhibition in the visual cortex. *Experimental Brain Research*, 1975, *22*, 415–419.

34   BRUNO G. BREITMEYER AND LEO GANZ

Hoffman, K.-P. Conduction velocity in pathways from retina to superior colliculus in the cat: A correlation with receptive field properties. *Journal of Neurophysiology*, 1973, *36*, 409–424.

Hoffman, K.-P., & Stone, J. Conduction velocity of afferents to cat visual cortex: A correlation with receptive field properties. *Brain Research*, 1971, *32*, 460–466.

Hoffman, K.-P., Stone, J., & Sherman, S. M. Relay of receptive-field properties in dorsal lateral geniculate nucleus of the cat. *Journal of Neurophysiology*, 1972, *35*, 518–531.

Holst, E. von, & Mittelstadt, H. Das Reafferenzprinzip. *Die Naturwissenschaften*, 1950, *20*, 464–467.

Hood, D. C. The effects of edge sharpness and exposure duration on detection threshold. *Vision Research*, 1973, *13*, 759–766.

Hubel, D. H., & Wiesel, T. N. Integrative action in cat's lateral geniculate body. *Journal of Physiology*, 1961, *155*, 385–398.

Hubel, D. H., & Wiesel, T. N. Receptive fields, binocular interaction and functional architecture in the cat's visual cortex. *Journal of Physiology*, 1962, *160*, 106–154.

Hubel, D. H., & Wiesel, T. N. Receptive fields and functional architecture of monkey striate cortex. *Journal of Physiology*, 1968, *195*, 215–243.

Hubel, D. H., & Wiesel, T. N. Stereoscopic vision in macaque monkey. *Nature* (London), 1970, *225*, 41–42.

Hubel, D. H., & Wiesel, T. N. Sequence regularity and geometry of orientation columns in monkey striate cortex. *Journal of Comparative Neurology*, 1974, *158*, 267–294.

Ikeda, H., & Wright, M. J. Differential effects of refractive errors and receptive field organization of central and peripheral ganglion cells. *Vision Research*, 1972, *12*, 1465–1476. (a)

Ikeda, H., & Wright, M. J. Receptive field organization of "sustained" and "transient" retinal ganglion cells which subserve differential functional roles. *Journal of Physiology*, 1972, *227*, 769–800. (b)

Ikeda, H., & Wright, M. J. Evidence for "sustained" and "transient" neurones in the cat's visual cortex. *Vision Research*, 1974, *14*, 133–136.

Ikeda, H., & Wright, M. J. Retinotopic distribution, visual latency and orientation tuning of "sustained" and "transient" cortical neurones in area 17 of the cat. *Experimental Brain Research*, 1975, *22*, 385–398. (a)

Ikeda, H., & Wright, M. J. Spatial and temporal properties of "sustained" and "transient" neurones in area 17 of the cat's visual cortex. *Experimental Brain Research*, 1975, *22*, 363–383. (b)

Jeannerod, M., & Chouvet, G. Saccadic displacement of the retinal image: Effects on the visual system in the cat. *Vision Research*, 1973, *13*, 161–169.

Julesz, B. *Foundations of cyclopean perception*. Chicago: University of Chicago Press, 1971.

Kahneman, D. Temporal summation in an acuity task at different energy levels—A study of the

determinants of summation. *Vision Research*, 1964, *4*, 557–566.

Kahneman, D. An onset–onset law for one case of apparent motion and metacontrast. *Perception & Psychophysics*, 1967, *2*, 577–584.

Kahneman, D. Method, findings, and theory in studies of visual masking. *Psychological Bulletin*, 1968, *70*, 404–425.

Kahneman, D., & Norman, J. The time-intensity relation in visual perception as a function of observer's task. *Journal of Experimental Psychology*, 1964, *68*, 215–220.

Keck, M. J., Pallela, T. D., & Pantle, A. Motion after effect as a function of the contrast of sinusoidal gratings. *Vision Research*, in press.

Keesey, U. T. Flicker and pattern detection: A comparison of thresholds. *Journal of the Optical Society of America*, 1972, *62*, 446–448.

Kinsbourne, M., & Warrington, E. K. Further studies on the masking of brief visual stimuli by a random pattern. *Quarterly Journal of Experimental Psychology*, 1962, *14*, 235–245.

Kolers, P. A. Intensity and contour effects in visual masking. *Vision Research*, 1962, *2*, 277–294.

Kolers, P. A. Some differences between real and apparent visual movement. *Vision Research*, 1963, *3*, 191–206.

Kolers, P. A., & Rosner, B. S. On visual masking (metacontrast): Dichoptic observations. *American Journal of Psychology*, 1960, *73*, 2–21.

Kuffler, S. W. Discharge patterns and functional organization of mammalian retina. *Journal of Neurophysiology*, 1953, *16*, 37–68.

Kulikowski, J. J. Human averaged occipital potentials evoked by pattern and movement. *Journal of Physiology*, 1974, *242*, 70–71P.

Kulikowski, J. J., & Tolhurst, D. J. Psychophysical evidence for sustained and transient detectors in human vision. *Journal of Physiology*, 1973, *232*, 149–162.

La Berge, D. Identification of the time to switch attention: A test of a serial and parallel model of attention. In S. Kornblum (Ed.), *Attention and performance* (Vol. 4). New York: Academic Press, 1973.

Lefton, L. A. Metacontrast: A review. *Perception & Psychophysics*, 1973, *13*, 161–171.

Liss, P. Does backward masking by visual noise stop stimulus processing? *Perception & Psychophysics*, 1968, *4*, 328–330.

MacKay, D. Elevation of visual threshold by displacement of retinal image. *Nature* (London), 1970, *225*, 90–92. (a)

MacKay, D. Interocular transfer of suppressive effects of retinal image displacement. *Nature* (London), 1970, *225*, 872–873. (b)

Maffei, L., Cervetto, L., & Fiorentini, A. Transfer characteristics of excitation and inhibition in cat retinal ganglion cells. *Journal of Neurophysiology*, 1970, *33*, 276–284.

Maffei, L., & Fiorentini, A. Processes of synthesis in visual perception. *Nature* (London), 1972, *240*, 479–481. (a)

Maffei, L., & Fiorentini, A. Retinogeniculate convergence and analysis of contrast. *Journal of Neurophysiology*, 1972, *35*, 65–72. (b)

Maffei, L., & Fiorentini, A. The visual cortex as a spatial frequency analyzer. *Vision Research*, 1973, *13*, 1255–1267.

Matin, E. Saccadic suppression: A review and analysis. *Psychological Bulletin*, 1974, *81*, 899–917.

Matin, E., Clymer, A., & Matin, L. Metacontrast and saccadic suppression. *Science*, 1972, *178*, 179–182.

Mayzner, M. S., et al. A U-shaped backward masking function in vision: A partial replication of the Weisstein and Haber study with two ring sizes. *Psychonomic Science*, 1965, *3*, 79–80.

Mayzner, M. S., & Tresselt, M. E. Visual information processing with sequential inputs: A general model for sequential blanking, displacement, and overprinting phenomena. *Annals of the New York Academy of Sciences*, 1970, *169*, 599–618.

McFadden, D., & Gummerman, K. Monoptic and dichoptic metacontrast across the vertical meridian. *Vision Research*, 1973, *13*, 185–196.

Michael, C. R. Opponent-color and opponent-contrast cells in the lateral geniculate of ground squirrel. *Journal of Neurophysiology*, 1973, *36*, 536–550.

Michaels, C. F., & Turvey, M. T. Hemiretinae and nonmonotonic masking functions with overlapping stimuli. *Bulletin of the Psychonomic Society*, 1973, *2*, 163–164.

Neisser, U. *Cognitive psychology*. New York: Appleton-Century-Crofts, 1967.

Palmer, L. A., & Rosenquist, A. C. Visual receptive fields of single striate cortical units projecting to the superior colliculus of the cat. *Brain Research*, 1974, *67*, 27–42.

Pantle, A. J. Adaptation to pattern spatial frequency effects on visual movement sensitivity in humans. *Journal of the Optical Society of America*, 1970, *60*, 1120–1124.

Poggio, G. B., Baker, F. H., Lamarre. Y., & Sanseverino, E. R. Afferent inhibition at input to visual cortex of the cat. *Journal of Neurophysiology*, 1969, *32*, 916–929.

Pollen, D. A., Lee, J. R., & Taylor, J. H. How does the striate cortex begin the reconstruction of the visual world? *Science*, 1971, *173*, 74–77.

Pollen, D. A., & Ronner, S. F. Periodic excitability of changes across the receptive fields of complex cells in the striate and parastriate cortex of the cat. *Journal of Physiology*, 1975, *245*, 667–697.

Purcell, D. G., & Stewart, A. L. U-shaped backward masking functions with nonmetacontrast paradigms. *Psychonomic Science*, 1970, *21*, 361–363.

Purcell, D. G., Stewart, A. L., & Dember, W. N. Spatial effectiveness of the mask: Lateral inhibition in visual backward masking. *Perception & Psychophysics*, 1968, *4*, 344–346.

Riggs, L., Merton, P., & Morton, H. Suppression of visual phophenes during saccadic eye movements. *Vision Research*, 1974, *14*, 997–1011.

Scharf, B., & Lefton, L. A. Backward and forward masking as a function of stimulus and task parameters. *Journal of Experimental Psychology*, 1970, *84*, 331–338.

Scheerer, E. Integration, interruption and processing rate in visual backward masking. *Psychologische Forschung*, 1973, *36*, 71–93.

Schiller, P. Forward and backward masking as a function of relative overlap and intensity of test and masking stimuli. *Perception & Psychophysics*, 1966, *1*, 161–164.

Schiller, P., & Smith, M. C. A comparison of forward and backward masking. *Psychonomic Science*, 1965, *3*, 77–78.

Schiller, P., & Smith, M. C. Detection in metacontrast. *Journal of Experimental Psychology*, 1966, *71*, 32–39.

Schiller, P., & Smith, M. C. Monoptic and dichoptic metacontrast. *Perception & Psychophysics*, 1968, *3*, 237–239.

Schneider, G. E. Contrasting visuomotor functions of tectum and cortex in the golden hamster. *Psychologische Forschung*, 1967, *31*, 52–62.

Schober, H. A. W., & Hilz, R. Contrast sensitivity of the human eye for square-wave gratings. *Journal of the Optical Society of America*, 1965, *55*, 1086–1091.

Sekuler, R., Pantle, A., & Levinson, E. Physiological bases of motion perception. In R. Held, H. Liebowitz, & H.-L. Teuber (Eds.), *Handbook of sensory physiology* (Vol. 8). New York: Springer, in press.

Sherrick, M. F., Keating, J. K., & Dember, W. N. Metacontrast with black and white stimuli. *Canadian Journal of Psychology*, 1974, *28*, 439–445.

Shipley, W. C., Kenney, F. A., & King, M. E. Beta apparent movement under binocular, monocular, and interocular stimulation. *American Journal of Psychology*, 1945, *58*, 545–549.

Singer, W., & Bedworth, N. Inhibitory interaction between X and Y units in the cat lateral geniculate nucleus. *Brain Research*, 1973, *49*, 291–307.

Singer, W., & Creutzfeldt, O. D. Reciprocal lateral inhibition of on- and off-center neurones in the lateral geniculate body of the cat. *Experimental Brain Research*, 1970, *10*, 311–330.

Singer, W., Pöppel, E., & Creutzfeldt, O. Inhibitory interaction in the cat's lateral geniculate nucleus. *Experimental Brain Research*, 1972, *14*, 210–226.

Smith, M. C., & Schiller, P. Forward and backward masking: A comparison. *Canadian Journal of Psychology*, 1966, *20*, 191–197.

Spencer, T. J. Some effects of different masking stimuli on iconic storage. *Journal of Experimental Psychology*, 1969, *81*, 132–140.

Spencer, T. J., & Shuntich, R. Evidence for an interruption theory of backward masking. *Journal of Experimental Psychology*, 1970, *85*, 198–203.

Sperling, G. The information available in brief visual presentations. *Psychological Monographs*, 1960, *74*(11, Whole No. 498).

Sperling, G. A model for visual memory tasks. *Human Factors*, 1963, *5*, 19–31.

36   BRUNO G. BREITMEYER AND LEO GANZ

Sperling, G. Temporal and spatial visual masking: I. Masking by impulse flashes. *Journal of the Optical Society of America*, 1965, *55*, 541–559.

Sperling, G. Successive approximations to a model for short-term memory. In *Proceedings of the Eighteenth International Congress of Psychology*. Amsterdam: North-Holland, 1967.

Sprague, J. M., Berlucchi, G., & Rizzolatti, G. The role of the superior colliculus and pretectum in vision and visually guided behavior. In R. Jung (Ed.), *Handbook of sensory physiology* (Vol. 7, part 3, *Central processing of visual information*). New York: Springer-Verlag, 1973.

Stewart, A. L., & Purcell, D. G. U-shaped masking functions in visual backward masking: Effects of target configuration and retinal position. *Perception & Psychophysics*, 1970, *7*, 253–256.

Stigler, R. Chronophotische Studien uber den Umgebungskontrast. *Pflügers Archiv für die gesamte Physiologie*, 1910, *134*, 365–435.

Stone, J., & Dreher, B. Projection of X- and Y-cells of the cat's lateral geniculate nucleus to areas 17 and 18 of visual cortex. *Journal of Neurophysiology*, 1973, *36*, 551–567.

Stone, J., & Hoffman, K.-P. Conduction velocity as a parameter in the organization of the afferent relay in the cat's lateral geniculate nucleus. *Brain Research*, 1971, *32*, 454–459.

Stromeyer, C. F., & Julesz, B. Spatial-frequency masking in vision: Critical bands and spread of masking. *Journal of the Optical Society of America*, 1972, *62*, 1221–1232.

Sukale-Wolf, S. U. *Prediction of the metacontrast phenomenon from simultaneous brightness contrast.* Unpublished doctoral dissertation, Stanford University, 1971.

Tinker, M. A. Recent studies of eye movements in reading. *Psychological Bulletin*, 1958, *55*, 215–231.

Toch, H. H. The perceptual elaboration of stroboscopic presentations. *American Journal of Psychology*, 1956, *69*, 345–358.

Tolhurst, D. J. Separate channels for the analysis of the shape and the movement of a moving visual stimulus. *Journal of Physiology*, 1973, *231*, 385–402.

Toyama, K., Matsunami, K., Ohno, T., & Tokoshiki, S. An intracellular study of neuronal organization in the visual cortex. *Experimental Brain Research*, 1974, *21*, 45–66.

Trevarthen, C. B. Two mechanisms of vision in primates. *Psychologische Forschung*, 1968, *31*, 299–337.

Turvey, M. T. On peripheral and central processes in vision: Inferences from an information-processing analysis of masking with patterned stimuli. *Psychological Review*, 1973, *80*, 1–52.

Turvey, M. T., Michaels, C. F., & Kewley-Port, D. Visual storage or visual masking? An analysis of the "retroactive contour enhancement" effect. *Quarterly Journal of Experimental Psychology*, 1974, *26*, 74–81.

Uttal, W. R. On the physiological basis of masking with dotted visual noise. *Perception & Psychophysics*, 1970, *7*, 321–327.

Uttal, W. R. The psychobiological silly season—or—what happens when neurophysiological data become psychological theories. *Journal of General Psychology*, 1971, *84*, 151–166.

Verhoeff, F. H. Phiphenomenon and anomalous projection. *Archives of Ophthalmology* (Chicago), 1940, *24*, 247–251.

Volkmann, F. Vision during voluntary saccadic eye movements. *Journal of the Optical Society of America*, 1962, *52*, 571–578.

Volkmann, F., Schick, A., & Riggs, L. Time course of visual inhibition during voluntary saccades. *Journal of the Optical Society of America*, 1968, *58*, 562–569.

Wanatabe, S., Konishi, M., & Creutzfeldt, O. Postsynaptic potentials in the cat's visual cortex following electrical stimulation of afferent pathways. *Experimental Brain Research*, 1966, *1*, 272–283.

Weiskrantz, L. The interaction between occipital and temporal cortex in vision: An overview. In F. O. Schmitt & F. G. Worden (Eds.), *The neurosciences third study program.* Cambridge, Mass.: MIT Press, 1974.

Weisstein, N. Backward masking and models of perceptual processing. *Journal of Experimental Psychology*, 1966, *72*, 232–240.

Weisstein, N. A Rashevsky-Landahl neural net: Simulation of metacontrast. *Psychological Review*, 1968, *75*, 494–521.

Weisstein, N. W-shaped and U-shaped functions obtained for monoptic and dichoptic disk-disk masking. *Perception & Psychophysics*, 1971, *9*, 275–278.

Weisstein, N. Metacontrast. In D. Jameson & L. M. Hurvich (Eds.), *Handbook of sensory physiology* (Vol. 7, part 4, *Visual psychophysics*). New York: Springer-Verlag, 1972.

Weisstein, N., & Growney, R. Apparent movement and metacontrast: A note on Kahneman's formulation. *Perception & Psychophysics*, 1969, *5*, 321–328.

Weisstein, N., & Haber, R. N. A U-shaped backward masking function in vision. *Psychonomic Science*, 1965, *2*, 75–76.

Weisstein, N., Ozog, G., & Szoc, R. A comparison and elaboration of two models of metacontrast. *Psychological Review*, 1975, *82*, 325–343.

Werner, H. Studies of contour: I. Qualitative analysis. *American Journal of Psychology*, 1935, *47*, 40–64.

Werner, H. Studies on contour strobostereoscopic phenomena. *American Journal of Psychology*, 1940, *53*, 418–422.

Wertheimer, M. Experimentalle Studien uber das Sehen von Bewegung. *Zeitschrift fur Psychologie*, 1912, *61*, 161–265.

Zeki, S. M. Cortical projections from two prestriate areas in the monkey. *Brain Research*, 1971, *34*, 19–35.

Zinchenko, V. P., & Vergiles, N. Y. *Formation of visual images.* New York: Consultants Bureau, 1972.

(Received May 23, 1975)

[6]

Neuronal Correlates of Subjective Visual Perception

NIKOS K. LOGOTHETIS AND JEFFREY D. SCHALL*

Neuronal activity in the superior temporal sulcus of monkeys, a cortical region that plays an important role in analyzing visual motion, was related to the subjective perception of movement during a visual task. Single neurons were recorded while monkeys (*Macaca mulatta*) discriminated the direction of motion of stimuli that could be seen moving in either of two directions during binocular rivalry. The activity of many neurons was dictated by the retinal stimulus. Other neurons, however, reflected the monkeys' reported perception of motion direction, indicating that these neurons in the superior temporal sulcus may mediate the perceptual experience of a moving object.

N EURONS IN THE VISUAL CORTEX of higher mammals respond only to specific properties of visual stimuli (1). One way to distinguish neuronal activity related to perceptual processes rather than to physical stimulus characteristics is to expose the visual system to stimuli that allow more than one percept. When the visual cues provided are enough to dictate one description of the visual scene, perception is unique and stable. But when the sensory data are insufficient for just one interpretation, rival possibilities are entertained and perception becomes ambiguous, switching between the alternatives. Binocular rivalry, a percept that ensues when dissimilar stimuli are presented to the two eyes, is a typical instance of perceptual instability (2). Because such stimuli cannot be fused by the cyclopean visual system, the perception alternates between the stimulus seen by the right eye alone or the left eye alone. For example, when the right eye is presented with upward movement and the left eye with downward movement, the perceived motion alternates between up and down.

The middle temporal (MT) and medial superior temporal areas in the superior temporal sulcus (STS) contain neurons that analyze visual motion (3), but it is not known whether such activity can be directly related to the conscious perception of movement. To investigate this possibility, we used rhesus monkeys because they experience binocular rivalry (4).

Three rhesus monkeys were trained in a motion discrimination task. Two vertically drifting horizontal gratings were generated on a video monitor and presented independently to the two eyes through a stereoscopic viewer. Eye movements were monitored with a scleral search coil, and a disparity calibration was performed to position the

Department of Brain and Cognitive Sciences, Massachusetts Institute of Technology, Cambridge, MA 02139.

*Present address: Department of Psychology, Vanderbilt University, Nashville, TN 37240.

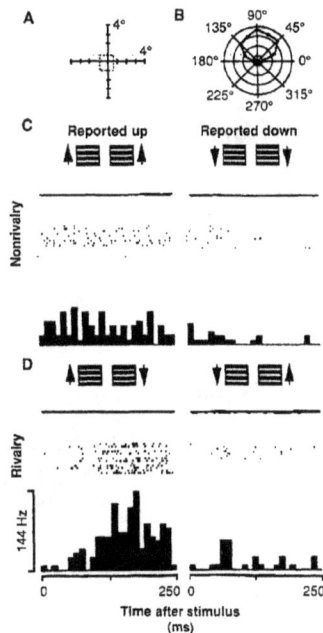

Fig. 1. Response of single unit in the STS to nonrivalrous and rivalrous stimuli. (**A**) Receptive field position. This cell had a small central receptive field. (**B**) Direction tuning curve. Each point represents the average discharge rate in response to drifting gratings. Each concentric circle represents 30 spikes per second. The cell preferred upward motion. (**C** and **D**) Responses during nonrivalrous (C) and rivalrous (D) grating presentation when the monkey reported seeing up (left) and down (right). The gratings depict the type of motion presented to each eye. Beneath the gratings, the vertical eye movement traces are superimposed for each trial. Single unit activity is illustrated by rasters and time histograms of the average firing rate. The eye position traces, rasters, and histograms are aligned on the onset of the nonrivalrous or rivalrous grating presentations.

gratings so that they overlapped (5). A trial began with the appearance of a fixation spot. After the monkey fixated on the spot, drifting gratings were presented for 400 to 1500 ms. The gratings were replaced by two spots on the left and right of the fixation spot. If the monkey perceived upward motion, he was required to execute a saccade (quick eye movement) to the right spot; a saccade to the left spot was required after downward movement. In half of the trials the gratings drifted in the same direction, and in the other half they were rivalrous, containing an equal number of up-down and down-up presentations. In the rivalrous trials the monkeys were rewarded for either response. Also, in half of the trials the fixation spot was removed when the gratings appeared to allow optokinetic responses. The various trial types were pseudorandomly interleaved.

Overall, the perceptual choice in rivalrous trials was as likely to correspond to the stimulus presented to one eye as to the other. As observed in humans (6), in 93% of the rivalry trials in which the monkeys exhibited measurable pursuit (7), its direction corresponded to the reported perceived

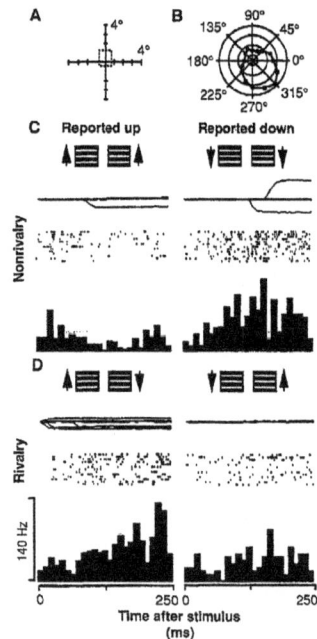

movement. The gain of pursuit during rivalry was significantly lower (mean ± SEM = 0.30 ± 0.01 for rivalry versus 1.00 ± 0.01 for nonrivalry), and the latency was significantly longer than normal (average of 296 ± 1.9 ms for rivalry versus 189 ± 2.5 ms for nonrivalry).

A total of 66 neurons were recorded from two monkeys (8). Seven had receptive fields that did not include the fovea; therefore, they were not used in this analysis. The remaining units exhibited directional specificity, and even if their preferred direction was not vertical on initial inspection, they had unequal responses for upward versus downward motion. Their receptive fields included the fovea, and their size was comparable to their eccentricity. According to these receptive field properties, these units were probably in MT. All of the neurons

analyzed in this report were binocular and approximately equally driven by stimulation of either eye.

A variety of neuronal responses was observed in STS, and different populations of neurons could be distinguished by comparing their modulation during nonrivalrous and rivalrous trials. The responses of one neuron with activity that was correlated with the perceived direction of motion during rivalry is shown in Fig. 1. When the gratings were moving in the same direction, the response of the cell reflected its upward preference. However, when the gratings presented to each eye were moving in opposite directions (that is, the grating presented to one eye moved downward and that presented to the other eye moved upward), then the cell discharged on those trials in which the monkey indicated that he per-

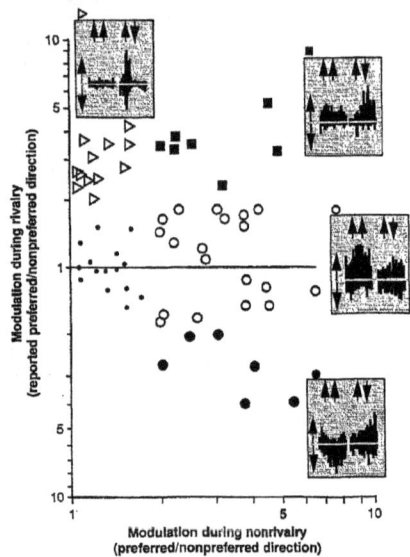

Fig. 2. Response of another STS unit during nonrivalrous and rivalrous grating presentation. Conventions are as in Fig. 1.

Fig. 3. Scatter plot of the directional modulation with nonrivalrous and rivalrous stimulus presentation. The response of each neuron (n = 59) was defined as the number of spikes discharged in the first 100 ms after grating presentation in each trial. The abscissa represents the ratio of the average response of a cell in a block of nonrivalrous trials to gratings in its preferred direction divided by the average response to gratings in its nonpreferred direction. The ordinate represents the modulation of the cell during rivalrous stimulus presentation. This modulation was defined as the ratio of the average response in trials in which the monkey reported seeing the direction of motion corresponding to the preferred direction of the cell divided by the average response in trials in which the monkey reported seeing the direction of motion in the nonpreferred direction. Values in the upper half indicate that the response of the cell was greater when the perceptual choice corresponded to the preferred direction. Values in the lower half indicate that the neuronal response was greater when the behavioral choice was in the nonpreferred direction. This analysis does not reflect the overall level of activity of the cells but rather the ratio of activities for the two directions. Lower half of the ordinate is a mirror image of the upper half and reflects movement preference in the opposite direction. A *t* test was used to determine whether the directional modulation of a cell was significant. All of the cells in the plot were derived from the same sample, but symbols illustrate the different types of modulation. Small solid dots (●) represent cells that were not directional in the vertical access during either the nonrivalrous or the rivalrous trials. The open triangles (△) represent cells that were not significantly directional during the nonrivalrous presentation but were directional during rivalry. Hence, the assignment of these points to the upper half of the plot was arbitrary. The open circles (○) represent cells that exhibited significant directional modulation during the nonrivalrous presentation, but during rivalry their response was independent of the perceptual choice of the monkey. The solid squares (■) and circles (●) signify cells that exhibited significant directionality during both rivalrous and nonrivalrous trials. Cells designated by solid squares responded more during rivalry when the perceptual choice of the monkeys corresponded to the preferred direction of the cell, while those signified with solid circles responded more when the perceptual choice corresponded to the nonpreferred direction. (Insets) Spike histograms of examples of the four modulated cell classes. The type of symbol at the upper left of each inset indicates the cell class. The arrows at the top of each panel indicate the nonrivalrous and rivalrous trial types, and the arrows on the left indicate trials in which the monkey reported upward or downward motion.

ceived upward movement. In contrast, this unit did not discharge on trials in which the monkey responded that he perceived downward motion, even though the optimal, upward-moving stimulus was being presented to one or the other eye. Although only 250 ms of activity is shown in Fig. 1, the differential activity was present as long as the gratings were presented (up to 1500 ms). The activity of another STS unit is shown in Fig. 2. This unit was more active in rivalry trials in which the monkey reported the direction of motion corresponding to the nonpreferred direction of the cell.

A quantitative analysis of the modulation of each neuron was performed (Fig. 3). Twenty-five percent of the neurons showed insignificant directionality in the vertical axis; another 21% of the cells, which had horizontal or oblique preferred directions, displayed directionality during rivalrous but not nonrivalrous trials. Thirty-two percent of the units exhibited directionality for nonrivalrous gratings, but their response during rivalry was independent of the perceptual choice of the monkeys; these units discharged whenever their optimal stimulus was present. Finally, 22% of the cells were modulated during rivalry according to their direction preference exhibited during nonrivalry. Half of these units responded when the perceptual choice of the monkey corresponded to the preferred direction of the cell (Fig. 1), and the other half responded when the preferred direction of motion was present in the suppressed eye (Fig. 2).

Because neuronal activity related to pursuit eye movements has been recorded in STS (9), the modulation of this last class of neuron could be a consequence of the pursuit eye movements, which are themselves correlated with the perceived direction of motion. Several arguments refute this interpretation. First, during trials in which the fixation spot was visible, the monkey did not exhibit measurable nystagmus, but the pattern of neuronal response was the same as that elicited in trials in which no fixation spot appeared. Second, the quantitative analysis of neuronal modulation (Fig. 3) included only the first 100 ms after grating presentation, well before pursuit was initiated. Finally, the relation of neuronal onset time to stimulus or pursuit onset was determined (10); this analysis confirmed that the neuronal discharge was related to stimulus presentation and not the execution of pursuit eye movements. Hence, the differential neuronal activity of these units during rivalry reflects a perceptual and not an oculomotor process. Studies reveal comparable prop-

erties of MT neurons in a different visual task (11).

During rivalry the stimulus presented to one eye is periodically invisible even though it still impinges on the retina. Psychoanatomical experiments have shown that this suppression occurs at a relatively advanced station in the visual pathway (12). Our results provide information about the site and mechanism of binocular rivalry by indicating that the STS contains elements that might mediate the periodic suppression and dominance characterizing binocular rivalry.

The neurons that discharged regardless of whether their optimal stimulus was in the suppressed or the dominant eye may be first-order neurons receiving afferents that are not inhibited during rivalry suppression. When the neurons that were differentially responsive in the vertical axis only during rivalry were mapped conventionally, they had a horizontal or oblique preferred direction. Thus, their directional tuning might be dynamic and adaptable to the perceptual requirements. The units that were specifically active when the optimal stimulus was present in the dominant eye (Fig. 1) could mediate the perception of motion that was expressed in the behavioral response of the monkeys. Finally, the neurons that were active when their optimal stimulus was present in the suppressed eye (Fig. 2) might provide the inhibition to lower or higher visual centers to suppress the view of one eye during rivalry.

This interpretation of the results is by no means conclusive. The differential modulation of these STS neurons in response to rivalrous stimuli was evident much earlier than subjects typically resolve the rivalrous perception. Thus, further processing is clearly involved, and the data do not exclude the possibility that the perception-related modulation observed in these neurons may be a result of feedback from higher centers.

In conclusion, the results of this study suggest the possibility of experimentally relating the activity of single neurons in the visual system to the internal perceptual state of the subjects. Such experiments may lead to a better understanding of how the processes that result in an internal representation of the visual world are instantiated in the structure and function of the visual pathways.

REFERENCES AND NOTES

1. D. H. Hubel and T. N. Wiesel, *J. Physiol. (London)* 195, 215 (1968).
2. P. Walker, *Psychol. Bull.* 85, 376 (1978); J. M. Wolfe, *Psychol. Rev.* 93, 269 (1986); R. Blake, *ibid.* 96, 145 (1989).

3. D. C. Van Essen, in *Cerebral Cortex*, vol. 3, *Visual Cortex*, A. Peters and E. G. Jones, Eds. (Plenum, New York, 1985), pp. 259–329; J. H. R. Maunsell and W. T. Newsome, *Annu. Rev. Neurosci.* 10, 363 (1987); W. T. Newsome and R. H. Wurtz, *Trends Neurosci.* 11, 394 (1988).
4. J. Myerson *et al.*, *Behav. Anal. Lett.* 1, 149 (1981).
5. The monkey was required to fixate on a spot that was presented to each eye sequentially. The location of the spot was adjusted for each eye so that the monkey made no saccade to refixate on it when the presentation was changed from one eye to the other. This approach allowed us to align the fixation target within the limits of resolution of our system (0.4°). The gratings were centered on the fused points. Separate psychophysical tests with random dot stereograms revealed that each monkey had normal stereoscopic fusion.
6. R. Fox *et al.*, *Vision Res.* 15, 849 (1975).
7. The onset and the gain of pursuit were determined by computer. All saccades were detected and excised. The onset of pursuit was computed by detecting a monotonic change in eye position of the appropriate speed (20 to 130% of the grating speed) and direction that moved the gaze at least 3 SD from the initial fixation position. The eye velocity was obtained by computing the slope of the regression line between the onset of pursuit and end of stimulus presentation. Eye velocity divided by the target velocity defined the pursuit gain.
8. The monkeys were prepared for recording with sterile surgical technique under pentobarbital anesthesia. Single units were recorded and isolated conventionally. Receptive fields were mapped with computer-generated gratings and spots that could be removed by hand with a joystick interface or that automatically drifted at different locations or directions while the monkey maintained fixation on a spot. A grating was positioned at the most sensitive region of the receptive field of a cell and drifted in 8 to 16 different directions to determine the directional tuning curve. After determination of the preferred direction, a grating was drifted in that direction in different locations of the monitor to map the borders of the receptive field.
9. W. T. Newsome *et al.*, *J. Neurophysiol.* 60, 604 (1988).
10. The neuronal latencies were determined from spike density functions that were derived by convolving the spike train with a Gaussian filter [J. M. MacPherson and J. W. Aldridge, *Brain Res.* 175, 183 (1979)]. The SD of the filter was the maximum of the video frame duration or the average interspike interval during the fixation period. The onset of activation was defined at the time when the spike density function deviated from the baseline before the stimulus by 3 SD. A statistical analysis of the relations between the neuronal response latency (NL), the pursuit latency (PL), and their difference (PL − NL) was performed [D. Commenges and J. Seal, *Brain Res.* 383, 350 (1986)]. There was essentially no relation between NL and PL (the average slope ± SE for the $n = 10$ cells was − 0.019 ± 0.021); in contrast there was a strong linear relation between PL − NL and PL (average slope ± SE = 1.132 ± 0.046 for the 10 cells). Furthermore, the ratio of the variance of NL to the variance of PL − NL was 17.84 ± 2.31 for $n = 10$ cells.
11. W. T. Newsome, K. H. Britten, J. A. Movshon, *Soc. Neurosci. Abstr.* 14, 458 (1988); K. H. Britten, W. T. Newsome, J. A. Movshon, *ibid.*, p. 458.
12. R. Blake and R. Overton, *Perception (London)* 8, 143 (1979).
13. We thank P. H. Schiller for his support; J. H. R. Maunsell, C. F. Stromeyer, J. Wu, J. M. Wolfe, and the reviewers for comments on the manuscript; E. Charles and D. Poeppel for participating in some recording; and M. E. Flynn-Sullivan for skilled technical assistance. N.K.L. was supported by NIH grant EY00676 and Office of Naval Research grant N00014-88-K-0164 to PHS, and J.D.S. was supported by NIH grant EY05959.

15 February 1989; accepted 31 May 1989

[7]

Separate visual pathways for perception and action

Melvyn A. Goodale and A. David Milner

Melvyn A. Goodale is at the Dept of Psychology, University of Western Ontario, London, Ontario N6A 5C2, Canada, and A. David Milner is at the Dept of Psychology, University of St Andrews, St Andrews KY16 9JU, UK.

Accumulating neuropsychological, electrophysiological and behavioural evidence suggests that the neural substrates of visual perception may be quite distinct from those underlying the visual control of actions. In other words, the set of object descriptions that permit identification and recognition may be computed independently of the set of descriptions that allow an observer to shape the hand appropriately to pick up an object. We propose that the ventral stream of projections from the striate cortex to the inferotemporal cortex plays the major role in the perceptual identification of objects, while the dorsal stream projecting from the striate cortex to the posterior parietal region mediates the required sensorimotor transformations for visually guided actions directed at such objects.

In an influential article that appeared in *Science* in 1969, Schneider[1] postulated an anatomical separation between the visual coding of the location of a stimulus and the identification of that stimulus. He attributed the coding of the location to the ancient retinotectal pathway, and the identification of the stimulus to the newer geniculostriate system; this distinction represented a significant departure from earlier monolithic descriptions of visual function. However, the notion of 'localization' failed to distinguish between the many different patterns of behaviour that vary with the spatial location of visual stimuli, only some of which turn out to rely on tectal mechanisms[2-4]. Nevertheless, even though Schneider's original proposal is no longer generally accepted, his distinction between object identification and spatial localization, between 'what' and 'where', has persisted in visual neuroscience.

Two cortical visual systems

In 1982, for example, Ungerleider and Mishkin[5] concluded that 'appreciation of an object's qualities and of its spatial location depends on the processing of different kinds of visual information in the inferior temporal and posterior parietal cortex, respectively.' They marshalled evidence from a number of electrophysiological, anatomical and behavioural studies suggesting that these two areas receive independent sets of projections from the striate cortex. They distinguished between a 'ventral stream' of projections that eventually reaches the inferotemporal cortex, and a 'dorsal stream' that terminates finally in the posterior parietal region. The proposed functions of these two streams were inferred largely from behavioural evidence derived from lesion studies. They noted that monkeys with lesions of the inferotemporal cortex were profoundly impaired in visual pattern discrimination and recognition[6], but less impaired in solving 'landmark' tasks, in which the location of a visual cue determines which of two alternative locations is rewarded. Quite the opposite pattern of results was observed in monkeys with posterior parietal lesions[7-9].

So, according to Ungerleider and Mishkin's 1982 version of the model of two visual systems, the inferotemporal lesions disrupted circuitry specialized for identifying objects, while the posterior parietal lesions interfered with neural mechanisms underlying spatial perception. Thus, within the visual domain, they made much the same functional distinction between identification and localization as Schneider, but mapped it onto the diverging ventral and dorsal streams of output from the striate cortex. Since 1982, there has been an explosion of information about the anatomy and electrophysiology of cortical visual areas[10,11] and, indeed, the connectional anatomy among these various areas largely confirms the existence of the two broad 'streams' of projections proposed by Ungerleider and Mishkin (see Fig. 1)[12,13].

It has recently been suggested[14] that these two streams can be traced back to the two main cytological subdivisions of retinal ganglion cells: one of these two subdivisions terminates selectively in the parvocellular layer, while the other terminates in the magnocellular layer of the lateral geniculate nucleus (LGN)[14-16]. Certainly, these 'parvo' and 'magno' subdivisions remain relatively segregated at the level of the primary visual cortex (V1) and in the adjacent visual area V2. They also appear to predominate, respectively, the innervation of area V4 and the middle temporal area (MT), which in turn provide the major visual inputs to the inferotemporal and posterior parietal cortex, respectively. However, it is becoming increasingly clear that the separation between magno and parvo information in the cortex is not as distinct as initially thought. For example, there is recent evidence for a parvo input into a subset of MT neurones[17] as well as for a large contribution from the magno pathway to V4 neurones[18] and to the 'blobs' in V1 (Ref. 19). In short, it now appears that the dorsal and the ventral streams each receive inputs from both the magno and the parvo pathways.

Two visuomotor systems: 'what' versus 'how'

Our alternative perspective on modularity in the cortical visual system is to place less emphasis on input distinctions (e.g. object location versus object qualities) and to take more account of output requirements[20,21]. It seems plausible from a functional standpoint that separate processing modules would have evolved to mediate the different uses to which vision can be put. This principle is already generally accepted in relation to 'automatic' types of behaviour such as saccadic eye movements[22], and it is possible that it could be extended to other systems for a range of behavioural skills such as visually guided reaching and grasping, in which close coordination is required between movements of the fingers, hands, upper limbs, head and eyes.

It is also our contention that the inputs and transformations required by these skilled visuomotor acts differ in important respects from those leading to what is generally understood as 'visual perception.' Indeed, as has been argued elsewhere, the functional modules supporting perceptual experience of the world may have evolved much more recently than those controlling actions within it[21]. In this article, it is proposed that this distinction ('what' versus 'how') – rather than the distinction between object vision and spatial vision ('what' versus 'where') – captures more appropriately the functional dichotomy between the ventral and dorsal projections.

Dissociation between prehension and apprehension

Neuropsychological studies of patients with damage to one projection system but not the other have also been cited in support of the model proposed by Ungerleider and Mishkin[5,23]. Patients with visual agnosia following brain damage that includes, for example, the occipitotemporal region, are often unable to recognize or describe common objects, faces, pictures, or abstract designs, even though they can navigate through the everyday world – at least at a local level – with considerable skill[24]. Conversely, patients suffering from optic ataxia following damage to the posterior parietal region are unable to reach accurately towards visual targets that they have no difficulty recognizing[25]. Such observations certainly appear to provide support in humans for an occipitotemporal system mediating object vision but not spatial vision, and a parietal system mediating spatial vision but not object vision.

Closer examination of the behaviour of such patients, however, leads to a different conclusion. Patients with optic ataxia not only have difficulty reaching in the right direction, but also in positioning their fingers or adjusting the orientation of their hand when reaching toward an object that can be oriented at different angles[25]. Such patients may also have trouble adjusting their grasp to reflect the size of the object they are asked to pick up.

Visually guided grasping was recently studied in a patient who had recovered from Balint's syndrome, in which bilateral parietal damage causes profound disorders of spatial attention, gaze and visually guided reaching[26]. While this patient had no difficulty in recognizing line drawings of common objects, her ability to pick up such objects remained quite impaired. For example, when she reached out for a small wooden block that varied in size from trial to trial, there was little relationship between the magnitude of the aperture between her index finger and thumb and the size of the block as the movement unfolded. Not only did she fail to show normal scaling of the grasping movement; she also made a large number of adjustments in her grasp as she closed in on the object – adjustments rarely observed in normal subjects. Such studies suggest that damage to the parietal lobe can impair the ability of patients to use information about the size, shape and orientation of an object to control the hand and fingers during a grasping movement, even though this same information can still be used to identify and describe the objects. Clearly, a 'disorder of spatial vision' fails to capture this range of visuomotor impairments.

There are, of course, other kinds of visuospatial disorders, many of which are associated with parietal lobe damage, while others are associated with temporal lobe lesions[27,28]. Unfortunately, we lack detailed analyses of the possible specificity of most such disorders: in many, the deficit may be restricted to particular behavioural tasks. For example, a recently described patient with a parietal injury performed

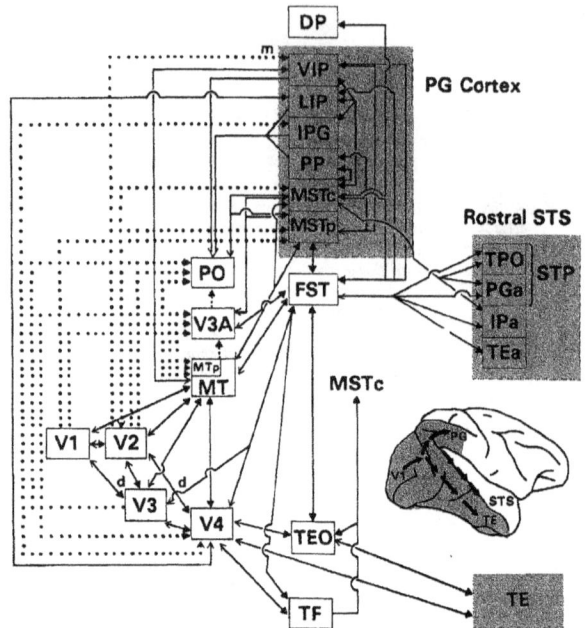

Fig. 1. *The 1982 version of Ungerleider and Mishkin's[5] model of two visual systems is illustrated in the small diagram of the monkey brain inset into the larger box diagram. In the original model, V1 is shown sending a dorsal stream of projections to the posterior parietal cortex (PG), and a ventral stream of projections to the inferotemporal cortex (TE). The box diagram illustrates one of the most recent versions of the interconnectivity of the visual cortical areas, showing that they can still be broadly segregated into dorsal and ventral streams. However, there is crosstalk between the different areas in the two streams, and there may be a third branch of processing projecting into the rostral superior temporal sulcus (STS) that is intimately connected with both the dorsal and ventral streams. (This is illustrated in both the brain and box diagrams.) Thus, the proposed segregation of input that characterized the dorsal and ventral streams in the original model is not nearly as clear cut as once was thought. (Modified, with permission, from Ref. 11.)*

poorly on a task in which visual guidance was needed to learn the correct route through a small ten-choice maze by moving a hand-held stylus[23]. However, he was quite unimpaired on a locomotor maze task in which he was required to move his whole body through space when working from a two-dimensional visual plan. Moreover, he had no difficulty in recalling a complex geometrical pattern, or in carrying out a task involving short-term spatial memory[29]. Such dissociations between performance on different 'spatial' tasks show that after parietal damage spatial information may still be processed quite well for some purposes, but not for others. Of course, the fact that visuospatial deficits can be fractionated in humans does not exclude combinations of such impairments occurring after large lesions, nor would it exclude possible selective input disorders occurring after smaller deafferentation lesions close to where the dorsal stream begins.

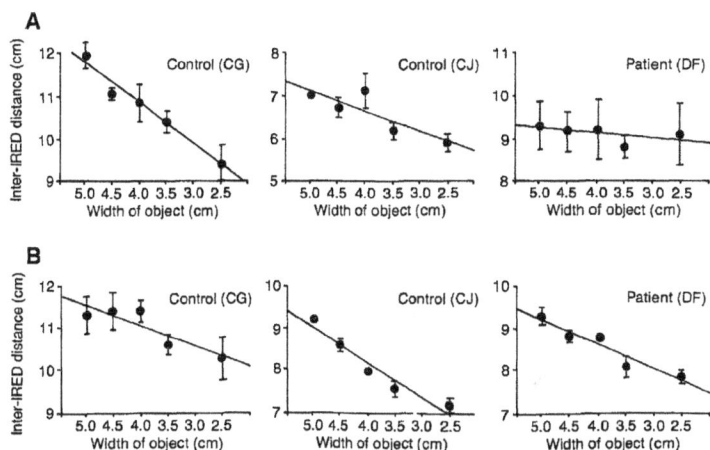

Fig. 2. *In both (A) the manual matching task and (B) the grasping task, five white plaques (each with an overall area of 25 cm² on the top surface, but with dimensions ranging from 5 × 5 cm to 2.5 × 10 cm) were presented, one at a time, at a viewing distance of approximately 45 cm. Diodes emitting infrared light (IREDs) were attached to the tips of the index finger and thumb of the right hand and were tracked with two infrared-sensitive cameras and stored on a WATSMART computer (Northern Digital Inc., Waterloo, Canada). The three-dimensional position of the IREDs and the changing distance between them were later reconstructed off line. (A) In the manual matching task, DF and two control subjects were instructed to indicate the width of each plaque over a series of randomly ordered trials by separating the index finger and thumb of their right hand. In DF, unlike the controls (CG and CJ), the aperture between the finger and thumb was not systematically related to the width of the target. DF also showed considerable trial to trial variability. (B) In contrast, when they were instructed to reach out and pick up each plaque, DF's performance was indistinguishable from that of the control subjects. The maximum aperture between the index finger and thumb, which was achieved well before contact, was systematically related to the width of the plaques in both DF and the two control subjects. In interpreting all these graphs, it is the slope of the function that is important rather than the absolute values plotted, since the placement of the IREDs and the size of the hand and fingers varied somewhat from subject to subject. Bars represent means ± SE. (Modified, with permission, from Ref. 31.)*

Complications also arise on the opposite side of the equation (i.e. in relation to the ventral stream), when the behaviour of patients with visual agnosia is studied in detail. The visual behaviour of one patient (DF) who developed a profound visual-form agnosia following carbon monoxide poisoning was recently studied. Although MRI revealed diffuse brain damage consistent with anoxia, most of the damage in the cortical visual areas was evident in areas 18 and 19, with area 17 apparently remaining largely intact. Despite her profound inability to recognize the size, shape and orientation of visual objects, DF showed strikingly accurate guidance of hand and finger movements directed at the very same objects[30,31]. Thus, when she was presented with a pair of rectangular blocks of the same or different dimensions, she was unable to distinguish between them. When she was asked to indicate the width of a single block by means of her index finger and thumb, her matches bore no relationship to the dimensions of the object and showed considerable trial to trial variability (Fig. 2A). However, when she was asked simply to reach out and pick up the block, the aperture between her index finger and thumb changed systematically with the width of the object, just as in normal subjects (Fig. 2B). In other words, DF scaled her grip to the dimensions of the objects she was about to pick up, even though she appeared to be unable to 'perceive' those dimensions.

A similar dissociation was seen in her responses to the orientation of stimuli. Thus, when presented with a large slot that could be placed in one of a number of different orientations, she showed great difficulty in indicating the orientation either verbally or manually (i.e. by rotating her hand or a hand-held card). Nevertheless, she was as good as normal subjects at reaching out and placing her hand or the card into the slot, turning her hand appropriately from the very onset of the movement[30,31].

These disparate neuropsychological observations lead us to propose that the visual projection system to the human parietal cortex provides action-relevant information about the structural characteristics and orientation of objects, and not just about their position. On the other hand, projections to the temporal lobe may furnish our visual perceptual experience, and it is these that we postulate to be severely damaged in DF.

Dorsal and ventral systems in the monkey

How well do electrophysiological studies of the two projection systems in the visual cortex of the monkey support the distinction we are making? While any correlations between human neuropsychology and monkey neurophysiology should only be made with caution, it is likely that humans share many features of visual processing with our primate relatives – particularly with the Old World monkeys in which most of the electrophysiology has been carried out. Furthermore, lesion studies of the two projection systems in the monkey should show parallels with the results of work done on human patients.

It was noted earlier that although there are differences in the major retinal origins of inputs to the dorsal and ventral systems in the monkey brain, there is subsequently a good deal of pooling of information. Moreover, there are convergent similarities in what is extracted within the two systems. For example, both orientation and disparity selectivity are present in neurones in both the magno and parvo systems within cortical areas V1 and V2 (Ref. 15).

Nevertheless, there are special features in the properties of individual neurones in the posterior parietal cortex (and in its major input areas V3A and MT) that are not found in the ventral system. The most striking feature of neurones in the posterior parietal region is not their spatial selectivity (indeed, like those of inferotemporal cells, their receptive fields are typically large), but rather the fact that their responses depend greatly on the concurrent behaviour of the animal with respect to the stimulus. Separate subsets of cells in the posterior parietal cortex have been shown to be implicated in visual fixation, pursuit and saccadic eye movements, eye–hand coordination, and visually guided reaching movements[32]. Many cells in the posterior parietal region have gaze-dependent responses; i.e. where the animal is looking determines the response amplitude of the cell (although not the retinal location of its receptive field)[33]. In reviewing these studies, Andersen[32] emphasizes that most neurones in this area 'exhibit both sensory-related and movement-related activity.' In a particularly interesting recent development, Taira *et al.*[34] have shown that some parietal cells are sensitive to those visual qualities of an object that determine the posture of the hand and fingers during a grasping movement. They studied neurones selectively associated with hand movements made by the monkey in reaching and picking up solid objects. Many of these cells were selective for the visual appearance of the object that was to be manipulated, including its size and in several cases its orientation.

The posterior parietal cortex may receive such form information from one or both of the areas V3 or V4, both of which project to area MT[35]. Other visual inputs pass through area MT and the adjacent medial superior temporal (MST) area, both of which contain cells variously selective for object motion in different directions, including rotation and motion in depth[32]. Thus, the posterior parietal cortex appears to receive the necessary inputs for continually updating the monkey's knowledge of the disposition and structural qualities of objects in its three-dimensional ego-space. Also, many motion-sensitive cells in the posterior parietal cortex itself appear to be well suited for the visual monitoring of limb position during reaching behaviour[36]; in contrast, motion-sensitive cells in the temporal lobe have been reported not to respond to such self-produced visual motion[37]. As for the output pathways, the posterior parietal region is strongly linked with those pre-motor regions of the frontal cortex directly implicated in ocular control[33,38], reaching movements of the limb[39], and grasping actions of the hand and fingers[39].

Thus, the parietal cortex is strategically placed to serve a mediating role in the visual guidance and integration of prehensile and other skilled actions (see Ref. 40 for a detailed account of this argument). The results of behavioural analyses of monkeys with posterior parietal damage support this further. Like patients with optic ataxia, such animals fail to reach correctly for visual targets[41], and they also have difficulty in shaping and orienting their hands when attempting to retrieve food[42,43]. Their reaching impairment is, therefore, one symptom of a wider visuomotor disorder, and most of the deficits that have been reported on 'maze' tasks following posterior parietal damage may also be visuomotor in nature[9,40].

Nonetheless, neurones in the dorsal stream do not show the high-resolution selectivity characteristic of neurones in the inferotemporal cortex, which are strikingly sensitive to form, pattern and colour[10]. In this and in neighbouring temporal lobe areas, some cells respond selectively to faces, to hands, or to the appearance of particular actions in others[44]. There-

fore, it is unsurprising that monkeys with inferotemporal lesions have profound deficits in visual recognition; however, as noted by Pribram[45], they remain highly adept at the visually demanding skill of catching flies!

A further peculiarity of many visual cells in the temporal cortex is that they continue to maintain their selective responsiveness over a wide range of size, colour, optical and viewpoint transformations of the object[44,46]. Such cells, far from providing the momentary information necessary for guiding action, specifically ignore such changing details. Consistent with this, behavioural studies have shown that by lesioning the inferotemporal cortex (but not the posterior parietal cortex), a monkey is less able to generalize its recognition of three-dimensional shape across viewing conditions[47,48].

Visual and attentional requirements for perception and action

As DeYoe and Van Essen[15] have suggested, 'parietal and temporal lobes could both be involved in shape analysis but associated with different computational strategies.' For the purposes of identification, learning and distal (e.g. social) transactions, visual coding often (though not always[44,46]) needs to be 'object-centred'; i.e. constancies of shape, size, colour, lightness, and location need to be maintained across different viewing conditions. The above evidence from behavioural and physiological studies supports the view that the ventral stream of processing plays an important role in the computation of such object-specific descriptions. In contrast, *action* upon the object requires that the location of the object and its particular disposition and motion with respect to the observer is encoded. For this purpose, coding of shape would need to be largely 'viewer-centred'[49], with the egocentric coordinates of the surface of the object or its contours being computed each time the action occurs. We predict that shape-encoding cells in the dorsal system should predominantly have this property. Nevertheless, certain constancies, such as size, would be necessary for accurate scaling of grasp aperture, and it might therefore be expected that the visual properties of the manipulation cells found by Taira *et al.*[34] in the posterior parietal region would have this property.

It is often suggested that the neuronal properties of the posterior parietal cortex qualify it as the prime mediator of visuospatial attention[50]. Certainly, many cells (e.g. in area 7a) are modulated by switches of attention to different parts of the visual field[51]. (Indeed, the 'landmark' disorder that follows posterior parietal damage in monkeys may be primarily due to a failure to attend or orient rather than a failure to localize[9,40,52].) However, it is now known that attentional modulation occurs in neurones in many parts of the cortex, including area V4 and the inferotemporal region within the ventral stream[53,54]. This might explain the occurrence of landmark deficits after inferotemporal as well as posterior parietal damage[7,8].

In general terms, attention needs to be switched to particular locations and objects whenever they are the targets either for intended action[51,55] or for identification[54]. In either case, this selection seems typically to be spatially based. Thus, human subjects performing manual aiming movements have a predilection to attend to visual stimuli that occur within the 'action space' of the hand[56]. In this instance the attentional facilitation might be mediated by mechanisms within the dorsal projection system; in other instances it is probably mediated by the ventral system. Indeed, the focus of lesions causing the human attentional disorder of 'unilateral neglect' is parietotemporal (unlike the superior parietal focus for optic ataxia[25]), as is the focus for object constancy impairments[57]. We conclude that spatial attention is physiologically non-unitary[55], and may be as much associated with the ventral system as with the dorsal.

A speculation about awareness

The evidence from the brain-damaged patient DF described earlier suggests that the two cortical pathways may be differentiated with respect to their access to consciousness. DF certainly appears to have no conscious perception of the orientation or dimensions of objects, although she can pick them up with remarkable adeptness. It may be that information can be processed in the dorsal system without reaching consciousness, and that this prevents interference with the perceptual constancies intrinsic to many operations within the ventral system that do result in awareness. Intrusions of viewer-centred information could disrupt the continuity of object identities across changing viewpoints and illumination conditions.

If this argument is correct, then there should be occasions when normal subjects are unaware of changes in the visual array to which their motor system is expertly adjusting. An example of such a dissociation has been reported in a study on eye–hand coordination during visually guided aiming[58]. Subjects were unable to report, even in forced-choice testing, whether or not a target had changed position during a saccadic eye movement, although correction saccades and manual aiming movements directed at the target showed near-perfect adjustments for the unpredictable target shift. In other words, an illusory perceptual constancy of target position was maintained in the face of large amendments in visuomotor control. In another recent example, it has been reported that the compelling illusion of slowed motion of a moving coloured object that is experienced at equiluminance does not prevent accurate ocular pursuit under the same conditions (see Ref. to Lisberger and Movshon, cited in Ref. 59). Such observations may illustrate the independent functioning of the ventral and dorsal systems in normal humans.

We do not, however, wish to claim that the division of labour we are proposing is an absolute one. In particular, the above suggestion does not imply that visual inputs are necessarily blocked from awareness during visuomotor acts, although that may be a useful option to have available. Rather, we assume that the two systems will often be simultaneously activated (with somewhat different visual information), thereby providing visual experience during skilled action. Indeed, the two systems appear to engage in direct crosstalk; for example, the posterior parietal and inferotemporal cortex themselves interconnect[33,60] and both in turn project to areas in the superior temporal sulcus[11–13]. There, cells that are highly form selective lie close to others that have motion specificity[44], thus providing scope for cooperation

between the two systems (see Fig. 1). In addition, there are many polysensory neurons in these areas, so that not only visual but also cross-modal interaction between these networks may be possible. This may provide some of the integration needed for the essential unity and cohesion of most of our perceptual experience and behaviour, although overall control of awareness may ultimately be the responsibility of superordinate structures in the frontal cortex[61]. Nevertheless, it is feasible to maintain the hypothesis that a *necessary condition* for conscious visual experience is that the ventral system be activated.

Concluding remarks

Despite the interactions between the dorsal and ventral systems, the converging lines of evidence reviewed above indicate that each stream uses visual information about objects and events in the world in different ways. These differences are largely a reflection of the specific transformations of input required by perception and action. Functional modularity in cortical visual systems, we believe, extends from input right through to output.

Selected references
1 Schneider, G. E. (1969) *Science* 163, 895–902
2 Ingle, D. J. (1982) in *Analysis of Visual Behavior* (Ingle, D. J., Goodale, M. A. and Mansfield, R. J. W., eds), pp. 67–109, MIT Press
3 Goodale, M. A. and Murison, R. (1975) *Brain Res.* 88, 243–255
4 Goodale, M. A. and Milner, A. D. (1982) in *Analysis of Visual Behavior* (Ingle, D. J., Goodale, M. A. and Mansfield, R. J. W., eds), pp. 263–299, MIT Press
5 Ungerleider, L. G. and Mishkin, M. (1982) in *Analysis of Visual Behavior* (Ingle, D. J., Goodale, M. A. and Mansfield, R. J. W., eds), pp. 549–586, MIT Press
6 Gross, C. G. (1973) *Prog. Physiol. Psychol.* 5, 77–123
7 Pohl, W. (1973) *J. Comp. Physiol. Psychol.* 82, 227–239
8 Ungerleider, L. G. and Brody, B. A. (1977) *Exp. Neurol.* 56, 265–280
9 Milner, A. D., Ockleford, E. M. and Dewar, W. (1977) *Cortex* 13, 350–360.
10 Desimone, R. and Ungerleider, L. G. (1989) in *Handbook of Neuropsychology*, Vol. 2 (Boller, F. and Grafman, J., eds), pp. 267–299, Elsevier
11 Boussaoud, D., Ungerleider, L. G. and Desimone, R. (1990) *J. Comp. Neurol.* 296, 462–495
12 Morel, A. and Bullier, J. (1990) *Visual Neurosci.* 4, 555–578
13 Baizer, J. S., Ungerleider, L. G. and Desimone, R. (1991) *J. Neurosci.* 11, 168–190
14 Livingstone, M. and Hubel, D. (1988) *Science* 240, 740–749
15 DeYoe, E. A. and Van Essen, D. C. (1988) *Trends Neurosci.* 11, 219–226
16 Schiller, P. H. and Logothetis, N. K. (1990) *Trends Neurosci.* 13, 392–398
17 Maunsell, J. H. R., Nealy, T. A. and De Priest, D. D. (1990) *J. Neurosci.* 10, 3323–3334
18 Nealey, T. A. and Maunsell, J. H. R. (1991) *Invest. Ophthalmol. Visual Sci.* 32 (Suppl.) 1117
19 Ferrera, V. P., Nealey, T. A. and Maunsell, J. H. R. (1991) *Invest. Ophthalmol. Visual Sci.* 32 (Suppl.) 1117
20 Goodale, M. A. (1983) in *Behavioral Approaches to Brain Research* (Robinson, T. E., ed.), pp. 41–61, Oxford University Press
21 Goodale, M. A. (1988) in *Computational Processes in Human Vision: An Interdisciplinary Perspective* (Pylyshyn, Z., ed.), pp. 262–285, Ablex
22 Sparks, D. L. and May, L. E. (1990) *Annu. Rev. Neurosci.* 13, 309–336
23 Newcombe, F., Ratcliff, G. and Damasio, H. (1987) *Neuropsychologia* 25, 149–161
24 Farah, M. (1990) *Visual Agnosia*, MIT Press
25 Perenin, M-T. and Vighetto, A. (1988) *Brain* 111, 643–674
26 Jakobson, L. S., Archibald, Y. M., Carey, D. and Goodale, M. A. (1991) *Neuropsychologia* 29, 803–809
27 Milner, B. (1965) *Neuropsychologia* 3, 317–338.

28 Smith, M. L. and Milner, B. (1989) *Neuropsychologia* 27, 71–81
29 Ettlinger, G. (1990) *Cortex* 26, 319–341
30 Milner, A. D. *et al.* (1991) *Brain* 114, 405–428
31 Goodale, M. A., Milner, A. D., Jakobson, L. S. and Carey, D. P. (1991) *Nature* 349, 154–156
32 Andersen, R. A. (1987) in *Higher Functions of the Brain, Part 2 (The Nervous System, Vol. V, Handbook of Physiology, Section 1)* (Mountcastle, V. B., Plum, F. and Geiger, S. R., eds), pp. 483–518, American Physiological Association
33 Andersen, R. A., Asanuma, C., Essick, G. and Siegel, R. M. (1990) *J. Comp. Neurol.* 296, 65–113
34 Taira, M., Mine, S., Georgopoulos, A. P., Murata, A. and Sakata, H. (1990) *Exp. Brain Res.* 83, 29–36
35 Felleman, D. J. and Van Essen, D. C. (1987) *J. Neurophysiol.* 57, 889–920
36 Mountcastle, V. B., Motter, B. C., Steinmetz, M. A. and Duffy, C. J. (1984) in *Dynamic Aspects of Neocortical Function* (Edelman, G. M., Gall, W. E. and Cowan, W. M., eds), pp. 159–193, Wiley
37 Perrett, D. I., Mistlin, A. J., Harries, M. H. and Chitty, A. J. (1990) in *Vision and Action: The Control of Grasping* (Goodale, M. A., ed.), pp. 163–180, Ablex
38 Cavada, C. and Goldman-Rakic, P. S. (1989) *J. Comp. Neurol.* 287, 422–445
39 Gentilucci, M. and Rizzolatti, G. (1990) in *Vision and Action: The Control of Grasping* (Goodale, M. A., ed.), pp. 147–162, Ablex
40 Milner, A. D. and Goodale, M. A. *Prog. Brain Res.* (in press)
41 Bates, J. A. V. and Ettlinger, G. (1960) *Arch. Neurol.* 3, 177–192
42 Faugier-Grimaud, S., Frenois, C. and Stein, D. G. (1978) *Neuropsychologia* 16, 151–168
43 Haaxma, R. and Kuypers, H. G. J. M. (1975) *Brain* 98, 239–260
44 Perrett, D. I., Mistlin, A. J. and Chitty, A. J. (1987) *Trends Neurosci.* 10, 358–364
45 Pribram, K. H. (1967) in *Brain Function and Learning* (Lindsley, D. B. and Lumsdaine, A. A., eds), pp. 79–122, University of California Press
46 Perrett, D. I. *et al.* (1991) *Exp. Brain Res.* 86, 159–173
47 Humphrey, N. K. and Weiskrantz, L. (1969) *Quart. J. Exp. Psychol.* 21, 225–238
48 Weiskrantz, L. and Saunders, R. C. (1984) *Brain* 107, 1033–1072
49 Marr, D. (1982) *Vision*, Freeman
50 Goldberg, M. E. and Colby, C. L. (1989) in *Handbook of Neuropsychology* (Vol. 2) (Boller, F. and Grafman, J., eds), pp. 301–315, Elsevier
51 Bushnell, M. C., Goldberg, M. E. and Robinson, D. L. (1981) *J. Neurophysiol.* 46, 755–772
52 Lawler, K. A. and Cowey, A. (1987) *Exp. Brain Res.* 65, 695–698
53 Fischer, B. and Boch, R. (1981) *Exp. Brain Res.* 44, 129–137
54 Moran, J. and Desimone, R. (1985) *Science* 229, 782–784
55 Rizzolatti, G., Gentilucci, M. and Matelli, M. (1985) in *Attention and Performance XI* (Posner, M. I. and Marin, O. S. M., eds), pp. 251–265, Erlbaum
56 Tipper, S., Lortie, C. and Baylis, G. *J. Exp. Psychol. Human Percept. Perform.* (in press)
57 Warrington, E. K. and Taylor, A. M. (1973) *Cortex* 9, 152–164
58 Goodale, M. A., Pelisson, D. and Prablanc, C. (1986) *Nature* 320, 748–750
59 Sejnowski, T. J. (1991) *Nature* 352, 669–670
60 Cavada, C. and Goldman-Rakic, P. S. (1989) *J. Comp. Neurol.* 287, 393–421
61 Posner, M. I. and Rothbart, M. K. (1991) in *The Neuropsychology of Consciousness* (Milner, A. D. and Rugg, M. D., eds), pp. 91–111, Academic Press

Acknowledgements
The authors are grateful to D. Carey, L. Jakobson and D. Perrett for their comments on a draft of this paper.

Part III
Object Interpolation and Completion

[8]

Subjective Contours

Certain combinations of incomplete figures give rise to clearly visible contours even when the contours do not actually exist. It appears that such contours are supplied by the visual system

by Gaetano Kanizsa

If we examine the conditions that give rise to visible contours, we usually find that a contour is perceived when there is a jump in the stimulation between adjacent areas. The jump may be due to a difference in brightness or a difference in color. There are conditions, however, that cause us to perceive contours in visual areas that are completely homogeneous. For example, in the illustration below the solid triangles in the center of each figure appear to have well-defined contours, but close examination of the contours where they cross an open area reveals that they have no physical

basis. If you fix your gaze on one of these contours, it disappears, yet if you direct your gaze to the entire figure, the contours appear to be real.

The phenomenon of contours that appear in the absence of physical gradients has aroused considerable interest among psychologists on both the experimental and the theoretical level. A number of variants of the effect have been discovered, and several explanations have been proposed for it. Here I shall describe some of the more interesting properties of the effect and examine some of the attempted explanations.

First, however, let us consider a related visual phenomenon: the phenomenon of virtual lines.

When we view three dots that are equidistant from one another and are not in a straight line, the visual system spontaneously organizes the dots into a triangle. In addition the three dots appear to be connected by three straight lines. These lines are called virtual, and although they are not actually seen, they are a real presence in our visual experience. They are far more compelling than other connecting lines that can be imagined. For example, the three dots

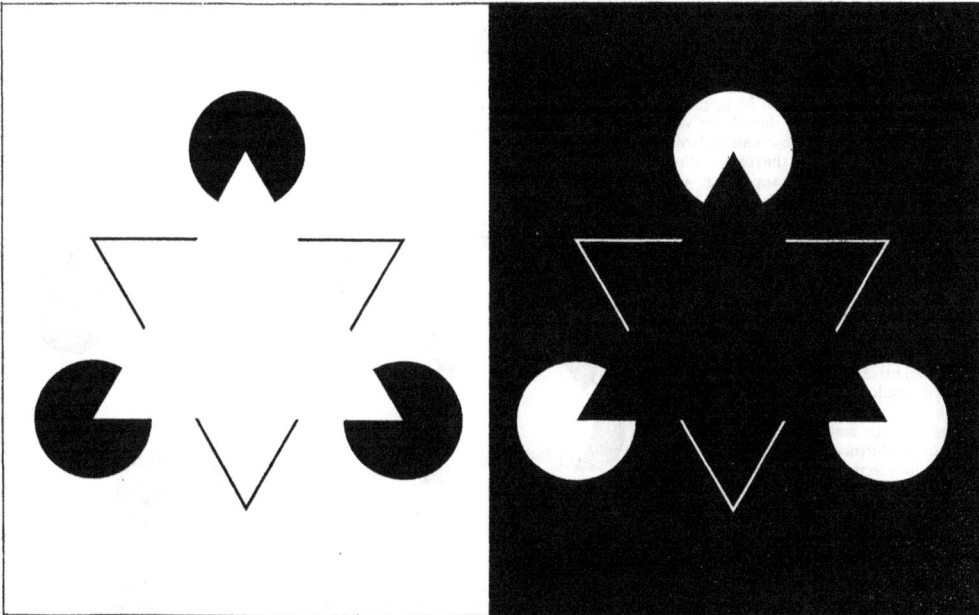

TWO SUBJECTIVE TRIANGLES, one whiter than white and the other blacker than black, appear to have distinct contours, but when the contours are examined closely, they disappear. The contours are subjective and have no physical reality. The region bounded by the subjective contours appears to be more intense than the background even though the color of the inner and the outer regions is identical.

could just as readily be points on a circle, but the curved connecting lines of the circle are more difficult to "see" than the straight lines of the triangle.

Because virtual lines are only phenomenally present and do not have a sensory modality, one may speak of them as being "amodal." Another kind of amodal contour is found in partially hidden figures [*see top illustration at right*]. Consider a black rectangle that has a gray ring behind it and a colored ring in front of it. Although the missing contours of the rectangle are not actually seen, they nonetheless have a strong phenomenal presence. If the two rings in the illustration are now made black, a new effect results. Both black rings complete themselves behind the black rectangle in an amodal manner, but the contours of the rectangle are visible in their entirety. Even in the homogeneous black regions where the rings overlap, the contours of the rectangle are visible. In other words, the contours have acquired a visual modality.

This "modal" presence is also found in the contours of the central triangles in the illustration on the opposite page. Since those contours appear in the absence of the gradients that normally produce modal, or visible, contours, the situation is clearly anomalous. For that reason I prefer to call such contours anomalous contours. In order to emphasize the fact that the contours have no physical basis over most of their length, other investigators have called them subjective contours. They are also known as illusory contours. Whatever term is used, the phenomenon is the same.

What factors are involved in the formation of subjective contours? Analysis of many examples of the phenomenon yields the following common characteristics. First, the region that is bounded by the subjective contours appears to be brighter than the background, even though the visual stimulation provided by both regions is exactly the same. Second, the region within the subjective contours appears as an opaque surface that is superposed on the other figures in the illustration.

The subjective contours we have considered up to this point have all been straight lines. Is it possible to create curved subjective contours? As the middle and bottom illustrations at the right demonstrate, there are a variety of ways for generating such subjective contours. Indeed, even amorphous subjective figures can be created.

The strength of the phenomenon of subjective contours can be measured in part by determining the resistance such contours show to interference by real lines. When a real line intersects a subjective contour, the contour in that region disappears, indicating that it has a relatively low degree of resistance to interference. On the other hand, the opaque subjective surface displays surprising resistance: it appears to pass under lines that intersect it [*see top illustration on page 51*]. The subjective sur-

AMODAL AND MODAL CONTOURS are found in overlapping figures. Amodal contours are not actually seen, but they have a strong phenomenal presence. For example, the missing contours of the black rectangle complete themselves behind the colored ring in an amodal manner. Modal contours, on the other hand, appear to be visible. For example, the contours of the rectangle at the right are visible even in the regions where they overlap the black rings.

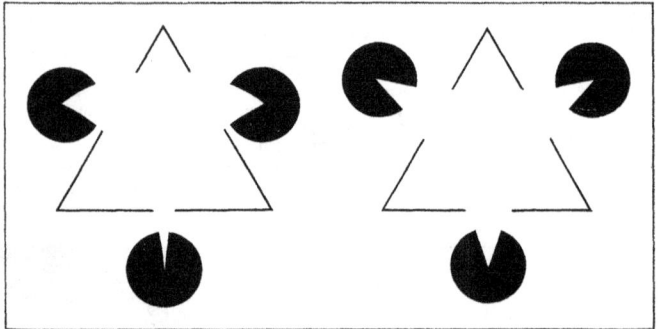

CURVED SUBJECTIVE CONTOURS are created by sectors with curved angles (*left*). Sectors with straight angles can create curved contours if angles are not aligned with one another.

GEOMETRIC REGULARITY is not a necessary condition for the formation of subjective surfaces and contours. Amorphous shapes are possible and irregular figures can generate contours.

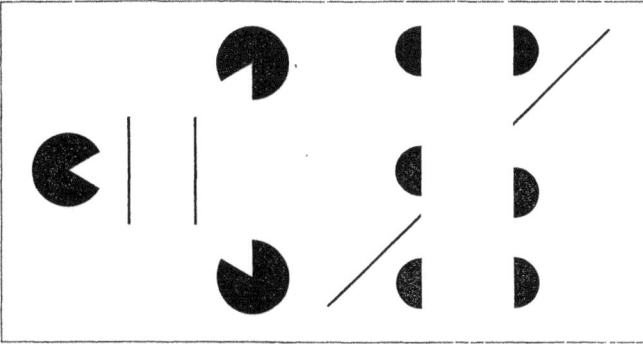

OPTICAL ILLUSIONS show that subjective contours have the same functional effects as real contours. In the Ponzo illusion (*left*), although both vertical lines are the same length, the effect of the subjective triangle is to make the line at the left appear to be longer. In the Poggendorf illusion the subjective surface gives rise to an apparent displacement of the slanted line.

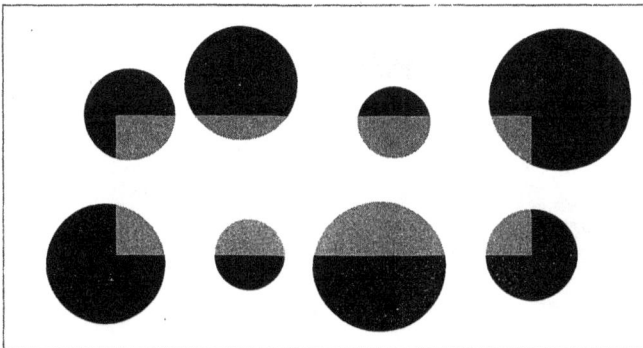

TRANSPARENT SUBJECTIVE SURFACES, as well as opaque ones, can be produced. The transparent surface, with clearly visible contours, seems to lie in a plane in front of black disks.

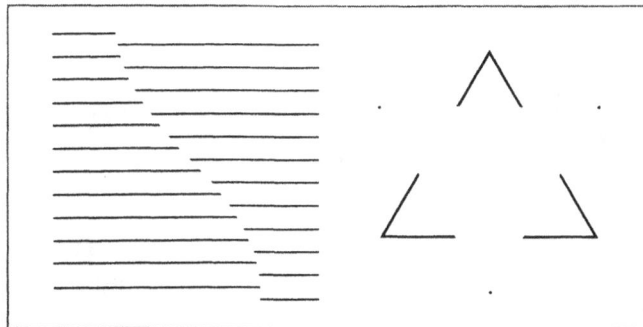

CONTOUR-DETECTOR HYPOTHESIS states that subjective contours are generated by partial activation of contour detectors in the visual system by short line segments in the stimulus. Subjective contours, however, can have an orientation completely different from that of the line segments (*left*). Furthermore, line segments are not necessary for generation of subjective contours (*right*). Curved subjective contour formed by line segments also demonstrates that differences in brightness due to contrast are not needed for formation of subjective contours.

face also displays strong resistance to interference within its borders. If large dark spots are placed inside the borders, the spots do not become part of the background but rather appear to be on the subjective surface. What happens when the background, instead of being homogeneous, has a texture? It turns out that a texture does not impede the formation of subjective contours or surfaces.

A number of optical illusions are produced by the reciprocal action between lines and surfaces. These optical illusions offer an opportunity to ascertain whether subjective contours and shapes have the same functional effects as objective, or real, contours and shapes. In many instances subjective contours and shapes are able to duplicate the illusion created by objective ones. As the top illustration at the left demonstrates, subjective contours and surfaces will interact with physically real lines to give rise to familiar optical illusions.

As we have seen, one of the characteristics of subjective surfaces is that they appear to be superposed on the other figures in the illustration. We have also seen that the subjective surface appears to be opaque. It is not difficult, however, to produce transparent subjective surfaces with distinct subjective contours [*see middle illustration at left*].

In most of the situations we have been examining the subjective surface appears to be brighter than the background, even though the two regions are identical in brightness and color. It is possible that the brightness of the subjective surface is due to contrast enhancement. Such enhancement is generally found when a light surface is adjacent to one dark surface or more. The intensity of the effect depends on the extent of the dark surface. Although the brightness-contrast effect may play a role in creating subjective surfaces, it is not a necessary condition for the formation of such surfaces or contours. This is readily demonstrated in the middle illustration on the opposite page, where a substantial reduction in the amount of black does not diminish the effect. A decisive item of evidence that contrast is not necessary for the formation of a subjective contour is presented in the figure at the left in the bottom illustration at the left. In this figure there are no differences in brightness that could be attributed to contrast, yet a curved subjective contour between the line segments is clearly visible.

It has been suggested by some investigators that subjective contours can be explained in terms of the partial activation of contour-detector cells in the visual system. According to this hypothesis, the short line segments in the visual stimulus activate some of the contour detectors, and signals from the activated detectors are interpreted as being a stimulus from a continuous line. The hypothesis does not stand up to careful examination, however. In many cases a subjective contour does not continue in the same direction as the stimulus line seg-

RESISTANCE TO INTERFERENCE is a measure of the perceptual strength of subjective surfaces. A subjective surface appears to pass under lines that intersect with it (*left*), but subjective contours are destroyed by the line. Spots inside the borders of the subjective surface become part of it (*middle*). The formation of subjective contours or surfaces is not impeded by the presence of a texture (*right*).

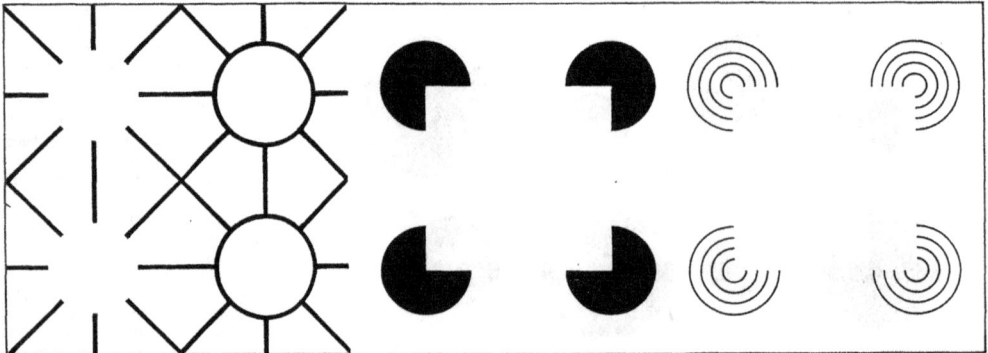

ENHANCED BRIGHTNESS of subjective surfaces is not due to contrast. If contrast were a primary condition of the effect, the black-ringed circles should appear to be brighter than the subjective circles (*left*). Reducing amount of black does not diminish the effect (*right*).

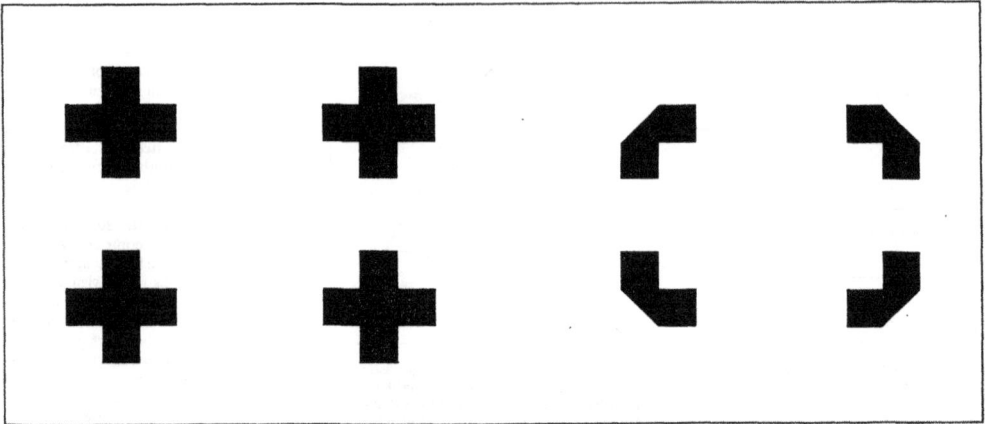

COMPLETE FIGURES do not generate subjective surfaces. Although crosses provide outlines of a rectangle, the rectangle is not perceived as a surface. When crosses are cut in half, a subjective rectangle is perceived and the half crosses are now seen as mutilated hexagons.

51

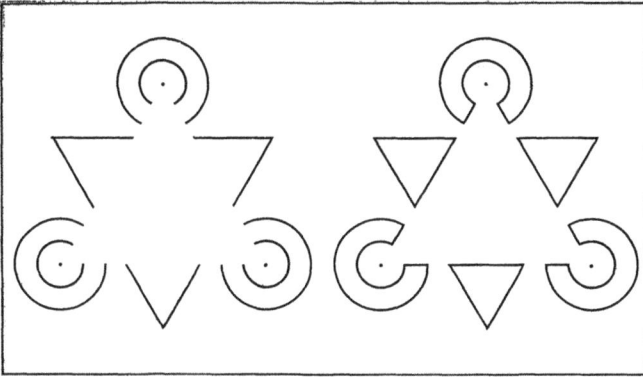

FIGURES WITH OPEN BORDERS appear to be incomplete. In order to complete the figures the visual system superposes an opaque surface that fills the gaps in the figures. Because the surface must have borders the necessary contours are also supplied by the visual system. If borders of figures are closed, there is no further need for completion and contours disappear.

ments. Moreover, line segments are not necessary for the generation of subjective contours. In some instances the line segments can be replaced by dots and subjective contours will still be perceived [*see figure at right in bottom illustration on page 50*].

There is one condition, I have found, that is always present in the formation of subjective contours That condition is the presence in the visual field of certain elements that are incomplete, which on completion are transformed into simpler stable and regular figures. For example, it could be said that the figure at the left in the illustration on page 48 consists of three black sectors and three angles. Each of these figural elements is incomplete in some way. Most observers, however, report that they see a white triangle covering three black disks and another triangle with a black border. This perceptual organization has obvious advantages from the standpoint of simplicity and stability The three angles become a

triangle, a stabler and more balanced figure. The three circular sectors acquire completeness and regularity by becoming disks In order for this perceptual organization to materialize, however, the white area in the center must be seen as an opaque triangle that is superposed on the other figures. And since the triangle must have a border, the necessary contours are supplied by the visual system. The contours are therefore the result of perceiving a surface and not vice versa. The subjective surface in turn is generated by the tendency of the visual system to complete certain figural elements

If these assertions are correct, we should be able to demonstrate that subjective contours and shapes will not be perceived when the visual field does not contain incomplete figural elements Since figures with open borders tend to appear incomplete, it is not difficult to create subjective contours with them If we close the borders on these figures and make no other changes, the subjec-

tive contours disappear [*see top illustration on this page*].

The following, I believe, offers further confirmation of the completion hypothesis. At the left in the bottom illustration on the preceding page there are four black crosses on a white field. In spite of the fact that the crosses provide the outlines of a rectangle in the central region, we do not perceive the rectangle as a subjective surface The reason is that the crosses are balanced and self-sufficient figures and do not require completion. When the crosses are cut in half, however, a subjective surface appears in the central area. The half crosses are in this case more likely to be seen as mutilated hexagons.

We have seen that irregularly shaped subjective figures can be produced In most of my examples the incomplete figures I have used to create subjective contours have been regular and symmetrical. Although geometric figures may enhance the effect, however, they are by no means necessary [*see bottom illustration on page 49*].

Finally, is it possible to generate subjective contours that meet and form a subjective angle? Paolo Sambin of the University of Padua found that an incomplete cross gives rise to such an effect [*see bottom illustration on this page*]. According to Sambin, the rectangular shape of the subjective surface that is perceived is produced by the resistance of the arms of the cross to invasion by the subjective surface. Without such resistance the subjective contour would assume the shape of a circle. The validity of his hypothesis can be demonstrated by narrowing the arms of the cross to the point where the invasion of the internal area is minimal. Under those conditions the subjective surface that is perceived has the form of a circle

Another example of contour perception in the absence of brightness gradients is found in the random-dot stereograms created by Bela Julesz of Bell Laboratories These stereograms do not reveal any contours when they are viewed monocularly, but when they are viewed with a stereoscope, they combine to form three-dimensional shapes and contours. Stanley Coren of the New School for Social Research has advanced the hypothesis that the perceptual mechanism giving rise to subjective contours and shapes is the same as the mechanism giving rise to three-dimensional depth perception

Since the formation of subjective contours is usually connected with the generation of surfaces and their stratification, or apparent layering, the line of reasoning proposed by Coren may be valid. On the other hand, in all the cases that we have examined stratification depends on the completion of some figural elements When there is no need for completion, stratification does not occur and there are no subjective contours Once more the primary factor seems to be the tendency to completion. Stratification seems to arise as a function of this completion

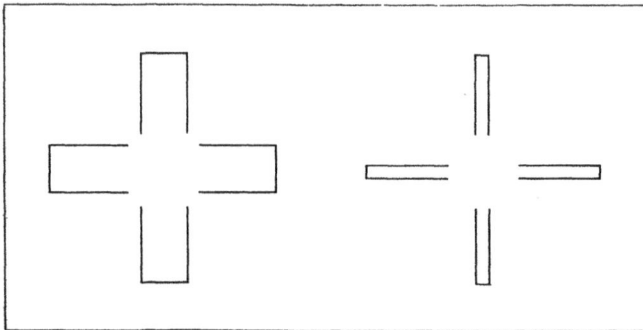

INCOMPLETE CROSS (*left*) gives rise to the unusual phenomenon of subjective angles. The angles are formed by the contours of the subjective square that covers central portion of the cross. Rectangular shape of the subjective surface is attributed to the resistance of arms of cross to invasion by the surface. If arms of cross are narrowed, circular subjective surface results.

[9]

Perceiving Objects Across Gaps in Space and Time

Philip J. Kellman and Thomas F. Shipley

Looking through a dense hedge, an observer may see only scattered spots of color from the scene behind. When the same observer looks while walking, however, the scene becomes clear. Somehow, the human visual system integrates spatially fragmentary information over time to achieve perception of objects and spatial layout. Such representations of bounded objects and surfaces in the three-dimensional (3-D) world are among the most remarkable products of visual perception. Obtaining them requires the solution of several difficult problems by the visual system.

One problem is detecting, from spatial variation in luminance, chromaticity, or texture, the projections of object boundaries. Work on edge-

Philip J. Kellman is Associate Professor of Psychology at Swarthmore College and Adjunct Professor at the University of Pennsylvania. His research focuses on perception of objects, motion, and space in human adults and infants. **Thomas F. Shipley** is Assistant Professor of Psychology at the University of Georgia in Athens. Address correspondence to Philip J. Kellman, Department of Psychology, Swarthmore College, Swarthmore, PA 19081.

detection has produced a number of proposals about specific variables that might be useful and how they might be detected.[1] The outputs of such processing, however, are surprisingly remote from a description of the objects and boundaries in the world. The primary culprit, as in the hedge example, is occlusion. In the 3-D world, projection of an object to the eyes of an observer is more often than not interrupted by nearer objects. As a consequence, rarely do the projected shapes reaching the observer include all the surfaces of an object oriented toward the observer. Another consequence is that most projected edges mark locations where one surface ends, but the other passes behind the first. Locating edges, by itself, does not indicate which side is bounded.

Occlusion often causes a single object to project to the eyes in multiple, spatially separated regions. Conversely, sometimes homogeneous areas in the optical projection come from separate objects in the world. Figure 1 contains examples of both of these effects. The situation is complicated further when objects or observers move. Parts of an object that project to an observer's eyes at one moment become occluded, whereas previously hidden areas become visible. The momentary

shapes of these projected areas bear little similarity to the shapes of the objects in the scene.

Despite the fragmentary nature of the input, human perceivers ordinarily have little difficulty detecting the unity and boundaries of objects. Explanations for this ability have been elusive. On some accounts, factors outside the stimulus, such as influences of familiarity, expectation, probability, or simplicity, are required. In terms of process, it is sometimes claimed that objects are determined by cognitive activity resembling general inference or problem-solving processes.[2] Our investigations of how spatial and temporal gaps are overcome in the perception of objects and boundaries offer support for a different perspective: Perception of objects and boundaries depends on particular stimulus relationships and a determinate process.[3]

The research points to a process common to a number of phenomena that on the surface seem diverse. We have identified the information used in the process and suggested a tentative account of the steps involved. The model applies to boundary interpolation in 2-D displays, but it also appears to extend straightforwardly to interpolation between surface boundaries in arbitrary 3-D positions. Some natural assumptions about visual processing of time-varying displays allow the model to account neatly for a number of results in spatiotemporal object perception, in which information is carried by motion. What follows is a

Fig. 1. The model of the space shuttle is visible despite projecting to the eyes from multiple locations interrupted by nearer objects. Also, parts of the fence in front and the structures behind have color and brightness similar to adjacent projected areas of the shuttle, yet are not seen as connected to it.

brief description of each of these aspects of the work.

DIVERSE PHENOMENA, SINGLE PROCESS

Perception of objects under partial occlusion is not the only case in which boundaries are perceived across gaps. Two others are shown in Figure 2, along with an example of partial occlusion (Fig. 2a). Figure 2b illustrates illusory contours. The perceived (interpolated) edges between the black inducing patterns are not defined by any physical gradient. The illusory figure seen in front of the inducing patterns is an example of what Michotte[4] termed *modal completion. Completion* refers to the perception of the whole object despite the gaps in the physical stimulus. The term *modal* signifies that the edges and surfaces supplied by the visual system come complete with sensory properties. One could, for example, judge the brightness of the interpolated white surface in the figure. In contrast, per-

ception of occluded regions is *amodal*, lacking sensory attributes or modes. The black object in Figure 2a is perceived as a unit, but its occluded region produces no local sensations.

One key to our approach to understanding boundary interpolation is the idea that modal and amodal completion are not different processes. Instead, partly occluded boundaries and illusory contours are different-looking manifestations of an identical underlying process. When first proposed, this notion was

surprising to some researchers because processes dealing with occlusion were often considered cognitive, whereas illusory figures, with their sensory accompaniments, were viewed as truly perceptual or sensory phenomena. In our view, the difference in appearance is superficial. What differs between illusory figures and partly occluded figures is whether the interpolated boundaries appear in front of or behind other surfaces in the scene. This difference in depth arrangement of perceived surfaces depends not on the process of unit formation,[5] but on depth information in the scene.

One argument in favor of this idea comes from figures in which, because of weak information about depth ordering, edges switch from illusory contours to partly occluded boundaries, and vice versa. An example is the type of display we have called a spontaneously splitting object (SSO). Figure 2c shows an SSO.[6] Although the entire black region is homogeneous, the visual system carves it into two objects. The intersecting boundaries of these objects are illusory contours and partly occluded edges. If the vertically elongated object is seen in front, its edges are illusory contours, while the edges of the horizontally extended object are partly occluded edges. With prolonged viewing, however, something curious hap-

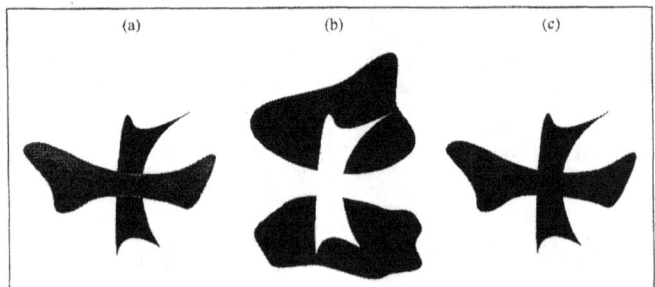

Fig. 2. Example of equivalent occlusion (a), illusory-figure (b), and spontaneously splitting object (c) displays.

pens. The object seen in front switches to behind, and vice versa. The shapes remain unchanged; what changes is their depth ordering. It would be possible, but cumbersome, to argue that there are two separate processes of modal and amodal completion involved. One would have to claim that at random times, each stops operating on one figure and switches to the other with perfect complementarity. A simpler interpretation is that the figural boundaries are given by a single interpolation process whose results do not change. What randomly alternates is the depth ordering of the figures, reminiscent of displays that undergo figure–ground reversals. Depth alternation is not surprising because there is no depth information specifying which object is in front. Such alternation does suggest that the visual system obeys the constraint that two different objects cannot occupy the same space at the same time.

Observations such as these led to the original proposal that these different examples of unit formation are manifestations of a single underlying process.[7] Empirical research has yielded strong support for the hypothesis. In brief, boundary interpolation seems to occur in virtually identical fashion in theoretically equivalent displays of illusory and occluded figures.[8] A number of variables, such as edge alignment, orientation, and spacing, affect edge interpolation equivalently in the two cases, across both simple and highly complex, randomly generated displays. Whether and how interpolation occurs depends on the relative positions of physically specified edges in the display, not on whether they are part of occlusion or illusory-figure displays. The phenomenological difference in these cases—what has been called amodal versus modal completion—has to do with the depth ordering of interpolated boundaries and other edges in the scene. Depth ordering, in turn, depends on available depth information. A striking consequence of the hypothesis is that it should be possible to construct displays in which an illusory contour connects to a partly occluded edge.[9] This is indeed the case, as Figure 3 illustrates.

CONDITIONS GOVERNING BOUNDARY INTERPOLATION

What relations among physically specified edges allow the visual system to interpolate new edges? A major issue among theories of visual completion is whether the relevant determinants are global or local. Global information might include the symmetry or simplicity of an object's overall shape. There is not, however, much evidence for global influences in unit formation, and we believe it to be primarily a local phenomenon.[10] Specifically, boundary interpolation depends on local edge orientations and their relations.

Some clues about the relevant information come from the ecology of perception. Of the several kinds of interpolated boundaries, partly occluded edges are most common in ordinary perception. Illusory contours, for example, are relatively rare outside perception laboratories. It is likely that the boundary interpo-

Fig. 3. Example of illusory contours joining partly occluded contours. The egg-shaped object has interpolated boundaries combining illusory-contour and partly occluded portions. Although the effect is visible in either the left or the right display, the depth relationships may be stabilized, and the effect made more striking, by viewing the two displays stereoscopically. The two views may be placed in a stereoscope or free-fused by crossing the eyes, so that each eye receives one of the two views.

lation process exists to deal with occlusion. Thus, the search for information governing the process might profitably consider the optics of occlusion.

A particularly helpful fact comes from projective geometry. Whenever one object partly occludes another, the optical projection contains sharp corners at the points of overlap. For example, in Figure 2a, there are four such sharp corners where the projected boundaries of black and gray regions meet. Formally, these corners are first-order, or tangent, discontinuities in the orientations of projected edges.

We have proposed that detection of this particular feature of optical projections is the starting point of the boundary interpolation process. The relevant tangent discontinuities (TDs) are those along the edges of extended regions.[11] The importance of TDs as starting points for the interpolation process has been supported by empirical findings.[12] The presence of TDs enhances the frequency of reports of illusory contours and the clarity of perceived contours, whereas smoothing TDs reduces or eliminates illusory contours.

TDs provide only the starting point, however. Although all occlusions give rise to TDs, not all TDs arise from occlusion. Some objects' shapes simply include sharp corners. What information could distinguish TDs arising from these two sources?

The visual system seems to solve this problem in combination with the problem of determining where occluded boundaries are located. Specifically, the solution depends on relative positions and orientations of the edges leading into TDs. When certain relations hold, edges are interpolated. We have labeled these relationships *conditions of relatability*. Two edges are relatable if they can be connected by a smooth (at least once differentiable), monotonic curve whose endpoints match the two edge tangents. We have proposed a formal criterion of relatability to express these relationships, which can be understood with reference to Figure 4a. If E_1 and E_2 are the edges of projected areas, leading into TDs, the tangent of each edge at the point where it meets the TD governs its relatability. If R and r are constructed, perpendicular to the tangents of E_1 and E_2, such that $R \geq r$ and θ is the angle between R and r, then E_1 and E_2 are relatable if and only if

$$0 \leq R \cos \theta \leq r$$

Figure 4b gives an example of two relatable edges; Figure 4c shows a pair of nonrelatable ones.

The relatability criterion embodies several principles. It implies that the visual system represents hidden edges according to a smoothness constraint[1] and in general does not construct corners or double inflections. Such a constraint exploits the ecological fact that objects tend to have (relatively) smooth boundaries and perhaps the fact that departures from smoothness in hidden edges

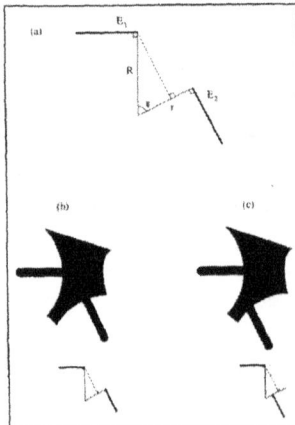

Fig. 4. Conditions of relatability. (a) Construction defining relatability (see text). (b) Example of relatable edges. (c) Example of nonrelatable edges.

would be difficult to anticipate. The utility of the criterion also depends on another principle from projective geometry: The optical projections of smooth curves and straight edges in the boundaries of objects will in general be smooth curves and straight edges. Thus, boundaries that are smoothly connected in the 3-D world will be relatable in their optical projections, even when partly occluded. Formally, the relatability criterion comprises necessary and sufficient conditions for a smooth (at least once differentiable) and monotonic curve to be constructed tangent to each of the two supporting edges.

The relatability criterion also contains the constraint that edges whose orientations differ by less than 90 deg ($R \cos \theta < 0$) are not relatable, a condition derived from empirical observation. There is little evidence that the boundary interpolation process creates edges bending through more than 90 deg. It should be noted that the limits of interpolation given formally are subject to perceptual thresholds. For example, misaligned parallel edges should not support interpolation, according to the model, but experimental evidence indicates that the process tolerates a small amount of misalignment, about 15 min of visual arc, before interpolation breaks down.

THE PROCESS OF UNIT FORMATION

Figure 5 summarizes our model of the process by which boundaries are interpolated and combined with locally specified boundaries to produce new perceived objects. The first two steps are not part of the model per se; they involve two earlier stages of visual processing that provide the input representation. The first, yielding a representation like Marr's primal sketch,[1] locates edges based on certain luminance changes across the optical projection. The second, as in Marr's 2.5-D sketch, assigns depth information to each point. Step 3 is the search of this representation for TDs, and orientations of edges leading into TDs are determined in Step 4. The test for relatability occurs in Step 5, and, in Step 6, smooth, monotonic connections are constructed between edge pairs passing the test.[13] Construction of an edge has the consequence that some TDs in the optical projection are perceived as loci of occlusion rather than as sharp corners of objects. Step 7 tests whether locally given plus interpolated edges form an enclosed area, in which case a unit (object, figure, or aperture) is perceived. Formation of such an area can lead to altered depth relations among surfaces at similar depths (Step 8), as a result of the operation of certain depth cues. In particular, the depth cue of interposition can be formalized as a set of rules operating on physically given and interpolated edges.[3]

BOUNDARY INTERPOLATION IN THREE-DIMENSIONAL SPACE

Interpolation processes have most often been illustrated and studied in 2-D, pictorial contexts. Recent observations and experiments suggest that depth information in the input representations plays an important role, however.[3,14] First, a pair of edges might line up in a 2-D projection, but, because of differences in their depth, they might not be smoothly connectable in 3-D. Interpolation does not seem to occur in these cases. Second, the interpolation process can produce edges that extend or curve in depth. These have been produced for both occluded objects and illusory contours, indicating that the process is sensitive to the 3-D orientations of the input edges. An example is

Published by Cambridge University Press

Locating Physically Specified Edges (Primal Sketch)
⇓
Assigning Depth Values to Edges of Surface Regions (2.5-D Sketch)
⇓
Locating Tangent Discontinuities in Edges of Surface Regions
⇓
Assigning Orientations (Tangents) to Edges Leading Into Discontinuities
⇓
Testing Relatability of Edge Pairs (For R, r perpendiculars (R ≥ r) to two edge tangents E1, E2, with angle of intersection Θ, E1 and E2 are relatable iff 0≤ R cos Θ ≤ r.)
⇓
Constructing Edges (Connection by at least once differentiable, monotonic edge, matching physically given edge tangents at endpoints)
⇓
Detecting Enclosed Regions (Delimited by physically specified plus interpolated edges)
⇓
Assigning Final Depth (Determination of depth relations among new enclosed regions and projectively adjacent surfaces)

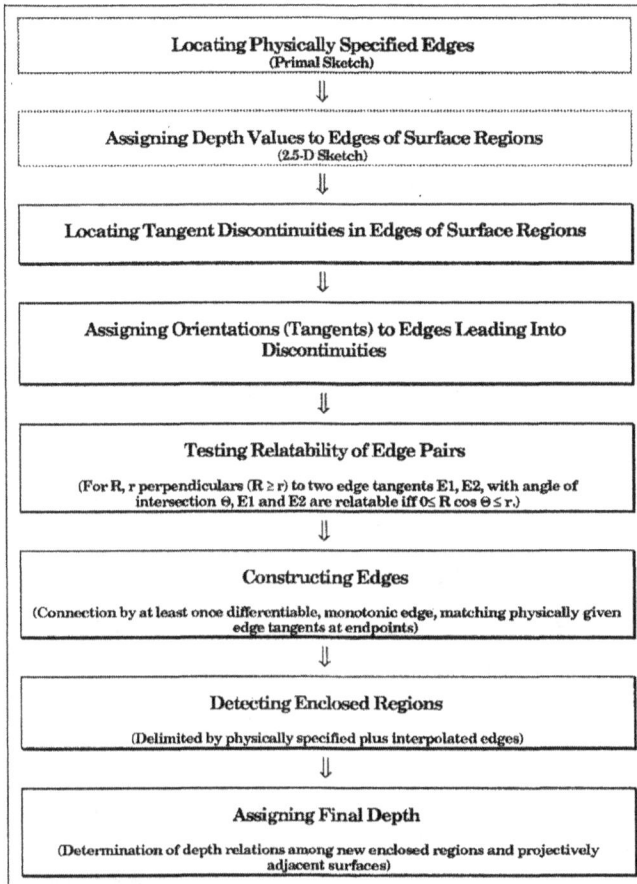

Fig. 5. Schematic of the unit formation model. (See text.)

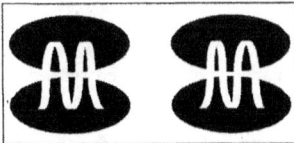

Fig. 6. Example of three-dimensional interpolation. The two views may be placed in a stereoscope or free-fused by crossing (or diverging) the eyes, so that each eye receives one of the two views.

shown in Figure 6. Third, work in progress suggests that subjects perceive interpolated edges in 3-D only when relatively little torsion (twisting) is required to connect surface edges.

A simple generalization of the model allows it to apply to surface edges in 3-space. The same relatability criterion determines whether two surface edges can connect, but the criterion can apply to edges in any plane, not just a frontoparallel plane. It follows that 3-D interpola-

tion should not occur between two edges that lie beyond some relatively small deviation (i.e., some threshold) from co-planarity. Although further study is needed, this generalization fits available data.

SPATIOTEMPORAL UNIT FORMATION

Perception of hidden edges and surfaces in ordinary circumstances often involves the relative motions of objects and observers. When motion and occlusion combine, perceiving objects requires the integration of fragmentary information over time. Consider the case of a stationary observer viewing a stationary target while objects move in between. (This case also approximates that of a moving observer viewing a distant scene through foliage.) In this case, there is no relative motion between the occluded scene and the observer, but various parts of the scene become visible at different times, and perhaps some parts never become visible. How might the visual system produce a representation of objects and surfaces by integrating available surface and edge fragments? A straightforward extension of our model might explain perception across time: Edge parts accumulated over time support interpolation when they meet the relatability criterion.

A second integration problem arises when objects move relative to the observer. Consider a running dog seen through a hedge. Partial information is given not only at different times, but in constantly changing locations. How can these fragments be pieced together? Perhaps the simplest possibility is that velocity information is used to infer where moving edge pieces will be later in time. If so, our model could be applied to the updated (extrapolated) positions of the fragments tracked over time. The latter process would require stimulus information about velocity as a basis for the temporal extrapolation.

Both of these extensions of the model have been confirmed empirically.[3] One line of studies involved the experimental apparatus shown schematically in Figure 7a. A moving occluding surface contained two slits, and displays were placed behind the occluding panel. Any momentary view provided minimal information about the figures behind the occluder, and a section between the two slits was always occluded. Using displays like those in Figures 7b and 7c, we varied edge relatability. Back-and-forth movement of the occluding panel, above a threshold speed, readily allowed subjects to detect the figural areas behind the occluder. The crucial question was how these edges would be used to interpolate form and boundaries across the vertical gap between the two slits. Subjects' responses about unity (forced choice—one vs. two display objects) and perceived form were predicted accurately by the relatability criterion applied to the

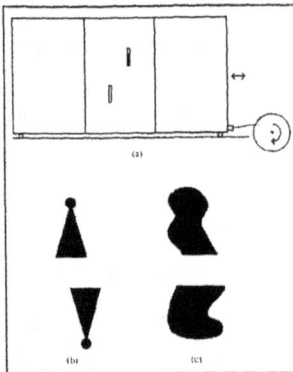

Fig. 7. Experimental investigation of spatiotemporal unit formation. (a) Schematic of apparatus used. Edge parts are revealed over time through two slits in a moving occluder. No object information is available at any time in the area between slits. (b) Nonrelatable display. (c) Relatable display.

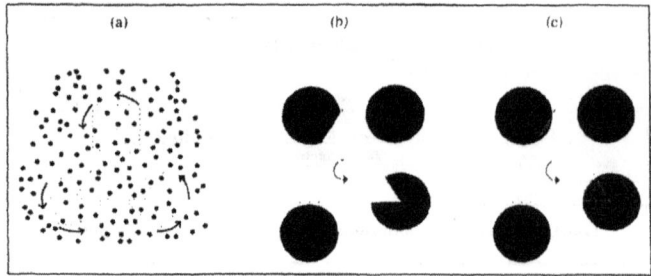

Fig. 8. Spatiotemporal unit formation phenomena. (a) Diagram of an illusory figure with motion-specified inducing elements. When the display is stationary, no figures are visible. When the square areas indicated by dotted lines rotate around their centers, they become visible as a result of accretion and deletion of background texture. The corners of the central triangle indicated by dotted lines then become visible because they lie in front of the squares and cause their own accretion and deletion of texture. Finally, these corner edges support interpolation of unspecified edges between them to make the complete triangle visible. (b) Schematic of kinetic illusory figure. The dotted lines indicate boundaries of a white triangle that is not visible against the white background. When the triangle rotates, sequential interruptions in the black circles allow the triangle to be perceived. (c) Schematic of kinetic occlusion. The same sequential interruptions in the black circles as in (b) appear as gray areas, rather than white, causing a gray rotating triangular figure to appear to be behind the white surface, and to be visible through holes or windows in that surface.

physically specified edges accumulated over time.

A related finding is that the physically specified edges participating in boundary interpolation can be defined exclusively by information given over time. Figure 8a shows a schematic of an illusory-figure display in which the input edges are given by accretion and deletion of texture elements, and no edge orientation information is available in any momentary projection.

Other research has involved moving objects revealed in fragments over time. In this case, the visual system appears to extrapolate the position of briefly given edge pieces over time, and relationships between these support interpolation. Examples of equivalent kinetic illusory-figure and kinetic occlusion displays[15] are shown in Figures 8b and 8c. In the case of the illusory figure (Fig. 8b), a rotating triangle of the background brightness and color is defined only by sequential partial occlusion of the separated circles. The result of these changes is perception of a unitary, rotating triangle

with crisp edges. In the occlusion case (Fig. 8c), the gray pieces are seen as parts of a triangle rotating behind a white surface with holes in it. The spatial relations given in the model together with the assumption of spatiotemporal tracking of the briefly given edge parts give a good account of these phenomena.

Although many motion phenomena remain to be investigated, available evidence supports the idea that spatiotemporal unit formation relies on the same basic process that accomplishes spatial interpolation. The additional requirements of spatiotemporal unit formation involve the accumulation of inputs to the interpolation process over time. Our investigations to date suggest three ways in which this accumulation occurs: (a) The edges on which interpolation is based can be created by motion-carried information, such as accretion and deletion of background texture. (b) Interpolation occurs between edges that are not specified simultaneously; that is, input edges can be registered sequentially. (c) A process of edge extrapolation in space allows the relatability criterion to be applied to the current positions of moving edges rather than their locations at the time they were registered.

CONCLUSION

Perception of objects from information that is fragmentary in space and time tells much about the character of perception generally. It illustrates, as the gestalt psychologists emphasized, that the outputs of perceptual processes do not mirror the local sensory inputs. Perception of unitary objects and continuous boundaries despite occlusion depends on spatial and temporal relationships in the input, and leads to abstract representations (completed objects and boundaries) in the output. Until recently, however, ideas about the process have been vague. Claims that perception involves simplicity, inference, hypothesis testing, or prior knowledge, or a combination of these, have placed few bounds on the processes and knowledge potentially involved.

Our work suggests that a number of object perception phenomena can be explained in terms of certain spatial and temporal relationships and a relatively local, autonomous process that progresses from these inputs to bounded objects in determinate ways. Although simple shapes and smooth boundaries can be outcomes of this process, simplicity and regularity principles are not its causes, except, perhaps, in a deeper sense. Perceived objects correspond to physical objects because visual processing exploits regularities about the physical world and laws determining its projection to the observer.

Acknowledgments—This research was supported by National Science Foundation Research Grant BNS 89-13707 to the authors. We thank Ken Nakayama and an anonymous reviewer for helpful comments.

Notes

1. D. Marr, *Vision* (Freeman, San Francisco, 1982); R.J. Watt, *Visual Processing: Computational, Psychophysical and Cognitive Research* (Erlbaum, London, 1988); J. Beck, Textural segmentation, in *Organization and Representation in Perception*, J. Beck, Ed. (Erlbaum, Hillsdale, NJ, 1982).

2. See, e.g., R.L. Gregory, *The Intelligent Eye* (McGraw-Hill, New York, 1970); I. Rock, *The Logic of Perception* (Bradford Books/MIT Press, Cambridge, MA, 1983).

3. P.J. Kellman and T.F. Shipley, A theory of visual interpolation in object perception, *Cognitive Psychology, 23,* 141–221 (1991).

4. A. Michotte, G. Thines, and G. Crabbe, *Les complements amodaux des structures perceptives; Studia Psycologica* (Publications Universitaires de Louvain, Louvain, Belgium, 1964); see also G. Kanizsa, *Organization in Perception* (Praeger, New York, 1979).

5. We use the phrase *unit formation* after Koffka

to encompass the connecting of visible parts into unitary objects, but also more generally, because the results of boundary interpolation can also be completion of holes in surfaces or single contours; K. Koffka, *Principles of Gestalt Psychology* (Harcourt Brace, New York, 1935).

6. A number of interesting examples of this type of display can be found in Kanizsa, note 4.

7. P. Kellman and M. Loukides, An object perception approach to static and kinetic subjective contours, in *The Perception of Illusory Contours*, S. Petry and G. Meyer, Eds. (Springer-Verlag, New York, 1987).

8. T.F. Shipley and P.J. Kellman, Perception of partially occluded objects and illusory figures: Evidence for an identity hypothesis, *Journal of Experimental Psychology: Human Perception and Performance, 18,* 106–120 (1992).

9. We thank Nancy Kanwisher for suggesting this possibility.

10. Global (or top-down) influences may have a much larger role in object recognition. Recognition from partial information, as when one recognizes a moving blur underneath the sofa as one's pet cat, is separable, conceptually and psychologically, from perception of boundaries and shape (Marr, note 1), although studies have often confounded the two processes.

11. Corners formed by thin lines, although useful for representing some aspects of shape, do not trigger the interpolation process.

12. T.F. Shipley and P.J. Kellman, The role of discontinuities in the perception of subjective contours, *Perception & Psychophysics, 48,* 259–270 (1990).

13. A specific form of edge arising naturally from the model extends one physically specified edge as a straight line and the other as an arc of constant curvature to a point where their tangents match. Thus, the predicted curve is once differentiable but not twice differentiable (the second derivative is undefined at the point of intersection between curved and straight segments). An alternative form of the connection would be a cubic spline, which by definition is everywhere twice differentiable. There are not currently precise enough data allowing a choice between these possibilities.

14. K. Nakayama and S. Shimojo, Toward a neural understanding of visual surface representation, *Cold Spring Harbor Symposia on Quantitative Biology, 40,* 911–924 (1990).

15. P.J. Kellman and M.H. Cohen, Kinetic subjective contours, *Perception & Psychophysics, 35,* 237–244 (1984).

[10]
Infants' Physical World

Renée Baillargeon

University of Illinois

ABSTRACT—*Investigations of infants' physical world over the past 20 years have revealed two main findings. First, even very young infants possess expectations about physical events. Second, these expectations undergo significant developments during the first year of life, as infants form event categories, such as occlusion, containment, and covering events, and identify the variables relevant for predicting outcomes in each category. A new account of infants' physical reasoning integrates these findings. Predictions from the account are examined in change-blindness and teaching experiments.*

KEYWORDS—*infant cognition; physical reasoning; explanation-based learning*

Over the past 20 years, my collaborators and I have been studying how infants use their developing physical knowledge to predict and interpret the outcomes of events. This article focuses on infants' knowledge about three event categories: *occlusion* events, which are events in which an object is placed or moves behind a nearer object, or occluder; *containment* events, which are events in which an object is placed inside a container; and *covering* events, which are events in which a rigid cover is lowered over an object (Baillargeon & Wang, 2002). I first summarize two relevant bodies of developmental findings, and then point out discrepancies between these findings. Next, I outline a new account of infants' physical reasoning that attempts to make sense of these discrepancies. Finally, I describe new lines of research that test predictions from this account.

All of the research reviewed here used the violation-of-expectation method. In a typical experiment, infants see an *expected* event, which is consistent with the expectation examined in the experiment, and an *unexpected* event, which violates this expectation. With appropriate controls, evidence that infants look reliably longer at the unexpected than at the expected event indicates that they possess the expectation under investigation, detect the violation in the unexpected event, and respond to this violation with increased attention.

PRIOR FINDINGS

Beginnings
Infants as young as 2.5 months of age (the youngest tested to date) can detect some violations in occlusion, containment, and covering events (see Fig. 1). For example, in one occlusion experiment, 2.5-month-old

Address correspondence to Renée Baillargeon, Psychology Department, University of Illinois, 603 E. Daniel, Champaign, IL 61820; e-mail: rbaillar@s.psych.uiuc.edu.

infants saw a toy mouse disappear behind one screen and reappear from behind another screen. The infants detected the violation in this event, suggesting that they believed that the mouse continued to exist after it became hidden, and realized that it could not disappear behind one screen and reappear from behind another screen without appearing in the gap between them (Aguiar & Baillargeon, 1999).

In a containment experiment, 2.5-month-old infants saw an experimenter lower an object inside a container; the experimenter then slid the container forward and to the side to reveal the object standing in the container's initial position. The infants responded to this event with increased attention, suggesting that they believed that the object continued to exist after it became hidden, and realized that it could not pass through the closed walls of the container (Hespos & Baillargeon, 2001b).

In a covering experiment, infants aged 2.5 to 3 months saw a toy duck resting on the left end of a platform; the middle of the platform was hidden by a screen slightly taller than the duck. An experimenter lowered a cover over the duck, slid the cover behind the left half of the screen, lifted it above the screen, moved it to the right, lowered it behind the right half of the screen, slid it past the screen, and finally lifted it to reveal the duck. The infants detected the violation in this event, suggesting that they believed that the duck continued to exist after it became hidden, and expected it to move with the cover when the cover was slid but not lifted to a new location (Wang, Baillargeon, & Paterson, in press).

How do 2.5-month-old infants detect these and other (e.g., Luo & Baillargeon, in press; Spelke, Breinlinger, Macomber, & Jacobson, 1992; Wilcox, Nadel, & Rosser, 1996) occlusion, containment, and covering violations? It does not seem likely that very young infants would have repeated opportunities to observe all of these (or similar) events and to learn to associate each event with its outcome. Rather, it seems more likely, as suggested by Spelke (1994), that from an early age infants interpret physical events in accord with general principles of *continuity* (objects exist continuously in time and space) and *solidity* (for two objects to each exist continuously, the two cannot exist at the same time in the same space). Later in this review, I return to the question of whether these principles are likely to be innate or learned.

Developments
Although by 2.5 months of age infants already possess expectations about occlusion, containment, and covering events, much development must still take place in these expectations. Recent research has revealed two main findings. First, for each event category, infants identify a series of variables that enables them to predict outcomes more and more accurately over time. For example, at about 3.5 months of age, infants identify height as an occlusion variable: They now

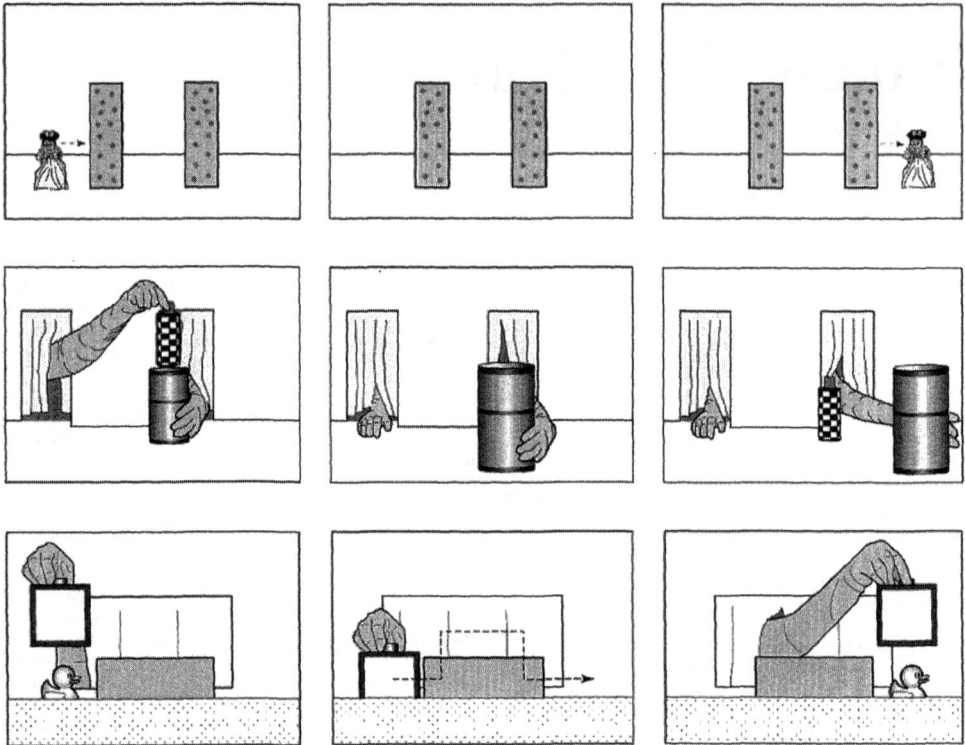

Fig. 1. Examples of violations detected by very young infants. The top row illustrates an occlusion violation: The toy mouse disappears behind one screen and reappears from behind the other screen without appearing in the gap between them (Aguiar & Baillargeon, 1999). The middle row illustrates a containment violation: The checkerboard object is lowered inside the container, which is then slid forward and to the side to reveal the object standing in the container's initial position (Hespos & Baillargeon, 2001b). The bottom row illustrates a covering violation: The cover is lowered over the toy duck, slid behind the left half of the screen, lifted above the screen, moved to the right, lowered behind the right half of the screen, slid past the screen, and finally lifted to reveal the duck (Wang, Baillargeon, & Paterson, in press).

expect tall objects to remain partly visible when behind short occluders (Baillargeon & DeVos, 1991). At about 7.5 months of age, infants identify another occlusion variable, transparency: They now expect an object to remain visible when behind a clear, transparent occluder (Luo & Baillargeon, 2004).

Second, infants do not generalize variables across event categories: They learn separately about each category. When infants identify a variable in one event category weeks or months before they identify it in another category, striking lags can be observed in their responses to similar events from the two categories (see Fig. 2). For example, in one series of experiments, 4.5-month-old infants saw an experimenter lower a tall object either behind (occlusion condition) or inside (containment condition) a short container until only the knob at the top of the object remained visible above the container. The infants detected the violation in the occlusion but not the containment condition; further results indicated that only infants ages 7.5 months and older detected the violation in the containment condition (Hespos &

Baillargeon, 2001a). In other experiments, 9-month-old infants watched an experimenter either lower a tall object inside a short container until it became fully hidden (containment condition) or lower a short cover—the container turned upside down—over the same object until it became fully hidden (covering condition). The infants detected the violation in the containment but not the covering condition; further results revealed that only infants ages 12 months and older detected the violation in the covering condition (Wang et al., in press). In yet other experiments, 7.5-month-old infants saw an object standing next to a transparent occluder (occlusion condition) or container (containment condition). Next, a large screen hid the occluder or container, and then an experimenter lifted the object and lowered it behind the occluder or inside the container. Finally, the screen was lowered to reveal only the transparent occluder or container. The infants detected the violation in the occlusion but not the containment condition; only infants ages 10 months and older detected the violation in the containment condition (Luo & Baillargeon, 2004).

Renée Baillargeon

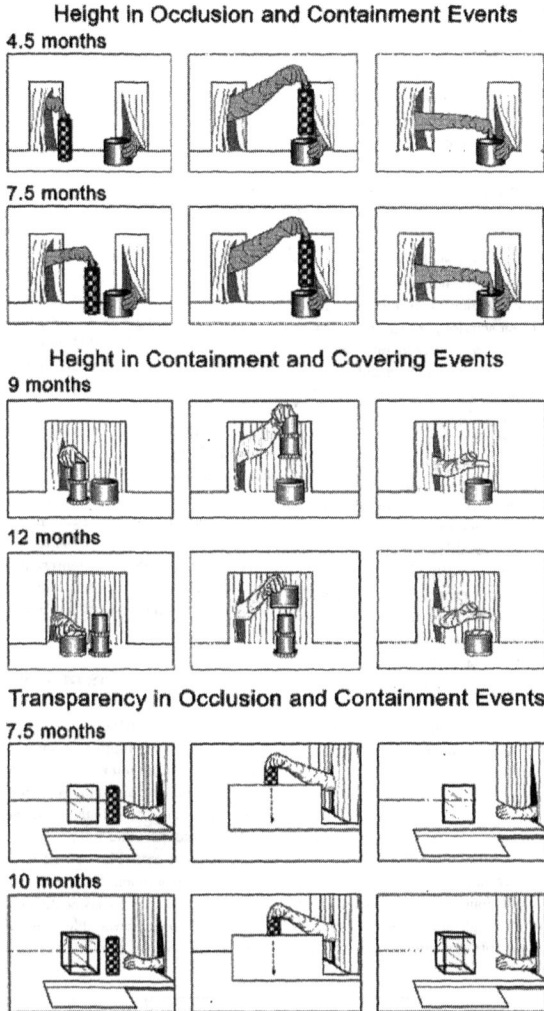

Height in Occlusion and Containment Events
4.5 months

7.5 months

Height in Containment and Covering Events
9 months

12 months

Transparency in Occlusion and Containment Events
7.5 months

10 months

Fig. 2. Examples of lags in infants' reasoning about the same variable in different event categories. The top two rows illustrate the lag in infants' identification of the height variable in containment as opposed to occlusion events. Although 4.5-month-old infants detect the violation in the occlusion event, it is not until infants are about 7.5 months old that they detect the violation in the containment event (Hespos & Baillargeon, 2001a). The middle two rows illustrate the lag in infants' identification of the height variable in covering as opposed to containment events: Although 9-month-old infants detect the violation in the containment event, it is not until infants are about 12 months old that they detect the violation in the covering event (Wang, Baillargeon, & Paterson, in press). The bottom two rows illustrate the lag in infants' identification of the transparency variable in containment as opposed to occlusion events: Although 7.5-month-old infants detect the violation in the occlusion event, it is not until infants are about 10 months old that they detect the violation in the containment event (Luo & Baillargeon, 2004).

These results indicate that infants do not generalize variables from occlusion to containment or covering events, but learn separately about each event category. Thus, the height variable is identified at about 3.5 months in occlusion events, but only at about 7.5 months in containment events and 12 months in covering events. Similarly, the transparency variable is identified at about 7.5 months in occlusion events, but only at about 10 months in containment events.

A NEW ACCOUNT OF INFANTS' PHYSICAL REASONING

Discrepancies

The developmental evidence I have just discussed suggests that the expectations infants acquire about events are not event-general expectations that are applied broadly to all relevant events, but rather *event-specific* expectations. Infants do not acquire general principles of height or transparency: They identify these variables separately in each event category. But if infants are capable of acquiring only event-specific expectations, how could they possess event-general principles of continuity and solidity, and as early as 2.5 months of age? One possibility is that infants' learning mechanism is initially geared toward acquiring event-general expectations, but soon evolves into a different mechanism capable of acquiring only event-specific expectations. Another possibility, which I think more likely, is that infants' general principles of continuity and solidity are innate (Spelke, 1994).

Whichever possibility one chooses, difficulties remain. If infants interpret events in accord with general continuity and solidity principles (whether learned or innate), one might expect them to detect *all* salient violations of these principles. However, we saw that although some continuity and solidity violations are detected as early as 2.5 months, others are not detected until much later: Recall, for example, that infants younger than 7.5 months do not respond with increased attention when a tall object becomes hidden inside a short container, and that infants younger than 12 months do not respond with increased attention when a tall object becomes hidden under a short cover.

A New Account

A new account of physical reasoning (see Fig. 3) attempts to make sense of infants' early successes and late failures at detecting continuity and solidity violations (Baillargeon, 2002; Wang et al., in press). This account rests on four assumptions. First, when watching a physical event, infants build a specialized physical representation of the event that is used to predict and interpret its outcome. Second, all

of the information, but only the information, included in the physical representation becomes subject to infants' general principles. Third, in the first weeks of life, infants' physical representations are rather impoverished: When representing an event, infants typically include only basic spatial and temporal information about it. For example, when watching a containment event, infants represent that an object is being lowered inside a container. This information captures the essence of the event, but leaves out most of its details: whether the container is taller or wider than the object, whether it is transparent or opaque, and so on.

Fourth, as infants form event categories and learn what variables to consider in each category, they include information about these variables in their physical representations. When watching an event, infants represent the basic information about the event and use this information to categorize it. They then access their knowledge of the event category selected; this knowledge specifies the variables that have been identified as relevant to the category and hence that should be included in the physical representation. Going back to our example, infants who have identified height as a containment variable would include information about the relative heights of the object and container in their representation of the event; this information would then become subject to their general principles, enabling them to detect violations involving tall objects and short containers.

Thus, according to this reasoning account, even very young infants should detect continuity and solidity violations that involve only the basic information they can represent; and much older infants should fail to detect continuity and solidity violations that involve information about variables they do not yet include in their physical representations.

TESTS OF THE ACCOUNT

Change-Blindness Effects

According to the reasoning account, infants who have not yet identified a variable as relevant to an event category, and hence do not include information about this variable when representing events from the category, should be unable to detect surreptitious changes involving the variable; in other words, they should be blind to these changes. An experiment with 11- and 12-month-old infants tested this prediction; this experiment built on the findings that height is identified at about 3.5 months as an occlusion variable but only at about 12 months as a covering variable. The infants watched an experimenter lower a tall cover in front of (occlusion condition) or over (covering

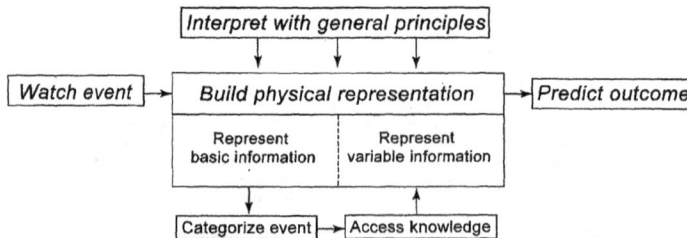

Fig. 3. A new account of physical reasoning in infancy (Baillargeon, 2002; Wang, Baillargeon, & Paterson, in press).

Renée Baillargeon

condition) a short object; next, the cover was removed to reveal an object as tall as the cover. Both the 11- and the 12-month-olds detected the change in the occlusion condition, but only the 12-month-olds detected the change in the covering condition. As predicted by the reasoning account, the 11-month-olds in the covering condition were blind to the surreptitious change in the height of the object (Wang & Baillargeon, 2004a).

Teaching Effects

Another prediction from the reasoning account concerns teaching effects. If infants could be taught a new variable in an event category, then they would include information about this variable when representing novel events from the category, enabling them to detect violations involving the variable earlier than they would otherwise. Wang and I recently attempted to teach 9.5-month-old infants the height variable in covering events (Wang & Baillargeon, 2004b).

What might be the key ingredients in a successful teaching experiment? The process by which infants typically identify a new variable in an event category is assumed to be one of explanation-based learning and to involve three main steps (e.g., Baillargeon, 2002). First, infants notice contrastive outcomes for the variable (e.g., they notice that when a cover is placed over an object, the object is sometimes fully and sometimes only partly hidden). Second, infants search for the conditions that relate to these outcomes (e.g., they detect that the object becomes fully hidden when it is shorter than the cover, and becomes partly hidden when it is taller than the cover). Finally, infants build an explanation for these condition-outcome data using their prior knowledge (e.g., infants' continuity and solidity principles specify that a tall object can extend to its full height inside a tall but not a short cover).

In line with this analysis, the infants in our experiment received three pairs of teaching trials. Each pair consisted of a tall- and a short-cover event. In each event, an experimenter rotated the cover forward to show its hollow interior, placed the cover next to a tall object (to facilitate height comparisons), and then lifted and lowered the cover over the object. The object became fully hidden in the tall-cover event, and partly hidden in the short-cover event. Different covers were used in the three pairs of trials. The infants next saw test events in which a novel tall (expected event) or short (unexpected event) cover was lowered over a novel tall object until it became fully hidden. The infants detected the violation in the short-cover event, suggesting that they were able to identify the height variable in covering events during the teaching trials. Positive results were also obtained when a 24-hr delay separated the teaching and test trials.

Subsequent experiments examined some of the assumptions behind our teaching trials. As expected, infants showed no evidence of learning when the teaching trials were modified so that they provided either no contrastive outcomes (the object was shorter and became fully hidden under the tall and short covers), no condition information (the cover was never placed next to the tall object on the apparatus floor, making it difficult for infants to compare their heights), or no explanation (false bottoms inside the covers—revealed when the covers were rotated forward—rendered them all equally shallow). The infants tested with the shallow covers were exposed to the same condition-outcome data as in our original teaching experiment, but could not make sense of the fact that the tall object became fully hidden under the tall but shallow covers.

FUTURE DIRECTIONS

I have focused on a small portion of infants' physical world: their knowledge of occlusion, containment, and covering events. Similar analyses can be offered for infants' knowledge of other event categories, such as support and collision events (e.g., Baillargeon, 2002). Together, this evidence provides strong support for the account of infants' physical reasoning presented here, and more generally for the notion that both event-general and event-specific expectations contribute to infants' responses to physical events.

In future research, my collaborators and I plan to expand our reasoning account in several directions. Infants recognize that events involving inert and self-moving objects may have different outcomes, so a complete account should explain infants' reasoning about both event and object categories. Furthermore, to make sense of events as they unfold, infants must not only represent individual events but also integrate successive events, so a complete account should specify how infants link successive physical representations.

We are also beginning to explore possible connections between infants' physical reasoning system and other cognitive systems. For example, infants can at first include in their physical representations only objects they directly see or have seen; only after some time are they able to infer the presence of additional objects, perhaps when connections are forged with a separate problem-solving system. Similarly, infants are at first limited to reasoning qualitatively about continuous variables (e.g., height or width); only after some time do they become able to engage in quantitative reasoning about these variables, perhaps when connections are formed with a system for representing absolute spatial information. Finally, infants may not reveal some of their physical knowledge in action (as opposed to violation-of-expectation) tasks until suitable connections are established with the system responsible for planning and executing actions (Berthier et al., 2001).

As researchers continue to make progress in understanding how infants attain and use their physical knowledge, we come closer to unveiling the complex architecture that makes it possible for them to learn, so very rapidly, about the world around them.

Recommended Reading

Baillargeon, R. (2002). (See References)

Leslie, A.M. (1994). ToMM, ToBY, and agency: Core architecture and domain specificity. In L.A. Hirschfeld & S.A. Gelman (Eds.), *Mapping the mind* (pp. 119–148). Cambridge, England: Cambridge University Press.

Spelke, E.S. (1994). (See References)

Acknowledgments—This research was supported by the National Institute of Child Health and Human Development (Grant HD-21104).

REFERENCES

Aguiar, A., & Baillargeon, R. (1999). 2.5-month-old infants' reasoning about when objects should and should not be occluded. *Cognitive Psychology, 39*, 116–157.

Baillargeon, R. (2002). The acquisition of physical knowledge in infancy: A summary in eight lessons. In U. Goswami (Ed.), *Handbook of childhood cognitive development* (pp. 47–83). Oxford, England: Blackwell.

Baillargeon, R., & DeVos, J. (1991). Object permanence in 3.5- and 4.5-month-old infants: Further evidence. *Child Development, 62,* 1227–1246.

Baillargeon, R., & Wang, S. (2002). Event categorization in infancy. *Trends in Cognitive Sciences, 6,* 85–93.

Berthier, N.E., Bertenthal, B.I., Seaks, J.D., Sylvia, M.R., Johnson, R.L., & Clifton, R.K. (2001). Using object knowledge in visual tracking and reaching. *Infancy, 2,* 257–284.

Hespos, S.J., & Baillargeon, R. (2001a). Infants' knowledge about occlusion and containment events: A surprising discrepancy. *Psychological Science, 12,* 140–147.

Hespos, S.J., & Baillargeon, R. (2001b). Knowledge about containment events in very young infants. *Cognition, 78,* 204–245.

Luo, Y., & Baillargeon, R. (2004). *Infants' reasoning about occlusion and containment events: Further evidence of décalages.* Unpublished manuscript, University of Illinois, Urbana-Champaign.

Luo, Y., & Baillargeon, R. (in press). When the ordinary seems unexpected: Evidence for rule-based physical reasoning in young infants. *Cognition.*

Spelke, E.S. (1994). Initial knowledge: Six suggestions. *Cognition, 50,* 431–445.

Spelke, E.S., Breinlinger, K., Macomber, J., & Jacobson, K. (1992). Origins of knowledge. *Psychological Review, 99,* 605–632.

Wang, S., & Baillargeon, R. (2004a). *Change blindness in infants: Event category effects.* Unpublished manuscript, University of California, Santa Cruz.

Wang, S., & Baillargeon, R. (2004b). *Teaching infants the variable height in covering events.* Unpublished manuscript, University of California, Santa Cruz.

Wang, S., Baillargeon, R., & Paterson, S. (in press). Detecting continuity violations in infancy: A new account and new evidence from covering and tube events. *Cognition.*

Wilcox, T., Nadel, L., & Rosser, R. (1996). Location memory in healthy preterm and fullterm infants. *Infant Behavior and Development, 19,* 309–323.

Part IV
Object Recognition and Classification

[11]

Objects, Parts, and Categories

Barbara Tversky and Kathleen Hemenway
Stanford University

SUMMARY

Concepts may be organized into taxonomies varying in inclusiveness or abstraction, such as *furniture, table, card table* or *animal, bird, robin*. For taxonomies of common objects and organisms, the basic level, the level of *table* and *bird*, has been determined to be most informative (Rosch, Mervis, Gray, Johnson, & Boyes–Braem, 1976). Psychology, linguistics, and anthropology have produced a variety of measures of perception, behavior, and communication that converge on the basic level. Here, we present data showing that the basic level differs qualitatively from other levels in taxonomies of objects and of living things and present an explanation for why so many measures converge at that level.

We have found that part terms proliferate in subjects' listings of attributes characterizing category members at the basic level, but are rarely listed at a general level. At a more specific level, fewer parts are listed, though more are judged to be true. Basic level objects are distinguished from one another by parts, but members of subordinate categories share parts and differ from one another on other attributes. Informants agree on the parts of objects, and also on relative "goodness" of the various parts. Perceptual salience and functional significance both appear to contribute to perceived part goodness. Names of parts frequently enjoy a duality not evident in names of other attributes; they refer at once to a particular appearance and to a particular function.

We propose that part configuration underlies the various empirical operations of perception, behavior, and communication that converge at the basic level. Part configuration underlies the perceptual measures because it determines the shapes of objects to a large degree. Parts underlie the behavioral tasks because most of our behavior is directed toward parts of objects. Labeling appears to follow the natural breaks of perception and behavior; consequently, part configuration also underlies communication measures. Because elements of more abstract taxonomies, such as scenes and events, can also be decomposed into parts, this analysis provides a bridge to organization in other domains of knowledge.

Knowledge organization by parts (partonomy) is contrasted to organization by kinds (taxonomy). Taxonomies serve to organize numerous classes of entities and to allow inference from larger sets to sets included in them. Partonomies serve to separate entities into their structural components and to organize knowledge of function by components of structure. The informativeness of the basic level may originate from the availability of inference from structure to function at that level.

170   BARBARA TVERSKY AND KATHLEEN HEMENWAY

Gallia est omnis divisa in partes tres. Gaul as a whole is divided into three parts. How many essays, since Caesar's account of his European campaign, have begun by decomposing the subject matter into parts? Knowing the parts of a topic and their interrelationship seems to be fundamental to comprehending the topic, whether the topic is a country under siege, a scientific discipline, or an automobile in need of repair. In this article, we examine the special role of parts in determining the *basic* or preferred level of abstraction in a taxonomy.

The world is filled with an overwhelming variety of objects and living things. One of the most fundamental aspects of human thought is the ability to perceive similarities and differences in objects and organisms, and to thereby group or classify them. Grouping individuals into categories gives us a basis for treating different objects and organisms as equivalent and enables us to reduce the numbers of entities in the world to manageable proportions. Classification also allows us to infer properties of individuals from knowledge of the category and to communicate information economically by category labels. The utility of categories can be further increased by organizing them into taxonomies of inclusiveness or abstraction. The animal taxonomy is a classic example. Robins, for example, are included in the class of birds, and birds are included in the class of vertebrates. The more inclusive classes are more abstract in that the features characterizing the class are more general and less concrete. Such structures allow succinct representation of knowledge and provide powerful potential for inference.

This research was supported by National Science Foundation Grant BNS 8002012 and National Institute of Mental Health Grant MH 34248 to Stanford University. Kathleen Hemenway was supported by a National Science Foundation Fellowship. Portions of this research were reported in a dissertation by Hemenway in partial fulfillment of the doctorate degree. Kathleen Hemenway is now at Bell Laboratories, Murray Hill, New Jersey.

We would like to express our gratitude to Barbara Malt, Edward Smith, Carolyn Mervis, and Eleanor Rosch for generously providing us with data to analyze, and to Allan Collins, Herbert Clark, Joachim Hoffman, Ellen Markman, Edward Smith, and Ewart Thomas for helpful discussion.

Requests for reprints should be sent to Barbara Tversky, Department of Psychology, Building 420, Stanford University, Stanford, California 94305.

What determines how different entities are grouped into categories, or how a general category is divided into subcategories? At one time, it was thought that category groupings were arbitrary, a matter of convention, different from culture to culture. Recent research in anthropology, linguistics, philosophy, and psychology has uncovered regularities in classification across languages and has linked characteristics of natural categories to structure in the perceived world (e.g., Berlin, 1972; Berlin, Breedlove, & Raven, 1966, 1973; Berlin & Kay, 1969; C. H. Brown, 1977, 1979; Hampton, 1979, 1981; Rosch & Mervis, 1975; Rosch, Mervis, Gray, Johnson, & Boyes–Braem, 1976). In their investigation of the internal structure of natural categories, Rosch and Mervis (1975) observed that attributes aren't evenly distributed over objects in the world; some attributes tend to co-occur with certain other attributes. For example, the attribute *has a beak* tends to co-occur with the attributes *flies, has wings, eats worms* and *builds nests.* Consequently, there are groups of entities, like birds, sharing many attributes with one another, and sharing few attributes with other entities. Rosch and Mervis showed that natural categories reflect this structure in the world: Categories group things that share attributes.

A preferred level of reference, or basic level of categorization, is a second characteristic of natural categories that has been linked to structure in the perceived world (Berlin, 1972; Berlin et al., 1973; Rosch et al., 1976). In essence, the basic level phenomenon is that categories at one level of specificity in a taxonomy are psychologically and linguistically more primary than more general and more specific categories. Relative informativeness has been used by Rosch et al. (1976) to identify the basic level. This has been operationalized as a relatively steep rise in the number of attributes listed by subjects for objects described at several levels of abstraction. For instance, subjects list very few attributes for *vehicles, furniture,* and *tools,* but list a far greater number of attributes for *car, table,* and *hammer.* Only a few additional attributes are listed for *two-door car, card table,* and *ball-peen hammer.* It has been suggested (Rosch, 1978) that basic level categories are most informative because, given our perceptual apparatus and the structure in the world, this is the level at which the natural correlations and discontinuities among features are most salient. Presumably, where informativeness is greatest, so is the inferential power of categorization.

Many empirical operations converge at the basic level in common taxonomies of objects and organisms. Basic level categories are the most general categories having members with similar and recognizable shapes; they are also the most abstract categories for which a single image can be formed for the category (Rosch et al., 1976). Basic level categories are the most general categories having members that are interacted with in the same ways (Rosch et al., 1976). In labeling an object, basic level terms are preferred (R. Brown, 1958; Cruse, 1977; Rosch et al., 1976), and in verification, basic level labels are verified most rapidly (Murphy & Smith, 1982; Rosch et al., 1976). Basic level terms tend to be the first categories named and understood by children (Mervis & Rosch, 1981), the first terms to enter a lexicon, shorter and less derived terms (Berlin, 1972; Rosch et al., 1976), and contextually neutral (Cruse, 1977). The first two measures reflect our perception of objects, the next measure reflects our behavior toward objects, and the final measures reflect our communication about them. It remains to be explained why so many different and significant operations converge at the same level.

Although the basic level of reference has been defined quantitatively, there seem to be qualitative differences among the levels of abstraction in common taxonomies (Rosch et al., 1976; Smith, Balzano, & Walker, 1978). Specifically, superordinate categories seem to primarily share functional features—vehicles are for transporting, and tools are for fixing. They do not seem to share perceptual features, in sharp contrast to objects belonging to the same basic level category, which appear to share both perceptual and functional features. On closer examination of the attributes listed by subjects, it appeared to us that one kind of feature especially predominates at the basic level of reference, namely, parts. Attributes listed for *screwdriver* include *handle* and *blade,* and attributes listed for *chair* include *seat, back,* and *legs.* Although object parts are portions of wholes, and therefore perceptual features, many names of parts seem to have a

special status in that they are at once perceptual and functional. They refer to both a perceptually identifiable segment of an object and to a specialized function of the object. A *handle,* for instance, is typically long, thin, and of a size compatible with the human hand; a handle is used for grasping. Likewise, a *blade* is also elongated, with one of its long edges thinner and sharper than the other; it is used for cutting. Similarly, a *seat* is a squarish, horizontal surface, of a size and height to be compatible with humans; it is used for sitting. The other sorts of attributes generated by subjects, for instance, *red, found in water, heavy, used for fixing,* do not have this dual character. Thus part names, in contrast to names of other attributes describing objects and organisms, have two faces: one toward appearance, the other toward function.

In these studies, we garner evidence supporting the proposal that it is the psychological prevalence of parts that grants special status to the basic level; that parts underlie the distinctiveness of objects from one another at the basic level, and that parts underlie each of the types of converging operations, and thereby account for their convergence. These claims entail three predictions, to be examined empirically. First, knowledge about parts is expected to underlie the superior informativeness of the basic level. Second, because part structure is expected to underlie the natural breaks or discontinuities at the basic level, different objects at the basic level should differ on parts and share other attributes. Third, different subordinate objects belonging to the same basic level category should share parts and differ on other attributes. Following Rosch (1978), we refer to issues concerning inclusion and abstraction relations between categories as the *vertical* dimension of categorization, and to issues concerning the relations among subcategories at the same level of analysis as the *horizontal* dimension of categorization. The first prediction, then, is a prediction about representation of vertical relations among categories, and the next two predictions are about representation of the horizontal relations.

These predictions were explored for categories of plants and animals as well as for categories of common objects. Although it is difficult to identify defining characteristics of members of object categories, functional characteristics are probably at least as important as form and structure in determining membership in those categories. For example, functional *sit-on-able-ness* is at least as important a determinant of membership in the chair category as is possessing a chairlike shape. In contrast, biological categories at all taxonomic levels are morphologically based: Membership in the most general categories is determined by gross morphological features, whereas membership in the most specific categories is determined by fine structural details (Dougherty, 1978; Hunn, 1976). Because biological categories at all taxonomic ranks are morphologically based, it is not likely that basic level categories are the most general categories having members with the same parts. Members of all categories, even very general ones, probably share some parts. Even so, the extent of perceived differentiation in terms of parts and other attributes may vary with taxonomic level.

The biological categories, then, are an especially important test of our predictions because they have a part structure even at all levels of description. If we can demonstrate in biological categories a level of abstraction for which few, if any, parts are listed, followed by a level for which many parts are listed, this is strong evidence for our claim that it is the psychological salience of parts that underlies the basic level of reference. Biological categories are also important because they are cultural universals and were present during the evolution of humankind, in contrast to object categories, which may differ from culture to culture.

STUDY 1: PARTS PREVAIL AT THE BASIC LEVEL

In this study, we demonstrate that the sharp increase in attributes listed from the superordinate to the basic level is accounted for by one kind of attribute listed by subjects, namely, parts. In this and subsequent studies, we follow the methods of Rosch et al. (1976) in many cases, reanalyzing their data by separating attributes into parts and nonparts. In reporting our results, we separate findings for object categories from findings for biological categories. One reason for this was that Rosch et al. did not find direct evidence for a basic level for biological categories. Another reason for treating objects separately from biological en-

tities was the possibility, discussed earlier, that perceived parts would play a role in determining the basic level for objects, but not for living things.

Object Categories

Method

Collection of Attributes

Criteria of frequency and depictability of instances led Rosch et al. (1976) to select six superordinate categories (clothing, fruit, furniture, musical instruments, tools, and vehicles), three basic level categories from each superordinate, and two subordinates from each basic level category. Although *fruit* is in some sense a biological category, it can also be regarded as an object category, since it is a human-defined part of a tree, engineered, packaged, and marketed much like a manufactured object. Rosch and her colleagues collected attribute norms according to a three-phase procedure described briefly here. In Phase 1, a large number of subjects were given 90 s to list attributes for each category; each subject listed attributes for categories at only one level of abstraction, and for only one category from each superordinate. In Phase 2, the attributes were tallied, and every attribute listed by less than one third of the subjects was eliminated, removing idiosyncratic responses. In Phase 3, other subjects, "judges," amended the attribute lists. The judges removed attributes they felt were not true of all category members, and added attributes if they felt the attributes were true of all category members; however, they could only add an attribute if it was already included in the list. Additions and deletions made by all 7 judges were included in the final tally. These two procedures—adding and deleting attributes—made the attribute lists logically consistent, so that properties attributed to a category were also attributed to all its subcategories.

Separating Parts From Other Attributes

Both the judge-amended and the nonamended attribute norms collected by Rosch et al. (1976) were separated into "parts" and "other attributes" according to three coinciding criteria. These norms were obtained through the good graces of Mervis and Rosch, and are used with permission. One criterion was a dictionary definition criterion. Several themes were repeated in the dictionaries we consulted: A part is one of the segments or portions into which something is regarded as divided; a part is less than a whole; together, parts constitute a whole. A second criterion was derived from Miller and Johnson-Laird's (1976) lucid discussion of relations that generate hierarchies. They distinguish a *taxonomic, or kind of* relation, from a *partonomic, or part of* relation. Whereas a taxonomic relation is expressed in an *is a* sentence frame, as in, A dog is an animal, a partonomic relation is expressed in a *has a* sentence frame, as in, A dog has a leg. This is not to say that all *is a* sentences express taxonomic relations or to say that all *has a* sentences express partonomic relations. However, for the attributes actually obtained, those that fit into a *has a* sentence frame were parts. Thus, the attributes *handle, teeth, blade,* and *edge,* listed for saw fit into a *has a* sentence frame, whereas *cuts* and *sharp* do not. A third criterion was the majority judgment of naive subjects who were asked to designate which of the attributes listed for 80 objects they regarded as parts. All of the attributes judges determined to be parts fit into a *has a* sentence frame, with the addition of material composition. Judges determined that attributes having an *is made of* or *is partially made of* relation to the object were also parts. These constituted only 9% of the parts attributes. The attribute *wood* listed for guitar is an example. *Wood* seems to be in lieu of *frame* or *body* in this instance and in others like it. Note here that *wood* also fits the dictionary definition of part. Additional justification for including material composition as parts comes from a separate study in which subjects, asked to list parts of objects, frequently listed parts by the materials they are made of. For example, *wood* and *metal* were commonly listed as parts of a screw-driver, instead of *handle* and *blade*. Finally, the form class of the attribute was helpful for distinguishing parts from other attributes. All of the parts listed were nouns, and most of the nouns listed were parts; the nouns that were not parts were *driver* and *passenger* for car and bus, and *chairs* for kitchen table. The nonpart attributes were adjectives (*loud, crispy, green, comfortable*) or else verb phrases or sentence fragments (*you eat on it, gives light, requires gas, lives in water*). Attributes considered to be parts, then, refer to segments of wholes that are less than wholes; they are judged by a majority of naive informants to be parts, and they fit into a *has a* or *is made of* or *is partially made of* sentence frame.

In Table 1 the attributes from some of the categories reported in Rosch et al. (1976) are displayed, separated into parts and nonparts. The careful reader will notice that *keys, black keys,* and *white keys* are all listed for piano, and *legs* and *four legs* for chair. Since the judges passed on these attributes, we had no choice but to leave them in as well. Redundant attributes constituted a small portion of the attributes, and leaving them out does not change the pattern of findings.

Results

Judge-Amended Tallies

In order to give equal weight to each category (because some categories elicit more attributes than others), the number of part and nonpart attributes were computed for each category and averaged over categories for each level of analysis. This technique was adopted throughout the research. Overall, 58% of the attributes were parts; however, the percentage varied with taxonomic level, as predicted. Parts were infrequent at the superordinate level and frequent at the basic and subordinate levels: Only 20% of the superordinate level attributes were parts, whereas 64% of the basic level attributes were parts, and 60% of the subordinate level attributes were parts.

In Figure 1 the mean numbers of parts and

other attributes in the judge-amended tally are displayed as a function of level of abstraction. For both parts and other attributes, the difference between the superordinate and basic levels is significantly larger than the difference between the basic and subordinate levels, $t(5) = 3.89$, $p < .01$; $t(5) = 3.48$, $p < .01$, and this disparity is more marked for parts than for other attributes, as predicted, $t(5) = 2.82$, $p < .01$. Also, the difference between the basic and subordinate levels is larger for other attributes than for parts, $t(5) = 2.77$, $p < .025$.

Nonamended Tallies

Numbers of parts and nonparts were averaged over categories for each level of abstraction, as before, to equalize the contribution of each category to the part partition. Overall, 57% of the attributes were parts; again, the proportion of parts to other attributes varied with level of abstraction. Thirty-eight percent of the superordinate level attributes were parts, 66% of the basic level attributes were parts, and 58% of the subordinate level attributes were parts.

In Figure 2 the mean numbers of parts and other attributes occurring at each level of abstraction are displayed. Subjects listed more parts at the basic level than at the subordinate level. The number of parts listed for each basic level category was significantly higher than the mean number listed for its subordinates (sign test $z = 2.58$, $p < .005$).

Biological Categories

Method

Selection of Categories

The superordinate categories used were plant and animal. The basic categories bird, fish, tree, and flower were chosen because attribute lists for 15 subordinates of each of those categories had been collected by Malt and Smith (1982), and they kindly allowed us to reanalyze their data. We asked 30 undergraduates at Stanford to rate the subordinates for familiarity, and selected 4 subordinates from each set of 15 on this basis.

Attribute Listing

Subjects. In this and subsequent studies, unless noted otherwise, subjects were Stanford introductory psychology students participating for course credit, or infrequently, for pay. Subjects were run in small or large groups, and sometimes participated in other, unrelated experiments in

174   BARBARA TVERSKY AND KATHLEEN HEMENWAY

Table 1
Judge-Amended Attributes Divided Into Parts and Other Attributes

Musical instrument
Makes sound

Guitar	Piano	Drum
Strings*	Keys*	Sticks*
Tuning keys*	Foot pedals*	Skins*
Neck*	Strings*	Round
Hole*	Legs*	Loud
Wood*	Lid*	Used by music groups
Makes music	Wood*	
You strum it	Black keys*	
Used by music groups	White keys*	
	Makes music	
Classical guitar	Upright piano	Kettle drum
(No additional)	(No additional)	(No additional)
Folk guitar	Grand piano	Bass drum
(No additional)	Large	(No additional)
	Used in concert halls	

Fruit
Seeds*
Sweet
You eat it

Apple	Peach	Grapes
Stem*	Pit*	Juicy
Core*	Skin*	Bunches
Skin*	Yellow–Orange	Makes wine
Juicy	Fuzzy	Grows on vine
Round	Soft	
Grows on trees	Grows on trees	
Delicious apple	Freestone peach	Concord grapes
Red	(No additional)	Purple
Crisp		
Shiny		
Tasty		
Macintosh apple	Cling peach	Green seedless grapes
(No additional)	Juicy	Green
	Canned	Small

Furniture
(No attributes)

Table	Lamp	Chair
Legs*	Light bulb*	Legs*
Top*	Shade*	Seat*
Surface*	Cord*	Back*
Wood*	Switches*	Arms*
You eat on it	Base*	Comfortable
You put things on it	Gives light	Four legs*
	You read by it	Wood*
		Holds people
		You sit on it
Kitchen table	Floor lamp	Kitchen chair
Chairs	(No additional)	(No additional)
Dining room table	Desk lamp	Living room chair
Four legs*	(No additional)	Large
		Soft
		Cushion*

Note. Judge-amended attributes selected from "Basic objects in natural categories" by E. Rosch, C. B. Mervis, W. Gray, D. Johnson, and P. Boyes–Braem, 1976, *Cognitive Psychology, 8,* pp. 435–436. Copyright 1976 by Academic Press. Adapted by permission. Lower levels include all attributes listed at higher levels. Parts are indicated by *.

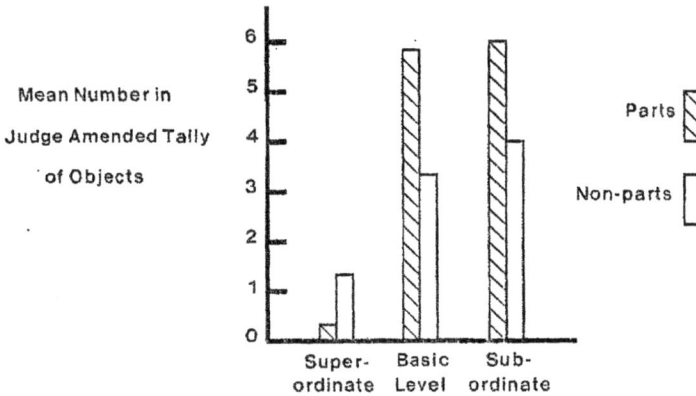

Figure 1. Mean number of parts and other attributes listed by subjects and amended by judges for object categories at three levels of abstraction.

the same session. There were 45 subjects in the present experiment; 15 subjects listed attributes for each super-ordinate and basic level category. In Malt and Smith's (1982) experiment there were 240 subjects, and 16 subjects listed attributes for each subordinate category. To make their data comparable to previous data, 1 of their subjects was randomly eliminated.

Materials. The booklets used in the present experiment were identical in format to those used by Rosch et al. (1976) and by Malt and Smith (1982). The booklets con-sisted of an instruction page, and several pages, each of which had a category label, either plant and animal or one kind of plant (tree or flower) and one kind of animal (bird or fish) at the top and was blank otherwise. Each booklet in Malt and Smith's experiment included four subordinate category labels (one kind of bird, one kind of fish, one kind of flower, and one kind of tree) as well as four unrelated basic category labels. Pages were collated in random order for each subject.

Procedure. The instructions were read aloud to subjects,

and then the subjects were timed while they listed attributes for each category. The attributes were tallied and attributes listed by a third or more of the subjects were included in the final nonamended lists. These lists were used in the judge-amending phase. The instructions and procedure were similar to those used by Rosch et al. (1976). Malt and Smith (1982) also used the Rosch procedure, except that they allowed subjects only 75 s per item for listing attributes.

Judgment of Attributes

Subjects. Another group of 10 students judged the truth of the attributes.

The following methods were used in this and subsequent judge-amending phases.

Materials and procedure. Booklets consisted of an in-struction page, followed by separate pages for each basic category. The attributes listed by 2 or more subjects for a basic level category, its superordinate, or its subordinates

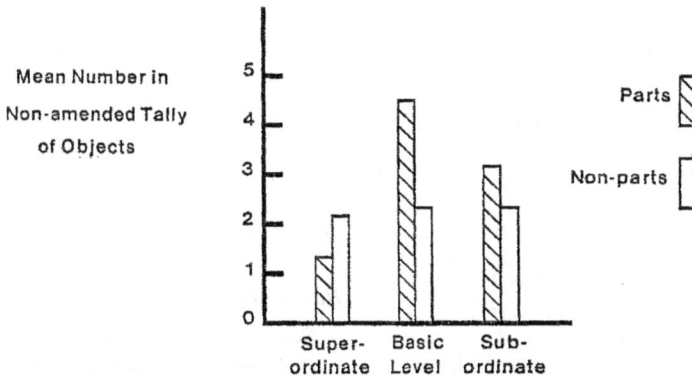

Figure 2. Mean number of parts and other attributes listed by subjects for object categories at three levels of abstraction.

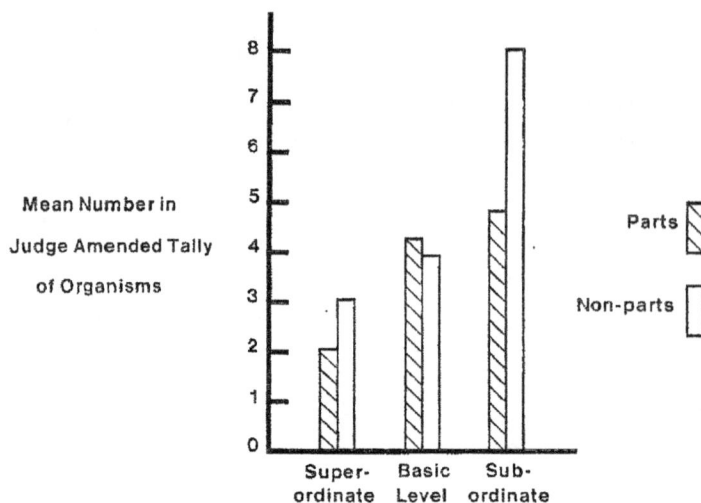

Figure 3. Mean number of parts and other attributes listed by subjects and amended by judges for biological categories at three levels of abstraction.

were typed in random order down the side of a page. The superordinate, basic, and subordinate category names were typed across the top of the page. Pages were collated randomly for each subject.

The experimenter read the instructions aloud to subjects while they read along silently. The instructions were very similar to those used by Rosch et al. (1976) and asked subjects to judge whether each attribute was true of each category listed across the top of the pages. The task was self-paced.

An attribute was included in the judge-amended norms for a category if a majority of the judges indicated possession. Logical consistency was not enforced; that is, an attribute was included for a category if a majority of the judges indicated possession, regardless of whether the attribute was included in the lists for all subcategories.

Results

Judge-Amended Attribute Tallies

As before, numbers of parts and nonparts were averaged over categories at each level of analysis. Overall, 42.7% of the attributes were parts. As before, the percentage varied with taxonomic level. Forty percent of the superordinate attributes were parts, whereas 52% of the basic level attributes were parts. The proportion of parts declined to 38% for subordinate level categories. In Figure 3 the mean numbers of parts and other attributes as a function of taxonomic level are displayed. As expected, biological categories are perceived to share parts even at the superordinate level.

Stem and *roots* were listed for plants, whereas *tail* and *eyes* were listed for animals. Some of the judge-amended norms are reported in Appendix A.

Nonamended Attribute Tallies

Numbers of parts and nonparts were averaged over categories at each level of analysis. Overall, 49.6% of the attributes were parts. For the nonamended tallies, the variation in proportion of parts with taxonomic level is even more striking: Parts constituted only 25% of superordinates, 70% of basic level attributes, and 46% of subordinate attributes. The decrease in number of parts listed from basic level to subordinate level was significant, $t(3) = 9.52$, $p < .005$. At the superordinate level, subjects listed significantly fewer parts than other attributes, for example, plants: $t(14) = 6.44$, $p < .005$; animals: $t(14) = 2.90$, $p < .01$. The mean numbers of part and nonpart attributes listed at each taxonomic level are displayed in Figure 4.

Raw Attribute Lists

Two analyses of the attribute lists obtained from Phase 1 shed light on the role of knowledge of parts in taxonomically organized categories. Parts were separated into modified

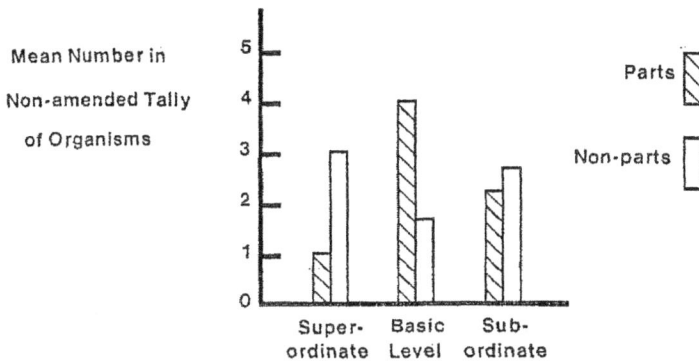

Figure 4. Mean number of parts and other attributes listed by subjects for biological categories at three levels of abstraction.

(e. g., *red petals*) or unmodified (e. g., *petals*). Quantified parts (e. g., *two eyes*) were infrequent and were excluded from the analysis. At the superordinate and basic levels, 12% and 10% of the parts were modified, respectively, whereas at the subordinate level, 34% were modified. Although, overall, fewer parts were listed at the subordinate level than at the basic level, more than twice as many modified parts were listed at the subordinate level. This result is consistent with the hypothesis that characteristics of parts are distinctive of contrasting subordinates.

The order in which subjects list attributes should be indicative of the relative importance of the attributes for the categories. If parts are particularly salient at the basic level, they should be listed earlier than other attributes. Attribute lists for each subject were split in half by order of output, and the percentage of parts listed in each half were computed. At the superordinate level, 48.5% of the parts were listed in the first half of the output, and at the subordinate level, 53% of the parts were listed in the first half of the output. In contrast, 71% of the parts in the basic level occurred in the first half of the output. Matched pairs t tests revealed a significant bias to name parts earlier for each basic level category; flower: $t(14) = 5.68$, tree: $t(14) = 3.59$, fish: $t(14) = 2.83$, and bird: $t(14) = 3.31$, all $ps < .005$; no bias for either of the superordinate categories ($t < .2$); and no bias for 14 out of 16 of the subordinate categories (for 13 categories, $t < 1$; for sparrow, $t = 2.20$, $p < .05$; for chicken, $t = 2.70$, $p < .02$).

Discussion

Parts dominate attribute lists at the basic level for amended and nonamended norms, for object and biological categories. Although parts are a minority of superordinate attributes, the majority of attributes listed at the basic level are parts. The proportion of parts listed decreases from the basic to the subordinate levels, becoming a minority of the attributes for biological categories. Only the parts attributes show the sharp rise in numbers from the superordinate to the basic level, taken as the definition of the basic level. Inclusion of other attributes attenuates this effect, especially in the biological categories. The comparison between the amended and nonamended norms is instructive. The amended norms force or encourage consistency on the tallies; attributes included in categories were also usually included for subcategories, because they were usually true of subcategories. This is consistent with the notion that more specific categories carry more information. However, the nonamended tallies tell a different story. More attributes are listed at the basic level than at the superordinate level, but fewer attributes are listed at the subordinate level than at the basic level. This drop in accessed knowledge with increasing specificity of category is completely attributable to the drop in numbers of parts listed. A desk lamp contains the same parts as a lamp, and double-knit pants contain the same parts as pants; however, subjects list fewer parts for desk lamp than lamp and fewer for double-knit pants than for pants. Moreover, a larger share of the parts listed at the subordinate level are modified parts, such as *white petals*. Because when judges amend the tallies, they add attributes (particularly parts) to the subordinate categories, we can infer that subjects know that sedans have carburetors and pine trees have trunks, even if the subordinate label fails to elicit them. Thus, the amended norms reflect the knowledge subjects have, whereas the nonamended norms reflect subjects' performance in this sort of task.

What determines the sorts of attributes subjects list for objects and entities? Despite the popularity of category and attribute norms (e.g., Ashcraft, 1978; Hampton, 1979, 1981; Malt & Smith, 1982; Rosch et al., 1976), their status has not received much discussion. How can we account for the failure to list parts and other attributes for objects, especially at the subordinate level of specificity, in spite of the fact that subjects judge these attributes to be true for those objects? Observation of the attribute lists suggests that in listing attributes, subjects attempt to be informative about the objects (Grice, 1975) to convey the knowledge they have about the categories. They give us good clues as to how to recognize the objects and as to what the objects are used for. Subjects also attempt to be relevant, for they do not say all they know about the objects. They tell attributes important for distinguishing the appearance or function of the object, so the smell of flowers and taste of fruit are mentioned, but not the smell or taste of clothing. They list fewer attributes at the subordinate level than at the basic level in spite of the fact that they know more attributes at the subordinate level. Subjects don't list *molecules* or *inanimate* or *cells* or *animate*, although the former two are properties of objects and the latter two are properties of living things. Subjects, then, are informative and relevant, but in the context of an implicit contrast set (see Garner, 1974; see also the discussion of contrastive field properties in Miller & Johnson–Laird, 1976). Interestingly, the implicit contrast set seems to be other objects at the same level of abstraction. More general features seem to be presupposed, and go unmentioned. So, it is more informative to mention *trunk* for tree than for pine tree, because tree contrasts with grass or bush or perhaps even more remote entities, and *trunk* is a property of trees, but not of these contrasting entities. Because the

implicit contrast set for *pine tree* will include other trees, listing *trunk* is not as informative, as it is shared by all trees, but listing *needles* is informative.

The parts norms (but not the nonparts norms) for biological categories establish directly that the basic level for biological categories for American college students is the level of tree, flower, fish, and bird, with plant and animal as superordinates. Previous work had shown that the level found to be basic (generic) in folk taxonomies (Berlin, 1978), namely, pine, bass, was not basic according to the Rosch et al. (1976) criterion. In fact, the data for object and biological categories look remarkably similar, despite the fact that biological categories are defined morphologically at all levels of abstraction, whereas superordinate object categories appear to carry functional meaning as well. Superordinate biological categories are judged to share a few parts, whereas superordinate object categories are not; however, the nonamended norms do not show this difference. For the biological categories, the basic level is less sharply defined. Inclusion of other attributes in addition to the parts attributes so attenuates the relationship of attributes to taxonomic level as to preclude establishment of a basic level for biological categories.

Although these studies have been directed at a vertical analysis of categories related by inclusiveness in a taxonomy, the results are suggestive of phenomena occurring horizontally, or between categories at the same level of analysis. We have seen that the attributes subjects list for categories are informative and relevant within an implicit contrast set, that is, characteristic and distinctive of the object in comparison to objects it is not. The prevalence of parts at the basic level suggests that, especially at that level, objects should differ from one another on the basis of parts and share other attributes. This is tested directly in the next set of studies.

STUDY 2: BASIC LEVEL CATEGORIES DIFFER BY PARTS

To test that basic objects differ from one another by parts and share other features, we examined attribute lists for a large number of basic level entities for each of four object and two biological categories. Finding that categories at the basic level differ from one another on the basis of parts but share other attributes would indicate that the perceived natural breaks among categories at that level are between clusters of shared parts.

Because a large number of basic and subordinate categories are needed for this analysis, it could not be performed on the data from Study 1. The attributes for 20 kinds of clothing, furniture, vehicles, and weapons were generously contributed by Rosch and Mervis (1975). Their data were collected using the three-phase procedure described earlier. These instances varied considerably in absolute frequency, production frequency (to superordinate name), and typicality vis-à-vis the superordinate category. No such lists of instances or of attributes existed for animals and plants, so we collected them. Interestingly, the six plant categories produced by our subjects (flower, tree, fern, grass, bush, vine) correspond closely to the life-form categories found in a large number of folk botanical taxonomies by Witkowski and C. H. Brown (reported in C. H. Brown, 1977). The animal categories selected were also at the life-form level as determined by cross-cultural ethnological studies (Berlin, 1978).

Object Categories

Method

Subjects

The subjects were 10 naïve staff persons in the Department of Psychology at Stanford who completed the booklets at their leisure.

Materials and Procedure

Booklets were compiled according to the following procedure. Separate forms were used for each superordinate category. The 20 basic categories from a superordinate were listed at the top of each page, and the attributes from the corresponding composite attribute list were typed, in a random order, below the list of categories. The pages were collated in a different random order for each subject (with the constraint that all the pages for one superordinate always occurred together). The subjects were instructed to circle all the attributes they considered to be parts on each of the pages. They were not told what a part is: However, they were told that *ears* and *trunk* are parts of an elephant, whereas *large, gray,* and *eats peanuts* are not.

Results and Discussion

Every attribute circled by a majority of the subjects was considered to be a part. Then, each attribute was assigned a weight equal to

Table 2

Median Number of Basic Level Categories Sharing Parts and Other Attributes

Type of category	Median weight	
	Parts	Other attributes
Object		
Clothing	3	5
Furniture	1	2
Vehicles	3	6
Weapons	1	2.5
Biological		
Animals	2.5	4
Plants	2.5	3

the number of basic level categories from the same superordinate possessing the attribute. Because of the high variability of these weights, the median (rather than the mean) weights for parts and nonparts were computed. Displayed in the top section of Table 2 are the median weights for parts and nonparts. For each category, the parts median is smaller than the nonparts median, $t(3) = 5.14$, $p < .01$. This result indicates that parts are more distinctive of contrasting basic categories than are nonparts, confirming our hypothesis that subjects list more parts at the basic level because parts are the distinctive features of objects at that level. Thus, parts contribute more than nonparts to the naturalness of basic level category cuts.

This result may also seem to imply that parts are working against the integrity of superordinate categories. After all, shared features are what "glue" a category together, and shared features are associated with the prototypicality of a category member (Rosch & Mervis, 1975). Because nonparts are more likely to be shared than parts, one may infer that sharing nonparts would be more predictive of prototypicality than sharing parts. To answer this question, separate family resemblance scores were computed on parts and nonparts, and each family resemblance score was correlated with typicality. The parts and the nonparts family resemblance scores correlated equally and highly with typicality, and with each other. So, although for these natural categories, parts and other attributes are equally associated with the typicality of instances of the same superordinate, only parts distinguish instances from one another.

Biological Categories: Elicitation of Instances

Method

Forty-one subjects were given small booklets with a cover page that the experimenter read aloud. The rest of the booklet consisted of a page titled "Plants" and another page titled "Animals," collated in random order. The instructions informed the subjects that each page of their booklets named a kind of thing, and that they would have 60 s to write down "items people commonly give as belonging to various categories or classes." The instructions also included an example.

Results

From the animals listed by 2 or more subjects, 20 animal categories were selected so that no category included another and so that the entire range of production frequency and produced genera were sampled. Thus, the list contained bee, ant, fish, snake, frog, bird, turtle, and alligator, as well as 12 mammals varying in familiarity. From the plants listed by 2 or more subjects, only six plant categories (flower, tree, fern, grass, bush, and vine) met the criteria.

Biological Categories: Attribute Listing

Method

Ten subjects listed attributes for the six plant categories and 10 other subjects listed attributes for the 20 animal categories. They were directed to list "characteristics and attributes that people feel are common to and characteristic of different kinds of ordinary everyday animals (plants)." The instructions also included a number of examples. To expedite collection of attribute norms, these subjects both generated and judged the truth of attributes. Malt & Smith (1982) compared attributes listed for common categories (e.g., lemon) when they were in the context of other categories from the same superordinate and when they were in the context of other categories from different superordinates. There were essentially no differences in the attributes produced in the two contexts, broad and narrow.

Results and Discussion

Those attributes listed by more than three judges were divided into parts and nonparts by the usual criteria. The median weights for parts and other attributes were computed, and are displayed in Table 2. Just as in the object categories, the median weights for nonparts are higher than the median weights for parts for biological categories, indicating that basic level plants and animals are perceived to share nonparts and to differ from one another on the basis of parts.

STUDY 3: SUBORDINATE LEVEL CATEGORIES SHARE PARTS

Parts, more than other attributes, distinguish one basic level entity from another. Reflection on the nature of subordinate categories as well as the decrease in parts listed at the subordinate level suggest that subordinate level categories may share the same parts and differ from one another on other attributes. We next examine that conjecture, first for object categories, and then for biological categories.

Object Categories

Attribute norms for 10 subordinates from each of four basic categories, chair, table, shirt, and pants, were compiled and analyzed. These categories were used because they were the only ones for which a substantial number of familiar subordinate category labels could be found.

Method

Subjects

There were 40 subjects in all; 10 subjects listed attributes for each set of subordinate categories.

Materials

In order to select subordinate categories, two judges (the authors) listed all the subordinate labels they could think of or find in catalogs. Brand names and unfamiliar labels were excluded from the lists. When near synonyms occurred in a list, only the more specific synonym was included. Where two labels applied to a single exemplar, one of the labels was excluded from the list whenever possible. Because many object subordinates don't form contrast sets, it was not possible to exclude all noncontrasting labels. The subordinate categories are displayed in Table 3.

Four different kinds of booklets were compiled, one for each set of subordinates. The booklets consisted of an instruction page followed by four identical forms. The 10 subordinates were listed across the top right-hand side of the forms, and blank space was left on the left-hand side for subjects to list attributes. For each attribute subjects listed, they put xs below the subordinates possessing the attribute.

Procedure

The written instructions were read aloud to subjects. They were asked to list "attributes, properties, and characteristics true of all the things listed across the top of the page, as well as attributes, properties, and characteristics true of only one or a few of them." Subjects worked at their own pace, listing all the attributes they could think of in 15 min.

Table 3
Nonbiological Subordinate Categories

Pants	Shirts
Corduroy pants	Dress shirt
Double-knit pants	Flannel shirt
Flared pants	Knit shirt
Levi pants	Long-sleeved shirt
Overalls	Sweat shirt
Pleated pants	T-shirt
Riding pants	Turtleneck shirt
Ski pants	V-neck shirt
Straight-leg pants	Western shirt
Sweat pants	Work shirt

Chairs	Tables
Beanbag chair	Card table
Dining room chair	Coffee table
Director's chair	Conference table
Easy chair	Dining room table
Folding chair	Drafting table
High chair	End table
Kitchen chair	Kitchen table
Reclining chair	Picnic table
Rocking chair	Ping pong table
Swivel chair	Typewriter table

Scoring

A subordinate category was considered to possess an attribute if at least 3 subjects indicated that the subordinate possessed it. The attributes were classified as parts and nonparts in the usual way. The parts were further classified as unmodified parts (called *parts*) and modified parts (e.g., *long sleeves, flat top*). Two of the parts in the lists occurred with quantifiers (i.e., *two legs, four legs*) and these parts were excluded from the tallies. Finally, a weight equal to the number of subordinates possessing an attribute was calculated for each attribute.

Results and Discussion

The median weights for parts and nonparts are given in Table 4. For each category the median parts weight is larger than the median nonparts weight. This result is significant, $t(3) = 3.70$, $p < .025$, and it is consistent with the other results indicating that the distinctive features of subordinate categories are nonparts. The modified parts medians were not included because so few modified parts occurred.

Biological Categories

Subordinate object categories share parts and differ from one another on other attributes. To examine the hypothesis that the distinctive features associated with biological subordi-

nates are mostly nonparts and, to a lesser extent, modifications on parts, attribute lists for many contrasting subordinate categories were analyzed.

Method

Attribute Listing

Based on the study of familiarity of subordinates described earlier, attribute lists of Malt and Smith (1982) for the 10 most familiar subordinates from each basic category were used. The resulting set of subordinate categories is displayed in Table 5.

To match the sample size in this experiment to the sample size in the corresponding study of object subordinates, 6 of Malt and Smith's (1982) 16 subjects were randomly selected and their data were eliminated. Every attribute listed for a category by 2 or more of the remaining 10 subjects was included in the next phase of the experiment.

Judgment of Attributes

Nine subjects judged the truth of the attributes according to the usual procedure. A subordinate was considered to possess an attribute if a majority of the 9 subjects indicated possession. A weight equal to the total number of subordinates possessing an attribute was computed for each attribute. The attributes were separated into parts and nonparts according to the usual criteria. The parts were further separated into three classes: modified, unmodified, and quantified parts. As before, the number of quantified parts was too small to be analyzed.

Results and Discussion

The median weights for parts, nonparts, and modified parts are displayed in the bottom

Table 4
*Median Number of Subordinate Categories
Sharing Parts, Modified Parts,
and Other Attributes*

Type of category	Median weight		
	Parts	Other attributes	Modified*
Object			
Pants	6	3	
Shirts	6	3	
Chairs	5.5	3	
Tables	9	2	
Biological			
Flowers	10	2	4
Trees	3	3	3
Birds	10	2	2
Fish	10	2	1

Note. * These numbers were inconsequential for object categories.

Table 5
Biological Subordinate Categories

Flowers	Trees
African violet	Bamboo
Azalea	Elm
Cherry blossom	Maple
Daisy	Oak
Iris	Palm tree
Lilac	Peach tree
Lily	Pear tree
Marigold	Pine
Poppy	Redwood
Rose	Sequoia

Birds	Fish
Blue jay	Carp
Chicken	Eel
Crow	Goldfish
Duck	Minnow
Hawk	Salmon
Mockingbird	Sardine
Owl	Shark
Pelican	Sunfish
Robin	Trout
Sparrow	Tuna

section of Table 4. The parts median is larger than both the nonparts median, $t(3) = 3.27$, $p < .025$, and the modified parts median, $t(3) = 2.85$, $p < .05$. The latter two medians don't differ from one another, $t(3) = .397$, *ns*. Seventy-five percent of the attributes in the norms are nonparts, 15% are parts, 9% are modified parts, and 1% are quantified parts.

On the whole, biological subordinate categories, like object subordinate categories, share parts and differ from one another on other attributes. To a certain extent, they also differ from one another in variations on parts.

DISCUSSION OF STUDIES 1–3

Taken together, these three studies indicate that parts are significantly linked to basic level category cuts: Subjects associate few, if any, part attributes with superordinate level categories, but associate a large number of part attributes with basic level concepts. Few, if any, additional parts are associated with subordinate level categories. Most of the features shared by (subordinate) members of a basic category are parts, and most of the features distinguishing one basic category from another are parts. In contrast, the features that differ-

entiate subordinates of a basic category are mostly nonparts. Unlike at other levels of abstraction, at the basic level parts are both (a) the features common to members of a category and (b) the features distinctive of contrasting categories. Thus, the perceived natural breaks among basic level categories occur between clusters of parts, whereas the perceived natural breaks among subordinate level categories occur between other attributes. These results extend and clarify Rosch et al.'s (1976) assertion that basic level categories are more effective than categories at other levels in grouping entities that share many features and separating entities that are distinguished by many features. Parts are a better index of "basicness" than are other, purely functional or perceptual attributes; in fact, these only attenuate the diagnosis of the basic level.

The predominance of parts listed at the basic level suggests, in addition to a quantitative diagnosis, a qualitative explanation of why members of basic level categories have very similar shapes, and why they are interacted with in the same ways (Rosch et al., 1976). Because that is what the task demands, subjects give lists of parts, but in actuality, parts are organized in specific configurations. The configuration of parts, or structural description, determines the shape of objects to a large degree. Moreover, because they have virtually no distinctive parts, members of different subordinate categories don't have distinctive shapes. Similarly because we typically interact with the parts of an object (we grasp *handles*, sit on *seats*, push *buttons*, etc.), objects that have the same parts are interacted with in the same ways. We return to this analysis in the final discussion. But first, let us have a closer look at parts themselves.

STUDY 4: GOODNESS OF PARTS

We have examined the role of parts in the vertical organization of categories, in distinguishing the basic or preferred level of reference. We have also examined the role of parts in the horizontal organization of categories, in distinguishing one basic level category from another. Another way of examining the horizontal role of parts is to investigate the different parts of a particular object. Until now, we have treated all parts associated with an object as equal. However, even casual perusal of the lists of parts suggests that there is variability in the "goodness" of the parts associated with an object or organism. The *trunk* of an elephant, for instance, seems to be a very good part of an elephant. It is a perceptually salient extension of the body and has functional significance for the elephant as well as for its human caretakers and perceivers. Furthermore, the trunk is a distinctive feature of an elephant, serving to distinguish elephants from other members of the animal kingdom. Similarly, the *screen* of a television is both a perceptually salient and functionally significant part of a television, as well as a part that distinguishes it from other furniture or appliances. Other parts, including many not even mentioned by our informants, seem to be less good, because they lack functional significance or perceptual salience, or object distinctiveness, or some combination of the above. For instance, optional parts, like the *cuffs* of pants or the *buttons* of a shirt lack functional significance or perceptual salience.

Goodness of parts of an object can be viewed as analogous to typicality of members of a category, in that both are ratings reflecting the perceived internal structure of elements related to a higher-level structure. In the case of goodness of parts, the relation is a partonomic, or part–whole relation, where the elements are the parts and the higher level structure is the whole object. In the case of typicality of members, the relation is a taxonomic, or class-inclusion relation, where the elements are categories at one level of abstraction and the higher order structure is a category at a higher level of abstraction. Some category members are perceived as better exemplars of the category than others (Rosch & Mervis, 1975; Mervis & Rosch, 1981); *car* is a better vehicle than *boat*, and *couch* is a better piece of furniture than *lamp*. Subjects' ratings of typicality of member have been used to describe the internal structure of categories, to reflect the fact that some members of a category are regarded as "better" than others. If the analogy holds, subjects' ratings of goodness of part should describe the internal structure of parts and reflect the fact that some parts of an object are seen as better than others.

The study reported here is an attempt to verify the intuition that parts vary in perceived

goodness, that people agree on which parts are better, and that good parts are more frequently mentioned. At the moment, the notion of good part is kept vague; this is an exploratory study, and part goodness is evaluated, not manipulated. The actual ratings prompt further discussion.

Parts Listing

Method

Subjects

The subjects were 30 students in introductory psychology at Stanford who participated for course credit.

Materials and Procedure

The booklets were identical to those used in the attribute listing study of biological categories except that the categories differed. The categories were: apple, car, chair, drum, grape, lamp, lettuce, onion, pants, piano, saw, screwdriver, shirt, and truck. Each booklet included only 7 of the 14 categories, one from each of the 7 superordinates. Each subject completed one booklet, so that 15 subjects listed parts for each category. The procedure was also identical to the procedure used in the attribute listing study of biological categories, except that subjects were asked to list parts only.

Results

The parts were tallied, and each part listed by 2 or more subjects was included in the rating experiment, described next. The low criterion of mention by 2 or more subjects was adopted to increase the range of goodness of parts. This resulted in the inclusion of parts that had been excluded from previous studies. So the list of parts (with goodness ratings) included in Appendix B is not the same list as the list used in Study 1, where parts were shown to be diagnostic of the basic level.

Goodness of Parts Ratings

Method

Materials

A separate form was made for each basic category. The category label was typed at the top of the page, and the parts were listed, in random order, down the left side. Next to each part was a 7-point scale ranging from *very good part* (1) to *not a good part* (7). The pages were collated randomly for each subject. The first page had the instructions on it.

184   BARBARA TVERSKY AND KATHLEEN HEMENWAY

Procedure

The instructions were read aloud to subjects while they read along silently. They were asked to judge the goodness of each part listed for the relevant object. Subjects weren't told what a good part meant; however, they were given several examples of good and bad parts. For example, they were told that *wings* are very good parts of an airplane, and that the *floor* of an airplane isn't a good part. They were also told that *hands* are good parts of a clock, while the *back* of a clock is not. Each of the 15 subjects judged parts for all 14 basic categories.

Results

The mean goodness rating was found for each part (see Appendix B for examples). The data for fruit are omitted from the analyses because several nonparts were inadvertently included. Intraclass correlations were computed on the ratings for each object; these reflect the degree of consensus among all 15 subjects. The correlations shown in Table 6 were good: They ranged from .21 to .66, indicating that people agree in the extent to which a given part is a good part.

The mean goodness ratings were also correlated with frequency of mention of the parts. Signs were reversed so that positive correlations indicate that part goodness and frequency of mention increase together. Only 7 of the 12 correlations were significant; however, the nonsignificant correlations occurred for the items having the fewest parts. These correlations are also displayed in Table 6. The correlations indicate that the parts people listed most frequently were perceived as good parts and provide some validation for the construct, goodness of part.

Both sets of correlations are probably attenuated by including only the parts listed by subjects when asked to list parts of objects, in other words, by including mainly good and "halfway decent" parts. The lists did not include, for instance, parts of other related objects, or technical part terms, or ubiquitous parts, such as molecules. Consistent with this interpretation, the goodness ratings were highly skewed, with more parts rated toward the good end of the scale. Forty-nine percent of the parts received ratings toward the good end (ratings less than or equal to 3), but only 5% of the parts received ratings toward the poor end (ratings greater than or equal to 5).

The reader may wonder why subjects gave

Table 6

Goodness Ratings: Agreement Among Subjects and Correlations With Frequency of Mention

Category	Number of parts	Intraclass correlation	Pearson P-M correlation
Clothing			
Pants	21	.32	.44**
Shirt	16	.24	.21
Furniture			
Chair	16	.33	.50**
Lamp	17	.38	.42*
Musical instruments			
Drum	16	.32	.38
Piano	20	.51	.50**
Tools			
Saw	10	.66	.36
Screwdriver	6	.39	.45
Vegetables			
Lettuce	11	.66	.53*
Onion	6	.35	.09
Vehicles			
Car	48	.25	.42***
Truck	33	.21	.39**

* $p < .05$. ** $p < .025$. *** $p < .01$.

such high goodness ratings to *light* for lamp and to *head* for lettuce, when neither *light* nor *head* passed the criteria for inclusion in the list of parts for Study 1. We believe the explanation lies in the demand characteristic of the rating task. When confronted with *head* in a list of parts for lettuce, the subject may think something like, "Well, *head* isn't really a *part* of *lettuce*, at least not as it appears in the supermarket. So, they must mean *lettuce* as a plant, in which case, it probably has roots and a stem of sorts, so *head* would be a very important part of *lettuce*."

Discussion

To a large degree, our subjects agreed on which parts are good parts of an object. Goodness ratings also predicted frequency of mention by other subjects asked to list parts of an object. The good parts, or for that matter, all the parts in these norms and in the attribute norms as well, are at the same level of analysis, the level of *seat* and *engine* and *wheel*. Subjects list parts, but not parts of parts. Appropriately configured, the parts listed form whole objects. Both perceptual salience and functional significance seem to play a role in goodness ratings. The best part of a chair is a *seat*, the best part of pants are *legs*, the best part of a saw is a *blade*, the best part of a piano is *keys*, and so on. In each of these examples, a case can be made that the best part is among the most perceptually salient and the functionally most important parts. Similarly, the parts receiving especially low ratings seem to be unimportant both to the perception of and the function of the object. The following examples illustrate this point: for lamp, the parts *gas, screws*, and *plastic;* for saw the *rust;* for lettuce, the parts *root, stem, dirt*, and *bug*. Another factor that appears to be correlated with part goodness is the prevalence of the part among the category members, or its essentialness. Optional or less essential parts, such as *stuffing* for chair and *radio* for car are viewed as less good parts than more prevalent and essential parts. Essentialness or prevalence seems to be related to functional significance; a chair without a *seat* wouldn't function as a chair, but a chair without *stuffing* would just be less comfortable. Ethnological evidence from universals in body-part naming corroborate these observations (Andersen, 1978; C. H. Brown, 1976). Body parts enjoying perceptual salience and functional significance are named earlier in the development of terminology and receive more distinctive names. A reasonable question to raise at this point would be, which contributes more to part goodness, perceptual salience, functional significance, or even frequency or essentialness. People could be asked to rate parts on each of these attributes separately, and those ratings could be correlated with goodness ratings. Examination of the goodness ratings discourages such an undertaking. Not only do perceptual salience and functional significance seem to be highly correlated themselves, but there is also an inherent ambiguity or duality in many of the part names themselves. To return to our old example, *seat* may refer to a perceptually distinct segment of a chair, but it also may refer to a distinct function.

For specially selected natural objects and for artificial objects, it seems possible to separate functional significance from perceptual salience. In artificial stimuli, there is usually no function to contend with. There is some evidence that for children, perceptual salience,

particularly in the contour of an artificial object, highly determines parsing an object into its parts (Kosslyn, Heldmeyer, & Glass, 1980). Young children fail to notice parts of natural objects that are functionally significant but perceptually small (Tversky & Bassok, 1978). This suggests that perceptual salience will influence perceived goodness of part at an earlier stage of development or of knowledge acquisition than functional significance. Elsewhere (Melkman, Tversky, & Baratz, 1981) it has been argued that perceptual properties are more immediate than functional properties. Perceptual properties may be known simply from observation of a static object, but knowledge of functional significance, of behavioral properties, seems to require observation of an object in use or in motion.

Recently, there have been several interesting attempts to account for the way we parse forms into parts, usually phrased in terms of the geometry of the forms or the surface appearance of the objects (Bower & Glass, 1976; Hoffman & Richards, 1982; Kosslyn et al., 1980; Palmer, 1977). Local minima in contours, changes in color or texture, "wholeness" of the part (tendency toward closed contour) have been suggested as characteristics of forms that determine parsing. Parts obtained through these perceptual principles have consequences for other tasks: They are better cues to memory for the whole form (Bower & Glass, 1976); they are more quickly identified as being part of the whole (Palmer, 1977). In recent artificial intelligence models, they have played an important role in the structural descriptions of objects (Hoffman & Richards, 1982). All of this research has explored artificial stimuli, where perceptual properties are manipulated but where functional or behavior properties are absent. The connection of parts parsing to function has only now been suggested.

Many metaphoric extensions of parts labels are evident in the list of object parts. Labels for body parts are broadly extended: many objects have *arms, legs, feet, heads*, and *bodies*. Both perceptual and functional similarity to the anthropomorphic parts affect metaphoric extensions. The arms and legs of objects, for instance, are long, thin extensions of objects, arms usually exending from the middle, legs extending at the bottom. But, arms and legs of objects also serve a similar function in objects as in people, that of support (for both) and of manipulation (for arms, viz., *arm* of a phonograph). Some object part labels seem to derive from the human parts with which they interact. *Handles* may look and function like hands, but also, they are interacted with by hands, and shirt *backs* and chair *backs* are at the rear sides of objects, but also are interacted with by the *backs* of people.

GENERAL DISCUSSION

Review of Findings

In taxonomies of common objects and organisms, one level of reference appears to have a privileged status in many diverse cognitive tasks. This level, called the basic level (Rosch et al., 1976), has been identified primarily using a quantitative index of informativeness. Our work has demonstrated a qualitative difference in categories at the basic level and has offered an explanation for the convergence of so many measures at that level. We have shown that one type of knowledge is particularly salient at the basic level, namely, knowledge about parts. Names of parts frequently enjoy a duality not apparent in other attributes; they refer both to a perceptual entity and to a functional role. The *leg* of a chair or the *handle* of a screwdriver have a particular appearance, but they also have a particular function. The prevalence of parts in subjects' attribute lists appears to be particularly diagnostic of the basic level. When asked to characterize entities at the superordinate level, subjects produce few, if any, parts, even for biological categories. Relatively many parts are produced at the basic level, the majority of attributes listed. The proportion of attributes that are parts (and, for nonamended norms, the absolute numbers) decreases at the subordinate level. Thus, part terms play a special role in the vertical organization of categories, that of distinguishing the basic level of reference. Parts play a role in the horizontal organization of categories, too. Different subordinate entities belonging to the same basic level category are perceived to share parts and to differ on other attributes. Similarly, different basic level categories are seen to share other attributes and to differ from one another on the basis of parts. So, the natural breaks among basic level categories

are between clusters of parts, but the natural breaks between subordinate or superordinate level categories are not based on parts. There is a horizontal organization or internal structure to the parts belonging to a particular object, as well. Parts differ in perceived goodness. Subjects agree on which parts of an object are relatively good parts of the object, and goodness is correlated with frequency of mention. Parts that are good appear to have both functional significance and perceptual salience, such as the *leg* of pants, or the *seat* of a chair. Good parts also seem to be shared by many category members and seem to have distinctive labels. None of these variables seems to be primary; rather, their intercorrelation seems to be a fact about the objects and organisms in the world.

Parts and the Convergence of Cognitive Tasks at the Basic Level

There is a long and growing list of cognitive tasks, reviewed earlier, that converge on the basic level. Some of these tasks reflect the appearance of objects, the way objects are perceived and represented. For instance, the basic level is the highest level of abstraction for which a generalized outline form can be recognized and the highest level for which an image can be generated. It is the level at which pictures of objects are identified most rapidly. Some of the tasks pertain to our behavior or responses to the objects, or, more teleologically, to the functions objects serve us. Thus, the basic level is the most abstract level for which motor programs directed toward the objects share elements. Some of the tasks relate to the way we label objects, to our communication about them. Thus, the basic level is the first level to be developed in the evolution of a taxonomy, and the level at which differentiations abound. Basic level terms tend to be shorter and more frequent than either more abstract or more specific terms. They are the terms first taught to and used by children.

Part configuration, we submit, forms the conceptual skeleton underlying and accounting for the convergence of so many different measures at the same level of abstraction. The configuration of parts, or structural description, accounts for the shapes objects may take, thus for our perceptual representations of the appearance of objects. When we interact with objects, our behavior is typically directed toward their parts. Different parts appear to have different functions, or to elicit different behaviors. We sit on the *seat* of a chair and lean against the *back,* we remove the *peel* of a banana, and eat the *pulp.* All other things being equal, entities distinguished in perception or behavior should also be distinguished in language, so breaks in communication should follow the natural breaks in perception. Our terms of reference are selected to pick out an entity in a context. Linguists have argued that basic level terms are contextually neutral (Cruse, 1977). So, saying, "Put out the dog" is fine, but when we say, "Put out the animal," we communicate something more than a simple request. Similarly, when we tell a friend we've acquired a new, pedigree, Hungarian straight-eared toy poodle, we convey something more than when we say we've gotten a new dog. Elsewhere (Tversky & Hemenway, 1983) we have argued that the ordinary context for an object is the scene in which it typically appears; scenes are, to a large degree, composed of basic level objects. So, *chairs* appear in houses and in schools and need to be distinguished from other objects appearing in those situations, particularly, other furniture. *Socks* appear in stores and houses and need to be distinguished from other objects appearing in those contexts, particularly, other clothing. Thus, parts and part configuration form a natural bridge connecting perception of objects and behavior toward them, and in turn, communication about them.

Two aspects of this argument are in need of elaboration. The first concerns the perceptual side, the second, the behavioral side. It might be argued that many of the tasks converging on the basic level concern the appearance, perception, and identification of objects, and that underlying these operations is simply the shapes of objects. Although shape undoubtedly contributes a great deal to the appearance, perception, and identification of objects, it simply does not go far enough. Shape is not unique. Objects are three-dimensional and appear to have different shapes from different points of view. Many objects have moving parts and appear differently in motion. Part configuration accounts for the different shapes objects may have when viewed from

different perspectives and when in motion as well. Many of the parts subjects regard as good parts of objects are enclosed parts, with no consequences for the shapes of objects. These enclosed parts, however, can affect appearance without affecting shape (e.g., the *screen* of a television set) and frequently have important functions. Will a television without a screen or a bureau without drawers be easily and reliably identified? And, only the Tin Woodsman could function without a heart. Shapes, too, cannot account for behavioral measures. Finally, other kinds of categories, such as scenes and events, have parts or components, but do not have shapes, so an analysis based on parts can be generalized to other hierarchies, whereas an analysis based on shape cannot. For these reasons, we believe parts and part configuration to be a more powerful theoretical concept than shape.

Others have argued that the proliferation of sensorial attributes distinguishes the basic level (Denis, 1982; Hoffmann, 1982). Of course, most sensorial attributes are parts, and most parts are sensorial, making it difficult to decide between them. The notable exceptions are internal parts, which are not sensorial, and colors, which are not parts. Would a lemon still be a lemon if it weren't yellow? If it didn't have pulp? Would a fire engine be a fire engine if it weren't red? If it didn't have an engine? Like shapes, sensorial features bear no relation to function and an account of the basic level based on sensorial features cannot be generalized to nonperceptual categories. For some tasks that depend on speeded visual recognition, there may be an advantage to color over internal parts, though for many objects and organisms, color is not a distinguishing feature at all. For other tasks, such as those that depend on function, uses, behavior, or relations to other categories, internal parts seem more important. Thus, sensorial features that are not parts may be more important in the identification procedure associated with a concept, whereas parts may be more important to the conceptual core (Smith & Medin, 1981).

Now, some comments on parts and function. The motor program norms collected by Rosch et al. (1976) used objects, mostly manufactured, as stimuli. These norms reflect human interaction with objects designed for human use. But, parts and function, or parts and behavior seem to be related independent of human users: Thus, the leaves and trunk of a tree have different functions for the tree, the legs and trunk of an elephant behave differently and have different functions for the elephant. Because cars are inanimate, we are less likely to talk about the function of the wheels or engine for the car, but we can say that these different parts of the car are associated with different behaviors. So we would like to argue that parts underlie function for human users, but that they are also related to functions or behaviors in a nonteleological sense, regarding the organism or object as a closed, self-contained system.

Parts and Other Kinds of Categories

Part configuration is especially important because of its role as a bridge between appearance and activity, between perception and behavior, between structure and function. Because structure is related to function via part configuration, part configuration underlies the informativeness of basic level categories. Is the prevalence of parts diagnostic of a privileged level in nonobject categories and hierarchies? Categories of scenes have a basic level, characterized by a proliferation of parts (Tversky & Hemenway, 1983). There is some preliminary evidence for a basic level in categories of events (Rosch, 1978; Rifkin, 1981), or scripted activities. Events, too, can be said to have parts or components. Eating at a restaurant, then, is composed of being seated, ordering food, eating, paying, and leaving. Note that the components of the restaurant script differ perceptually as well as functionally. More generally, it may be the case that perceived part structure is the basis for a privileged status in a taxonomy, that without a level of abstraction where component structure is particularly salient, there will not be a basic level of categorization where so many varied tasks and operations converge.

Parts and Principles of Categorization

The basic level of reference is the starting point for building a taxonomy both phylogenetically, in a community of speakers of the same language (Berlin, 1978), and ontogenetically, in the developing speech of children

(Clark, 1983; Mervis & Crisafi, 1982). There are indications that the principles of classification are not the same at other levels. Rosch and her colleagues (Rosch et al., 1976) have argued that category cuts are determined by the structure of the world. Primary cuts are made at the basic level because, for this level in particular, attributes are correlated. Our work suggests that part configuration, because of its role in relating structure, function, and communication, underlies the correlated attributes or high cue validity present at the basic level. Unlike many categories at other levels, basic level categories seem to be mutually exclusive. Entities seem to belong to no more than one basic level category, though they may belong to more than one superordinate or subordinate category. Subordinate categories, in fact, seem to be designed to cross-classify members of basic object categories. So we have straight-leg pants that may or may not be denim pants and also may or may not be striped pants and even may or may not be wash-and-wear pants. Kitchen chairs may be wooden chairs and may be armless chairs and may be Breuer chairs. Moreover, in general, straight-leg pants and wooden chairs differ from other pants and chairs only on that single feature. The principles governing the construction of subordinate categories in artifacts do not seem to be principles of mutual exclusion. Of course, biological categories are necessarily mutually exclusive, but human beings frequently destroy their elegance by using such categories as farm animals or shade trees or drought-resistant flowers or tropical fish, that cross-cut the biologically rooted categories. In a less flagrant way, superordinate categories can also violate mutual exclusion. Cars and roller skates may be vehicles as well as toys. Knives may be tools and weapons and kitchen utensils. A recorder may be a musical instrument and a toy. We do not balk at these exceptions to mutual exclusion. Not so for basic level concepts. Something isn't both a cantaloupe and a ball. It can be a cantaloupe that looks like a ball, or a ball that looks like a cantaloupe, but isn't both. Sometimes, at the boundaries, it's hard to tell the cups from the mugs or the stools from the chairs, but these are recognized as marginal examples, where both appearance and function are similar. Knives, however, are central tools and central kitchen utensils and central weapons. In folk taxonomies (Berlin et al., 1973), the basic level is the first and most richly differentiated. Other levels are differentiated later, but optionally. Young children, too, appear to break up the world's objects and organisms on one level, the basic level, and show resistance, verbally and conceptually, to higher level categories that include more than one basic level category (Clark, 1983; Inhelder & Piaget, 1964). Children find part–whole relations easier than class inclusion (Markman, 1981), which may explain why their first classifications are at the basic level.

Thus, for object and biological categories, primary or basic category cuts seem to follow natural breaks in the correlational structure of attributes in the world. These breaks, we have argued, are determined by part configuration. Grouping and differentiation at other levels of abstraction need not follow the same principles as categorization at the basic level. Basic categories come first, and are based primarily on parts. Then, we form higher-order, superordinate groupings, that are typically based on function, not perception, where function is rather abstractly conceived. At the same time, we also subdivide basic level categories into more specific categories, on the basis of one (or very few) perceptual or functional features. In contrast to basic level categories, both more general and more specific categories do not have a basis in part configuration, nor do they always conform to mutual exclusivity.

Taxonomy and Partonomy

Sedans and station wagons are kinds of automobiles, while engines, wheels, and doors are parts of automobiles. Both these relations, *kind of* and *part of*, are asymmetric and transitive and can form hierarchies (Miller & Johnson–Laird, 1976). Hierarchies of kinds form the familiar object and organism taxonomies where lower levels are related to upper levels by class inclusion. Hierarchies of parts form partonomies. A familiar one is the body part partonomy, where body is divided into head, trunk, arms, and legs, and each of these is, in turn, divided into its subparts. Abstract concepts can also be represented as partonomies. In eighth-grade civics, for instance, we

all learn that the government consists of legislative, judicial, and executive branches, each of which is further divided into its subcomponents. Taxonomies have been recommended for their cognitive economy (e. g., Collins & Quillian, 1969); not only do they provide a structure for a large body of knowledge, reducing the number of categories with which we ordinarily need to deal, but they also generally allow inference of properties from higher level nodes to the categories included in them. If having wheels or running on land are properties of cars, then we can infer that they will hold for any kind of car. In general, *part of* relations do not allow such inference; it is not the case that all parts of cars have wheels or run on land.

Parts and Naive Induction

Part configuration seems to serve a very different role in the organization of knowledge. Put directly, part decomposition appears to be a way of relating structure to function. Our exploration of goodness of part led us to the conclusion that parts that are perceived to be good are, in general, those that enjoy both perceptual salience and functional significance. This intuition, in fact, seems to be the basis for naive induction, for initial mental models of the physical (and metaphysical) world, for intuitive science. Preliminary investigations of many phenomena are often guided by these working assumptions: that separate parts will have separate functions, that similar parts will have similar functions, that more salient parts will have more important functions, that, together, parts form an organized, integrated, functioning whole. These initial assumptions may turn out to be wrong, but they nevertheless characterize initial explorations. Biology abounds with examples where structural parts guided the search for function. Phrenology, where separate parts of the skull were assumed to have separate cognitive functions, stands as a classic example of a failure of this approach. But it was eventually replaced by neuroanatomy, which has succeeded in relating different brain structures to different cognitive functions. In his dramatic account of the revolution in microbiology, Judson (1979) showed how at many stages, new techniques for "seeing" structure and determining components led to major advances in the discovery of function. In their rudimentary, intuitive attempts to account for physical phenomena, children, too, often explain function or behavior by reference to parts, of objects, situations, or events (for instance, Bullock, Gelman, & Baillargeon, 1983). Our mental models for comprehending physical systems typically divide them into separate parts having separate functions (see examples in Anderson, 1981, and Gentner & Stevens, 1983). Designers of complex systems for human use, such as computer systems, are often explicitly advised to conform to these working assumptions, of separate parts for separate functions, of similar parts for similar functions, of large parts for important functions, and so on (Norman, 1982). Perceived part configuration, then, underlies both perceived structure and perceived function. As such, it seems to form the basis for intuitive causal reasoning and naive induction.

We began with Caesar's campaign on Gaul, with the observation that in describing or comprehending some body of knowledge or set of phenomena, we often begin by decomposing the thing to be understood into separate parts. This "divide-and-conquer" strategy is invoked not just because smaller parts are easier to deal with, but also because different parts are to be dealt with differently. Each part has a different story. How does this relate to the phenomenon of a basic level, to a preferred level of reference or abstraction, to a level more informative than others, to a level where the primary categories of objects and organisms, scenes and events are carved out? Our work has shown that one particular kind of information is more salient in the minds of people when they think about entities at the basic level, namely, information about parts. Through parts, we link the world of appearance to the realm of action. Through parts, we use structure to comprehend, infer, and predict function. This, then, seems to be the knowledge that makes the basic level the most informative level: the knowledge of function that can be inferred from structure.

References

Andersen, E. S. (1978). Lexical universals in body-part terminology. In J. H. Greenberg (Ed.), *Universals of Human Language* (pp. 335–368). Stanford, CA: Stanford University Press.

Anderson, J. R. (Ed.). (1981). *Cognitive skills and their acquisition*. Hillsdale, NJ: Erlbaum.

Ashcraft, M. H. (1978). Property norms for typical and atypical items from 17 categories: A description and discussion. *Memory & Cognition, 6,* 227–232.

Berlin, B. (1972). Speculations on the growth of ethnobotanical nomenclature. *Language in Society, 1,* 51–86.

Berlin, B. (1978). Ethnobiological classification. In E. Rosch & B. B. Lloyd (Eds.), *Cognition and categories* (pp. 9–26). Hillsdale, NJ: Erlbaum.

Berlin, B., Breedlove, D. E., & Raven, P. H. (1966). Folk taxonomies and biological classification. *Science, 154,* 273–275.

Berlin, B., Breedlove, D. E., & Raven, P. H. (1973). General principles of classification and nomenclature in folk biology. *American Anthropologist, 75,* 214–242.

Berlin, B., & Kay, P. (1969). *Basic color terms: Their universality and evolution.* Berkeley and Los Angeles: University of California Press.

Bower, G. H., & Glass, A. (1976). Structural units and the redintegrative power of picture fragments. *Journal of Experimental Psychology: Human Learning and Memory, 2,* 456–466.

Brown, C. H. (1976). General principles of human anatomical partonomy and speculations on the growth of partonomic nomenclature. *American Ethnologist, 3,* 400–424.

Brown, C. H. (1977). Folk botanical life-forms: Their universality and growth. *American Anthropologist, 79,* 317–342.

Brown, C. H. (1979). Folk zoological life-forms: Their universality and growth. *American Anthropologist, 81,* 791–817.

Brown, R. (1958). How shall a thing be called? *Psychological Review, 65,* 14–21.

Bullock, M., Gelman, R., & Baillargeon, R. (1983). The development of causal reasoning. In W. Friedman (Ed.), *The developmental psychology of time* (pp. 209–254). New York: Academic Press.

Clark, E. (1983). Meanings and concepts. In J. H. Flavell & E. M. Markman (Eds.), *Handbook of child psychology: Vol. 3. Cognitive Development* (4th ed., pp. 787–840). New York: Wiley.

Collins, A. M., & Quillian, M. R. (1969). Retrieval time from semantic memory. *Journal of Verbal Learning and Verbal Behavior, 8,* 240–247.

Cruse, D. A. (1977). The pragmatics of lexical specificity. *Journal of Linguistics, 13,* 153–164.

Denis, M. (1982). Images and semantic representations. In J-F Le Ny & W. Kintsch (Eds.), *Language and comprehension* (pp. 17–27). Amsterdam: North-Holland.

Dougherty, J. W. D. (1978). Salience and relativity in classification. *American Ethnologist, 5,* 66–80.

Garner, W. R. (1974). *The processing information and structure.* Potomac, MD: Erlbaum.

Gentner, D., & Stevens, A. L. (Eds.). (1983). *Mental models.* Hillsdale, NJ: Erlbaum.

Grice, H. P. (1975). Logic and conversation. In P. Cole & J. L. Morgan (Eds.), *Syntax and semantics: Speech acts* (Vol. 3, pp. 41–58). New York: Academic Press, 1975.

Hampton, J. A. (1979). Polymorphous concepts in semantic memory. *Journal of Verbal Learning and Verbal Behavior, 18,* 441–461.

Hampton, J. A. (1981). An investigation of the nature of abstract concepts. *Memory & Cognition, 9,* 149–156.

Hoffman, D. D., & Richards, W. A. (1982). *Representing plane curves for recognition* (AI Memo No. 630). Cambridge, MA: MIT, Artificial Intelligence Laboratory.

Hoffmann, J. (1982). Representations of concepts and the classification of objects. In R. Klix, J. Hoffmann, & E. van der Meer (Eds.), *Cognitive research in psychology: Recent approaches, designs and results* (pp. 72–89). Amsterdam: North-Holland.

Hunn, E. (1976). Toward a perceptual model of folk biological classification. *American Ethnologist, 3,* 508–524.

Inhelder, B., & Piaget, J. (1964). *The early growth of logic in the child.* New York: Norton.

Judson, H. F. (1979). *The eighth day of creation.* New York: Simon & Schuster.

Kosslyn, S. M., Heldmeyer, K. H., & Glass, A. L. (1980). Where does one part end and another begin? A developmental study. In J. Becker, F. Wilkening, & T. Trabasso (Eds.), *Information integration in children* (pp. 147–168). Hillsdale, NJ: Erlbaum.

Malt, B. C., & Smith, E. E. (1982). The role of familiarity in determining typicality. *Memory & Cognition, 10,* 69–75.

Markman, E. M. (1981). Two different principles of conceptual organization. In M. E. Lamb & A. L. Brown (Eds.), *Advances in developmental psychology* (pp. 199–236). Hillsdale, NJ: Erlbaum.

Melkman, R., Tversky, B., & Baratz, D. (1981). Developmental trends in the use of perceptual and conceptual attributes in grouping, clustering, and retrieval. *Journal of Experimental Child Psychology, 31,* 470–486.

Mervis, C. B., & Crisafi, M. A. (1982). Order of acquisition of subordinate-, basic-, and superordinate-level categories. *Child Development, 53,* 258–266.

Mervis, C. B., & Rosch, E. (1981). Categorization of natural objects. *Annual Review of Psychology, 32,* 89–115.

Miller, G. A., & Johnson-Laird, P. N. (1976). *Language and perception.* Cambridge, MA: Harvard University Press.

Murphy, G. L., & Smith, E. E. (1982). Basic-level superiority in picture categorization. *Journal of Verbal Learning and Verbal Behavior, 21,* 1–20.

Norman, D. A. (1982). Steps toward a cognitive engineering: Design rules based on analyses of human errors. *Proceedings of the conference on human factors in computer systems.* Gaithersburg, MD.

Palmer, S. E. (1977). Hierarchical structure in perceptual representation. *Cognitive Psychology, 9,* 441–474.

Rifkin, A. J. (1981). *Event categories, event taxonomies, and basic level events.* Unpublished manuscript, New York University, New York.

Rosch, E. (1978). Principles of categorization. In E. Rosch & B. Lloyd (Eds.), *Cognition and categorization* (pp. 27–48). Hillsdale, NJ: Erlbaum.

Rosch, E., & Mervis, C. B. (1975). Family resemblances: Studies in the internal structure of categories. *Cognitive Psychology, 7,* 573–605.

Rosch, E., Mervis, C. B., Gray, W., Johnson, D., & Boyes-Braem, P. (1976). Basic objects in natural categories. *Cognitive Psychology, 8,* 382–439.

Smith, E. E., & Medin, D. L. (1981). *Categories and concepts.* Cambridge, MA: Harvard University Press.

Smith, E. E., Balzano, G. J., & Walker, J. (1978). Nominal, perceptual, and semantic codes in picture categorization. In J. W. Cotton & R. L. Klatzky (Eds.), *Semantic factors in cognition* (pp. 137–167). Hillsdale, NJ: Erlbaum.

Tversky, B., & Bassok, M. (1978). *What's missing?* Unpublished manuscript, Stanford University, Stanford, CA.

Tversky, B., & Hemenway, K. (1983). Categories of environmental scenes. *Cognitive Psychology, 15,* 121–149.

(Appendixes follow on next page)

Appendix A

Table A1
Attributes Included in Judge-Amended Tally for Some Biological Categories at Three Levels

Category	Parts	Nonparts	Category	Parts	Nonparts
Animal	Tail Eyes	Moves Living Eats	Plant (*continued*)		Needs water Green
Bird	Two legs Wings Feathers Beak	Lays eggs Living Builds nests Eats Moves	Flower	Petals Stem Leaves	Needs carbon dioxide Needs water Pretty Green
Chicken	Two legs Wings Feathers Beak	Brown Lays eggs Eats worms Living Eaten by humans Builds nests Eats Moves	Rose	Petals Thorns Stem Leaves	Needs carbon dioxide Needs water Red Pretty Yellow Grows on bushes Colorful Pink

Robin	Two legs
	Wings
	Red breast
	Feathers
	Beak
		Chirps
		Flies
		Lays eggs
		Eats worms
		Small
		Living
		Builds nests
		Eats
		Moves
			Poppy	Petals
				Stem
				Leaves
					Needs carbon
					  dioxide
					Needs water
					Pretty
					California state
					  flower
					Opium
					White
					Colorful

Fish	Tail Fins Eyes Gills Scales	Moves Living Eats Swims	Tree	Bark Trunk Wood Branches Roots	Green Needs carbon dioxide Needs water

Goldfish	Tail
	Fins
	Eyes
	Gills
	Scales
		Small
		Orange
		Moves
		Living
		Kept in small bowl
		Swims
		Eats
			Palm tree	Trunk
				Leaves
				Coconuts
				Wood
				Branches
				Branches all at
				  top
				Roots
				Bark
					Warm climate
					Green
					Large
					Tall
					Needs carbon
					  dioxide
					Needs water
					Very tall

Salmon	Tail Fins Eyes Gills Scales	Used in salads Comes in cans Moves Lives in streams Living Used in sandwiches Swims Eats Swims upstream Ocean	Pine	Trunk Wood Branches Roots Needles Cones Bark	Green Large Tall Needs carbon dioxide Forest Needs water Fragrant Very tall Used for furniture
Plant	Stem Roots	Needs carbon dioxide			

Appendix B

Table B1
Selected Mean Goodness Ratings of Parts of Objects

Part	M	Part	M	Part	M	Part	M
		Clothing: Pants				Tools: Saw (*continued*)	
Leg	1.9	Snaps	3.9	Metal blade	1.5	Wood (parts)	4.0
Pockets	2.1	Inseam	4.0	Teeth	1.9	Screws	4.3
Seat	2.2	Hem	4.3	Metal	2.3	Rust	6.2
Zipper	2.5	Buttons	4.3				
Material	2.6	Label	4.5			Vegetables: Lettuce	
Crotch	3.1	Stitching	4.6				
Waist band	3.1	Bell bottoms	4.6	Head	1.0	Core	4.5
Belt loops	3.4	Cuff	4.8	Green	1.8	Root	5.3
Belt	3.7	Elastic	4.9	Leaf	1.8	Stem	5.5
Thread	3.7	Patches	5.3	Cellulose	3.2	Dirt	6.5
Seam	3.9			Water	3.5	Bug	6.7
				Vein	3.8		
		Furniture: Chair				Vehicles: Car	
Seat	1.6	Cloth, material	3.1				
Arms	1.9	Legs	3.3	Engine	1.5	Mirror	2.7
Back	2.2	Foot rest	3.5	Steering wheel	1.6	Chassis	2.7
Cushion	2.3	Leg rest	3.5	Brakes	1.6	Lights	2.8
Back rest	2.4	Wood	3.5	Wheels	1.9	Axle	2.8
Arm rests	2.5	Stuffing	3.6	Seats	1.9	Speedometer	2.9
Upholstery	2.9	Feet	4.7	Tires	2.0	Side view mirror	2.9
Head rest	3.0	Buttons	5.9	Headlights	2.1	Radiator	2.9
				Transmission	2.1	Hood	3.1
		Musical instruments: Piano		Gear shift	2.1	Horn	3.1
				Windshield	2.1	Fender	3.3
Keys	1.1	Legs	3.4	Pedals	2.2	Exhaust pipe	3.3
Keyboard	1.1	Wood	3.5	Pistons	2.3	Spare tire	3.4
White keys	1.2	Cover	3.8	Carburetor	2.3	Roof	3.6
Black keys	1.5	Lid	4.1	Fuel tank	2.3	Dashboard	3.6
Music	1.7	Music stand	4.3	Gasoline	2.3	Trunk	3.6
Pedals	1.8	Screws	4.7	Battery	2.4	Radio	3.7
Strings	1.9	Brand name	4.7	Spark plugs	2.5	Door handles	3.9
Hammers	2.7	plate		Rearview mirror	2.5	Paint	4.0
Bench	2.9	Hinges	4.7	Drive shaft	2.5	Glove	4.1
Wood body	3.0	Wheels	5.8	Seat belt	2.5	compartment	
Stool	3.1			Body	2.6	Hubcaps	4.4
				Bumpers	2.6	Carpeting	4.7
		Tools: Saw		Window	2.7	Rugs	4.8
				Wipers	2.7	Handle	4.9
Blade	1.1	Handle	2.6	Door	2.7		
Sharp teeth	1.2	Motor	3.3				

Received March 25, 1983
Revision received September 1, 1983 ■

[12]

Parts of recognition*

D.D. HOFFMAN

University of California, Irvine

W.A. RICHARDS

Massachusetts Institute of Technology

Abstract

We propose that, for the task of object recognition, the visual system decomposes shapes into parts, that it does so using a rule defining part boundaries rather than part shapes, that the rule exploits a uniformity of nature—transversality, and that parts with their descriptions and spatial relations provide a first index into a memory of shapes. This rule allows an explanation of several visual illusions. We stress the role inductive inference in our theory and conclude with a précis of unsolved problems.

1. Introduction

Any time you view a statue, or a simple line drawing, you effortlessly perform a visual feat far beyond the capability of the most sophisticated computers today, through well within the capacity of a kindergartener. That feat is shape recognition, the visual identification of an object using only its shape. Figure 1 offers an opportunity to exercise this ability and to make several observations. Note first that, indeed, shape alone is sufficient to recognize the objects; visual cues such as shading, motion, color, and texture are not present in the figure. Note also that you could not reasonably predict the contents of the figure before looking at it, yet you recognized the objects.

*We are grateful to Thomas Banchoff, Aaron Bobick, Mike Brady, Carmen Egido, Jerry Fodor, Jim Hodgson, Jan Koenderink, Jay Lebed, Alex Pentland, John Rubin, Joseph Scheuhammer, and Andrew Witkin for their helpful discussions and, in some cases, for reading earlier drafts. We are also grateful to Alan Yuille for comments and corrections on the mathematics in the appendices. Preparation of this paper was supported in part by NSF and AFOSR under a combined grant for studies in Natural Computation, grant 79-23110-MCS, and by the AFOSR under an Image Understanding contract F49620-83-C-0135. Technical support was kindly provided by William Gilson; artwork was the creation of Julie Sandell and K. van Buskirk. Reprints may be obtained from D. Hoffman, School of Social Sciences, University of California, Irvine, CA 92717, U.S.A.

Figure 1.   *Some objects identifiable entirely from their profiles.*

Clearly your visual system is equipped to describe the shape of an object and to guess what the object is from its description. This guess may just be a first guess, perhaps best thought of as a first index into a memory of shapes, and might not be exactly correct; it may simply narrow the potential matches and trigger visual computations designed to narrow them further.

This first guess is more precisely described as an inference, one the truth of whose premises—the descriptions of shape—does not logically guarantee the truth of its conclusion—the identity of the object. Because the truth of the conclusion does not follow logically from the truth of the premises, the strength of the inference must derive from some other source. That source, we claim, is the regularity of nature, its uniformities and general laws. The design of the visual system exploits regularities of nature in two ways: they underlie the mental categories used to represent the world and they permit inferences from impoverished visual data to descriptions of the world.

Regularities of nature play both roles in the visual task of shape recognition, and both roles will be examined. We will argue that, just as syntactic analysis decomposes a sentence into its constituent structure, so the visual system decomposes a shape into a hierarchy of parts. Parts are not chosen arbitrarily; the mental category 'part' of shapes is based upon a regularity of nature discovered by differential topologists—transversality. This is an example of a regularity in the first role. The need arises for a regularity in the second role because although parts are three-dimensional, the eye delivers only a two-dimensional projection. In consequence the three-dimensional parts must be inferred from their two-dimensional projections. We propose that this inference is licensed by another regularity, this time from the field of singularity theory.

2. Why parts?

Before examining a part definition and its underlying regularity, we should ask: Given that one wants to recognize an object from its shape, why partition the shape at all? Could template matching or Fourier descriptors rise to the occasion? Possibly. What follows is not so much intended to deny this as to indicate the usefulness of parts.

To begin, then, an articulation of shapes into parts is useful because one never sees an entire shape in one glance. Clearly the back side is never visible (barring transparent objects), but even the front side is often partially occluded by objects interposed between the shape and the observer. A Fourier approach suffers because all components of a Fourier description can change radically as different aspects of a shape come into view. A part theory, on the other hand, can plausibly assume that the parts delivered by early vision correspond to the parts stored in the shape memory (after all, the contents of the shape memory were once just the products of early visual processing), and that the shape memory is organized such that a shape can be addressed by an inexhaustive list of its parts. Then recognition can proceed using the visible parts.

Parts are also advantageous for representing objects which are not entirely rigid, such as the human hand. A template of an outstretched hand would correlate poorly with a clenched fist, or a hand giving a victory sign, etc. The proliferation of templates to handle the many possible configurations of the hand, or of any articulated object, is unparsimonious and a waste of memory. If part theorists, on the other hand, pick their parts prudently (criteria for prudence will soon be forthcoming), and if they introduce the notion of spatial relations among parts, they can decouple configural properties from the shape of an object, thereby avoiding the proliferation of redundant mental models.

The final argument for parts to be considered here is phenomenological: we see them when we look at shapes. Figure 2, for instance, presents a cosine surface, which observers almost uniformly see organized into ring-like parts. One part stops and another begins roughly where the dotted circular contours are drawn. But if the figure is turned upside down the organization changes such that each dotted circular contour, which before lay between parts, now lies in the middle of a part. Why the parts change will be explained by the partitioning rule to be proposed shortly; the point of interest here is simply that our visual systems do in fact cut surfaces into parts.

68   *D.D. Hoffman and W.A. Richards*

Figure 2.   *The cosine surface at first appears to be organized into concentric rings, one*
ring terminating and the next beginning approximately where the dashed
circular contours are drawn. But this organization changes when the figure
is turned upside down.

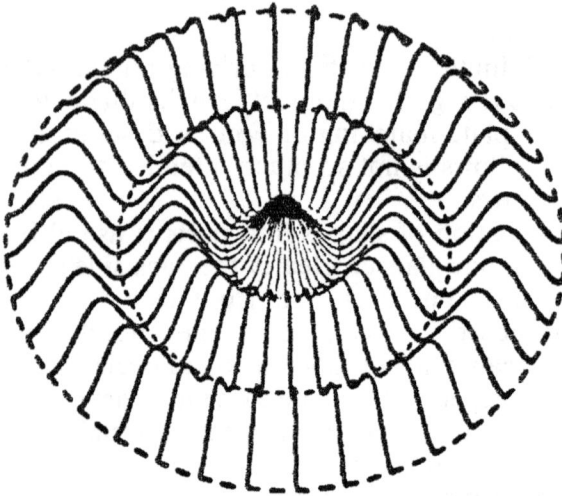

3. Parts and uniformities of nature

Certainly any proper subset of a surface is a part of that surface. This definition of part, however, is of little use for the task of shape recognition. And
although the task of shape recognition constrains the class of suitable part
definitions (see Section 5), it by no means forces a unique choice. To avoid
an *ad hoc* choice, and to allow a useful correspondence between the world
and mental representations of shape, the definition of part should be motivated by a uniformity of nature.[1]

One place not to look for a defining regularity is in the shapes of a part.
One could say that all parts are cylinders, or cones, or spheres, or polyhedra,
or some combination of these; but this is legislating a definition, not discovering a relevant regularity. And such a definition would have but limited
applicability, for certainly not all shapes can be decomposed into just cylinders, cones, spheres, and polyhedra.

If a defining regularity is not to be found in part shapes, then another place

---

[1]Unearthing an appropriate uniformity is the most creative, and often most difficult, step in devising an
explanatory theory for a visual task. Other things being equal, one wants the most general uniformity of nature
possible, as this grants the theory and the visual task the broadest possible scope.

Figure 3.   *An illustration of the transversality regularity. When any two surfaces inter-*
penetrate at random they always meet in concave discontinuities, as indicated
by the dashed contours.

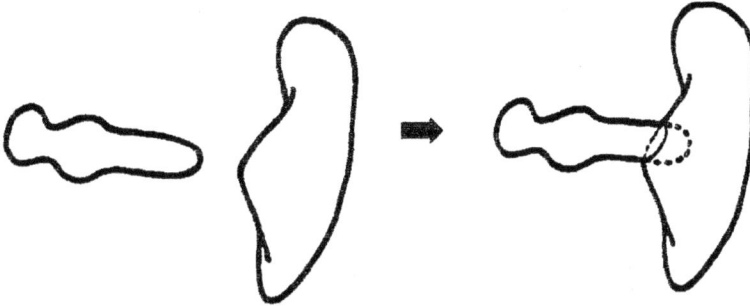

to look is part intersections. Consider the two three-dimensional blobs depicted in the left of Fig. 3. Certainly these two spatially separated shapes are
different parts of this figure. Indeed, each spatially distinct object in a visual
scene is a part of that scene. Now if two such separate objects are interpenetrated to form one new composite object, as shown in the right of Fig. 3, then
the two objects, which were before separate parts of the visual scene, are
surely now prime candidates to be parts of the new composite shape. But can
we tell, simply by examining the new composite shape, what the original
parts are? That is, is there a way to tell where one part stops and the next
part begins on the new composite shape? Fortunately there is a way, one
which depends on a regularity in the way two shapes generically intersect.
This regularity is called transversality (for a detailed discussion of transversality see Guillemin and Pollack (1974)).

- *Transversality regularity.* When two arbitrarily shaped surfaces are made
  to interpenetrate they always[2] meet in a contour of concave discontinuity
  of their tangent planes.

To see this more clearly, observe the silhouette of the composite shape
shown in the right of Fig. 3. Notice that this composite silhouette is not
smooth at the two points where the silhouette of one of its parts intersects
the silhouette of the other part. At these two points the direction of the
silhouette's outline (i.e., its tangent direction) changes abruptly, creating a
concave cusp (i.e., a cusp which points into the object, not into the

---

[2]The word *always* is best interpreted "with probability one assuming the surfaces interpenetrate at random".

background) at each of the two points. In fact, such concave discontinuities arise at every point on the surface of the composite shape where the two parts meet. These contours of concave discontinuity of the tangent plane of the composite shape will be the basis for a partitioning rule in the next section. But three observations are in order.

First, though it may sound esoteric, transversality is a familiar part of our everyday experience. A straw in a soft drink forms a circular concave discontinuity where it meets the surface of the drink. So too does a candle in a birthday cake. The tines of a fork in a piece of steak, a cigarette in a mouth, all are examples of this ubiquitous regularity.

Second, transversality does not double as a theory of part growth or part formation (D'Arcy Thompson, 1968). We are not claiming, for example, that a nose was once physically separated from the face and then got attached by interpenetration. We simply note that when two spatially separated shapes are interpenetrated, their intersection is transversal. Later we will see how this regularity underlies the visual definition of separate parts of any composite shape, such as the nose of a face or a limb of a tree, regardless of how the composite shape was created.

Finally, transversality does encompass movable parts. As mentioned earlier, one attraction of parts is that, properly chosen, they make possible a decoupling of configuration and shape in descriptions of articulated objects. But to do this the parts must cut an object at its articulations; a thumb–wrist part on the hand, for instance, would be powerless to capture the various spatial relations that can exist between the thumb and the wrist. Now the parts motivated by transversality will be the movable units, fundamentally because a transversal intersection of two surfaces remains transversal for small pertubations of their positions. This can be appreciated by reviewing Fig. 3. Clearly the intersection of the two surfaces remains a contour of concave discontinuity even as the two surfaces undergo small independent rotations and translations.

4. Partitioning: The minima rule

On the basis of the transversality regularity we can propose a first rule for dividing a surface into parts: divide a surface into parts along all contours of concave discontinuity of the tangent plane. Now this rule cannot help us with the cosine surface because this surface is entirely smooth. The rule must be generalized somewhat, as will be done shortly. But in its present form the rule can provide insight into several well-known perceptual demonstrations.

4.1. Blocks world

We begin by considering shapes constructed from polygons. Examine the staircase of Fig. 4. The rule predicts that the natural parts are the steps, and not the faces on the steps. Each step becomes a 'part' because it is bounded by two lines of concave discontinuity in the staircase. (A face is bounded by a concave and a convex discontinuity.) But the rule also makes a less obvious prediction. If the staircase undergoes a perceptual reversal, such that the 'figure' side of the staircase becomes 'ground' and *vice versa*, then the step boundaries must change. This follows because only *concave* discontinuities define step boundaries. And what looks like a concavity from one side of a surface must look like a convexity from the other. Thus, when the staircase reverses, convex and concave discontinuities must reverse roles, leading to new step boundaries. You can test this prediction yourself by looking at the step having a dot on each of its two faces. When the staircase appears to reverse note that the two dots no longer lie on a single step, but lie on two adjacent steps (that is, on two different 'parts').

Similar predictions from the rule can also be confirmed with more complicated demonstrations such as the stacked cubes demonstration shown in Fig. 5. The three dots which at first appear to lie on one cube, lie on three different cubes when the figure reverses.

Still another quite different prediction follows from our simple partitioning rule. If the rule does not define a unique partition of some surface, then the division of that surface into parts should be perceptually ambiguous (unless,

Figure 4. *The Schroder staircase, published by H. Schroder in 1858, shows that part boundaries change when figure and ground reverse. The two dots which at first appear to lie on one step suddenly seem to lie on two adjacent steps when the staircase reverses.*

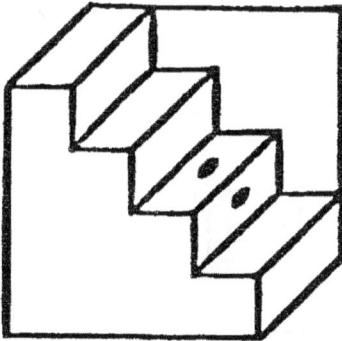

of course, there are additional rules which can eliminate the ambiguity). An elbow-shaped block provides clear confirmation of this prediction (see Fig. 6). The only concave discontinuity is the vertical line in the crook of the elbow; in consequence, the rule does not define a unique partition of the block. Perceptually, there are three plausible ways to cut the block into parts (also shown in Fig. 6). All three use the contour defined by the partitioning rule, but complete it along different paths.

Figure 5.   *Stacked cubes also show that parts change when figure and ground reverse. Three dots which sometimes lie on one cube will lie on three different cubes when the figure reverses.*

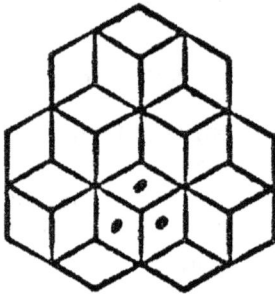

Figure 6.   *Elbow-shaped blocks show that a rule partitioning shapes at concave discontinuities is appropriately conservative. The rule does not give a closed contour on the top block, and for good reason. Perceptually, three different partitions seem reasonable, as illustrated by the bottom three blocks.*

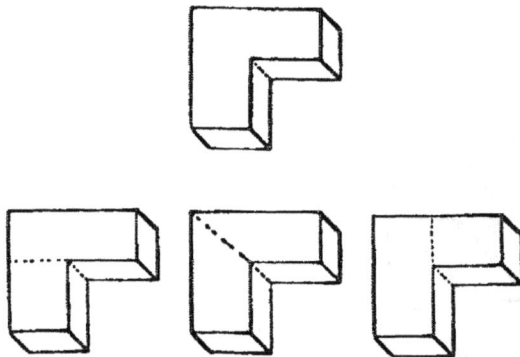

4.2. Generalization to smooth surfaces

The simple partitioning rule directly motivated by transversality leads to interesting insights into our perception of the parts of polygonal objects. But how can the rule be generalized to handle smooth surfaces, such as the cosine surface? To grasp the generalization, we must briefly digress into the differential geometry of surfaces in order to understand three important concepts: surface normal, principal curvature, and line of curvature. Fortunately, although these concepts are quite technical, they can be understood intuitively.

The surface normal at a point on a surface can be thought of as a unit length needle sticking straight out of (orthogonal to) the surface at that point, much like the spines on a sea urchin. All the surface normals at all points on a surface are together called a field of surface normals. Usually there are two possible fields of surface normals on a surface—either outward pointing or inward pointing. A sphere, for instance, can either have the surface normals all pointing out like spines, or all pointing to its center. Let us adopt the convention that the field of surface normals is always chosen to point into the figure (i.e., into the object). Thus a baseball has inward normals whereas a bubble under water, if the water is considered figure, has outward normals. Reversing the choice of figure and ground on a surface implies a concomitant change in the choice of the field of surface normals. And, as will be discussed shortly, a reversal of the field of surface normals induces a change in sign of each principal curvature at every point on the surface.

It is often important to know not just the surface normal at a point but also how the surface is curving at the point. The Swiss mathematician Leonhard Euler discovered around 1760 that at any point on any surface there is always a direction in which the surface curves least and a second direction, always orthogonal to the first, in which the surface curves most. (Spheres and planes are trivial cases since the surface curvature is identical in all directions at every point.) These two directions at a point are called the principal directions at that point and the corresponding surface curvatures are called the principal curvatures. Now by starting at some point and always moving in the direction of the greatest principal curvature one traces out a line of greatest curvature. By moving instead in the direction of the least principal curvature one traces out a line of least curvature. On a drinking glass the family of lines of greatest curvature is a set of circles around the glass. The lines of least curvature are straight lines running the length of the glass (see Fig. 7).

With these concepts in hand we can extend the partitioning rule to smooth surfaces. Suppose that wherever a surface has a concave discontinuity we smooth the discontinuity somewhat, perhaps by stretching a taut skin over it.

74   *D.D. Hoffman and W.A. Richards*

Figure 7.   *Lines of curvature are easily depicted on a drinking glass. Lines of greatest curvature are circles. Lines of least curvature are straight lines.*

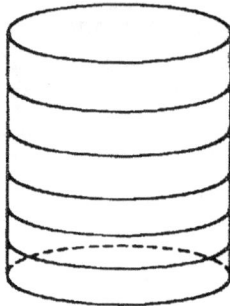

Lines of greatest curvature   Lines of least curvature

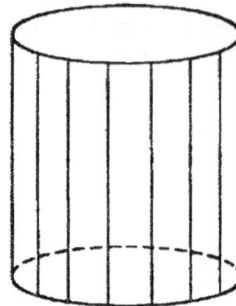

Then a concave discontinuity becomes a contour where, locally, the surface has greatest negative curvature. In consequence we obtain the following generalized partitioning rule for surfaces.

- *Minima rule.* Divide a surface into parts at loci of negative minima of each principal curvature along its associated family of lines of curvature.

The minima rule is applied to two surfaces in Fig. 8. The solid contours indicate members of one family of lines of curvature, and the dotted contours are the part boundaries defined by the minima rule. The bent sheet of paper on the right of Fig. 8 is particularly informative. The lines of curvature shown for this surface are sinusoidal, whereas the family of lines not shown are perfectly straight and thus have zero principal curvature (and no associated minima). In consequence, the product of the two principal curvatures at each point, called the *Gaussian curvature*, is always zero for this surface. Now if the Gaussian curvature is always zero on this surface, then the Gaussian curvature cannot be used to divide the surface into parts. But we see parts on this surface. Therefore whatever rule our visual systems use to partition surfaces cannot be stated entirely in terms of Gaussian curvature. In particular, the visual system cannot be dividing surfaces into parts at loci of zero Gaussian curvature (parabolic points) as has been proposed by Koenderink and van Doorn (1982b).

The minima rule partitions the cosine surface along the circular dotted contours shown in Fig. 2. It also explains why the parts differ when figure and ground are reserved. For when the page is turned upside down the visual system reverses its assignment of figure and ground on the surface (perhaps

Figure 8. *Part boundaries, as defined by the smooth surface partitioning rule, are indicated by dashed lines on several different surfaces. The families of solid lines are the lines of curvature whose minima give rise to the dashed partitioning contour.*

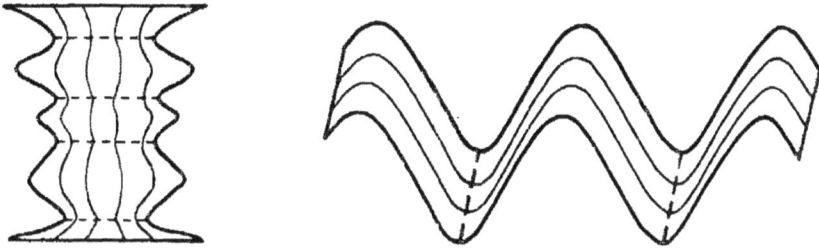

due to a preference for an interpretation which places the object below rather than overhead). When figure and ground reverse so does the field of surface normals, in accordance with the convention mentioned earlier. But simple calculations show that when the normals reverse so too does the sign of the principal curvatures. Consequently minima of the principal curvatures must become maxima and *vice versa*. Since minima of the principal curvatures are used for part boundaries, it follows that these part boundaries must also move. In sum, parts appear to change because the partitioning rule, motivated by the transversality regularity, uses minima of the principal curvatures, and because these minima relocate on the surface when figure and ground reverse. A more rigorous treatment of the partitioning rule is provided in Appendix 1.

5. Parts: Constraints from recognition

The task of visual recognition constrains one's choice of parts and part descriptions. We evaluate the part scheme proposed here against three such constraints—*reliability, versatility,* and *computability*—and then note a non-constraint, *information preservation.*

Reliability. Recognition is fundamentally a process of matching descriptions of what one sees with descriptions already in memory. Imagine the demands on memory and on the matching process if every time one looked at an object one saw different parts. A face, for example, which at one instant appeared to be composed of eyes, ears, a nose, and a mouth, might at a later instant metamorphose into a potpourri of eye–cheek, nose–chin, and mouth–

ear parts—a gruesome and unprofitable transmutation. Since no advantage accrues for allowing such repartitions, in fact since they are uniformly deleterious to the task of recognition, it is reasonable to disallow them and to require that the articulation of a shape into parts be invariant over time and over change in viewing geometry. This is the constraint of reliability (see Marr, 1982; Marr and Nishihara, 1978; Nishihara, 1981; Sutherland, 1968); the parts of a shape should be related reliably to the shape. A similar constraint governs the identification of linguistic units in a speech stream (Liberman *et al*, 1967; Fodor, 1983). Apparently the shortest identifiable unit is the syllable; shorter units like phones are not related reliably to acoustic parameters.

The minima rule satisfies this reliability constraint because it uses only surface properties, such as extrema of the principal curvatures, which are independent (up to a change in sign) of the coordinate system chosen to parametrize the surface (Do Carmo, 1976). Therefore the part boundaries do not change when the viewing geometry changes. (The part boundaries do change when figure and ground reverse, however.)

Versatility. Not all possible schemes for defining parts of surfaces are sufficiently versatile to handle the infinite variety in shape that objects can exhibit. Other things being equal, if one of two partitioning schemes is more versatile than another, in the sense that the class of objects in its scope properly contains the class of objects in the scope of the other scheme, the more versatile scheme is to be preferred. A partitioning scheme which can be applied to any shape whatsoever is most preferable, again other things being equal. This versatility constraint can help choose between two major classes of partitioning schemes: boundary-based and primitive-based. A *boundary-based* approach defines parts by their contours of intersection, not by their shapes. A *primitive-based* approach defines parts by their shapes, not by their contours of intersection (or other geometric invariants, such as singular points).

Shape primitives currently being discussed in the shape representation literature include spheres (Badler and Bajcsy, 1978; O'Rourke and Badler, 1979), generalized cylinders (Binford, 1971; Brooks *et al*., 1979; Marr and Nishihara, 1978; Soroka, 1979), and polyhedra (Baumgart, 1972; Clowes, 1971; Guzman, 1969; Huffman, 1971; Mackworth, 1973; Waltz, 1975), to name a few (see Ballard and Brown, 1982). The point of interest here is that, for all the interesting work and conceptual advances it has fostered, the primitive-based approach has quite limited versatility. Generalized cylinders, for instance, do justice to animal limbs, but are clearly inappropriate for faces, cars, shoes, ... the list continues. A similar criticism can be levelled against each proposed shape primitive, or any conjunction of shape primitives. Perhaps a large enough conjunction of primitives could handle most shapes we do in fact encounter, but the resulting proposal would more resemble a restaurant menu than a theory of shape representation.

A boundary-based scheme on the other hand, if its rules use only the geometry (differential or global) of surfaces, can apply to any object whose bounding surface is amenable to the tools of differential geometry—a not too severe restriction.[3] Boundary rules simply tell one where to draw contours on a surface, as if with a felt marker. A boundary-based scheme, then, is to be preferred over a primitive-based scheme because of its greater versatility.

The advantage of a boundary-based scheme over a primitive-based scheme can also be put this way: using a boundary-based scheme one can locate the parts of an object without having any idea of what the parts look like. This is not possible with the primitive-based scheme. Of course one will want descriptions of the parts one finds using a boundary-based scheme, and one may (or may not) be forced to a menu of shapes at this point. Regardless, a menu of part shapes is not necessary for the task of locating parts. In fact a menu-driven approach restricts the class of shapes for which parts can be located. The minima rule, because it is boundary-based and uses only the differential geometry of surfaces, satisfies the versatility constraint—all geometric surfaces are within its scope.[4]

Computability. The partitioning scheme should in principle be computable using only information available in retinal images. Otherwise it is surely worthless. This is the constraint of *computability.* Computability is not to be confused with efficiency. Efficiency measures how quickly and inexpensively something can be computed, and is a dubious criterion because it depends not only on the task, but also on the available hardware and algorithms. Computability, on the other hand, states simply that the scheme must in principle be realizable, that it use only information available from images.

We have not yet discussed whether our parts are computable from retinal

---

[3]Shapes outside the purview of traditional geometric tools might well be represented by fractal-based schemes (Mandelbrot, 1982; Pentland 1983). Candidate shapes are trees, shrubs, clouds—in short, objects with highly crenulate or ill-defined surfaces.

[4]One must, however, discover the appropriate scales for a natural surface (Hoffman, 1983a, b; Witkin, 1983). The locations of the part boundaries depend, in general, on the scale of resolution at which the surface is examined. In consequence an object will not receive a single partitioning based on the minima rule, but will instead receive a nested hierarchy of partitions, with parts lower in the hierarchy being much smaller than parts higher in the hierarchy. For instance, at one level in the hierarchy for a face one part might be a nose. At the next lower level one might find a wart on the nose. The issue of scale is quite difficult and beyond the scope of this paper.

images (but see Appendix 2). And indeed, since minima of curvature are third derivative entities, and since taking derivatives exaggerates noise, one might legitimately question whether our part boundaries are computable. This concern for computability brings up an important distinction noted by Marr and Poggio (1977), the distinction between theory and algorithm. A theory in vision states what is being computed and why; an algorithm tells how. Our partitioning rule is a theoretical statement of what the part boundaries should be, and the preliminary discussion is intended to say why. The rule is not intended to double as an algorithm so the question of computability is still open. Some recent results by Yuille (1983) are encouraging though. He has found that directional zero-crossings in the shading of a surface are often located on or very near extrema of one of the principal curvatures along its associated lines of curvature. So it might be possible to read the part boundaries directly from the pattern of shading in an image, avoiding the noise problems associated with taking derivatives (see also Koenderink and van Doorn, 1980, 1982a). It is also possible to determine the presence of part boundaries directly from occluding contours in an image (see Appendix 2).

Information preservation: A non-constraint. Not just any constraints will do. The constraints must follow from the visual task; otherwise the constraints may be irrelevant and the resulting part definitions and part descriptions inappropriate. Because the task of recognition involves classification, namely the assignment of an individual to a class or a token to a type, not all the information available about the object is required. Indeed, in contrast to some possible needs for machine vision (Brady, 1982b, 1982c), we stress that a description of a shape for recognition need not be information preserving, for the goal is not to reconstruct the image. Rather it is to make explicit just what is key to the recognition process. Thus, what is critical is the form of the representation, what it makes explicit, how well it is tailored to the needs of recognition. Raw depth maps preserve all shape information of the visible surfaces, but no one proposes them as representations for recognition because they are simply not tailored for the task.

6. Projection and parts

We have now discussed how 'parts' of shapes may be defined in the three-dimensional world. However the eye sees only a two-dimensional projection. How then can parts be inferred from images? Again, we proceed by seeking a regularity of nature. As was noted earlier, the design of the visual system exploits regularities of nature in two ways: they underlie the mental categories used to represent the world and they license inferences from impoverished visual data to descriptions of the world. The role of transversality in the design of the mental category 'part' of shape is an example of the first case. In this section we study an example of the second case. We find that lawful properties of the singularities of the retinal projection permit an inference from retinal images to three-dimensional part boundaries. For simplicity we restrict attention to the problem of inferring part boundaries from silhouettes.

Consider first a discontinuous part boundary (i.e., having infinite negative curvature) on a surface embedded in three dimensions (Fig. 3). Such a contour, when imaged on the retina, induces a concave discontinuity in the resulting silhouette (notice the concave cusps in the silhouette of Fig. 3). Smooth part boundaries defined by the minima partitioning rule can also provide image cusps, as shown in the profiles of Fig. 1. It would be convenient to infer the presence of smooth and discontinuous part boundaries in three dimensions from concave discontinuities in the two-dimensional silhouette, but unfortunately other surface events can give rise to these discontinuities as well. A torus (doughnut), for instance, can have two concave discontinuities in its silhouette which do not fall at part boundaries defined by the minima rule (see Fig. 9).

Fortunately, it is rare that a concave discontinuity in the silhouette of an object does not indicate a part boundary, and when it does not this can be detected from the image data. So one can, in general, correctly infer the presence or absence of part boundaries from these concave discontinuities. The proof of this useful result (which is banished to Appendix 2) exploits regularities of the singularities of smooth maps between two-dimensional manifolds. We have seen how a regularity of nature underlies a mental category, *viz.*, 'part' of shape; here we see that another regularity (e.g., a singularity regularity) licenses an inference from the retinal image to an instance of this category.

Figure 9. *A torus can have concave discontinuities (inducated by the arrows) which do not correspond to part boundaries.*

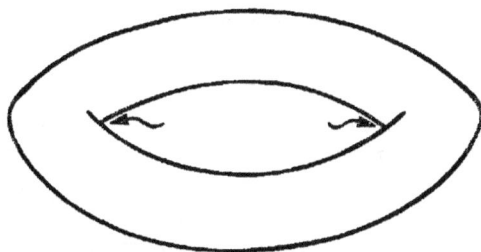

80   *D.D. Hoffman and W.A. Richards*

Figure 10. *A reversing figure, similar to Attneave (1974), appears either as an alternating chain of tall and short mountains or as a chain of tall mountains with twin peaks.*

The singularity regularity, together with transversality, motivates a first partitioning rule for plane curves: *Divide a plane curve into parts at concave cusps.* Here the word *concave* means concave with respect to the silhouette (figure) side of the plane curve. A concavity in the figure is, of course, a convexity in the ground.

This simple partitioning rule can explain some interesting perceptual effects. In Fig. 10, for instance, the same wiggly contour can look either like valleys in a mountain range or, for the reversed figure–ground assignment, like large, twin-peaked mountains. The contour is carved into parts differently when figure and ground reverse because the partitioning rule uses only concave cusps for part boundaries. And what is a concave cusp if one side of the contour is figure must become a convex cusp when the other side is figure, and *vice versa*. There is an obvious parallel between this example and the reversible staircase discussed earlier.

6.1. Geometry of plane curves

Before generalizing the rule to smooth contours we must briefly review two concepts from the differential geometry of place curves: principal normal and curvature. The principal normal at a point on a curve can be thought of as a unit length needle sticking straight out of (orthogonal to) the curve at that point, much like a tooth on a comb. All the principal normals at all points on a curve together form a field of principal normals. Usually there are two possible fields of principal normals—either leftward pointing or rightward pointing. Let us adopt the convention that the field of principal normals is always chosen to point into the figure side of the curve. Reversing the choice of figure and ground on a curve implies a concomitant change in the choice of the field of principal normals.

Curvature is a well-known concept. Straight lines have no curvature, circles have constant curvature, and smaller circles have higher curvature than larger circles. What is important to note is that, because of the convention forcing the principal normals to point into the figure, concave portions of a smooth curve have negative curvature and convex portions have positive curvature.

6.2. Parts of smooth curves

It is an easy matter now to generalize the partitioning rule. Suppose that wherever a curve has a concave cusp we smooth the curve a bit. Then a concave cusp becomes a point of negative curvature having, locally, the greatest absolute value of curvature. This leads to the following generalized partitioning rule: *Divide a plane curve into parts at negative minima of curvature.*[5]

Several more perceptual effects can be explained using this generalized partitioning rule. A good example is the reversing figure devised by Attneave (see Fig. 11). He found that by simply scribbling a line through a circle and separating the two halves one can create two very different looking contours. As Attneave (1971) points out, the appearance of the contour depends upon

Figure 11. *Attneave's reversing figure, constructed by scribbling a line down a circle. The apparent shape of a contour depends on which side is perceived as figure.*

---

[5]Transversality directly motivates using concave cusps as part boundaries. Only by smoothing do we include minima as well (both in the case of silhouette curves and in the case of part boundaries in three dimensions). Since the magnitude of the curvature at minima decreases with increased smoothing, it is useful to introduce the notion of the strength or goodness of a part boundary. The strength of a part boundary is higher the more negative the curvature of the minimum. Positive minima have the least strength, and deserve to be considered separately from the negative minima, a possibility suggested to us by Shimon Ullman.

which side is taken to be part of the figure, and does not depend upon any prior familiarity with the contour.

Now we can explain why the two halves of Attneave's circle look so different. For when figure and ground reverse, the field of principal normals also reverses in accordance with the convention. And when the principal normals reverse, the curvature at every point on the curve must change sign. In particular, minima of curvature must become maxima and *vice versa*. This repositioning of the minima of curvature leads to a new partitioning of the curve by the partitioning rule. In short, the curve looks different because it is organized into fundamentally different units or chunks. Note that if we chose to define part boundaries by inflections (see Hollerbach, 1975; Marr, 1977), or by both maxima and minima of curvature (see Duda and Hart, 1973), or by all tangent and curvature discontinuities (Binford, 1981), then the chunks would not change when figure and ground reverse.

A clear example of two very different chunkings for one curve can be seen in the famous face–goblet illusion published by Turton in 1819. If a face is taken to be figure, then the minima of curvature divide the curve into chunks corresponding to a forehead, nose, upper lip, lower lip, and chin. If instead the goblet is taken to be figure then the minima reposition, dividing the curve into new chunks corresponding to a base, a couple of parts of the stem, a bowl, and a lip on the bowl. It is probably no accident that the parts defined by minima are often easily assigned verbal labels.

Demonstrations have been devised which, like the face–goblet illusion, allow more than one interpretation of a single contour but which, unlike the face–goblet illusion, do not involve a figure–ground reversal. Two popular examples are the rabbit–duck and hawk–goose illusions (see Fig. 13). Because these illusions do not involve a figure–ground reversal, and because in consequence the minima of curvature never change position, the partitioning rule

Figure 12. *The reversing goblet can be seen as a goblet or a pair of facial profiles (adapted from Turton, 1819). Defining part boundaries by minima of curvature divides the face into a forehead, nose, upper lip, lower lip, and chin. Minima divide the goblet into a base, a couple parts of the stem, a bowl, and a lip on the bowl.*

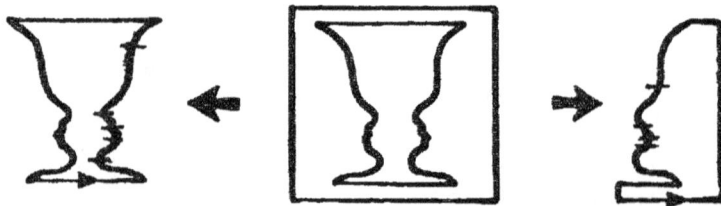

Figure 13. *Some ambiguous shapes do not involve a reversal of figure and ground. Consequently, the part boundaries defined by minima of curvature do not move when these figures change interpretations. In this illustration, for instance, a rabbit's ear turns into a duck's bill without moving, and a hawk's head turns into a goose's tail, again without moving.*

must predict that the part boundaries are identical for both interpretations of each of these contours. This prediction is easily confirmed. What is an ear on the rabbit, for instance, becomes an upper bill on the duck.

If the minima rule for partitioning is really used by our visual systems, one should expect it to predict some judgments of shape similarity. One case in which its prediction is counterintuitive can be seen in Fig. 14. Look briefly at the single half-moon on the right of the figure. Then look quickly at the two half-moons on the left and decide which seems more similar to the first (go ahead). In an experiment performed on several similar figures, we found that nearly all subjects chose the bottom half-moon as more similar. Yet if you look again you will find that the bounding contour for the top half-moon is identical to that of the right half-moon, only figure–ground reversed. The bounding contour of the bottom half-moon, however, has been mirror reversed, and two parts defined by minima of curvature have been swapped. Why does the bottom one still look more similar? The minima rule gives a simple answer. The bottom contour, which is not figure–ground reversed from the original contour, has the same part boundaries. The top contour, which is figure–ground reversed from the original, has entirely different part boundaries.

7. Holes: A second type of part

The minima rule for partitioning surfaces is motivated by a fact about generic intersections of surfaces: surfaces intersect transversally. As Fig. 3 illustrates, this implies that if two surfaces are interpenetrated and left together to form a composite object then the contour of their intersection is a contour of

Figure 14. *A demonstration that some judgments of shape similarity can be predicted by the minima partitioning rule. In a quick look, the bottom left half-moon appears more similar to the right half-moon than does the top left one. However the bounding contour of the top left half-moon is identical to that of the right half-moon, whereas the bounding contour of the bottom left half-moon has been mirror reversed and has had two parts interchanged.*

figure-ground reversed

reference

mirror reversed

concave discontinuity on the composite surface. Now suppose instead that after the two surfaces are interpenetrated one surface is pulled out of the other, leaving behind a depression, and then discarded. The depression created in this manner has just as much motivation for being a 'part' on the basis of transversality as the parts we have discussed up to this point.

As can be seen by examining the right side of Fig. 3, the contour that divides one part from the other on the composite object is precisely the same contour that will delimit the depression created by pulling out the penetrating part. But whereas in the case of the composite object this contour is a contour of *concave* discontinuity, in the case of the depression this contour is a contour of *convex* discontinuity. And smoothing this contour leads to positive extrema of a principal curvature for the case of a depression. We are led to conclude that a shape can have at least two kinds of parts—'positive parts' which are bounded by negative extrema of a principal curvature, and 'negative parts' (holes) bounded by positive extrema of a principal curvature.

This result presents us with the task of finding a set of rules that determine when to use positive extrema or negative extrema as part boundaries. We do not have these rules yet, but here is an example of what such rules might look like. If a contour of negative extrema of a principal curvature is not a closed contour, and if it is immediately surrounded (i.e., no intervening extrema) by a closed contour of positive extrema of a principal curvature, then take the contour of positive extrema as the boundary of a (negative) part.

Note in any case that what we will not have are single parts bounded by both negative and positive extrema of a principal curvature.

8. Perception and induction

Inferences and regularities of nature have cropped up many times in the theory and discussions presented here. It is useful to explore their significance more fully.

Perceptual systems inform the perceiver about properties of the world she needs to know. The need might be to avoid being eaten, to find what is edible, to avoid unceremonious collisions, or whatever. The relevant knowledge might be the three-dimensional layout of the immediate surrounds, or that ahead lies a tree loaded with fruit, or that crouched in the tree is an unfriendly feline whose perceptual systems are also at work reporting the edible properties of the world. Regardless of the details, what makes the perceptual task tricky is that the data available to a sensorium invariably underdetermine the properties of the world that need to be known. That is, in general there are infinitely many states of the world which are consistent with the available sense data. Perhaps the best known example is that although the world is three-dimensional, and we perceive it as such, each retina is only two-dimensional. Since the mapping from the world to the retina is many-to-one, the possible states of the world consistent with a retinal image, or any series of retinal images, are many. The upshot of all this is that knowledge of the world is inferred. Inference lies at the heart of perception (Fodor and Pylyshyn, 1981; Gregory, 1970; Helmholtz, 1962; Hoffman, 1983b; Marr, 1982).

An inference, reduced to essentials, is simply a list of premises and a conclusion. An inference is said to be *deductively valid* if and only if the conclusion is logically guaranteed to be true given that the premises are true. So, for example, the following inference, which has three premises and one conclusion, is deductively valid: "A mapping from 3-D to 2-D is many-to-one. The world is 3-D. A retinal image is 2-D. Therefore a mapping from the world to a retinal image is many-to-one." An inference is said to be *inductively strong* if and only if it is unlikely that the conclusion is false while its premises are true, and it is not deductively valid (see Skyrms, 1975).[6] So the following inference is inductively strong: "The retinal disparities across my visual field are highly irregular. Therefore whatever I am looking at is not flat." Though this inference is inductively strong, it can prove false, as is in fact the case whenever one views a random dot stereogram.

In perceptual inferences the sensory data play the role of the premises, and the assertions about the state of the world are the conclusions. Since the state of the world is not logically entailed by the sensory data, perceptual inferences are not of the deductive variety—therefore they are inductive.

This is not good news. Whereas deductive inference is well understood, inductive inference is almost not understood at all. Induction involves a morass of unresolved issues, such as projectibility (Goodman, 1955), abduction (Levi, 1980; Peirce, 1931), and simplicity metrics (Fodor, 1975). These problems, though beyond the scope of this paper, apply with unmitigated force to perceptual inferences and are thus of interest to students of perception (Nicod, 1968).

But, despite these difficulties, consider the following question: If the premises of perceptual inferences are the sensory data and the conclusion is an assertion about the state of the world, what is the evidential relation between perceptual premises and conclusions? Or to put it differently, how is it possible that perceptual interpretations of sensory data bear a nonarbitrary (and

---

[6]The distinction between deductively valid and inductively strong inferences is not mere pedantry; the distinction has important consequences for perception, but is often misunderstood. Gregory (1970, p. 160), for instance, realizes the distinction is important for theories of perception, but then claims that "Inductions are generalizations of instances." This is but partly true. Inductive inferences may proceed from general premises to general conclusions, from general premises to particular conclusions, as well as from particular premises to general conclusions (Skyrms, 1975). The distinction between inductive and deductive inferences lies in the evidential relation between premises and conclusions.

even useful) relation to the state of the world? Or to put it still differently, why are perceptual inferences inductively strong?

Surely the answer must be, at least in part, that since the conclusion of a perceptual inference is a statement about the world, such an inference can be inductively strong only if it is motivated by laws, regularities, or uniformities of nature. To see this in a more familiar context, consider the following inductively strong inference about the world: "If I release this egg, it will fall". The inference here is inductively strong because it is motivated by a law of nature—gravity. Skeptics, if there are any, will end up with egg on their feet.

Laws, regularities, and uniformities in the world, then, are crucial for the construction of perceptual inferences which have respectable inductive strength. Only by exploiting the uniformities of nature can a perceptual system overcome the paucity of its sensory data and come to useful conclusions about the state of the world.

If this is the case, it has an obvious implication for perceptual research: identifying the regularities in nature which motivate a particular perceptual inference is not only a good thing to do, but a *sine qua non* for explanatory theories of perception.[7] An explanatory theory must state not only the premises and conclusion of a particular perceptual inference, but also the lawful properties of the world which license the move from the former to the latter. Without all three of these ingredients a proposed theory is incomplete.

---

[7]At least two conditions need to be true of a regularity, such as rigidity, for it to be useful: (1) It should in fact be a regularity. If there were not rigid objects in the world, rigidity would be useless. (2) It should allow inductively strong inferences from images to the world, by making the 'deception probability', to be defined shortly, very close to zero. For instance, let w (world) stand for the following assertion about four points in the world: "are in rigid motion in 3-D". Let i (image) stand for the following assertion about the retinal images of the same four points: "have 2-D positions and motions consistent with being the projections of rigid motion in 3-D". Then what is the probability of w given i? The existence of rigid objects does not in itself make this conditional probability high. Using Bayes' theorem we find that $P(w|i) = P(w) \cdot P(i|w)/[P(w) \cdot P(i|w) + P(-w) \cdot P(i|-w)]$. Since the numerator and the first term of the denominator are identical, this conditional probability is near one only if $P(w) \cdot P(i|w) \gg P(-w) \cdot P(i|-w)$. And since $P(-w)$, though unknown is certainly much greater than zero, $P(w|i)$ is near one only if $P(i|-w)$—let's call this the 'deception probability'—is near zero. Only if the deception probability is near zero can the inference from the image to the world be inductively strong. A major goal of 'structure from motion' proofs (Bobick, 1983; Hoffman and Flinchbaugh, 1982; Longuet-Higgins and Prazony, 1981; Richards *et al.*, 1983; Ullman, 1979) is to determine under what conditions this deception probability is near zero. Using an assumption of rigidity, for instance, Ullman has found that with three views of three points the deception probability is one, but with three views of four points it is near zero.

9. Conclusion

The design of the visual system exploits regularities of nature in two ways: they underlie the mental categories used to represent the world and they license inferences from incomplete visual data to useful descriptions of the world. Both uses of regularities underlie the solution to a problem in shape recognition. Transversality underlies the mental category 'part' of shape; singularities of projection underlie the inference from images to parts in the world.

The partitioning rules presented in this paper are attractive because (1) they satisfy several constraints imposed by the task of shape recognition, (2) they are motivated by a regularity of nature, (3) the resulting partitions look plausible, and (4) the rules explain and unify several well-known visual illusions.

Remaining, however, is a long list of questions to be answered before a comprehensive, explanatory theory of shape recognition is forthcoming. A partial list includes the following. How are the partitioning contours on surfaces to be recovered from two-dimensional images? How should the surface parts be described? All we have so far is a rule for cutting out parts. But what qualitative and metrical descriptions should be applied to the resulting parts? Can the answer to this question be motivated by appeal to uniformities and regularities in the world? What spatial relations need to be computed between parts? Although the part definitions don't depend upon the viewing geometry, is it possible or even necessary that the predicates of spatial relations do (Rock, 1974; Yin, 1970)? How is the shape memory organized? What is the first index into this memory?

The task of vision is to infer useful descriptions of the world from changing patterns of light falling on the eye. The descriptions can be reliable only to the extent that the inferential processes which build them exploit regularities in the visual world, regularities such as rigidity and transversality. The discovery of such regularities, and the mathematical investigation of their power in guiding particular visual inferences, are promising directions for the researcher seeking to understand human vision.

Appendix 1

Surface partitioning in detail

This appendix applies the surface partitioning rule to a particular class of surfaces: surfaces of revolution. The intent is to convey a more rigorous understanding of the rule and the partitions it yields. Since this section is quite mathematical, some readers might prefer to look at the results in Fig. 16 and skip the rest.

Notation. Tensor notation is adopted in this section because it allows concise expression of surface concepts, (see Dodson and Poston, 1979; Hoffman, 1983a; Lipschutz, 1969). A vector in $\Re^3$ is $\mathbf{x} = (x^1, x^2, x^3)$. A point in the parameter plane is (u^1, u^2). A surface patch is $\mathbf{x} = \mathbf{x}(u^1, u^2) = (x^1(u^1, u^2), x^2(u^1, u^2), x^3(u^1, u^2))$. Partial deriviatives are denoted by subscripts:

$$\mathbf{x}_1 = \frac{\partial \mathbf{x}}{\partial u^1}, \mathbf{x}_2 = \frac{\partial \mathbf{x}}{\partial u^2}, \mathbf{x}_{12} = \frac{\partial^2 \mathbf{x}}{\partial u^1 \partial u_2}, \text{etc.}$$

A tangent vector is $d\mathbf{x} = \mathbf{x}_1 du^1 + \mathbf{x}_2 du^2 = \mathbf{x}_i du^i$ where the Einstein summation convention is used. The first fundamental form is

$$\mathbf{|} = d\mathbf{x} \cdot d\mathbf{x} = \mathbf{x}_i \cdot \mathbf{x}_j du^i du^j = g_{ij} du^i du^j$$

where the g_{ij} are the first fundamental coefficients and $i, j = 1, 2$.

The differential of the normal vector is the vector $d\mathbf{N} = \mathbf{N}_i du^i$ and the second fundamental form is

$$\mathbf{\|} = d^2\mathbf{x} \cdot \mathbf{N} = \mathbf{x}_{ij} \cdot \mathbf{N} du^i du^j = b_{ij} du^i du^j$$

where the b_{ij} are the second fundamental coefficients and $i, j = 1, 2$.

A plane passing through a surface S orthogonal to the tangent plane of S at some point P and in a direction $du^i:du^j$ with respect to the tangent plane intersects the surface in a curve whose curvature at P is the *normal curvature* of S at P in the direction $du^i:du^j$. The normal curvature in a direction $du^i:du^j$ is $k_n = \mathbf{\|}/\mathbf{|}$. The two perpendicular directions for which the values of k_n take on maximum and minimum values are called the *principal directions*, and the corresponding curvatures, k_1 and k_2, are called the *principal curvatures*. The *Gaussian curvature* at P is $K = k_1 k_2$. A *line of curvature* is a curve on a surface whose tangent at each point is along a principal direction.

Partitions of a surface of revolution. A surface of revolution is a set $S \subset \Re^3$ obtained by rotating a regular plane curve α about an axis in the plane which does not meet the curve. Let the $x^1 x^3$ plane be the plane of α and the x^3 axis the rotation axis. Let

$$\alpha(u^1) = (x(u^1), z(u^1)), \, a < u^1 < b, \, z(u^1) > 0.$$

Let u^2 be the rotation angle about the x^3 axis. Then we obtain a map

$$\mathbf{x}(u^1, u^2) = (x(u^1)\cos(u^2), x(u^1)\sin(u^2), z(u^1))$$

Figure 15. *Surface of revolution.*

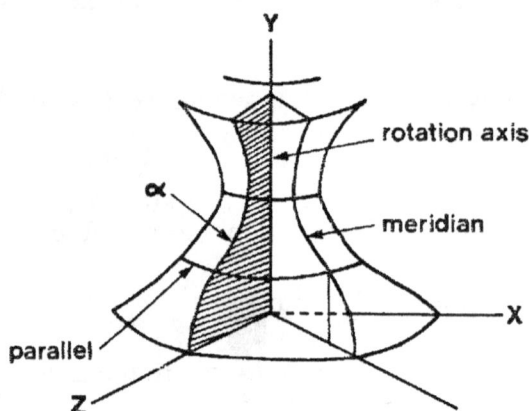

from the open set $U = \{(u^1, u^2) \in \Re^2; 0 < u^2 < 2\pi, a < u^1 < b\}$ into S (Fig. 15). The curve α is called the *generating curve* of S, and the x^3 axis is the *rotation axis* of S. The circles swept out by the points of α are called the *parallels* of S, and the various placements of α on S are called the *meridians* of S.

Let $\cos(u^2)$ be abbreviated as c and $\sin(u^2)$ as s. Then $\mathbf{x}_1 = (x_1 c, x_1 s, z_1)$ and $\mathbf{x}_2 = (-xs, xc, 0)$. The first fundamental coefficients are then

$$g_{ij} = \mathbf{x}_i \cdot \mathbf{x}_j = \begin{pmatrix} x_1^2 + z_1^2 & 0 \\ 0 & x^2 \end{pmatrix}.$$

The surface normal is

$$\mathbf{N} = \frac{\mathbf{x}_1 \times \mathbf{x}_2}{|\mathbf{x}_1 \times \mathbf{x}_2|} = \frac{(z_1 c, z_1 s, -x_1)}{\sqrt{z_1^2 + x_1^2}}.$$

If we let u be arc length along α then $\sqrt{z_1^2 + x_1^2} = 1 = g_{11}$ and

$$\mathbf{N} = (z_1 c, z_1 s, -x_1).$$

The second fundamental coefficients are

$$b_{ij} = \mathbf{x}_{ij} \cdot \mathbf{N} = \begin{pmatrix} x_{11} z_1 - x_1 z_{11} & 0 \\ 0 & -x z_1 \end{pmatrix}.$$

Since $g_{12} = b_{12} = 0$ the principal curvatures of a surface of revolution are

$$k_1 = b_{11}/g_{11} = x_{11}z_1 - x_1 z_{11}$$
$$k_2 = b_{22}/g_{22} = -z_1/x.$$

The expression for k_1 is identical to the expression for the curvature along α. In fact the meridians (the various positions of α on S) are lines of curvature, as are the parallels. The curvature along the meridians is given by the expression for k_1 and the curvature along the parallel is given by the expression for k_2. The expression for k_2 is simply the curvature of a circle of radius x multiplied by the cosine of the angle that the tangent to α makes with the axis of rotation.

Observe that the expressions for k_1 and k_2 depend only upon the parameter u^1, not u^2. In particular, since k_2 is independent of u^2 there are no extrema or inflections of the normal curvature along the parallels. The parallels are circles. Consequently no segmentation contours arise from the lines of curvature associated with k_2. Only the minima of k_1 along the meridians are used for segmentation. Fig. 16 shows several surfaces of revolution with the

Figure 16. *Partitions on surfaces of revolution.*

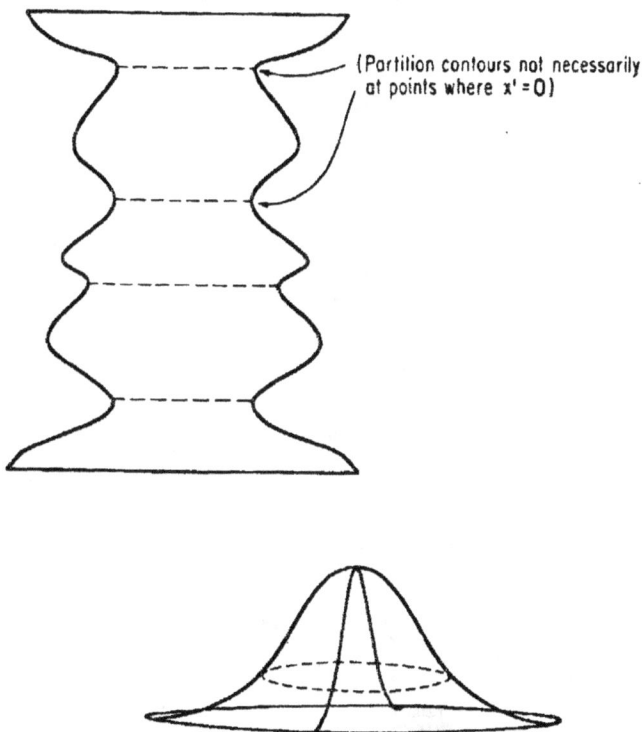

(Partition contours not necessarily
at points where x' = 0)

minima of curvature along the meridians marked. The resulting segmentation contours appear quite natural to human observers.

As a surface of revolution is flattened along one axis, the partitioning contours which are at first circles become, in general, more elliptical and bow slightly up or down.

Appendix 2

Inferring part boundaries from image singularities

In general, a concave discontinuity in a silhouette indicates a part boundary (as defined by the minima rule) on the imaged surface. This appendix makes this statement more precise and then examines a special case.

Only two types of singularity can arise in the projection from the world to the retina (Whitney, 1955). These two types are *folds* and *spines* (see Fig. 17). Intuitively, folds are the contours on a surface where the viewer's line of sight would just graze the surface, and a spine separates the visible portion of a fold from the invisible. A contour on the retina corresponding to a fold on a surface is called an *outline* (Koenderink and van Doorn, 1976, 1982b). A *termination* is a point on the retina corresponding to a spine on a surface. A *T-junction* (see Fig. 17) occurs where two outlines cut each other.

We wish to determine the conditions in which a T-junction indicates the presence of a part boundary. Two results are useful here. First, the sign of curvature of a point on an outline (projection of a fold) is the sign of the Gaussian curvature at the corresponding surface point (Koenderink and van Doorn, 1976, 1982b). Convex portions of the outline indicate positive Gaussian curvature, concave portions indicate negative Gaussian curvature, and inflections indicate zero Gaussian curvature. Second, the spine always occurs

Figure 17. *Singularities of the retinal projection.*

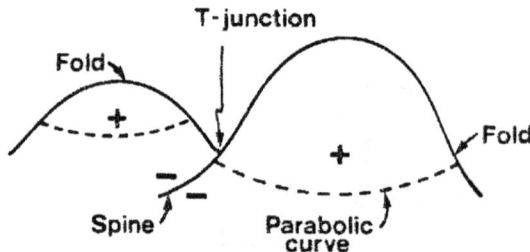

at a point of negative Gaussian curvature. That is, the visible portion of a fold always ends in a segment whose projected image is concave (Koenderink and van Doorn, 1982b).

The scheme of the proof is the following. Suppose that the folds on both sides of a T-junction have convex regions, as shown in Fig. 17. Then the sign of the Gaussian curvature is positive, and in fact both principal curvatures are positive, in these two regions. Now the presence of a spine indicates that these regions of positive Gaussian curvature are separated by a region of negative Gaussian curvature. This implies that the principal curvature associated with one family of lines of curvature is negative in this region. But then the principal curvature along this family of lines of curvature must go from positive to negative and back to positive as the lines of curvature go from one hill into the valley and back up the other hill. If this is true, then in the generic case the principal curvature will go through a negative minimum somewhere in the valley—and we have a part boundary.

There are two cases to consider. In the first the loci where one principal curvature goes from positive to negative (parabolic curves) surround each hill. In the second case the parabolic curve surrounds the valley between the two hills. We consider only the first case.

In the first case there are two ways that the lines of curvature entering the valley from one parabolic curve might fail to connect smoothly with lines of curvature entering the valley from the other parabolic curve: they might intersect orthogonally or not at all. If they intersect orthogonally then the two principal curvatures must both be negative, and the Gaussian curvature, which is the product of the two principal curvatures, must be positive. But the valley between the parabolic contours has negative Gaussian curvature, a contradiction.

If the lines of curvature fail to intersect then there must be a singularity in the lines of curvature somewhere in the region having negative Gaussian curvature. However, "The net of lines of curvature may have singular properties at umbilical points, and at them only." (Hilbert and Cohn-Vossen, 1952, p. 187). Umbilical points, points where the two principal curvatures are equal, can only occur in regions of positive Gaussian curvature—again a contradiction. (Here we assume the surface is smooth. A singularity could also occur if the surface were not smooth at one point in the valley. But in the generic case part boundaries would still occur.)

This proof requires that the two folds of a T-junction each have a convex region. The two folds of T-junctions on a torus do not satisfy this condition—they are always concave. Thus it is a simple matter to determine from an image when a T-junction warrants the inference of a part boundary.

The proof outlined here is a special case. A general proof is needed which

94   *D.D. Hoffman and W.A. Richards*

specifies when a concave cusp in a silhouette indicates the presence of a part boundary or two different objects. The more general proof would not use the relation between spine points and Gaussian curvature. The proof might run roughly as follows: a concave cusp is a double point in the projection. A line connecting the two points on the surface which project to the cusp necessarily lies outside the surface between the two points. But then the surface is not convex everywhere between these two points. Consequently there is a concave discontinuity (part boundary) between the points or the Gaussian curvature must go negative. If the Gaussian curvature goes from positive (convex) to negative and then back to positive (convex), one of the principal curvatures must also. But this implies it has a negative minimum, in the general case, and so we have a smooth part boundary.

References

Attneave, F. (1974) Multistability in perception, *Scient. Am.*, *225*, 63–71.

Badler, N. and Bajcsy, R. (1978) Three-dimensional representations for computer graphics and computer vision. *Comp. Graph.*, *12*, 153–160.

Ballard, D. and Brown, C. (1982) *Computer Vision*, Englewood Cliffs, N.J., Prentice-Hall.

Baumgart, B. (1972) *Winged edge polyhedron representation*. STAN-CS-320, AIM-179, Stanford AI Lab.

Binford, T. (1971) Visual perception by computer. IEEE Conf. Syst. Cont., Miami.

Binford, T. (1981) Inferring surfaces from images. *Art. Intell.*, *17*, 205–244.

Bobick, A. (1983) A hybrid approach to structure-from-motion. Association for Computing Machinery Workshop on Motion: Representation and Perception.

Brady, J.M. (1982a) Parts description and acquisition using vision. *Proc. Soc. Photo-opt. Instrument. Eng.*

Brady, J.M. (1982b) Criteria for representations of shape. In A. Rosenfeld and J. Beck (eds.), *Human and Machine Vision*.

Brady, J.M. (1982c) Describing visible surfaces. In A. Hanson and E. Riseman (eds.), *Computer Vision Systems*.

Brooks, R., Greiner Russell, and Binford, T. (1979) The ACRONYM model based vision system. *Proc. Int. Joint Conf. Art. Intell.*, *6*, 105–113.

Clowes M. (1971) On seeing things. *Art. Intell.*, *2*, 79–116.

Dennett, D. (1978) Intentional systems. In *Brainstorms*. Montgomery, VT, Bradford.

Do Carmo, M. (1976) *Differential Geometry of Curves and Surfaces*. Englewood Cliffs, NJ, Prentice-Hall.

Dodson, D. and Poston, T. (1977) *Tensor Geometry*. London, Pitman.

Duda, R. and Hart, P. (1973) *Pattern Classification and Scene Analysis*. New York, Wiley.

Fodor, J. (1975) *The Language of Thought*, Cambridge, MA, Harvard University Press.

Fodor, J. (1983) *The Modularity of Mind*, Cambridge, MA, MIT Press.

Fodor, J. and Pylyshyn, Z. (1981) How direct is visual perception?: Some reflections on Gibson's "Ecological Approach". *Cog.*, *9*, 139–196.

Goodman, N. (1955) *Fact, Fiction and Forecast*. Cambridge, MA, Harvard University Press.

Gregory, R. (1970) *The Intelligent Eye*. New York, McGraw-Hill.

Guillemin, V. and Pollack, A. (1974) *Differential Topology*. Englewood Cliffs, NJ, Prentice-Hall.

Guzman, A. (1969) Decomposition of a visual scene into three-dimensional bodies. In A. Grasseli (ed.), *Automatic Interpretation and Classification of Images*, New York, Academic Press.

Helmholtz, H. (1962) *Treatise on Physiological Optics, Volume 3*, Dover reprint.

Hilbert, D. and Cohn-Vossen, S. (1952) *Geometry and the Imagination*, New York, Chelsea.

Hoffman, D. (1983a) Representing Shapes for Visual Recognition. MIT Ph.D. thesis.

Hoffman, D. (1983b) The interpretation of visual illusions, *Scient. Am.*, *249*, 154–162.

Hoffman D. and Flinchbaugh, B. (1982) The interpretation of biological motivation, *Biol. Cybernet.*, *42*, 195–204.

Hoffman, D. and Richards, W. (1982) Representing smooth plane curves for visual recognition: Implications for figure–ground reversal. *Proc. Am. Ass. Art. Intell.*, 5–8.

Hollerbach, J. (1975) *Hierarchical Shape Description of Objects by Selection and Modification of Prototypes*, MIT AI-TR-346.

Huffman, D. (1971) Impossible objects as nonsense sentences. *Mach. Intell.*, *6*.

Koenderink, J. and van Doorn, A. (1976) The singularities of the visual mapping. *Biol. Cybernet.*, *24*, 51–59.

Koenderink, J. and van Doorn, A. (1979) The internal representation of solid shape with respect to vision. *Biol. Cybernet.*, *32*, 211–216.

Koenderink, J. and van Doorn, A. (1980) Photometric invariants related to solid shape. *Optica Acta*, *7*, 981–996.

Koenderink, J. and van Doorn, A. (1982a) Perception of solid shape and spatial lay-out through photometric invariants. In R. Trappl (ed.), *Cybernetics and Systems Research*, Amsterdam, North-Holland.

Koenderink, J. and van Doorn, A. (1982b) The shape of smooth objects and the way contours end. *Perception*, *11*, 129–137.

Levi, I. (1980) *The Enterprise of Knowledge*, Cambridge, MA, MIT Press.

Liberman, A., Cooper, F., Shankweiler, D., and Studdert-Kennedy, M. (1967) The perception of the speech code. *Psychol. Rev.*, *74*, 431–461.

Lipschutz, M. (1969) *Differential Geometry*, (Schaum's Outline), New York, McGraw-Hill.

Longuet-Higgins, H.C. and Prazdny, K. (1981) The interpretation of a moving retinal image. *Proc. R. Soc. Lond.*, *B208*, 385–397.

Mackworth, A. (1973) Interpreting pictures of polyhedral scenes. *Art. Intell.*, *4*, 121–137.

Mandelbrot, B. (1982) *The Fractal Geometry of Nature*. San Francisco, Freeman.

Marr, D. (1977) Analysis of occluding countour. *Proc. R. Soc. Lond.*, *B197*, 441–475.

Marr, D. (1982) *Vision*. San Francisco, Freeman.

Marr, D. and Nishihara, H.K. (1978) Representation and recognition of the spatial organization of three-dimensional shapes. *Proc. R. Soc. Lond.*, *B200*, 269–294.

Marr, D. and Poggio, T. (1977) From understanding computation to understanding neural circuitry, *Neurosci. Res. Prog. Bull.*, *15*, 470–488.

Nicod, J. (1968) *Geometry and Induction*, Berkeley, University of California Press.

Nishihara, H.K. (1981) Intensity, visible-surface, and volumetric representations. *Art. Intell.*, *17*, 265–284.

O'Rourke, J. and Badler, N. (1979) Decomposition of three-dimensional objects into spheres. *IEEE Trans. Pattern Anal. Mach. Intell.*, *1*.

Pentland, A. (1983) Fractal-based description. *Proc. Int. Joint Conf. Art. Intell.*

Peirce, C. (1931) *Collected Papers*, Cambridge, MA, Harvard University Press.

Richards, W., Rubin, J.M. and Hoffman, D.D. (1983) Equation counting and the interpreation of sensory data. *Perception*, *11*, 557–576, and MIT AI Memo 618 (1981).

Rock, I. (1974) The perception of disoriented figures. *Scient. Am. 230*, 78–85.

Skyrms, B. (1975) *Choice and Chance*. Belmont, Wadsworth Publishing Co.

Soroka, B. (1979) Generalized cylinders from parallel slices. *Proc. Pattern Recognition and Image processing*, 421–426.

Spivak, M. (1970) *Differential Geometry, Volume 2*, Berkeley, Publish or Perish.

96   *D.D. Hoffman and W.A. Richards*

Sutherland, N.S. (1968) Outlines of a theory of visual pattern recognition in animals and man. *Proc. R. Soc. Lond., B171*, 297-317.

Thompson, D'Arcy (1968) *On Growth and Form*, Cambridge, University of Cambridge Press.

Turton, W. (1819) *A Conchological Dictionary of the British Islands*, (frontispiece), printed for John Booth, London. [This early reference was kindly pointed out to us by J.F.W. McOmie.]

Ullman, S. (1979) *The Interpretation of Visual Motion*. Cambridge, MA, MIT Press.

Waltz, D. (1975) Understanding line drawings of scenes with shadows. In P. Winston (ed.), *The Psychology of Computer Vision*, New York, McGraw-Hill.

Whitney, H. (1955) On singularities of mappings of Euclidean spaces. I. Mappings of the plane into the plane. *Ann. Math., 62*, 374–410.

Witkin, A.P. (1983) Scale-space filtering. *Proc. Int. Joint Conf. Artificial Intelligence.*

Yin, R. (1970) Face recognition by brain-injured patients: A dissociable ability? *Neuropsychologia, 8*, 395–402.

Yuille, A. (1983) *Scaling theorems for zero-crossings*. MIT AI Memo 722.

Résumé

Les auteurs suggèrent que le système visuel pour la reconnaissance des objets, décompose les formes en éléments et qu'il utilise pour cela une règle définissant les frontères de ces éléments plutôt que leurs formes. Cette règle exploite une régularité de la nature: la transversalité. Les éléments, leurs descriptions et leurs relations spatiales fournissent un premier index dans la mémoire des formes. On peut avec cette règle rendre compte de plusieurs illusions visuelles. Les auteurs insistent sur le rôle de l'inférence inductive et concluent en indiquant les problèmes non résolus.

[13]

Recognition-by-Components: A Theory of Human Image Understanding

Irving Biederman
State University of New York at Buffalo

The perceptual recognition of objects is conceptualized to be a process in which the image of the input is segmented at regions of deep concavity into an arrangement of simple geometric components, such as blocks, cylinders, wedges, and cones. The fundamental assumption of the proposed theory, recognition-by-components (RBC), is that a modest set of generalized-cone components, called geons ($N \leq 36$), can be derived from contrasts of five readily detectable properties of edges in a two-dimensional image: curvature, collinearity, symmetry, parallelism, and cotermination. The detection of these properties is generally invariant over viewing position and image quality and consequently allows robust object perception when the image is projected from a novel viewpoint or is degraded. RBC thus provides a principled account of the heretofore undecided relation between the classic principles of perceptual organization and pattern recognition: The constraints toward regularization (Pragnanz) characterize not the complete object but the object's components. Representational power derives from an allowance of free combinations of the geons. A Principle of Componential Recovery can account for the major phenomena of object recognition: If an arrangement of two or three geons can be recovered from the input, objects can be quickly recognized even when they are occluded, novel, rotated in depth, or extensively degraded. The results from experiments on the perception of briefly presented pictures by human observers provide empirical support for the theory.

Any single object can project an infinity of image configurations to the retina. The orientation of the object to the viewer can vary continuously, each giving rise to a different two-dimensional projection. The object can be occluded by other objects or texture fields, as when viewed behind foliage. The object need not be presented as a full-colored textured image but instead can be a simplified line drawing. Moreover, the object can even be missing some of its parts or be a novel exemplar of its particular category. But it is only with rare exceptions that an image fails to be rapidly and readily classified, either as an instance of a familiar object category or as an instance that cannot be so classified (itself a form of classification).

A Do-It-Yourself Example

Consider the object shown in Figure 1. We readily recognize it as one of those objects that cannot be classified into a familiar category. Despite its overall unfamiliarity, there is near unanimity in its descriptions. We parse—or segment—its parts at regions of deep concavity and describe those parts with common,

This research was supported by the Air Force Office of Scientific Research Grants F4962083C0086 and 86-0106.

I would like to express my deep appreciation to Thomas W. Blickle and Ginny Ju for their invaluable contributions to all phases of the empirical research described in this article. Thanks are also due to Elizabeth A. Beiring, John Clapper, and Mary Lloyd for their assistance in the conduct of the experimental research. Discussions I had with James R. Pomerantz, John Artim, and Brian Fisher helped improve aspects of the manuscript.

Correspondence concerning this article should be addressed to Irving Biederman, Department of Psychology, State University of New York at Buffalo, Park Hall, Amherst, New York 14260.

simple volumetric terms, such as "a block," "a cylinder," "a funnel or truncated cone." We can look at the zig-zag horizontal brace as a texture region or zoom in and interpret it as a series of connected blocks. The same is true of the mass at the lower left: we can see it as a texture area or zoom in and parse it into its various bumps.

Although we know that it is not a familiar object, after a while we can say what it resembles: "A New York City hot dog cart, with the large block being the central food storage and cooking area, the rounded part underneath as a wheel, the large arc on the right as a handle, the funnel as an orange juice squeezer and the various vertical pipes as vents or umbrella supports." It is not a good cart, but we can see how it might be related to one. It is like a 10-letter word with 4 wrong letters.

We readily conduct the same process for any object, familiar or unfamiliar, in our foveal field of view. The manner of segmentation and analysis into components does not appear to depend on our familiarity with the particular object being identified.

The naive realism that emerges in descriptions of nonsense objects may be reflecting the workings of a representational system by which objects are identified.

An Analogy Between Speech and Object Perception

As will be argued in a later section, the number of categories into which we can classify objects rivals the number of words that can be readily identified when listening to speech. Lexical access during speech perception can be successfully modeled as a process mediated by the identification of individual primitive elements, the phonemes, from a relatively small set of primitives (Marslen-Wilson, 1980). We only need about 44 phonemes to code all the words in English, 15 in Hawaiian, 55 to represent virtually all the words in all the languages spoken around the world. Because the set of primitives is so small and each pho-

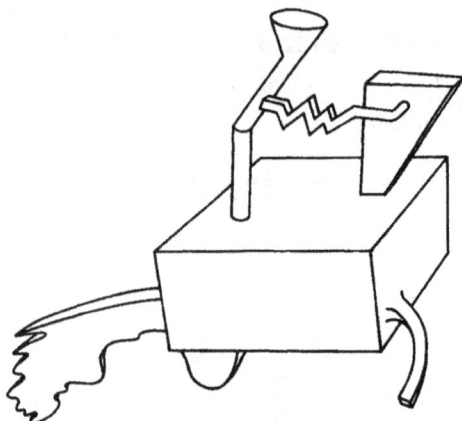

Figure 1. A do-it-yourself object. (There is strong consensus in the segmentation loci of this configuration and in the description of its parts.)

neme specifiable by dichotomous (or trichotomous) contrasts (e.g., voiced vs. unvoiced, nasal vs. oral) on a handful of attributes, one need not make particularly fine discriminations in the speech stream. The representational power of the system derives from its permissiveness in allowing relatively free combinations of its primitives.

The hypothesis explored here is that a roughly analogous system may account for our capacities for object recognition. In the visual domain, however, the primitive elements would not be phonemes but a modest number of simple geometric components—generally convex and volumetric—such as cylinders, blocks, wedges, and cones. Objects are segmented, typically at regions of sharp concavity, and the resultant parts matched against the best fitting primitive. The set of primitives derives from combinations of contrasting characteristics of the edges in a two-dimensional image (e.g., straight vs. curved, symmetrical vs. asymmetrical) that define differences among a set of simple volumes (viz., those that tend to be symmetrical and lack sharp concavities). As in speech perception, these contrasts need only be dichotomous or trichotomous rather than quantitative, so that the human's limited capacities for absolute judgment are not taxed. The particular properties of edges that are postulated to be relevant to the generation of the volumetric primitives have the desirable properties that they are invariant over changes in orientation and can be determined from just a few points on each edge. Consequently, they allow a primitive to be extracted with great tolerance for variations of viewpoint, occlusion, and noise.

Just as the relations among the phonemes are critical in lexical access—"fur" and "rough" have the same phonemes but are not the same words—the relations among the volumes are critical for object recognition: Two different arrangements of the same components could produce different objects. In both cases, the representational power derives from the enormous number of combinations that can arise from a modest number of primitives. The relations in speech are limited to left-to-right

(sequential) orderings; in the visual domain a richer set of possible relations allows a far greater representational capacity from a comparable number of primitives. The matching of objects in recognition is hypothesized to be a process in which the perceptual input is matched against a representation that can be described by a few simple categorized volumes in specified relations to each other.

Theoretical Domain: Primal Access to Contour-Based Perceptual Categories

Our theoretical goal is to account for the initial categorization of isolated objects. Often, but not always, this categorization will be at a basic level, for example, when we know that a given object is a typewriter, a banana, or a giraffe (Rosch, Mervis, Gray, Johnson, & Boyes-Braem, 1976). Much of our knowledge about objects is organized at this level of categorization: the level at which there is typically some readily available name to describe that category (Rosch et al., 1976). The hypothesis explored here predicts that when the componential description of a particular subordinate differs substantially from a basic-level prototype, that is, when a subordinate is perceptually nonprototypical, categorizations will initially be made at the subordinate level. Thus, we might know that a given object is a floor lamp, a penguin, a sports car, or a dachshund more rapidly than we know that it is a lamp, a bird, a car, or a dog (e.g., Jolicoeur, Gluck, & Kosslyn, 1984). (For both theoretical and expository purposes, these readily identifiable nonprototypical members [subordinates] of basic level categories will also be considered basic level in this article.)

Count Versus Mass Noun Entities: The Role of Surface Characteristics

There is a restriction on the scope of this approach of volumetric modeling that should be noted. The modeling has been limited to concrete entities with specified boundaries. In English, such objects are typically designated by count nouns. These are concrete objects that have specified boundaries and to which we can apply the indefinite article and number. For example, for a count noun such as "chair" we can say "a chair" or "three chairs." By contrast, mass nouns are concrete entities to which the indefinite article or number cannot be applied, such as water, sand, or snow. So we cannot say "a water" or "three sands," unless we refer to a count noun shape, as in "a drop of water," "a bucket of water," "a grain of sand," or "a snowball," each of which does have a simple volumetric description. We conjecture that mass nouns are identified primarily through surface characteristics such as texture and color, rather than through volumetric primitives.

Primal Access

Under restricted viewing and uncertain conditions, as when an object is partially occluded, texture, color, and other cues (such as position in the scene and labels) may constitute part or all of the information determining memory access, as for example when we identify a particular shirt in the laundry pile from seeing just a bit of fabric. Such identifications are indirect, typically the result of inference over a limited set of possible objects. (Additional analyses of the role of surface features is presented later in the discussion of the experimental comparison of the perceptibility of color photography and line drawings.) The goal of the present effort is to account for what can be called *primal access:* the first contact of a perceptual input from an isolated, unanticipated object to a representation in memory.

Basic Phenomena of Object Recognition

Independent of laboratory research, the phenomena of everyday object identification provide strong constraints on possible models of recognition. In addition to the fundamental phenomenon that objects can be recognized at all (not an altogether obvious conclusion), at least five facts are evident. Typically, an object can be recognized rapidly, when viewed most from novel orientations, under moderate levels of visual noise, when partially occluded, and when it is a new exemplar of a category.

The preceding five phenomena constrain theorizing about object interpretation in the following ways:

1. Access to the mental representation of an object should not be dependent on absolute judgments of quantitative detail, because such judgments are slow and error prone (Garner, 1962; Miller, 1956). For example, distinguishing among just several levels of the degree of curvature or length of an object typically requires more time than that required for the identification of the object itself. Consequently, such quantitative processing cannot be the controlling factor by which recognition is achieved.

2. The information that is the basis of recognition should be relatively invariant with respect to orientation and modest degradation.

3. Partial matches should be computable. A theory of object interpretation should have some principled means for computing a match for occluded, partial, or new exemplars of a given category. We should be able to account for the human's ability to identify, for example, a chair when it is partially occluded by other furniture, or when it is missing a leg, or when it is a new model.

Recognition-by-Components: An Overview

Our hypothesis, recognition-by-components (RBC), bears some relation to several prior conjectures for representing objects by parts or modules (e.g., Binford, 1971; Brooks, 1981; Guzman, 1971; Marr, 1977; Marr & Nishihara, 1978; Tversky & Hemenway, 1984). RBC's contribution lies in its proposal for a particular vocabulary of components derived from perceptual mechanisms and its account of how an arrangement of these components can access a representation of an object in memory.

Stages of Processing

Figure 2 presents a schematic of the presumed subprocesses by which an object is recognized. These stages are assumed to be arranged in cascade. An early edge extraction stage, responsive to differences in surface characteristics namely, luminance, texture, or color, provides a line drawing description of the object. From this description, nonaccidental properties of image

edges (e.g., collinearity, symmetry) are detected. Parsing is performed, primarily at concave regions, simultaneously with a detection of nonaccidental properties. The nonaccidental properties of the parsed regions provide critical constraints on the identity of the components. Within the temporal and contextual constraints of primal access, the stages up to and including the identification of components are assumed to be bottom-up.[1] A delay in the determination of an object's components should have a direct effect on the identification latency of the object.

The arrangement of the components is then matched against a representation in memory. It is assumed that the matching of the components occurs in parallel, with unlimited capacity. Partial matches are possible with the degree of match assumed to be proportional to the similarity in the components between the image and the representation.[2] This stage model is presented to provide an overall theoretical context. The focus of this article is on the nature of the units of the representation.

When an image of an object is painted on the retina, RBC assumes that a representation of the image is segmented—or parsed—into separate regions at points of deep concavity, particularly at cusps where there are discontinuities in curvature (Marr & Nishihara, 1978). In general, paired concavities will arise whenever convex volumes are joined, a principle that Hoffman and Richards (1985) term *transversality.* Such segmentation conforms well with human intuitions about the boundaries of object parts and does not depend on familiarity

---

[1] The only top-down route shown in Figure 2 is an effect of the nonaccidental properties on edge extraction. Even this route (aside from collinearity and smooth curvature) would run counter to the desires of many in computational vision (e.g., Marr, 1982) to build a completely bottom-up system for edge extraction. This assumption was developed in the belief that edge extraction does not depend on prior familiarity with the object. However, as with the nonaccidental properties, a top-down route from the component determination stage to edge extraction could precede independent of familiarity with the object itself. It is possible that an edge extraction system with a competence equivalent to that of a human—an as yet unrealized accomplishment—will require the inclusion of such top-down influences. It is also likely that other top-down routes, such as those from expectancy, object familiarity, or scene constraints (e.g., Biederman, 1981; Biederman, Mezzanotte, & Rabinowitz, 1982), will be observed at a number of the stages, for example, at segmentation, component definition, or matching, especially if edges are degraded. These have been omitted from Figure 2 in the interests of simplicity and because their actual paths of influence are as yet undetermined. By proposing a general account of object recognition, it is hoped that the proposed theory will provide a framework for a principled analysis of top-down effects in this domain.

[2] Modeling the matching of an object image to a mental representation is a rich, relatively neglected problem area. Tversky's (1977) contrast model provides a useful framework with which to consider this similarity problem in that it readily allows distinctive features (components) of the image to be considered separately from the distinctive components of the representation. This allows principled assessments of similarity for partial objects (components in the representation but not in the image) and novel objects (containing components in the image that are not in the representation). It may be possible to construct a dynamic model based on a parallel distributed process as a modification of the kind proposed by McClelland and Rumelhart (1981) for word perception, with components playing the role of letters. One difficulty of such an effort is that the set of neighbors for a given word is well specified and readily available from a dictionary; the set of neighbors for a given object is not.

Stages in Object Perception

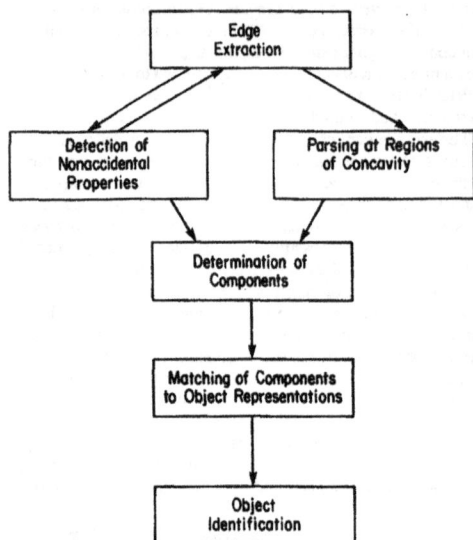

Figure 2. Presumed processing stages in object recognition.

with the object, as was demonstrated with the nonsense object in Figure 1.

Each segmented region is then approximated by one of a possible set of simple components, called *geons* (for "geometrical ions"), that can be modeled by generalized cones (Binford, 1971; Marr, 1977, 1982). A generalized cone is the volume swept out by a cross section moving along an axis (as illustrated in Figure 5). (Marr [1977, 1982] showed that the contours generated by any smooth surface could be modeled by a generalized cone with a convex cross section.) The cross section is typically hypothesized to be at right angles to the axis. Secondary segmentation criteria (and criteria for determining the axis of a component) are those that afford descriptions of volumes that maximize symmetry, axis length, and constancy of the size and curvature of the cross section of the component. Of these, symmetry often provides the most compelling subjective basis for selecting subparts (Brady & Asada, 1984; Connell, 1985). These secondary bases for segmentation and component identification are discussed below.

The primitive components are hypothesized to be simple, typically symmetrical volumes lacking sharp concavities, such as blocks, cylinders, spheres, and wedges. The fundamental perceptual assumption of RBC is that the components can be differentiated on the basis of perceptual properties in the two-dimensional image that are readily detectable and relatively independent of viewing position and degradation. These perceptual properties include several that traditionally have been thought of as principles of perceptual organization, such as

good continuation, symmetry, and Pragnanz. RBC thus provides a principled account of the relation between the classic phenomena of perceptual organization and pattern recognition: Although objects can be highly complex and irregular, the units by which objects are identified are simple and regular. The constraints toward regularization (Pragnanz) are thus assumed to characterize not the complete object but the object's components.

Color and Texture

The preceding account is clearly edge-based. Surface characteristics such as color, brightness, and texture will typically have only secondary roles in primal access. This should not be interpreted as suggesting that the perception of surface characteristics per se is delayed relative to the perception of the components (but see Barrow & Tenenbaum, 1981), but merely that in most cases the surface characteristics are generally less efficient routes for accessing the classification of a count object. That is, we may know that a chair has a particular color and texture simultaneously with its componential description, but it is only the volumetric description that provides efficient access to the mental representation of "chair."[3]

Relations Among the Components

Although the components themselves are the focus of this article, as noted previously the arrangement of primitives is necessary for representing a particular object. Thus, an arc side-connected to a cylinder can yield a cup, as shown in Figure 3C. Different arrangements of the same components can readily lead to different objects, as when an arc is connected to the top of the cylinder to produce a pail (Figure 3D). Whether a component is attached to a long or short surface can also affect classification, as with the arc producing either an attaché case (Figure 3A) or a strongbox (Figure 3B).

The identical situation between primitives and their arrangement exists in the phonemic representation of words, where a given subset of phonemes can be rearranged to produce different words.

The representation of an object would thus be a structural description that expressed the relations among the components (Ballard & Brown, 1982; Winston, 1975). A suggested (minimal) set of relations will be described later (see Table 1). These

---

[3] There are, however, objects that would seem to require both a volumetric description and a texture region for an adequate representation, such as hairbrushes, typewriter keyboards, and corkscrews. It is unlikely that many of the individual bristles, keys, or coils are parsed and identified prior to the identification of the object. Instead those regions are represented through the statistical processing that characterizes their texture (for example, Beck, Prazdny, & Rosenfeld, 1983; Julesz, 1981), although we retain a capacity to zoom down and attend to the volumetric nature of the individual elements. The structural description that would serve as a representation of such objects would include a statistical specification of the texture field along with a specification of the larger volumetric components. These compound texture–componential objects have not been studied, but it is possible that the characteristics of their identification would differ from objects that are readily defined solely by their arrangement of volumetric components.

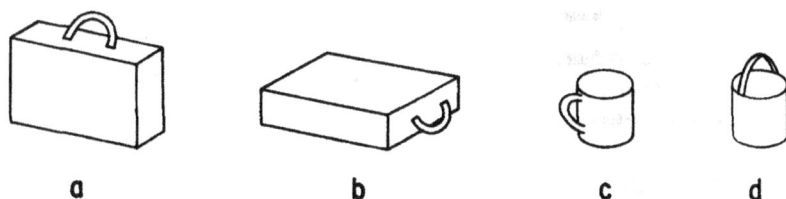

Figure 3. Different arrangements of the same components can produce different objects.

relations include specification of the relative sizes of the components, their orientation and the locus of their attachment.

Nonaccidental Properties: A Perceptual Basis for a Componential Representation

Recent theoretical analyses of perceptual organization (Binford, 1981; Lowe, 1984; Rock, 1983; Witkin & Tenenbaum, 1983) provide a perceptual basis for generating a set of geons. The central organizational principle is that certain properties of edges in a two-dimensional image are taken by the visual system as strong evidence that the edges in the three-dimensional world contain those same properties. For example, if there is a straight line in the image (*collinearity*), the visual system infers that the edge producing that line in the three-dimensional world is also straight. The visual system ignores the possibility that the property in the image might be a result of a (highly unlikely) accidental alignment of eye and curved edge. Smoothly curved elements in the image (*curvilinearity*) are similarly inferred to arise from smoothly curved features in the three-dimensional world. These properties, and the others described later, have been termed *nonaccidental* (Witkin & Tenenbaum, 1983) in that they would only rarely be produced by accidental alignments of viewpoint and object features and consequently are generally unaffected by slight variations in viewpoint.

If the image is symmetrical (*symmetry*), we assume that the object projecting that image is also symmetrical. The order of symmetry is also preserved: Images that are symmetrical under both reflection and 90° increments of rotation, such as a square or circle, are interpreted as arising from objects (or surfaces) that are symmetrical under both rotation and reflection. Although skew symmetry is often readily perceived as arising from a tilted symmetrical object or surface (Palmer, 1983), there are cases where skew symmetry is not readily detected (Attneave, 1982). When edges in the image are parallel or coterminate we assume that the real-world edges also are parallel or coterminate, respectively.

These five nonaccidental properties and the associated three-dimensional inferences are described in Figure 4 (adapted from Lowe, 1984). Witkin and Tenenbaum (1983; see also Lowe, 1984) argue that the leverage provided by the nonaccidental relations for inferring a three-dimensional structure from a two-dimensional image edges is so great as to pose a challenge to the effort in computational vision and perceptual psychology that assigned central importance to variation in local surface characteristics, such as luminance gradients, from which surface

curvature could be determined (as in Besl & Jain, 1986). Although a surface property derived from such gradients will be invariant over some transformations, Witkin and Tenenbaum (1983) demonstrate that the suggestion of a volumetric component through the shape of the surface's silhouette can readily override the perceptual interpretation of the luminance gradient. The psychological literature, summarized in the next section, provides considerable evidence supporting the assumption that these nonaccidental properties can serve as primary organizational constraints in human image interpretation.

Psychological Evidence for the Rapid Use of Nonaccidental Relations

There can be little doubt that images are interpreted in a manner consistent with the nonaccidental principles. But are these relations used quickly enough to provide a perceptual basis for the components that allow primal access? Although all the principles have not received experimental verification, the available evidence strongly suggests an affirmative answer to the preceding question. There is strong evidence that the visual system quickly assumes and uses collinearity, curvature, symmetry, and cotermination. This evidence is of two sorts: (a) demonstrations, often compelling, showing that when a given two-dimensional relation is produced by an accidental alignment of object and image, the visual system accepts the relation as existing in the three-dimensional world; and (b) search tasks showing that when a target differs from distractors in a nonaccidental property, as when one is searching for a curved arc among straight segments, the detection of that target is facilitated compared to conditions where targets and background do not differ in such properties.

Collinearity versus curvature. The demonstration of the collinearity or curvature relations is too obvious to be performed as an experiment. When looking at a straight segment, no observer would assume that it is an accidental image of a curve. That the contrast between straight and curved edges is readily available for perception was shown by Neisser (1963). He found that a search for a letter composed only of straight segments, such as a Z, could be performed faster when in a field of curved distractors, such as C, G, O, and Q, then when among other letters composed of straight segments such as N, W, V, and M.

Symmetry and parallelism. Many of the Ames demonstrations (Ittleson, 1952), such as the trapezoidal window and Ames room, derive from an assumption of symmetry that includes parallelism. Palmer (1980) showed that the subjective directionality of arrangements of equilateral triangles was based on the

120   IRVING BIEDERMAN

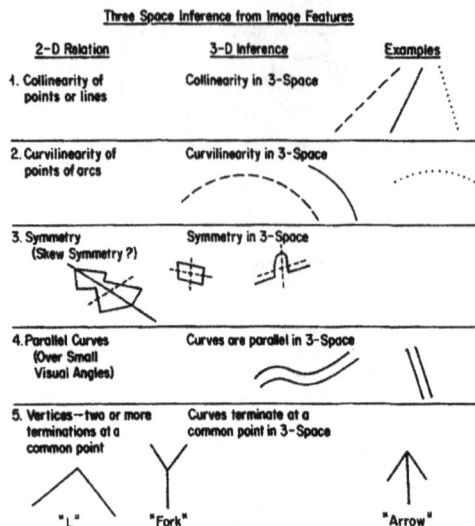

Three Space Inference from Image Features

2-D Relation	3-D Inference	Examples
1. Collinearity of points or lines	Collinearity in 3-Space	
2. Curvilinearity of points of arcs	Curvilinearity in 3-Space	
3. Symmetry (Skew Symmetry ?)	Symmetry in 3-Space	
4. Parallel Curves (Over Small Visual Angles)	Curves are parallel in 3-Space	
5. Vertices—two or more terminations at a common point	Curves terminate at a common point in 3-Space	

"L"   "Fork"   "Arrow"

Figure 4. Five nonaccidental relations. (From Figure 5.2, *Perceptual organization and visual recognition* [p. 77] by David Lowe. Unpublished doctorial dissertation, Stanford University. Adapted by permission.)

derivation of an axis of symmetry for the arrangement. King, Meyer, Tangney, and Biederman (1976) demonstrated that a perceptual bias toward symmetry contributed to apparent shape constancy effects. Garner (1974), Checkosky and Whitlock (1973), and Pomerantz (1978) provided ample evidence that not only can symmetrical shapes be quickly discriminated from asymmetrical stimuli, but that the degree of symmetry was also a readily available perceptual distinction. Thus, stimuli that were invariant under both reflection and 90° increments in rotation could be rapidly discriminated from those that were only invariant under reflection (Checkosky & Whitlock, 1973).

Cotermination. The "peephole perception" demonstrations, such as the Ames chair (Ittleson, 1952) or the physical realization of the "impossible" triangle (Penrose & Penrose, 1958), are produced by accidental alignment of the ends of noncoterminous segments to produce—from one viewpoint only—L, Y, and arrow vertices. More recently, Kanade (1981) has presented a detailed analysis of an "accidental" chair of his own construction. The success of these demonstrations document the immediate and compelling impact of cotermination.

The registration of cotermination is important for determining vertices, which provide information that can serve to distinguish the components. In fact, one theorist (Binford, 1981) has suggested that the major function of eye movements is to determine coincidence of segments. "Coincidence" would include not only cotermination of edges but the termination of one edge on another, as with a T vertex. With polyhedra (volumes produced by planar surfaces), the Y, arrow, and L vertices allow

inference as to the identity of the volume in the image. For example, the silhouette of a brick contains a series of six vertices, which alternate between Ls and arrows, and an internal Y vertex, as illustrated in Figure 5. The Y vertex is produced by the cotermination of three segments, with none of the angles greater than 180°. (An arrow vertex, also formed from the cotermination of three segments, contains an angle that exceeds 180°; an L vertex is formed by the cotermination of two segments.) As shown in Figure 5, this vertex is not present in components that have curved cross sections, such as cylinders, and thus can provide a distinctive cue for the cross-section edge. (The curved Y vertex present in a cylinder can be distinguished from the Y or arrow vertices in that the termination of one segment in the curved Y is tangent to the other segment [Chakravarty, 1979].)

Perkins (1983) has described a perceptual bias toward parallelism in the interpretation of this vertex.[4] Whether the presence of this particular internal vertex can facilitate the identification of a brick versus a cylinder is not yet known, but a recent study by Biederman and Blickle (1985), described below, demonstrated that deletion of vertices adversely affected object recognition more than deletion of the same amount of contour at midsegment.

The T vertex represents a special case in that it is not a locus of cotermination (of two or more segments) but only the termination of one segment on another. Such vertices are important for determining occlusion and thus segmentation (along with concavities), in that the edge forming the (normally) vertical segment of the T cannot be closer to the viewer than the segment forming the top of the T (Binford, 1981). By this account, the T vertex might have a somewhat different status than the Y, arrow, and L vertices, in that the T's primary role would be in segmentation, rather than in establishing the identity of the volume.[5]

Vertices composed of three segments, such as the Y and ar-

_____

[4] When such vertices formed the central angle in a polyhedron, Perkins (1983) reported that the surfaces would almost always be interpreted as meeting at right angles, as long as none of the three angles was less than 90°. Indeed, such vertices cannot be projections of acute angles (Kanade, 1981) but the human appears insensitive to the possibility that the vertices could have arisen from obtuse angles. If one of the angles in the central Y vertex was acute, then the polyhedra would be interpreted as irregular. Perkins found that subjects from rural areas of Botswana, where there was a lower incidence of exposure to carpentered (right-angled) environments, had an even stronger bias toward rectilinear interpretations than did Westerners (Perkins & Deregowski, 1982).

[5] The arrangement of vertices, particularly for polyhedra, offers constraints on "possible" interpretations of lines as convex, concave, or occluding (e.g., Sugihara, 1984). In general, the constraints take the form that a segment cannot change its interpretation, for example, from concave to convex, unless it passes through a vertex. "Impossible" objects can be constructed from violations of this constraint (Waltz, 1975) as well as from more general considerations (Sugihara, 1982, 1984). It is tempting to consider that the visual system captures these constraints in the way in which edges are grouped into objects, but the evidence would seem to argue against such an interpretation. The impossibility of most impossible objects is not immediately registered, but requires scrutiny and thought before the inconsistency is detected. What this means in the present context is that the visual system has a capacity for classifying vertices locally, but no perceptual routines for determining the global consistency of a set of vertices.

Some Nonaccidental Differences Between a Brick and a Cylinder

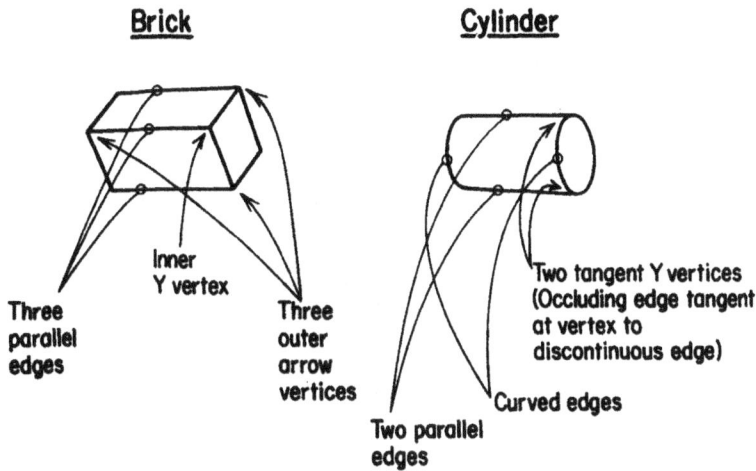

Figure 5. Some differences in nonaccidental properties between a cylinder and a brick.

row, and their curved counterparts, are important determinants as to whether a given component is volumetric or planar. Planar components (to be discussed later) lack three-pronged vertices.

The high speed and accuracy of determining a given nonaccidental relation (e.g., whether some pattern is symmetrical) should be contrasted with performance in making absolute quantitative judgments of variations in a single physical attribute, such as length of a segment or degree of tilt or curvature. For example, the judgment as to whether the length of a given segment is 10, 12, 14, 16, or 18 cm is notoriously slow and error prone (Beck, Prazdny, & Rosenfeld, 1983; Fildes & Triggs, 1985; Garner, 1962; Miller, 1956; Virsu, 1971a, 1971b). Even these modest performance levels are challenged when the judgments have to be executed over the brief 100-ms intervals (Egeth & Pachella, 1969) that are sufficient for accurate object identification. Perhaps even more telling against a view of object recognition that postulates the making of absolute judgments of fine quantitative detail is that the speed and accuracy of such judgments decline dramatically when they have to be made for multiple attributes (Egeth & Pachella, 1969; Garner, 1962; Miller, 1956). In contrast, object recognition latencies for complex objects are reduced by the presence of additional (redundant) components (Biederman, Ju, & Clapper, 1985, described below).

Geons Generated From Differences in Nonaccidental Properties Among Generalized Cones

I have emphasized the particular set of nonaccidental properties shown in Figure 4 because they may constitute a perceptual basis for the generation of the set of components. Any primitive

that is hypothesized to be the basis of object recognition should be rapidly identifiable and invariant over viewpoint and noise. These characteristics would be attainable if differences among components were based on differences in nonaccidental properties. Although additional nonaccidental properties exist, there is empirical support for rapid perceptual access to the five described in Figure 4. In addition, these five relations reflect intuitions about significant perceptual and cognitive differences among objects.

From variation over only two or three levels in the nonaccidental relations of four attributes of generalized cylinders, a set of 36 geons can be generated. A subset is illustrated in Figure 6.

Six of the generated geons (and their attribute values) are shown in Figure 7. Three of the attributes describe characteristics of the cross section: its shape, symmetry, and constancy of size as it is swept along the axis. The fourth attribute describes the shape of the axis. Additional volumes are shown in Figures 8 and 9.

Nonaccidental Two-Dimensional Contrasts Among the Geons

As indicated in the above outline, the values of the four generalized cone attributes can be directly detected as contrastive differences in nonaccidental properties: straight versus curved, symmetrical versus asymmetrical, parallel versus nonparallel (and if nonparallel, whether there is a point of maximal convexity). Cross-section edges and curvature of the axis are distinguishable by collinearity or curvilinearity. The constant versus expanded size of the cross section would be detectable through parallelism; a constant cross section would produce a general-

122   IRVING BIEDERMAN

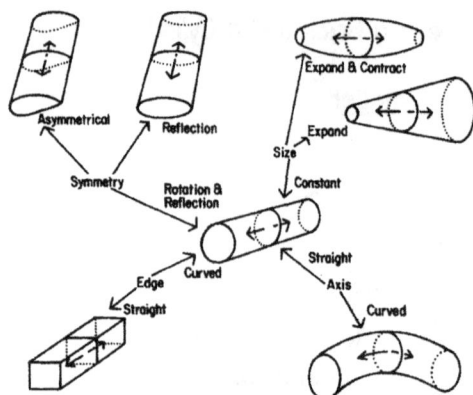

Figure 6. An illustration of how variations in three attributes of a cross section (curved vs. straight edges; constant vs. expanded vs. expanded and contracted size; mirror and rotational symmetry vs. mirror symmetry vs. asymmetrical) and one of the shape of the axis (straight vs. curved) can generate a set of generalized cones differing in nonaccidental relations. (Constant-sized cross sections have parallel sides; expanded or expanded and contracted cross sections have sides that are not parallel. Curved versus straight cross sections and axes are detectable through collinearity or curvature. The three values of cross-section symmetry [symmetrical under reflection & 90° rotation, reflection only, or asymmetrical] are detectable through the symmetry relation. Neighbors of a cylinder are shown here. The full family of geons has 36 members.)

ized cone with parallel sides (as with a cylinder or brick); an expanded cross section would produce edges that were not parallel (as with a cone or wedge). A cross section that expanded and then contracted would produce an ellipsoid with nonparallel sides and extrema of positive curvature (as with a lemon). Such extrema are invariant with viewpoint (e.g., Hoffman & Richards, 1985) and actually constitute a sixth nonaccidental relation. The three levels of cross-section symmetry are equivalent to Garner's (1974) distinction as to the number of different stimuli produced by increments of 90° rotations and reflections of a stimulus. Thus, a square or circle would be invariant under 90° rotation and reflection, but a rectangle or ellipse would be invariant only under reflection, as 90° rotations would produce another figure in each case. Asymmetrical figures would produce eight different figures under 90° rotation and reflection.

Specification of the nonaccidental properties of the three attributes of the cross section and one of the axis, as described in the previous paragraph, is sufficient to uniquely classify a given arrangement of edges as one of the 36 geons. These would be matched against a structural description for each geon that specified the values of these four nonaccidental image properties. But there are actually more distinctive nonaccidental image features for each geon than the four described in the previous paragraph (or indicated in Figures 7, 8, and 9). In particular, the arrangement of vertices, both of the silhouette and the presence of an interior Y vertex, and the presence of a discontinuous (third) edge along the axis (which produces the interior

Y vertex) provide a richer description for each component than do the four properties of the generating function. This point can be readily appreciated by considering, as an example, some of the additional nonaccidental properties differentiating the brick from the cylinder in Figure 5. Each geon's structural description would thus include a larger number of contrastive image properties than the four that were directly related to the generating function.

Consideration of the featural basis for the structural descriptions for each geon suggests that a similarity measure can be defined on the basis of the common versus distinctive image features for any pair of components. The similarity measure would permit the promotion of alternative geons under conditions of ambiguity, as when one or several of the image features were undecidable.

Is geon identification two-dimensional or three-dimensional? Although the 36 geons have a clear subjective volumetric interpretation, it must be emphasized they can be uniquely specified from their two-dimensional image properties. Consequently, recognition need not follow the construction of an "object centered" (Marr, 1982) three-dimensional interpretation of each volume. It is also possible that, despite the subjective componential interpretation given to the arrangement of image features as simple volumes, it is the image features themselves, in specified relationships, that mediate perception. These alternatives remain to be evaluated.

Additional Sources of Contour and Recognition Variation

RBC seeks to account for the recognition of an infinitely varied perceptual input with a modest set of idealized primitives.

Partial Tentative Geon Set Based on Nonaccidentalness Relations

CROSS SECTION

Geon	Edge Straight S Curved C	Symmetry Rot & Ref ++ Ref + Asymm −	Size Constant ++ Expanded − Exp & Cont −−	Axis Straight + Curved −
	S	+ +	+ +	+
	C	+ +	+ +	+
	S	+	−	+
	S	+ +	+	−
	C	+ +	−	+
	S	+	+	+

Figure 7. Proposed partial set of volumetric primitives (geons) derived from differences in nonaccidental properties.

Geons with Expanded and Contracted Cross Sections (--)

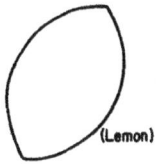

Cross Section:
Edge: Curved (C)
Symmetry: Yes (+)
Size: Expanded & Contracted: (--)
Axis: Straight (+)

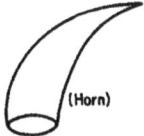

(Lemon)

Cross Section:
Edge: Curved (C)
Symmetry: Yes (+)
Size: Expanded (+)
Axis: Curved (-)

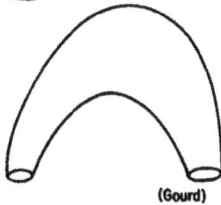

(Horn)

Cross Section:
Edge: Curved (C)
Symmetry: Yes (+)
Size: Expanded & Contracted (--)
Axis: Curved (-)

(Gourd)

Figure 8. Three curved geons with curved axes or expanded and/or contracted cross sections. (These tend to resemble biological forms.)

A number of subordinate and related issues are raised by this attempt, some of which will be addressed in this section. This section need not be covered by a reader concerned primarily with the overall gist of RBC.

Asymmetrical cross sections. There are an infinity of possible cross sections that could be asymmetrical. How does RBC represent this variation? RBC assumes that the differences in the departures from symmetry are not readily available and thus do not affect primal access. For example, the difference in the shape of the cross section for the two straight-edged volumes in Figure 10 might not be apparent quickly enough to affect object recognition. This does not mean that an individual could not store the details of the volume produced by an asymmetrical cross section. But the presumption is that the access for this detail would be too slow to mediate primal access. I do not know of any case where primal access depends on discrimination among asymmetrical cross sections within a given component type, for example, among curved-edged cross sections of constant size, straight axes, and a specified aspect ratio. For instance, the curved cross section for the component that can model an airplane wing or car door is asymmetrical. Different wing designs might have different shaped cross sections. It is likely that most people, including wing designers, will know that the object is an airplane, or even an airplane wing, before they know the subclassification of the wing on the basis of the asymmetry of its cross section.

A second way in which asymmetrical cross sections need not

be individually represented is that they often produce volumes that resemble symmetrical, but truncated, wedges or cones. This latter form of representing asymmetrical cross sections would be analogous to the schema-plus-correction phenomenon noted by Bartlett (1932). The implication of a schema-plus-correction representation would be that a single primitive category for asymmetrical cross sections and wedges might be sufficient. For both kinds of volumes, their similarity may be a function of the detection of a lack of parallelism in the volume. One would have to exert scrutiny to determine whether a lack of parallelism had originated in the cross section or in a size change of a symmetrical cross section. In this case, as with the components with curved axes described in the preceding section, a single primitive category for both wedges and asymmetrical straight-edged volumes could be postulated that would allow a reduction in the number of primitive components. There is considerable evidence that asymmetrical patterns require more time for their identification than symmetrical patterns (Checkosky & Whitlock, 1973; Pomerantz, 1978). Whether these effects have consequences for the time required for object identification is not yet known.

One other departure from regular components might also be noted. A volume can have a cross section with edges that are both curved and straight, as would result when a cylinder is sectioned in half along its length, producing a semicircular cross section. The conjecture is that in such cases the default cross section is the curved one, with the straight edges interpreted as slices off the curve, in schema-plus-correction representation (Bartlett, 1932).

CROSS SECTION

Geon	Edge Straight S Curved C	Symmetry Rot & Ref ++ Ref + Asymm -	Size Constant ++ Expanded - Exp & Cont --	Axis Straight + Curved -
	S	+	++	-
	C	+	++	-
	S	++	-	-
	C	++	-	-
	S	+	-	-
	C	+	-	-

Figure 9. Geons with curved axis and straight or curved cross sections. (Determining the shape of the cross section, particularly if straight, might require attention.)

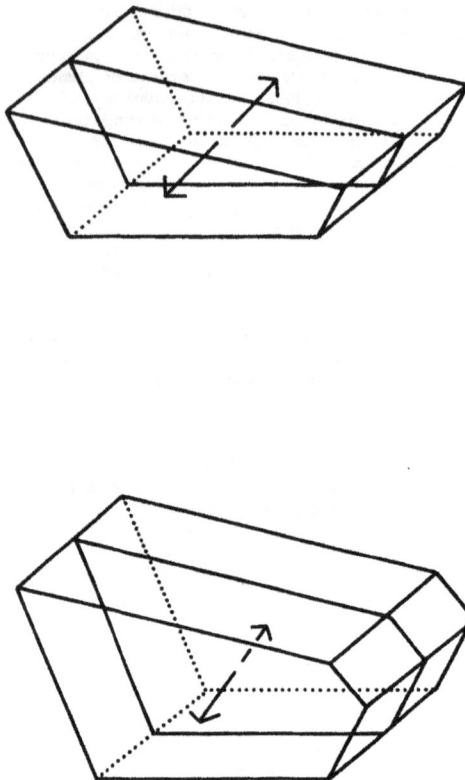

Figure 10. Volumes with an asymmetrical, straight-edged, cross section. (Detection of differences between such volumes might require attention.)

Component terminations. When a cross section varies in size, as with a cone, it can converge to a point, as with the horn in Figure 8, or appear truncated, as with the cone in Figure 7. Such termination differences could be represented as independently specified characteristics of the structural description for the geon, determinable in the image by whether the termination was a single L vertex (with a point) or two tangent Y vertices (with a truncated cone).

Another case arises when a cylinder has a cross section that remains constant for part of its length but then tapers to produce a point, as with a sharpened pencil. Such objects could be modeled by joining a cylinder to a cone, with the size of the cross sections matched so that no concavity is produced. The parsing point in this case would be the join where different nonaccidental properties were required to fit the volumes, namely, the shift from parallel edges with the cylinder to converging edges with the cone. Such joins provide a decidedly weaker basis—subjectively—for segmentation than joins producing

cusps. The perceptual consequences of such variation have not been studied.

Metric variation. For any given geon type, there can be continuous metric variation in aspect ratio, degree of curvature (for curved components), and departure from parallelism (for nonparallel components). How should this quantitative variation be conceptualized? The discussion will concentrate on aspect ratio, probably the most important of the variations. But the issues will be generally applicable to the other metric variations as well.[6]

One possibility is to include specification of a range of aspect ratios in the structural description of the geons of an object as well as the object itself. It seems plausible to assume that recognition can be indexed, in part, by aspect ratio in addition to a componential description. An object's aspect ratio would thus play a role similar to that played by word length in the tachistoscopic identification of words, where long words are rarely proffered when a short word is flashed. Consider an elongated object, such as a baseball bat, with an aspect ratio of 15:1. When the orientation of the object is orthogonal to the viewpoint, so that the aspect ratio of its image is also 15:1, recognition might be faster than when presented at an orientation where the aspect ratio of its image differed greatly from that value, say 2:1. One need not have a particularly fine-tuned function for aspect ratio as large differences in aspect ratio between two components would, like parallelism, be preserved over a large proportion of arbitrary viewing angles.

Another way to incorporate variations in the aspect ratio of an object's image is to represent only qualitative differences, so that variations in aspect ratios exert an effect only when the relative size of the longest dimensions undergo reversal. Specifically, for each component and the complete object, three variations could be defined depending on whether the axis was much smaller, approximately equal to, or much longer than the longest dimension of the cross section. For example, for a geon whose axis was longer than the diameter of the cross section (which would be true in most cases), only when the projection of the cross section became longer than the axis would there be an effect of the object's orientation, as when the bat was viewed almost from on end so that the diameter of the handle was greater than the projection of its length.

A close dependence of object recognition performance on the preservation of the aspect ratio of a geon in the image would challenge RBC's emphasis on dichotomous contrasts of nonaccidental relations. Fortunately, these issues on the role of aspect ratio are readily testable. Bartram's (1976) experiments, described later in the section on orientation variability, suggest that sensitivity to variations in aspect ratio need not be given heavy weight: Recognition speed is unaffected by variation in aspect ratio across different views of the same object.

Planar geons. When a three-pronged vertex (viz., Y, tangent Y, or arrow) is not present in a parsed region, the resultant region appears planar, as with the flipper of the penguin in Figure

---

[6] Aspect ratio is a measure of the elongation of a component. For constant-sized cross sections and straight axes, it can be expressed as the width-to-height ratio of the smallest bounding rectangle that would just enclose the component. More complex functions are needed expressing the change in aspect ratio as a function of axis position when the cross section varies in size or the axis is curved.

10 or the eye of the elephant in Figure 11. Such shapes can be conceptualized in two ways. The first (and less favored) is to assume that these are just quantitative variations of the volumetric components, but with an axis length of zero. They would then have default values of a straight axis (+) and a constant cross section (+). Only the edge of the cross section and its symmetry could vary.

Alternatively, it might be that a planar region is not related perceptually to the foreshortened projection of the geon that could have produced it. Using the same variation in cross-section edge and symmetry as with the volumetric components, seven planar geons could be defined. For ++symmetry there would be the square and circle (with straight and curved edges, respectively) and for +symmetry the rectangle, triangle, and ellipse. Asymmetrical (−) planar geons would include trapezoids (straight edges), and drop shapes (curved edges). The addition of these seven planar geons to the 36 volumetric geons yields 43 components (a number close to the number of phonemes required to represent English words). The triangle is here assumed to define a separate geon, although a triangular cross section was not assumed to define a separate volume under the intuition that a prism (produced by a triangular cross section) is not quickly distinguishable from a wedge. My preference for assuming that planar geons are not perceptually related to their foreshortened volumes is based on the extraordinary difficulty of recognizing objects from views that are parallel to the axis of the major components so that foreshortening projects only the planar cross section, as shown in Figure 27. The presence of three-pronged vertices thus provides strong evidence that the image is generated from a volumetric rather than a planar component.

Selection of axis. Given that a volume is segmented from the object, how is an axis selected? Subjectively, it appears that an axis is selected that would maximize the axis's length, the symmetry of the cross section, and the constancy of the size of the cross section. By maximizing the length of the axis, bilateral symmetry can be more readily detected because the sides would be closer to the axis. Often a single axis satisfies all three criteria, but sometimes these criteria are in opposition and two (or more) axes (and component types) are plausible (Brady, 1983). Under such conditions, axes will often be aligned to an external frame, such as the vertical (Humphreys, 1983).

Negative values. The plus values in Figures 7, 8, and 9 are those favored by perceptual biases and memory errors. No bias is assumed for straight and curved edges of the cross section. For symmetry, clear biases have been documented. For example, if an image could have arisen from a symmetrical object, then it is interpreted as symmetrical (King et al., 1976). The same is apparently true of parallelism. If edges could be parallel, then they are typically interpreted as such, as with the trapezoidal room or window.

Curved axes. Figure 8 shows three of the most negatively marked primitives with curved crossed sections. Such geons often resemble biological entities. An expansion and contraction of a rounded cross section with a straight axis produces an ellipsoid (lemon), an expanded cross section with a curved axis produces a horn, and an expanded and contracted cross section with a rounded cross section produces a banana slug or gourd.

In contrast to the natural forms generated when both cross section and axis are curved, the geons swept by a straight-edged cross section traveling along a curved axis (e.g., the components on the first, third, and fifth rows of Figure 9) appear somewhat less familiar and more difficult to apprehend than their curved counterparts. It is possible that this difficulty may merely be a consequence of unfamiliarity. Alternatively, the subjective difficulty might be produced by a conjunction–attention effect (CAE) of the kind discussed by Treisman (e.g., Treisman & Gelade, 1980). (CAEs are described later in the section on attentional effects.) In the present case, given the presence in the image of curves and straight edges (for the rectilinear cross sections with curved axis), attention (or scrutiny) may be required to determine which kind of segment to assign to the axis and which to assign to the cross section. Curiously, the problem does not present itself when a curved cross section is run along a straight axis to produce a cylinder or cone. The issue as to the role of attention in determining geons would appear to be empirically tractable using the paradigms created by Treisman and her colleagues (Treisman, 1982; Treisman & Gelade, 1980).

Conjunction–attentional effects. The time required to detect a single feature is often independent of the number of distracting items in the visual field. For example, the time it takes to detect a blue shape (a square or a circle) among a field of green distractor shapes is unaffected by the number of green shapes. However, if the target is defined by a conjunction of features, for example, a blue square among distractors consisting of green squares and blue circles, so that both the color and the shape of each item must be determined to know if it is or is not the target, then target detection time increases linearly with the number of distractors (Treisman & Gelade, 1980). These results have led to a theory of visual attention that assumes that humans can monitor all potential display positions simultaneously and with unlimited capacity for a single feature (e.g., something blue or something curved). But when a target is defined by a conjunction of features, then a limited capacity attentional system that can only examine one display position at a time must be deployed (Treisman & Gelade, 1980).

The extent to which Treisman and Gelade's (1980) demonstration of conjunction–attention effects may be applicable to the perception of volumes and objects has yet to be evaluated. In the extreme, in a given moment of attention, it may be the case that the values of the four attributes of the components are detected as independent features. In cases where the attributes, taken independently, can define different volumes, as with the shape of cross sections and axes, an act of attention might be required to determine the specific component generating those attributes: Am I looking at a component with a curved cross section and a straight axis or is it a straight cross section and a curved axis? At the other extreme, it may be that an object recognition system has evolved to allow automatic determination of the geons.

The more general issue is whether relational structures for the primitive components are defined automatically or whether a limited attentional capacity is required to build them from their individual-edge attributes. It could be the case that some of the most positively marked geons are detected automatically, but that the volumes with negatively marked attributes might require attention. That some limited capacity is involved in the perception of objects (but not necessarily their components) is documented by an effect of the number of distracting objects on perceptual search (Biederman, Blickle, Teitelbaum, Klatsky,

& Mezzgnotte, in press). In their experiment, reaction times and errors for detecting an object such as a chair increased linearly as a function of the number of nontarget objects in a 100-ms presentation of nonscene arrangements of objects. Whether this effect arises from the necessity to use a limited capacity to construct a geon from its attributes or whether the effect arises from the matching of an arrangement of geons to a representation is not yet known.

Relations of RBC to Principles of Perceptual Organization

Textbook presentations of perception typically include a section of Gestalt organizational principles. This section is almost never linked to any other function of perception. RBC posits a specific role for these organizational phenomena in pattern recognition. As suggested by the section on generating geons through nonaccidental properties, the Gestalt principles, particularly those promoting Pragnanz (Good Figure), serve to determine the individual geons, rather than the complete object. A complete object, such as a chair, can be highly complex and asymmetrical, but the components will be simple volumes. A consequence of this interpretation is that it is the components that will be stable under noise or perturbation. If the components can be recovered and object perception is based on the components, then the object will be recognizable.

This may be the reason why it is difficult to camouflage objects by moderate doses of random occluding noise, as when a car is viewed behind foliage. According to RBC, the geons accessing the representation of an object can readily be recovered through routines of collinearity or curvature that restore contours (Lowe, 1984). These mechanisms for contour restoration will not bridge cusps (e.g., Kanizsa, 1979). For visual noise to be effective, by these considerations, it must obliterate the concavity and interrupt the contours from one geon at the precise point where they can be joined, through collinearity or constant curvature, with the contours of another geon. The likelihood of this occurring by moderate random noise is, of course, extraordinarily low, and it is a major reason why, according to RBC, objects are rarely rendered unidentifiable by noise. The consistency of RBC with this interpretation of perceptual organization should be noted. RBC holds that the (strong) loci of parsing is at cusps; the geons are organized from the contours between cusps. In classical Gestalt demonstrations, good figures are organized from the contours between cusps. Experiments subjecting these conjectures to test are described in a later section.

A Limited Number of Components?

According to the prior arguments, only 36 volumetric components can be readily discriminated on the basis of differences in nonaccidental properties among generalized cones. In addition, there are empirical and computational considerations that are compatible with a such a limit.

Empirically, people are not sensitive to continuous metric variations as evidenced by severe limitations in humans' capacity for making rapid and accurate absolute judgments of quantitative shape variations.[7] The errors made in the memory for shapes also document an insensitivity to metric variations.

Computationally, a limit is suggested by estimates of the number of objects we might know and the capacity for RBC to readily represent a far greater number with a limited number of primitives.

Empirical Support for a Limit

Although the visual system is capable of discriminating extremely fine detail, I have been arguing that the number of volumetric primitives sufficient to model rapid human object recognition may be limited. It should be noted, however, that the number of proposed primitives is greater than the three—cylinder, sphere, and cone—advocated by some "How-to-Draw" books. Although these three may be sufficient for determining relative proportions of the parts of a figure and can aid perspective, they are not sufficient for the rapid identification of objects.[8] Similarly, Marr and Nishihara's (1978) pipe-cleaner (viz., cylinder) representations of animals (their Figure 17) would also appear to posit an insufficient number of primitives. On the page, in the context of other labeled pipe-cleaner animals, it is certainly possible to arrive at an identification of a particular (labeled) animal, for example, a giraffe. But the thesis proposed here would hold that the identifications of objects that were distinguished only by the aspect ratios of a single component type would require more time than if the representation of the object preserved its componential identity. In modeling only animals, it is likely that Marr and Nishihara capitalized on the possibility that appendages (such as legs and some necks) can often be modeled by the cylindrical forms of a pipe cleaner. By contrast, it is unlikely that a pipe-cleaner representation of a desk would have had any success. The lesson from Marr and Nishihara's demonstration, even when limited to animals, may be that an image that conveys only the axis structure and axes length is insufficient for primal access.

As noted earlier, one reason not to posit a representation system based on fine quantitative detail, for example, many variations in degree of curvature, is that such absolute judgments are notoriously slow and error prone unless limited to the 7 ± 2 values argued by Miller (1956). Even this modest limit is challenged when the judgments have to be executed over a brief 100-ms interval (Egeth & Pachella, 1969) that is sufficient for accurate object identification. A further reduction in the capacity for absolute judgments of quantitative variations of a simple

---

[7] Absolute judgments are judgments made against a standard in memory, for example, that Shape A is 14 cm. in length. Such judgments are to be distinguished from comparative judgments in which both stimuli are available for simultaneous comparison, for example, that Shape A, lying alongside Shape B, is longer than B. Comparative judgments appear limited only by the resolving power of the sensory system. Absolute judgments are limited, in addition, by memory for physical variation. That the memory limitations are severe is evidenced by the finding that comparative judgments can be made quickly and accurately for differences so fine that thousands of levels can be discriminated. But accurate absolute judgments rarely exceed 7 ± 2 categories (Miller, 1956).

[8] Paul Cezanne is often incorrectly cited on this point. "Treat nature by the cylinder, the sphere, the cone, *everything in proper perspective so that each side of an object or plane is directed towards a central point*" (Cezanne, 1904/1941, p. 234, italics mine). Cezanne was referring to perspective, not the veridical representation of objects.

shape would derive from the necessity, for most objects, to make simultaneous absolute judgments for the several shapes that constitute the object's parts (Egeth & Pachella, 1969; Miller, 1956). This limitation on our capacities for making absolute judgments of physical variation, when combined with the dependence of such variation on orientation and noise, makes quantitative shape judgments a most implausible basis for object recognition. RBC's alternative is that the perceptual discriminations required to determine the primitive components can be made categorically, requiring the discrimination of only two or three viewpoint-independent levels of variation.[9]

Our memory for irregular shapes shows clear biases toward "regularization" (e.g., Woodworth, 1938). Amply documented in the classical shape memory literature was the tendency for errors in the reproduction and recognition of irregular shapes to be in a direction of regularization, in which slight deviations from symmetrical or regular figures were omitted in attempts at reproduction. Alternatively, some irregularities were emphasized ("accentuation"), typically by the addition of a regular subpart. What is the significance of these memory biases? By the RBC hypothesis, these errors may have their origin in the mapping of the perceptual input onto a representational system based on regular primitives. The memory of a slight irregular form would be coded as the closest regularized neighbor of that form. If the irregularity was to be represented as well, an act that would presumably require additional time and capacity, then an additional code (sometimes a component) would be added, as with Bartlett's (1932) "schema with correction."

Computational Considerations: Are 36 Geons Sufficient?

Is there sufficient representational power in a set of 36 geons to express the human's capacity for basic-level visual categorizations? Two estimates are needed to provide a response to this question: (a) the number of readily available perceptual categories, and (b) the number of possible objects that could be represented by 36 geons. The number of possible objects that could be represented by 36 geons will depend on the allowable relations among the geons. Obviously, the value for (b) would have to be greater than the value for (a) if 36 geons are to prove sufficient.

How many readily distinguishable objects do people know? How might one arrive at a liberal estimate for this value? One estimate can be obtained from the lexicon. There are less than 1,500 relatively common basic-level object categories, such as chairs and elephants.[10] If we assume that this estimate is too small by a factor of 2, allowing for idiosyncratic categories and errors in the estimate, then we can assume potential classification into approximately 3,000 basic-level categories. RBC assumes that perception is based on a particular componential configuration rather than the basic-level category, so we need to estimate the mean number of readily distinguishable componential configurations per basic-level category. Almost all natural categories, such as elephants or giraffes, have one or only a few instances with differing componential descriptions. Dogs represent a rare exception for natural categories in that they have been bred to have considerable variation in their descriptions. Categories created by people vary in the number of allowable types, but this number often tends to be greater than the natural categories. Cups, typewriters, and lamps have just a few

(in the case of cups) to perhaps 15 or more (in the case of lamps) readily discernible exemplars.[11] Let us assume (liberally) that the mean number of types is 10. This would yield an estimate of 30,000 readily discriminable objects (3,000 categories × 10 types/category).

A second source for the estimate derives from considering plausible rates for learning new objects. Thirty thousand objects would require learning an average of 4.5 objects per day, every day for 18 years, the modal age of the subjects in the experiments described below.

[9] This limitation on our capacities for absolute judgments also occurs in the auditory domain in speech perception, in which the modest number of phonemes can be interpreted as arising from dichotomous or trichotomous contrasts among a few invariant dimensions of speech production (Miller, 1956). Examples of invariant categorized speech features would be whether transitions are "feathered" (a cue for voicing) or the formants "murmured" (a cue for nasality). That these features are dichotomous allows the recognition system to avoid the limitations of absolute judgment in the auditory domain. It is possible that the limited number of phonemes derives more from this limitation for accessing memory for fine quantitative variation than it does from limits on the fineness of the commands to the speech musculature.

[10] This estimate was obtained from three sources: (a) several linguists and cognitive psychologists, who provided guesses of 300 to 1,000 concrete noun object categories; (b) the average 6-year-old child, who can name most of the objects seen in his or her world and on television and has a vocabulary of less than 10,000 words, about 10% of which are concrete count nouns; and (c) a 30-page sample from Webster's Seventh New Collegiate Dictionary, which provided perhaps the most defensible estimate; I counted the number of readily identifiable, unique concrete nouns that would not be subordinate to other nouns. Thus, "wood thrush" was not included because it could not be readily discriminated from "sparrow," but "penguin" and "ostrich" were counted as separate noun categories, as were borderline cases. The mean number of such nouns per page was 1.4, so given a 1,200 page dictionary, this is equivalent to 1,600 noun categories.

[11] It might be thought that faces constitute an obvious exception to the estimate of a ratio of ten exemplars per category presented here, in that we can obviously recognize thousands of faces. But can we recognize individual faces as rapidly as we recognize differences among basic level categories? I suspect not. That is, we may know that it is a face and not a chair in less time than that required for the identification of any particular face. Whatever the ultimate data on face recognition, there is evidence that the routines for processing faces have evolved to differentially respond to cuteness (Hildebrandt, 1982; Hildebrandt & Fitzgerald, 1983), age (e.g., Mark & Todd, 1985), and emotion and threats (e.g., Coss, 1979; Trivers, 1985). Faces may thus constitute a special stimulus case in that specific mechanisms have evolved to respond to biologically relevant quantitative variations and caution may be in order before results with face stimuli are considered characteristic of perception in general. Another possible exception to the exemplar/category ratio presented here occurs with categories such as lamps, which could have an arbitrarily large number of possible bases, shade types, and so on. But these variations may actually serve to hinder recognition. In a number of experiments in our laboratory, we have noted that highly stylized or unusual exemplars of a category are extremely difficult to identify under brief exposures (and out of context). The elements producing the variation in these cases may thus be acting as noise (or irrelevant components) in the sense that they are present in the image but not present in the mental representation for that category. These potential difficulties in the identification of faces or objects may not be subjectively apparent from the casual perusal of objects on a page, particularly when they are in a context that facilitates their classification.

Table 1
Generative Power of 36 Geons

Value	Component
36	First component (G_1)
×	×
36	Second component (G_2)
×	×
3	Size ($G_1 \gg G_2$, $G_1 \ll G_2$, $G_1 = G_2$)
×	×
2.4	G_1 top or bottom or side (represented for 80% of the objects)
×	×
2	Nature of join (end-to-end [off center] or end-to-side [centered])
×	×
2	Join at long or short surface of G_1
×	×
2	Join at long or short surface of G_2
	Total: 74,649 possible two-geon objects

Note. With three geons, 74,649 × 36 × 57.6 = 154 million possible objects. Equivalent to learning 23,439 new objects every day (approximately 1465/waking hr or 24/min) for 18 years.

Although the value of 4.5 objects learned per day seems reasonable for a child in that it approximates the maximum rates of word acquisition during the ages of 2–6 years (Carey, 1978), it certainly overestimates the rate at which adults develop new object categories. The impressive visual recognition competence of a 6-year-old child, if based on 30,000 visual categories, would require the learning of 13.5 objects per day, or about one per waking hour. By the criterion of learning rate, 30,000 categories would appear to be a liberal estimate.

Componental Relations: The Representational Capacity of 36 Geons

How many objects could be represented by 36 geons? This calculation is dependent upon two assumptions: (a) the number of geons needed, on average, to uniquely specify each object; and (b) the number of readily discriminable relations among the geons. We will start with (b) and see if it will lead to an empirically plausible value for (a). A possible set of relations is presented in Table 1. Like the components, the properties of the relations noted in Table 1 are nonaccidental in that they can be determined from virtually any viewpoint, are preserved in the two-dimensional image, and are categorical, requiring the discrimination of only two or three levels. The specification of these five relations is likely conservative because (a) it is certainly a nonexhaustive set in that other relations can be defined; and (b) the relations are only specified for a pair, rather than triples, of geons. Let us consider these relations in order of their appearance in Table 1.

1. Relative size. For any pair of geons, G_1 and G_2, G_1 could be much greater than, smaller than, or approximately equal to G_2.

2. Verticality. G_1 can be above or below or to the side of G_2, a relation, by the author's estimate, that is defined for at least 80% of the objects. Thus giraffes, chairs, and typewriters have a top-down specification of their components, but forks and

knives do not. The handle of a cup is side-connected to the cylinder.

3. Centering. The connection between any pair of joined geons can be end-to-end (and of equal-sized cross section at the join), as the upper and lower arms of a person, or end-to-side, producing one or two concavities, respectively (Marr, 1977). Two-concavity joins are far more common in that it is rare that two arbitrarily joined end-to-end components will have equal-sized cross sections. A more general distinction might be whether the end of one geon in an end-to-side join is centered or off centered at the side of the other component. The end-to-end join might represent only the limiting, albeit special, case of off-centered joins. In general, the join of any two arbitrary volumes (or shapes) will produce two concavities, unless an edge from one volume is made to be joined and collinear with an edge from the other volume.

4. Relative size of surfaces at join. Other than the special cases of a sphere and a cube, all primitives will have at least a long and a short surface. The join can be on either surface. The attaché case in Figure 3A and the strongbox in Figure 3B differ by the relative lengths of the surfaces of the brick that are connected to the arch (handle). The handle on the shortest surface produces the strongbox; on a longer surface, the attaché case. Similarly, the cup and the pail in Figures 3C and 3D, respectively, differ as to whether the handle is connected to the long surface of the cylinder (to produce a cup) or the short surface (to produce a pail). In considering only two values for the relative size of the surface at the join, I am conservatively estimating the relational possibilities. Some volumes such as the wedge have as many as five surfaces, all of which can differ in size.

Representational Calculations

The 1,296 different pairs of the 36 geons (i.e., 36^2), when multiplied by the number of relational combinations, 57.6 (the product of the various values of the five relations), gives us 74,649 possible two-geon objects. If a third geon is added to the two, then this value has to be multiplied by 2,073 (36 geons × 57.6 ways in which the third geon can be related to one of the two geons), to yield 154 million possible three-component objects. This value, of course, readily accommodates the liberal estimate of 30,000 objects actually known.

The extraordinary disparity between the representational power of two or three geons and the number of objects in an individual's object vocabulary means that there is an extremely high degree of redundancy in the filling of the 154 million cell geon-relation space. Even with three times the number of objects estimated to be known by an individual (i.e., 90,000 objects), we would still have less than $\frac{1}{10}$ of 1% of the possible combinations of three geons actually used (i.e., over 99.9% redundancy).

There is a remarkable consequence of this redundancy if we assume that objects are distributed randomly throughout the object space. (Any function that yielded a relatively homogeneous distribution would serve as well.) The sparse, homogeneous occupation of the space means that, on average, it will be rare for an object to have a neighbor that differs only by one geon or relation.[12] Because the space was generated by considering only the number of possible two or three component objects, a constraint on the estimate of the average number of components per object that are sufficient for unambiguous identification is implicated. If objects were distributed relatively homogeneously among combinations of relations and geons, then only two or three geons would be sufficient to unambiguously represent most objects.

Experimental Support for a Componential Representation

According to the RBC hypothesis, the preferred input for accessing object recognition is that of the volumetric geons. In most cases, only a few appropriately arranged geons would be all that is required to uniquely specify an object. Rapid object recognition should then be possible. Neither the full complement of an object's geons, nor its texture, nor its color, nor the full bounding contour (or envelope or outline) of the object need be present for rapid identification. The problem of recognizing tens of thousands of possible objects becomes, in each case, just a simple task of identifying the arrangement of a few from a limited set of geons.

Several object-naming reaction time experiments have provided support for the general assumptions of the RBC hypothesis, although none have provided tests of the specific set of geons proposed by RBC or even that there might be a limit to the number of components.[13]

In all experiments, subjects named or quickly verified briefly presented pictures of common objects.[14] That RBC may provide a sufficient account of object recognition was supported by experiments indicating that objects drawn with only two or three of their components could be accurately identified from a single 100-ms exposure. When shown with a complete complement of components, these simple line drawings were identified almost as rapidly as full colored, detailed, textured slides of the same objects. That RBC may provide a necessary account of object recognition was supported by a demonstration that degradation (contour deletion), if applied at the regions that prevented recovery of the geons, rendered an object unidentifiable. All the original experimental results reported here have received at least one, and often several, replications.

Perceiving Incomplete Objects

Biederman, Ju, and Clapper (1985) studied the perception of briefly presented partial objects lacking some of their components. A prediction of RBC was that only two or three geons would be sufficient for rapid identification of most objects. If there was enough time to determine the geons and their relations, then object identification should be possible. Complete objects would be maximally similar to their representation and should enjoy an identification speed advantage over their partial versions.

Stimuli

The experimental objects were line drawings of 36 common objects, 9 of which are illustrated in Figure 11. The depiction of the objects and their partition into components was done subjectively, according to generally easy agreement among at least three judges. The artists were unaware of the set of geons described in this article. For the most part, the components corresponded to the parts of the object. Seventeen geon types (out of the full set of 36), were sufficient to represent the 180 components comprising the complete versions of the 36 objects.

The objects were shown either with their full complement of components or partially, but never with less than two components. The first two or three components that were selected were almost always the largest components from the complete object, as illustrated in Figures 12 and 13. For example, the airplane (Figure 13), which required nine components to look complete, had the fuselage and two wings when shown with three of its nine components. Additional components were added in decreasing order of size, subject to the constraint that additional components be connected to the existing components. Occasionally the ordering of large-to-small was altered when a smaller component, such as the eye of an animal, was judged to be highly diagnostic. The ordering by size was done under the assumption that processing would be completed earlier for larger components and, consequently, primal access would be controlled by those parts. However, it might be the case that a smaller part, if it was highly diagnostic, would have a greater role in controlling access than would be expected from its small size. The objects were displayed in black line on a white background and averaged 4.5° in greatest extent.

---

[12] Informal demonstrations suggest that this is the case. When a single component or relation of an object is altered, as with the cup and the pail, only with extreme rarity is a recognizable object from another category produced.

[13] Biederman (1985) discusses how a limit might be assessed. Among other consequences, a limit on the number of components would imply categorical effects whereby quantitative variations in the contours of an object, for example, degree of curvature, that did not alter a component's identity would have less of an effect on the identification of the object than contour variations that did alter a component's identity.

[14] Our decision to use a naming task with which to assess object recognition was motivated by several considerations. Naming is a sure sign of recognition. Under the conditions of these experiments, if an individual could name the object, he or she must have recognized it. With other paradigms, such as discrimination or verification, it is difficult (if not impossible) to prevent the subject from deriving stimulus selection strategies specific to the limited number of stimuli and distractors. Although naming RTs are relatively slow, they are remarkably well behaved, with surprisingly low variability (given their mean) for a given response and few of the response anticipation or selection errors that occur with binary responses (especially, keypresses). As in any task with a behavioral measure, one has to exert caution in making inferences about representations at an earlier stage. In every experiment reported here, whenever possible, the same objects (with the same name) served in all conditions. The data from these experiments (e.g., Figures 19 and 20) were so closely and reasonably associated with the contour manipulations as to preclude accounts based on a late name-selection stage. Moreover, providing the subjects with the set of possible names prior to an experiment, which might have been expected to affect response selection, had virtually no effect on performance. When objects could not be used as their own controls, as was necessary in studies of complexity, it was possible to experimentally or statistically control naming-stage variability because the determinants of this variability—specifically, name familiarity (which is highly correlated with frequency and age of acquisition) and length—are well understood.

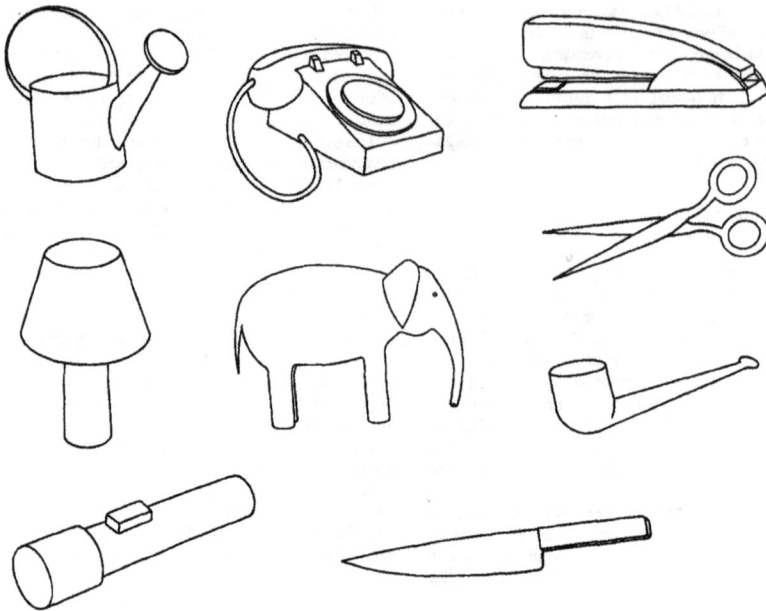

Figure 11. Nine of the experimental objects.

The purpose of this experiment was to determine whether the first few geons that would be available from an unoccluded view of a complete object would be sufficient for rapid identification of the object. We ordered the components by size and diagnosticity because our interest, as just noted, was on primal access in recognizing a complete object. Assuming that the largest and most diagnostic components would control this access, we studied the contribution of the *n*th largest and most diagnostic component, when added to the *n*−1 already existing components, because this would more closely mimic the contribution of that component when looking at the complete object. (Another kind of experiment might explore the contribution of an "average" component by balancing the ordering of the components. Such an experiment would be relevant to the recognition of an object that was occluded in such a way that only the displayed components would be available for viewing.)

Complexity

The objects shown in Figure 11 illustrate the second major variable in the experiment. Objects differ in complexity; by RBC's definition, the differences are evident in the number of components they require to look complete. For example, the lamp, the flashlight, the watering can, the scissors, and the elephant require two, three, four, six, and nine components, respectively. As noted previously, it would seem plausible that partial objects would require more time for their identification than complete objects, so that a complete airplane of nine com-

ponents, for example, might be more rapidly recognized than only a partial version of that airplane, with only three of its components. The prediction from RBC was that complex objects, by furnishing more diagnostic combinations of components that could be simultaneously matched, would be more rapidly identified than simple objects. This prediction is contrary to models that assume that objects are recognized through a serial contour tracing process such as that studied by Ullman (1983).

General Procedure

Trials were self-paced. The depression of a key on the subject's terminal initiated a sequence of exposures from three projectors. First, the corners of a 500-ms fixation rectangle (6° wide) that corresponded to the corners of the object slide were shown. This fixation slide was immediately followed by a 100-ms exposure of a slide of an object that had varying numbers of its components present. The presentation of the object was immediately followed by a 500-ms pattern mask consisting of a random appearing arrangement of lines. The subject's task was to name the object as fast as possible into a microphone that triggered a voice key. The experimenter recorded errors. Prior to the experiment, the subjects read a list of the object names to be used in the experiment. (Subsequent experiments revealed that this procedure for name familiarization produced no effect. When subjects were not familiarized with the names of the experimental objects, results were virtually identical to

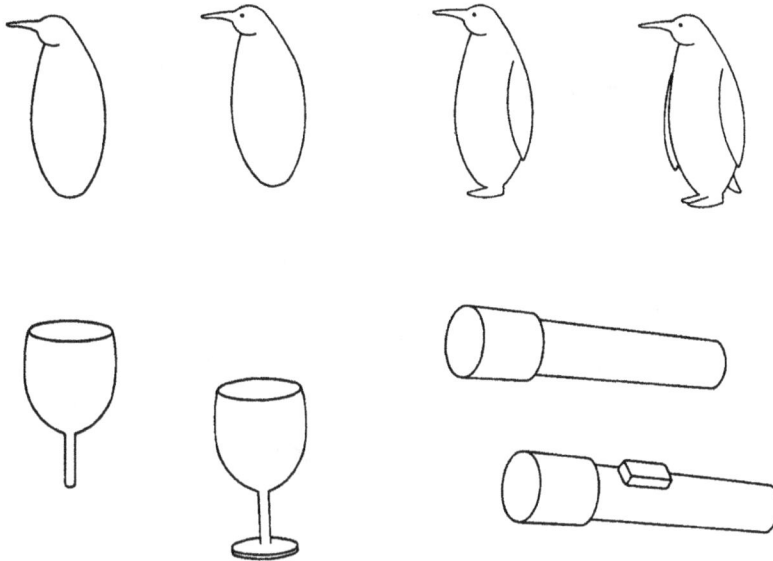

Figure 12. Illustration of the partial and complete versions of 2 three-component objects (the wine glass and flashlight) and 1 nine-component object (the penguin).

when such familiarization was provided. This finding indicates that the results of these experiments were not a function of inference over a small set of objects.) Even with the name familiarization, all responses that indicated that the object was identified were considered correct. Thus "pistol," "revolver," "gun," and "handgun" were all acceptable as correct responses for the same object. Reaction times (RTs) were recorded by a microcomputer that also controlled the projectors and provided speed and accuracy feedback on the subject's terminal after each trial.

Objects were selected that required two, three, six, or nine components to look complete. There were 9 objects for each of these complexity levels, yielding a total set of 36 objects. The various combinations of the partial versions of these objects brought the total number of experimental trials (slides) to 99. Each of 48 subjects viewed all the experimental slides, with balancing accomplished by varying the order of the slides.

Results

Figure 14 shows the mean error rates as a function of the number of components actually displayed on a given trial for the conditions in which no familiarization was provided. Each function is the mean for the nine objects at a given complexity level. Although each subject saw all 99 slides, only the data for the first time that a subject viewed a particular object will be discussed here. For a given level of complexity, increasing numbers of components resulted in better performance, but error rates overall were modest. When only three or four components of the complex objects (those with six or nine components to

look complete) were present, subjects were almost 90% accurate. In general, the complete objects were named without error, so it is necessary to look at the RTs to see if differences emerge for the complexity variable.

Mean correct RTs, shown in Figure 15, provide the same general outcome as the errors, except that there was a slight tendency for the more complex objects, when complete, to have shorter RTs than the simple objects. This advantage for the complex objects was actually underestimated in that the complex objects had longer names (three and four syllables) and were less familiar than the simple objects. Oldfield (1966) and Oldfield and Wingfield (1965) showed that object-naming RTs were longer for names that have more syllables or are infrequent. This effect of slightly shorter RTs for naming complex objects has been replicated, and it seems safe to conclude, conservatively, that complex objects do not require more time for their identification than simple objects. This result is contrary to what would be expected from a serial contour-tracing process (e.g., Ullman, 1984). Serial tracing would predict that complex objects would require more time to be seen as complete compared to simple objects, which have less contour to trace. The slight RT advantage enjoyed by the complex objects is an effect that would be expected if their additional components were affording a redundancy gain from more possible diagnostic matches to their representations in memory.

Line Drawings Versus Colored Photography

The components that are postulated to be the critical units for recognition are edge-based and can be depicted by a line

Figure 13. Illustration of partial and complete versions of a nine-component object (airplane).

drawing. Color, brightness, and texture would be secondary routes for recognition. From this perspective, Biederman and Ju (1986) reasoned that naming RTs for objects shown as line drawings should closely approximate naming RTs for those objects when shown as colored photographic slides with complete detail, color, and texture. This prediction would be true of any model that posited an edge-based representation mediating recognition.

In the Biederman and Ju experiments, subjects identified brief presentations (50–100 ms) of slides of common objects.[15] Each object was shown in two versions: professionally photographed in full color or as a simplified line drawing showing only the object's major components (such as those in Figure 11). In three experiments, subjects named the object; in a fourth experiment a yes–no verification task was performed against a target name. Overall, performance levels with the two types of stimuli were equivalent: mean latencies in identifying images presented by color photography were 11 ms shorter than the drawing but with a 3.9% higher error rate.

A previously unexplored color diagnosticity distinction among objects allowed us to determine whether color and lightness was providing a contribution to primal access independent of the main effect of photos versus drawings. For some kinds of objects, such as bananas, forks, fishes, or cameras, color is diagnostic to the object's identity. For other kinds, such as chairs, pens, or mittens, color is not diagnostic. The detection of a yellow region might facilitate the perception of a banana, but the detection of the color of a chair is unlikely to facilitate its identification, because chairs can be any color. If color was

contributing to primal access, then the former kinds of objects, for which color is diagnostic, should have enjoyed a larger advantage when appearing in a color photograph, but this did not happen. Objects with a diagnostic color did not enjoy any advantage when they were displayed as color slides compared with their line-drawing versions. That is, showing color-diagnostic objects such as a banana or a fork as a color slide did not confer any advantage over the line-drawing version compared with objects such as a chair or mitten. Moreover, there was no color

---

[15] An oft-cited study, Ryan and Schwartz (1956), did compare photography (black & white) against line and shaded drawings and cartoons. But these investigators did not study basic-level categorization of an object. Subjects had to determine which one of four configurations of three objects (the positions of five double-throw electrical knife switches, the cycles of a steam valve, and the fingers of a hand) was being depicted. The subjects knew which object was to be presented on a given trial. For two of the three objects, the cartoons had lower thresholds than the other modes. But stimulus sampling and drawings and procedural specifications render interpretation of this experiment problematical; for example, the determination of the switch positions was facilitated in the cartoons by filling in the handles so they contrasted with the background contacts. The variability was enormous: Thresholds for a given form of depiction for a single object ranged across the four configurations from 50 to 2,000 ms. The cartoons did not have lower thresholds than the photographs for the hands, the stimulus example most frequently shown in secondary sources (e.g., Neisser, 1967; Hochberg, 1978; Rock, 1984). Even without a mask, threshold presentation durations were an order of magnitude longer than was required in the present study.

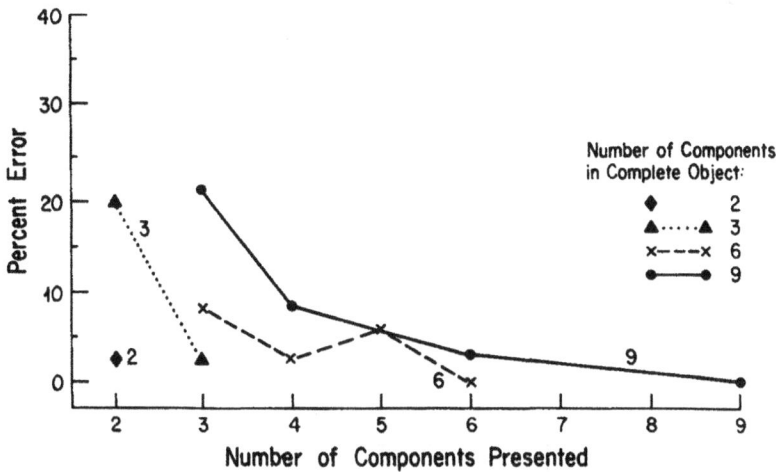

Figure 14. Mean percent error as a function of the number of components in the displayed object (abscissa) and the number of components required for the object to appear complete (parameter). (Each point is the mean for nine objects on the first occasion when a subject saw that particular object.)

diagnosticity advantage for the color slides on the verification task, where the color of the to-be-verified object could be anticipated.

This failure to find a color diagnosticity effect, when combined with the finding that simple line drawings could be identified so rapidly as to approach the naming speed of fully detailed, textured, colored photographic slides, supports the premise that the earliest access to a mental representation of an object can be modeled as a matching of an edge-based representation of a few simple components. Such edge-based descriptions are thus sufficient for primal access.

The preceding account should not be interpreted as suggesting that the perception of surface characteristics per se are delayed relative to the perception of the components but merely that in most cases surface cues are generally less efficient routes for primal access. That is, we may know that an image of a chair has a particular color and texture simultaneously with its volumetric description, but it is only the volumetric description that provides efficient access to the mental representation of "chair."

It should be noted that our failure to find a benefit from color photography is likely restricted to the domain whereby the edges are of high contrast. Under conditions where edge extraction is difficult, differences in color, texture, and luminance might readily facilitate such extraction and result in an advantage for color photography.

There is one surface characteristic that deserves special note: the luminance gradient. Such gradients can provide sufficient information as to a region's surface curvature (e.g., Besl & Jain, 1986) from which the surface's convexity or concavity can be determined. Our outline drawings lacked those gradients. Consider the cylinder and cone shown in the second and fifth rows, respectively, of Figure 7. In the absence of luminance gradients, the cylinder and cone are interpreted as convex (not hollow).

Yet when the cylinder is used to make a cup and a pail in Figure 3, or the cone used to make a wine glass in Figure 12, the volumes are interpreted as concave (hollow). It would thus seem to be the case that the interpretation of hollowness—an interpretation that overrides the default value of solidity—of a volume can be readily accomplished top-down once a representation is elicited.

The Perception of Degraded Objects

RBC assumes that certain contours in the image are critical for object recognition. Several experiments on the perception of objects that have been degraded by deletion of their contour (Biederman & Blickle, 1985) provide evidence that these contours are necessary for object recognition (under conditions where contextual inference is not possible).

RBC holds that parsing of an object into components is performed at regions of concavity. The nonaccidental relations of collinearity and curvilinearity allow filling-in: They extend broken contours that are collinear or smoothly curvilinear. In concert, the two assumptions of (a) parsing at concavities and (b) filling-in through collinearity or smooth curvature lead to a prediction as to what should be a particularly disruptive form of degradation: If contours were deleted at regions of concavity in such a manner that their endpoints, when extended through collinearity or curvilinearity, bridge the concavity, then the components would be lost and recognition should be impossible. The cup in the right column of the top row of Figure 16 provides an example. The curve of the handle of the cup is drawn so that it is continuous with the curve of the cylinder forming the back rim of the cup. This form of degradation, in which the components cannot be recovered from the input through the nonaccidental properties, is referred to as *nonrecov-*

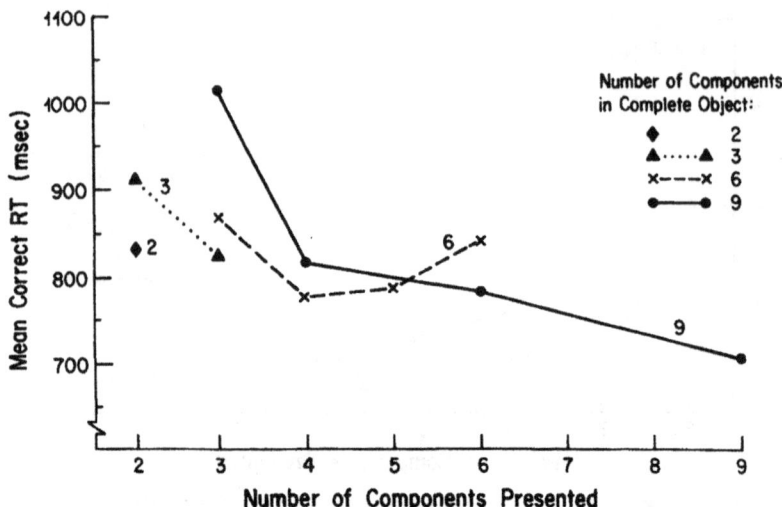

Figure 15. Mean correct reaction time as a function of the number of components in the displayed object (abscissa) and the number of components required for the object to appear complete (parameter). (Each point is the mean for nine objects on the first occasion when a subject saw that particular object.)

erable degradation and is illustrated for the objects in the right column of Figure 16.

An equivalent amount of deleted contour in a midsection of a curve or line should prove to be less disruptive as the components could then be restored through collinearity or curvature. In this case the components should be recoverable. Example of recoverable forms of degradation are shown in the middle column of Figure 16.

In addition to the procedure for deleting and bridging concavities, two other applications of nonaccidental properties were used to prevent determination of the components: vertex alteration and misleading symmetry or parallelism.

Vertex Alteration

When two or more edges terminate at the same point in the image, the visual system assumes that they are terminating at the same point in depth and a vertex is present at that point. Vertices are important for determining the nature of a component (see Figure 5). As noted previously, volumetric components will display at least one three-pronged vertex.

There are two ways to alter vertices. One way is by deleting a segment of an existing vertex. For example, the T-vertex produced by the occlusion of one blade of the scissors by the other has been converted into an L-vertex, suggesting that the boundaries of the region in the image are the boundaries of that region of the object. In the cup, the curved-T-vertex produced by the joining of a discontinuous edge of the front rim of the cup with the occlusional edge of the sides and back rim has been altered to an L-vertex by deleting the discontinuous edge. With only L-vertices, objects typically lose their volumetric character and appear planar.

The other way to alter vertices is to produce them through misleading extension of contours. Just as approximate joins of interrupted contours might be accepted to produce continuous edges, if three or more contours appear to meet at a common point when extended then a misleading vertex can be suggested. For example, in the watering can in the right column of Figure 11, the extensions of the contour from the spout attachment and sprinkler appear to meet the contours of the handle and rim, suggesting a false vertex of five edges. (Such a multivertex is nondiagnostic to a volume's three-dimensional identity [e.g., Guzman, 1968; Sugihara, 1984].)

Misleading Symmetry or Parallelism

Nonrecoverability of components can also be produced by contour deletion that produces symmetry or parallelism not characteristic of the original object. For example, the symmetry of oval region in the opening of the watering can suggests a planar component with that shape.

Even with these techniques, it was difficult to remove contours supporting all the components of an object, and some remained in nominally nonrecoverable versions, as with the handle of the scissors.

Subjects viewed 35 objects, in both recoverable and nonrecoverable versions. Prior to the experiment, all subjects were shown several examples of the various forms of degradation for several objects that were not used in the experiment. In addition, familiarization with the experimental objects was manipulated between subjects. Prior to the start of the experimental trials, different groups of six subjects (a) viewed a 3-sec slide of the intact version of the objects, for example, the objects in the left column of Figure 16, which they named; (b) were provided with the names of the objects on their terminal; or (c) were given no familiarization. As in the prior experiment, the subject's task was to name the objects.

A glance at the second and third columns in Figure 16 is sufficient to reveal that one does not need an experiment to show that the nonrecoverable objects would be more difficult to identify than the recoverable versions. But we wanted to determine if the nonrecoverable versions would be identifiable at extremely long exposure durations (5 s) and whether the prior exposure to the intact version of the object would overcome the effects of the contour deletion. The effects of contour deletion in the recoverable condition was also of considerable interest when compared with the comparable conditions from the partial object experiments.

Results

The error data are shown in Figure 17. Identifiability of the nonrecoverable stimuli was virtually impossible: The median error rate for those slides was 100%. Subjects rarely guessed wrong objects in this condition; most often they merely said that they "didn't know." When nonrecoverable objects could be identified, it was primarily for those instances where some of the components were not removed, as with the circular rings of the handle of the scissors. When this happened, subjects could name the object at 200-ms exposure duration. For the majority of the objects, however, error rates were well over 50% with no gain in performance even with 5 s of exposure duration. Objects in the recoverable condition were named at high accuracy at the longer exposure durations.

As in the previous experiments, familiarizing the subjects with the names of the objects had no effect compared with the condition in which the subjects were given no information about the objects. There was some benefit, however, in providing intact versions of the pictures of the objects. Even with this familiarity, performance in the nonrecoverable condition was extraordinarily poor, with error rates exceeding 60% when subjects had a full 5 s to decipher the stimulus. As noted previously, even this value underestimated the difficulty of identifying objects in the nonrecoverable condition, in that identification was possible only when the contour deletion allowed some of the components to remain recoverable.

The emphasis on the poor performance in the nonrecoverable condition should not obscure the extensive interference that was evident at the brief exposure durations in the recoverable condition. The previous experiments had established that intact objects, without picture familiarization, could be identified at near perfect accuracy at 100 ms. At this exposure duration in the present experiment, error rates for the recoverable stimuli, whose contours could be restored through collinearity and curvature, averaged 65%. These high error rates at 100-ms exposure duration suggest that the filling-in processes require an image (retinal or iconic)—not merely a memory representation—and sufficient time (on the order of 200 ms) to be successfully executed.

A Parametric Investigation of Contour Deletion

The dependence of componential recovery on the availability and locus of contour and time was explored parametrically by

Figure 16. Example of five stimulus objects in the experiment on the perception of degraded objects. (The left column shows the original intact versions. The middle column shows the recoverable versions. The contours have been deleted in regions where they can be replaced through collinearity or smooth curvature. The right column shows the nonrecoverable versions. The contours have been deleted at regions of concavity so that collinearity or smooth curvature of the segments bridges the concavity. In addition, vertices have been altered, for example, from Ys to Ls, and misleading symmetry and parallelism have been introduced.)

Biederman and Blickle (1985). In the previous experiment, it was necessary to delete or modify the vertices in order to produce the nonrecoverable versions of the objects. The recoverable versions of the objects tended to have their contours deleted in midsegment. It is possible that some of the interference in the nonrecoverable condition was a consequence of the removal of vertices per se, rather than the production of inappropriate components. Contour deletion was performed either at the vertices or at midsegments for 18 objects, but without the accidental bridging of components through collinearity or curvature that was characteristic of the nonrecoverable condition. The amount of contour removed varied from 25%, 45%, and 65%, and the objects were shown for 100, 200, or 750 ms. Other aspects of the procedure were identical to the previous experiments with only name familiarization provided. Figure 18 shows an example for a single object.

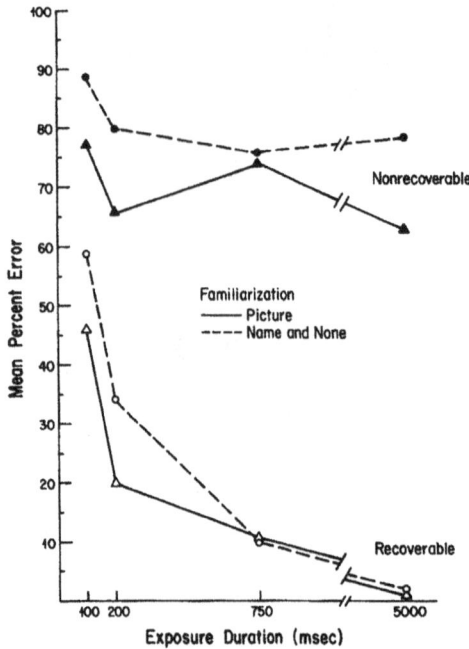

Figure 17. Mean percent errors in object naming as a function of exposure duration, nature of contour deletion (recoverable vs. nonrecoverable components), and familiarization (none, name, or picture). (No differences were apparent between the none and name pretraining conditions, so they have been combined into a single function.)

The mean percent errors are shown in Figure 19. At the briefest exposure duration and the most contour deletion (100-ms exposure duration and 65% contour deletion), removal of the vertices resulted in considerably higher error rates than the midsegment removal, 54% and 31% errors, respectively. With less contour deletion or longer exposures, the locus of the contour deletion had only a slight effect on naming accuracy. Both types of loci showed a consistent improvement with longer exposure durations, with error rates below 10% at the 750-ms duration. By contrast, the error rates in the nonrecoverable condition in the prior experiment exceeded 75%, even after 5 s. Although accuracy was less affected by the locus of the contour deletion at the longer exposure durations and the lower deletion proportions, there was a consistent advantage on naming latencies of the midsegment removal, as shown in Figure 20. (The lack of an effect at the 100-ms exposure duration with 65% deletion is likely a consequence of the high error rates for the vertex deletion stimuli.) This result shows that if contours are deleted at a vertex they can be restored, as long as there is no accidental filling-in. The greater disruption from vertex deletion is expected on the basis of their importance as diagnostic image features for the components. Overall, both the error and RT data document a striking dependence of object identification on

what RBC assumes to be a prior and necessary stage of componential determination.

We conclude that the filling-in of contours, whether at midsegment or vertex, is a process that can be completed within 1 s. But the suggestion of a misleading component that bridges a concavity through collinearity or curvature produces an image that cannot index the original object, no matter how much time there is to view the image. Figure 21 compares a nonrecoverable version of an object (on the left) with a recoverable version, with considerably less contour available in the latter case. That the recoverable version is still identifiable shows that the recoverable objects would retain an advantage even if they had less contour than the nonrecoverable objects. Note that only four of the components in the recoverable version can be restored by the contours in the image, yet this is sufficient for recognition (although with considerable costs in time and effort). The recoverable version can be recognized despite the extreme distortion in the bounding contour and the loss of all the vertices from the right side of the object.

Perceiving Degraded Versus Partial Objects

Consider Figure 22 that shows, for some sample objects, one version in which whole components are deleted so that only three (of six or nine) of the components remain and another version in which the same amount of contour is removed, but in midsegment distributed over all of the object's components. With objects with whole components deleted, it is unlikely that the missing components are added imaginally, prior to recognition. Logically, one would have to know what object was being recognized to know what parts to add. Instead, the activation

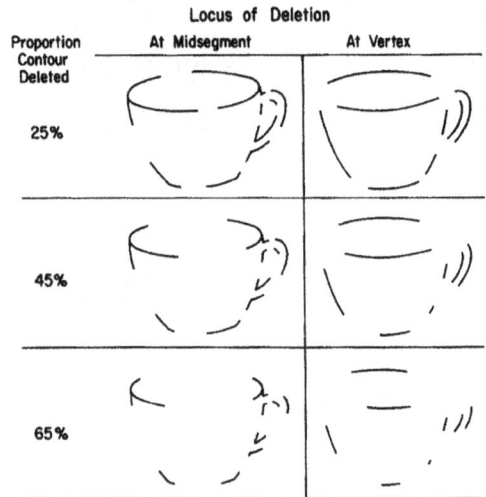

Figure 18. Illustration for a single object of 25, 45, and 65% contour removal centered at either midsegment or vertex. (Unlike the nonrecoverable objects illustrated in Figure 16, vertex deletion does not prevent identification of the object.)

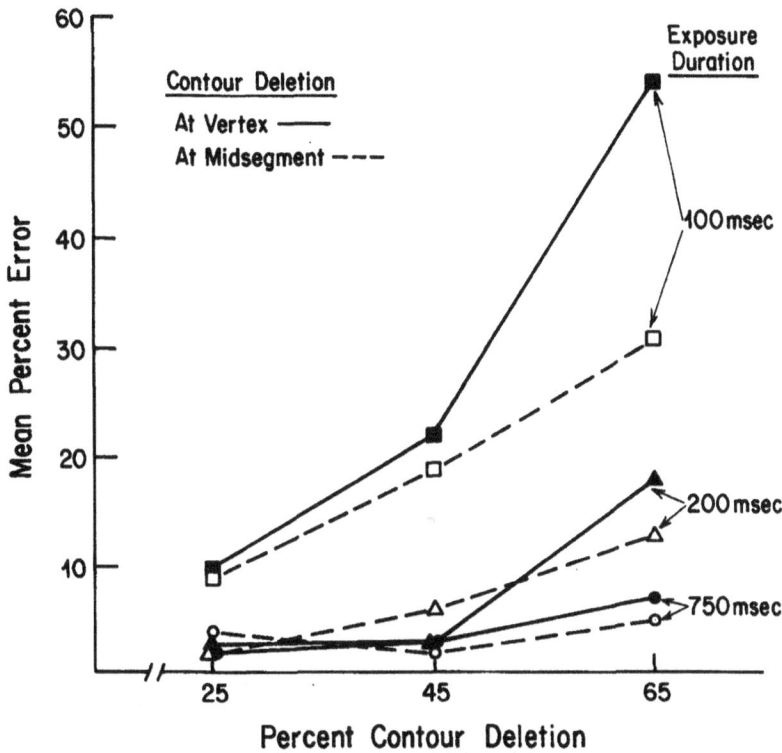

Figure 19. Mean percent object naming errors as a function of locus of contour removal (midsegment or vertex), percent removal, and exposure duration.

of a representation most likely proceeds in the absence of the parts, with weaker activation the consequence of the missing parts. The two methods for removing contour may thus be affecting different stages. Deleting contour in midsegment affects processes prior to and including those involved in the determination of the components (see Figure 2). The removal of whole components (the partial object procedure) is assumed to affect the matching stage, reducing the number of common components between the image and the representation and increasing the number of distinctive components in the representation. Contour filling-in is typically regarded as a fast, low-level process. We (Biederman, Beiring, Ju, & Blickle, 1985) studied the naming speed and accuracy of six- and nine-component objects undergoing these two types of contour deletion. At brief exposure durations (e.g., 65 ms) performance with partial objects was better than objects with the same amount of contour removed in midsegment both for errors (Figure 23) and RTs (Figure 24). At longer exposure durations (200 ms), the RTs reversed, with the midsegment deletion now faster than the partial objects.

Our interpretation of this result is that although a diagnostic subset of a few components (a partial object) can provide a sufficient input for recognition, the activation of that representation is not optimal compared with a complete object. Thus, in the partial object experiment described previously, recognition RTs were shortened with the addition of components to an already recognizable object. If all of an object's components were degraded (but recoverable), recognition would be delayed until contour restoration was completed. Once the filling-in was completed and the complete complement of an object's geons was activated, a better match to the object's representation would be possible (or the elicitation of its name) than with a partial object that had only a few of its components. The interaction can be modeled as a cascade in which the component-deletion condition results in more rapid activation of the geons but to a lower asymptote (because some geons never get activated) than the midsegment-deletion condition.

More generally, the finding that partial complex objects—with only three of their six or nine components present—can be recognized more readily than objects whose contours can be restored through filling-in documents the efficiency of a few components for accessing a representation.

138   IRVING BIEDERMAN

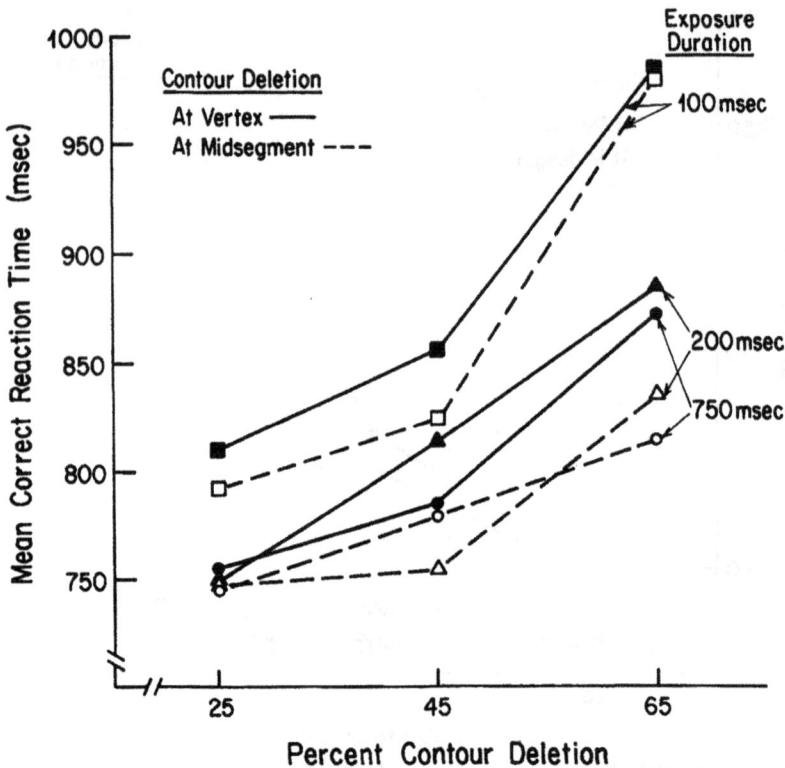

Figure 20. Mean correct object-naming reaction time (in milliseconds) as a function of locus of contour removal (midsegment or vertex), percent removal, and exposure duration.

Contour Deletion by Occlusion

The degraded recoverable objects in the right column of Figure 16 have the appearance of flat drawings of objects with interrupted contours. Biederman and Blickle (1985) designed a demonstration of the dependence of object recognition on componential identification by aligning an occluding surface so that it appeared to produce the deletions. If the components were responsible for an identifiable volumetric representation of the object, we would expect that with the recoverable stimuli the object would complete itself under the occluding surface and assume a three-dimensional character. This effect should not occur in the nonrecoverable condition. This expectation was met, as shown in Figures 25 and 26. These stimuli also provide a demonstration of the time (and effort?) requirements for contour restoration through collinearity or curvature. We have not yet obtained objective data on this effect, which may be complicated by masking effects from the presence of the occluding surface, but we invite the reader to share our subjective impressions. When looking at a nonrecoverable version of an object

in Figure 25, no object becomes apparent. In the recoverable version in Figure 26, an object does pop into a three-dimensional appearance, but most observers report a delay (our own estimate is approximately 500 ms) from the moment the stimulus is first fixated to when it appears as an identifiable three-dimensional entity.

This demonstration of the effects of an occluding surface to produce contour interruption also provides a control for the possibility that the difficulty in the nonrecoverable condition was a consequence of inappropriate figure–ground groupings, as with the stool in Figure 16. With the stool, the ground that was apparent through the rungs of the stool became figure in the nonrecoverable condition. (In general, however, only a few of the objects had holes in them where this could have been a factor.) Figure–ground ambiguity would not invalidate the RBC hypothesis but would complicate the interpretation of the effects of the nonrecoverable noise, in that some of the effect would derive from inappropriate grouping of contours into components and some of the effect would derive from inappropriate figure–ground grouping. That the objects in the nonre-

Figure 21. A comparison of a nonrecoverable version of an object (on the left) with a recoverable version (on the right) with half the contour of the nonrecoverable. Despite the reduction of contour the recoverable version still enjoys an advantage over the nonrecoverable.

| Complete | Component Deletion | Midsegment Deletion |

Figure 22. Sample stimuli with equivalent proportion of contours removed either at midsegments or as whole components.

coverable condition remain unidentifiable when the contour interruption is attributable to an occluding surface suggests that figure–ground grouping cannot be the primary cause of the interference from the nonrecoverable deletions.

Summary and Implications of the Experimental Results

The sufficiency of a component representation for primal access to the mental representation of an object was supported by two results: (a) that partial objects with two or three components could be readily identified under brief exposures, and (b) that line drawings and color photography produced comparable identification performance. The experiments with degraded stimuli established that the components are necessary for object perception. These results suggest an underlying principle by which objects are identified.

Principle of Componential Recovery

The results and phenomena associated with the effects of degradation and partial objects can be understood as the workings of a single Principle of Componential Recovery: If the components in their specified arrangement can be readily identified, object identification will be fast and accurate. In addition to those aspects of object perception for which experimental research was described above, the principle of componential recovery might encompass at least four additional phenomena in object perception: (a) objects can be more readily recognized from some orientations than from others (orientation variability); (b) objects can be recognized from orientations not previously experienced (object transfer); (c) articulated (or deformable) objects, with variable componential arrangements, can be recognized even when the specific configuration might not have been experienced previously (deformable object invariance); and (d) novel instances of a category can be rapidly classified (perceptual basis of basic-level categories).

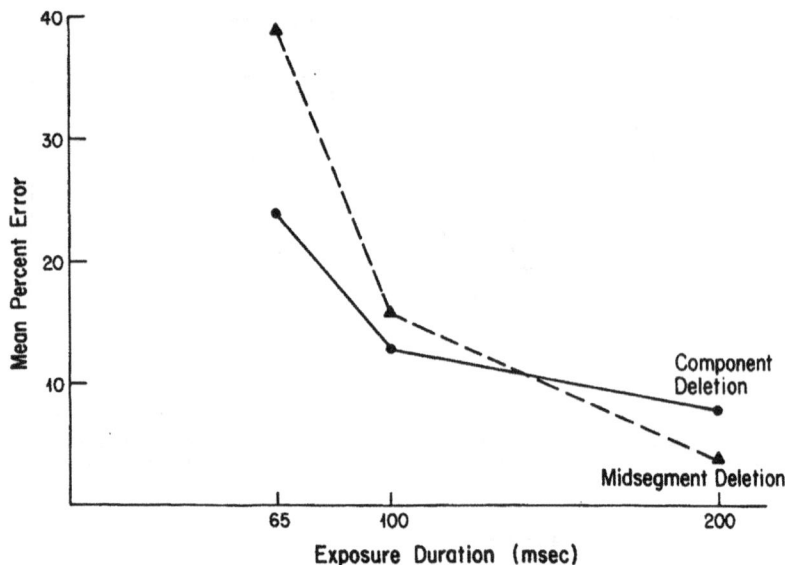

Figure 23. Mean percent errors of object naming as a function of the nature of contour removal (deletion of midsegments or components) and exposure duration.

Orientation Variability

Objects can be more readily identified from some orientations compared with others (Palmer, Rosch, & Chase, 1981). According to the RBC hypothesis, difficult views will be those in which the components extracted from the image are not the components (and their relations) in the representation of the object. Often such mismatches will arise from an "accident" of viewpoint where an image property is not correlated with the property in the three-dimensional world. For example, when the viewpoint in the image is along the axis of the major components of the object, the resultant foreshortening converts one or some of the components into surface components, such as disks and rectangles in Figure 27, which are not included in the componential description of the object. In addition, as illustrated in Figure 27, the surfaces may occlude otherwise diagnostic components. Consequently, the components extracted from the image will not readily match the mental representation of the object and identification will be much more difficult compared to an orientation, such as that shown in Figure 28, which does convey the components.

A second condition under which viewpoint affects identifiability of a specific object arises when the orientation is simply unfamiliar, as when a sofa is viewed from below or when the top–bottom relations among the components are perturbed as when a normally upright object is inverted. Jolicoeur (1985) recently reported that naming RTs were lengthened as a function of an object's rotation away from its normally upright position. He concluded that mental rotation was required for the identification of such objects, as the effect of X–Y rotation on RTs was similar for naming and

mental rotation. It may be that mental rotation—or a more general imaginal transformation capacity stressing working memory—is required only under the (relatively rare) conditions where the relations among the components have to be rearranged. Thus, we might expect to find the equivalent of mental paper folding if the parts of an object were rearranged and the subject's task was to determine if a given object could be made out of the displayed components. RBC would hold that the lengthening of naming RTs in Jolicoeur's (1985) experiment is better interpreted as an effect that arises not from the use of orientation dependent features but from the perturbation of the "top-of" relations among the components.

Palmer et al. (1981) conducted an extensive study of the perceptibility of various objects when presented at a number of different orientations. Generally, a three-quarters front view was most effective for recognition, and their subjects showed a clear preference for such views. Palmer et al. (1981) termed this effective and preferred orientation of the object its *canonical orientation.* The canonical orientation would be, from the perspective of RBC, a special case of the orientation that would maximize the match of the components in the image to the representation of the object.

Transfer Between Different Viewpoints

When an object is seen at one viewpoint or orientation it can often be recognized as the same object when subsequently seen at some other orientation in depth, even though there can be extensive differences in the retinal projections of the two views. The principle of componential recovery would hold that trans-

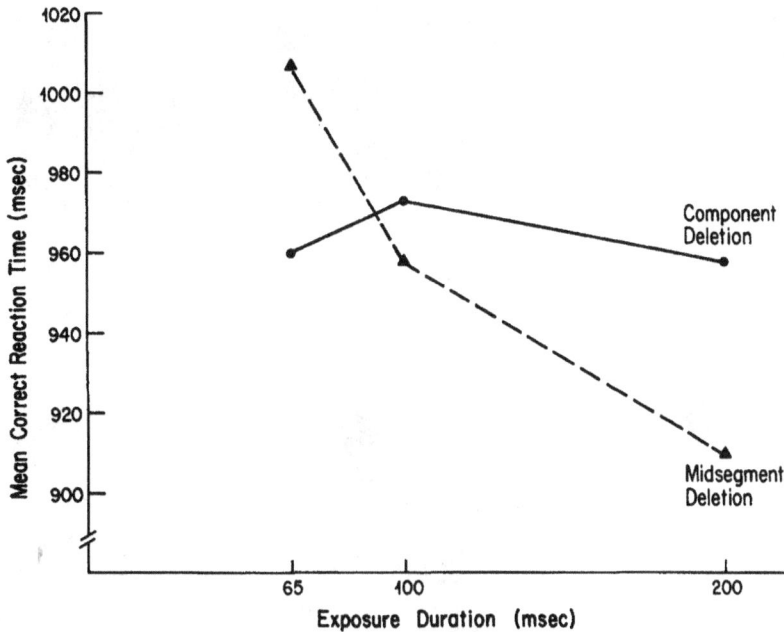

Figure 24. Mean correct reaction time (in milliseconds) in object naming as a function of the nature of contour removal (deletion at midsegments or components) and exposure duration.

fer between two viewpoints would be a function of the componential similarity between the views, as long as the relations among the components were not altered. This could be experimentally tested through priming studies with the degree of priming predicted to be a function of the similarity (viz., common minus distinctive components) of the two views. If two different views of an object contained the same components, RBC would predict that, aside from effects attributable to variations in aspect ratio, there should be as much priming as when the object was presented at an identical view. An alternative possibility to componential recovery is that a presented object would be mentally rotated (Shepard & Metzler, 1971) to correspond to the original representation. But mental rotation rates appear to be too slow and effortful to account for the ease and speed with which transfer occurs between different orientations in depth of the same object.

There may be a restriction on whether a similarity function for priming effects will be observed. Although unfamiliar objects (or nonsense objects) should reveal a componential similarity effect, the recognition of a familiar object, whatever its orientation, may be too rapid to allow an appreciable experimental priming effect. Such objects may have a representation for each orientation that provides a different componential description. Bartram's (1974) results support this expectation that priming effects might not be found across different views of familiar objects. Bartram performed a series of studies in which subjects named 20 pictures of objects over eight blocks

of trials. (In another experiment [Bartram, 1976], essentially the same results were found with a same–different name-matching task in which pairs of pictures were presented.) In the *identical* condition, the pictures were identical across the trial blocks. In the *different view* condition, the same objects were depicted from one block to the next but in different orientations. In the *different exemplar* condition, different exemplars, for example, different instances of a chair, were presented, all of which required the same response. Bartram found that the naming RTs for the identical and different view conditions were equivalent and both were shorter than control conditions, described below, for concept and response priming effects. Bartram theorized that observers automatically compute and access all possible three-dimensional viewpoints when viewing a given object. Alternatively, it is possible that there was high componential similarity across the different views and the experiment was insufficiently sensitive to detect slight differences from one viewpoint to another. However, in four experiments with colored slides, we (Biederman & Lloyd, 1985) failed to obtain any effect of variation in viewing angle and have thus replicated Bartram's basic effect (or lack of effect). At this point, our inclination is to agree with Bartram's interpretation, with somewhat different language, but restrict its scope to familiar objects. It should be noted that both Bartram's and our results are inconsistent with a model that assigned heavy weight to the aspect ratio of the image of the object or postulated an underlying mental rotation function.

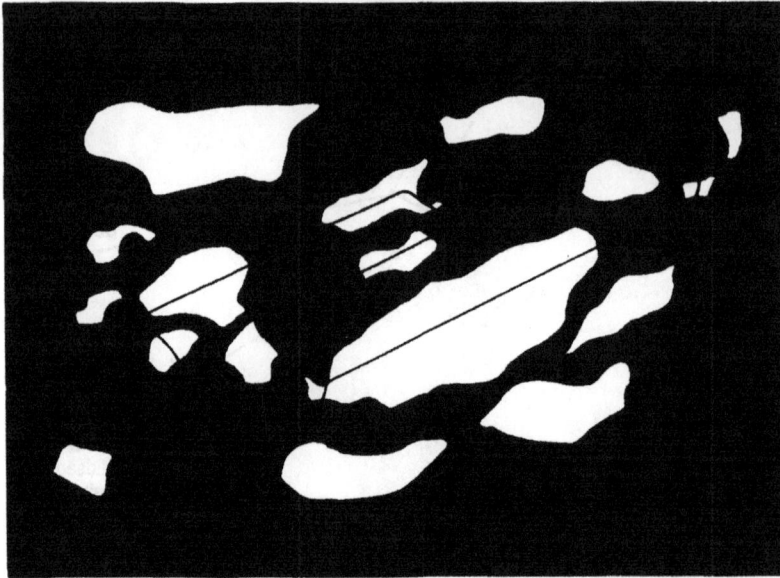

Figure 25. Nonrecoverable version of an object where the contour deletion
is produced by an occluding surface.

Different Exemplars Within an Object Class

Just as we might be able to gauge the transfer between two
different views of the same object based on a componential-
based similarity metric, we might be able to predict transfer
between different exemplars of a common object, such as two
different instances of a lamp or chair.

As noted in the previous section, Bartram (1974) also included a different exemplar condition, in which different objects with the same name—different cars, for example—were
depicted from block to block. Under the assumption that
different exemplars would be less likely to have common components, RBC would predict that this condition would be slower
than the identical and different view conditions but faster than
a different object control condition with a new set of objects
that required different names for every trial block. This was
confirmed by Bartram.

For both different views of the same object as well as different
exemplars (subordinates) within a basic-level category, RBC predicts that transfer would be based on the overlap in the components between the two views. The strong prediction would be that
the same similarity function that predicted transfer between
different orientations of the same object would also predict the
transfer between different exemplars with the same name.

The Perceptual Basis of Basic Level Categories

Consideration of the similarity relations among different exemplars with the same name raises the issue as to whether objects are most readily identified at a basic, as opposed to a subordinate or superordinate, level of description. The componential
representations described here are representations of specific,
subordinate objects, although their identification was often
measured with a basic-level name. Much of the research suggesting that objects are recognized at a basic level have used
stimuli, often natural, in which the subordinate-level exemplars
had componential descriptions that were highly similar to those
for a basic-level prototype for that class of objects. Only small
componential differences, or color or texture, distinguished the
subordinate-level objects. Thus distinguishing Asian elephants
from African elephants or Buicks from Oldsmobiles requires
fine discrimination for their verification. The structural descriptions for the largest components would be identical. It is
not at all surprising that in these cases basic-level identification
would be most rapid. On the other hand, many human-made
categories, such as lamps, or some natural categories, such as
dogs (which have been bred by humans), have members that
have componential descriptions that differ considerably from
one exemplar to another, as with a pole lamp versus a ginger jar
table lamp, for example. The same is true of objects that differ
from their basic-level prototype, as penguins or sport cars. With
such instances, which unconfound the similarity between basic-
level and subordinate-level objects, perceptual access should be
at the subordinate (or instance) level, a result supported by a
recent report by Jolicoeur, Gluck, and Kosslyn (1984). In general, then, recognition will be at the subordinate level but will
appear to be at the basic level when the componential descrip-

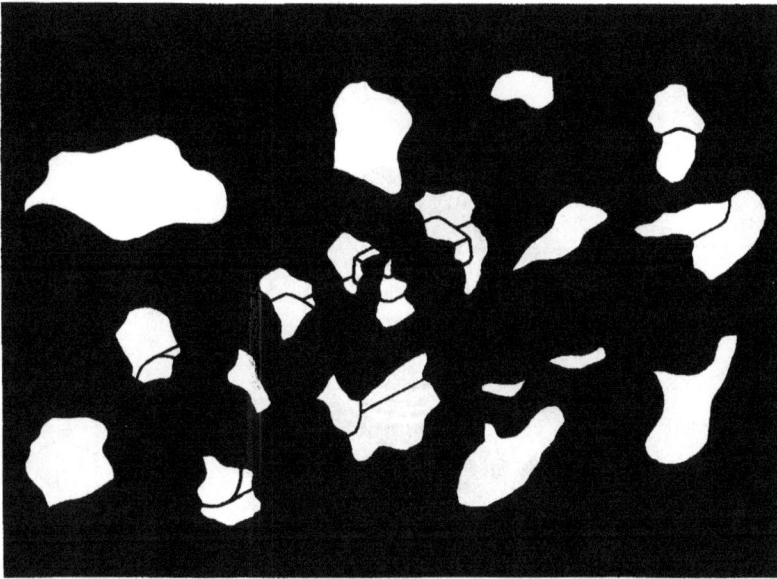

Figure 26. Recoverable version of an object where the contour deletion is produced by an occluding surface. (The object, a flashlight, is the same as that shown in Figure 25. The reader may note that the three-dimensional percept in this figure does not occur instantaneously.)

tions are the same at the two levels. However, the ease of perceptual recognition of nonprototypical exemplars, such as penguins, makes it clear that recognition will be at the level of the exemplar.

The kinds of descriptions postulated by RBC may play a central role in children's capacity to acquire names for objects. They may be predisposed to employ different labels for objects that have different geon descriptions. When the perceptual system presents a new description for an arrangement of large geons, the absence of activation might readily result in the question "What's that?"

For some categories, such as chairs, one can conceive of an extraordinarily large number of instances. Do we have a priori structural descriptions for all these cases? Obviously not. Although we can recognize many visual configurations as chairs, it is likely that only those for which there exists a close structural description in memory will recognition be rapid. The same caveat that was raised about the Marr and Nishihara (1978) demonstrations of pipe-cleaner animals in an earlier section must be voiced here. With casual viewing, particularly when supported by a scene context or when embedded in an array of other chairs, it is often possible to identify unusual instances as chairs without much subjective difficulty. But when presented as an isolated object without benefit of such contextual support, we have found that recognition of unfamiliar exemplars requires markedly longer exposure durations than those required for familiar instances of a category.

It takes but a modest extension of the principle of componen-

tial recovery to handle the similarity of objects. Simply put, similar objects will be those that have a high degree of overlap in their components and in the relations among these components. A similarity measure reflecting common and distinctive components (Tversky, 1977) may be adequate for describing the similarity among a pair of objects or between a given instance and its stored or expected representation, whatever their basic- or subordinate-level designation.

The Perception of Nonrigid Objects

Many objects and creatures, such as people and telephones, have articulated joints that allow extension, rotation, and even separation of their components. There are two ways in which such objects can be accommodated by RBC. One possibility, as described in the previous section on the representation for variation within a basic-level category, is that independent structural descriptions are necessary for each sizable alteration in the arrangement of an object's components. For example, it may be necessary to establish a different structural description for the left-most pose in Figure 29 than in the right-most pose. If this was the case, then a priming paradigm might not reveal any priming between the two stimuli. Another possibility is that the relations among the components can include a range of possible values (Marr & Nishihara, 1978). For a relation that allowed complete freedom for movement, the relation might simply be "joined." Even that might be relaxed in the case of objects with separable parts, as with the handset and base of a

Figure 27. A viewpoint parallel to the axes of the major components of a common object.

Figure 28. The same object as in Figure 27, but with a viewpoint not parallel to the major components.

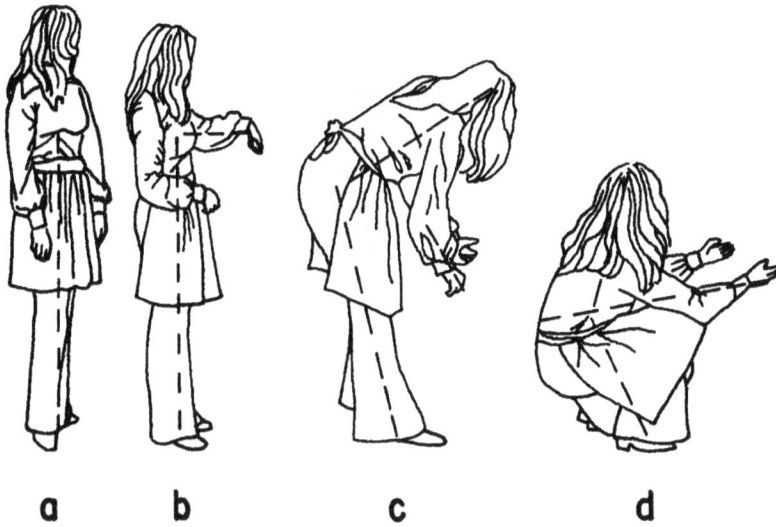

Figure 29. Four configurations of a nonrigid object.

telephone. In that case, it might be either that the relation is "nearby" or else different structural descriptions are necessary for attached and separable configurations. Empirical research needs to be done to determine if less restrictive relations, such as "join" or "nearby," have measurable perceptual consequences. It may be the case that the less restrictive the relation, the more difficult the identifiability of the object. Just as there appear to be canonical views of rigid objects (Palmer et al., 1981), there may be a canonical "configuration" for a nonrigid object. Thus, the poses on the right in Figure 29 might be identified as a woman more slowly than would the poses on the left.

Conclusion

To return to the analogy with speech perception, the characterization of object perception provided by RBC bears a close resemblance to some current views as to how speech is perceived. In both cases, the ease with which we are able to code tens of thousands of words or objects is solved by mapping that input onto a modest number of primitives—55 phonemes or 36 components—and then using a representational system that can code and access free combinations of these primitives. In both cases, the specific set of primitives is derived from dichotomous (or trichotomous) contrasts of a small number (less than ten) of independent characteristics of the input. The ease with which we are able to code so many words or objects may thus derive less from a capacity for coding continuous physical variation than it does from a perceptual system designed to represent the free combination of a modest number of categorized primitives based on simple perceptual contrasts.

In object perception, the primitive components may have their origins in the fundamental principles by which inferences

about a three-dimensional world can be made from the edges in a two-dimensional image. These principles constitute a significant portion of the corpus of Gestalt organizational constraints. Given that the primitives are fitting simple parsed parts of an object, the constraints toward regularization characterize not the complete object but the object's components. RBC thus provides, for the first time, an account of the heretofore undecided relation between these principles of perceptual organization and human pattern recognition.

References

Attneave, F. (1982). Pragnanz and soap bubble systems. In J. Beck (Ed.) *Organization and representation in visual perception* (pp. 11–29). Hillsdale, NJ: Erlbaum.

Ballard, D., & Brown, C. M. (1982). *Computer vision*. Englewood Cliffs, NJ: Prentice-Hall.

Barrow, H. G., & Tenenbaum, J. M. (1981). Interpreting line-drawings as three-dimensional surfaces. *Artificial Intelligence, 17*, 75–116.

Bartlett, F. C. (1932). *Remembering: a study in experimental and social psychology.* New York: Cambridge Univ. Press.

Bartram, D. (1974). The role of visual and semantic codes in object naming. *Cognitive Psychology, 6*, 325–356.

Bartram, D. (1976). Levels of coding in picture-picture comparison tasks. *Memory & Cognition, 4*, 593–602.

Beck, J., Prazdny, K., & Rosenfeld, A. (1983). A theory of textural segmentation. In J. Beck, B. Hope, & A. Rosenfeld (Eds.), *Human and machine vision* (pp. 1–38). New York: Academic Press.

Besl, P. J., & Jain, R. C. (1986). Invariant surface characteristics for 3D object recognition in range images. *Computer Vision, Graphics, and Image Processing, 33*, 33–80.

Biederman, I. (1981). On the semantics of a glance at a scene. In M. Kubovy & J. R. Pomerantz (Eds.), *Perceptual organization* (pp. 213–253). Hillsdale, NJ: Erlbaum.

Biederman, I. (1985). Human image understanding: Recent experiments and a theory. *Computer Vision, Graphics, and Image Processing, 32,* 29–73.

Biederman, I., Beiring, E., Ju, G., & Blickle, T. (1985). *A comparison of the perception of partial vs. degraded objects.* Unpublished manuscript, State University of New York at Buffalo.

Biederman, I., & Blickle, T. (1985). *The perception of objects with deleted contours.* Unpublished manuscript, State University of New York at Buffalo.

Biederman, I., Blickle, T. W., Teitelbaum, R. C., Klatsky, G. J., & Mezzanotte, R. J. (in press). Object identification in multi-object, non-scene displays. *Journal of Experimental Psychology: Learning, Memory, and Cognition.*

Biederman, I., & Ju, G., (in press). Surface vs. edge-based determinants of visual recognition. *Cognitive Psychology.*

Biederman, I., Ju, G., & Clapper, J. (1985). *The perception of partial objects.* Unpublished manuscript, State University of New York at Buffalo.

Biederman, I., & Lloyd, M. (1985). *Experimental studies of transfer across different object views and exemplars.* Unpublished manuscript, State University of New York at Buffalo.

Biederman, I., Mezzanotte, R. J., & Rabinowitz, J. C. (1982). Scene perception: Detecting and judging objects undergoing relational violations. *Cognitive Psychology, 14,* 143–177.

Binford, T. O. (1971, December). *Visual perception by computer.* Paper presented at the IEEE Systems Science and Cybernetics Conference, Miami, FL.

Binford, T. O. (1981). Inferring surfaces from images. *Artificial Intelligence, 17,* 205–244.

Brady, M. (1983). Criteria for the representations of shape. In J. Beck, B. Hope, & A. Rosenfeld (Eds.), *Human and machine vision* (pp. 39–84). New York: Academic Press.

Brady, M., & Asada, H. (1984). Smoothed local symmetries and their implementation. *International Journal of Robotics Research, 3,* 3.

Brooks, R. A. (1981). Symbolic reasoning among 3-D models and 2-D images. *Artificial Intelligence, 17,* 205–244.

Carey, S. (1978). The child as word learner. In M. Halle, J. Bresnan, & G. A. Miller (Eds.), *Linguistic theory and psychological reality* (pp. 264–293). Cambridge, MA: MIT Press.

Cezanne, P. (1941). Letter to Emile Bernard. In J. Rewald (Ed.), *Paul Cezanne's letters* (translated by M. Kay, pp. 233–234). London: B. Cassirrer. (Original work published 1904).

Chakravarty, I. (1979). A generalized line and junction labeling scheme with applications to scene analysis. *IEEE Transactions PAMI,* April, 202–205.

Checkosky, S. F., & Whitlock, D. (1973). Effects of pattern goodness on recognition time in a memory search task. *Journal of Experimental Psychology, 100,* 341–348.

Connell, J. H. (1985). *Learning shape descriptions: Generating and generalizing models of visual objects.* Unpublished master's thesis, Massachusetts Institute of Technology, Cambridge.

Coss, R. G. (1979). Delayed plasticity of an instinct: Recognition and avoidance of 2 facing eyes by the jewel fish. *Developmental Psychobiology, 12,* 335–345.

Egeth, H., & Pachella, R. (1969). Multidimensional stimulus identification. *Perception & Psychophysics, 5,* 341–346.

Fildes, B. N., & Triggs, T. J. (1985). The effect of changes in curve geometry on magnitude estimates of road-like perspective curvature. *Perception & Psychophysics, 37,* 218–224.

Garner, W. R. (1962). *Uncertainty and structure as psychological concepts.* New York: Wiley.

Garner, W. R. (1974). *The processing of information and structure.* New York: Wiley.

Guzman, A. (1968). Decomposition of a visual scene into three-dimensional bodies. *AFIRS Fall Joint Conferences, 33,* 291–304.

Guzman, A. (1971). Analysis of curved line drawings using context and

global information. *Machine intelligence* 6 (pp. 325–375). Edinburgh: Edinburgh University Press.

Hildebrandt, K. A. (1982). The role of physical appearance in infant and child development. In H. E. Fitzgerald, E. Lester, & M. Youngman (Eds.), *Theory and research in behavioral pediatrics* (Vol. 1, pp. 181–219). New York: Plenum.

Hildebrandt, K. A., & Fitzgerald, H. E. (1983). The infant's physical attractiveness: Its effect on bonding and attachment. *Infant Mental Health Journal, 4,* 3–12.

Hochberg, J. E. (1978). *Perception* (2nd ed.). Englewood Cliffs, NJ: Prentice-Hall.

Hoffman, D. D., & Richards, W. (1985). Parts of recognition. *Cognition, 18,* 65–96.

Humphreys, G. W. (1983). Reference frames and shape perception. *Cognitive Psychology, 15,* 151–196.

Ittleson, W. H. (1952). *The Ames demonstrations in perception.* New York: Hafner.

Jolicoeur, P. (1985). The time to name disoriented natural objects. *Memory & Cognition, 13,* 289–303.

Jolicoeur, P., Gluck, M. A., & Kosslyn, S. M. (1984). Picture and names: Making the connection. *Cognitive Psychology, 16,* 243–275.

Julesz, B. (1981). Textons, the elements of texture perception, and their interaction. *Nature, 290,* 91–97.

Kanade, T. (1981). Recovery of the three-dimensional shape of an object from a single view. *Artificial Intelligence, 17,* 409–460.

Kanizsa, G. (1979). *Organization in vision: Essays on Gestalt perception.* New York: Praeger.

King, M., Meyer, G. E., Tangney, J., & Biederman, I. (1976). Shape constancy and a perceptual bias towards symmetry. *Perception & Psychophysics, 19,* 129–136.

Lowe, D. (1984). *Perceptual organization and visual recognition.* Unpublished doctoral dissertation, Stanford University, Stanford, CA.

Mark, L. S., & Todd, J. T. (1985). Describing perception information about human growth in terms of geometric invariants. *Perception & Psychophysics, 37,* 249–256.

Marr, D. (1977). Analysis of occluding contour. *Proceedings of the Royal Society of London, Series B, 197,* 441–475.

Marr, D. (1982). *Vision.* San Francisco: Freeman.

Marr, D., & Nishihara, H. K. (1978). Representation and recognition of three dimensional shapes. *Proceedings of the Royal Society of London, Series B, 200,* 269–294.

Marslen-Wilson, W. (1980). *Optimal efficiency in human speech processing.* Unpublished manuscript, Max-Planck-Institut für Psycholinguistik, Nijmegen, The Netherlands.

McClelland, J. L., & Rumelhart, D. E. (1981). An interactive activation model of context effects in letter perception, Part I: An account of basic findings. *Psychological Review, 88,* 375–407.

Miller, G. A. (1956). The magical number seven, plus or minus two: Some limits on our capacity for processing information. *Psychological Review, 63,* 81–97.

Neisser, U. (1963). Decision time without reaction time: Experiments in visual scanning. *American Journal of Psychology, 76,* 376–385.

Neisser, U. (1967). *Cognitive Psychology.* New York: Appleton.

Oldfield, R. C. (1966). Things, words, and the brain. *Quarterly Journal of Experimental Psychology, 18,* 340–353.

Oldfield, R. C., & Wingfield, A. (1965). Response latencies in naming objects. *Quarterly Journal of Experimental Psychology, 17,* 273–281.

Palmer, S. E. (1980). What makes triangles point: Local and global effects in configurations of ambiguous triangles. *Cognitive Psychology, 12,* 285–305.

Palmer, S., Rosch, E., & Chase, P. (1981). Canonical perspective and the perception of objects. In J. Long & A. Baddeley (Eds.), (pp. 135–151). *Attention & performance IX.* Hillsdale, NJ: Erlbaum.

Penrose, L. S., & Penrose, R. (1958). Impossible objects: A special type of illusion. *British Journal of Psychology, 49,* 31–33.

Perkins, D. N. (1983). Why the human perceiver is a bad machine. In

J. Beck, B. Hope, & A. Rosenfeld, (Eds.), *Human and machine vision* (pp. 341–364). New York: Academic Press.

Perkins, D. N., & Deregowski, J. (1982). A cross-cultural comparison of the use of a Gestalt perceptual strategy. *Perception, 11,* 279–286.

Pomerantz, J. R. (1978). Pattern and speed of encoding. *Memory & Cognition, 5,* 235–241.

Rock, I. (1983). *The logic of perception.* Cambridge, MA: MIT Press.

Rock, I. (1984). *Perception.* New York: W. H. Freeman.

Rosch, E., Mervis, C. B., Gray, W., Johnson, D., & Boyes-Braem, P. (1976). Basic objects in natural categories. *Cognitive Psychology, 8,* 382–439.

Ryan, T., & Schwartz, C. (1956). Speed of perception as a function of mode of representation. *American Journal of Psychology, 69,* 60–69.

Shepard, R. N., & Metzler, J. (1971). Mental rotation of three dimensional objects. *Science, 171,* 701–703.

Sugihara, K. (1982). Classification of impossible objects. *Perception, 11,* 65–74.

Sugihara, K. (1984). An algebraic approach to shape-from-image problems. *Artificial Intelligence, 23,* 59–95.

Treisman, A. (1982). Perceptual grouping and attention in visual search for objects. *Journal of Experimental Psychology: Human Perception and Performance, 8,* 194–214.

Treisman, A., & Gelade, G. (1980). A feature integration theory of attention. *Cognitive Psychology, 12,* 97–136.

Trivers, R. (1985). *Social evolution.* Menlo Park, CA: Benjamin/Cummings.

Tversky, A. (1977). Features of similarity. *Psychological Review, 84,* 327–352.

Tversky, B., & Hemenway, K. (1984). Objects, parts, and categories. *Journal of Experimental Psychology: General, 113,* 169–193.

Ullman, S. (1984). Visual routines. *Cognition, 18,* 97–159.

Virsu, V. (1971a). Tendencies to eye movement, and misperception of curvature, direction, and length. *Perception & Psychophysics, 9,* 65–72.

Virsu, V. (1971b). Underestimation of curvature and task dependence in visual perception of form. *Perception & Psychophysics, 9,* 339–342.

Waltz, D. (1975). Generating semantic descriptions from drawings of scenes with shadows. In P. Winston (Ed.), *The psychology of computer vision* (pp. 19–91). New York: McGraw-Hill.

Winston, P. A. (1975). Learning structural descriptions from examples. In P. H. Winston (Ed.), *The psychology of computer vision* (pp. 157–209). New York: McGraw-Hill.

Witkin, A. P., & Tenenbaum, J. M. (1983). On the role of structure in vision. In J. Beck, B. Hope, & A. Rosenfeld (Eds.), *Human and machine vision* (pp. 481–543). New York: Academic Press.

Woodworth, R. S. (1938). *Experimental psychology.* New York: Holt.

Received June 28, 1985
Revision received June 3, 1986 ■

Part V
Different Types of Objects

[14]

What Is "Special" About Face Perception?

Martha J. Farah and Kevin D. Wilson
University of Pennsylvania

Maxwell Drain
University of Michigan

James N. Tanaka
Oberlin College

There is growing evidence that face recognition is "special" but less certainty concerning the way in which it is special. The authors review and compare previous proposals and their own more recent hypothesis, that faces are recognized "holistically" (i.e., using relatively less part decomposition than other types of objects). This hypothesis, which can account for a variety of data from experiments on face memory, was tested with 4 new experiments on face perception. A selective attention paradigm and a masking paradigm were used to compare the perception of faces with the perception of inverted faces, words, and houses. Evidence was found of relatively less part-based shape representation for faces. The literatures on machine vision and single unit recording in monkey temporal cortex are also reviewed for converging evidence on face representation. The neuropsychological literature is reviewed for evidence on the question of whether face representation differs in degree or kind from the representation of other types of objects.

Several lines of research have suggested that face recognition is "special." Neuropsychological studies have demonstrated that face recognition can be selectively impaired relative to the recognition of objects of equivalent difficulty, implying that people use different brain areas for face recognition and other types of object recognition (Farah, Klein, & Levinson, 1995). Single unit recordings in monkeys have revealed a population of cells in the temporal cortex that respond selectively to faces, in some cases responding differentially to particular faces, suggesting a role for these cells in face recognition (e.g., see Desimone, 1991, for a recent review). Although cells have also been found that respond to nonface objects, the selectivity and strength of such responses are weaker (Baylis, Rolls, & Leonard, 1985). Developmentally, face recognition appears to have an innate component. At just 30 min of age, infants will track a moving face farther than other moving patterns of comparable contrast, complexity, and spatial frequency (Johnson, Dziurawiec, Ellis, & Morton, 1991). The face inversion effect, discussed in more detail later, provides another indication that face recognition is different from other kinds of object recognition. Whereas most objects are somewhat harder to recognize upside down

than rightside up, inversion makes faces dramatically harder to recognize (see Valentine, 1988, for a review).

The question of how face recognition is special has received less attention. How is shape represented for purposes of face recognition, and how does this differ from the representations of shape used for object recognition? Of course, it is possible that there are no differences and that face recognition is equivalent to other forms of visual pattern recognition in terms of the underlying visual information processing involved. Nevertheless, the differences just reviewed in neural implementation, developmental course, and sensitivity to orientation make it reasonable to suspect that differences also exist in the way faces and objects are represented and to inquire into those differences.

Hypotheses About Face Representation

Most hypotheses about face representation highlight the importance of the overall structure or "gestalt" of faces relative to other kinds of objects that people recognize. This general idea has been subjected to a variety of specific formulations and operationalizations. Here we review a number of these formulations, briefly mentioning the type of experimental paradigm by which each formulation has been operationalized. We also note briefly the weaknesses of each approach, which have motivated continued attempts to frame and test new hypotheses concerning face perception.

Bradshaw and Wallace (1971) formulated the hypothesis that faces are perceived as gestalts in terms of Sternberg's (1969) distinction between parallel and serial processing. They tested the hypothesis that facial features are perceived simultaneously or *in parallel* using an adaptation of the short-term memory scanning paradigm: Each participant's task was to compare sequentially presented faces and judge them same or different. Pairs that were different could differ in one or more (up to a total of seven) of their features, and the question of interest was

Martha J. Farah and Kevin D. Wilson, Department of Psychology, University of Pennsylvania; Maxwell Drain, Department of Psychology, University of Michigan; James N. Tanaka, Department of Psychology, Oberlin College.

This research was supported by National Institutes of Health Grants R01 NS34030, R01 AG14082, K02 AG00756, and R15 HD30433. We thank Don Hoffman and Jim Johnston for helpful comments on an earlier version of this article.

Correspondence concerning this article should be addressed to Martha J. Farah, Department of Psychology, University of Pennsylvania, 3815 Walnut Street, Philadelphia, Pennsylvania 19104-6196.

whether reaction times to these pairs would vary as a result of the number of features that differed. Bradshaw and Wallace found that the number and identity of differing features did affect reaction time, consistent with a serial self-terminating search for differences, and concluded that faces in their experiment were not perceived as unitary gestalts. The Bradshaw and Wallace experiment was one of several conducted in the 1970s using speeded "same" – "different" paradigms in which it was assumed that if the features of faces are processed in parallel, there should be no effect of number of differing features (e.g., Matthews, 1978; Smith & Nielsen, 1970). This seems a questionable assumption, because the greater the number of differing features, the more dissimilar the two faces will be overall and the easier it will be to detect the difference, no matter how they are represented. In addition, Bradshaw and Wallace (1971) themselves pointed out the possibility that their experimental task may have induced special strategies (p. 447).

Rhodes (1988) formulated the issue in terms of what she labeled first versus second order, or *configurational*, features. First order features were taken to be the appearance of relatively discrete facial features labeled with common words such as *eye, nose, chin,* and so on. Second order features were defined by Rhodes as having configurational properties, under which she included spatial relations among first order features and the position of first order features, along with information about face shape. The hypothesis tested by Rhodes was that face perception involves second order features and is hence at least partly configurational. To determine which types of features predict perceived facial similarity, Rhodes used multidimensional scaling of similarity ratings among a set of faces and then regressed a large set of both first and second order features on the scaling solution. Her results indicated that both first and second order features were relevant determinants of facial appearance. Although this work represents a milestone in methodological sophistication, a drawback is that the concept of configuration was not explicitly defined. For example, is eye tilt, which was included in the analysis, a first order shape feature or a second order position feature? From the point of view of recasting the intuitive concept of gestalt face processing into more explicit information-processing terms, the concept of configuration is not a tremendous improvement. In addition, because Rhodes did not conduct similar analyses with patterns other than faces, she did not draw any conclusions about how face perception differs from the perception of other patterns.

Yet another formulation of the idea that overall structure or gestalt is important in face perception comes from Sergent (1984), who applied Garner's (1974) framework of dependence versus independence of stimulus feature processing to faces and suggested that the perception of facial features shows *dependency* or mutual influence. She analyzed participants' performance in a speeded matching task and a similarity rating task and found that the effects of combinations of features could not always be predicted by the effects of the features individually. Furthermore, this conclusion held only for upright faces. A limitation of these results pointed out by Bruce (1988) is that only one facial feature displayed this pattern of nonindependence with the other features, the feature termed "internal space." This refers to how closely grouped the features are toward the center of the face, which is a more relational property than what

one normally thinks of as an individual feature. Nevertheless, the finding cannot simply be a trivial consequence of labeling the relations among a set of features as a feature, because the same feature did not interact with the others in inverted faces.

Another well-known attempt at formulating what is special about face perception is in terms of spatial frequency. Harmon (1973) and Ginsburg (1978) demonstrated that *low spatial frequency information* may be particularly important in face recognition and that the high spatial frequencies may be of only marginal additional use. Because low spatial frequencies represent the large-scale structure of the face, this hypothesis provides another explicit version of the general idea that faces are represented as gestalts. Again, Bruce (1988) provided a useful critique of this hypothesis, including a review of subsequent empirical work that challenges the special role of low spatial frequencies in face perception using filtered images.

The final hypothesis discussed here is based on an analogy with the word superiority effect in reading (Reicher, 1969; Wheeler, 1970; this hypothesis was suggested to us by Don Hoffman, personal communication, 1995). Perhaps faces are represented in terms of parts and wholes to the same degree as other visual patterns, but the whole-level representations are particularly important in encoding the part representations.

The foregoing hypotheses are different, but they have in common an emphasis on the overall structure of the face, above and beyond its more local featural information. The hypothesis of Bradshaw and Wallace (1971), that face perception involves parallel perception of features, captures the idea that all parts of the face are perceived simultaneously. However, this is a weaker notion of overall structure or gestalt than the hypothesis of Sergent (1984), in which the parts are not only perceived together but influence one another so that, in effect, the "whole is more than the sum of its parts." Rhodes's (1988) concept of configurational information captures yet another way in which face perception might transcend local feature perception, by involving nonlocal features consisting of relations among local features. This is distinct from the parallel processing hypothesis, which does not broach the topic of relations among features being processed in parallel, and is at least formally distinct from the interdependence hypothesis, which concerns the interactions among features rather than the features themselves. The spatial frequency hypothesis describes the difference between local features and overall structure in terms of the different spatial scales at which such information is typically available. The facilitation of part encoding by whole context emphasizes the importance of overall structure in deriving a part-based representation. The hypothesis presented shortly is yet another attempt to capture the notion of gestalt face representation in explicit terms from cognitive psychology. Before presenting our hypothesis, we review one last alternative, one that is quite distinct from the rest and that has become perhaps the best-known hypothesis about the distinctive nature of face recognition.

Diamond and Carey (1986) distinguished between what they termed *first order relational information,* which is sufficient to recognize most objects, and *second order relational information,* which is needed for face recognition. They defined these terms explicitly, and their meanings appear to be quite distinct from Rhodes's (1988) similar terminology. First order relational information consists of the spatial relations of the parts of an object with respect to one another. In contrast, second order relational information exists only for objects whose parts share a general spatial configuration, and it consists of the spatial relations of the parts relative to the prototypical arrangement of the parts. For a face, the first order relational information would include the spatial relations among the eyes, nose, and mouth, for example. The second order relational information would include the spatial locations of these parts relative to the prototypical arrangement of eyes, nose, and mouth. Diamond and Carey also suggested that the use of prototypes and second order relational information is not unique to face recognition but underlies all "expert" recognition of objects with prototypical spatial configurations. In support of their hypothesis, they demonstrated that dog recognition by dog experts showed an inversion effect comparable in magnitude to the face inversion effect, whereas nonexperts, who had developed prototypes for human faces but not for dogs, showed only a face inversion effect.

Although Diamond and Carey's (1986) results show that pronounced inversion effects are not necessarily limited to faces and that expertise may be an important factor in determining the mode of encoding, these results do not directly address the role of first versus second order relational information per se in face recognition. Diamond and Carey's data do not reveal the types of visual information processing that their dog experts were using when recognizing dogs or the types that all of their participants were using when recognizing faces.

Tanaka and Farah (1991) conducted a direct test of the hypothesis that second order relational information is particularly sensitive to inversion and that this sensitivity underlies the face inversion effect. They reasoned that the strongest and most direct test of such a hypothesis would involve nonface stimuli and would consist of varying the relative importance of first and second order relational information for stimulus recognition while holding other aspects of the stimuli and task constant. To this end, they taught participants to identify dot patterns that either shared a common configuration (each pattern having been generated from a prototype by small changes in dot position) or did not. In two experiments, they obtained a moderate inversion effect for the dot patterns, but there was no difference between the two types of patterns. They concluded that relatively greater reliance on second order relational information does not necessarily result in greater sensitivity to pattern inversion. The implication of this finding for the face inversion effect and the nature of face recognition more generally is that the face inversion effect is probably not caused by reliance on second order relational information, and therefore the underlying difference between face and object recognition is probably not the degree to which they rely on second order relational information.

Holistic Face Representation: Evidence of Minimal Part Decomposition in Memory Representations of Faces

Our alternative hypothesis about the difference between face and object recognition concerns the degree of part decomposition used in representing the two types of stimuli. In many current theories of object recognition, stimulus shape is represented in terms of explicitly represented parts, such that parts are represented as shapes in their own right (e.g., Biederman, 1987; Hoffman & Richards, 1985; Marr, 1982; Palmer, 1975).

Our hypothesis is that face recognition differs from other types of recognition in that it involves relatively little part decomposition. For example, according to most theories of vision, recognizing a particular house involves explicitly representing at least some of the parts of the house, such as the door, window, front steps, and so forth, whereas, according to our hypothesis, recognizing a particular face does not involve (or involves to a lesser extent) explicit representations of the eyes, nose, and mouth. Instead, we hypothesize that faces are recognized primarily as undifferentiated wholes. Note that we do not deny the possibility of a mixed population of representations, some of which are holistic and some of which feature explicitly represented parts. Indeed, people's ability to recognize and distinguish isolated parts of faces, even if it is less proficient than their corresponding ability with whole faces, suggests that they must have access to explicit representations of facial parts under at least some circumstances. Such part representations might bear a hierarchical relation to people's whole face representations, analogous to the relation between letter and word representations, or might simply constitute an independent population of representations. Our claim is that, to the extent that this is true, face recognition involves disproportionately more holistic representations than the recognition of other types of patterns.

We previously tested this hypothesis with two types of experiments. The first was based on an approach developed by cognitive psychologists in the 1970s to the question of which portions of a visual pattern are psychologically real parts and which are not. Bower and Glass (1976) demonstrated that some portions of a pattern provided an effective retrieval cue for drawing the pattern from memory and others did not. This distinction corresponded to whether the portions were "good" parts according to Gestalt principles. Reed (1974) found that participants were more likely to be able to verify that pattern fragments that were "good" parts were contained in a mentally imaged pattern. Palmer (1977) obtained ratings of the goodness or naturalness of different ways of parsing patterns and showed that participants were better able to recognize that a pattern fragment came from a previously studied pattern if it was independently rated a good or natural part.

These studies all demonstrate that when a portion of a pattern corresponds to a part in the natural parse of the pattern by the visual system, it will be better remembered. They thus provide an assay for the degree to which a portion of a pattern is treated as a psychologically real part by the viewer. In our initial experiments, we relied most directly on Palmer's (1977) approach, reasoning that if a portion of a pattern is explicitly represented as a part in the visual representation of the stimulus that underlies recognition, then it should be identified more accurately when presented in isolation from the rest of the pattern than when it does not have the status of a part in the pattern representation. In contrast to Palmer's (1977) research, which focused on memory for geometric patterns, ours involved realistic drawings.

Tanaka and Farah (1993) taught participants to identify faces and various contrasting classes of nonface stimuli and then assessed the degree to which the parts of these stimuli were explicitly represented in participants' memories. For example, in one experiment, participants learned to name a set of faces (e.g., Joe or Larry), as well as a set of houses (e.g., Bill's house or Tom's house). They were then given two-alternative forced-choice tests of the identity of isolated parts (e.g., "Which is Joe's nose?" or "Which is Bill's door?") or whole patterns in which the correct and incorrect choices differed only by a single part (e.g., "Which is Joe?" [when confronted with Joe and a version of Joe with the alternative nose from the isolated part test pair] or "Which is Bill's house?" [when confronted with Bill's house and a version of Bill's house with the alternative door from the isolated test pair]). It was found that, relative to their ability to recognize whole faces and houses, subjects were impaired at recognizing parts of faces as compared with parts of houses. Could the difference have been caused by the nature of the parts themselves? No, because the same pattern of results was obtained when faces were compared with scrambled faces and inverted faces, whose parts are identical. These results are consistent with the hypothesis that during the learning and subsequent recognition of the houses, scrambled faces, and inverted faces, participants explicitly represented their parts, whereas during the learning and subsequent recognition of the intact upright faces, they did not, or they did so to a lesser extent.

Tanaka and Sengco (1997) showed that these results should not be interpreted simply in terms of a part-based representation in which, for faces, the configuration of parts is particularly important. If this were the case, changes in configuration would affect overall face recognition, but so long as individual parts are explicitly represented, this manipulation should not affect recognition of the individual parts per se. Testing this prediction by comparing upright faces with inverted faces and houses, they again found evidence of holistic coding of upright faces.

This operationalization of holistic representation has also been used with members of two special populations. Tanaka, Kay, Grinnel, and Stansfield (in press) have shown that children as young as 6 years old show a disadvantage for isolated parts of faces, whether tested for their long-term memory for faces in the same way as the adult participants described earlier or tested with an immediate memory paradigm in which a pair of test faces or face parts is presented immediately after the study face. Farah, Tanaka, and Drain (unpublished data, described in Farah, 1996) tested a prosopagnosic participant (i.e., an individual who has lost the ability to recognize faces) on short-term memory for faces presented in a normal format or "exploded" so that the parts of the face were presented separately. Whereas normal participants performed better with the normal faces, presumably because they could encode them as wholes, the prosopagnosic participants performed roughly equivalently whether given the opportunity to encode the faces as wholes or forced to encode them as parts. This result is consistent with the hypothesis that the face recognition ability that has been lost in prosopagnosia involves the representation of faces as wholes.

Recent work by Moscovitch, Winocur, and Behrmann (1997) complements these findings by showing that a patient whose face recognition was disproportionately spared, relative to object recognition, could not recognize photographs of faces that had been cut into separate parts. The results of this and numerous other experiments with this patient led the authors to conclude that face and object recognition differ in their reliance on part representations, although their operationalization of "part" appears to include arbitrary fragments as well as structural components in a shape hierarchy (e.g., see Experiment 14).

Another way in which we have tested the holistic representation hypothesis is by determining whether it could explain the face inversion effect (Farah, Tanaka, & Drain, 1995). If face recognition differs from other forms of object recognition by the use of relatively undecomposed or holistic representations, then perhaps the face inversion effect results from the use of holistic, or non-part-based, representation. In the first experiment, we taught participants to identify random dot patterns and later tested their recognition of the patterns either upright or inverted. Half of the patterns learned by participants were presented in a way that encouraged parsing the pattern into parts: Each portion of the pattern corresponding to a part was made from a distinctive color, so grouping by color defined parts. The other half of the patterns learned were presented in all black, and the test stimuli for all patterns were presented in black. When participants had been induced to see the patterns in terms of parts during learning, their later performance in identifying the patterns showed no effect of orientation. In contrast, when they were not induced to encode the patterns in terms of parts, they showed an inversion effect in later recognition. In a second experiment, we manipulated participants' encoding of faces and then tested their ability to recognize the faces upright and inverted. They were induced to learn half of the faces in a partwise manner (in the "exploded" format described earlier), whereas the other half of the faces to be learned were presented in a normal format. All faces were tested in a normal format. For the faces that were initially encoded in terms of parts, there was no inversion effect. In contrast, faces encoded normally showed a normal inversion effect. These results suggest that what is special about face recognition, by virtue of which it is so sensitive to orientation, is that it involves representations with relatively little or no part decomposition.

Are Perceptual Representations of Faces Holistic?

Each of these earlier lines of research was relevant to testing the hypothesis that faces are stored in a relatively holistic form in memory. Strictly speaking, they do not address the question of whether faces are perceived holistically. This question is of interest because some of the evidence reviewed earlier suggests that the "special" status of faces extends to the visual representations that are initially constructed during perception. For example, patients who are impaired at face recognition appear to perceive faces abnormally (Farah, 1990). In addition, the face inversion effect can be obtained in tasks that are free of any long-term memory component (e.g., matching of sequentially presented faces; Valentine, 1988). These considerations suggest that the memory representations of faces, studied in our previous research, are holistic because faces are initially encoded holistically during perception. However, the hypothesis that faces are perceived holistically has not been tested directly. That was the goal of the present experiments.

In these experiments, we assessed the degree of part decomposition on-line, during the perception of faces, using two types of experimental paradigms. In the first, we measured the relative availability of part and whole representations by requiring participants to compare single features of simultaneously presented pairs of faces and observed the influence of irrelevant features on their ability to judge the similarity or difference of the probed feature. For example, they might be asked whether two faces have the same or different noses. To the extent that participants have explicit representations of the separate features of a face, they should be able to compare them with one another. To the extent that they do not have explicit representations of these features, but rather, only a holistic representation of the entire face, they should suffer cross talk from irrelevant features when judging the probed feature. The amount of cross talk with upright faces can be compared with that with inverted faces to measure the relative availability of parts and wholes in the representations of the two kinds of stimuli. In the subsequent three experiments, we explored the effect on face perception of masks composed of face parts or whole faces. As Johnston and McClelland (1980) reasoned in their experiments on word perception, to the extent that masks contain shape elements similar to those used in representing the stimulus, the mask will interfere with perception of the stimulus. The effects of part and whole masks on the perception of upright faces were compared with their effects on the perception of words, inverted faces, and houses.

Experiment 1

The degree to which people explicitly represent the parts of faces during face perception was investigated with a *same–different* matching paradigm in which particular parts of the face were to be compared. On each trial, a pair of faces was briefly presented, one beside the other, followed immediately by the name of a facial part. Participants were to decide whether the two faces shared the same exemplar of the named part (e.g., the same nose). To the extent that the parts of the face are explicitly represented in immediate visual memory as units of shape in their own right, participants should be able to compare them with one another independently of the other separately represented face parts. To the extent that participants have only a unitary, undecomposed representation of each face, they should be able to judge only the overall similarity or difference between the faces, and their judgment of the similarity of any individual part will be contaminated by the amount of similarity between the other parts.

Of course, face representations are unlikely to be either pure holistic representations with no explicit part-level representations (especially in the context of the present task's demands) or pure collections of parts with no explicit whole-level representation. The present experiment was therefore designed to compare the relative contributions of part and whole representations with the perception of upright and inverted faces. That is, the prediction was neither that faces are perceived only as wholes nor that nonfaces are perceived only as parts; rather, a differential weighting of parts and wholes for faces relative to nonfaces was predicted. Because the hypothesis that face perception is holistic pertains only to the perception of upright faces, inverted faces provide control stimuli that are geometrically identical to upright faces (except for orientation), and therefore have the same partwise and holistic similarity relations, but are predicted to have less holistic perceptual representations.

Method

Participants. Twenty-four undergraduate students at Carnegie Mellon University participated in exchange for course credit. All participants had normal or corrected-to-normal vision.

Materials. Six faces were created with the Mac-A-Mug (Macintosh) program. All of the internal features of the faces (eyes, nose, and mouth) were distinctive, and all of the external features (facial outline, chin, ears, and hair) were the same. Each of these faces was presented side by side with an identical copy of itself and with copies in which one or more features differed. Specifically, each face was paired with a face differing in eyes only, nose only, mouth only, eyes and nose, eyes and mouth, nose and mouth, and eyes, nose, and mouth. For each of the six original faces, there were 8 face pairs, 1 composed of an identical pair and 7 composed of pairs with one or more features changed as just described. This resulted in 48 different face pairs. Three of the original six faces appeared to the left of their different versions, and three appeared to the right. Each face measured 10.5 × 14.5 cm and subtended about 12° × 16.5° at the average participant viewing distance.

Procedure. Stimuli were presented, and responses collected, on a Macintosh II computer. On each trial, after the offset of a central fixation dot, a pair of faces was presented for 1 s, followed immediately by one of the words *eyes, nose, mouth,* or *all.* Participants were instructed to judge whether or not the named parts of the two faces were identical or, if probed with *all,* to judge whether the two faces were identical. Although we have no theoretically motivated predictions for the results of the *all* probe condition, we included it to weaken the implicit task demand to view the faces as collections of unrelated distinct parts (a task demand that might increase the likelihood of an artifactual null result). Participants responded using the computer keyboard, pressing "z" for *same* and "/" for *different.* Response latencies were not recorded. Approximately 12–16 practice trials were given.

The part probes followed face pairs that were either identical or differed by either just the named part or all parts. This resulted in equal numbers of trials on which the correct answer was *same* and *different* for each part probe, along with 72 trials with part probes. The *all* probe followed all pairs, resulting in fewer *same* than *different* trials by a 1:7 ratio, along with 48 trials with *all* probes. The combined 120 trials were presented once with the faces upright and once with the faces inverted; half of the participants performed the task with the upright faces first, and half performed it with the inverted faces first. There was a 5-min break between the two blocks of trials.

Results and Discussion

The results of the part probe conditions are of primary interest, because they are relevant to confirming or disconfirming the holistic perception hypothesis. Thus, they are discussed first. As can be seen in Table 1, the compatibility of the probed and irrelevant parts had an effect on response accuracy, and the effect was larger for upright faces than for inverted faces. For upright faces, when the irrelevant parts were compatible with the probed part (i.e., the probed part was the same and the irrelevant features were also the same, or the probed part was different and the irrelevant features were also different), participants achieved an average rate of 74.6% correct; when the irrelevant parts were not compatible with the probed part (i.e., the probed part was the same and irrelevant parts were different, or the probed part was different and the irrelevant parts were the same), participants achieved only 61.8% correct. The corresponding means for the inverted faces were 66.6% and 62.2% correct. This pattern of results was predicted by the hypothesis that face perception is holistic. Figure 1 shows the means of the

Table 1

Percentage Correct Facial Matching in Experiment 1 for Upright and Inverted Faces: Same or Different Probed Parts and Compatible or Incompatible Nonprobed Parts

	Upright		Inverted	
Probed feature	Irrelevant features compatible	Irrelevant features incompatible	Irrelevant features compatible	Irrelevant features incompatible
Same	91.5	71.6	86.6	74.7
Different	57.6	51.9	46.5	49.6

compatible and incompatible conditions for upright and inverted faces. Figure 2 shows the effect of compatibility for upright and inverted faces.

A planned comparison was carried out to test the prediction that compatible irrelevant parts will facilitate performance relative to incompatible parts and that this effect will be greater for the upright faces than for the inverted faces. The corresponding weights for the upright and inverted faces with compatible and incompatible irrelevant parts were set at .67, −.67, .33, and −.33, respectively, yielding a value of $F(1, 23) = 35.10$, $p < .0001$.

A repeated measures analysis of variance was performed on participants' percentage correct rates in each of the part probe conditions of interest; the following crossed variables were used: probed part (same or different), irrelevant part (compatible or incompatible with probed feature), and orientation (upright or inverted). The hypothesis that face perception is relatively holistic predicts that the compatibility of the irrelevant parts will have a larger effect on judgments about upright faces than on judgments about inverted faces. The corresponding interaction, between compatibility and orientation, was significant, $F(1, 23) = 6.85$, $p < .02$. In addition, there were three significant main effects and one other significant interaction. *Same* responses were more accurate than *different* responses (81.1% vs. 51.4%

correct), $F(1, 23) = 106.94$, $p < .001$; performance was more accurate with compatible than incompatible irrelevant parts (70.6% vs. 62% correct), $F(1, 23) = 20.80$, $p < .001$; upright faces were compared more accurately than inverted faces (68.2% vs. 64.4% correct), $F(1, 23) = 4.23$, $p < .05$; and the effect of compatibility was greater for *same* trials than for *different* trials (89.1% and 73.2% correct for compatible and incompatible *same* trials and 52.1% and 50.8% correct for compatible and incompatible *different* trials), $F(1, 23) = 29.05$, $p < .001$. No other effects were significant ($ps > .1$ in all cases). Separate analyses of variance testing the simple effects of compatibility on upright and inverted faces revealed a significant effect for the upright faces, $F(1, 23) = 31.92$, $p < .0001$, and a borderline significant effect for inverted faces, $F(1, 23) = 3.79$, $p = .064$.

Examination of the means in Table 1 suggests that participants were more likely to respond "same" than "different" in this experiment, and indeed accuracy on *different* trials was at chance. We therefore repeated the critical planned comparison with only the data from *same* trials and confirmed that the predicted pattern of results was obtained with this subset of the data, $F(1, 23) = 52.88$, $p < .0001$.

In the *all* probe condition, participants were to respond "same" only if all of the parts of the faces matched. Mean percentage correct rates for the conditions of interest are shown in Table 2. The only significant effect was that of response, with

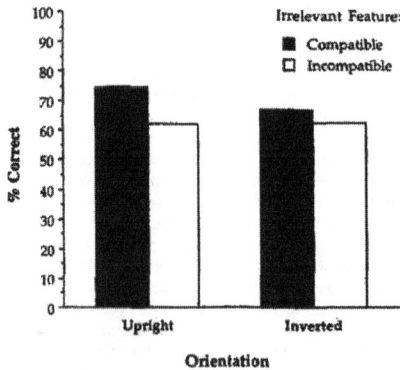

Figure 1. Percentage correct facial part matching in Experiment 1 for upright and inverted faces as a function of the compatibility between the probed parts and the nonprobed, or irrelevant, parts.

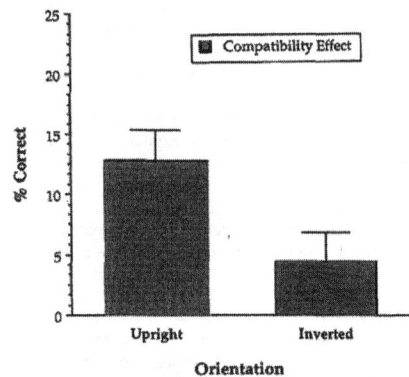

Figure 2. Effect of compatibility for upright and inverted faces in Experiment 1.

Table 2

Percentage Correct Whole Face Matching in Experiment 1 for Upright and Inverted Faces: Same or Different Faces

Whole face	Upright	Inverted
Same	80.6	82.6
Different	69.1	62.8

same responses more accurate than *different* responses (81.6% vs. 66.0% correct), $F(1, 23) = 15.04$, $p < .001$. No other effects were significant ($ps > .1$).

The prediction of the holistic face perception hypothesis was borne out by the results of this experiment. We reasoned that if perceived faces were represented as undifferentiated whole shapes, without explicitly represented parts, then it would be difficult for participants to compare parts independent of the whole. We found that this was indeed the case when the difficulty of comparing parts of upright faces was compared with the difficulty of comparing the same parts of the same faces inverted, which do not engage face-specific representations (or do so to a lesser extent). Of course, this result is susceptible to the alternative explanation that both upright and inverted faces are represented to the same degree in terms of parts but that, for some reason, the individual parts are less accessible when faces are upright. However, in the absence of an independent reason to believe that there is differential part accessibility, rather than differential representation of parts, with upright faces, the holistic perception hypothesis provides the most straightforward account of these data.

This experiment tested the holistic perception hypothesis with the representations of faces in immediate visual memory. Participants could begin their comparisons of the faces as soon as they read the probe words, which appeared at the same instant that the faces disappeared. In Experiment 2, we manipulated perceptual encoding per se using different kinds of pattern masks, thereby studying the roles of part and whole representations in the initial construction of face representations during perception. This increases the number of qualitatively different experimental paradigms that have been used to test the hypothesis of holistic face representation and, in particular, helps to rule out the alternative hypothesis that parts are represented but merely less available for access during explicit comparisons. It also provides the most direct test of the holistic representation hypothesis as applied to perception.

Experiment 2

One way of stating the holistic representation hypothesis is that, in the course of constructing a perceptual representation of a face, it is not necessary to construct explicit representations of its parts. This formulation of the issue highlights its similarity to an issue addressed by Johnston and McClelland (1980) in their research on word recognition. They hypothesized that word recognition involves a hierarchical recognition process in which letters are explicitly recognized before words. They tested this hypothesis by assessing the relative effects of different kinds of masks on word perception. Although they interpreted their re-

sults using a detailed quantitative model, the qualitative gist of their reasoning was as follows: If the explicit representation of letters is a necessary stage leading up to word recognition, then masks made up of letters should have a more detrimental effect on word recognition than masks made up of letter fragments. Their results supported this prediction.

We used a simple version of the Johnston and McClelland paradigm to address the question of whether face recognition requires explicit representation of facial parts. If faces are recognized as a whole and part representation plays a relatively small role in face recognition, then a mask made of face parts should be less detrimental than a mask consisting of a whole face. In this experiment, we used words as the contrasting nonface stimulus set, because Johnston and McClelland's earlier work had suggested that they are recognized via part representations.

Participants performed a sequential same–different matching task in which a stimulus was presented briefly, followed by a mask, a blank interstimulus interval, and a second stimulus. By varying the nature of the mask, we could assess the effects of interfering with part and whole representations on the quality of perception of the first stimulus. Part and whole word masks consisted of nonwords and words, respectively, as in the original experiments of Johnston and McClelland. These masks were composed of letters not present in the word stimuli, and nonword masks were scrambled versions of the word masks. Examples are shown in the Appendix. By analogy, part and whole face masks were composed of facial parts not used in the stimulus faces, and part face masks were scrambled versions of whole face masks, as shown in Figure 3. The question of whether the part face masks are equivalent to the part word masks for purposes of this experiment is discussed in the *Results and Discussion* section.

Method

Participants. Sixteen students from Carnegie Mellon University and the University of Pennsylvania were paid for their participation in this study. All participants had normal or corrected-to-normal vision. Five were replaced because their performance in one or more conditions was below 55% correct or above 95% correct.

Materials. We created a set of 36 four-letter words using 14 target letters (*c, d, e, f, h, j, l, m, o, p, s, t, u,* and *z*) in 18-point Courier font. These words were 3 cm long and subtended an angle of about 3.5° at the average participant viewing distance. Each of the words was paired with a copy of itself and with another word. The other word differed by a single letter (e.g., *most* was changed to *must*), thus producing 36 same-word pairs and 36 different-word pairs. The changed letter occurred equally often in each of the four letter positions. Nine 4-letter word masks, or whole masks, were created from 11 mask letters (*a, b, g, i, k, n, r, v, w, x,* and *y*). As in Johnston and McClelland (1980), *q* was not used in any of the target or mask words. Part masks were created by scrambling the positions of the letters within each of the whole masks, resulting in nine whole masks and nine part masks. Examples are shown in the Appendix.

A set of 36 faces was created with the Mac-A-Mug software. The faces measured 10.5 × 14.5 cm and subtended about 12° × 16.5° at the average participant viewing distance. Each of these faces was paired with a copy of itself and with a similar-appearing but different face to create 36 same-face and 36 different-face pairs. As in the previous experiment, faces shared the same facial outline (hair, ears, chin, and shoulders); only the internal features (eyes, nose, and mouth) differed

Whole Mask   Part Mask

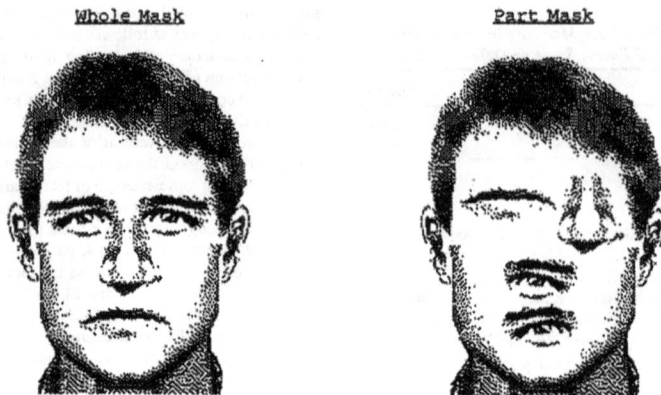

-Figure 3. Examples of whole and part masks for face stimuli.

between faces. Whereas *different* word pairs differed by only one part, *different* face pairs differed by all three internal parts so as to be roughly equivalent in difficulty. Subsequent experiments provide evidence that the nature of *different* pair construction is not responsible for the results to be reported. Nine additional faces, different from those used in the stimuli pairs, were used as whole masks. As with the word masks, part masks for faces were created by scrambling the positions of the parts within the face (e.g., placing the mouth in the normal position of the nose, the eyes in the normal position of the mouth, and the nose in the normal position of the eyes). An example is shown in Figure 3.

For each set of stimuli, words and faces, the 36 basic items were repeated four times, twice paired with their corresponding *different* version and twice paired with themselves for *same* trials. This resulted in 144 word trials and 144 face trials, which were blocked. Whole and part masks were randomly assigned to trials. Trial order was randomized with the restriction that no more than three consecutive trials could include the same type of mask or require the same response.

Procedure. A Macintosh II computer was used to present stimuli and record responses. The contrast on the Macintosh's monitor was set to approximately one half full brightness and two thirds full contrast. All trials began with the presentation of a fixation dot for 500 ms, followed by the first stimulus of a pair. After an interstimulus interval of 100 ms, a mask was exposed for 300 ms. After a 2-s delay, the second stimulus of the pair was presented. In setting exposure durations for the two types of stimuli, we were forced to choose between equating accuracy and equating exposure duration. Because sensitivity to manipulations of perceptual difficulty is known to depend on overall performance levels (with the greatest sensitivity at levels of performance that are intermediate between poor and excellent), we chose to equate accuracy at the expense of equating exposure duration. (Note that both accuracy and exposure duration were equated for upright and inverted faces in subsequent experiments.) The exposure duration for the first and second word stimuli was 17 ms, and the duration for first and second face stimuli was 200 ms. Participants responded using the computer keyboard, pressing "z" for *same* and "/" for *different.* Both responses and response latencies were recorded. After each response, a "Ready?" prompt appeared, and participants, when ready, initiated the next trial by pushing the space bar. Twelve practice trials, with equal numbers of *same, different,* part, and whole mask trials, were included, and feedback

concerning accuracy was given. Half of the participants performed the block of face trials first, and the other half performed the block of word trials first. There was a 5-min rest break between blocks.

Results and Discussion

We focus our attention on the analysis of accuracy, because error rates are high for conventional reaction time analysis. We therefore begin our discussion of the results with the accuracy measures. As can be seen in Table 3 and Figure 4, whole masks interfered more with perception of faces than part masks (73.1% vs. 77.6% correct), but there was little difference apparent in word perception (77.0% vs. 77.8% correct for the corresponding conditions). Figure 5 shows the effect for type of mask on word and face matching accuracy.

A planned comparison was carried out to test the prediction that whole masks would be more disruptive than part masks and that this difference would be greater for face perception than word perception. The corresponding weights for the whole and

Table 3

Face and Word Matching in Experiment 2 With Part or Whole Masks: Same or Different Stimuli

Mask type	Faces		Words	
	Same	Different	Same	Different
	Percentage correct			
Part	80.7	74.5	75.7	79.9
Whole	77.6	68.6	74.5	79.5
	Response time (ms)			
Part	1,123.6	1,100.5	1,011.4	1,228.0
Whole	1,184.0	1,146.1	1,042.5	1,225.4

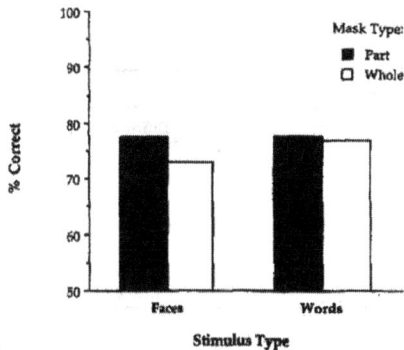

Figure 4. Percentage correct face and word matching in Experiment 2 with whole and part masks.

part face mask and whole and part word masks were set at −.67, .67, −.33, and .33, respectively, yielding a value of $F(1, 15) = 11.58$, $p < .005$.

A repeated measures analysis of variance was conducted on participants' number correct performance in each of the conditions of interest, and the following crossed variables were used: stimulus type (word or face), mask type (part or whole), and response type (same or different). There was a significant interaction between stimulus type and response, with higher accuracy for *different* than for *same* word pairs and the opposite trend with faces, $F(1, 15) = 6.31$, $p < .05$. Participants achieved average rates of 75.1% and 79.7% correct for *same* and *different* word pairs and 79.2% and 71.5% correct for the corresponding face pairs. The interaction between stimulus type and mask type narrowly missed the .05 significance level, $F(1, 15) = 4.20$, $p = .058$. Finally, the effect of mask type was of borderline significance, with whole masks being more detrimental to performance, $F(1, 15) = 3.94$, $p = .066$. No other effects were significant ($ps > .1$ in all cases). Separate analyses of variance were carried out to test the simple effects of mask type on face and word matching. The effect on face perception was significant, $F(1, 15) = 6.58$, $p < .05$, and the effect on word perception was not, $F(1, 15) = 0.29$, $p > .1$.

Response times were also analyzed after removal of response times from incorrect trials and those that were more than 3 standard deviations above the mean of other reaction times in the same cell for the participant. The same planned comparison was performed on the response time data, and a significant result was obtained, $F(1, 15) = 5.89$, $p < .05$. With part and whole face masks, participants responded in an average of 1,112 and 1,165 ms; with part and whole word masks, the corresponding means were 1,120 and 1,134 ms. In a repeated measures analysis of variance with the same variables used in the analysis of accuracy data, only the interaction between stimulus type and response was significant; participants responded to *same* and *different* word pairs in 1,027 and 1,227 ms and to *same* and *different* face pairs in 1,154 and 1,123 ms, $F(1, 15) = 11.26$, $p < .005$. No other effects were significant ($ps > .1$ in all

cases). As with the accuracy data, separate analyses of variance were performed on the reaction time data for the word and face conditions to assess the simple effects of mask type on each type of stimulus. Neither effect was significant ($ps > .1$ in both cases).

Although there was a trend for the perception of both types of stimuli to be more impaired by whole masks than by part masks, this trend was much more pronounced for faces than for words. This is consistent with the hypothesis that there is less need for the parts of the face to be explicitly represented during face perception than there is for the parts of words to be represented during word perception. We now consider some alternative explanations for this result.

The face and word stimuli differed from one another in a variety of ways other than their identities as faces and words. For example, the words were smaller than the faces. As noted in the *Materials* section, the way in which *different* stimuli were derived from *same* stimuli differed. To obtain comparable levels of accuracy for faces and words, we used different exposure durations. Perhaps the greater susceptibility of faces to whole masking results not from a basic difference in the nature of face and word representation but, rather, from their larger size, more distributed differences, or longer exposures. Other differences between the two sets of stimuli in the present experiment pertain to the nature of their part masks. Whereas the parts of the word part masks were perfectly superimposed on the parts of the word they masked, the parts of the face part masks were not. For example, even when a mouth is centered on a nose, some of the nose is left unmasked. Also, whereas each of the letters in the word part masks occurs in a realistic position (e.g., there are four-letter words that begin with the letter *a*, as shown in the first part word mask in the Appendix), the eyes, noses, and mouths of the face part masks occur in unrealistic positions. Perhaps the relatively greater effect of whole masks for faces is due to the incomplete masking of the face part masks or their more artificial nature relative to the word part masks.

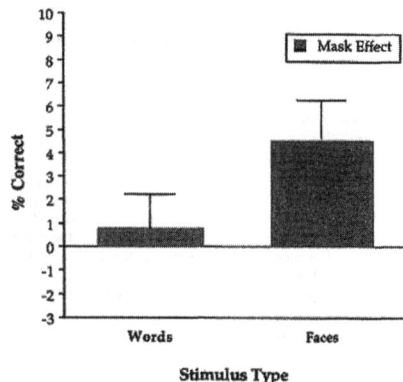

Figure 5. Effect of part versus whole masking on accuracy of matching faces and words in Experiment 2.

Table 4

Upright Face, Inverted Face, and Word Matching in Experiment 3 With Part or Whole Masks: Same or Different Stimuli

Mask type	Upright faces		Inverted faces		Words	
	Same	Different	Same	Different	Same	Different
	Percentage correct					
Part	79.0	80.3	78.4	72.1	72.8	88.2
Whole	73.1	77.8	80.5	68.4	71.2	89.0
	Response time (ms)					
Part	1,054.5	1,029.2	1,094.6	1,022.1	932.0	1,084.7
Whole	1,066.6	1,060.0	1,080.2	1,101.1	992.2	1,132.6

These possibilities can all be addressed by comparing the effects of part and whole masks on the perception of upright and inverted faces. Inverted faces are equivalent to upright faces in their size, in the nature of their "different" stimuli, and in their exposure duration. They are also subject to the same amount of overlap with inverted part masks as upright faces are with upright part masks, and the inverted part face masks are similarly unrealistic.

Experiment 3

In this experiment, we replicated Experiment 2 with words and upright faces and also included inverted faces. If the differences between the effects of part and whole masks on face and word perception are due to the kinds of low-level differences between the face and word stimuli discussed earlier, then the effects of masking inverted faces should be similar to the effects of masking upright faces. In contrast, if the greater effect of whole masking on upright faces is due to face-specific perceptual representations, then inverted faces should not be disproportionately sensitive to whole masks.

Method

Participants. Twenty-four new participants were recruited for this study. All were undergraduate students from the University of Pennsylvania who were paid for their participation. Participants had normal or corrected-to-normal vision. Seven were replaced because their performance in one or more conditions was either below 55% correct or above 95% correct.

Materials. The materials were the same as in the previous experiment, with the exception of a new block of trials created by inverting the same face stimuli and masks used in the upright face condition.

Procedure. The procedure was the same as that used in the first experiment, with the addition of a third block of trials for the inverted face condition. The order of blocks was counterbalanced over participants so that each block occurred equally often in each ordinal position. In addition, participants completed 20 practice trials for each block, and we used their performance during practice to adjust the brightness of the monitor so as to equate as much as possible the difficulty of the three blocks.

Results and Discussion

Table 4 and Figure 6 show the mean accuracy of participants in the conditions of interest. As in the previous experiment,

whole masks interfered more with perception of faces than part masks (75.6% vs. 79.7% correct), but there was again little difference apparent in word perception (80.1% and 80.5% correct for the corresponding conditions). In addition, inverted faces failed to show a large difference between whole and part masks (74.5% and 75.3% correct, respectively). This is consistent with the hypothesis that the difference observed with upright faces is indicative of a form of face-specific representation. Although upright and inverted faces share low-level perceptual features, inverted faces do not engage specialized face perception mechanisms or do so to a lesser extent than upright faces. Figure 7 shows the effects of mask type in the three conditions of interest.

A planned comparison was carried out to test the prediction that whole masks are more disruptive than part masks and that this difference will be greater for upright face perception than for inverted face or word perception. The corresponding weights for the whole and part upright face masks, whole and part inverted face masks, and whole and part word masks, derived from the ratios of the means of Experiment 2, were −.74, .74, −.13, .13, −.13, and .13, respectively, yielding a value of $F(2, 46) = 9.21, p < .005$.

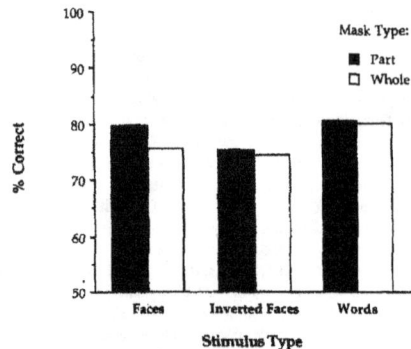

Figure 6. Percentage correct upright face, inverted face, and word matching in Experiment 3 with whole and part masks.

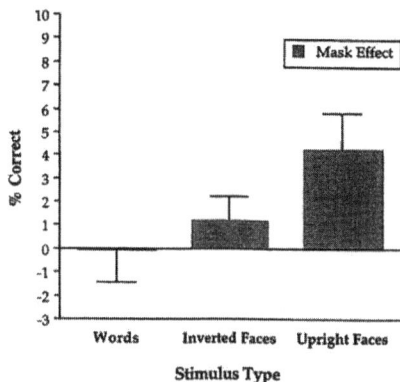

Figure 7. Effect of part versus whole masking on accuracy of matching faces, words, and inverted faces in Experiment 3.

A repeated measures analysis of variance was conducted on participants' number correct performance in each of the conditions of interest; the following crossed variables were used: stimulus type (word, inverted face, or upright face), mask type (part or whole), and response type (same or different). There was again a significant interaction between stimulus type and response, although the form of the interaction differed from that observed in Experiment 2, with lower accuracy for *same* than *different* word pairs (72.0% vs. 88.6% correct) and faces (76.1% vs. 79.0% correct) and inverted faces showing a pattern of higher accuracy for *same* than *different* pairs (79.5% vs. 73.0% correct), $F(1, 15) = 32.34$, $p < .001$. We cannot offer any hypotheses to explain this pattern or the difference between the present outcome and the outcome of Experiment 2. However, note that the response times showed a different pattern (described subsequently). Mask type had a significant effect, with higher accuracy for part than whole masks (78.5% vs. 76.7%), $F(1, 23) = 8.95$, $p < .01$. Finally, two effects were of borderline significance: *Different* responses were more accurate than *same* responses, $F(1, 23) = 3.16$, $.05 < p < .1$, and there was a trend toward a three-way interaction among stimulus type, mask type, and response type, $F(2, 46) = 2.63$, $.05 < p < .1$. No other effects, including the overall interaction between mask type and stimulus type, were significant ($ps > .1$ in all cases). Separate analyses of variance were carried out to assess the simple effects of mask type on each of the stimulus types. Mask type had a significant effect on face matching accuracy, $F(1, 23) = 7.04$, $p < .02$, but not on word matching or inverted face matching ($ps > .1$ in both cases).

Response times were analyzed as before. Initially, a planned comparison on the six relevant means was carried out, as with the accuracy data from this experiment, but this failed to produce significant results, $F(2, 46) = 2.41$, $p > .1$. A repeated measures analysis of variance was also carried out, with the same variables used in the analysis of accuracy data. Participants were faster with part than with whole masks (1,036 vs. 1,072 ms), $F(1, 23) = 4.40$, $p < .05$. Also, there was an interaction

between stimulus type and response type, with *same* words being particularly fast (1,061 and 1,045 ms for *same* and *different* faces, 1,087 and 1,062 ms for *same* and *different* inverted faces, and 962 and 1,109 ms for *same* and *different* words), $F(1, 23) = 10.45$, $p < .001$. There was a trend of borderline significance for faster responses to *same* than to *different* trials, $F(1, 23) = 3.65$, $.05 < p < .1$, which was opposite to the borderline significant trend in accuracy for better performance on *different* trials. No other effects were significant ($ps > .1$ in all cases). Separate analyses of variance on matching reaction time for faces, words, and inverted faces failed to reveal any significant effects ($ps > .1$ in all cases).

In sum, the predicted pattern of results was obtained in the accuracy data of this experiment. Specifically, the perception of upright faces was more disrupted by the use of a whole mask than by the use of a part mask. In contrast, neither words nor inverted faces showed this pattern. The difference in efficacy of part and whole masking for upright and inverted faces rules out the alternative hypothesis that part face masks are ineffective because of imperfect superposition of patterned regions in the mask and stimulus.

Experiment 4

The previous two experiments used the relative effects of part and whole masks to measure the degree of holistic representation in face perception and compare it with the degree of holistic representation in the perception of words and inverted faces. The goal of Experiment 4 was to extend this contrast to a kind of concrete object viewed in a normal orientation. We chose houses as our contrast objects.

On the basis of neuropsychological dissociations among disorders of face, word, and object recognition, we have previously hypothesized that objects are intermediate between faces and words in their reliance on holistic representations (Farah, 1991). In the present experiment, we therefore predicted that the difference in efficacy between part and whole masks would be larger for faces than for houses and larger for houses than for words.

Method

Participants. To resolve the smaller differences predicted to be found between faces and houses than between faces and words or faces and inverted faces, we increased by 50% the number of participants included in this study. Thirty-six undergraduate students from the University of Pennsylvania were paid for their participation. Participants had normal or corrected-to-normal vision. Six were replaced because their performance in one or more conditions fell below 55% correct or above 95% correct.

Materials. The word and face materials from Experiment 2 were used again. In addition, a set of 36 houses was created with architectural design software for Macintosh. Each of these houses was paired with a copy of itself and with a similar-appearing but different house to create 36 *same* and 36 *different* pairs. All houses shared the same external frame, but the internal features (door, bay window, and second story windows) differed between houses. Nine additional houses, different from those used in the stimulus pairs, were used as whole masks. As a means of creating part masks, the locations of the windows and door were scrambled, with each part in another part's position. This procedure is exactly analogous to the procedure for making part masks for the faces. Figure 8 shows typical whole house and part house masks.

Whole Mask   Part Mask

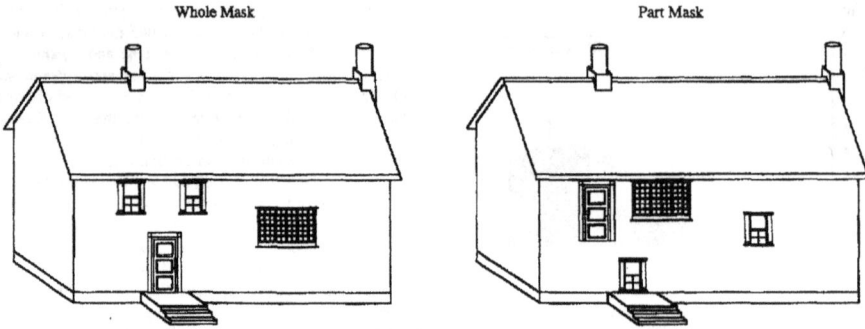

Figure 8. Examples of whole and part masks for house stimuli.

Procedure. The procedure was the same as that used in Experiment 3, with houses replacing inverted faces.

Results and Discussion

Table 5 and Figure 9 show the mean accuracy of participants in the conditions of interest. As in the previous experiments, whole masks interfered more with perception of faces than part masks (75% vs. 78.5% correct), and there was again little difference apparent in word perception (79.2% and 78.0% correct for the corresponding conditions). In addition, houses showed an intermediate-sized difference between whole and part masks (83.2% vs. 85% correct). This is consistent with the hypothesis that face perception is more holistic than house perception and house perception is more holistic than word perception. Figure 10 shows the mask effect for the three types of stimuli.

A planned comparison was carried out to test the prediction that whole masks are more disruptive than part masks and that this difference will be greatest for face perception, intermediate for house perception, and smallest for word perception. The corresponding weights for the whole and part upright face masks, whole and part house masks, and whole and part word masks, derived from the mean ratios of Experiment 2 with the

assumption that houses would be intermediate between faces and words, were $-.567$, $.567$, $-.333$, $.333$, $-.100$, and $.100$, respectively, yielding a value of $F(1, 70) = 15.82$, $p < .0005$.

A repeated measures analysis of variance was conducted on participants' number correct performance in each of the conditions of interest, and the following crossed variables were used: stimulus type (word, house, or face), mask type (part or whole), and response type (same or different). There was a significant effect of stimulus type, with highest accuracy for houses (84.1%), followed by words (78.6%) and faces (76.7%), $F(2, 35) = 13.29$, $p < .0001$. There was also a significant effect of mask type, with slightly better performance with part masks than whole masks (80.5% vs. 79.1% correct), $F(1, 35) = 7.10$, $p < .02$. Overall, performance on *different* pairs was more accurate than performance on *same* pairs (81.5% vs. 78.1% correct), $F(1, 35) = 5.32$, $p < .05$. The interaction of interest, between stimulus type and mask type, was significant, $F(2, 70) = 6.77$, $p < .005$. There was also a significant interaction between stimulus type and response type, with *same* trials less accurate than *different* trials for words (70.3% vs. 86.9% correct) and *same* trials more accurate for both houses (86.9% vs. 81.3% correct) and faces (77.2% vs. 76.3% correct), $F(2, 70) = 33.10$, $p <$

Table 5

Face, House, and Word Matching in Experiment 4 With Part or Whole Masks: Same or Different Stimuli

Mask type	Faces		Houses		Words	
	Same	Different	Same	Different	Same	Different
		Percentage correct				
Part	78.5	78.6	87.4	82.5	70.2	85.7
Whole	75.9	74.0	86.3	80.1	70.4	88.1
		Response time (ms)				
Part	1,207.0	1,106.8	1,187.9	1,092.4	1,105.0	1,199.9
Whole	1,190.7	1,155.3	1,208.5	1,103.3	1,173.4	1,245.7

494 FARAH, WILSON, DRAIN, AND TANAKA

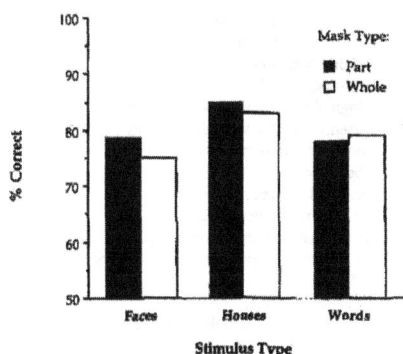

Figure 9. Percentage correct face, house, and word matching in Experiment 4 with whole and part masks.

.0001. No other effects were significant ($ps > .1$ in all cases). As usual, separate analyses of variance were performed to assess the simple effects of mask type on each type of stimulus. Both face and house perception were significantly affected by mask type, $F(1, 35) = 12.11, p < .002$, and $F(1, 35) = 4.56, p < .05$, respectively, but word perception was not ($p > .1$).

The data from just the house and face conditions were also analyzed separately to allow a direct comparison between the effects of part and whole masking on faces and on another type of concrete object in a normal orientation. A planned comparison was carried out with the following weights for part and whole masked faces and houses, respectively: $.67, -.67, .33,$ and $-.33$. This yielded $F(1, 35) = 29.83, p < .0001$. A repeated measures analysis of variance was also carried out, revealing significant effects of stimulus type, $F(1, 35) = 34.76, p < .0001$, and mask type, $F(1, 35) = 11.86, = p = .002$. There was a borderline significant effect of response type, $F(1, 35) = 3.29, p = .08$. Finally, the interaction between stimulus type and mask was also of borderline significance, $F(2, 35) = 3.15, p = .08$. No other effects were significant ($ps > .1$ in all cases).

Response times were analyzed as before. Initially, a planned comparison on the six relevant means was carried out, as with the accuracy data from this experiment, $F(2, 70) = 2.30, p > .1$. A repeated measures analysis of variance was also carried out, with the same variables used in the analysis of accuracy data. There was a significant effect of mask type, part masks allowing faster responses than whole masks (1,150 vs. 1,179 ms), $F(1, 35) = 5.15, p < .05$. There was also a significant interaction between stimulus type and response type, with *same* responses faster than *different* responses for words (1,139 vs. 1,223 ms) and the opposite for both faces (1,199 vs. 1,131 ms) and houses (1,198 vs. 1,098 ms), $F(2, 70) = 11.02, p < .0001$. No other effects were significant ($ps > .1$ in all cases). Separate analyses of variance revealed no significant effects of mask type for face and house perception ($ps > .1$ in both cases) and a borderline significant effect of mask type for word perception, $F(1, 35) = 3.71, p = .06$.

General Discussion

The present experiments add to a growing body of evidence in cognitive psychology suggesting that faces are represented holistically (i.e., with little or no part decomposition) relative to objects and patterns other than faces. Previous research has compared face representation with the representation of scrambled faces, inverted faces, and houses and assessed the role of parts versus holistic representation in both long-term and short-term memory for faces. It has also tested the generality of holistic face representation across developmental stages and showed that an individual with a neurological impairment in terms of face recognition did not benefit from the opportunity to represent faces holistically. Finally, previous research has also obtained an inversion effect with dot patterns, but only if they were initially encoded holistically, and shown that the face inversion effect can be eliminated for face stimuli if the faces were initially encoded in terms of separate parts. In sum, memory for faces has been shown to be holistic in the context of a number of different experimental paradigms and relative to a number of different comparison stimuli.

In the present studies, we showed that faces are represented more holistically than other stimuli in immediate perceptual memory and during perception. Comparison stimuli included inverted faces, words, and houses. In the remainder of this article, we discuss the relation of our hypothesis to previous claims about face representation and to perspectives on face representation derived from neurophysiology and computational vision. Also, we consider the question of how uniquely "special" is face representation.

Holistic Face Representation and Earlier Claims

As we noted earlier, our hypothesis has much in common with earlier ones about face representation, in that it gives special importance to the overall structure or gestalt of the face relative to local features. However, each of the hypotheses is reasonably

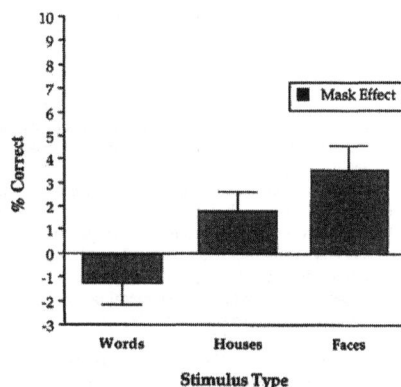

Figure 10. Effect of part versus whole masking on accuracy of matching faces, houses, and words in Experiment 4.

distinct in terms of the way in which information about overall structure is represented. In the case of our hypothesis, faces are represented holistically, which we define as meaning without explicitly representing (or relying to a lesser degree on explicit representations of) the local features themselves. In the framework of structural descriptions, we hypothesize that there is relatively little part decomposition for faces relative to other objects or patterns.

An undecomposed representation is essentially a template. In measuring the fit of a stimulus to a template representation, it is the overall best fit that is important rather than some summation of the fits of particular regions of the input pattern with explicitly defined parts of the internal representation. This is not to say that different regions of the template might not be differentially weighted in computing fit; rather, their heavier contribution to the fit equation is not a function of part identity per se but spatial location within the overall pattern. Consistent with this, Tanaka and Farah (1993) found that the eye region was more heavily weighted than others in people's judgments of facial identity only when the face was upright and intact and that eyes per se showed no special weighting in the inverted and scrambled faces conditions.

How does this hypothesis differ from earlier claims, and how well does it account for the data marshalled in support of earlier claims? The contrast between the idea of holistic face representation and the parallel processing hypothesis of the 1970s resides in the role of part-based representation: Whereas part-based representation is relegated to a lesser or possibly even nonexistent role according to the holistic face perception hypothesis, the parallel processing hypothesis maintains that the representation of faces is as part based as the representation of other objects but that these psychologically real parts are processed in parallel rather than serially. As for the evidence showing serial processing of parts, it is possible that this results from a strategy specific to the experimental task, as Bradshaw and Wallace (1971) themselves suggested.

The claim put forth by Rhodes (1988), that configurational features are important in face representation, differs more subtly from our hypothesis. Representations that include configurational features such as distances between first order features will behave in many ways like holistic face representations, in that a holistic representation of a face with particular features in a particular spatial arrangement will contain the information coded in the configurational feature for that spatial arrangement. However, the difference is that the features, first order and configurational, are psychologically real or explicit according to Rhodes's hypothesis, whereas in ours they are not. One could, of course, extract such features from a holistic representation, and in this sense holistic representations implicitly contain both first order and configurational features. To make an analogy with early vision, the retinal image implicitly contains information about edges without explicitly representing them. The finding that shared first and second order features are predictive of participants' similarity ratings does not imply that participants explicitly represent them. To continue the analogy, similarity, as measured by overlap of retinal images, will be predicted by similar edge maps. Therefore, the results of Rhodes (1988) are not inconsistent with holistic face representation.

Sergent's (1984) claim that the features of faces are not processed independently is essentially a claim about the stimulus properties of faces that are predictive of human sorting and similarity-rating behavior, following Garner's (1974) taxonomy of stimulus properties. Her conclusion puts constraints on possible psychological representations but is not itself a specific claim about representation. As with the Rhodes (1988) findings, the holistic representation hypothesis accommodates these findings naturally, because facial features are not hypothesized to be independent units of representation and would therefore not be expected to combine independently.

Like the holistic representation hypothesis, the spatial frequency hypothesis is an explicit claim about the representations underlying face recognition. The two hypotheses are also similar in that the spatial frequency spectrum of a pattern is not decomposed in terms of the spatially delimited parts of the pattern (e.g., eyes and nose) but is matched with other candidate patterns holistically. However, the hypotheses differ in that the spatial frequency hypothesis, as put forth by Harmon (1973) and Ginsburg (1978), emphasizes the contributions of low spatial frequencies to face perception, whereas the holistic representation hypothesis makes no distinction between different frequency bands in face recognition. The latter hypothesis is therefore able to accommodate (although it does not predict) the finding that disconfirmed the spatial frequency hypothesis, that different ranges of spatial frequency are critical to face perception in different task contexts.

The idea that face representation involves parts but that the derivation of part-based representations is sensitive to top-down support from whole representations, as in the word superiority effect, is similar to the holistic representation hypothesis in its emphasis on the whole-level representation. One point of difference from our hypothesis is the assumption that part-level representations are necessarily computed during face perception and recognition. A more critical difference is that word superiority and face superiority effects are limited to threshold viewing conditions (Homa, Haver, & Schwartz, 1976; Mermelstein, Banks, & Prinzmetal, 1979) and do not manifest themselves in the full range of tasks in which holistic face representation has been found.

In sum, although there is considerable similarity and overlap between the predictions of earlier hypotheses and the holistic face representation hypothesis, the hypotheses themselves are distinct. The holistic face perception hypothesis is consistent with the findings of earlier research and, in addition, has generated a number of new predictions about memory for faces and perception of faces that have been confirmed in experiments reviewed and reported here.

Can the results of our experiments be accounted for by the earlier hypotheses? Given that most of the hypotheses include explicit, psychologically real representations of parts (parallel processing, first order and configurational features, nonindependently processed features, and even the second order relational hypothesis of Diamond & Carey, 1986, for which no independent empirical support exists), they cannot easily account for the findings reported here: specifically, participants' disproportionately poor ability to compare parts within whole faces in immediate visual memory and their disproportionately good ability to perceive a face that has been masked by face parts. The spatial frequency hypothesis, which does not include explicit representations of parts, can account for these findings. However, as noted earlier, it has suffered direct disconfirmation in research using filtered face images.

Face Recognition by Monkeys and Machines: Converging Evidence

A relatively new source of evidence on face representation is single cell recordings in monkey temporal cortex (see Desimone, 1991, for a review). Some neurons in this area respond selectively to faces, relative to other patterns, and some even respond differentially to different faces. Moreover, this selectivity in responding is maintained over changes in size, position, and contrast, consistent with a primary role for these cells in face recognition. A discrepant finding concerns the effect of lesions to the superior temporal sulcus, which did not abolish the ability of monkeys to recognize faces despite the high concentration of face-selective cells in this area (Heywood & Cowey, 1993). However, the face-selective cells in this particular region of temporal cortex are tuned more sharply to emotional expression than facial identity, whereas the cells in more inferior areas of temporal cortex are tuned more sharply for identity than expression (Hasselmo, Rolls, & Baylis, 1989). It is therefore reasonable to suppose that the inferior temporal cortex is indeed the locus of face recognition in monkeys. Given the high degree of similarity between the human and monkey visual systems, the so-called "face cells" of monkeys may provide additional clues to the nature of human face recognition.

The holistic face representation hypothesis predicts that face cells should function essentially as templates relative to a normalized stimulus pattern. That is, scrambling the features of a face should not just reduce a cell's response but should abolish it, even though there remains partial similarity between the intact and the scrambled face at the level of features. In contrast, deleting a feature should not have a dramatic effect on the cell's response, because only one region of the pattern has been changed. Both of these predictions are borne out by recordings from face cells (Desimone, Albright, Gross, & Bruce, 1984).

Evidence concerning a role for part representations in the face perception of monkeys has been discussed by Perrett, Mistlin, and Chitty (1987), who pointed out that the temporal cortex contains cells responsive to eyes and mouths as well as faces. They suggested that these facial feature cells may provide the input to face cells, so that face representations are built up from representations of face parts. Although it is indeed tempting to conjecture that the part cells provide input to the face cells, two considerations weigh in favor of caution before accepting this interpretation of the part cells. First, Desimone (1991) has pointed out that the selectivity of the part cells for face parts per se has been less well established than the selectivity of face cells for faces. That is, the possibility remains that these cells may represent more elementary visual attributes such as dark spots surrounded by bits of white rather than eyes. Second, only eye and mouth cells have been reported, and these parts of the face convey expressions that are important social cues for primates. In the absence of nose cells, chin cells, and so forth, it seems more likely that the eye and mouth cells form part of a system for nonverbal communication rather than facial identity recognition. The hypothesis that the part cells are the input to

the face cells could be tested by analysis of response latencies. Although the finding that the earliest part responses occurred earlier than the earliest face responses would be ambiguous, the reverse finding would decisively rule out the hierarchical hypothesis.

Several computer systems have been developed for face recognition, and the types of representations they use may provide insights into the computational pressures toward different ways of representing faces. Although early systems used representations in which facial features were explicitly represented for recognition (e.g., Goldstein, Harmon, & Lesk, 1972; Kanade, 1977), Yuille (1991) pointed out that such representations are extremely difficult to extract from a gray scale image of a face. His "deformable template" approach uses facial features only as anchor points at which the image and stored template are brought into register; the overall fit is what determines recognition.

Turk and Pentland (1991) sought an efficient representation for faces on which to base an automatic face recognition system. Using principal-components analysis of gray scale images of faces, they found that a population code of whole faces, rather than facial features, best captured the differences among faces in a concise format. In their system of "eigenfaces," a given face is represented by weights denoting the overall similarity of the face to an ensemble of other whole faces. A related way of identifying efficient codes for representing patterns is by forcing an artificial neural network to represent patterns using limited numbers of neuronlike units and analyzing what the individual units come to represent. Such networks have been trained to classify gray scale images of faces by identity and expression (Fleming & Cottrell, 1990) as well as by sex (Golomb, Lawrence, & Sejnowski, 1991). In all of these cases, the units in the networks' hidden layer, which represent the face in a compressed form, generally correspond to whole faces rather than facial features.

In sum, recent work in computational vision has favored holistic representations of faces. It would be of great interest to compare the performance of a given system with faces and with some large and relatively homogeneous-appearing set of nonface objects. Would "eigenchair" representations be more efficient than representations based on a set of "eigenseats," "eigenlegs," and so on? Such a comparison could potentially illuminate the computational basis for holistic face representations.

Holistic Representation: Unique to Faces?

We began this article with the assertion that face recognition is "special" and went on to pose the question of how it is special, in terms of the shape representations used in recognition. There are two possible interpretations of the word *special* in this context. Faces could be special in degree or special in kind. In closing, we attempt to address the question of whether face recognition is the extreme end of a continuum of part-based to more holistic representation or whether holistic representation is confined, categorically, to faces. The evidence currently at hand does not allow a decisive answer to this question. Nevertheless, some clues are available.

The comparison among faces, houses, and words in Experiment 4 suggests that houses are intermediate between faces and words in their susceptibility to part masks. This finding is consistent with the idea of a continuum of representation, with faces the most holistic, words the most part based, and objects such as houses intermediate. We predicted this pattern of results on the basis of previously observed patterns of association and dissociation among visual recognition impairments after brain damage. Whereas face, object, and word recognition are all pairwise doubly dissociable after brain damage (i.e., for any two of these abilities, patients exist for whom one is impaired and the other preserved), it is unclear whether all three-way combinations of ability and deficit can occur. In a 1991 review of 99 published cases, Farah found no unambiguous cases of intact object recognition with impaired face and word recognition or of impaired object recognition with intact face and word recognition (see Rumiati, Humphreys, Riddoch, & Bateman, 1994, and Farah, 1997, for an updated discussion). What type of underlying organization would impose these constraints on patterns of co-occurrence among visual recognition impairments?

The simplest solution involves two underlying representational abilities, one that is essential for face recognition, useful for object recognition, and not used for word recognition and another that is essential for word recognition, useful for object recognition, and not used for face recognition. The work of Johnston and McClelland (1980) with normal participants, discussed earlier, suggests that word recognition requires the construction of a part-based (specifically, letter-based) representation. Work with an alexic patient suggests that a problem underlying selective impairments in visual word recognition is an impairment in representing multiple parts, be they letters in a word or complex nonorthographic stimuli (Farah & Wallace, 1991). Taking these findings together with the evidence of holistic face representation, a plausible inference is that the two representational abilities uncovered in the analysis of co-occurrence correspond to holistic and part-based representation. More specifically, the ability to represent complex wholes with little or no part decomposition may be the ability required for face recognition, useful for object recognition, and not needed for word recognition, and the ability to represent a number of distinct parts may be the ability required for word recognition, useful for object recognition, and not needed for face recognition. This interpretation of the data suggests that faces are special in degree, not in kind. Specifically, it suggests that they constitute an extreme case of stimuli that rely on holistic shape representation but are not necessarily discontinuous from other types of objects in their reliance on holistic representation.

References

Baylis, G. C., Rolls, E. T., & Leonard, C. M. (1985). Selectivity between faces in the responses of a population of neurons in the cortex in the superior temporal sulcus of the monkey. *Brain Research, 342,* 91–102.

Biederman, I. (1987). Recognition-by-components: A theory of human image understanding. *Psychological Review, 94,* 115–147.

Bower, G. H., & Glass, A. L. (1976). Structural units and the reintegrative power of picture fragments. *Journal of Experimental Psychology, 2,* 456–466.

Bradshaw, J. L., & Wallace, G. (1971). Models for the processing and identification of faces. *Perception & Psychophysics, 9,* 443–448.

Bruce, V. (1988). *Recognizing faces.* Hove, England: Erlbaum.

Desimone, R. (1991). Face-selective cells in the temporal cortex of monkeys. *Journal of Cognitive Neuroscience, 3,* 1–8.

Desimone, R., Albright, T. D., Gross, C. D., & Bruce, C. (1984). Stimulus-selective responses of inferior temporal neurons in the macaque. *Journal of Neuroscience, 4,* 2051–2062.

Diamond, R., & Carey, S. (1986). Why faces are and are not special: An effect of expertise. *Journal of Experimental Psychology: General, 115,* 107–117.

Farah, M. J. (1990). *Visual agnosia: Disorders of object recognition and what they tell us about normal vision.* Cambridge, MA: MIT Press/Bradford Books.

Farah, M. J. (1991). Patterns of co-occurrence among the associative agnosias: Implications for visual object representation. *Cognitive Neuropsychology, 8,* 1–19.

Farah, M. J. (1996). Is face recognition 'special'? Evidence from neuropsychology. *Behavioral Brain Research, 76,* 181–189.

Farah, M. J. (1997). Distinguishing perceptual and semantic impairments affecting visual object recognition. *Visual Cognition, 4,* 199–206.

Farah, M. J., Klein, K. L., & Levinson, K. L. (1995). Face perception and within-category discrimination in prosopagnosia. *Neuropsychologia, 33,* 661–674.

Farah, M. J., Tanaka, J. N., & Drain, M. (1995). What causes the face inversion effect. *Journal of Experimental Psychology: Human Perception and Performance, 21,* 628–634.

Farah, M. J., & Wallace, M. A. (1991). Pure alexia as a visual impairment: A reconsideration. *Cognitive Neuropsychology, 8,* 313–334.

Fleming, M., & Cottrell, G. W. (1990). Categorization of faces using unsupervised feature extraction. *Proceedings of IJCNN-90, 2,* 65–70.

Garner, W. R. (1974). *The processing of information and structure.* Potomac, MD: Erlbaum.

Ginsburg, A. (1978). *Visual information processing based on spatial filters constrained by biological data.* Unpublished doctoral dissertation, Cambridge University, Cambridge, England.

Goldstein, A. J., Harmon, J. D., & Lesk, A. B. (1972). Identification of human faces. *Proceedings of the IEEE, 59,* 748–760.

Golomb, B. A., Lawrence, D. T., & Sejnowski, T. J. (1991). *SexNet: A neural network identifies sex from human faces.* San Mateo, CA: Morgan Kaufmann.

Harmon, L. D. (1973). The recognition of faces. *Scientific American, 227,* 71–82.

Hasselmo, M. E., Rolls, E. T., & Baylis, G. C. (1989). The role of expression and identity in the face-selective responses of neurons in the temporal visual cortex of the monkey. *Behavioral Brain Research, 32,* 203–218.

Heywood, C. A., & Cowey, A. (1993). The role of "face-cell" area in the discrimination and recognition of faces by monkeys. *Philosophical Transactions of the Royal Society of London, Series B: Biological Sciences, 335,* 31–38.

Hoffman, D. D., & Richards, W. (1985). The parts of recognition. *Cognition, 18,* 65–96.

Homa, D., Haver, B., & Schwartz, T. (1976). Perceptibility of schematic face stimuli: Evidence for a perceptual Gestalt. *Memory & Cognition, 4,* 176–185.

Johnson, M. H., Dziurawiec, S., Ellis, H. D., & Morton, J. (1991). Newborns' preferential tracking of face-like stimuli and its subsequent decline. *Cognition, 40,* 1–19.

Johnston, J. C., & McClelland, J. C. (1980). Experimental tests of a hierarchical model of word identification. *Journal of Verbal Learning and Verbal Behavior, 19,* 503–524.

Kanade, T. (1977). *Computer recognition of human faces.* Basel, Switzerland: Birkhauser Verlag.

Marr, D. (1982). *Vision.* San Francisco: Freeman.

498 FARAH, WILSON, DRAIN, AND TANAKA

Matthews, M. L. (1978). Discrimination of identikit construction of faces: Evidence for a dual processing strategy. *Perception & Psychophysics, 23,* 153–161.

Mermelstein, R., Banks, W., & Prinzmetal, W. (1979). Figural goodness effects in perception and memory. *Perception & Psychophysics, 26,* 472–480.

Moscovitch, M., Winocur, G., & Behrmann, M. (1997). What is special about face recognition? Nineteen experiments on a person with visual object agnosia and dyslexia but normal face recognition. *Journal of Cognitive Neuroscience, 9,* 555–604.

Palmer, S. E. (1975). The effects of contextual scenes on the identification of objects. *Memory & Cognition, 3,* 519–526.

Palmer, S. E. (1977). Hierarchical structure in perceptual representation. *Cognitive Psychology, 9,* 441–474.

Perrett, D. I., Mistlin, A. J., & Chitty, A. J. (1987). Visual neurones responsive to faces. *Trends in Neuroscience, 10,* 358–364.

Reed, S. K. (1974). Structural descriptions and the limitations of visual images. *Memory & Cognition, 2,* 329–336.

Reicher, B. M. (1969). Perceptual recognition as a function of meaningfulness of stimulus material. *Journal of Experimenal Psychology, 81,* 275–280.

Rhodes, G. (1988). Looking at faces: First-order and second-order features as determinates of facial appearance. *Perception, 17,* 43–63.

Rumiati, R. I., Humphreys, G. W., Riddoch, M. J., & Bateman, A. (1994). Visual object recognition without prosopagnosia or alexia: Evidence for hierarchical theories of object recognition. *Visual Cognition, 1,* 181–225.

Sergent, J. (1984). An investigation into component and configural processes underlying face perception. *British Journal of Psychology, 75,* 221–242.

Smith, E. E., & Nielsen, G. D. (1970). Representations and retrieval processes in short-term memory: Recognition and recall of faces. *Journal of Experimental Psychology, 85,* 397–405.

Sternberg, S. (1969). The discovery of processing stages: Extensions of Donders' method. *Acta Psychologica, 30,* 276–315.

Tanaka, J. W., & Farah, M. J. (1991). Second-order relational properties and the inversion effect: Testing a theory of face perception. *Perception & Psychophysics, 50,* 367–372.

Tanaka, J. W., & Farah, M. J. (1993). Parts and wholes in face recognition. *Quarterly Journal of Experimental Psychology, 46,* 225–245.

Tanaka, J. W., Kay, J. B., Grinnell, E., & Stansfield, B. (in press). Face recognition in young children: When the whole is greater than the sum of its parts. *Visual Cognition.*

Tanaka, J. W., & Sengco, J. A. (1997). Features and their configuration in face recognition. *Memory & Cognition, 25,* 583–592.

Turk, M., & Pentland, A. (1991). Eigenfaces for recognition. *Journal of Cognitive Neuroscience, 3,* 71–86.

Valentine, T. (1988). Upside-down faces: A review of the effects of inversion upon face recognition. *British Journal of Psychology, 79,* 471–491.

Wheeler, D. D. (1970). Processes in word recognition. *Cognitive Psychology, 1,* 59–85.

Yuille, A. L. (1991). Deformable templates for face recognition. *Journal of Cognitive Neuroscience, 3,* 59–70.

Appendix

Examples of Whole and Part Masks for Word Stimuli

Whole masks	Part masks
brag	arbg
rank	nkar
baby	abyb
king	nikg
bark	abkr
gang	ngag
ring	gnri
wing	nigw
wink	wkni

Received March 24, 1995
Revision received November 26, 1997
Accepted December 26, 1997 ■

[15]

The Reviewing of Object Files: Object-Specific Integration of Information

DANIEL KAHNEMAN AND ANNE TREISMAN

University of California, Berkeley

AND

BRIAN J. GIBBS

Stanford University

A series of experiments explored a form of object-specific priming. In all experiments a preview field containing two or more letters is followed by a target letter that is to be named. The displays are designed to produce a perceptual interpretation of the target as a new state of an object that previously contained one of the primes. The link is produced in different experiments by a shared location, by a shared relative position in a moving pattern, or by successive appearance in the same moving frame. An object-specific advantage is consistently observed: naming is facilitated by a preview of the target, if (and in some cases only if) the two appearances are linked to the same object. The amount and the object specificity of the preview benefit are not affected by extending the preview duration to 1 s, or by extending the temporal gap between fields to 590 ms. The results are interpreted in terms of a reviewing process, which is triggered by the appearance of the target and retrieves just one of the previewed items. In the absence of an object link, the reviewing item is selected at random. We develop the concept of an object file as a temporary episodic representation, within which successive states of an object are linked and integrated.

INTRODUCTION

This paper brings together techniques and ideas from two fields that are traditionally separate: (1) the study of object perception and of the con-

This research was supported partly by grants from the Canadian Natural Sciences and Engineering Research Council to Daniel Kahneman and to Anne Treisman, and partly by the Air Force Office of Scientific Research, Air Force Systems Command, USAF, under Grant AFOSR 88-0206 to Daniel Kahneman and Grant AFOSR 87-0125 to Anne Treisman. The manuscript is submitted for publication with the understanding that the U.S. Government is authorized to reproduce and distribute reprints for governmental purposes, notwithstanding any copyright notation thereon. We are grateful to Roger Browse, Michael Satterfield, and Ephram Cohen for the development of our software, to Diane Chajczyk, Sharon Sato, and Amy Hayes for their help in programming and running the experiments, to Irvin Rock for helpful comments, to Sherlyn Jimenez, Kathleen Miszuk, and Julia Simovsky for help in preparing the manuscript, and to Marcia Grabowecky for making the figures. Requests for reprints should be addressed to Daniel Kahneman, Department of Psychology, University of California, Berkeley, CA 94720.

tinuity of object identity through change and motion; and (2) the study of preview or priming effects, where the identification of a stimulus is facilitated if it matches a prime previously seen in the same context. We describe an initial set of studies of an *object-specific preview effect,* so called because the effect of a preview depends on whether the target and the prime are both seen as states of the same perceived object. Two theoretical ideas guided the research: a belief that perceptual objects are essential units of information processing, and the notion that the context within which a stimulus is processed is frequently evoked by the stimulus itself.

Some time ago we proposed an account of object perception as the process of setting up and utilizing temporary "episodic" representations of real world objects, which we call *object files* (Kahneman & Treisman, 1984). These are separate from the representations stored in a long-term recognition network, which are used in identifying and classifying objects. Several lines of evidence motivate this theoretical separation of object files or tokens from the stored types used to label their identity. One is the primacy of objects in determining the allocation of attention. Attention to any one property of an object causes even irrelevant properties of that object to be attended, as in the familiar Stroop effect. Moreover, the division of attention between relevant attributes is facilitated if the attributes belong to the same object (Treisman, Kahneman, & Burkell, 1983). The finding of an object-specific matching effect is a natural extension of these observations: we show that the focusing of attention on a target object not only enhances the salience of all its current properties—it also selectively reactivates the recent history of that object.

The maintenance of the perceived continuity of objects as they move, change, or momentarily disappear requires operations that relate the current state of the object to its prior history. When an object appears in a complex scene, a correspondence process attempts to match it to a particular object seen in the immediately preceding moments. We use the term *reviewing* to refer to the process in which a current target item evokes an item previewed in an earlier visual field. Reviewing facilitates recognition when the current and previous states of the object match, hampers it otherwise.

The next sections develop the theoretical notions of object file and reviewing. We then describe three experimental situations in which object-specific preview effects are observed, and report initial results. The paper concludes with a brief review of related research and theoretical ideas in the recent literature.

Object Files, Movement, and Change

Imagine watching a strange man approaching down the street. As he reaches you and stops to greet you he suddenly becomes recognizable as a familiar friend whom you had not expected to meet in this context. Throughout the episode, there was no doubt that a single individual was present; he preserved his unity (in the sense that he remained the *same* individual), although neither his retinal size, his shape, nor his mental label remained constant. Perception appears to define objects more by spatiotemporal constraints than by their sensory properties or by their labeled identity. The perceptual system is also capable of restoring continuity that has been briefly broken in the stream of sensory inputs. The man who reappears after walking behind a car will normally be treated as the same individual who was seen to disappear, provided that the disappearance was short and that the parameters of motion remain more or less constant.

Discontinuities of sensory input are also produced by movements of the observer—most obviously by movements of the eyes. The issue of object identity and continuity arises at every saccade. When the sensory stimuli change abruptly because of an eye or body movement, the perceptual system faces the task of matching each old object to its immediate history. People's unawareness of their saccades is a testimony to the success with which this task of restoring continuity is performed.

The experienced continuity of a changing object highlights the distinction between two senses of the term "identity." In one sense, the identity of an object is the label conferred on it when it is identified. In that sense, of course, the approaching man does not have the same identity when recognized as a friend as he had when he was assumed to be a stranger. In the other sense of the term, his identity and perceived continuity are precisely what he retains even as his properties and the label or name we give him vary. The ascription of continuity through change is essential to this second notion of identity.

The distinction between the two meanings of identity is related to a contrast between two views of perception (Kahneman & Treisman, 1984). In one view, perception is equated to recognition or identification. A stimulus is said to be perceived when it activates a set of nodes in long-term memory that represent its parts, properties, and categories of membership. (Whether this representation uses distributed or localized codes, and whether it conforms to symbolic or connectionist principles, is largely irrelevant to our discussion). We have called this view the "*display-board model*" of perception; perceptual experience is seen as depending on a succession of states of activation of units in semantic memory—rather like the display board used in some offices to identify the employees currently at work. The display-board model does not provide a natural way of representing the maintained perceptual identity of an object that is successively assigned different labels.

The object-centered approach that will be developed here emphasizes the distinction between identifying and seeing. We adopt the common notion that the visual field is parsed into perceptual objects and a relatively undifferentiated perceptual ground. We then assume that the main end product of perceptual processing of a stationary scene is a set of *object files*, each containing information about a particular object in the scene. Each object file is addressed by its location at a particular time, not by any feature or identifying label. It collects the sensory information that has so far been received about the object at that location. This information can be matched to stored descriptions to identify or classify the object, but it need not be. We can normally see completely novel objects with little difficulty, without knowing what they are. When the sensory situation changes, the information in the files is updated, yielding the perceptual experience of changing or moving objects. A file is kept open so long as its object is in view, and may be discarded shortly thereafter. The system bridges over the discontinuities produced by temporary occlusion, or by saccades, assigning current information to preexisting files whenever possible.

Visual objects are hierarchically organized; a group of dancers can be a visual object, as can an individual dancer, or her right hand. At any instant one of these levels may be dominant in the parsing of the scene. Tentatively, we assume that object files are set up at the preferred level, which is determined by the controlled allocation of attention (LaBerge, 1983; Navon, 1977) or by the automatic effect of bottom-up constraints and grouping factors. We also assume that there is some limit to the number of object files that can be maintained at once, so that the focusing of attention at the lower level causes more of the scene to be pushed into the perceptual ground. Attention to a higher level also has its costs, because the resolution of information within an object file is limited. The file for a complex object will represent its parts and the relations among them, but we surmise that the representation of a part is sketchier than if this part had been allocated an object file of its own, and also that the representation of relations among parts is more detailed than relations among separate objects.

Explicit recognition occurs at the level at which object files are currently set up. To mediate recognition, the sensory description in the object file is compared to stored representations of known objects. If and when a match is found, the identification of the object is entered in the file, together with information predicting other characteristics, its likely behavior, and the responses it should appropriately evoke, both affective and cognitive. The system of episodic object tokens is distinct from the semantic network of nodes and connections that mediates recognition. The identity of a changing object is carried by the assignment of information about its successive states to the same temporary file, rather than by its name or by its properties. Two identical red squares in successive fields may be perceived as distinct objects if the spatial/temporal gap between them cannot be bridged, but the transformation of frog into prince is seen as a change in a single visual object.

Reviewing, Correspondence, and Apparent Motion

Whenever a change in visual input is detected, current information about changing or reappearing objects must be assigned to existing object files; if this fails, a new file must be set up. Three distinct operations are needed to provide perceptual continuity through change. (1) A *correspondence* operation determines, for each object in the terminal display, whether it is "new" or whether it is an object recently perceived, now at a different location (Ullman, 1979); (2) a *reviewing* process retrieves the characteristics of the initial object, now no longer in view; (3) an *impletion* process uses current and reviewed information to produce a percept of change or motion that links the two views (Shepard, 1984).

The phenomenon of apparent motion provides significant information about the functioning of object files. In the basic demonstration of apparent motion a single object is presented at t_0, removed, and eventually replaced at t_1 by a single object in another location. When the spatial and temporal intervals fall within a critical range the perceptual impression is that a single object moves smoothly from the original location to the terminal one. When the exposure of the first stimulus is brief (<130 ms) the object is perceived as moving as soon as it appears. The normal percept of a brief stationary appearance is suppressed in the context of motion.

A critical observation is that in the classroom demonstration of apparent motion the percept of an object moving from one position to another can only be constructed from two successive stationary stimuli *after* the information about the second stimulus is presented. There may be no way of anticipating where the motion will go, or indeed that there will be motion. The object presented in the second display must retrieve (review) a trace of the object in the preceding one. If a close match is found, simple object continuity is perceived. If a physically plausible displacement or transformation could result in a match, the relevant object file may be updated and the transformation may be seen to occur (Shepard, 1984; Warren, 1977). However, if the new stimulus is sufficiently different from all its predecessors, or if the change in location is incompatible with the time interval or with any previous trajectory, a new object file may be opened and the sudden appearance of a new object will be consciously experienced.

When more than one object is present, there is a problem of *correspon-*

dence to be solved before apparent motion can be seen (Ullman, 1979). It is of interest that the similarity of such attributes as shape or color carries relatively little weight in the correspondence process, which is dominated by spatiotemporal contiguity of low-frequency information (Kolers, 1972; but see Green, 1986, 1989). This fits our notion that object files are addressed primarily by spatiotemporal characteristics rather than by properties or labels. It is also important that the set of rules that governs the assignment of histories to current objects is carried out under constraints of coherence: Whenever possible, a one-to-one mapping is preferred, and an object is not necessarily assigned to its nearest neighbor in the previous scene. In the Ternus effect, the perceived direction of movement of several objects can be determined by the location of one newly appearing object, plus the constraint that each object must occupy a location in both displays and be seen in coherent motion between them (Ternus, 1938).

Successive stimuli can be assigned to the same object file even when they are separated by an ISI and a spatial gap that exceed the range of apparent motion. The best example is the amodal completion observed by Michotte in what he called the "tunnel effect." If an object is seen to disappear (with gradual occlusion) and then to reappear some distance away (with gradual disocclusion) subjects report a compelling impression that a single object disappeared into a tunnel or behind a wall, traveled invisibly in the interval, and finally reappeared at the other end. Here again, the perceptual interpretation that bridges the gap between disappearance and reappearance can only be generated after the second event.

The Reviewing Paradigm

The present experiments explore a new paradigm to throw light on the temporal integration of information about objects that move or change. We use evidence of facilitation in naming latency to a repeated letter as a way to investigate how newly appearing objects are matched to possible past appearances within continuing object files.

The general features of the paradigm are the following. A typical experiment consists of two successive displays, respectively labeled the preview field and the target field. The preview field contains two or more different letters. The target field contains a single letter, which is to be named as quickly as possible. The successive displays for several variants of the paradigm are illustrated in Figs. 1–3. In each case, the target is selectively connected to one of the items in the preview field, because they are successively shown in the same place (Fig. 1; Studies 1 and 2), because the target is seen to arrive in apparent motion from the position of one of the preview letters (Fig. 2; Study 3), or because the target is presented in a frame which moved from another location in which it had originally contained one of the preview letters (Fig. 3; Studies 4–7). On

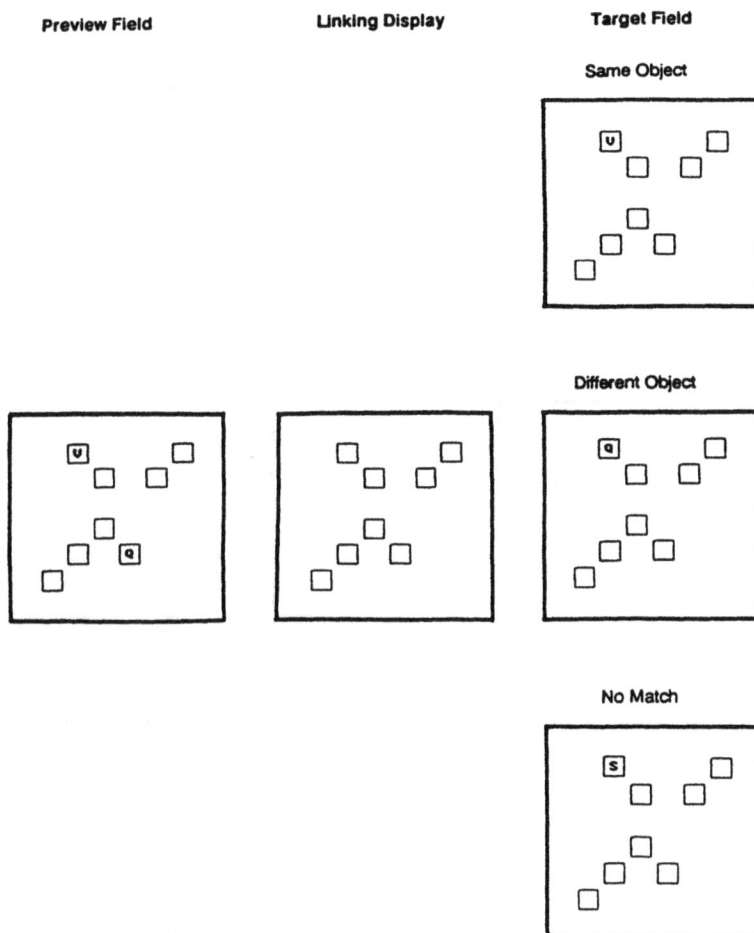

FIG. 1. Examples of displays used in Experiment 1 to test objective-specific reviewing effects. The three headings (Preview Field, Linking Display, and Target Field) show three successive displays, shown at different time intervals. The three vertically aligned displays under Target Field in each case show examples illustrating the three main relations between the previous field and the target field.

some trials, the target letter matches one of the items in the preview field. Three experimental conditions are defined as follows:

Same object (SO)—the target letter matches the preview letter seen as belonging to the same object (or in Experiment 3 as being the same object).

Different object (DO)—the target matches the preview letter seen as belonging to (or being) another object.

No match (NM)—the target matches neither of the preview letters.

Preview Field   Linking Display   Target Field

Same Object

Different Object

No Match

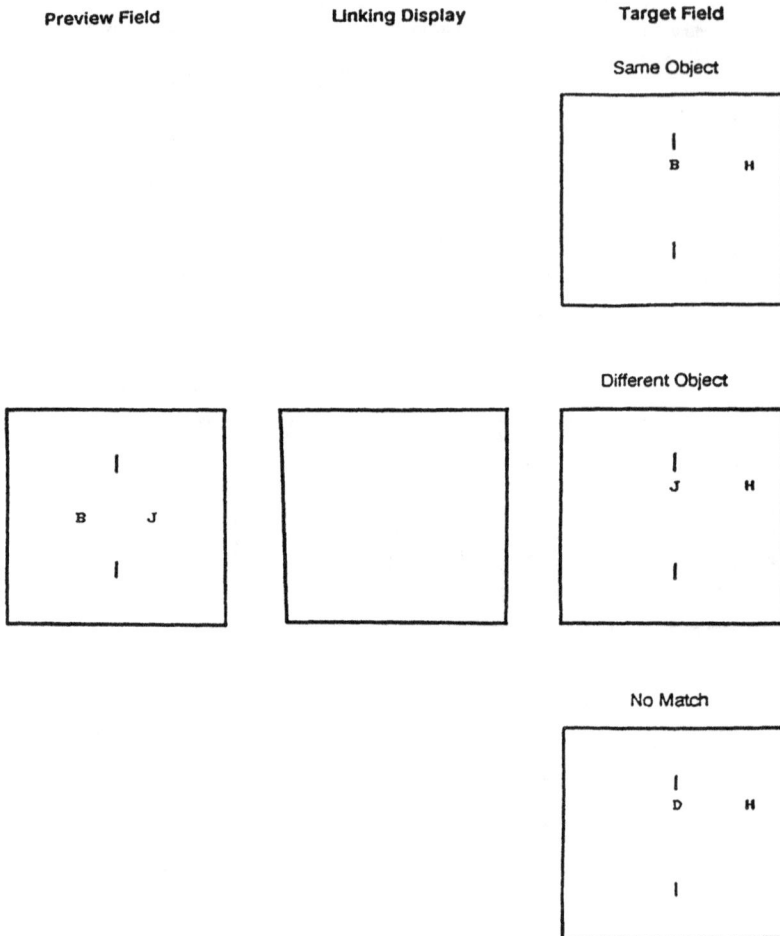

FIG. 2. Examples of displays used in Experiment 3 with apparent motion.

The comparisons of naming latencies in the three conditions yield several useful indices:

The *same-object preview effect* is the difference between naming times in the SO and NM conditions.

The *nonspecific preview effect* is the difference between the DO and NM conditions.

The *object-specific preview advantage* is the difference between the SO and DO conditions.

For most statistical analyses we focus on the last two indices (the first is their sum). The standard result that defines object-specific preview effects is that the latencies are quite similar in conditions DO and NM, and significantly faster in condition SO.

REVIEWING OBJECT FILES 183

Preview Field   Linking Display   Target Field

Same Object

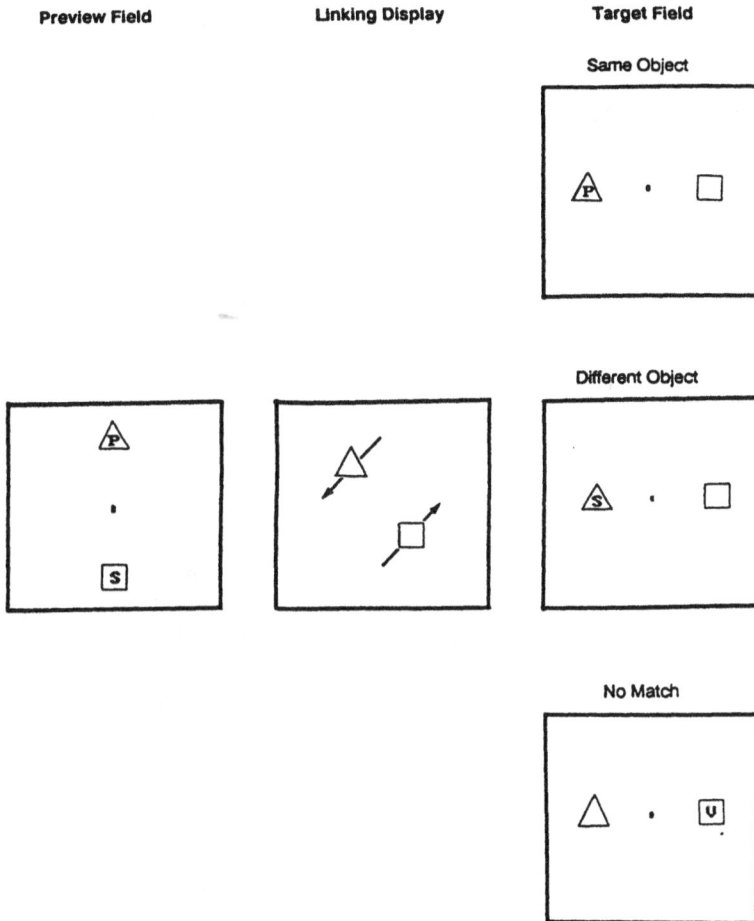

Different Object

No Match

FIG. 3. Examples of displays used in Experiment 4 with real motion in the linking display.

We speak of preview effects rather than priming effects, because the label "priming" can be misleading in several ways. It suggests a beneficial effect of the presentation of a first stimulus on the processing of a subsequent one; but in fact a match between successive stimuli can produce interference as well as facilitation. Furthermore, the facilitation or interference are not necessarily produced by an activation process that is instigated by the "prime" and continues during the ISI between this stimulus and the subsequent target. Matching effects can be produced by the process we call reviewing, a retrieval process triggered by the target, which picks out the trace of a particular past episode (Glucksberg, Kreuz, & Rho, 1986; Kirsner, Dunn, & Standen, 1987; Koriat & Norman, 1988, 1989). The reviewing process described in this paper appears to involve the retrieval by a current stimulus of a plausible prior instantiation, which speeds up or impedes the identification of the current stimulus and the response to it. We test the assumption that, when a match is found within the same single object file, perception of the new stimulus will be faster than when a new object file must be created, or a radical and physically implausible change made to a previously existing file. Matching a previously perceived frog to the prince currently in view may require a few extra milliseconds.

We now turn to a description of a set of experiments using the reviewing paradigm. The experiments were conducted over a period of several years, at the University of British Columbia and at the University of California. Several of the seven studies described below bring together for expository purposes a number of separate experiments, which were most often planned and executed sequentially, and sometimes vary slightly in procedural details.

STUDY 1: REVIEWING WITH STATIONARY DISPLAYS

This study had three goals: the first was to look for object specificity in the letter matching benefit across two displays separated by a temporal interval. (Later experiments add spatial to temporal separation, using moving rather than stationary objects). The second aim was to distinguish the reviewing of object files from node priming, by varying the number of letter tokens independently of the number of letter types. The object-reviewing effect was expected to vary inversely with the number of objects presented (i.e., the number of letter tokens, independent of whether they are instances of the same letter), whereas the amount of node priming might be expected to increase with the number of repetitions of each prime. The third goal was to see whether the duration of the preview display had any effect. Would there be some minimal time required to set up the initial object representations tying the letters to the frames?

We presented eight square frames, and in two, four, or all eight of them flashed a letter either for 250 ms or for 100 ms (see Fig. 1). After an interval of 300 ms, a single letter appeared in one of the previously filled frames. The task was to name this target letter as quickly as possible. In one condition (with a 250-ms initial exposure), all the letters in the preview display were different from each other; in the other two conditions (one with 250 ms and one with 100 ms initial exposure), only two different letters were used, with one, two, or four tokens of each. The main questions were (1) whether the naming latency would be shorter when the target letter matched the letter that had previously appeared in the same frame, compared to when it matched a letter that had appeared in a different frame, (2) whether this object-specific effect depended on the initial exposure duration, and (3) whether the difference in latency to name a matching letter and a different letter in the same frame would depend on the number of letter types or on the number of letter tokens in the first display.

Method

Stimuli. The stimuli were shown on a Mitsubishi G479 monitor controlled by an IBM AT computer and Artist 1 Plus color graphics board. The technical specification of the phosphors, confirmed by direct measurements, indicates decay to 1% of original luminance in less than 30 ms. Subjects were shown a sequence of different displays. In the first display, eight red squares (luminance 9 cd/m^2) were shown on a black background; they were randomly located in a 6 × 6 matrix. Each square subtended 1.1° and the complete matrix subtended 8.9°. The squares remained visible throughout the sequence of events in a trial. After 166 ms, two, four, or eight white letters (luminance 37 cd/m^2) were flashed up inside two, four, or eight of the squares. The letters subtended 0.6° and were shown for 250 or 100 ms, followed by an interval of 300 ms with only the squares present. Then in the final display, a single letter was shown in one of the squares that had earlier contained a letter. In Experiment 1(a) on letter types, each letter in the initial display was different; in Experiments 1(b) and 1(c) on letter tokens, only two letter types were used in the initial display, and each was present as one, two, or four tokens. So a display of eight letter tokens might consist of four L's and four Q's. The preview field was shown for 250 ms in Experiments 1(a) and 1(b), and for 100 ms in Experiment 1(c). Letters were shown in uppercase and were selected from the following set: C,K,L,M,P,Q,S,T,V.

Procedure. Subjects were asked to watch the displays and to name the final letter on each trial as quickly as possible. A voice key detected the response and the computer registered the latency from the onset of the letter. There were three kinds of trials: on same-object (SO) trials, the target letter was the same as the letter that had previously appeared in the same frame; on different-object (DO) trials, the target letter was the same as a letter that had initially appeared in a different frame; on no-match (NM) trials, the final target letter differed from all the initial letters. The target letter never appeared in a previously empty frame. There were nine conditions in each of the three experiments, defined by three display sizes (two, four, and eight letter tokens) and three types of trials (SO, DO, and NM). Each experiment consisted of 12 blocks of 45 trials, giving a total of 60 trials per condition, run in one session lasting about 1 h.

Errors were monitored during the practice trials. They were rare. In the experimental trials the subjects were asked to score their own errors by pressing a key which caused the reaction time to be ignored both for that trial and for the next.

Subjects. Twelve paid subjects (9 women, all students at the University of California) were tested in Experiment 1(a) with two, four, or eight letter types and a 250-ms exposure. Twelve other subjects (8 women) were tested in Experiment 1(b) with two, four, or eight letter tokens, also at a 250-ms exposure, and 12 more (8 women) in Experiment 1(c) with two, four, or eight letter tokens and a 100-ms exposure.

Results and Discussion

The latencies for the various conditions are shown in Table 1, together with two difference measures: the *object-specific advantage* is the difference between naming latency in the same-object (SO) and different-object (DO) conditions; the *nonspecific preview effect* is the difference between the DO condition and the no-match (NM) condition. As is commonly the case in studies of priming, these difference measures do not necessarily reflect a single effect. The object-specific advantage combines a possible benefit of a match between the target and the letter that preceded it, and a possible cost of a mismatch between them. The nonspecific preview measure combines a possible facilitating effect of the prior presentation of the target and a possible reaction of surprise at its appearance in the wrong frame.

In this and in subsequent studies, we carried out three separate ANOVA's: on the mean RT across priming conditions, and on the two preview effects, respectively labeled the object-specific advantage (the difference between SO and DO latencies) and the nonspecific preview benefit (the difference between DO and NM latencies). The two preview effects are not independent, because they share the DO condition, but the separate analyses help the exposition. For convenience, the table also includes the results of a simple t test of each preview effect against zero.

In the ANOVA on mean RT, the main effect of experimental groups (the major columns in Table 1) was not significant [$F(2,33) = 2.23$]. There was a significant effect of display size [$F(2,66) = 84.81, p < .001$] but no interaction ($F < 1$).

The object-specific preview benefit was highly significant overall ($M = 16$ ms; $F(1,33) = 88.37, p < .001$). The effect of display size was significant [$F(2,66) = 26.69, p < .001$] reflecting a steep decrease of preview benefits as the number of previewed letters increased from two to eight. There was also a significant effect of groups [$F(2,66) = 3.68, p < .05$], indicating some reduction of object specificity with the short exposure duration.

TABLE 1
Mean Naming Latencies and Preview Effects in Study 1

Preview letters: Preview duration:	1(a) types 250 ms			1(b) tokens 250 ms			1(c) tokens 100 ms		
Display size:	2	4	8	2	4	8	2	4	8
Same object	474	500	517	473	495	513	520	540	552
Different object	509	517	523	504	517	517	536	552	551
No match	501	519	525	508	521	521	549	560	562
Mean RT	495	512	522	495	511	517	535	551	555
Preview effects									
Object specific	35**	17**	6	31**	22**	4	16	12	−1
Nonspecific	−8*	2	2	4	4	4	13	8	11

** These values are significant at $p < .01$.
* These values are significant at $p < .05$.

The nonspecific preview effect (DO–NM) was slight, but significant overall [$M = 4$ ms; $F(1,33) = 5.37, p < .05$]. There was no significant effect of display size and the effect of groups did not quite reach significance [$F(2,33) = 2.90, p < .07$].

The central result of these experiments is the finding of a substantial object-specific preview advantage. The response to a target letter was speeded when it appeared in a frame that had contained the same letter in the preview display. With preview displays of two items, the overall advantage of presenting preview letter and target in the same frame rather than in a different one was 27 ms. In contrast, the benefit of presenting the target letter in the "wrong" frame (compared to not showing it at all) was only 3 ms overall. There is some suggestion that the nonspecific benefit from a letter in a different frame was greater at the shorter exposure duration; the average nonspecific preview benefit did reach significance in that group [$t(11) = 2.59, p < .05$]. On the other hand, with 250 ms preview, the preview effect is almost entirely object specific. It seems that the specificity may in some conditions take time to become fully established.

A standard account of priming in terms of activation of nodes in semantic memory would predict no difference in priming from the letter in the same and in a different frame. In each case, the nodes for the priming letters would be equally primed, as would the locations in which letters had appeared. Only the specific combination of letter and location was changed in the different-object condition. To explain our results by node priming would require nodes that are specific for every letter in every possible location. Such a model has indeed been proposed by McClelland and Rumelhart (1981) and by Fukushima (1988). However, the experiments we describe later are not amenable to this account, because we observe preview benefits that are object specific without being location specific.

Our form of location-specific priming differs from two other reports which used consistent long-term associations between letters and positions (Banks & Krajicek, 1990; Lambert & Hockey, 1986). Their results demonstrated a tonic effect of expectancy, rather than the phasic integration of information in a temporary representation suggested by the present experiment.

The virtual absence of nonspecific priming in this experiment is a robust observation which recurs in most of our experiments with letters. In view of the ubiquity of repetition priming effects, this is a puzzling result: Why does the advance presentation of the target letter confer no general advantage in naming it, due to preactivation of the relevant nodes in a recognition network? The answer, we suppose, is that the vocabulary of stimuli and responses was quite small; it seems possible that all the items were primed to ceiling by the frequent repetition. In a subsequent experiment that used a large set of words as stimuli, the nonspecific priming was quite strong, although an additional object-specific advantage was still present (Treisman & Kahneman, manuscript in preparation).

The second important finding of our study is that the object-specific advantage was sharply reduced as the number of preview letters increased, and that this display size or load effect was about the same for repeated letter tokens as for different letter types. Although only two different letter types were present in the repeated token displays, the advantage of the same-object over the no-match condition was reduced from 35 ms with two tokens to 8 ms with eight tokens [Experiment 1(b)]. The limit seems to be set by the number of tokens that must be located in their respective frames, not by the number of different letter types to be identified. This result is consistent with the idea that separate object representations must be created for the separate perceptual entities present in the display. When the target letter appears, it is matched only to the earlier letter that formed part of the same object representation. The steep decrease of the object-specific benefit with display size and the reduced specificity with a short preview could reflect a limited rate at which object files can be established. Alternatively, there may be difficulties of retrieval with the more complex displays. The finding of an object-specific preview benefit suggests the existence of a specific, visual memory that preserves the spatial configuration of the initial display. Yet the interval between preview and target (an ISI of 300 ms) should be sufficient to eliminate iconic memory as a factor, according to the usual estimates.

The limited capacity of the memory that is probed in this experiment suggests a relatively long-lived form of postcategorical storage that is nevertheless still visual and object or location specific. However, it is possible that the longer persistence can be explained simply because the criterion for memory is less stringent in our experiment than in a partial report procedure; it is analogous to a measure of "savings" rather than of recall. In the following experiment we attempt to clarify the relation of these results to iconic storage, by comparing an ISI of 700 ms with an ISI of 300 ms.

STUDY 2: EFFECTS OF ISI

In this experiment we used two letter types and two, four, or eight tokens in each display, and tested two ISI's in a within-subject design. The method and stimuli were otherwise identical to those of Experiment 1(b). Eighteen subjects [two of whom had participated in Experiment 1(a)] were given 12 blocks of 45 trials at each ISI, in separate sessions. The order of ISI was counterbalanced. Two subjects were discarded because of exceptionally high error rates (up to 14% in some conditions) and highly variable reaction times. The mean error rate for the remaining 16 subjects was 1.1%.

The results are shown in Table 2. As before, we conducted separate analyses of the mean reaction time and the two preview effects. Reaction time was significantly faster at the longer ISI [$F(1,15) = 28.72, p < .001$] and increased with the size of the preview display [$F(2,30) = 95.49, p < .001$], but the two variables did not interact [$F(2,30) = 2.20$, NS].

The object-specific advantage (DO–SO) was significant overall [$F(1,15) = 36.62, p < .001$]; it decreased significantly with the number of items in the priming field [$F(2,30) = 6.83, p < .01$], but neither the effect of ISI nor the interaction of ISI with display size were significant [$F(1,15) = 0.15$ and $F(2,30) = 0.96$, respectively]. The lack of effect of ISI on object specificity would seem to rule out iconic memory as a factor in the reviewing benefits. Whatever visual trace mediates the reviewing effect remains equally effective across an interval within which iconic memory is thought to have completely disappeared.

The nonspecific preview effect (NM–DO) was significant overall [$M = 4.5$ ms, $F(1,15) = 8.69, p < .01$], indicating a slight benefit from a preview of the target in a different object. The main effect of ISI was significant [$F(1,15) = 7.49, p < .05$]. The linear trend relating increasing nonspecific benefit to increasing display size was not quite significant [$F(1,30) = 3.58, p < .06$]. This marginal trend is due mainly to an unusually large increase of naming latency in the NM condition with a long ISI. We surmise that when the subject has had 700 ms to consider a display that consists, say,

TABLE 2
Mean Naming Latencies and Preview Benefits in Experiment 2

Preview duration:	300 ms			700 ms		
Display size:	2	4	8	2	4	8
Same object	527	540	555	506	527	533
Different object	549	554	556	526	534	539
No match	543	556	556	528	546	555
Mean	540	550	556	520	536	542
		Preview effects				
Object specific	22**	14**	1	20**	7	6
Nonspecific	−6	2	0	2	12*	16**

** These values are significant at $p < .01$.
 * These values are significant at $p < .05$.

of four K's and four T's, the appearance of a new letter as a target could be somewhat disconcerting.

The main finding of both Studies 1 and 2 is a robust object-specific preview benefit which diminishes sharply with increasing display size. This effect involves a spatial representation of objects, with a sharply limited capacity or limitation on access, but with considerably longer persistence than that attributed to iconic memory. Other researchers have based similar proposals on different lines of empirical evidence. Coltheart (1972), Phillips (1974), Sternberg, Knoll and Turock (1986), and DiLollo and Dixon (1988) all distinguish a schematic short-term visual memory from sensory or iconic storage. Together with ours, their evidence suggests the existence of at least one form of short-term visual storage which, unlike iconic memory, is not tied to spatial position, not subject to masking, and remains available for at least 600 ms. However, the great variety of experimental methods makes it difficult to ascertain whether a single process is involved in all their experiments, and in the priming effects that we observe.

STUDY 3: OBJECT SPECIFICITY IN THE PREVIEW EFFECT WITH OBJECTS IN APPARENT MOTION

Our next concern is to distinguish the existence of object-specific perceptual representations ("object files") from the persistence of information tied to particular visual locations. We dissociate these effects by using objects in real or apparent motion, presenting the target letter in a different location from the matching letter in the initial display. We describe first an experiment in which we used apparent motion to link one of the items in the preview field to the target.

The stimuli in this experiment were two successive displays, each containing two letters, with the second pair displaced diagonally either above or below the first pair (see Fig. 2). No frames were used in this experiment. The preview display was centered between the fixation marks. The target display always included a letter just below the top fixation bar or just above the bottom one, with a second letter either to its right or to its left. The time intervals we used gave viewers a clear impression that a single pair of letters moved coherently from the initial to the final locations. Thus, the two letters in the first display were integrated perceptually with the two in the second display. In Fig. 2, the B in the first frame turns into B in the SO condition, J in the DO condition, and D in the NM condition; the J in the first frame becomes H in all these conditions. Ternus (1938) first described a similar display in which global apparent motion is seen, its direction determined by the relative location of the peripheral item in the second display. This happens whether the shapes are the same or not. Kolers (1972) showed that shape has little influence on apparent motion when the spatial and temporal intervals are optimal.

In our displays too the perceived direction of motion was determined by the location of the peripheral letter in the second display. Nothing in the initial display indicated which of the two previewed letters would be seen to move into the target location and thus to "become" the target letter. We were interested in discovering whether there would be a preview benefit when the target matched one of the initial letters and if so whether it would be object specific, occurring only when the target was perceptually integrated with the matching prime. In this experiment, differences in location could play no role in selective preview effects, since the two preview letters were equidistant from the location of the target. Only the illusory motion linked the target to one previewed letter rather than the other, and the motion was determined only after the appearance of the target. Lingering activation in particular spatial locations could generate only nonspecific benefits.

Method

Stimuli. The apparatus used to control and display the stimuli was the same as in Experiment 1. The letters were red, the fixation marks were white, and the background field was dark. The letters shown on each trial were chosen randomly from the set B,C,D,F,H,J,K,S. Viewed from a distance of 60 cm, each letter subtended 0.9°. Two vertical bars, each subtending 0.4° in length and separated vertically by 3.9°, were used to control fixation. Each trial began with presentation of these bars for 100 ms. Two letters were then shown 1.5° to the left and right of the center of the display, for 100 ms in one session and 1 s in another session. After an ISI of 33 ms (for the 100-ms preview) or 0 ms (for the 1-s preview), two new letters were shown. One of these letters, the target, was presented just below the top fixation bar or just above the bottom one. The other letter in the target field was 3.1° either to the left or right of the target. The target field remained in view until the subject responded.

Procedure. There were eight types of trials in each session, four conditions with the display arriving at the target position from the left side, and the same four conditions with the target display arriving from the right. On SO trials, the target letter was the same as the preview letter that appeared to fuse with it perceptually; on DO trials, the target letter was the same as the preview letter that appeared to move to the more peripheral location; on NM trials the target letter differed from both the initial letters; on asterisks trials, the preview display consisted of two asterisks. The peripheral letter in the final display always differed from the other three. The conditions were randomly mixed in each block of trials. The two sessions with different preview durations were run on separate days in counterbalanced order in a within-subject design. Each session lasted about 1 h.

Subjects were asked to name the letter that appeared between the bar markers as quickly as they could without making errors. Their response times were measured from the triggering of a voice key. Naming latencies were collected in 36 trials in each of the eight conditions. Subjects were given one block of practice trials before each experiment began. As in the previous experiments, they scored their own responses. The correct letter was presented in the center of the screen on each trial, after the experimental displays. Subjects pressed a right-hand key if their response matched the correct letter and a left-hand key if they were incorrect, or if some other sound triggered the voice key before they spoke (a rare event).

192   KAHNEMAN, TREISMAN, AND GIBBS

Subjects. Thirteen paid subjects (all students at the University of California, 5 women)
participated in this experiment.

Results and Discussion

Errors averaged 1.6% across all conditions. The reaction time data are
shown in Table 3.

The ANOVA on mean RT showed no effect of either duration of the
priming field or the direction of motion, and no interaction [$F(1,12)$ =
0.32, and $F(1,12)$ = 2.95, respectively]. Separate ANOVA's were run as
before on the two preview effects, and a separate ANOVA on the difference between the no-match and the asterisks conditions.

The object-specific benefit was significant overall [M = 15 ms, $F(1,12)$
= 24.44, $p < .001$]. There was no main effect of either prime duration or
direction of apparent motion [$F(1,12)$ = 0.37 and $F(1,12)$ = 1.35, respec-
tively], but the interaction of these variables was highly reliable [$F(1,12)$
= 11.28, $p < .01$]. Leftward movement gave more object-specific benefit
at the short preview exposure and rightward movement gave more at the
long. A likely explanation for this interaction is that subjects attended to
the letters in the preview field in a left to right order, giving an advantage
to the left letter, read first, when the exposure was brief and to the right
letter, read last, when the exposure was long.

The nonspecific preview effect was actually a small cost [M = 4 ms;
$F(1,12)$ = 5.89, $p < .05$] incurred when the target letter was previewed in
the wrong location, relative to not previewed at all. The cost may be due
to some conflict in the observed direction of motion between the global

TABLE 3
Mean Naming Latencies and Preview Benefits in Experiment 3

Preview duration:	100 ms		1000 ms	
Motion direction:	L	R	L	R
Same object	462	472	467	465
Different object	488	482	473	485
No match	479	479	472	479
Asterisks	467	471	465	468
Mean	474	476	469	474
Preview effects				
Object specific	26**	10	6	20**
Nonspecific	-9	-3	-1	-6
New letter vs asterisks	12**	8**	7	11*

** These values are significant at $p < .01$.
 * These values are significant at $p < .05$.

Ternus effect and a weak tendency to match shapes and reverse the Ternus motion in the DO conditions. There was no significant effect of experimental conditions on the nonspecific preview effect.

The asterisks gave significantly faster latencies than the new letters [M = 10 ms, $F(1,12)$ = 18.70, $p < .001$] indicating that the object-specific benefit, at least in this display, was due to a cost of assigning different letter identities to the same object, rather than to the benefit of a match. The asterisks were clearly irrelevant to the task and may have been filtered out. Later experiments test the effects of blank previews and of digit previews.

The central finding, as with stationary displays, was the object-specific effect of the preview field. An account in terms of lingering activation in a location can now be ruled out, because the target appeared in a different location from the preview letters, and equally far from the matching letter in SO and in DO trials. The link between target and prime was determined entirely by the location of the irrelevant letter which selected the direction of the illusory motion attributed to the whole display. The processing of the target was selectively affected by the initial letter that was perceptually integrated with it, and largely unaffected by the other letter in the preview field.

A second important conclusion from the present experiment is that the preview effect is determined in a backward process, which is controlled by the target display. The initial displays on SO and DO trials were identical in terms of any forward effect of priming or interference. In both cases two letters were presented, of which one was then repeated as a target. The difference between the conditions arose only after the onset of the target field, because the object correspondence between the two fields was only determined at that time. The preview effect observed in the present study was therefore a "backward" effect (Glucksberg et al., 1986; Kahneman & Miller, 1986; Kiger & Glass, 1983; Koriat, 1981; Seidenberg, Waters, Sanders, & Langer, 1984). A characteristic of the second display (in this case the position of the irrelevant letter) controls the selection of the preview item with which the target will interact. The term "priming" is clearly awkward to describe what is going on here, because it suggests a forward effect from prime to target, rather than a backward selective process.

The results do more than indicate that the target selects the earlier item with which it will interact. They also pin down the basis of selection, and eliminate some plausible alternatives. For example, it would be theoretically possible for the target letter to select the item in the preview field that most closely resembles it; selection by similarity is invoked in many accounts of priming and of episodic retrieval (e.g., Kahneman & Miller, 1986; Kirsner et al., 1987; McClelland & Rumelhart, 1985). In the present

experiment, however, selection by similarity would produce equal priming benefits for the SO and DO conditions, since the target-to-be is
present in the preview field in both. The absence of any preview benefit
in the DO condition shows that similarity played no role at all in this
experiment. The position of the letters in the simple configuration to
which they belong appears to be the sole basis for selective interaction. It
is this spatial property that defines the object file to which successive
items are assigned. The rules of correspondence that govern apparent
motion in complex displays (Ullman, 1979) also govern the reviewing
process that yields object specific preview benefits in the present experiment.

STUDY 4: REVIEWING WITH MOVING FRAMES

In the remaining studies to be described in this paper, we used moving
frames to create selective links between items in the preview and target
fields. In a typical experiment, the computer presented two outline shapes
(frames), then two letters inside the frames (see Fig. 3); the letters then
disappeared and the frames moved to new positions, equidistant from the
initial positions; finally a single target letter appeared in one of the frames.
Reaction time for naming the letter was, as before, the dependent variable. As in the previous experiments, there were three types of display,
labeled SO, DO, and NM. A cue (vertical bar markers) appeared during
the trial to indicate the position of the target letter.

In Study 4 (which was actually run as a series of experiments with
different groups of subjects), we tested a number of variations on the
same basic paradigm. We varied the duration of the preview field, the
duration of the motion of the empty frames, the contents of the preview
display, and the timing of the cue that indicated the position of the target.
Most of our studies in this paradigm have used an "early" cue, in which
the bars that indicated the position of the target appeared simultaneously
with the onset of the motion of the frames. The purpose of the early cue
was to direct attention immediately to the target position, to prevent as far
as possible selective attention to one of the two preview letters. To check
on the possibility that an early cue might direct the subject's attention to
one of the moving frames even before the target arrived, we included
"late cue" conditions, in which the bars indicating the location of the
target appeared simultaneously with the target itself.

By varying the duration of the preview and the speed of motion we
explored the possibility that the temporal integration that mediates the
reviewing benefit depends on the preview still being only partially processed when the target appears. If the preview is seen as an event that is
clearly temporally separate from the target, the two might not be combined. On the other hand, if reviewing represents a retrieval by the later

input of its most likely prior instantiation, as we suggested in the Introduction, there is no reason to expect much effect of the preview duration.
So long as the preview letters are presented long enough to be identified
and linked in separate object files to the frames that contain them, the
critical variable should be whether the final letter is seen as a new instantiation of one of the earlier letters. This in turn will depend on whether
motion (real or apparent) has linked the appearances of the target and the
preview across space and time.

Method

Stimuli. The displays were presented in white on a dark field on a DEC VR17-LC graphics
terminal with P40 phosphor, controlled by a DEC PDP 11/34 computer. The display was
viewed through a blue filter (Kodak Wratten 47), which cut down visible persistence. Viewing distance was 60 cm.

The following sequence of stimuli was shown on each trial. First two outline shapes
appeared, a triangle and a square subtending 2.1° vertically and horizontally, centered 2.5°
above and below a fixation point (see Fig. 3). After a delay of 500 ms, capital letters (.6° tall)
appeared inside the two frames. The letters were selected from the set B,C,D,F,G,H,K,J,S.
They were presented for 20 ms in the "short exposure" conditions, or for 1 s in the "long"
conditions. The frames then moved in apparently smooth motion (new images were drawn
every 13 ms) to positions centered 4.2° to the left or right of fixation. The triangular frame
was always at the top of the display initially, and it moved equally often to the left and to the
right; the square frame always started at the bottom of the display and moved to the opposite
side. The motion lasted 130 ms in the "fast" conditions and 590 ms in the "slow" conditions. The location of the target was cued by bars above and below it, and the timing of that
cue was also a variable in these experiments. The "early" cue was shown with the onset of
the preview letters (with the short exposure) or when the frame began to move (with long
exposures); the "late" cue appeared at the same time as the target. There were six conditions defined by characteristics of the display sequence, four resulting from the combination
of long or short preview duration and early or late cue, and two more with the long preview
duration and with slow (590 ms) motion, again with either an early or a late cue. In the
conditions combining early cue and short exposure the preview field contained digits rather
than letters on a quarter of the trials. Nine subjects in the late-cue, long-exposure condition
and all eight subjects in the early-cue, slow-movement condition had empty frames in the
preview fields on a quarter of the trials.

Subjects and procedure. The six conditions were run as separate experiments, with some
overlap of participants. A total of 71 subjects took part in at least one experiment. Of these,
14 took part in two experiments. Each subject completed one block of 48 trials for practice,
followed by five experimental blocks, divided equally among the types of trials included in
that experiment.

Results and Discussion

The results of this set of experiments are presented in Table 4. When
the statistical analysis called for comparisons across experiments, we
treated the various groups as independent, in spite of some overlap of
membership. This is generally a conservative procedure.

We analyzed the set of six experiments as a 3×2 design with three
display types and two values of the timing of the cue that indicated the

TABLE 4
Mean Naming Latencies and Preview Benefits in Study 4

Motion: Preview duration: Cue	Fast 20 ms		Fast 1 sec		Slow 1 sec	
	Early	Late	Early	Late	Early	Late
N	(14)	(19)	(14)	(21)	(8)	(10)
Same object	484	531	495	543	445	531
Different object	515	544	518	557	486	550
No match	516	556	519	564	484	549
Mean	505	544	511	555	472	543
			Preview effects			
Object specific	31**	13**	23**	14**	41**	19*
Nonspecific	1	12**	1	7*	−2	−1

** These values are significant at $p < .01$.
  * These values are significant at $p < .05$.

target position. The analysis of mean RT yielded a highly significant effect of the timing of the cue—as might be expected, the early cue yielded shorter latencies [$M = 48$ ms, $F(1,80) = 20.31$, $p < .001$]. The three display types did not differ significantly [$F(2,80) = 1.45$], and did not interact with cue timing [$F(2,80) = 0.64$].

The object-specific benefit was highly significant in each group separately, and was, of course, significant overall. The benefit was significantly greater with the early cue than with the late cue [$F(1,80) = 15.70$, $p < .001$]. Again, the display types did not differ significantly [$F(2,80) = 2.23$], and did not interact with cue timing [$F(2,30) = 0.90$]. The nonspecific benefit was barely significant overall [$M = 4.5$ ms, $F(1,80) = 3.97$, $p < .05$], and marginally larger with the late than with the early cue [$F(1,80) = 3.67$, $p < .06$].

In summary, the results suggest that the object-specific effect is independent of preview duration, slightly increased with slower motion, and larger with an early cue than with a late cue. The nonspecific effect, in contrast, appears to be slightly larger with the late cue.

This pattern of results suggests that on some occasions the presentation of the target causes reviewing of a preview letter that was presented in the other object; the results suggest further that this failure of selectivity is very rare when the early cue is used, and somewhat more common with the late cue—at least with the present display. The early cue was designed to direct the subject's attention immediately to the position in which the target would appear. In the absence of such a cue, attention could be captured on some trials by one or another of the two moving frames, following that frame to its final position, and inducing a bias in favor of the letter it had contained. On one-third of these occasions, the target would actually appear in the frame that the subject did not follow or attend. The occasional captures of attention by the "wrong" frame can only lower performance in the SO condition, because the letter that is reviewed on these trials does not match the target. By the same logic, performance in the DO condition should improve when object selection fails, because the item reviewed will then match the target. In the NM condition, of course, · the direction of attention during motion should make little difference because both preview letters differ from the target.

An alternative interpretation of the difference between early and late cues is that presentation of the early cue quickly directs attention to the frame that is moving to the cued location, and thereby diverts it from the other frame and the letter it contains. This account is rather implausible, for several reasons. First, it requires exceptional agility of the mechanism that directs spatial attention. Note that the early cue is a pull cue (Jonides, 1981), of the kind that generally produces an automatic redirection of attention. Note as well that the duration of motion in the fast condition is only 130 ms, which appears too short to contain two movements of attention guided by an inference from the direction of motion. In another experiment with an early cue, we found perfect object specificity even when the duration of the motion was only 55 ms. The preview effect was also highly specific in the apparent motion design of Study 3, which was effectively a late cue situation.

The perfect object specificity of the preview effect with a long-duration preview and an early cue is a significant result. The two letters shown in that field were equal in potential relevance for a full second, regardless of the cueing condition. Although both letters were surely perceived and identified during that time, a preview of the target in the "wrong" object had no effect. This seems to us to be strong evidence against the idea that the preview benefit observed in these experiments is mediated by node activation, because both nodes should have been equally, and probably fully, activated. Note again that the results cannot be explained by location-specific nodes, because the target was never presented in the same location as the prime.

Our aim in varying the speed of motion was to push the boundary conditions still further from any iconic representation by extending the interval between the offset of the previewed letter and the appearance of the target. Would the two still be integrated when the linking motion took nearly 600 ms? The answer is clearly yes; with the early cue the object-specific preview benefit was somewhat larger with the slow than with the fast motion. There is no requirement that sensory traces of the preview letters remain active to ensure a preview benefit. With fast motion, subjects sometimes reported an illusion of seeing the preview letter move with the frame. When the motion took 590 ms, the letter did not remain phenomenologically visible; yet it was still just as likely to be integrated with the target in the process of reviewing.

In this experiment we used different outline shapes as frames, a triangle and a square. This could potentially have been relevant to the object specificity of the preview benefit. However, one condition in Experiment 6(b) replicates essentially the same conditions using identical square frames, and shows the same amount of object-specific benefit. What seems to matter is the perceptual continuity of the frame that links the preview to the target letter, rather than the association between its shape and the letter it contains.

Finally, four of the experiments had additional control conditions, as well as SO, DO, and NM trials: on 25% of trials, two experiments showed digits in the preview field and two experiments showed empty frames. The digits in the short-exposure conditions yielded significantly faster latencies than the no-match letters [$M = 8$ ms, $t(13) = 3.07$, $p < .01$ with the early cue; $M = 8$ ms, $t(18) = 2.51$, $p < .05$ with the late cue]. On the other hand, the advantage of the blank fields over the no-match letters did not reach significance (means of 7 ms for long-exposure, late-cue, and 0 ms for the slow-movement, early cue condition]. There seems in these experiments to be a small cost associated with reviewing a different letter rather than an irrelevant symbol or an empty frame, but the main reviewing effect here is due to the advantage of a matching preview letter in the same frame.

STUDY 5: MOVING FRAMES WITH TWO OR FOUR PREVIEW LETTERS

This experiment tests the effect of the number of items in the preview field with moving frames, and extends the comparison of early and late cues to a display that does not encourage attentional following of a particular frame. The experiment was designed to test the generality of the inverse relationship between the size of the object-specific and nonspecific preview effects, which was observed in some conditions of Study 4. We expected that an increase in the number of previewed letters might reduce the selectivity of the priming effect, as it appeared to do in Study 1.

Method

Stimuli. The displays were presented with the same computer and graphics terminal as those of Study 4. As shown in Fig. 4, the four frames that contained the letters were squares, 1.1° a side, which were initially centered at equal intervals on the circumference of an imaginary circle 4.0° in diameter. The position of the set of frames was randomly chosen from three possibilities (with a square at either 12:30, 1:30, or 2:30 on an imaginary clock). The letters shown on a trial were selected from the set of all consonants except G,N,Q,R,V, and W. On 25% of trials the preview letters were replaced by plus signs. The four frames were first shown alone for 500 ms, followed by a 30-ms exposure of either two or four letters (or plus signs). When two letters were shown, they were located at opposite ends of a diameter. The preview letters disappeared and the frames moved along straight lines to new positions, computed by combining an expansion of the circle to 64 mm diameter with a ⅛ turn in a clockwise or counterclockwise direction (see Fig. 4). The display created an impression of simultaneous expansion and rotation of the whole pattern. The frames retained their vertical orientation during the movement, which took 130 ms and consisted of 10 stops. A target letter then appeared in one of the frames. On SO trials the target matched the letter that had previously appeared in that frame; on DO trials it matched a letter previously shown in another frame, on NM trials it was a new letter; on the remaining trials the preview display contained two or four plus signs. Each of these trial types occurred

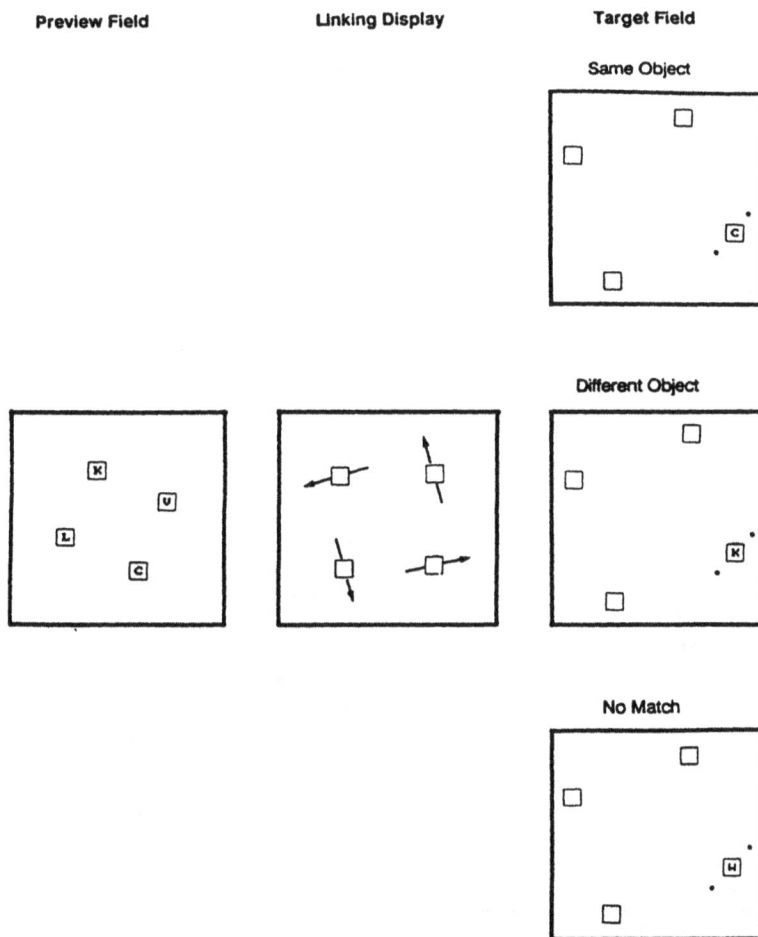

FIG. 4. Examples of displays used in Experiment 5.

200   KAHNEMAN, TREISMAN, AND GIBBS

equally often in randomized order. The cue consisted of two asterisks presented at opposite corners of the target frame.

Procedure. There were three groups of subjects. One group of 16 subjects was tested with the early cue and two or four preview letters. The other two groups were tested with a late cue; one group of 12 subjects had separate blocks with two or four preview letters, with order counterbalanced; finally, a group of 10 subjects encountered the two types of trials randomly mixed in each block. The aim was to see whether there were any strategic effects which would depend on knowing how many letters to expect.

Results

The results obtained with mixed and with blocked trials were essentially identical, and the data for the 22 subjects tested with the late cue were therefore pooled. The mean naming latencies and preview effects are shown in Table 5. (The final row of the Table is discussed later).

Naming latency was faster with an early cue than with a late cue [$M = 50$ ms, $F(1,36) = 6.14$, $p < .05$], and faster with two than with four items in the preview display [$M = 15$ ms, $F(1,36) = 50.17$]. The two variables did not interact ($F < 1$).

The object-specific preview benefit (DO–SO) was significantly greater with two than with four previewed letters [$M = 18$ ms, $F(1,36) = 10.12$], but there was no significant difference between early and late cue and no interaction between these variables ($F < 1$). The effect of display size is compatible with the findings of Experiment 1(a), with stationary objects.

The nonspecific preview effect (NM–DO) did not quite reach significance [$M = 4$ ms, $F(1,36) = 3.65$, $p = .07$]. There was no significant

TABLE 5
Mean Naming Latencies and Preview Benefits in Study 5

	Early cue		Late cue	
Number of preview items:	Two	Four	Two	Four
Same object	576	603	623	653
Different object	611	622	663	674
No match	611	626	667	682
Pluses	600	606	642	654
Mean	600	614	649	666
Cost of new letter vs plus	11	20**	25**	28**
Preview effects				
Object specific	35**	19**	40**	21**
Nonspecific	0	4	4	8*
Total benefit	35	35	48	53

** These values are significant at $p < .01$.
  * These values are significant at $p < .05$.

effect of display size [$F(1,36) = 0.46$], or of cue timing [$F(1,36) = 1.02$], and no sign of any interaction between these variables.

There is a notable difference between this study and Study 4 in the effects of cue timing. In the present results, unlike Study 4, the object specificity of preview benefits was hardly reduced by late cueing. We tentatively attribute this finding to the coherent motion of the four frames in the present experiment. The display induced a global percept of an expanding circle, and thereby reduced the tendency to follow one particular frame to its destination before the late cue appeared.

Finally, the comparison of NM trials with plus trials yielded a highly significant difference in favor of the latter [$M = 21$ ms, $F(1,36) = 72.38$, $p < .01$], and a significant interaction with early vs late cue [$F(1,36) = 5.06, p < .05$]. The cost of a new letter relative to a plus sign was greater for late cue trials. Thus, in this study there seems to be more interference from nameable letters than from an irrelevant symbol, perhaps because the letters were more perceptually confusable with the target and perhaps because of potential response conflict. However, there was also some facilitation from the identity match in the SO condition relative to the pluses, at least with two preview letters [$t(15) = 3.57, p < .01$ for the early cue and $t(21) = 6.62, p < .001$ for the late cue].

Discussion: A Model of Reviewing

The discussion of Study 4 introduced the notion of a reviewing process, which usually picks the item presented in the same object as the target, but sometimes selects another item. If we assume that the difference between reviewing a matching or a mismatching item is unaffected by the basis of selection, and that no more than one item is reviewed on any trial, the fraction p of trials on which reviewing is object specific can be estimated from the data for any experimental situation. With two items in the preview field, the object selectivity of reviewing in a particular experimental condition can be estimated by the following ratio, where the labels for experimental conditions denote the corresponding response latencies:

$p = (\text{NM–SO})/[(\text{NM–SO}) + (\text{NM–DO})]$.

Allowing for the effect of display size, this random selection model leads to the following expression for p when the preview field contains n items:

$p = (\text{NM–SO})/[(\text{NM–SO}) + (n-1)(\text{NM–DO})]$.

Applying this measure to the data of Table 4 yields a crude but suggestive indication of the effects of the timing of the location cue and of the number of priming items. The computed values for the proportions of object-specific reviewing trials are .95 and .66, respectively, for two and four items with an early cue, and .90 and .55 for two and four items with a late cue. Object selectivity is nearly perfect with two primes, substantially impaired with four. There seem to be limits to the number of letters that can be bound to specific frames, at least in the limited time available here.

Another measure of interest, labeled *total preview benefit* (TPB), is defined next. The following simple model provides a rationale for this measure. Assume that a single item is reviewed on a fraction r of trials, that no item is reviewed on the other trials, and that reaction time is A ms faster when the target matches the reviewed letter than when it does not. It is easily seen that in the case of a priming field with two items the following equations hold:

$$TPB = r.A = (SO-NM) + (DO-NM),$$

and also

$$(SO-NM) = p.r.A \text{ and } (DO-NM) = (1-p).r.A.$$

In the general case of n items in the preview field, these equations become

$$TPB = r.A = (SO-NM) + (n-1)(DO-NM)$$
$$(SO-NM) = p.r.A \text{ and } (DO-NM) = (1-p).r.A/(n-1).$$

The process model has three parameters, but our design provides no way of separating the true matching advantage A from the fraction r of trials on which an item is reviewed. We can estimate only the product of these values, which is our measure of total preview benefit, TPB.

We did not report the measures of selectivity and total preview benefits for previous studies, because the added expository burden would not have been rewarded by illuminating findings. First, there were several experiments in which a central assumption of the model appeared to be violated: the model assumes that a match of the target to the reviewed item yields the same benefit of A ms, regardless of whether the match occurs in the SO or DO conditions. This assumption is incompatible with the occasional finding (in Studies 1 and 3) of cases in which performance in the DO condition was reliably worse than in condition NM; we interpreted these results as indicating surprise at the appearance of the target letter in the "wrong" object. Second, the individual estimates of TPB are quite variable, precluding meaningful comparisons across groups.

In the present experiment, the values of TPB were 35 ms for both two and four primes, with an early cue. The corresponding values of TPB with the late cue were 48 and 53 ms. In both cases, the values of TPB appeared to remain constant across different levels of object specificity, induced by differences in the number of previewed letters. The difference in TPB between early and late cue was larger, but not significant in a between-group comparison [$M = 16$ ms, $t(36) = 1.38$]. The experiments reported iNEWn Study 6 were conducted specifically to test the constancy of total matching benefits in a within-subject design, which could be sufficiently sensitive to reject it. They explored two other ways of varying the degree of object specificity: in one case the linking motion was replaced by shared color as a possible basis for selective reviewing; in another, the frames moved but not to the final destination of the target.

STUDY 6: A TEST OF THE REVIEWING MODEL

In the model that was just introduced, a target may occasionally [with probability $(1-p)$] select for reviewing an item that was not presented in the same object. Thus, the process of reviewing is guided by the structure of object relations, but is not necessarily restricted to successive states of the same object. In the next experiment we examine pairs of closely similar displays which differ in the support they provide for object-guided reviewing. In the terms of the minimal formal model introduced above, we set out to create conditions in which the efficiency of selection by object (indexed by p in the model) would vary, in order to test whether total preview benefits (TPB) would remain approximately constant.

Experiment 6(a) used color as a possible basis for selective retrieval of the prime, to replace the linking motion used in Studies 3, 4, and 5. The preview field consisted of two stationary frames in which letters were shown, in two different colors. The target letter sometimes matched the preview letter shown in the same color (SO), sometimes the other letter (DO), and sometimes neither (NM). We compared the preview benefits in this situation to those produced, with a very similar display, where one of the preview letters was linked to the target by movement of its frame.

In Experiment 6(b), the two frames that contained the preview letters always moved, but on unlinked-motion trials the moving frames did not reach the box in which the target was eventually shown (see Fig. 5). This situation provides no obvious basis for selection. Will subjects still retrieve one of the two letters (at random) to match to the target, and if so will they do it less often than with a linking motion or color? Thus the three questions were whether (a) there would still be any reviewing benefit for letters presented in different locations in the absence of linking motion; (b) if so, whether this could be controlled by a shared property (color); (c) finally, whether total preview benefits would be approximately the same in matched conditions.

Stimuli and procedure. Experiment 6(a) was conducted with the color monitors used in Experiments 1–3. The letters in Experiment 6(a) were selected from the set C,K,L,P,Q,R,S,T,V. The sequence of events in the color conditions was the following: two white outline square frames subtending 1.1° a side appeared alone for 500 ms, above and below the center of the screen and separated vertically by 4.6°; characters were shown in the frames for 1 s; 87 ms after the characters disappeared from the frames,

204   KAHNEMAN, TREISMAN, AND GIBBS

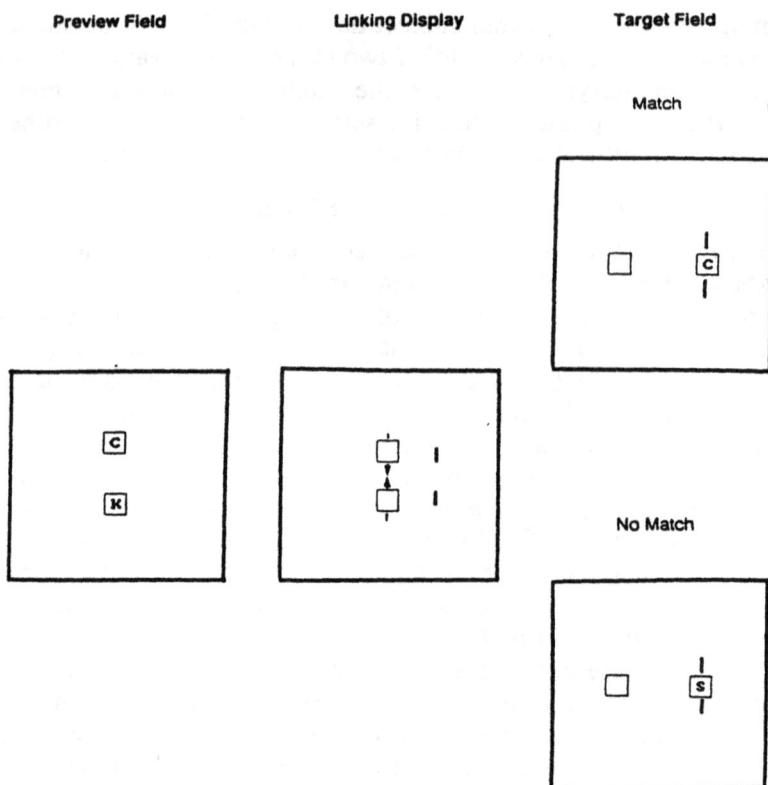

FIG. 5. Examples of displays used in Experiment 6(b).

two new frames appeared to the right and left of the center of the screen and separated by 4.6°; all four frames were present together for 87 ms, to inhibit apparent motion from the first to the second set of frames; the initial frames disappeared, and the new frames were shown alone for 87 ms, at which time a target letter appeared in one of them. No cue to target position was provided.

The sequence in the motion conditions was the same until the disappearance of the preview letters, at which time the frames started to move to their final positions. The motion was carried out in 15 steps and was completed in 250 ms. In the color conditions, one of the preview letters was greenish yellow and the other was purple; the target was shown in one of these colors. In the motion conditions all three letters shown on a trial were in the same color, and the color varied randomly over trials.

Experiment 6(b) was carried out with the same equipment as Experiments 4 and 5. The letters were selected from the set B,C,D,F,H,J,K,S. The frames and letters appeared in white on a dark background. The trial started with presentation of two outline frames, each subtending 2.1° a side, separated vertically (edge to edge) by 2.9°. After 500 ms, two letters appeared in the frames for 40 ms, then fixation bars appeared 3.1° to the left or right of the center of the display, and the empty squares began to move. There were two conditions. The linked motion condition was similar to the motion used in Study 4. In the unlinked motion case, the two frames moved toward the center of the display, until they were 0.8° apart (see Fig. 5). The movement lasted 400 ms. At that time, two frames appeared to the left and right of the center, separated by 4.2°. The frame cued by the fixation bars contained a letter.

Subjects. Two different groups of subjects were tested, 12 (7 women) in the color condition and 9 (5 women) in the nonspecific motion condition.

Results

The mean latencies and preview benefits are shown in Table 6. The standard linking-motion conditions gave the familiar pattern of significant object-specific benefit, and no significant priming in the DO condition.

The color condition of Experiment 6(a) showed significant preview benefit from both the matching and the mismatching colored letters, and no significant difference between the two. [Half the subjects showed more priming from the mismatched color, so the 5-ms difference did not approach significance, $t (11) = 1.13$]. The total benefits, 35 ms for motion and 29 ms for color, did not differ significantly ($t = 0.61$, ns).

In the unlinked motion condition of Experiment 6(b) there was no difference between the two objects in the degree to which they resembled or were linked to the target. The only measure of interest in that condition is the sum of preview effects over the two items, which is obtained by doubling the observed priming effect. The result, 29 ms, did not differ

TABLE 6
Mean Naming Latencies and Preview Effects in Studies 6(a) and 6(b)

	Color	Motion	Unlinked motion	Linked motion
Same object	527	544	536	476
Different object	532	561	537	505
No match	544	570	551	509
Preview effects				
Specific	5	17**	15**	29*
Nonspecific	12*	9		4
Total benefit	29	35	29	37

** These values are significant at $p < .01$.
* These values are significant at $p < .05$.

significantly from the sum of preview effects for the linked-motion condition [37 ms; $t(8) = 0.70$].

The algebraic model of reviewing was introduced quite tentatively in the discussion of Experiment 5, both because it appeared rather too simple to be true and because it did not give a good account of the effects of preview display size in some of the experiments reported in Studies 1 and 2. The nonspecific preview effect was negative in one condition of Study 1, apparently violating an assumption of the model. The results of Study 2 were quite erratic, because of an unusually steep effect of display size on the control condition NM, which provides the baseline for the estimation of nonspecific benefits. On the other hand, the reviewing model seemed to fit the results of Studies 4 and 5 rather well. The experiments of Study 6 were conducted to obtain a more conclusive test of the model, and their results support it.

The novel assumption of the reviewing model, which is compatible with the notion of a correspondence process, is that the processing of the target letter is affected at most by one item from the preview field. The selection of the preview item that will be reviewed is dominated by a linking motion, but is affected neither by a match of colors nor by a match of the letters across the two fields. We were apparently successful in the attempt to vary the selectivity of reviewing without affecting the total preview benefit. The important conclusion of these experiments is that a shared object is not a necessary condition for the type of preview benefit that we have observed. The object provides a powerful guide to the process of selective retrieval that we have called reviewing but, when no object continuity is present, a new item may retrieve any earlier item, apparently at random.

STUDY 7: RECENCY IN REVIEWING

The evidence presented so far indicates that, when the objects in successive fields are strongly linked, attention to the target letter brings about a reviewing of the immediate history of the corresponding object in the preview field. This reviewing can go back in time for at least 700 ms when no intervening events occur. What happens if intervening objects are presented? Can reviewing access an earlier state of an object that has recently been updated? Our hypothesis suggests this should not be possible. In an attempt to find out, an experiment was conducted in which two sets of letters were successively shown in stationary frames, before these began to move. The same frames were filled in both preview displays, so that the first set of preview letters was overwritten by the second.

Method

Stimuli. The displays were the same as those in Experiment 4 except that (1) the movement consisted of 6 exposures instead of 10 and lasted only 100 ms; (2) two successive pairs of initial letters were presented before the framing shapes moved. The frames were first presented for 300 ms. They remained visible while two pairs of letters were presented for 200 ms each with an ISI of 200 ms between them. The remaining sequence of events was as in Study 4. The cue indicating target position appeared at the same time as the first pair of letters and remained visible until the end of each trial.

Procedure. There were six conditions: (1) SO1: matching letter in first display in the same object as the target; (2) SO2: matching letter in the second display, in the same object as the target; (3) DO1: matching letter in the first display, in a different object from the target; (4) DO2: matching letter in the second display, in a different object from target; (5) NM: no-match with all different letters; (6) different digits (from the set 23457) in both preview displays. These conditions were randomly mixed within blocks. Subjects were given one block of practice and then six experimental blocks of 48 trials each, giving 48 reaction times per subject per condition.

Subjects. A total of 10 students at the University of British Columbia (6 women) participated as paid subjects.

Results and Discussion

The mean naming latencies and preview effects are given in Table 7. The results are clear: of the four items in the preview displays (two each in two consecutive fields), only one yielded a preview benefit. As expected, this was the last letter previewed in the frame that later contained the target [$M = 19$ ms, $t(9) = 3.41$, $p < .01$]. The results for condition SO1, in which the target was previewed earlier in the same object, indicate no benefit whatever ($M = 0$ ms). Since the preview benefit was present and undiminished with stationary objects in Experiment 2 across a blank interval between preview and target of 700 ms, and with moving objects in Experiment 4(b) across an interval of 590 ms, the absence of any benefit from the matching letter in the first field, presented 500 ms

TABLE 7
Mean Naming Latencies and Preview Effects in Experiment 7

Target shown in:	Recent field		Early field
Same object	510		529
Different object	533		532
No match		529	
Digits		525	
	Preview effects		
Object specific	23**		3
Nonspecific	−4		−3

** This value is significant at $p < .01$.

208   KAHNEMAN, TREISMAN, AND GIBBS

before the target, is unlikely to be due simply to decay over time. The
second letter in the same frame appears to wipe out the first, so far as the
reviewing process is concerned.

All this makes sense if the purpose of the underlying representation—
the object file—is to mediate perception and to control and integrate
response tendencies. This function is served economically by maintaining
a record of the current state of the environment. The most recent description of an object remains in force unless updated, and it is consulted when
the state of the object changes, in order to maintain perceptual continuity.
The pattern of results suggests that the information in the object file is
overwritten only when new and incompatible information is entered.
When the previous information simply disappears, the preview benefit
survives apparently intact for at least 600–700 ms, and perhaps much
longer.

It would be interesting to see whether the updating rule is strictly object
specific rather than location specific. When one object is temporarily
occluded by another object, the second should not overwrite the first, if
the updating operates on object files rather than physical locations. This
could be tested, for example, with displays like those that generate Michotte's tunnel effect (1963), or with displays in which a stationary object
is temporarily hidden by an object that appears closer to the observer.
Recent experiments suggest that cues to occlusion are available and can
be used to modify early visual processing, such as that involved in determining the direction of motion in small apertures (Shimojo, Silverman, &
Nakayama, 1988), or the perception of matching shapes (Sekuler &
Palmer, 1990).

GENERAL DISCUSSION

This series of experiments has established a robust object-specific benefit: when a new stimulus appears, it will be named faster if it physically
matches a previous stimulus seen as part of the same perceptual object. In
different experiments we used shared location, relative position in a pattern seen in apparent motion, or a shared frame to link the target selectively to one of the previewed letters. A significant difference between the
SO and the DO conditions was found in each case, although the preview
displays in these conditions contained the same information and should
have induced the same activation in semantic memory.

The most important results of these experiments were the following: (1)
with only two objects in the field, the benefit of prior presentation of the
target was almost entirely object specific, but selectivity was impaired
when the number of items was increased; (2) the limit on performance was
determined by the number of different tokens in the scene, not the number of types; (3) the specificity of the preview effect was unchanged when

the preview was presented for one full second; (4) the object-specific benefit was not reduced by much slower linking movement, resulting in an ISI of 590 ms; (5) the benefit was wiped out by the subsequent presentation of another letter in the same object; (6) similarity of color did not induce a selective link between the target and a prime; (7) in the absence of links through object identity, the same preview benefits appeared to be distributed equally among the items in the preview display, compatible with an essentially arbitrary process of selection.

Additional experiments to be reported separately produced the following findings: (8) when words from a large vocabulary are used instead of letters, there is a large nonspecific priming effect, as well as a significant object-specific benefit; (9) there is also substantial nonspecific priming, even with letters, when the preview field contains just one letter rather than two or more; (10) differences of case between the preview and the target letter reduced the object-specific preview benefit in some conditions but not in others.

Two further variants of the reviewing design were concerned with the level of information that is integrated in object representations. (11) Feature information as well as letter identity may be collected and integrated in object-specific representations. In one experiment, the priming field consisted of four frames, each containing a single vertical or horizontal line. The frames moved empty to new positions. Three of the frames in the target display contained a line; the fourth contained either a line or a plus sign. Subjects responded to the presence or absence of the plus. They were slowed significantly in responding to the absence of a plus when the two lines shown in each of the frames would have made a plus if superimposed. This result suggests genuine integration of feature information. (12) At the other extreme, we failed to get object-specific benefits in a letter classification task where only the responses were shared between preview and target. This suggests the accumulation and integration of perceptual information rather than the accumulation of response tendencies; however, we do not propose that the possibility of accumulating response tendencies in object files has been ruled out.

We interpret these findings in terms of two theoretical notions: a selective reviewing process, and the object files that are reviewed. Our hypothesis is that the allocation of attention to the target item evokes an automatic process of reviewing, which selects one of the current object files, resulting in facilitation when the target and the retrieved item match, interference when they do not. When the target is assigned by a correspondence process to a particular object in the preview field, this link controls reviewing. In the absence of selective perceptual factors a random item will be reviewed. The information that is retrieved and integrated by the reviewing process may range from elements of shape (the lines that make a plus) to more abstract letter identities. We distinguish the effects of reviewing from effects of node priming. In our account, node priming played no role in the present experiments, presumably because the vocabulary of stimuli and responses was so small that node priming for all items was permanently at ceiling. When we used words we found both an object-specific advantage of about 25 ms for the SO over the DO condition and a large nonspecific preview benefit of about 50 ms in the comparison of DO and NM conditions.

We have stressed three characteristics of the reviewing process that produces the object-specific preview benefits observed in our experiments: it operates backward, it selects only a single item, and it is guided mainly by the features that control the unity and continuity of an object over time, but not by the shape, color, or content of the target. Any priming effect logically involves both a memory trace and a probe, but alternative analyses may focus on one or the other. The present treatment focuses on the function of the target as a probe, rather than on the lingering memory trace produced by the preview. This emphasis is justified by the observation that the SO and DO conditions in several of our experiments are strictly identical until the appearance of the target. Consequently, both the object-specific advantage and the absence of nonspecific priming must be explained by events that occur after that time.

We consider the almost total absence of nonspecific preview benefits in most of the experiments to be a serendipitous outcome of our initial choice of an experimental vocabulary. As already noted, considerable nonspecific priming was obtained in the same design when the stimuli were words drawn from a large vocabulary. However, the recurrent null result obtained in the present studies is a highly instructive result, which seems unlikely to have arisen from a combination of facilitation and interference effects that just happened to cancel out in the DO condition. Instead of the target being primed by several previewed items, and more by the one shown in the same object than by others, we are led to the hypothesis that only one of the previewed items is reviewed, a hypothesis that gained substantial support from the near constancy of total preview benefits observed in Experiments 6(a) and 6(b). Once the hypothesis has been formulated, however, there is no reason to restrict its applications to situations in which nonspecific priming can be eliminated. To account for cases in which nonspecific preview advantages are found, as well as object-specific ones (as in some of our studies with late cues, with no linking motion and with words), we simply give up the assumption that the selection is completely controlled by object relations. Even if reviewing never picked out more than one previewed item, nonspecific benefits would be found whenever the shape or content of the target have a part in controlling the operation of selective retrieval, and also, of course, when cues to object continuity are weak or absent and the selection is made at random. How far this notion of backward processing can be pushed to account for priming effects that are usually attributed to residual or to spreading activation is a matter to be settled by future research. The relation of reviewing to so-called backward priming effects is also a matter to be explored further (Glucksberg et al., 1986; Koriat, 1981).

Related Research: (1) Reviewing and Repetition Priming

Koriat and Norman (1988, 1989) have reported a set of studies that are relevant to our story, and they develop a concept that appears related to the concept of reviewing. They looked at repetition effects across successive trials with an intertrial interval of 500 ms in a classification task involving mental rotation. Their subjects classified letters or digits presented singly or in pairs in different orientations relative to the normal upright. Koriat and Norman found that when a stimulus exactly matched the previous stimulus except for its orientation, classification reaction times were faster than when the stimuli differed. The facilitation decreased with increasing mismatch in orientation, even when the present stimulus was itself upright (although the backward alignment benefit was greater for stimuli that deviated most from the upright orientation). They describe this backward alignment as an automatic "stimulus-induced, perceptual process that responds to the visual congruence between successive stimuli" (p. 491). The match appears to be holistic, since there is no facilitation for two identical digit pairs when the order within pairs is reversed (e.g., 13 and 31). Koriat and Norman suggest that the backward alignment is "designed to detect transformational invariance across successive visual events without necessarily establishing their identities. Like apparent motion, it can rely strictly on the visual correspondence between successive stimuli" (p. 491). We would add the prediction that the benefits would be object specific if the letters or digits were presented in separate frames or locations. In Koriat and Norman's experiments, all the stimuli appeared at fixation.

Kirsner et al. (1987) have offered an account of long-term repetition effects that emphasizes the role of the target as a memory probe. The main interest of these authors is to explain the specificity, both featural and linguistic, of repetition priming in verbal memory tasks. Their theory attempts to account for the evidence that specific conjunctions of surface features and abstract identities are stored and retrieved, whether they are relevant to the task or not. They review evidence that repetition priming in word identification is typically increased when the probe stimuli match the previewed items in type font, in letter case, in phonological form, in modality, and in language; explicit memory for these attributes varies inversely with their importance in mediating priming, suggesting that the priming depends on a failure to differentiate the memory trace from the current probe.

Kirsner et al. (1987) attribute priming to a matching process linking the current stimulus description and the record of an earlier stimulus description. The match speeds up the identification process. They use the terms "description" and "record" to refer respectively to an object file representing a present stimulus and to the memory trace of a past stimulus. The "descriptions" are highly articulated structural descriptions of the object, reached through sensory analysis abstracting information about its physical properties, parsing it into components to give structural elements, and where applicable "redescribing" the object in alternative media such as a phonological code for a visually presented word. "Like object files, they provide a functional location where perceptual information can be stored and organized during interpretation" (p. 149). Kirsner et al. (1987) see word recognition as involving access to "an extremely detailed record of one or more instances" (p. 161). Access is achieved not by a search process but by direct addressing through "the particular combination of codes (i.e., pattern of activity) that constitute the record. When the stimulus description re-creates that combination, the record has been 'discovered' " (p. 161).

There is of course a critical difference between the situations we investigated and those with which Kirsner et al. (1987) were concerned: the continuity of object identity is not a relevant factor in studies of long-term priming, whereas it seems to be the dominant factor that controls reviewing in the present experiments. However, the process of retrieving records that they describe appears to be quite similar to the process of retrieving object files that we have discussed here, except for the change in the basis of selective retrieval.

(2)Trans-Saccadic Integration

The possibility of spatiotopic fusion has been the focus of much important research on the trans-saccadic integration of information (see Irwin, 1991 and Pollatsek & Rayner, 1990 for reviews). The hypothesis that the detailed retinotopic images of successive fixations are brought into register, then combined before being fully processed, was once quite popular, but recent evidence has cast much doubt on it (Irwin, 1991). A series of studies have shown that the information that is integrated across saccades can be moderately abstract. In particular, Pollatsek, Rayner, and Collins (1984) showed that replacing a picture by its mirror image or changing the size of a picture by 10% across fixations did not reduce the benefit of parafoveal preview, and McConkie and Zola (1979) showed that the benefit of parafoveal preview of words was not reduced by arbitrary changes of the case of constituent letters. However, there is also compelling evidence for the maintenance of visual, spatial information across saccades (Irwin, Zacks, & Brown, 1990; Pollatsek et al., 1984). Irwin (1991) opted for an interpretation involving two separate mechanisms. He attributes the more abstract, conceptual facilitation to priming of already existing word and object representations in long-term memory, and the more visual sensory facilitation to short-term visual memory. We offer the alternative suggestion that the object file contains information at several levels. The evidence of object-specific benefits at these levels, which we will present in a separate paper, supports this position.

A recent article by Pollatsek, Rayner, and Henderson (1990) used a design very similar to ours, in conjunction with a study of eye movements. The sequence of events on each trial was as follows: fixation, followed by the presentation of two pictures of easily nameable objects, next to each other, 5° and 10° from fixation; subjects were instructed to move fixation to a mark between the pictures; the onset of a saccade triggered a change in the display, leaving one of the original pictures in view, next to a larger checkerboard pattern. The subjects were instructed to name the remaining picture, and their reaction times were recorded. In the no-switch condition (similar to our SO condition) the picture to be named was in the same spatial location it had occupied in the preview, but its retinal location was changed. In the switch condition (similar to DO) it occupied the spatial location previously filled by the other object. The results indicated a location-specific benefit of 10 ms, and considerable nonspecific priming. The responses in the switch condition were faster by 48 ms than responses on trials where the target matched neither of the two previewed objects.

In terms of the present analysis, which does not assign a special role to location as against object identity, the procedure used by Pollatsek et al. (1990) is somewhat ambiguous—mainly because it is unlikely that the checkerboard was seen as a new state of the object whose position it occupied. If the checkerboard was seen as a new object, it is quite possible that the target object in the switch condition was not perceived as a new token, but as the same object previously shown in the location now occluded by the checkerboard pattern. A similar perceptual ambiguity may affect other experiments in that series, which duplicated the sequence of retinal stimulation of the original studies, with a stationary eye: one field was first shown to the parafovea for 200 ms, followed by the second field at fixation. In this experiment, the SO condition was actually slower than the DO condition, by 19 ms. Once again, there was considerable nonspecific advantage: the SO condition was 31 ms faster than the NM condition. We have not replicated this experiment in detail, but have generated similar displays: The apparent motion they yield appears to us to be ambiguous, with the preview picture often moving into the target

214   KAHNEMAN, TREISMAN, AND GIBBS

picture and the checkerboard appearing as a new object. There is no clear
Ternus effect like the global motion one gets with pairs of letters.

The large amount of nonspecific priming observed in these studies
could be due in part to this perceptual ambiguity. In addition, node priming was probably more important in that study than in our experiments
with letters. Although the vocabulary of pictures was quite small (20
objects were used), the task of naming pictures is harder than letter naming and the reaction times were accordingly much slower than in our
experiments. Finally, the correlation between the contents of the preview
and target fields was lower than in our studies, which generally used a
vocabulary of eight items. In both studies the probability of appearing as
the target was ⅓ for each previewed item, but the probability was ⅙ for
other items in our study, ¹/₁₈ in the study by Pollatsek et al. (1990), a
difference that might be reflected in more active processing of the previewed items in their study. The discrepancy between the results of the
Pollatsek et al. (1990) study and our own is instructive; follow-up work
will be needed to identify the boundary conditions for the object-specific
benefit we studied. If our conjectures about the relevant variables are
correct, there would be no reason to amend the interpretation offered for
our results.

(3) Object Tokens

In the introduction to this paper we contrasted two models of perception: a display-board model in which objects currently in view are represented by the activation of corresponding nodes in long-term semantic
memory, and a model in which perception consists of the construction
and utilization of the episodic representations that we have called object
files. Similar distinctions have been drawn by others, particularly in computational approaches to visual modeling. One early example was the
separation between different knowledge sources and the "blackboard"
through which they communicate (Reddy, Erman, Farrell, & Neely,
1973). This idea was extended by McClelland (1986) within the connectionist PDP framework to allow more than one word to be identified at a
time, using what he called "programmable blackboards." Another example is the idea of incremental representations used by Ullman (1984) in his
discussion of visual routines. The incremental representations are temporary structures to which new information is added as it is extracted by
visual operations such as boundary tracing, "coloring" or bounded activation, and indexing, at a level of processing that is intermediate between
parallel preattentive feature registration and object identification through
matching to stored object models.

There are also a few empirical studies that are relevant to the notion of
object files. The closest to our paradigm is a set of experiments by Tipper,

Brehaut, and Driver (1990) in which they explore the conditions under which inhibition or "negative priming" from a distractor in one display carries over to a target in the next display; in particular they test whether it depends on the two sharing the same location or on their being perceived as the same object. Between the preview and the probe displays, their stimuli appeared to pass behind an occluding surface and to emerge at different locations. The negative priming effect (slower responses to the target when it had previously been seen as a distractor) proved to be object centered rather than tied to either the retinal or the environmental location of the distractor in the preceding display. The authors suggest (p. 503) that "object files can survive occlusion and may be inhibited during selection of another object." Their finding complements ours: whereas we have demonstrated facilitation from a preview of the target, they show interference when a previously unattended (and therefore inhibited) object later becomes relevant. Both demonstrate that attentional effects are tied to objects rather than to locations.

Perhaps the most dramatic demonstration of the ability of the perceptual system to individuate and to track object tokens is described by Pylyshyn and Storm (1989). They presented subjects with either identical stimuli (small white pluses) moving in random directions at randomly varying speeds. Subjects were able to track up to four of these for several seconds with about 85% accuracy in the absence of any individuating properties other than the spatiotemporal continuity of the elements.[1] Pylyshyn (1989) explores the idea that we need the ability to index visual elements—features, locations, parts or objects—at some very early stage of processing before we can make any other information about their spatial relations explicit. He suggests that we have available about four visual indices or FINSTs (short for "fingers of instantiation") which we can attach to features or clusters of features and which can maintain access to these features as they move in space or as we define their relation to other features. These FINSTs are set up and maintained preattentively, and may in fact be used to determine where attention should be directed.

How do FINSTs relate to object files? We might think of them as the initial spatiotemporal label that is entered in the object file and that is used to address it. Our object files contain considerably more information; in fact all the information that defines and describes a particular perceived

---

[1] Pylyshyn and Storm's subjects may have coded the four moving pluses that they were tracking as the corners of a single global deforming shape. If so, they would, in our object file terms, have been entered into a file representing a single changing object, making their spatial relations explicit, and perhaps representing them as emergent features of the global shape such as its angles, its elongation, and its convexity or concavity. Yantis (1989) reported evidence consistent with this hypothesis.

object. So a FINST might be the initial phase of a simple object file before any features have been attached to it. The story is a little more complex, however, since several FINSTs are needed to define the structure of any object with parts whose spatial relations can vary; so there cannot be a one-to-one mapping between FINSTs and object file addresses. The problems that the two theories are designed to solve are not exactly matched, and, as a consequence, neither are the theoretical constructs. FINSTs are perhaps closer to Marr's concept of place tokens—abstract markers that allow the visual system to treat filled locations independently of the particular features or objects that occupy them. For example, place tokens allow certain spatial relations, such as colinearity, to be made explicit without reference to any other aspect of the elements between which they hold.

The most important perceptual phenomena which led us to postulate the existence of temporary, episodic representations of objects, separate from their descriptions in a long-term recognition network, are the following:

(1) *The feature-conjunction problem.* We are unlikely to have a node for the word "fox" written in green uppercase letters and another for the number "162" handwritten in red ink. It is easier to explain with object files than with a display board analogy how arbitrary sets of potentially interchangeable properties can be allocated to the correct objects in the perceptual representation (Treisman & Schmidt, 1982). This has been called the "binding problem," and has been discussed in the context of computational theories of vision that use distributed representations, for which the problem is particularly acute (Feldman & Ballard, 1982; Hinton, McClelland, & Rumelhart, 1986; Strong & Whitehead, 1989). Some way of representing temporary episodic associations of features is needed when several objects are present at once, and it is not immediately obvious how the activation of sets of long term memory nodes could mediate this information. As Hinton et al. (1986) point out, "In a conventional computer it is easy to solve the binding problem. We simply create two records in the computer memory. . . . In parallel networks it is much harder to solve the binding problem." The present results make it clear that, even with coarse coding of conjunctions, as suggested by Hinton et al. (1986), simple location-specific replication of shape or object detectors is insufficient to model human perception of dynamic displays. We suggest that separate records—object files in our terms—may still be necessary.

(2) *Constraints on visual attention.* In tasks requiring selective attention, performance is usually efficient when one object must be selected and another ignored as irrelevant. On the other hand, it is difficult to attend selectively to different properties of a single object, like the color

and word in the standard Stroop task (Kahneman & Henik, 1981). Display board models would have difficulty explaining why it should be easier to focus on one of two nodes when the properties they code happen to characterize two different objects in the field than when they belong to a single object. Conversely, divided attention is improved when two relevant items are phenomenologically grouped to form a single "perceptual object" (Duncan, 1984; Treisman et al., 1983), as if attention operates on object files as units. Finally, interference from distractors in a letter classification task (Eriksen & Eriksen, 1974) is determined more by grouping through shared motion than by spatial proximity (Driver & Baylis, 1989). Letters that move together may be assigned to a shared object file, making selective attention to one of them more difficult.

(3) *The type-token distinction.* When the scene contains several replicas of the same object, we must form separate identical tokens to represent each instance. If perception depended only on the level of activation of particular nodes for the identities of the objects currently visible, some additional way would be needed to distinguish many small dogs, or many atypical dogs, from one large or typical dog. Interestingly, it appears that the coding of repeated instances may fail with brief presentations or at high rates of sequential presentation, leading to "repetition blindness" (Kanwisher, 1987; Mozer, 1989).

(4) *The perception of moving, changing objects.* Perhaps the most compelling source of evidence that perception is object centered is the observation of continuity and unity across motion and change that we illustrated at the beginning of this paper. Onlookers in the movie can exclaim "It's a bird; it's a plane; it's Superman!" without any change of referent for the pronoun. If the appropriate constraints of spatiotemporal continuity are observed, objects retain their perceptual integrity and unity. Since neither spatial location, sensory properties, nor even the most appropriate label need remain constant, we are forced to attribute any object-specific perceptual phenomena to some form of object-specific representation, addressed by its present location and by its continuous history of travel and change through space over time.

REFERENCES

Driver, J., & Baylis, G. C. (1989). Movement and visual attention: The spotlight metaphor breaks down. *Journal of Experimental Psychology: Human Perception and Performance, 15*, 448–456.

Feldman, J. A., & Ballard, D. H. (1982). Connectionist models and their properties. *Cognitive Science, 6*, 205–254.

Glucksberg, S., Kreuz, R. J., and Rho, S. (1986). Context can constrain lexical access: Implications for models of language comprehension. *Journal of Experimental Psychology: Learning, Memory and Cognition, 12*, 323–335.

Green, M. (1986). What determines correspondence strength in apparent motion? *Vision Research, 26*, 599–607.

218   KAHNEMAN, TREISMAN, AND GIBBS

Green, M. (1989). Color correspondence in apparent motion. *Perception and Psychophysics*, **45**, 15–20.

Hinton, G. E., McClelland, J. L., & Rumelhart, D. E. (1986). Distributed representations. In D. E. Rumelhart, J. L. McClelland, & the PDP Research Group (Eds.), *Parallel distributed processing: Explorations in the microstructure of cognition: Vol. 1. Foundations.* Cambridge, MA: MIT Press/Bradford.

Irwin, D. (1991). Perceiving an integrated visual world. In D. Meyer & S. Kornblum (Eds.), *Attention and performance* (Vol. XIV), in press.

Irwin, D., Zacks, J. L., & Brown, J. S. (1990). Visual memory and the perception of a stable visual environment. *Perception and Psychophysics*, **47**, 35–46.

Jonides, J. (1981). Voluntary versus automatic control over the mind's eye movement. In J. Long & A. Baddeley (Eds.), *Attention and performance* (Vol. IX). Hillsdale, NJ: Erlbaum.

Kahneman, D., & Henik, A. (1981). Perceptual organization and attention. In M. Kubovy & J. R. Pomerantz (Eds.), *Perceptual organization.* Hillsdale, NJ: Erlbaum.

Kahneman, D., & Miller, D. (1986). Norm theory: Comparing reality to its alternatives. *Psychological Review*, **93**, 136–153.

Kahneman, D., & Treisman, A. (1984). Changing views of attention and automaticity. In R. Parasuraman and D. A. Davies (Eds.), *Varieties of attention.* New York: Academic Press.

Kanwisher, N. G. (1987). Repetition blindness: Type recognition without token individuation. *Cognition*, **27**, 117–143.

Kiger, J. I., and Glass, A. L. (1983). The facilitation of lexical decisions by a prime occurring after the target. *Memory and Cognition*, **11**, 356–365.

Kirsner, K., Dunn, J., & Standen, P. (1987). Record-based word recognition. In M. Coltheart (Ed.), *Attention and performance: Vol. XII. The psychology of reading.* London: Erlbaum.

Kolers, P. A. (1972). *Aspects of motion perception.* Elmsford, NY: Pergamon.

Koriat, A. (1981). Semantic facilitation in lexical decision as a function of prime-target association. *Memory and Cognition*, **9**, 587–598.

Koriat, A., & Norman, J. (1988). Frames and images: Sequential effects in mental rotation. *Journal of Experimental Psychology: Learning Memory and Cognition*, **14**, 93–111.

Koriat, A., & Norman, J. (1989). Establishing global and local correspondence between successive stimuli. *Journal of Experimental Psychology: Learning Memory and Cognition*, **15**, 480–494.

LaBerge, D. (1983). Spatial extent of attention to letters and words. *Journal of Experimental Psychology: Human Perception and Performance*, **3**, 371–379.

Lambert, A. & Hockey, R. (1986). Selective attention and performance with a multidimensional visual display. *Journal of Experimental Psychology: Human Perception and Performance*, **12**, 484–495.

McClelland, J. L. (1986). The programmable blackboard model of reading. In J. L. McClelland, D. E. Rumelhart, & the PDP Research Group (Eds.), *Parallel distributed processing: Vol. 2. Psychological and biological models.* Cambridge, MA: MIT Press.

McClelland, J. L., & Rumelhart, D. E. (1985). Distributed memory and the representation of general and specific information. *Journal of Experimental Psychology: General*, **114**, 159–188.

McConkie, G. W., & Zola, D. (1979). Is visual information integrated across successive fixations in reading? *Perception and Psychophysics*, **25**, 221–224.

Michotte, A. (1963). *The perception of causality.* (T. Miles and E. Miles, Trans.). London: Methuen. (Original work published 1946).

Mozer, M. C. (1989). Types and tokens in visual letter perception. *Journal of Experimental Psychology: Human Perception and Performance, 15,* 287–303.

Navon, D. (1977). Forest before trees: The precedence of global features in visual perception. *Cognitive Psychology, 9,* 353–363.

Pollatsek, A., & Rayner, K. (1990). What is integrated across fixations? In T. Weymouth & L. T. Maloney (Eds.), *Exploratory vision: The active eye.* New York: Springer-Verlag.

Pollatsek, A., Rayner, K., & Collins, W. E. (1984). Integrating pictorial information across eye movements. *Journal of Experimental Psychology: General,* 426–442.

Pollatsek, A., Rayner, K., & Henderson, J. M. (1990). Role of spatial location in integration of pictorial information across saccades. *Journal of Experimental Psychology: Human Perception and Performance, 16,* 199–210.

Pylyshyn, Z. (1989). The role of location indexes in spatial perception: A sketch of the FINST spatial index model. *Cognition, 32,* 65–97.

Pylyshyn, Z. W., & Storm, R. W. (1988). Tracking of multiple independent targets: Evidence for a parallel tracking mechanism. *Spatial Vision, 3,* 1–19.

Rayner, K. (1978). Foveal and parafoveal cues in reading. In J. Requin (Ed.), *Attention and performance* (Vol. VIII, pp. 149–161). Hillsdale, NJ: Erlbaum.

Rayner, K., McConkie, G. W., & Zola, D. (1980). Integrating information across eye movements. *Cognitive Psychology, 12,* 206–226.

Rayner, K., & Pollatsek, A. (1983). Is visual information integrated across saccades? *Perception and Psychophysics, 34,* 39–48.

Reddy, D. R., Erman, L. D., Farrell, R. D., & Neely, R. B. (1973). The Hearsay speech understanding system: An example of the recognition process. *Proceedings of the International Conference on Artificial Intelligence* (pp. 185–194).

Seidenberg, M. S., Waters, G. S., Sanders, M., & Langer, P. (1984). Pre- and postlexical loci of contextual effects on word recognition. *Memory & Cognition, 12,* 315–328.

Sekuler, A. B., & Palmer, S. E. (1990). Visual completion of partly occluded objects: A microgenetic analysis. Manuscript in preparation.

Shepard, R. (1984). Ecological constraints on internal representation: Resonant kinematics of perceiving, imagining, thinking, and dreaming. *Psychological Review, 91,* 417–447.

Shimojo, S., Silverman, G. H., & Nakayama, K. (1988). Occlusion and solutions to the aperture problem for motion. *Vision Research,* in press.

Sternberg, S., Knoll, R. K., & Turock, D. L. (1986). Direct access by spatial position in visual memory: 2. Visual location probes. *Bell Laboratories Technical Memorandum.*

Ternus, J. (1938). The problem of phenomenal identity. In W. D. Ellis (Ed.), *A source book of Gestalt psychology.* New York: Harcourt, Brace and Co.

Treisman, A., Kahneman, D., & Burkell, J. (1983). Perceptual objects and the cost of filtering. *Perception and Psychophysics, 33,* 527–532.

Treisman, A., & Schmidt, H. (1982). Illusory conjunctions in the perception of objects. *Cognitive Psychology, 14,* 107–141.

Ullman, S. (1979). *The interpretation of visual motion.* Cambridge, MA: MIT Press.

Ullman, S. (1984). Visual routines. *Cognition, 18,* 97–159.

Yantis, S. (1989). *Dynamic multielement attentional tracking.* Talk given at 30th annual meeting of the Psychonomic Society, Atlanta, GA.

(Accepted December 10, 1990)

[16]

Auditory and visual objects

Michael Kubovy*, David Van Valkenburg

University of Virginia, Charlottesville, VA, USA

Received 8 December 1999; accepted 17 November 2000

Abstract

Notions of objecthood have traditionally been cast in visuocentric terminology. As a result, theories of auditory and cross-modal perception have focused more on the differences between modalities than on the similarities. In this paper we re-examine the concept of an object in a way that overcomes the limitations of the traditional perspective. We propose a new, cross-modal conception of objecthood which focuses on the similarities between modalities instead of the differences. Further, we propose that the auditory system might consist of two parallel streams of processing (the 'what' and 'where' subsystems) in a manner analogous to current conceptions of the visual system. We suggest that the 'what' subsystems in each modality are concerned with objecthood. Finally, we present evidence for – and elaborate on – the hypothesis that the auditory 'where' subsystem is in the service of the visual-motor 'where' subsystem.

Keywords: Auditory; Visual; Objecthood

1. Introduction

In this article we argue for the concept of an *auditory object*. Although some have found such a concept so strange that they avoid the term altogether in favor of 'auditory event' (Blauert, 1997, p. 2), we are convinced that it is both a useful and important concept. To clarify it, we offer a distinction between an auditory 'what' subsystem and an auditory 'where' subsystem (in a manner analogous to

---

* Corresponding author. Department of Psychology, P.O. Box 400400, University of Virginia, Charlottesville, VA 22904-4400, USA. Fax: +1-804-982-4766.

E-mail addresses: kubovy@virginia.edu (M. Kubovy), dlv6b@virginia.edu (D. Van Valkenburg).

98   *M. Kubovy, D. Van Valkenburg / Cognition 80 (2001) 97–126*

Milner & Goodale, 1995), and argue that the 'what' subsystem forms auditory objects, and that the 'where' subsystem is in the service of vision.

The bias against the idea of auditory objecthood is embedded in folk ontology. Language itself[1] may lead us to believe that objects are visible by definition. For example, according to the *Oxford English Dictionary*, *object* means "Something placed before the eyes, or presented to the sight or other sense; an individual thing seen or perceived, or that may be seen or perceived; a material thing" (Object, 1993). The etymology of the word *object* explains the visuocentric connotation of the word: it derives from the Latin *ob-*, 'before' or 'toward', and *iacere*, 'to throw'. It used to mean, "Something 'thrown' or put in the way, so as to interrupt or obstruct the course of a person or thing; an obstacle, a hindrance" (Object, 1993). Indeed, most visible things are obstacles or a hindrance to sight; they prevent you from seeing something that lies behind them because they are opaque.[2]

In this paper we will deviate from our everyday notion of object in order to extend it to audition. We will do this by finding a different criterion for objecthood, one that does not rely on the notion of opacity. We must do this because the notion of opacity simply does not apply to auditory perception. Material things can of course be opaque to sound (Beranek, 1988, Chapter 3). But we do not listen to *material* things, we listen to *vibrating* things – *audible sources*. One sound source does not in general prevent you from hearing another: many natural sounds, especially biological ones, are composed of a fundamental frequency and discrete harmonics – i.e. they are sparse, like fences. Furthermore, masking is rare in nature because the masking sound must be considerably louder than the masked one (e.g. it takes the sound of a waterfall or thunder to mask our voices).

Although one sound can mask another, Bregman (1990), in his discussion of the auditory continuity illusion, shows that audible sources do not offer a natural analog to opacity. The auditory continuity illusion is created when one deletes part of a signal and replaces it with a louder sound: the signal is perceived to continue uninterrupted 'behind' the sound. Bregman compares this illusion with the visual experience of continuity behind an occluder (Fig. 1): "Let us designate the interrupted sound or visual surface as A, and consider it to be divided into A1 and A2 by B, the interrupting entity… [In vision one] object's surface must end exactly where the other begins and the contours of A must reach dead ends where they visually meet the outline of B. In the auditory modality, the evidence for the continuity occurs in the properties of B itself as well as in A1 and A2; B must give rise to a set of neural properties that contain those of the missing part of A. In vision, on the other hand, if objects are opaque, there is no hint of the properties of A in the visual region occupied by B" (p. 383).

We pointed out earlier that we do not listen to material things, but to audible sources. The auditory system is generally concerned with *sources* of sound (such as speech or music), not with *surfaces* that reflect the sound (Bregman, 1990, pp. 36–

---

[1] Indo-European languages in particular.

[2] There are two exceptions: things that are transparent and things that are sparse. There are two kinds of sparse things: things with holes in them (e.g. fences) and things that branch (e.g. plants).

M. Kubovy, D. Van Valkenburg / Cognition 80 (2001) 97–126 99

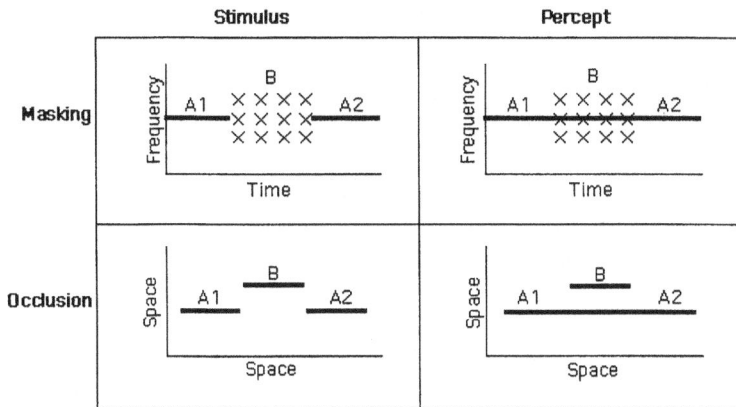

Fig. 1. The auditory continuity illusion (top) compared to the visual effect of continuity behind an occluder (bottom).

38). In a series of experiments, Watkins (Watkins, 1991, 1998, 1999; Watkins & Makin, 1996) has explored how the auditory system compensates for the distortion of spectral envelope (the major determinant of the perceived identity of many sounds) caused by factors such as room reverberation.

For the visual system just the opposite is true: it is generally concerned with *surfaces* of objects, not with the *sources* that illuminate them. As Mollon (1995) points out (giving credit to Monge, 1789):

> our visual system is built to recognise ... permanent properties of objects, their spectral reflectances, ... not ... the spectral flux ... (pp. 148–149).

These differences are summarized in Table 1.

For these reasons, we believe that to understand auditory objects we will have to rethink certain commonly accepted analogies between visual and auditory perception. In particular, we will show that both modalities are endowed with 'what' and 'where' subsystems, but that the relation between these four subsystems is complex. Obviously it is the 'what' subsystem of each modality that deals with objects, and so we will devote considerable attention to the auditory 'what' subsystem. But before we do, we must attend to the evidence connecting the auditory 'where' subsystem and the visuomotor orienting subsystem. We will claim that auditory localization is in the service of visual localization. This assertion is one of the cornerstones of our argument that space is not central to the formation of auditory objects.

Table 1
Comparison of vision and audition

Source of information	Vision	Audition
Primary	Surfaces	Sources
Secondary	Location and color of sources	Surfaces

2. Auditory 'where' in the service of visual 'where'

When two auditory sources appear to come from different spatial locations, shouldn't we say that they constitute different auditory objects, as do Wightman and Jenison (1995, pp. 371–372)? We prefer not to, because we believe that auditory localization is in the service of visual orienting, a hypothesis first formulated at the turn of the twentieth century by Angell: auditory "localisation occurs in the space world of vision–touch–movement... Most persons seem to make their localisation of sounds either in the form of visual imagery, or in the form of quasi-reflex localising movements of head and eye" (Angell, 1906, pp. 154–155). In this section we review the evidence supporting Angell's hypothesis.

The earliest sign of directional discrimination of sound in the human newborn is head orientation (Clifton, 1992), which suggests that the newborn is optimizing its head orientation to see the source.

Auditory localization is malleable, and can be influenced by the spatial location of a simultaneous visual stimulus. Bertelson and Aschersleben (1998) asked observers to judge whether the source of a sound was to the left or right of the median sagittal plane. When they presented the sound synchronously with an off-center flash, the sound appeared to be shifted in the direction of the light flash.

Sound localization itself is influenced by the act of visual orienting. Rorden and Driver (1999) presented observers with a noise burst from one of four speakers arranged in a fronto-parallel square array, and asked them to indicate whether the sound came from above or below their head. Before the noise was played, the observers were given a signal instructing them to move their eyes to the left or to the right. Reaction times (RTs) for correct up/down decisions were shorter when the direction of the intended eye movement was ipsilateral with the source of the noise than when it was contralateral to the source of the noise (regardless of whether the noise was heard before or after the eye movement was initiated).

Even clearer evidence of the role of auditory localization in visuomotor orientation is provided by Goldring, Dorris, Corneil, Balantyne, and Munoz (1996). On each trial they presented (for 1 s) either a visual target (an LED), an auditory target (broadband noise), or both, from a variety of azimuths. The participants' task was to turn their gaze towards the target as quickly as possible. When the targets were unimodal the relative eye–head latency depended on the eccentricity of the target: if eccentricity was less than 20° visual angle (dva), visual targets elicited a lower latency than auditory targets; beyond 20 dva, this order was reversed. For our purposes this result has one major implication: auditory localization is in the service of visual orientation where vision is weakest. (See also, Hughes, Nelson, and Aronchick (1998) who develop these findings further.)

To say that auditory localization is in the service of vision does *not* imply that auditory cueing is the most effective way to orient the visual system. Indeed, Jay and Sparks (1990) have shown that auditory-induced saccades are generally slower and less accurate than visually-induced saccades. Moreover, we are not arguing that auditory localization is equivalent to visual localization.

There is evidence of a one-way dependence of the visual modality on the auditory modality from studies of multimodal cueing. Spence and Driver (1997) presented observers with a light or sound (the target) from one of four positions in a fronto-parallel square array, and asked them to indicate whether the sound came from above or below their head. Some ISI before the target, observers were presented with an uninformative exogenous visual or auditory cue from either the left or right side. RTs for correct localization were compared across conditions. The results showed short-lived (ISI ≤ 200 ms) facilitated performance for valid auditory cues when the target was either visual or auditory. Visual cues, however, facilitated performance only for visual targets. Spence and Driver have since replicated this effect numerous times; they interpret their results as evidence for auditory localization in the service of vision: audition influences visual localization but *not* vice-versa (Spence & Driver, 1999).

The dominance of vision over audition is confirmed in a case of left visual neglect, i.e. a derangement of visual space representation (Ladavas & Pavani, 1998). The patient was asked to point to left, center or right acoustic stimuli under visual control or blindfolded. Her pointing to left auditory stimuli was influenced by visual spatial information, i.e. she manifested left neglect. But when she was blindfolded, she pointed to the previously ignored left space.

In macaque monkeys, Jay and Sparks (1984) found that the auditory receptive fields shifted with changes in eye position, allowing the auditory and visual maps to remain in register. Even in the barn owl, for which auditory localization is of primary importance in predation, Brainard and Knudsen (1993) found that individuals reared wearing prisms undergo visually-induced changes in the tuning for sound localization cues in the tectum and in the external nucleus of the inferior colliculus (see also Aitkin, 1990; Aronson & Rosenbloom, 1971; Stryker, 1999; Zheng & Knudsen, 1999).

If an auditory 'where' subsystem exists, it would have to combine spatial and somatosensory information. Young, Spirou, Rice, and Voigt (1992) have produced intriguing evidence on this matter. They suggested that the dorsal cochlear nucleus in the cat DGN is responsible for early analysis of sound source location on the basis of two observations: (1) the "DGN principal cells are exquisitely sensitive to spectral features of stimuli that carry sound localization information...", and (2) there is a somatosensory input to the DGN which may be providing information about the orientation of the cat's mobile pinnae, and thus allowing the DGN to integrate pinna-position information with sound localization cues. In humans, there are numerous subcortical areas that are believed to be responsible for cross-modal integration, and which possibly contain a supramodal representation of space (Andersen, Snyder, Bradley, & Xing, 1997; Stein & Meredith, 1993). Audio-visual speech integration studies using fMRI (Calvert, Campbell, & Brammer, 2000) as well as PET studies examining visual-tactile integration (Banati, Goerres, Tjoa, Aggleton, & Grasby, 2000; Macaluso, Frith, & Driver, 2000) provide converging evidence that the superior colliculus, as well as portions of the heteromodal cortex, are likely candidate areas. (See Spence and Driver (1997) for a more complete review of the neurological evidence supporting this idea.)

Let us summarize our argument to this point: (a) sound appears to inform us about

102   *M. Kubovy, D. Van Valkenburg / Cognition 80 (2001) 97–126*

● ● ●   ● ● ●   ● ● ●   ● ● ●   ● ● ●

Fig. 2. Grouping by proximity (after Wertheimer, 1923/1938).

○ ○ ● ● ○ ○ ● ● ○ ○ ● ● ○ ○ ● ● ○ ○ ● ●

Fig. 3. Grouping by similarity (after Wertheimer, 1923/1938).

sources and events rather than surfaces and material objects; (b) our language suggests to us that objects are visual; and (c) the visual objects we see have considerable control over what we hear. Wightman and Jenison (1995, pp. 371–372) distinguish between *concrete* auditory objects "formed by sounds emitted by real objects in the environment" (i.e. an orchestra) and *abstract* auditory objects, which "do not often correspond to real environmental objects" (i.e. a melody). We differentiate the auditory subsystem that processes these 'concrete' objects – the 'where' subsystem – from the auditory subsystem that processes 'abstract' auditory objects – the 'what' subsystem. To understand the auditory 'what' subsystem, we must abandon visuocentric notions of objecthood and offer a more general definition of perceptual object, be it visual or auditory.

3. 'What' subsystems: objects, grouping, figure-ground, and edges

A *perceptual object* is that which is susceptible to figure-ground segregation. This definition will allow us to develop a useful concept of auditory object. A critic who *defines* figure-ground segregation as a process applied to objects might claim that our definition is circular. But we believe that the benefit of the new definition outweighs the cost of abandoning the definition of figure-ground segregation in terms of objects. We believe that the process of grouping and most forms of feature integration are pre-attentive (Kubovy, Cohen, & Hollier, 1999; see also Bregman, 1990, pp. 206–209). We propose the following view of the relation between early processing, grouping, figure-ground segregation and attention. Early processing produces elements that require grouping. Grouping occurs following the principles described by the Gestalt psychologists (Figs. 2 and 3, from Wertheimer, 1923/1938, further developed by Kubovy, Holcombe, & Wagemans, 1998); it produces Gestalts, or perceptual organizations, which are also putative perceptual objects. Attention selects one putative object (or a small set of them) to become figure (Fig. 4) (Peterson & Gibson, 1994) and relegates all other information to ground (Fig. 5). The putative objects that become figure are perceptual objects, whereas the ground remains undifferentiated information (see Brochard, Drake, Botte, & McAdams, 1999 for evidence that the ground remains undifferentiated in audition).

There is little doubt that grouping and figure-ground segregation describe processes that are meaningful for auditory perception. Grouping is a well-estab-

M. Kubovy, D. Van Valkenburg / Cognition 80 (2001) 97–126 103

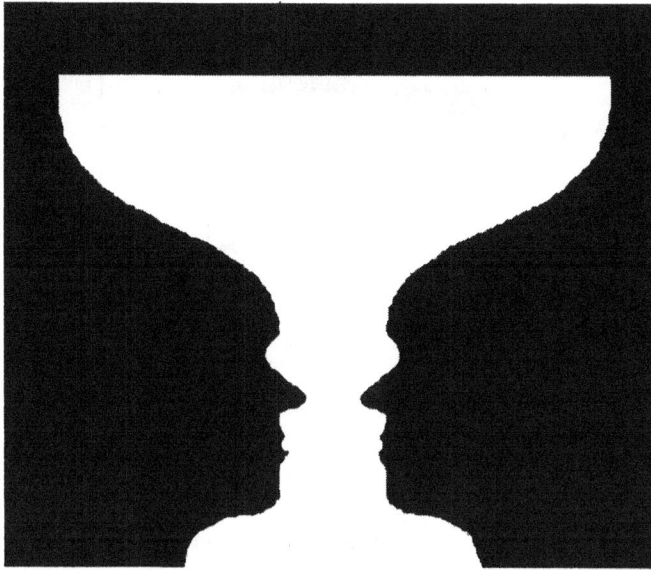

Fig. 4. Rubin vase/face.

lished auditory phenomenon. In particular, auditory stream formation – the auditory analog of visual grouping – has been studied in depth (Bregman, 1990; Handel, 1989, Chapter 7).

Figure-ground segregation is mentioned less frequently.[3] Nevertheless, in studies of streaming it has often been observed that when an auditory sequence breaks into two streams, we cannot pay attention to more than one of them at a time. For example, Bregman and Campbell (1971) presented observers with a repeating sequence of three high pitch notes (*ABC*) and three low pitch notes (123) in the order *A*–1–*B*–2–*C*–3. Observers typically reported the order of notes as *A*–*B*–*C*–1–2–3 or 1–2–3–*A*–*B*–*C*; they were able to attend to one stream or the other, but not both streams simultaneously. As in vision, whichever stream is being attended becomes the figure and the other the ground.

3.1. Plensensory functions and edges

Another phenomenon characterizes visual objects: the formation and assignment of edges. When the faces in Fig. 4 are seen in the foreground, they take ownership of

---

[3] Many forms of music use a drone, a low-pitched sustained tone that serves as an auditory background for music played at a higher pitch. The word suggests that a musical drone resembles the hum produced by bees. Drones were common in antiquity; today they appear in the music of the Balkans, Sardinia, Appalachia, and India, to name just a few.

104   *M. Kubovy, D. Van Valkenburg / Cognition 80 (2001) 97–126*

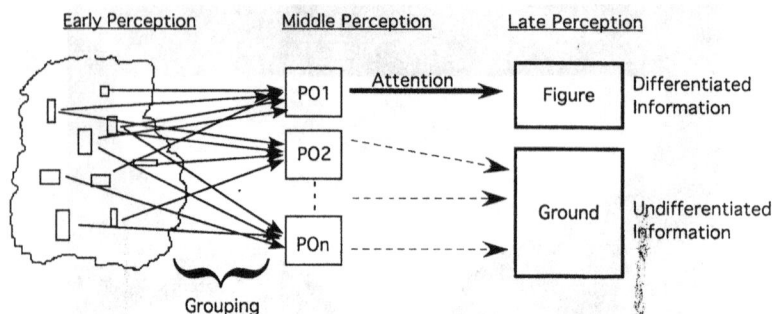

Fig. 5. A conservative view of the formation of perceptual objects. Early processing produces elements that undergo grouping to produce PO_1, PO_2, ..., PO_n, a set of perceptual organizations (or putative objects – recall that we have defined an object as the result of figure-ground segregation; therefore, these elements are merely *candidates* for objecthood). Attention is required to produce figure-ground segregation, which allocates processing capacity to the figure and leaves the ground relatively undifferentiated.

the two edges and the background appears to continue behind them. Let us suppose that *any object, be it visual or auditory, must have an edge or a boundary.*

What kinds of edges can be found in optic and acoustic information? To answer this question for vision, Adelson and Bergen (1991) developed the *plenoptic function*, which allows us to characterize edges in the optic information available at every point in space and time. But, as we will see, as soon as we try to construct an analogous *plenacoustic function*, we will face difficult theoretical questions, which we will try to answer in the course of this paper.

The plenoptic function (Fig. 6) is a formalized answer to the question, What can potentially be seen? It is the culmination of a line of thought that began with Leonardo da Vinci that was introduced into the study of perception by Gibson (1979) and further explored by Johansson and Orjesson (1989), who put the idea as follows:

> The central concept of ecological optics is the ambient optic array at a point of observation. To be an *array* means to have an arrangement, and to be *ambient at a point* means to surround a position in the environment that could be occupied by an observer. The position may or may not be occupied; for the present let us treat it as if it were not.[4] (p. 65)

The construction of the plenoptic function starts with a viewpoint, $V(x,y,z)$. We place a box with a pinhole (called a *pinhole camera*) at V, pointing in the direction (ϕ,θ)

---

[4] In this sense, our figures are slightly misleading because we have inserted pictures of eyes at points of observation in space.

M. Kubovy, D. Van Valkenburg / Cognition 80 (2001) 97–126 105

Fig. 6. Two points of the plenoptic function for viewpoints V_1 and V_2. Each arrow, light or dark, corresponds to a pencil of rays in direction (θ,ϕ). The dark arrows correspond to what might be seen by eyes at V_1 and V_2. (Slightly modified and redrawn from Fig. 1.3 in Adelson and Bergen (1991).)

(Fig. 7).[5] At the back of the camera is a spectrograph. We obtain a record of the intensity of light as a function of two variables: wavelength, λ, and time, t. Since we can change the viewpoint and rotate the camera in any direction, what can potentially be seen of a scene from any position is the plenoptic function, $P(\phi,\theta,\lambda,t,x,y,z)$.

Objects that reflect light readily create discontinuities in the plenoptic function: edges. By slicing the plenoptic function along various planes, as in Fig. 8, we can see how edges in these planes correspond to familiar features of the visual world. For example, Fig. 8a shows an edge that does not change in azimuth (ϕ); it is therefore vertical, whereas in Fig. 8b it does not change in tilt (θ), and it is therefore horizontal. Fig. 8h describes the effect of a horizontal movement of the viewpoint without changing either ϕ or θ.

We now turn to the plenacoustic function, in the hope that it will help us think about acoustic edges. But we encounter difficulties from the very outset. We are not sure how to illustrate it. Can we use Fig. 6, except that we replace the eyes with ears but leave the ecology (here, a tree) unchanged? That cannot be right. Even students of auditory navigation (Arias, Curet, Moyano, Joekes, & Blanch, 1993; Ashmead & Wall, 1999; Ashmead et al., 1998; Stoffregen & Pittenger, 1995) do not claim that a tree is a natural object of auditory perception. So we are reminded that the acoustic ecology differs from the optic ecology: as we pointed out earlier, auditory perception is more concerned with sources than with surfaces.

Should we then start from an illustration like Fig. 9? We think that even this

---

[5] We adopt the convention of Euler angles (Goldstein, 1980) according to which ϕ (azimuth) and θ (pitch or tilt) are successive counterclockwise rotations of the camera: ϕ is a rotation about the z-axis, and θ is a rotation about the ξ-axis of the camera in the xy plane.

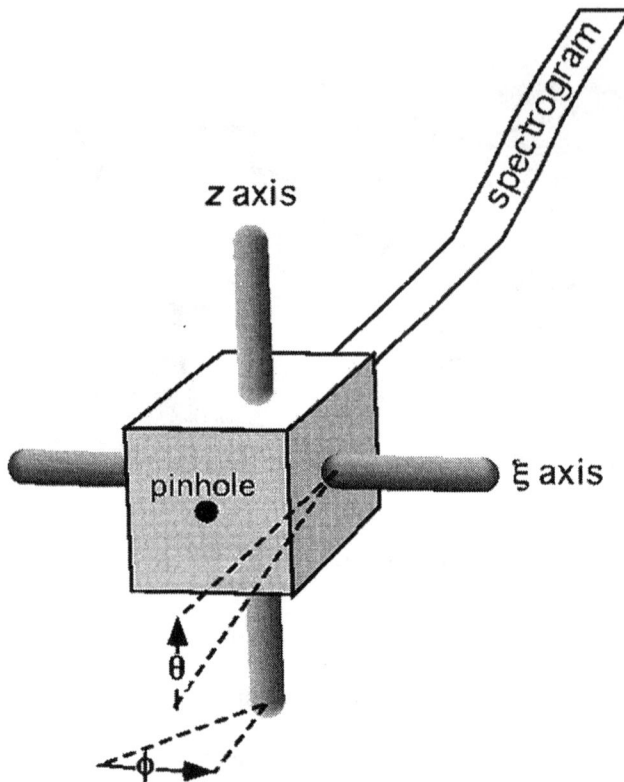

Fig. 7. The pinhole camera.

illustration is misleading, albeit subtly. It draws our attention to the 'where' aspect of audition: *Where* is the screaming boy? *Where* is the crying girl?

Before we can construct a plenacoustic function, we must think through the 'what' aspect of auditory perception. The Kubovy (1981) theory of indispensable attributes (TIA) will prove to be a useful tool in this endeavor.

3.2. Indispensable attributes, emergent properties, and grouping

Plensensory functions would suggest to us where edges might occur in the information available to an observer. Here we move beyond the perceptual ecology to examine the evidence that auditory objects are formed in pitch-time, whereas visual objects are formed in space-time. We begin with a series of thought experiments proposed by Kubovy to illustrate his TIA, after which we will present empirical evidence in support of this theory.

The TIA focuses on an important aspect of object formation: the aggregation of elements to form an emergent object. An emergent property is a property of an aggregate that is not present in the aggregated elements. For example, at room

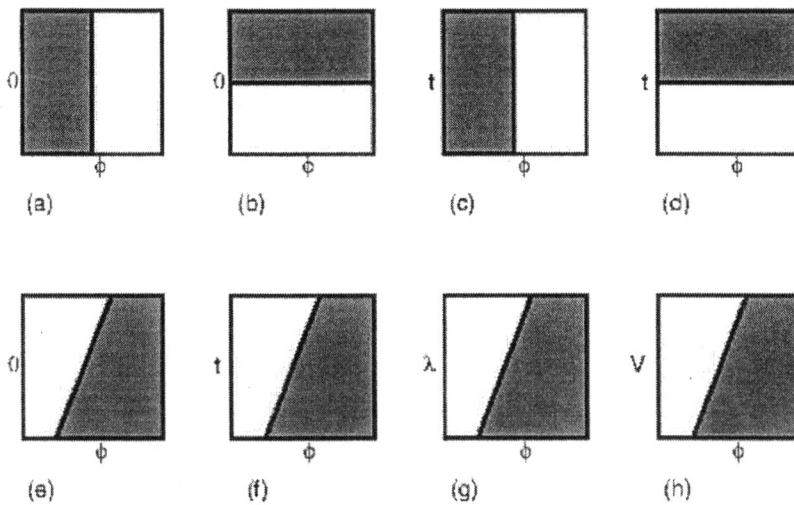

Fig. 8. Some edge-like structures that might be found along particular planes within the plenoptic function (note the varying axes, as labeled on each panel): (a) a vertical edge; (b) a horizontal edge; (c) a stationary edge; (d) a full-field brightening; (e) a tilting edge; (f) a moving edge; (g) a color sweep; (h) an edge with horizontal binocular parallax. (Slightly modified from Fig. 1.4 in Adelson and Bergen (1991).)

Fig. 9. Two points of the plenacoustic function for hearpoints H_1 and H_2. The dark arrows correspond to the sounds that might be least attenuated by the shadow of the head at H_1 and H_2.

temperature, water is a liquid, but the elements that compose it are both gasses. Thus, at room temperature, the property *liquid* is an emergent property of water. There are two kind of emergent properties: *eliminative* and *preservative*. When hydrogen and oxygen combine to form water, the properties of the elements (being gasses) are not observable; they are eliminated by the process of aggregation. In the human sciences such eliminative emergent properties are also common: we can mix two colored lights (say, red and yellow), and observers will not be able to tell whether the orange they see is a spectral orange or a mixture. Thus, color mixture is an eliminative emergent property. Preservative emergent properties were first noticed by Ehrenfels (1890/1988), who described a *melody* as being an emergent property of the set of notes comprising it. The notes can be heard; indeed they *must* be heard for the melody to be recognized. In a melody the elements are preserved in the process of aggregation; in fact the emergence of the melody is conditional upon the audibility of the elements.

The TIA offers a heuristic argument that suggests the conditions under which a perceptual aggregate will preserve the individuality of its elements. More simply, what are the features of stimuli that enable a perceptual system to determine that there is more than one entity in the environment? An attribute (or dimension) is defined as indispensable if and only if it is a prerequisite of perceptual numerosity. As we will show, these attributes are different for vision and for audition.

Spatial separation is an indispensable attribute for vision. Imagine presenting to an observer two spots of light on a surface (Fig. 10a). Both of them are yellow and they coincide; the observer will report one light. Now suppose we change the color of the lights, so that one spot is blue and the other is yellow, but they still coincide (Fig. 10b); the observer will report one white light. For the observer to see more than one light, they must occupy different spatial locations (Fig. 10c).

Pitch separation is an indispensable attribute for sound. Imagine simultaneously playing two 440 Hz sounds for a listener (Fig. 11a). Both of them are played over the same loudspeaker; the listener will report hearing one sound. Now suppose we play these two sounds over two loudspeakers (Fig. 11b); the listener will still report hearing one sound. For the listener to report more than one sound, they must be separated in frequency (Fig. 11c).

By analogous argument, time is an indispensable attribute for both vision and audition. Time thus takes on the role of a common indispensable attribute.

We would like to head off several possible misinterpretations of the TIA. (a) We do *not* claim that auditory spatial cueing is ineffective. On the contrary, we have no doubt that auditory spatial cueing gives rise to costs and benefits (Scharf, 1998). Our claim is that although spatial cueing may be sufficient to draw attention to a pitch, attention is allocated to the *pitch*, not to its *location*. (b) We do not claim that indispensable attributes are prerequisites of perceptual numerosity at every point. For example, consider Fig. 12. It would be foolish of us to claim that we do not see two planes at X. Rather, we see two overlapping objects, and we see them occupying different extensions in space. In audition, an analogous case is homophonic induction (Warren, 1982). Homophonic induction occurs when observers are played a long pure tone with periodic amplitude increases: we hear one continuous tone and a

M. Kubovy, D. Van Valkenburg / Cognition 80 (2001) 97–126 109

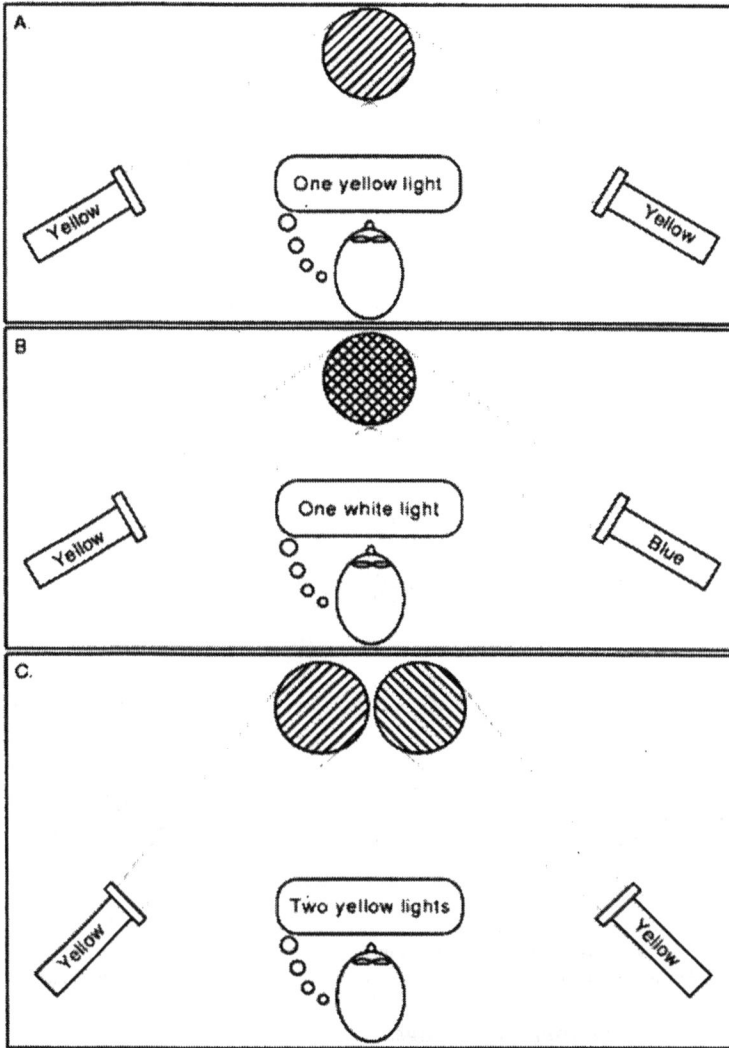

Fig. 10. (a) Two yellow spotlights create coincident spots. The observer sees one yellow spot. (b) One yellow spotlight and one blue spotlight create coincident spots. The observer sees one white spot. (c) Two spotlights create separate spots. Regardless of their color, the observer sees two spots.

second intermittent tone of the same pitch. Thus, we hear two overlapping objects, and we hear them occupying different extensions in time.

We draw the following conclusions from our thought experiments. (a) In vision space is an indispensable attribute for perceptual numerosity; color is not. (b) In audition frequency is an indispensable attribute for perceptual numerosity; space is not. (c) In both, time is an indispensable attribute.

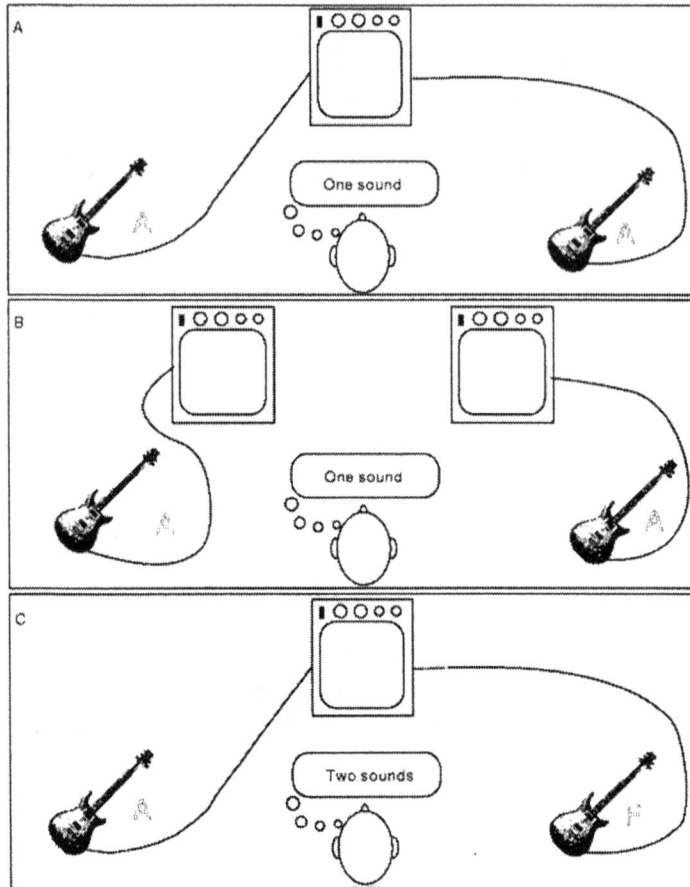

Fig. 11. (a) One loudspeaker plays two *A*s. The listener hears one *A* sound. (b) One loudspeaker plays an *A* while another speaker plays an *A*. The listener hears one *A* sound. (c) An *A* and an *F* are played. Regardless of whether they are played over one loudspeaker or two, the listener hears two sounds, an *A* and an *F*.

3.3. Indispensable attributes and edges

Earlier we could not construct a plenacoustic function because we did not know enough to map optics onto acoustics. With the TIA in hand, we can conjecture that we will find contours in the indispensable attributes of each modality. Looking back at Fig. 8 we observe that in each of the eight panels, one of the axes of the plane is spatial or temporal.

Likewise, in audition, we find edges in pitch, and edges in time, but not in space. The claim that there are edges in pitch may seem strange, but a moment's thought will show that the idea is quite natural. A biologically important source is periodic, at least over short periods of time. Therefore, it is characterized by a *fundamental frequency* that can be thought of as its lower edge in pitch. As we mentioned earlier,

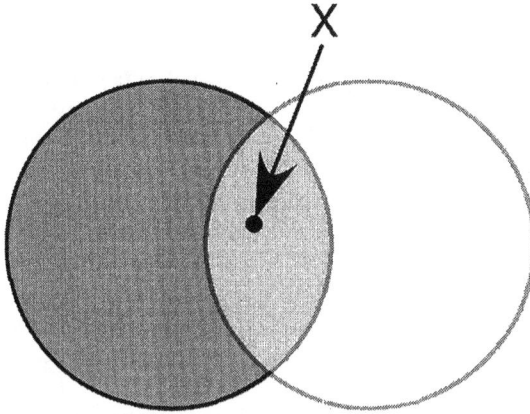

Fig. 12. Transparency: observers perceive two planes at X.

the object delimited can be schematically represented by its spectrum, as shown in Fig. 13. It is further characterized by the shape of its leading edge in pitch-time, its *attack*, and its trailing edge in pitch-time, its *decay*.

3.4. Interim conclusions

Up to here we have done two things. (a) We have argued in favor of an auditory 'where' subsystem that is linked to visuomotor orientation. (b) We have offered a new definition of perceptual objecthood, and we have shown that it implies a new way of thinking about auditory objects. We also made an assumption: in perceptual systems that have separate 'what' and 'where' subsystems, the 'what' subsystems are responsible for the generation of perceptual objects. We now turn to a fundamental question: what is the evidence for two auditory subsystems?

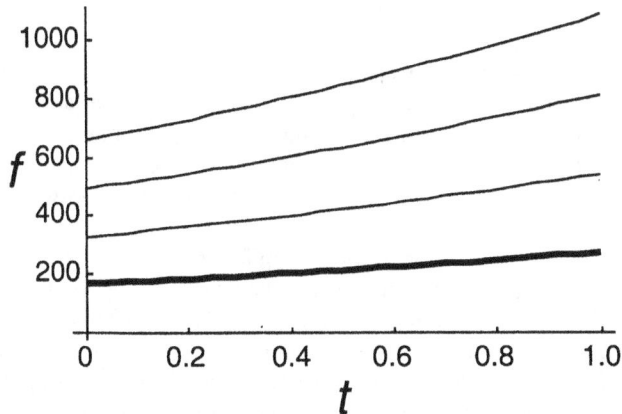

Fig. 13. An example of an auditory object. The first four harmonics of a tone gliding from 165 to 272 Hz over 1 s. The fundamental (the thick line) is the edge of the object.

112   *M. Kubovy, D. Van Valkenburg / Cognition 80 (2001) 97–126*

4. Evidence for two auditory subsystems

The idea of a parallel between the two visual subsystems and two auditory subsystems is gaining favor (Cisek & Turgeon, 1999). Unfortunately, the evidence for a separation of streams in the auditory system is scattered in the literature and may not be sufficiently strong to be conclusive. We turn first to behavioral evidence, and then present neurophysiological evidence.

It is possible to create an auditory illusion in which the 'what' of a stimulus is perceived correctly, but the 'where' is perceived incorrectly. Deustch and Roll (1976) created a stimulus that consists of a sequence of five pairs of concurrent dichotic tones. Let us denote by *A* a 400 Hz tone lasting 250 ms, and by *B* an 800 Hz tone of the same duration. The right ear receives *AAABB* (with 250 ms pauses between tones) and the other receives *BBBAA*. Right-handed listeners report hearing *AAABB*, but they hear the first three tones as if they came to the right ear and the remaining two as if they came to the left. Thus, they dissociated the two subsystems, because the dominant ear determines 'what' is heard, but the localization of the sounds (the 'where') is illusory.

Under some conditions, adaptation affects localization but not pitch perception. Hafter (1997) studied adaptation to trains of high-frequency clicks. He presented click trains in which the clicks had an inter-aural time disparity (ITD), so that listeners heard the clicks localized to the right or to the left. The listeners showed *binaural adaptation*: the effectiveness of the inter-aural information in the click train gradually diminished. He then presented listeners with trains of clicks that give rise to *periodicity pitch*, which is controlled by the inter-click interval (ICI). He asked listeners to discriminate changes in the pitch they heard when he changed the ICI. He found that the listeners suffered no adaptation in the performance of this task.

A somewhat indirect piece of behavioral evidence in favor of two auditory subsystems comes from experiments on the distribution of auditory response times. Wynn (1977) collected more than 300 000 response times from observers who were asked to tap in synchrony with a visual or auditory pulse. The distribution of RTs to visual pulses was unimodal. But the distribution of RTs to auditory pulses was bimodal, with many more fast responses than slow ones. As he increased the intensity of the sounds, three phenomena emerged: (a) the modes did not shift; (b) the humps became narrower; and (c) the mode of slow RTs diminished. From this Wynn concludes that there are two pathways in audition: one 'slow' and one 'fast'.

There also is neurophysiological evidence in favor of our hypothesis. On the basis of single-unit and tracer studies in cats and macaques as well as results from PET and fMRI experiments on humans, Rauschecker (1997, 1998a,b) argues that the auditory system has a dorsal 'where' stream and a ventral 'what' stream. Vocal communication sounds – presumably processed by a 'what' subsystem – project into areas of the lateral belt (and parabelt) of the superior temporal cortex. Auditory spatial information – presumably processed by a 'where' subsystem – projects into parietal areas. Studies of human patients with left hemispheric lesions provide a

M. Kubovy, D. Van Valkenburg / Cognition 80 (2001) 97–126 113

double dissociation between the two subsystems (Clarke, Bellmann, Meuli, Assal, & Steck, 2000). Patients with lesions in the medial, posterior auditory cortex (which Clarke et al., 2000 call the 'putative spatial pathway') exhibit localization deficits, whereas more lateral lesions (in the 'putative recognition pathway') cause recognition deficits.

5. Relations between 'what' and 'where' in vision and audition

We have suggested that the auditory 'where' subsystem is probably in the service of the visuomotor subsystem. The visual 'where' subsystem provides us with spatial information about the world in egocentric terms (Milner & Goodale, 1995). We believe the same to be true about the auditory 'where' subsystem. In other words, both the visual and the auditory 'where' subsystems may be thought of as being in the service of action.

It is harder to describe the relation between the visual and the auditory 'what' subsystems. We suggested earlier that they both are concerned with the segregation of figure from ground and the grouping of elements into objects. In vision this conception does not create a disjunction between the products of the 'what' and the 'where' subsystems, although the mechanisms are dissociable. Visual objects are extended in space, and they are located in space. So in vision the two subsystems seem to work to the same end: collecting information about a unified spatiotemporal reality.

In audition, however, distinguishing between the two subsystems creates what might be called an ontological chasm. The kinds of objects the auditory 'what' subsystem constructs need not be located in space, nor do they need to be defined in spatial terms. Nevertheless, if we surmise that the origin of the auditory 'what' subsystem is in vocal communication, then its non-spatiality becomes somewhat less puzzling.

The problem we encountered earlier, when we were considering the possibility of constructing a plenacoustic function, may be called the *dimension mapping question*: which dimensions of the optical input are analogous to which dimensions of the acoustic input? *The answer depends on our view of these inputs.* If we think of them in spatiotemporal terms, then the spatial and temporal dimensions in the two inputs will correspond to each other. Thus, six dimensions of the plenoptic function, ϕ, θ, t, V_x, V_y, V_z, map onto six dimensions of a putative plenacoustic function, ϕ, θ, t, H_x, H_y, H_z. We call this the *spatiotemporal mapping*. If, on the other hand, we think of the plensensory functions in terms of object formation, then the analogous dimensions in the two functions are those that allow for the formation of edges in the plenoptic and the plenacoustic functions. We call this mapping the *indispensable attributes mapping*.

5.1. The spatiotemporal mapping

Under the spatiotemporal mapping visual space and time are mapped onto auditory space and time. This is a natural view to take in the light of the assumptions made by Newton (1726/1999): "Absolute, true, and mathematical time, in and of itself and of its own nature, without reference to anything external, flows uniformly... Absolute space, of its own nature without reference to anything external, always remains homogeneous and immovable ... times and spaces are, as it were, the places of themselves and of all things" (pp. 408–410). In his *Critique of Pure Reason*, Kant (1787/1996) took Newton's idea further: "Space is not an empirical concept that has been abstracted from outer experiences. For the presentation of space must already lie at the basis in order for certain sensations to be referred to something outside of me..." (p. 77, B 38).[6] "Time is not an empirical concept that has been abstracted from any experience. For simultaneity or succession would not even enter our perception if the presentation of time did not underlie them a priori" (p. 85, B 46).

Newton and Kant were powerful influences. It was natural for early psychologists to adopt the spatiotemporal mapping. From this mapping they concluded that color gets mapped onto pitch, since they are non-spatial and non-temporal, and since they are both caused by waves. For example, we read a footnote by A.J. Ellis, translator of *Sensations of Tone* by Helmholtz (1885/1954):

> Assuming the undulatory theory, which attributes the sensation of light to the vibration of a supposed luminous 'ether', resembling air but more delicate and mobile, then the phenomena of 'interference' enables us to calculate the lengths of waves of light in empty space, &c., hence the numbers of vibrations in a second, and consequently the ratios of these numbers, which will then clearly resemble the ratios of pitch numbers that measure musical intervals. Assuming, then, that the yellow of the spectrum answers to the tenor *c* in music, and Fraunhaufer's 'line *A*' corresponds to the *G* below it, Prof. Helmholtz, in his *Physiological Optics* (*Handbuch der Physiologischen Optik*, 1867, p. 237), gives the following analogies between the notes of the piano and the colors of the spectrum:

G, Red,	*g*, Ultra-violet,
G#, Red,	*g#*, Ultra-violet,
A, Red	*a*, Ultra-violet,
A#, Orange-red,	*a#*, Ultra-violet,
B, Orange,	*b*, end of the solar spectrum.
c, Yellow,	The scale therefore
c#, Green,	extends to about a Fourth
d, Greenish-blue,	beyond the octave.
d#, Cyanogen-blue	
e, Indigo-blue,	
f, Violet,	

(p. 18)

---

[6] This is the traditional way to denote p. 38 in the second edition of the *Critique*.

M. Kubovy, D. Van Valkenburg / Cognition 80 (2001) 97–126 115

As profound differences between light and sound became clear in the twentieth century, psychologists abandoned the exploration of parallels between pitch and color. But the rest of the spatiotemporal mapping has been retained. Research on the 'cocktail party problem' is an excellent example. How do we segregate a speaker's voice from the voices of other concurrent speakers at a cocktail party? To Cherry (1959), who coined the term, the problem was a spatial one. All of his experiments involved dichotic listening: the listener hears a different message in each ear and has to report something from one or both. The assumption of the primacy of space in audition is even clearer in Broadbent (1958): "Sounds reaching the two ears are of course often perceived as coming from different directions ... and such sounds we will regard as arriving by different 'channels'" (p. 15). In this context the auditory system was considered to be a 'where' system, and auditory segregation was thought to be spatial in nature.

The implicit assumption of the auditory system as a 'where' system persists. For example, Handel (1988) criticized the original formulation of the TIA (Kubovy, 1981) for this very reason (for a reply, see Kubovy, 1988): "The auditory and visual worlds are inherently both temporal and spatial" (p. 315). For this reason, Handel opposed Kubovy's commitment to the TIA mapping and claimed that all mappings are possible and relevant, depending on the context. Although we have come somewhat closer to Handel's position by proposing two mappings, we are making a more specific claim. For the 'where' subsystems the spatiotemporal mapping is appropriate; for the 'what' subsystems the TIA mapping is appropriate.

5.2. The indispensable attributes mapping

We believe that the TIA mapping will allow researchers to formulate testable hypotheses about the nature of auditory objects and auditory object perception. The TIA is a heuristic tool for extending theories of visual perception into the domain of auditory perception (and perhaps vice-versa). Note that such extensions have been done in the past with considerable success. For example, Bregman (1990) has shown the similarities between the Gestalt principles in vision and in audition. Just as grouping by proximity functions in visual space (Kubovy et al., 1998), it also operates in auditory pitch (Bregman, 1990). McPherson, Ciocca, and Bregman (1994) have shown that good continuation operates in audition in an analogous way to vision. The concept of amodal completion as it is used in vision (Kanizsa, 1979) has been given a number of different names in audition: the acoustic tunnel effect (Vicario, 1960), perceptual restoration (Warren, 1970, 1984), the continuity effect (Bregman, 1990), and the phonemic restoration effect (Samuel, 1991). Since all of these phenomena abide by the same laws of grouping and organization, a desirable goal would be to have a theoretical framework which can account for this. The TIA is such a framework.

5.3. Implications for theories of attention

An attentional counterpart of TIA – which we will abbreviate to ATIA – could come in two versions: *strong* and *weak*. According to a strong ATIA, selective attention can *only* be directed to indispensable attributes, and not to other stimulus attributes. For example, the strong ATIA predicts that in vision you can pay attention to a region of space (or to an object defined by its spatial boundaries), but not to a part of color space. The work of Shih and Sperling (1996) favors such a position. They have shown that visual selective attention can be directed to space but not to color or size. On each trial of the experiment they presented a series of briefly presented frames (typically 27 of them). In each frame six letters were presented, equidistant from a fixation point. The characters in a frame were uniformly colored red or green. In one of these frames one letter was replaced with a digit. The observer's task was to report the digit's name, location, and color. The dependent variable was the observer's report accuracy. Before each trial the observer was given information (not always valid) about the color of the digit. The main result was this: the observers' accuracy was not affected by the validity of the cue. In a second experiment the color of the digit differed from the color of the letters, and observers did show a cost or benefit that depended on the validity of the cue. Thus, color can *draw* our attention to spatial locations, we cannot selectively attend to color – only to spatial locations.

According to a weak ATIA selective attention is generally directed towards indispensable attributes, but *can* be directed towards other attributes. For example, color is not an indispensable attribute, yet color-based inhibition of return (IOR) has been reported. Law, Pratt, and Abrams (1995) showed observers two successive color patches in the center of a monitor, with an ISI of 900 ms. They asked observers to respond as soon as they detected the second patch. When the two colors were the same, RTs were ≈ 5.5 ms longer than when the colors were different. We note, however, that the magnitude of the inhibition observed in this experiment is much lower than the effects observed with space-based IOR. The authors themselves acknowledge that "the color-based inhibition of return that we observed might be reduced or eliminated in situations with spatial uncertainty" (p. 407). We therefore await further progress on this topic before we retreat from the strong ATIA.

5.4. Costs of not adhering to indispensable attributes

The spatiotemporal mapping implies that space holds the same status in audition as it does in vision. Culling and Summerfield (1995) have argued the contrary: "the introspective impression that one can concentrate on a particular direction in order to pick out an attended voice from an interfering babble may be misleading. ...there is evidence that localization occurs after concurrent sounds have been separated by other processes" (p. 796). In other words, auditory objects are *not* formed in space. This assertion is supported by three experiments in which Culling and Summerfield explored the role of within-channel and across-channel processes in the perceptual separation of competing sounds that had different inter-aural phase spectra. A similar position is adopted by Darwin and Hukin (1999) in regards to speech sounds. They claim (on p. 622, illustrated in their Fig. 3, right-hand panel) that auditory objects are the result of non-spatial grouping processes (e.g. harmonicity and onset

M. Kubovy, D. Van Valkenburg / Cognition 80 (2001) 97–126 117

time). Once an object is formed, listeners can direct their attention to it, and even attend to its direction. This is precisely what we have been arguing.

Reliance on the spatiotemporal mapping may have led researchers to the erroneous conclusion that attention operates differently in vision and in audition. For example, Posner (1978) attempted to obtain spatial cueing effects in a variety of tasks, using endogenous, or top-down, cues. Even though his attempt failed, Spence and Driver (1994) determined that "it is clear that endogenous mechanisms of spatial auditory attention must exist at some level of processing: otherwise we could not achieve such textbook feats, such as selectively shadowing a message from one location while ignoring a message from a different location" (p. 557). So Spence and Driver do not believe Posner's data because they are not consistent with the spatio-temporal mapping. Butchel and Butter (1988) used exogenous spatial cues and found spatial cueing effects in vision but not in audition. They argue that due to the lack of a 'fovea-like' area in audition, there is no spatial attention in audition.

According to Spence and Driver (1994) there may be several reasons why Butchel and Butter (1988), Posner (1978), and Scharf, Quigley, Aoki, Peachey, and Reeves (1987) failed to find an auditory IOR. (a) Audition is poorer than vision with respect to spatial localization, and so maybe past experimenters failed to utilize sufficient angular separation. (b) The intensity of the peripheral cues may have been insufficient to draw attention. (c) Because RTs in auditory detection/ discrimination tasks are generally faster than in vision, the auditory response speeds may have been at ceiling because the tasks may not have been sufficiently demanding. (d) Perhaps the previous tasks were performed without engaging the spatial aspects of audition. In an extensive set of experiments, Spence and Driver showed that when the auditory spatial localization subsystem is engaged by the task, attentional effects appear. Observers were given exogenous cues at the lateral midline from either the left or the right with a sound that they were to ignore and which did not predict the lateralization of the target. Later observers were presented with a target sound on either the same side or the opposite side as the cue. Their task was to press one of two buttons as quickly as possible to indicate where the target was located. Targets were presented either in front of/behind (Experiment 1) or above/below the lateral midline (Experiment 2). They found an advantage for valid cues at ISI = 100 ms, but not at ISI = 400 ms or ISI = 1000 ms. There was no IOR. This was interpreted by Spence and Driver as being evidence for a short-lived advantage due to exogenous orientation. When the observers were required to make a frequency discrimination instead of a localization judgement (Experiment 3) the advantage on the cued side disappeared. Spence and Driver concluded that when the task demands are not based on localization, there is no attentional effect of spatial cueing in audition.

In a subsequent report, Spence and Driver (1998) argue that IOR operates differently in vision and audition. They showed that auditory RT *was not* affected by the location of the auditory target that appeared on the preceding trial, whereas visual detection RT *was* affected by the location of the visual target on the preceding trial. Only when targets were unpredictably auditory or visual did this effect occur between auditory targets presented on successive trials. Quinlan and Hill (1999)

118   *M. Kubovy, D. Van Valkenburg / Cognition 80 (2001) 97–126*

explained the auditory IOR in the modality-uncertain condition of Spence and Driver (1998) as a 'modality' switching effect. In a series of three experiments, observers made left/right localization judgments to either visual or auditory signals. In the first two experiments, observers were given a cue indicating the signal's modality, whereas in the third experiment the observers were not cued. The difference between the first and second experiments was the ISI between the modality cue and the subsequent presentation. The results of Experiment 1 (ISI = 50 ms) show that there is a cost to switching between modalities between trials. Observers were significantly slower when the modality changed between experimental trials. In Experiment 2 (ISI = 500 ms), where observers had time to prepare for the switch between modalities, the effect disappeared. Quinlan and Hill interpreted this result as an indication that the costs seen in Experiment 1 were due to the modality switching, and further, that modality switching requires attention. Finally, in Experiment 3, Quinlan and Hill showed that when there is no modality preparatory signal and ISI = 500 ms, the costs associated with modality switching re-emerge. They concluded that the effects seen in this and in Spence and Driver (1998) were the result of modality switching, not IOR. We believe that the above studies examined the 'where' component of the auditory system. Many researchers have hypothesized that this link occurs in the superior colliculus (Abrams & Dobkin, 1994; Goldring et al., 1996; Hughes et al., 1998; Spence & Driver, 1994; Tipper, Weaver, Jerreat, & Burak, 1994).

A TIA viewpoint would lead to a different experiment: instead of having tones vary in location, they would vary in pitch. Under *these* circumstances, we would expect to observe auditory IOR. (We are puzzled by the results of Mondor and Breau (1999) and Mondor, Breau, and Milliken (1998), who found frequency-based IOR, but also localization-based IOR. We are currently replicating their work.)

5.5. Benefits of indispensable attributes

When the TIA mapping is used, further analogies as well as an interesting separation between the auditory and the visual 'what' subsystems emerge. Duncan, Martens, and Ward (1997) report on experiments in which observers were asked to identify a stimulus shortly after they had deployed their attention to another stimulus (to study the so-called 'attentional blink', AB). In one experiment the stimuli were visual: they consisted of two streams of written trigrams ('xxx', 150 ms long, separated by an ISI of 100 ms). One stream consisted of a pair of trigrams above and below a fixation cross; the other consisted of a pair of trigrams to the right and the left of the fixation cross. One stream lagged behind the other by 125 ms. Each stream contained one target trigram ('nap', 'nab', 'cod', or 'cot'). The participants were asked to report which target trigrams they had seen. When the two target trigrams were 125 or 375 ms apart, the identification of the later trigram was depressed, i.e. an AB was observed. In a second experiment the stimuli were auditory: they consisted of two streams (one high-pitched, the other low-pitched) of spoken syllables ('guh', 150 ms long, separated by an ISI of 100 ms). One stream lagged behind the other by 125 ms. Each stream contained one target

M. Kubovy, D. Van Valkenburg / Cognition 80 (2001) 97–126 119

syllable ('nap', 'nab', 'cod', or 'cot'). The listeners were asked to report which target syllables they heard. If the two target syllables were 125 or 375 ms apart, the identification of the later syllable was depressed, i.e. an AB was observed. The auditory and the visual results were remarkably similar. In a third experiment one stream was visual and the other was auditory. No AB was observed. This result does not only fit what we would expect, given the TIA mapping, it also shows that the two 'what' subsystems are not linked. Despite these results, some research has shown that cross-modal AB can be elicited under certain circumstances (Arnell & Jolicoeur, 1999; Potter, Chun, Banks, & Muckenhoupt, 1998) – therefore tending to favor a weaker version of the ATIA. Arnell and Jolicoeur (1999), for example, have shown that if the target presentation rate is under 120 ms/item, then cross-modal AB is observable. Arnell and Jolicoeur argue that this cross-modal AB occurs because of a central processing limitation.

According to Treisman and Gelade (1980), if a target differs in one feature from a set of distracters (e.g. an O among Xs or a red O among green Os) the RT to find the target is independent of the number of distracters. If a difference between the target and the distracters is a conjunction of features (e.g. a green O among green Xs and red Os) then the RT varies with the number of distracters. It is as if targets in the single feature condition spontaneously segregated themselves from the other elements, but failed to do so when they were defined by a conjunction. An analogous phenomenon has been demonstrated by Lenoble (1986). Her work built upon a demonstration of concurrent-pitch segregation by Kubovy, Cutting, and McGuire (1974), in which listeners heard seven equal-intensity binaural tones. When the ITD of individual tones was manipulated, listeners were able to hear a melody segregated from the complex even though it was not audible in either ear alone. When Lenoble (1986) presented observers with tone complexes in which target tones were defined by a conjunction of ITD and amplitude or frequency modulation, concurrent-pitch segregation did not occur.

An interesting (and testable) hypothesis is that observers are only able to allocate voluntary attention to indispensable attributes. The Shih and Sperling (1996) results indicate that observers are able to voluntarily devote attention to space, but that only space could be attended to in this way. This would mean that in audition, observers would only be able to allocate attention to particular frequencies or pitch space and not to other features such as rise time, intensity, or space. While to our knowledge a critical test of this hypothesis has not been made, there are results which suggest that this may indeed be the case. Mondor and Terrio (1998) conducted a series of five experiments designed to examine the role of selective attention and pattern structure in audition. They presented observers with a sequence of ascending or descending tones and the observer was to make a speeded response to a target tone that differed from the non-targets in duration, rise time, or intensity, or the target tone contained a 1 ms gap. Target tones could be consistent with the overall pattern structure or inconsistent (in frequency). When targets fell on tones that were consistent with the overall pattern structure observers were not more sensitive or faster to make a response. When targets fell on tones inconsistent with the overall pattern structure, however, observers remained equally sensitive (as measured by d') but were significantly faster to detect the targets. Deviations in frequency from an established pattern were sufficient to draw attention and thus enhance the detection of these features when they fell on an inconsistent target. The implication of these studies is that frequency is more important than duration, rise time, intensity, or the presence of a gap for auditory selective attention mechanisms (although we acknowledge that the evidence would be stronger had Mondor and Terrio (1998) tested the analogous case – where pattern inconsistency is defined by, for example, duration or rise time).

The following experiment could serve as a critical test of the hypothesis that observers can only voluntarily allocate attention to indispensable attributes. We would place listeners in front of a linear array of four loudspeakers (i.e. two on each side of the observer's midline). We would use five different instrumental sounds: a target (i.e. a bassoon) and four distracters (i.e. a flute, a guitar, a piano, and a trumpet), chosen so that they are easily distinguishable. On each trial, we would play a series of brief 'frames' of sound, each of which would comprise the four distracter instruments. Each of the instruments would be played from a different speaker and at a different frequency. In one of the frames we would replace one of the distracters with the target instrument (the bassoon). We would ask the listeners to determine which frame contained the target. Before each trial we would give the listeners one of two types of cues: (a) a spatial cue (e.g. informing them that the target is 80% likely to come from the left), or (b) a pitch cue (e.g. informing them that the target is 80% likely to be high-pitched). According to the TIA there should be no cost or benefit from spatial cues, because listeners cannot allocate attention to a spatial location, but there should be costs and benefits associated with pitch cues.

6. Overview

In summary, consider Fig. 14. On the left side of the diagram we have set out the characteristics of audition, and on the right we have done so for vision. Each of the modalities is represented by two pathways, one labeled 'what' and the other labeled 'where'. We should stress that we are using the term 'where' as shorthand for the sense of Milner and Goodale (1995), i.e. a subsystem that maintains spatial information in egocentric coordinates for the purpose of controlling action. That is why we sometimes refer to it in this paper as a visuo*motor* system.

In the center of the diagram we show that the auditory and the visual 'where' subsystems are tightly linked. This is because of the evidence (see Section 2) that the auditory 'where' subsystem is in the service of the visual 'where' subsystem. We connected these two subsystems with a thick line to indicate their linkage, and added an arrow to this line to indicate the asymmetric relation between them (one is in the service of the other). The two subsystems are mapped onto each other with the traditional spatiotemporal mapping.

To either side of the 'where' subsystem(s) we represent the 'what' subsystems.

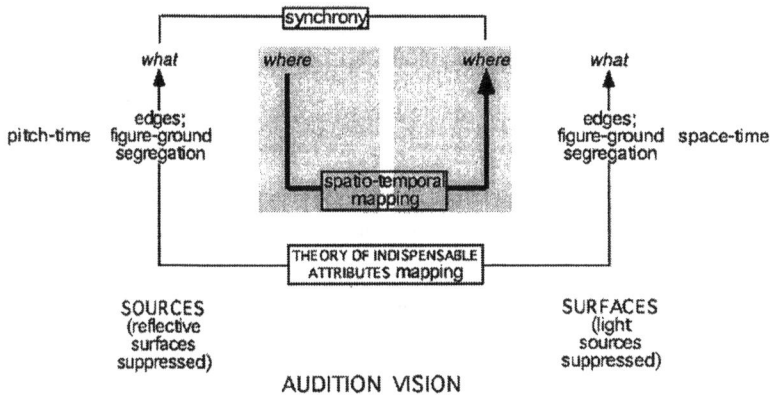

Fig. 14. Summary of the theory.

Here we show that the key operation of both the visual and the auditory 'what' subsystems is figure-ground segregation and edge formation (see Section 3.1). We also indicate that the auditory operation occurs in pitch-time, whereas the visual operation occurs in space-time (see Section 3.2). We connected these two subsystems with a thin line to indicate that they are analogous, and that the heuristic we offer to draw analogies between the two is the TIA. When we use the term 'analogy' we do not wish to take a stand on whether they are *merely* analogous, i.e. that they evolved separately, or whether they might be *homologous*, i.e. they have some common evolutionary origin.

We also note a link between the visual 'where' and auditory 'what' which represents the ventriloquism effect, in which synchronous visual and auditory events can determine the auditory localization.

Finally, we remind the reader (in the lower left and right corners of the auditory and visual boxes) of a fundamental difference between the two subsystems (summarized in Table 1).

7. Conclusion

The human cortex contains 10^{10} neurons. Up to half of these may be involved in visual function (Palmer, 1999, p. 24); the auditory system is much smaller. This seems to confirm that reality unfolds in space and time and that understanding is visual. But we believe that the main source of resistance to a non-visuocentric view of perception is the 'Knowing is Seeing' metaphor. According to Lakoff and Johnson (1999, Table 4.1, pp. 53–54) this metaphor (summarized in Table 2) is a tool all of us use to understand the idea of knowing.

We hope that our analysis will enable us to hear more clearly the polyphony between the two voices in the complex counterpoint between vision and audition.

Table 2
The Knowing is Seeing primary metaphor (Lakoff & Johnson, 1999, pp. 393–394)

Visual domain	Knowledge domain
Object seen	→ Idea
Seeing an object clearly	→ Knowing an idea
Person who sees	→ Person who knows
Light	→ 'Light' of reason
Visual focusing	→ Mental attention
Visual acuity	→ Intellectual acuity
Physical viewpoint	→ Mental viewpoint
Visual obstruction	→ Impediment to knowing

Acknowledgements

We wish to thank B.J. Scholl and J. Mehler for their superb editorial work on this paper. We are also grateful to those who contributed in various ways to this paper: A. Bregman, R.S. Bolia, C. Spence, S. Handel, C.L. Krumhansl, J.G. Neuhoff, B. Repp, M. Turgéon, and A.J. Watkins. Our work is supported by NEI grant No. R01 EY 12926-06.

References

Abrams, R. A., & Dobkin, R. S. (1994). Inhibition of return: effects of attentional cuing on eye movement latencies. *Journal of Experimental Psychology: Human Perception and Performance*, *20* (3), 467–477.

Adelson, E. H., & Bergen, J. R. (1991). The plenoptic function and the elements of early vision. In M. S. Landy, & J. A. Movshon (Eds.), *Computational models of visual processing* (pp. 3–20). Cambridge, MA: MIT Press.

Aitkin, L. (1990). Coding for auditory space. In M. J. Rowe, & L. Aitkin (Eds.), *Information processing in mammalian auditory and tactile systems* (pp. 169–178). New York: Wiley-Liss.

Andersen, R. A., Snyder, L. H., Bradley, D. C., & Xing, J. (1997). Multimodal representation of space in the posterior parietal cortex and its use in planning movements. *Annual Review of Neuroscience*, *20*, 303–330.

Angell, J. R. (1906). *Psychology: an introductory study of the structure and function of human conscious* (3rd ed., pp. 141–160). New York: Henry Holt.

Arias, C., Curet, C. A., Moyano, H. F., Joekes, S., & Blanch, N. (1993). Echolacation: a study of auditory functioning in blind and sighted subjects. *Journal of Visual Impairment & Blindness*, *87*, 73–77.

Arnell, K. A., & Jolicoeur, P. (1999). The attentional blink across stimulus modalities: evidence for central processing limitations. *Journal of Experimental Psychology: Human Perception and Performance*, *25* (3), 630–648.

Aronson, E., & Rosenbloom, S. (1971). Space perception in early infancy: perception within a common auditory-visual space. *Science*, *172*, 1161–1163.

Ashmead, D. H., & Wall, R. S. (1999). Auditory perception of walls via spectral variations in the ambient sound field. *Journal of Rehabilitation Research and Development*, *36*, 313–322.

Ashmead, D. H., Wall, R. S., Eaton, S. B., Ebinger, K. A., Snook-Hill, M.-M., Guth, D. A., & Yang, X. (1998). Echolocation reconsidered: using spatial variations in the ambient sound field to guide locomotion. *Journal of Visual Impairment & Blindness*, *92*, 615–632.

Banati, R. B., Goerres, G. W., Tjoa, C., Aggleton, J. P., & Grasby, P. (2000). The functional anatomy of visuo-tactile integration in man: a study using pet. *Neuropsychologia*, *38*, 115–124.

M. Kubovy, D. Van Valkenburg / Cognition 80 (2001) 97–126 123

Beranek, L. L. (1988). *Acoustical measurements* (Rev. ed.). Woodbury, NY: American Institute of Physics.

Bertelson, P., & Aschersleben, G. (1998). Automatic visual bias of perceived auditory location. *Psychonomic Bulletin & Review*, *5* (3), 482–489.

Blauert, J. (1997). *Spatial hearing: the psychophysics of human sound localization* (Rev. ed.). Cambridge, MA: MIT Press.

Brainard, M. S., & Knudsen, E. I. (1993). Experience-dependent plasticity in the inferior colliculus: a site for visual calibration of the neural representation of auditory space in the barn owl. *Journal of Neuroscience*, *13*, 4589–4608.

Bregman, A. (1990). *Auditory scene analysis: the perceptual organization of sound*. Cambridge, MA: MIT Press.

Bregman, A. S., & Campbell, J. (1971). Primary auditory stream segregation and perception of order in rapid sequences of tones. *Journal of Experimental Psychology*, *89*, 244–249.

Broadbent, D. E. (1958). *Perception and communication*. New York: Pergamon Press.

Brochard, R., Drake, C., Botte, M., & McAdams, S. (1999). Perceptual organization of complex auditory sequences: effects of number of simultaneous subsequences and frequency separation. *Journal of Experimental Psychology: Human Perception and Performance*, *25* (6), 1742–1759.

Butchel, H. A., & Butter, C. M. (1988). Spatial attentional shifts: implications for the role of polysensory mechanisms. *Neuropsychologia*, *26*, 499–509.

Calvert, G. A., Campbell, R., & Brammer, M. J. (2000). Evidence from functional magnetic resonance imaging of crossmodal binding in human heteromodal cortex. *Current Biology*, *10*, 649–657.

Cherry, C. (1959). *On human communication*. Cambridge, MA: MIT Press.

Cisek, P., & Turgeon, M. (1999). 'Binding through the fovea', a tale of perception in the service of action. *Psyche*, *5* http://psyche.cs.monash.edu.au/v5/psyche-5-34-cisek.html, accessed January 2000.

Clarke, S., Bellmann, A., Meuli, R. A., Assal, G., & Steck, A. J. (2000). Auditory agnosia and spatial deficits following left hemispheric lesions: evidence for distinct processing pathways. *Neuropsychologia*, *38*, 797–807.

Clifton, R. K. (1992). The development of spatial hearing in human infants. In L. A. Werner, & E. W. Rubel (Eds.), *Developmental psychoacoustics* (pp. 135–157). Washington, DC: APA Press.

Culling, J. F., & Summerfield, Q. (1995). Perceptual separation of concurrent speech sounds: absence of across-frequency grouping by common interaural delay. *Journal of the Acoustical Society of America*, *98* (2), 785–797.

Darwin, C. J., & Hukin, R. W. (1999). Auditory objects of attention: the role of interaural time differences. *Journal of Experimental Psychology: Human Perception and Performance*, *25* (3), 617–629.

Deustch, D., & Roll, P. (1976). Separate "what" and "where" decision mechanisms in processing a dichotic tonal sequence. *Journal of Experimental Psychology: Human Perception and Performance*, *2* (1), 23–29.

Duncan, J., Martens, S., & Ward, R. (1997). Restricted attentional capacity within but not between sensory modalities. *Nature*, *387*, 808–809.

Ehrenfels, C. von (1988). On 'gestalt qualities'. In B. Smith (Ed.), *Foundations of gestalt theory* (pp. 82–117). Munich, Germany: Philosophia Verlag. (Original work published 1890)

Gibson, J. J. (1979). *The ecological approach to visual perception*. Hillsdale, NJ: Lawrence Erlbaum.

Goldring, J., Dorris, M., Corneil, B., Balantyne, P., & Munoz, D. (1996). Combined eye-head gaze shifts to visual and auditory targets in humans. *Experimental Brain Research*, *111*, 68–73.

Goldstein, H. (1980). *Classical mechanics* (2nd ed.). Reading, MA: Addison-Wesley.

Hafter, E. R. (1997). Binaural adaptation and the effectiveness of a stimulus beyond its onset. In R. H. Gilkey, & T. R. Anderson (Eds.), *Binaural and spatial hearing in real and virtual environments* (pp. 211–232). Mahwah, NJ: Lawrence Erlbaum.

Handel, S. (1988). Space is to time as vision is to audition: seductive but misleading. *Journal of Experimental Psychology: Human Perception and Performance*, *14*, 315–317.

Handel, S. (1989). *Listening: an introduction to the perception of auditory events*. Cambridge, MA: MIT Press.

Helmholtz, H. L. F. (1954). *On the sensations of tone as a physiological basis for the theory of music* (2nd ed., A. J. Ellis, Trans.). New York: Dover. (Original work published 1885)

Hughes, H., Nelson, M., & Aronchick, D. (1998). Spatial characteristics of visual-auditory summation in human saccades. *Vision Research, 38*, 3955–3963.

Jay, M. F., & Sparks, D. L. (1984). Auditory receptive fields in primate superior colliculus shift with changes in eye position. *Nature, 309*, 345–347.

Jay, M. F., & Sparks, D. L. (1990). Localization of auditory and visual targets for the initialization of saccadic eye movements. In M. A. Berkley, & W. C. Stebbins (Eds.), *Comparative perception. Basic mechanisms*: Vol. 1. (pp. 351–374). New York: Wiley.

Johansson, G., & Orjesson, E. B. (1989). Toward a new theory of vision. Studies in wide-angle space perception. *Ecological Psychology, 1*, 301–331.

Kanizsa, G. (1979). *Organization in vision: essays on Gestalt perception.* New York: Praeger.

Kant, I. (1996). *Critique of pure reason* (W. S. Pluhar, Trans.). Indianapolis, IN: Hackett. (Original work published 1787)

Kubovy, M. (1981). Concurrent-pitch segregation and the theory of indispensable attributes. In M. Kubovy, & J. Pomerantz (Eds.), *Perceptual organization* (pp. 55–99). Hillsdale, NJ: Lawrence Erlbaum.

Kubovy, M. (1988). Should we resist the seductiveness of the space:time:vision:audition analogy? *Journal of Experimental Psychology: Human Perception and Performance, 14*, 318–320.

Kubovy, M., Cohen, D., & Hollier, J. (1999). Feature integration that routinely occurs without focal attention. *Psychonomic Bulletin & Review, 6*, 183–203.

Kubovy, M., Cutting, J. E., & McGuire, R. M. (1974). Hearing with the third ear: dichotic perception of a melody without monaural familiarity cues. *Science, 186*, 272–274.

Kubovy, M., Holcombe, A., & Wagemans, J. (1998). On the lawfulness of grouping by proximity. *Cognitive Psychology, 35*, 71–98.

Ladavas, E., & Pavani, F. (1998). Neuropsychological evidence of the functional integration of visual, auditory and proprioceptive spatial maps. *NeuroReport: an International Journal for the Rapid Communication of Research in Neuroscience, 9*, 1195–1200.

Lakoff, G., & Johnson, M. (1999). *Philosophy in the flesh: the embodied mind and its challenge to western thought.* New York: Basic Books.

Law, M. B., Pratt, J., & Abrams, R. A. (1995). Color-based inhibition of return. *Perception & Psychophysics, 57* (3), 402–408.

Lenoble, J. S. (1986). Feature conjunctions and the perceptual grouping of concurrent tones (Unpublished doctoral dissertation, Rutgers – The State University of New Jersey, New Brunswick, NJ, 1986). *Dissertation Abstracts International, 47-06B*, 2654.

Macaluso, E., Frith, C., & Driver, J. (2000). Selective spatial attention in vision and touch: unimodal and multimodal mechanisms revealed by PET. *Journal of Neurophysiology, 83*, 3062–3075.

McPherson, L., Ciocca, V., & Bregman, A. (1994). Organization in audition by similarity in rate of change: evidence from tracking individual frequency glides in mixtures. *Perception & Psychophysics, 55* (3), 269–278.

Milner, A. D., & Goodale, M. A. (1995). *The visual brain in action.* Oxford: Oxford University Press.

Mollon, J. (1995). Seeing colour. In T. Lamb, & J. Bourriau (Eds.), *Colour: art & science* (pp. 127–150). Cambridge: Cambridge University Press.

Mondor, T. A., & Breau, L. M. (1999). Facilitative and inhibitory effects of location and frequency cues: evidence of a modulation in perceptual sensitivity. *Perception & Psychophysics, 61* (3), 438–444.

Mondor, T. A., Breau, L. M., & Milliken, B. (1998). Inhibitory processes in auditory selective attention: evidence of location-based and frequency-based inhibition of return. *Perception & Psychophysics, 60* (2), 296–302.

Mondor, T. A., & Terrio, N. A. (1998). Mechanisms of perceptual organization and auditory selective attention: the role of pattern structure. *Journal of Experimental Psychology: Human Perception and Performance, 24* (6), 1628–1641.

Monge, G. (1789). Mémoire sure quelques phénomènes de la vision. *Annales de Chimie, 3*, 131–147.

Newton, I. (1999). *Mathematical principle of natural philosophy* (I. B. Cohen & A. Whitman, Trans.). Berkeley, CA: University of California Press. (Original work published 1726)

Object (1993). In *Oxford English Dictionary* (2nd ed.). (http://etext.lib.virginia.edu/etcbin/oedbin/

oed2www?specfile = /web/data/oed/oed.o2w&act =
text&offset = 287948343&textreg = 0&query = object, retrieved 1 October 1999)

Palmer, S. E. (1999). *Vision science: photons to phenomenology*. Cambridge, MA: MIT Press.

Peterson, M. A., & Gibson, B. S. (1994). Must figure-ground organization precede object recognition? An assumption in peril. *Psychological Science, 5*, 253–259.

Posner, M. I. (1978). *Chronometric explorations of the mind*. Hillsdale, NJ: Erlbaum.

Potter, M. C., Chun, M. M., Banks, B. S., & Muckenhoupt, M. (1998). Two attentional deficits in serial target search: the visual attentional blink and an amodal task-switch deficit. *Journal of Experimental Psychology: Learning, Memory and Cognition, 24* (4), 979–992.

Quinlan, P. T., & Hill, N. I. (1999). Sequential effects in rudimentary auditory and visual tasks. *Perception & Psychophysics, 61* (2), 375–384.

Rauschecker, J. P. (1997). Processing of complex sounds in the auditory cortex of cat, monkey, and man. *Acta Oto-Laryngologica – Supplement, 532*, 34–38.

Rauschecker, J. P. (1998a). Cortical processing of complex sounds. *Current Opinions in Neurobiology, 288*, 516–521.

Rauschecker, J. P. (1998b). Parallel processing in the auditory cortex of primates. *Audiology and Neurootology, 3*, 86–103.

Rorden, C., & Driver, J. (1999). Does auditory attention shift in the direction of an upcoming saccade? *Neuropsychologia, 37*, 357–377.

Samuel, A. G. (1991). A further examination of attentional effects in the phonemic restoration illusion. *Quarterly Journal of Experimental Psychology, 43A* (3), 679–699.

Scharf, B. (1998). Auditory attention: the psychoacoustical approach. In H. Pashler (Ed.), *Attention* (pp. 75–113). Hove: Psychology Press.

Scharf, B., Quigley, S., Aoki, C., Peachey, N., & Reeves, A. (1987). Focused auditory attention and frequency selectivity. *Perception & Psychophysics, 42*, 215–223.

Shih, S., & Sperling, G. (1996). Is there feature-based attentional selection in visual search? *Journal of Experimental Psychology: Human Perception and Performance, 22* (3), 758–779.

Spence, C., & Driver, J. (1994). Covert spatial orienting in audition: exogenous and endogenous mechanisms. *Journal of Experimental Psychology: Human Perception and Performance, 20* (3), 555–574.

Spence, C., & Driver, J. (1997). Audiovisual links in exogenous overt spatial orienting. *Perception & Psychophysics, 59* (1), 1–22.

Spence, C., & Driver, J. (1998). Auditory and audiovisual inhibition of return. *Perception & Psychophysics, 60* (1), 125–139.

Spence, C., & Driver, J. (1999). Cross-modal attention. In G. W. Humphreys, & A. Treisman (Eds.), *Attention, space, and action* (pp. 130–149). New York: Oxford University Press.

Stein, B. E., & Meredith, M. A. (1993). *The merging of the senses*. Cambridge, MA: MIT Press.

Stoffregen, T. A., & Pittenger, J. B. (1995). Human echolation as a basic form of perception and action. *Ecological Psychology, 7*, 181–216.

Stryker, M. P. (1999). Sensory maps on the move. *Science, 284*, 925–926.

Tipper, S. P., Weaver, B., Jerreat, L. M., & Burak, A. L. (1994). Object-based and environment-based inhibition of return of visual attention. *Journal of Experimental Psychology: Human Perception and Performance, 20* (3), 478–499.

Treisman, A. M., & Gelade, G. (1980). A feature-integration theory of attention. *Cognitive Psychology, 12*, 97–136.

Vicario, G. (1960). The acoustic tunnel effect. *Rivista da Psicologia, 54*, 41–52.

Warren, R. M. (1970). Perceptual restoration of missing speech sounds. *Science, 167*, 392–393.

Warren, R. M. (1982). *Auditory perception: a new synthesis*. New York: Pergamon Press.

Warren, R. M. (1984). Perceptual restoration of obliterated sounds. *Psychological Bulletin, 96*, 371–383.

Watkins, A. J. (1991). Central, auditory mechanisms of perceptual compensation for spectral-envelope distortion. *Journal of the Acoustical Society of America, 90*, 2942–2955.

Watkins, A. J. (1998). The precedence effect and perceptual compensation for spectral envelope distortion. In A. Palmer, A. Rees, A. Q. Summerfield, & R. Meddis (Eds.), *Psychophysical and physiological advances in hearing* (pp. 336–343). London: Whurr.

Watkins, A. J. (1999). The influence of early reflections on the identification and lateralization of vowels. *Journal of the Acoustical Society of America, 106*, 2933–2944.

Watkins, A. J., & Makin, S. J. (1996). Effects of spectral contrast on perceptual compensation for spectral-envelope distortion. *Journal of the Acoustical Society of America, 99*, 3749–3757.

Wertheimer, M. (1938). Laws of organization in perceptual forms. In W. Ellis (Ed.), *A source book of Gestalt psychology* (pp. 71–88). London: Routledge & Kegan Paul. (Original work published 1923)

Wightman, F. L., & Jenison, R. (1995). Auditory spatial layout. In W. Epstein, & S. J. Rogers (Eds.), *Perception of space and motion* (2nd ed. pp. 365–400). San Diego, CA: Academic Press.

Wynn, V. T. (1977). Simple reaction time – evidence for two auditory pathways to the brain. *Journal of Auditory Research, 17*, 175–181.

Young, E. D., Spirou, G. A., Rice, J. J., & Voigt, H. F. (1992). Neural organization and responses to complex stimuli in the dorsal cochlear nucleus. *Philosophical Transactions of the Royal Society of London, Series B, 336*, 407–413.

Zheng, W., & Knudsen, E. I. (1999). Functional selection of adaptive auditory space map by $GABA_A$-mediated inhibition. *Science, 284*, 962–965.

[17]

The shape of holes

Marco Bertamini[a,*], Camilla J. Croucher[b]

[a]*Department of Psychology, University of Liverpool, Eleanor Rathbone Building, Bedford Street South, Liverpool L69 7ZA, UK*
[b]*MRC Cognition and Brain Sciences Unit, University of Cambridge, Cambridge, UK*

Received 22 August 2001; received in revised form 12 June 2002; accepted 14 September 2002

Abstract

The shape of holes can be recognized as accurately as the shape of objects (Palmer, S. E. (1999). *Vision science: photons to phenomenology*. Cambridge, MA: MIT Press), yet the area enclosed by a hole is a background region, and it can be demonstrated that background regions are not represented as having shape. What is therefore the shape of a hole, if any? To resolve this apparent paradox, we suggest that the shape of a hole is available indirectly from the shape of the surrounding object. We exploited the fact that observers are faster at judging the position of convex vertices than concave ones (*Perception 30* (2001) 1295), and using a figural manipulation of figure/ground we found a reversal of the relative speeds when the same contours were presented as holes instead of objects. If contours were perceived as belonging to the hole rather than the surrounding object then there would have been no qualitative difference in responses to the object and hole stimuli. We conclude that the contour bounding a hole is automatically assigned to the surrounding object, and that a change in perception of a region from object to hole always drastically changes the encoded information. We discuss the many interesting aspects of holes as a subject of study in different disciplines and predict that much insight especially about shape will continue to come from holes.

Keywords: Holes; Figure/ground organization; Perception of shape; Contours

1. Introduction

When Ringo Starr in the animated movie Yellow Submarine picks up a round black hole and puts it in his pocket, we enjoy the joke and wit because holes have a special ontological status: they exist but they are not real objects (Casati & Varzi, 1994). From the point of view of how we perceive the shape of holes, Stephen Palmer (1999) has discussed an interesting paradox, which has its roots in the phenomenon of figure/ground organization

---

* Corresponding author.
   E-mail address: m.bertamini@liv.ac.uk (M. Bertamini).

described originally by the Danish Gestaltist Edgar Rubin (1921). In Palmer's words: "if the contour of the hole is assigned to the surrounding object [...] how can observers then see the hole itself as having a shape?" (Palmer, 1999, p. 286). A possible solution to the

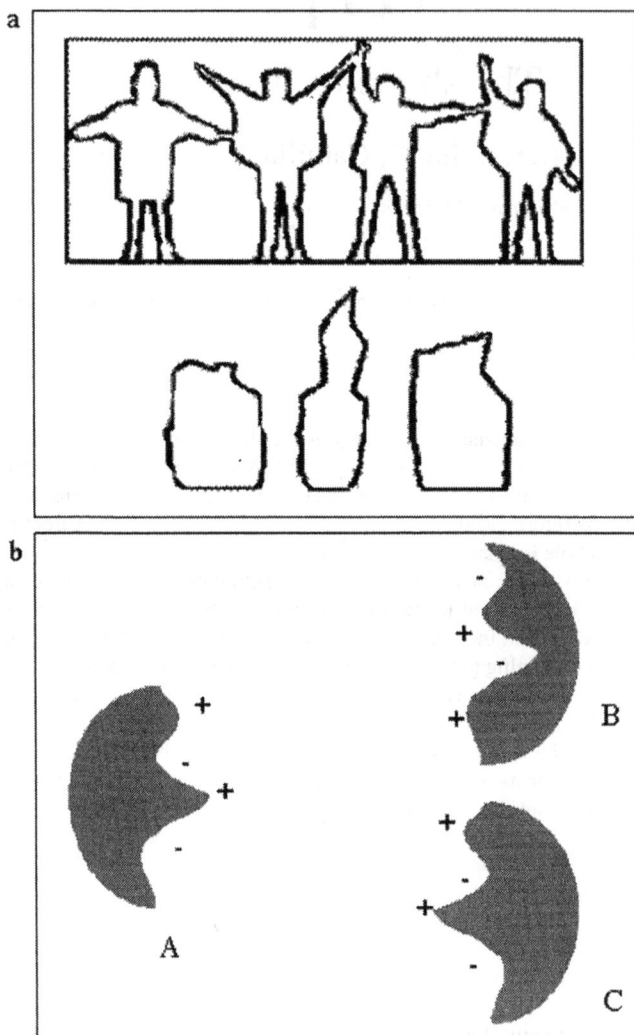

Fig. 1. (a) Because of how we organize the top scene into figures and background, the ground regions between the figures do not have shape. Notice how the regions of background isolated below are shapes that we do not perceive in the scene above (if this is parsed as a group of human semaphore signals). This demonstration is based on a similar one in Kanizsa (1979). (b) Two halves of a disk have different shapes, even though they share the same bounding contour. This demonstration is based on Attneave (1974). The positive and negative curvature of the contour has been labelled to show that when polarity changes from A to B (because of a change of where the inside of the figure is) the perceived shape is different.

paradox is that, in fact, holes do not have shape, but the surrounding object does. People may therefore judge many aspects of the hole indirectly, by looking at the object. In this paper we demonstrate this empirically by showing that the representation of a shape changes in a predicted way with a change in figure/ground organization, that is with a change from a figure to a hole.

In the introduction we will first discuss figure/ground organization and in particular the principle of unidirectional boundary belonging. There is an old Gestalt principle that says that boundaries belong to figures, and if a hole is not a figure it follows that it does not have boundaries. Next we briefly review the philosophical debate on the nature of holes, with respect in particular to the book by Casati and Varzi (1994). Casati and Varzi (1994) from a theoretical standpoint, and Palmer (1999) from a perceptual standpoint, are in agreement on the necessity to assign shape information to holes. The implication of this is that holes are qualitatively different from other background regions. We disagree with this view at least in so far as we believe in the generality of the principle that says that boundaries only belong to figures: this principle holds also in the case of holes.

1.1. Figure/ground organization and boundary belonging

When an ambiguous 2D image such as Rubin's vase is resolved into a figure and a background, the figure is thing-like, nearer the observer, closed, and its shape is clearly defined by the contour (Koffka, 1935; Rubin, 1921). The background on the other hand extends behind the figure and therefore has no shape. In other words, the contours always belong to the figure, and even when a display is ambiguous, it will never belong to both regions at the same time. In the famous vase example, the contour can belong to a vase in front of a uniform background, or to two faces in front of a uniform background. Fig. 1a is based on our favourite demonstration in Kanizsa (1979). When the scene is perceived as showing four people the space of background visible between the figures has no shape. When these regions of background are isolated as figures (as in Fig. 1a) we need to inspect the image carefully to notice that those contours were present in the scene all along.

The modern interpretation of this effect on the basis of a generic viewpoint assumption is that contours belonging to two objects are unlikely to coincide in the image. Given a cluttered world of opaque objects it is more reasonable for the visual system to interpret contours as the product of occlusion (Albert, 2000; Driver & Baylis, 1996; Hoffman, 1998). There are also theories that suggest inhibitory processes on opposite sides of a contour which would explain the fact that the ground appears shapeless (e.g. Peterson, de Gelder, Rapcsak, Gerhardstein, & Bachoud-Lévi, 2000).[1]

There is evidence to support the Gestalt principle that contours only belong to figures. In memory, people cannot recall as a shape the region that was seen as part of the background. To use again the example of the vase, people would not remember the vase if they

---

[1] In Peterson et al.'s model (Peterson et al., 2000; Peterson & Kim, 2001) the regions of background are processed and can affect figure/ground organization, for instance if they match memory traces. At the same time the inhibitory process may explain the fact that such regions are not consciously seen as having shape. However, the debate on how much the background regions are processed is not central to our paper. Peterson et al.'s model is in agreement with the Gestaltist position that the representation of a background region (and presumably holes) should always be weaker in a direct comparison with the representation of a figure.

36   *M. Bertamini, C.J. Croucher / Cognition 87 (2003) 33–54*

saw two faces, and vice versa (Rock, 1983), and people cannot easily match contours that have changed because of a change in figure/ground assignment, so that convexities and concavities have swapped (Driver & Baylis, 1996). Moreover, in ambiguous situations, border ownership is bistable, rather than leading to cue averaging (Albert, 2001).

The problem with holes, therefore, is that their shapes should not be perceived, and therefore should not be remembered, if they behave just like any other background region (see Fig. 1a). Contrary to this prediction, Rock, Palmer, and Hume (cited in Palmer, 1999) found that people remember the shape of holes *just as well* as the shape of an object. This is what Palmer calls a paradox. He suggests that a representation for the shape of the hole must exist, maybe because when an object has a hole in it we have a representation of a hole-less object plus a representation of the hole (Palmer, 1999).

1.2. The ontology of holes

Holes can be discussed in the context of ontology (do holes have existence in themselves?), topology[2] (how would a topological change, like acquiring a hole, change an object?), and even mereology (what role do holes play in part–whole relationships?). We do believe that the most relevant description of the visual world of humans is in terms of surfaces and media (as argued by Gibson, 1979), and we also accept that in the description of shapes a crucial role is played by part structure, and in this sense mereology is relevant. However, before we can deal with the role of parts, we need to discuss some basic ontological issues.

With respect to figure/ground organization we have seen that regions of ground are not perceived as having a shape. Holes are a type of regions of background, and all regions of background (including holes) do not exist as objects. Perhaps the human visual system simply did not have any reason to develop a machinery sensitive to the shape of non-existent things.

The essay by Lewis and Lewis (1983) is an excellent exploration of the controversy on the nature of holes. On the one side we have nominalistic materialism which suggests that nothing exists but concrete material objects, and on the other side we have those who believe that entities like holes exist even though they are neither material nor objects. The Lewis and Lewis (1983) solution is to equate holes with hole-linings which are material, and claim that the rest of the problem is about language. Casati and Varzi (1994) disagree and suggest that holes are *superficial particulars*. There is a similarity between this philosophical position and Palmer's suggestion that we must be able to perceive both the objects and the holes within the objects (Palmer, 1999).

Casati and Varzi's treatment of holes is interesting for us in our study of shapes, and in agreement with us they accept the central role of surfaces (Casati & Varzi, 1994). Surfaces belong to geometry, not physics (Koenderink, 1990), and in this sense holes cannot be treated in a purely materialistic way. However, in their book Casati and Varzi also formulated a question very similar to Palmer's paradox. Taken literally, the positions of both

---

[2] There is a debate on the usefulness of topology to describe how the visual system analyzes shape (e.g. Chen, 2001; Hecht & Bader, 1998) but this issue is not central for our argument. In the present work we exploit holes to manipulate a type of information, namely contour curvature, which is outside the realm of topology.

M. Bertamini, C.J. Croucher / Cognition 87 (2003) 33–54 37

Casati and Varzi and Palmer predict that the shape of a hole should be available to the observer, and they do not predict any qualitative difference between the perceived shape of a hole and the perceived shape of an object when such shapes are congruent. As we shall see, we do predict (and find) such a qualitative difference.

One last aspect of the Casati and Varzi (1994) analysis needs to be mentioned. On topological grounds they provide a classification of holes into hollows, tunnels, and cavities. The holes we are concerned with in this paper are tunnels, in that a background is always visible through our holes. Nevertheless, we would argue that our predictions apply to any holes in solid objects where the visible boundary of the hole is the projected rim of the surface as it turns inwards (self-occlusion). This will become clearer in the next section in which we set out the rationale for our predictions, but as an example one can think of the inside of a mouth. This is a hollow (if we ignore the digestive system) through which we do not see a background but rather the inside of the hole. The lips are the defining boundary of the hollow, but because the contours of the lips are concave (in the projected image) this hollow should behave like a tunnel in our analysis. We will now turn to this distinction between convex and concave contours, and an analysis based not on topology but on some simple considerations from differential geometry.

1.3. Holes and parts

It can be argued that there is an evolutionary progression from topology to affine geometry, to Euclidean geometry. Much progress has been made recently in artificial intelligence by considering the front-end visual system as a Geometer, or as a geometry engine (e.g. Koenderink, 1990; ter Haar Romeny & Florack, 2000). We do not have the space or the expertise to offer a review, but there is one specific contribution based on differential geometry which we need to introduce, because its implications will be the basis of our experiments.

Consider a world of surfaces defining solid shapes in 3D Euclidean space, and a projection onto a 2D image. At the end of the previous section we have started to use the word rim, which we need to define more clearly. A rim is the place on a surface where what is visible ends and the surface becomes invisible (due to self-occlusion). Therefore, although the rim is a specific boundary on the 3D surface, its location depends on the vantage point of the observer. Because at the rim the surface becomes invisible, the rim will project onto a 2D image as a contour. Taking a sphere as the simplest example, in parallel projection the rim corresponds to a great circle of the sphere, and the contour in the 2D image is a circle.

Importantly, Koenderink (1984) has shown that convex and concave regions of a contour arise respectively from the projection of convex and saddle regions of a smooth opaque surface.[3] The implication is that, because of how objects self-occlude, the convex-

---

[3] Convex, concave and saddle points on a surface are defined by their Gaussian curvature, but in this discussion it is sufficient to rely on the intuitive meaning of the words. Anticlastic or hyperbolic points are other words for saddle points, and synclastic or elliptic points are other words for both convex and concave points. If we throw a dart to a smooth surface we would land with probability 1 on one of these three types of locations (convex, concave, saddle). This means that they are fundamental in describing shape, although unfortunately curvature is not all that there is to solid shape (Koenderink, 1990).

ities and concavities of a 2D contour are informative about rims and therefore solid shape. We refer to this information also as contour polarity because if we compute curvature along the contour, the values for convex and concave regions have opposite sign.

A second important fact is that when arbitrary solid shapes meet and interpenetrate, they form concave creases. If one allows for some smoothing, the points along the crease are saddle points that can be seen in the image (i.e. 2D projection) as concavities (Hoffman & Richards, 1984). A crease is a concave discontinuity, but in the more general case of a smooth surface, this is a point where the curvature reaches a minimum. Hoffman and Richards (1984) consequently argue that the visual system should see shapes as composed of parts separated by minima of curvature. This part decomposition can be useful for the purpose of recognizing a complex shape on the basis of its structural description (Biederman, 1987; Marr & Nishihara, 1978).

In summary, although there is no a priori reason for the visual system to necessarily encode contour curvature information, there are good reasons rooted in geometry to expect that any system interested in solid shape should be attuned to such information.

Bertamini (2001) (starting from an effect noted by Gibson, 1994) has recently shown that observers are better at judging the position of a vertex if it is perceived as convex. That is, information about the position of convex vertices is more readily available than information about the position of concave vertices. This finding demonstrates the importance of the polarity of contour curvature, i.e. convexities and concavities. Bertamini argued that if objects are parsed into parts separated by concavities (minima of curvature; Hoffman & Richards, 1984), convex regions are represented as parts and have positions, whereas concave regions are boundaries between parts (see also Attneave, 1954). This is a novel approach to the issue of structural information and perceived parts. Computational considerations have long been used to argue for the existence of shape and volume primitives for object recognition (e.g. Biederman, 1987; Marr & Nishihara, 1978). However, in this paper and in Bertamini (2001) the task is not one of object recognition, yet parts play an important role because they are the by-product of how we represent solid shape, and by definition they have the property of having a position. To reiterate this concept, for us a part is by definition a shape with a position and (probably) an orientation.

It may be interesting to look at convexities and concavities from an historical perspective as well. Ibn al-Haytham (known in the West as Alhazen) was writing about the importance of this type of information for perception of shape about 1000 years ago (ca. 1030) in his book on Optics (as cited in Norman, Phillips, & Ross, 2001). Within the Gestalt school the manipulation of this variable was started very early by Bahnsen (1928), a student of Rubin, and especially by Kanizsa and Gerbino (1976), who confirmed that convexity contributed to prägnanz or good form. Much more recently, a paper by Norman et al. (2001) probably deserves mentioning for the ecological validity of their stimuli. They used silhouettes of potatoes (*Ipomoea batatas*) and asked people to reproduce their shapes on paper using only a limited number of points. People systematically chose the maxima of curvature.

For a more in depth discussion of the importance of curvature polarity for perceiving solid shape see Hoffman and Richards (1984), Hoffman (1998), and Koenderink (1984, 1990). For empirical evidence about the fast and obligatory encoding of curvature polarity see Baylis and Cale (2001), Baylis and Driver (1995, 2001a), Bertamini (2001), Bertamini,

M. Bertamini, C.J. Croucher / Cognition 87 (2003) 33–54 39

Friedenberg, and Argyle (2002), Hoffman and Singh (1997), Norman et al. (2001) and Singh, Seyranian, and Hoffman (1999).

1.4. A solution to the paradox

To try and draw together all of these issues, let us consider again Fig. 1a. One difficulty in remembering a background region is due to the different shape that the region would have had if it had been seen as a figure. Had it been a figure, curvature polarity would have been completely different. Another factor in Fig. 1a is that the uniform regions of background have boundaries that belong to more than one separate object. By avoiding this problem, perhaps a clearer example is given in Fig. 1b, based on an observation by Attneave (1974), as discussed in Hoffman (1998). The difference between two halves of a disk is perceptually strong, because convex regions on one side correspond to concave regions on the other. Note how hard it is to recognize that in A and B the two boundaries are in fact congruent, simply because the inside of the region has changed and with it the curvature polarity. On the other hand, A and C are not congruent (they match under a reflection only) and yet they look rather similar (because the curvature polarity is the same). Another way to describe this phenomenon is that it is difficult to judge the shape of contours (the line that divides the circle) and ignore the fact that those contours are the margins of different surfaces.

In summary, although a figure/ground reversal does not change the contours per se, it does change the information encoded. The inside becomes outside and curvature polarity is reversed. When the memory for a hole is tested using the same configuration (the same hole), there is no difficulty in remembering it (Palmer, 1999), not because the hole is represented as having its own shape, but because the shape of the overall figure (with a hole in it) has not changed. It is only when memory for a hole (ground) is tested using an object (figure) with an identical outline that the task becomes difficult, because their shapes are different in terms of curvature polarity (Fig. 1b).

In this paper we have exploited the convexity advantage discussed above (Bertamini, 2001) using a task in which observers had to judge the relative position of two vertices (task originally introduced by Baylis & Driver, 1993). We tested whether regions that are perceived as holes are processed in exactly the *opposite* way from regions that are perceived as objects.

Consider a simple circle seen as a figure; this region has a strictly convex contour (positive curvature). The same circle seen as a hole, by definition, has a strictly concave contour (negative curvature). Consider now the six-sided objects of Fig. 2. The task is to judge which of the two vertices on the side is lower (left or right). The comparison between the Barrel (convex vertices) and the Hourglass (concave vertices) shows that people are better in the case of the Barrel, even though the vertices are farther apart (because the areas of the two shapes is kept the same) (Gibson, 1994). To discover whether this is a consequence of a change in polarity of the contours we adopted a design that included Barrel- and Hourglass-shaped holes. We show that when simple shapes are depicted as holes there is a reversal of the pattern seen for objects with identical contours. It is easier to judge the position of the vertices for the Barrel-shaped object than the Barrel-shaped hole. Conversely, it is easier to judge the position of the vertices for the Hourglass-shaped hole than the

40

M. Bertamini, C.J. Croucher / Cognition 87 (2003) 33–54

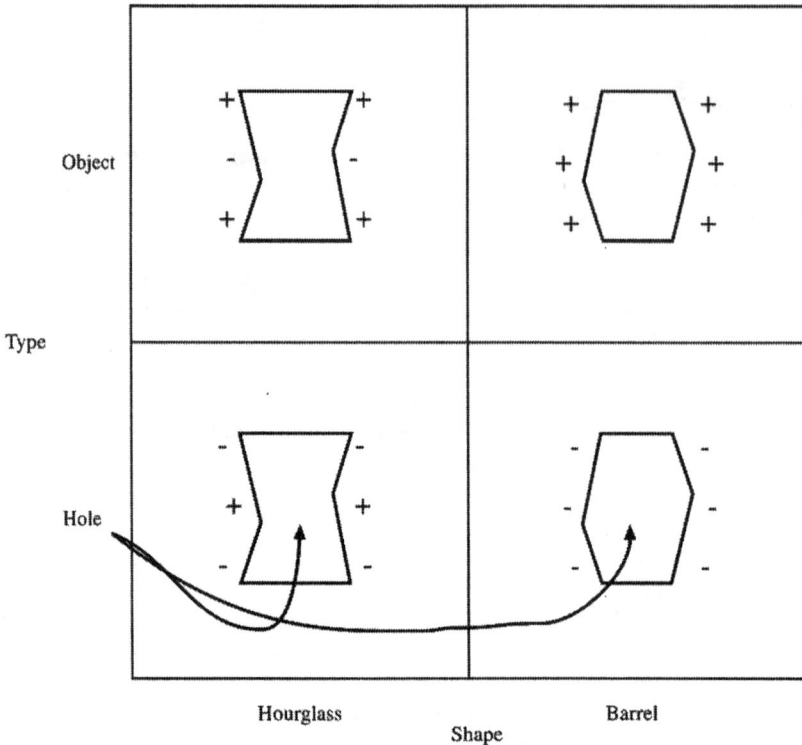

Fig. 2. Two shapes were used in all experiments. Both shapes were irregular hexagons; for mnemonic purposes we label the shape on the right Barrel and the one on the left Hourglass. In this figure we also label with + and − the convex and concave vertices, and in the bottom row we show how such information changes when the shapes are perceived as holes. Note in particular the change from convex to concave and vice versa of the two vertices at the side of the figures, as these are the only vertices carrying the information necessary to perform the task (i.e. one of these vertices was always vertically higher or lower than the other).

Hourglass-shaped object. This is a remarkable change that can only be explained on the basis of polarity inversion, since the geometry of the contours themselves remains unchanged.

Our conclusion is that the shape of a hole is known indirectly via the shape of the object enclosing it. Therefore, our representation of a hole is qualitatively different to our representation of a figure possessing the same contours, and this is due to the drastic differences in part structure between the two. Let us take the example of a fish-shaped hole (discussed in Casati & Varzi, 1994). It is true that people can recognize this as a fish, but our claim is that to do that people must be doing one of two things; either they enforce a figure/ground reversal so that they do not see this region as a hole, or, alternatively, they rely on a slower process that compensates by means of our vast cognitive resources for the fact that perceptually that figure is not the figure of a fish (albeit it is a figure containing enough information to infer the presence of a fish). We are aware that this is a strong claim. Put it in other words, the (perceived) shape of holes is different from the (perceived) shape of objects with the same (congruent) shape. The experiments presented in this paper support this claim. However, in this paper we do not tackle the role of familiarity, and therefore we use simple geometrical shapes.

Research on perception of holes in the literature is limited, with a few exceptions (Cavedon, 1980; Nelson & Palmer, 2001). In generating our stimuli we relied on Bozzi's observations (Bozzi, 1975). He has pointed out that for a hole to be perceived as such the figure that contains it should be perceived as a figure and should therefore have a visible outer boundary, in addition to the 'inner boundary' that forms the edges of the hole; there should be evidence that the background seen through the hole is the same as the background outside the figure; finally, the boundary of the hole should be related, or at least not completely unrelated, to the outer boundary of the figure (for a summary in English of Bozzi's observations see Palmer, 1999, p. 287). We therefore exploited these rules to create stimuli on a computer, reproduced in Fig. 3. The figure containing the hole was drawn in a solid green colour, and the background visible through the hole and outside the

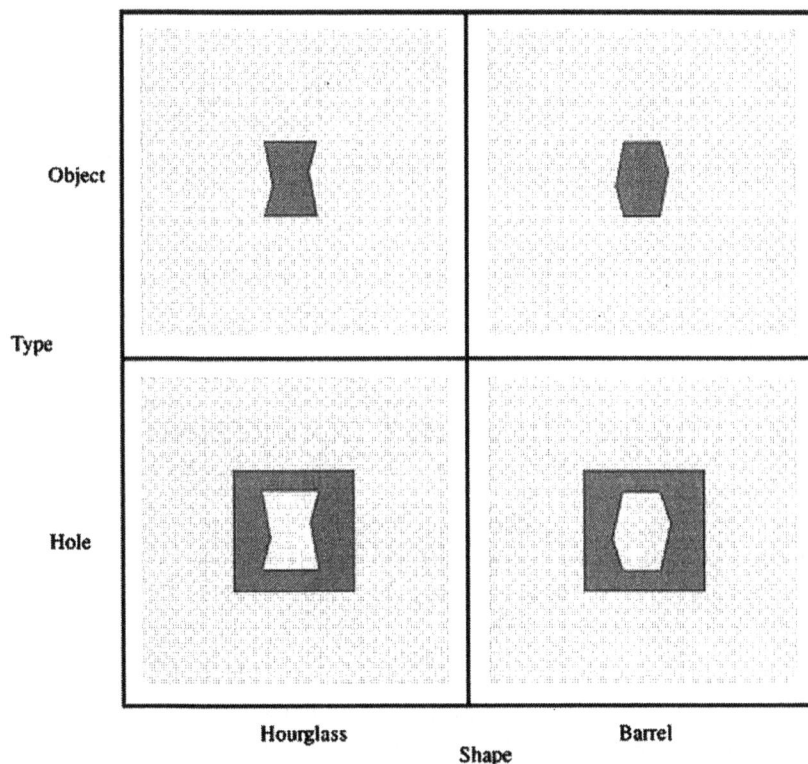

Fig. 3. Examples of stimuli used in Experiment 1. Note that the contours of the shapes themselves are unchanged in the Object and Hole conditions. The background had a texture composed of tiny red diamonds and was present on the screen throughout the experiment. The actual angle formed by the vertices was varied from trial to trial.

figure had a texture to promote the impression of a surface (Experiment 1). Moreover, the textured background was always present on the screen, i.e. was not erased after every trial. Finally, the hole was (roughly) centred on the figure.

Because it is easier to access positional information for convex vertices (Bertamini, 2001) we predicted and found a cross-over interaction between Shape (Barrel and Hourglass) and Type (Object and Hole).

2. General method

Participants sat in a quiet room under conditions of normal illumination. The stimuli were generated and presented by an Apple G4 computer connected to a 17 inch monitor (1250 × 980 pixels at 75 Hz). The computer also recorded whether each response was correct and the reaction time from stimulus onset in milliseconds using the VideoToolbox functions (Pelli, 1997). Each participant saw 24 practice trials, followed by five blocks of 160 trials each. They were encouraged to take breaks if necessary at the end of each block. All conditions were interleaved and the order of presentation of the trials was randomized for each participant.

The monitor was surrounded by a reduction screen to encourage perception of depth in the display, leaving a circular area of screen with a diameter of 22 degrees of visual angle visible. The average viewing distance was 57 cm. Fig. 3 shows the stimuli for Experiment 1, but the layout was similar in all experiments. A square area of background with a 10 degree side was always present on the screen. In Experiment 1 this area had a texture consisting of small dark red diamonds on a white background. Two shapes were compared, both irregular hexagons, but for illustrative purposes we used the term Barrel for the strictly convex shape, and the term Hourglass for the shape with concavities. In the Object condition, both shapes were 2.5 degrees of visual angle tall. In the Hole condition, the same shapes were holes in a larger square (4 degree side). On average over all the trials, the Barrel and Hourglass shapes had the same area. These shapes were chosen for two reasons. Firstly, they are among the simplest possible shapes in which there are two facing vertices, and secondly, they are similar to those used in previous literature (Baylis & Driver, 1993; Gibson, 1994). The solid colour used for the object was always green. Note that in the Hole condition the same regions, instead of being green objects, were presented as areas of background colour in a green square. However, the position was only approximately centred, because all objects and holes were presented at random small distances from the centre of the screen to (a) minimize visual aftereffects and (b) avoid a strategy of focusing always on one screen location.

The angles of the target vertices were randomly varied between 148 and 168 degrees (acute angle measures). This meant that the steepness of the sides of the shapes varied, as did the distance between the two vertices. This aspect of the stimuli is new with respect to similar displays used in the literature (e.g. Baylis & Driver, 1993) and was introduced to avoid possible learning effects that could take place when a given angle is presented in hundreds of trials.

The vertical offset between the right and left vertices was always fixed to 0.5 degrees of visual angle. Because the task was about which vertex was lower, this vertical offset was

M. Bertamini, C.J. Croucher / Cognition 87 (2003) 33–54   43

the only factor that determined whether 'left' or 'right' was the correct answer. The observers were instructed to look for this offset, and they were told to press the "z" key if the left vertex was lower and the "/" key if the right vertex was lower. The stimuli were verbally described as objects and objects with holes, but there was no pressure in the instructions to organize the stimuli in depth. At the end of the 24 practice trials observers were asked whether they had any questions or would like more practice, in which case a second practice session was started. Both accuracy and speed were stressed, and a brief sound immediately informed the participants of an incorrect response.

3. Experiment 1: the shape of objects and holes

We compared reaction times and errors for the stimuli shown in Fig. 3. We predicted a significant interaction, and more specifically we predicted the interaction to have the following critical aspect. Observers would be faster for the Barrel shape when it was depicted as an Object than when it was a Hole, because in the Object condition the vertices were convex and in the Hole condition they were concave (for evidence of a convexity advantage see Bertamini, 2001). The opposite should occur for the Hourglass shape, because when it was an Object the vertices were concave and when it was a Hole they were convex. Referring to Fig. 3, this means an opposite effect of Type for the two levels of Shape, and therefore the important comparison is within each column of the figure. A less critical aspect is the comparison within the rows of the figure. Responses to the Barrel should be faster than responses to the Hourglass in the Object condition, but the opposite should be true for the Hole condition. However, this second aspect of the interaction relies on Barrels and Hourglasses being roughly the same in difficulty, and this may not be the case. In other words there may be a main effect of Shape, with one shape faster than the other overall. For example, it has been suggested that the Hourglass has a more complex part structure because it is 'bisected' by two concave vertices (Gibson, 1994).

In summary, we predicted an interaction between Shape and Type, and a difference in the direction in which Type affected the two Shapes, with the change from Objects to Holes making the task harder for the Barrel but easier for the Hourglass, due to the polarity reversal.

In Experiment 1 we varied the Type factor according to the figural considerations discussed above (Bozzi, 1975), but in addition we manipulated whether the observers saw the stimuli monocularly or binocularly. This factor may affect depth stratification, as binocular viewing provides clues to the flatness of the display, and therefore may influence whether the objects with holes are seen in front of the background.

3.1. Method

Twenty-eight psychology undergraduates from the University of Liverpool participated in this experiment in return for course credit. Their average age was about 19 years and 25 were female. They all had normal or corrected vision. Fourteen participants did the task binocularly and 14 participants did the task monocularly.

44   *M. Bertamini, C.J. Croucher / Cognition 87 (2003) 33–54*

3.2. Results and discussion

Results are shown in Fig. 4. The graphs show the mean reaction times for the four combinations of factors (Barrel–Object, Barrel–Hole, Hourglass–Object, and Hourglass–Hole) averaged across all participants. The error bars are within-subjects standard errors computed according to Loftus and Masson (1994). The lower graphs show the mean percentage of errors for the same four conditions. For this and all subsequent analyses, responses above 3000 ms were excluded as outliers, and a logarithm transformation was used to normalize the distribution (Ulrich & Miller, 1993). For the reaction times analyses incorrect responses were also excluded.

In Fig. 4 we do not collapse the results from the monocular and binocular viewing conditions, but there was no difference between the two conditions according to the analyses of variance (ANOVAs) on reaction time and accuracy reported below.

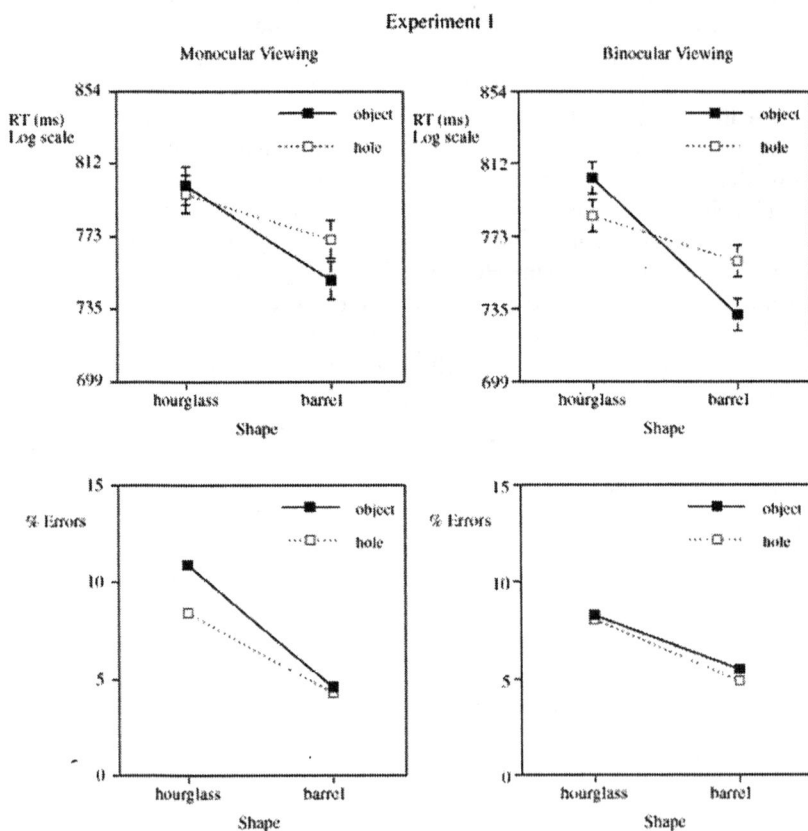

Fig. 4. Results from Experiment 1. Reaction time is at the top and percent error is at the bottom. The error bars are within-subjects standard errors (Loftus & Masson, 1994). We are presenting the monocular and binocular results separately for information, but the difference was not significant.

M. Bertamini, C.J. Croucher / Cognition 87 (2003) 33–54 45

3.2.1. Reaction times

A three-way mixed ANOVA on Shape (Barrel or Hourglass), Type (Object or Hole) and Viewing (binocular or monocular) showed that Shape was a significant factor ($F(1, 26) = 18.66$, $P < 0.001$), with participants faster on the Barrel. Type was also significant ($F(1, 26) = 4.92$, $P = 0.035$), with people being slightly quicker for the Object stimuli than the Hole stimuli. The interaction between Shape and Type was highly significant ($F(1, 26) = 25.19$, $P < 0.001$). A Scheffé post-hoc test showed that people were significantly faster on the Barrel when it was an Object than when it was a Hole ($P < 0.001$), but they were marginally slower on the Hourglass when it was an Object than when it was a Hole ($P = 0.057$). Finally, there was no effect of Viewing ($F(1, 26) = 0.18$, $P = 0.673$) and it did not interact with any of the other factors.

3.2.2. Accuracy

Fig. 4 also shows that accuracy was high. However, Shape was significant ($F(1, 26) = 25.78$, $P < 0.001$), with people being more accurate for the Barrel shape. There was a marginal effect of Type ($F(1, 26) = 3.92$, $P = 0.058$) and no interaction ($F(1, 26) = 1.06$, $P = 0.312$). Finally, Viewing condition had no effect on accuracy ($F(1, 26) = 0.22$, $P = 0.641$). An inspection of the graphs shows no sign of a speed–accuracy trade-off.

Experiment 1 confirmed that people were slower on the Hourglass than on the Barrel, across both Object and Hole conditions. People were also faster for Object than Hole stimuli, perhaps because of the different size of the green stimulus (larger in the Hole condition). Most interestingly for us, there was a cross-over interaction between the two factors: people were faster on the Barrel shape when it was presented as an Object than when it was presented as a Hole, and vice versa for the Hourglass (albeit marginally). Ideally we would have liked the reversal (cross-over interaction) to be as clear for the Barrel and for the Hourglass. Possibly this problem is related to the fact that the Hourglass was a harder condition overall. This factor was manipulated in a subsequent experiment (Experiment 3).

We suggest that this interaction is because the polarity of the vertices was reversed, i.e. for the Barrel the vertices were represented as convex parts in the Object trials but as concavities in the Hole trials. The vertices of the Hourglass were more difficult to judge in the Object trials, perhaps because concavities are represented as boundaries between parts, which are not perceived as having a position of their own (Bertamini, 2001). This suggests that the important factor in judging within-shape vertices is not the overall shape but whether those vertices are perceived as being concave or convex, and that this can be manipulated by changing figure and ground so that the shape is perceived as a hole.

Initially we were concerned that having participants view the displays binocularly would reduce their perception of depth in the displays due to binocular disparity information, leading to the hole regions being perceived not as holes but as flat shapes superimposed on rectangles. However, the data obtained with binocular viewing were remarkably consistent with those from the monocular viewing condition. Perhaps this should have been expected all along, because a significant difference in depth need not be necessary for the surface lying on the top to have a hole in it. The similarity between the two viewing conditions suggests that our manipulation of the display did in fact have the effect predicted by Bozzi (1975) in creating the impression of a hole on the basis of figural factors.

Our findings are consistent with those recently reported by Tsal, Lamy, and Ilan (2000), who used conditions similar to our Barrel–Object and Barrel–Hole. However, they were not investigating perception of contour polarity. Their interpretation of the poorer performance in the hole condition ("enclosure" in their terminology) is that it requires attention to spread over a larger area. This is possible, and is a factor that may have been confounded with the effect of number of objects in the past (Baylis & Driver, 1993). However, in this paper we remain neutral with respect to the debate about object-based versus space-based attention. By comparing the Barrel and Hourglass stimuli we have found an interaction which cannot be explained on the basis of either the number of objects (one in both the Object and Hole conditions) or the spatial extent of the area attended (the same in the Barrel and Hourglass conditions).

4. Experiment 2: solid colours

Although we used a textured background to encourage depth stratification for the Hole conditions, we wondered whether this might have affected the results in some unpredicted way. We therefore ran a control experiment using dark red shapes on a uniform green background, to see whether the interaction of Shape and Type would still occur under these conditions.

4.1. Method

Fourteen psychology undergraduates from the University of Liverpool participated in return for course credit. None had participated in Experiment 1. All participants did the task binocularly. The equipment and procedure were identical to those in Experiment 1 except that the texture was replaced by a solid green colour and the green figure was replaced by a solid red colour (see Fig. 5). The green was the same colour used for the figure in Experiment 1, and the red was the same colour used for the squares of the texture in Experiment 1. The background was darker than the old texture because it was now a solid colour. If our conclusions from Experiment 1 were correct we should again find a significant interaction between Shape and Type, notwithstanding the changes in colours.

4.2. Results and discussion

The results for both reaction times and errors can be seen in Fig. 6. We ran a series of ANOVAs using the same design as in Experiment 1.

4.2.1. Reaction times

Once again, Shape was a significant factor ($F(3, 13) = 24.35$, $P < 0.001$), with participants faster on the Barrel. There was no main effect of Type ($F(1, 13) = 0.85$, $P = 0.374$), but a significant interaction ($F(3, 13) = 5.67$, $P = 0.033$).

4.2.2. Accuracy

Accuracy was even higher than in the first experiment. However, there was a significant effect of Shape ($F(3, 13) = 21.07$, $P < 0.001$) but not of Type ($F(1, 13) = 1.89$,

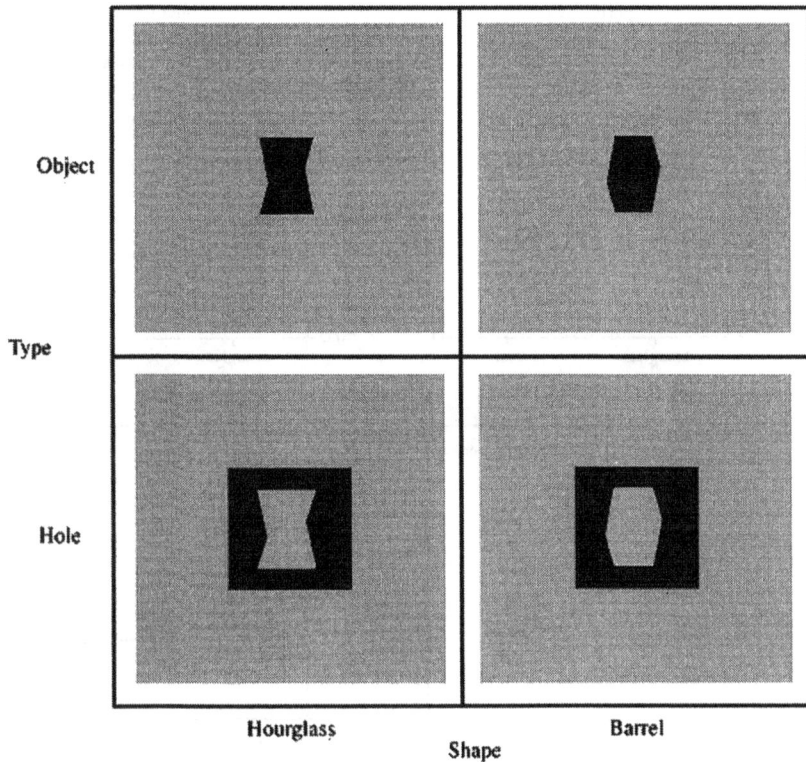

Fig. 5. Examples of stimuli used in Experiment 2. The only difference with respect to the stimuli in Experiment 1 was the elimination of the texture. The figure was always red and the background always green.

$P = 0.193$), and no interaction ($F(3, 13) = 2.70$, $P = 0.124$). An inspection of the graphs shows no sign of a speed–accuracy trade-off.

This experiment replicated the findings of Experiment 1, although it is interesting that the participants in this condition were faster than those in Experiment 1. The means differ from those of Experiment 1 by between 80 ms (for the Barrel–Object condition) and 150 ms (for the two Hourglass conditions). This may be because removing the texture decreased visual complexity and made the task simpler. However, this control experiment confirms that it is easier to compare two vertices within a shape if they are convex than if they are concave.

5. Experiment 3: adjustment of difficulty

Experiments 1 and 2 confirmed an interaction between Shape and Type, even when overall the task was easier. Nevertheless, in both experiments the effect of Shape was significant, showing that the Hourglass was in general harder than the Barrel. Because

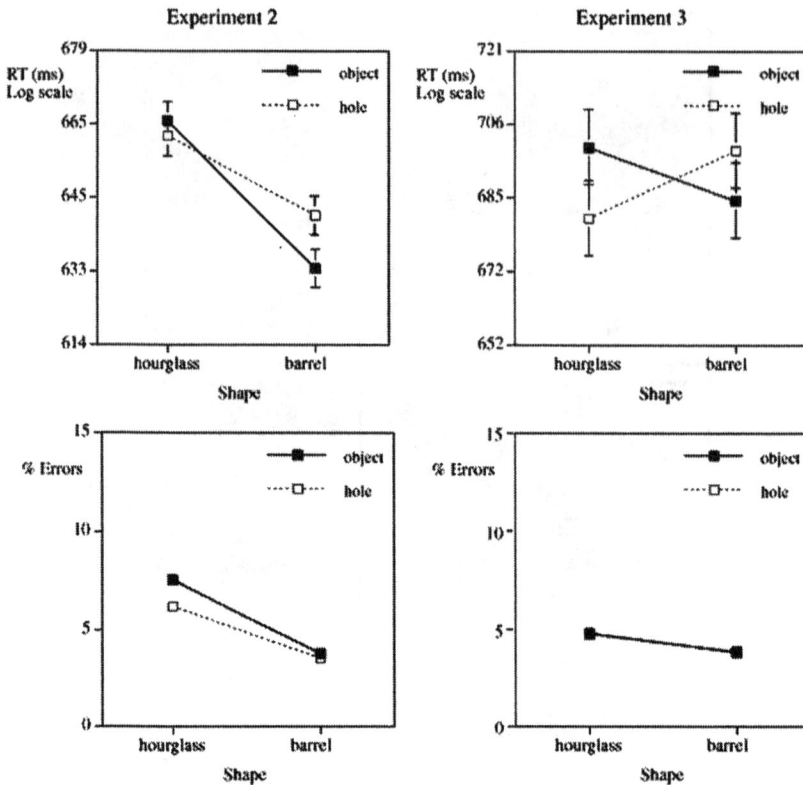

Fig. 6. Results from Experiment 2 (solid colours) and 3 (adjusted difficulty). Reaction time is at the top and percent error is at the bottom. The error bars are within-subjects standard errors.

comparing differences in performance at different points on a range of difficulty is problematic we wanted to ensure that the interaction was present when all conditions were in the same range. Therefore, Experiment 3 tested the hypothesis that the interaction would still be present if the relative difficulties of the two shapes were to be adjusted so as to require comparable reaction time. A change from Object to Hole should make the Barrel task harder and the Hourglass task easier, as before, but in this new scenario we also expect that a change from Barrel to Hourglass should make the Object task harder and the Hole task easier (an effect that in Experiments 1 and 2 was hidden by an overall difference in difficulty between the two shapes). As can be seen in Fig. 6, this type of cross-over interaction was indeed confirmed.

5.1. Method

Sixteen observers participated in return for course credit or a small monetary reward. The procedure was identical to Experiment 1 except that the process of generating the vertices was adjusted. As before there were two vertices on the sides of the shapes which participants had to look at in order to perform the task. The range of the angles formed by these vertices was reduced to only two values; for the Barrel they were 161 and 156 degrees, whilst for the Hourglass they were 156 and 152 degrees. The smaller angles (sharper vertices) used for the Hourglass should make the task easier in relative terms, and the exact values were chosen after piloting. We predict again a significant interaction between Shape and Type, but this time there should be no effect of Shape.

5.2. Results and discussion

The results for both reaction times and errors can be seen in Fig. 6. We ran an ANOVA using the same steps and design as in Experiments 1 and 2. Shape was not a significant factor ($F(1, 15) = 0.02$, $P = 0.897$), and neither was there an effect of Type ($F(1, 15) = 0.18$, $P = 0.675$). However, the interaction was significant ($F(1, 15) = 13.64$, $P = 0.002$). Post-hoc Scheffé tests on the means confirmed that for the Barrel, the Object condition was faster than the Hole condition ($P = 0.048$), whilst for the Hourglass the Object condition was significantly slower than the Hole condition ($P = 0.008$). Accuracy was again extremely high, and as a result no factor was significant. An inspection of the graphs in Fig. 6 shows no sign of a speed–accuracy trade-off.

This experiment replicated the findings of Experiments 1 and 2. The important contribution of Experiment 3 is that it proves that eliminating a difference in difficulty between the two shapes does not eliminate the cross-over interaction. On the contrary, it supports our original hypothesis that because convex vertices define the structural parts of an object, their position is always more readily available than the position of concave vertices.

6. General discussion

Although holes are very interesting entities for study in themselves, they become even more interesting with respect to the study of how shape information is encoded and represented. In this paper we found evidence to support the central role of curvature polarity in shape perception. By changing the nature of a given closed contour from an object to a hole we can achieve a reversal of curvature polarity without any change in the actual contours (i.e. edge information). This reversal is a special case of a figure/ground reversal, which has already been shown to affect performance in visual search (Humphreys & Müller, 2000), contour matching (Driver & Baylis, 1996) and judgements about position (Bertamini, 2001). Unlike other figure/ground reversals, holes are unique in that there is no change in the actual (and presumably the perceived) closure of the region. In fact, the figure/ground reversal in the present experiments was achieved purely on the basis of contextual information (Bozzi, 1975). Using holes, a curvature polarity reversal can be achieved without altering factors such as closure and number of objects.

The question arises of how a change of curvature polarity takes place. Is this inversion a slow and serial process, and does it require attention? The Barrel and the Hourglass have six vertices, but for the Barrel they are all convex, whilst for the Hourglass four are convex and two are concave (Fig. 2). We mentioned that it has been suggested that this makes the

Hourglass more complex and responses to it slower (Gibson, 1994). In our argument we have claimed that curvature polarity is a very basic aspect of shape, and it is extracted fast and obligatorily. However, the precise role of attention in curvature extraction is beyond the scope of the present paper. As for the complexity of the Hourglass shape, comparing the figures-with-holes reveals that the figure with Hourglass-shaped hole would still be more complex than the figure with Barrel-shaped hole, and therefore this difference cannot explain the interaction.

It is important to note that in all the experiments presented here, observers could have responded purely on the basis of the shape of contours disregarding which side of the contour was figure and which was ground. There was nothing in the task or in the instructions that forced observers to pay attention to figure/ground organization. But had they treated the contours as edges defined only by colour or luminance, no interaction between Shape and Type have been found. The interaction was present because figure/ground organization is obligatory and curvature polarity information cannot be ignored. This is consistent with what was found by Driver and Baylis (1996) and Bertamini et al. (2002).

What we call figures or objects in our experiments could be called *surfaces*, and in this sense our findings are also consistent with the evidence of a primary role of surfaces for the human visual system (e.g. Lappin & Craft, 2000; Nakayama, He, & Shimojo, 1995; Nakayama & Shimojo, 1992). Surfaces may be defined by contours and lines in the geometry we learn at school but this does not imply that they are secondary or that they are constructed from lines by the human visual system. If visual organisms have evolved to extract relevant visual information to survive in a world of solid shapes, then convex and concave regions of contours are directly informative about solid shape. This difference helps us to understand the phenomena described in Fig. 1a,b. Moreover, Bertamini (2001) suggested that convex regions define parts of solid objects that need a description in a way that is qualitatively different from the description of a concave region, namely positional information should be more directly available for convex parts. If this is true we can predict differences between two congruent outlines when they are perceived as figure and hole. In this paper we empirically confirmed these predictions.

Anecdotal support for this view that convexity is critical for how we represent shape can be found also in the following quote: "In general the surfaces of things growing or blown up from the inside tend to possess positive Gaussian curvature. [...] the sculpture of many cultures reveals this very clearly. Very often the negatively curved parts are reduced to narrow V-shaped grooves between the bulging ovoid parts. An extreme example is the famous "Venus of Willendorf" from paleolithic origin (ca. 11000 B.C.). Clearly this fact that we all seem to know from introspection is not a short-lived "cultural whim", but somehow pervades human visual perception throughout known history and over all cultures." (Koenderink, 1990, p. 251).

Note that simple contours and surfaces were used in our experiments, but the logic of the discussion relies on the fact that even such pictorial stimuli must be understood in the context of perceiving and representing solid shapes. Contours are informative about rims of self-occluding surfaces in space. In other words, the experimenter's choice of simple stimuli cannot turn off the sophisticated visual intelligence of a human observer, and the

M. Bertamini, C.J. Croucher / Cognition 87 (2003) 33–54 51

same machinery will be engaged by any visual task, although simple stimuli can reveal important underlying principles.

The importance of describing the information available to the observer in terms of surfaces and media (an idea first introduced by Gibson, 1979) can be further clarified by contrasting it with possible alternatives. As discussed in Section 1, much of the problems with holes stem from the fact that they are not objects whereas at the same time they are uniform connected regions (a concept introduced by Palmer & Rock, 1994). According to Palmer and Rock (1994) uniform connected regions are the initial units of perceptual organization. Both material objects and uniform connected regions have intuitive appeal as the basic units of perception. But a visual system interested in material objects is construed as a Physicist, and a visual system interested in uniform connected regions is construed as a serial Computer that has to start from a 2D image similar to a mosaic to recover 3D information (for a critique see, for example, Bruno, Bertamini, & Domini, 1997). As discussed earlier, we prefer to think of the visual system as a Geometer, interested first and foremost in solid shape.

It could be argued that in all our experiments there was some ambiguity in the display. This is true, however we have conducted a separate set of experiments in which the display was not ambiguous at all, because of binocular disparity. By using random dot stereograms we have presented surfaces at different depths with or without holes. The shapes are only visible after fusing the two stereograms so we can be confident that a hole in a surface is perceived as such. Consistent with this more powerful way in which a hole was created, we have found even stronger interactions than those reported in this paper (Bertamini & Mosca, 2002).

Many of the issues mentioned in this discussion can be followed up in future research, and some of this work is under way. Timing issues can be tested by varying presentation time or adopting a priming paradigm (e.g. Baylis & Cale, 2001). Issues to do with attention can be looked at, for example, with secondary tasks. The role of convexity in creating complete objects can be detected indirectly by tasks requiring fine shape judgements (e.g. Liu, Jacobs, & Basri, 1999). The basic difference in the representations of a figure and a hole even when their contours are congruent could be detected with imaging techniques which would show the important cortical regions involved in processing shape information modulated by figure/ground organization (e.g. Baylis & Driver, 2001b; Kourtzi & Kanwisher, 2001). Holes with meaningful shapes could be used to see whether recognition of a hole as a particular object will substantially affect its representation (e.g. Peterson et al., 2000).

There are even some perhaps more difficult philosophical questions that must be addressed. Should perception and ontology agree or can there exist fundamental differences between what holes are (a question of ontology), and what they are for the visual system?

7. Conclusions

The interaction reported in this paper is consistent with the hypothesis that the position of a convex region is more readily available to the observer (Bertamini, 2001; Gibson, 1994).

52   M. Bertamini, C.J. Croucher / Cognition 87 (2003) 33–54

Moreover, with respect to the paradox of how people can remember the shape of a hole, we conclude that a hole is defined by the contour of the enclosing object, rather than the hole itself possessing the contour. To repeat the argument, consider the case of a rectangle containing an Hourglass-shaped hole (Figs. 2 and 3): the object in this case has two contours – a square contour on the outside and the Hourglass contour which contains two protruding parts pointing inwards towards a central void. Even if this hole is always represented by the shape of the object-with-hole, this would not prevent observers from recognizing the shape of the hole when asked to remember it over time. This interpretation is therefore entirely consistent with the findings of Rock, Palmer, and Hume (cited in Palmer, 1999). In summary, because the shapes of holes and objects have curvature with opposite polarity (by definition) they are perceived as having different shapes. Therefore, we have demonstrated that (a) contour assignment and curvature polarity have a critical and obligatory role in the representation of shape in the human visual system, and that (b) holes are promising material for the empirical study of shape representation. However, none of what we have discovered so far contradicts the tenet of Gestalt theory that says that boundaries belong to the figure and only to the figure (Koffka, 1935; Rubin, 1921).

Acknowledgements

We thank Peter Giblin, Richard Latto, and Rebecca Lawson and three anonymous reviewers for comments on the manuscript, and Emily Deploe for help in running Experiment 1 as part of her undergraduate degree.

References

Albert, M. K. (2000). The generic-viewpoint assumption and Bayesian inference. *Perception, 29*, 601–608.
Albert, M. K. (2001). Cue interactions, border ownership and illusory contours. *Vision Research, 41*, 2827–2834.
Attneave, F. (1954). Some informational aspects of visual perception. *Psychological Review, 61*, 183–193.
Attneave, F. (1974). Multistability in perception. *Scientific American, 225*, 63–71.
Bahnsen, P. (1928). Eine untersuchung über symmetrie und asymmetrie bei visuellen wahrnehmungen. *Zeitschrift für Psychologie, 108*, 129–154.
Baylis, G. C., & Cale, E. M. (2001). The figure has a shape, but the ground does not: evidence from a priming paradigm. *Journal of Experimental Psychology: Human Perception and Performance, 27* (3), 633–643.
Baylis, G. C., & Driver, J. (1993). Visual attention and objects: evidence for hierarchical coding of location. *Journal of Experimental Psychology: Human Perception and Performance, 19*, 451–470.
Baylis, G. C., & Driver, J. (1995). Obligatory edge assignment in vision: the role of figure and part segregation in symmetry detection. *Journal of Experimental Psychology: Human Perception and Performance, 21*, 1323–1342.
Baylis, G. C., & Driver, J. (2001). Perception of symmetry and repetition within and across visual shapes: part-descriptions and object-based attention. *Visual Cognition, 8*, 163–196.
Baylis, G. C., & Driver, J. (2001). Shape-coding in IT cells generalizes over contrast and mirror reversal, but not figure-ground reversal. *Nature Neuroscience, 4*, 937–942.
Bertamini, M. (2001). The importance of being convex: an advantage for convexity when judging position. *Perception, 30*, 1295–1310.
Bertamini, M., Friedenberg, J., & Argyle, L. (2002). No within-object advantage for detection of rotational symmetry. *Acta Psychologica, 111*, 59–81.

Bertamini, M., & Mosca, F. (2002). Objects and holes have different perceived shape even when they are congruent, in preparation.

Biederman, I. (1987). Recognition-by-components: a theory of human image understanding. *Psychological Review, 94* (2), 115–147.

Bozzi, P. (1975). Osservazioni su alcuni casi di trasparenza fenomenica realizzabili con figure a tratto. In G. d'Arcais (Ed.), *Studies in perception: Festschrift for Fabio Metelli* (pp. 88–110). Milan: Martelli-Giunti.

Bruno, N., Bertamini, M., & Domini, F. (1997). Amodal completion of partly occluded surfaces: is there a mosaic stage? *Journal of Experimental Psychology: Human Perception and Performance, 23* (5), 1412–1426.

Casati, R., & Varzi, A. C. (1994). *Holes and other superficialities*. Cambridge, MA: MIT Press.

Cavedon, A. (1980). *Contorno e disparazione retinica come determinanti della localizzazione in profondità: le condizioni della percezione di un foro (Istituto di Psicologia Report 12)*, Padova: Università di Padova.

Chen, L. (2001). Perceptual organisation: to reverse back the inverted (upside-down) question of feature binding. *Visual Cognition, 8* (3–5), 287–303.

Driver, J., & Baylis, G. C. (1996). Edge-assignment and figure-ground segmentation in short-term visual matching. *Cognitive Psychology, 31*, 248–306.

Gibson, B. S. (1994). Visual attention and objects: one versus two or convex versus concave? *Journal of Experimental Psychology: Human Perception and Performance, 20* (1), 203–207.

Gibson, J. J. (1979). *The ecological approach to visual perception*. Boston, MA: Houghton Mifflin.

Hecht, H., & Bader, H. (1998). Perceiving topological structure of 2-D patterns. *Acta Psychologica, 99*, 255–292.

Hoffman, D. D. (1998). *Visual intelligence*, New York: W.W. Norton.

Hoffman, D. D., & Richards, W. (1984). Parts of recognition. *Cognition, 18*, 65–96.

Hoffman, D. D., & Singh, M. (1997). Salience of visual parts. *Cognition, 63*, 29–78.

Humphreys, G., & Müller, H. (2000). A search asymmetry reversed by figure-ground assignment. *Psychological Science, 11*, 196–201.

Kanizsa, G. (1979). *Organization in vision*. New York: Praeger.

Kanizsa, G., & Gerbino, W. (1976). Convexity and symmetry in figure-ground organization. In M. Henle, *Vision and artifact* (pp. 25–32). New York: Springer.

Koenderink, J. J. (1984). What does the occluding contour tell us about solid shape? *Perception, 13*, 321–330.

Koenderink, J. J. (1990). *Solid shape*. Cambridge, MA: MIT Press.

Koffka, K. (1935). *Principles of gestalt psychology*. New York: Harcourt Brace.

Kourtzi, Z., & Kanwisher, N. (2001). Representation of perceived object shape by the human lateral occipital complex. *Science, 293*, 1506–1509.

Lappin, J. S., & Craft, W. D. (2000). Foundations of spatial vision: from retinal images to perceived shapes. *Psychological Review, 107*, 6–38.

Lewis, D., & Lewis, S. (1983). Holes. In D. Lewis (Ed.), *Philosophical papers* (pp. 3–9), Vol. 1. New York: Oxford University Press.

Liu, Z., Jacobs, D. W., & Basri, R. (1999). The role of convexity in perceptual completion: beyond good continuation. *Vision Research, 39*, 4244–4257.

Loftus, G., & Masson, M. (1994). Using confidence intervals in within-subject designs. *Psychonomic Bulletin & Review, 1*, 476–490.

Marr, D., & Nishihara, H. (1978). Representation and recognition of the spatial organisation of three-dimensional shapes. *Proceedings of the Royal Society of London B, 200*, 269–294.

Nakayama, K., He, Z. J., & Shimojo, S. (1995). Visual surface representation: a critical link between lower-level and higher level vision. In S. M. Kosslyn & D. N. Osherson (Eds.), *Visual cognition. An invitation to cognitive science* (pp. 1–70). Cambridge, MA: MIT Press.

Nakayama, K., & Shimojo, S. (1992). Experiencing and perceiving visual surfaces. *Science, 257*, 1357–1363.

Nelson, R., & Palmer, S. E. (2001). Of holes and wholes: the perception of surrounded regions. *Perception, 30*, 1213–1226.

Norman, J. F., Phillips, F., & Ross, H. E. (2001). Information concentration along the boundary contours of naturally shaped solid objects. *Perception, 30*, 1285–1294.

Palmer, S. E. (1999). *Vision science: photons to phenomenology*. Cambridge, MA: MIT Press.

Palmer, S., & Rock, I. (1994). Rethinking perceptual organization: the role of uniform connectedness. *Psychonomic Bulletin & Review, 1* (1), 29–55.

Pelli, D. G. (1997). The VideoToolbox software for visual psychophysics: transforming numbers into movies. *Spatial Vision, 10*, 437–442.

Peterson, M. A., de Gelder, B., Rapcsak, S. Z., Gerhardstein, P. C., & Bachoud-Lévi, A. -C. (2000). Object memory effects on figure assignment: conscious object recognition is not necessary or sufficient. *Vision Research, 40*, 1549–1567.

Peterson, M. A., & Kim, J. H. (2001). On what is bound in figures and grounds. *Visual Cognition, 8*, 329–348.

Rock, I. (1983). *The logic of perception*. Cambridge, MA: MIT Press.

Rubin, E. (1921). *Visuell Wahrgenommene Figuren*, Kobenhaven: Glydenalske Boghandel.

Singh, M., Seyranian, G. D., & Hoffman, D. D. (1999). Parsing silhouettes: the short-cut rule. *Perception & Psychophysics, 61*, 636–660.

ter Haar Romeny, B. M., & Florack, L. M. J. (2000). Front-end vision: a multiscale geometry engine. *Lectures Notes in Computer Science, 1811*, 297–307.

Tsal, Y., Lamy, D., & Ilan, C. (2000). The two-object cost is a space-based phenomenon. *Abstracts of the Psychonomic Society, 5*, 33.

Ulrich, R., & Miller, J. (1993). Information processing models generating lognormally distributed reaction times. *Journal of Mathematical Psychology, 37* (4), 513–525.

Part VI
Information Processing and Models

[18]

THE DISCOVERY OF PROCESSING STAGES:
EXTENSIONS OF DONDERS' METHOD

SAUL STERNBERG [1]

Bell Telephone Laboratories, Murray Hill, N.J., U.S.A.

ABSTRACT

A new method is proposed for using reaction-time (RT) measurements to study stages of information processing. It overcomes limitations of Donders' and more recent methods, and permits the discovery of stages, assessment of their properties, and separate testing of the additivity and stochastic independence of stage durations. The main feature of the *additive-factor method* is the search for non-interacting effects of experimental factors on mean RT. The method is applied to several binary-classification experiments, where it leads to a four-stage model, and to an identification experiment, where it distinguishes two stages. The sets of stages inferred from both these and other data are shown to carry substantive implications. It is demonstrated that stage-durations may be additive without being stochastically independent, a result that is relevant to the formulation of mathematical models of RT.

1. INTRODUCTION

The work of DONDERS (1868) that we have been commemorating was based on the idea that the time between stimulus and response is occupied by a train of successive processes, or stages: each component process begins only when the preceding one has ended. Donders developed the *subtraction method* to measure the durations of some of these stages, and thereby study their properties; mean reaction-times (RTs) from two different tasks are compared, where one task is thought to require all the stages of the first, plus an additional stage. The difference between mean RTs is taken to be an estimate of the mean duration of the interpolated stage. The method was popular for several decades (see JASTROW, 1890) and then came into disfavor (see KÜLPE, 1895).

Although it has seen something of a revival in the last few years (e.g., NEISSER, 1963; STERNBERG, 1966; TAYLOR, 1966; POSNER and

[1] I am indebted to J. Krauskopf for several helpful suggestions. I also thank P. D. Bricker, C. S. Harris, R. S. Nickerson, and G. Sperling for criticisms of the manuscript, B. Barkow and B. A. Nasto for laboratory assistance, and D. S. Hougak, P. L. Moore, B. A. Nasto, and A. M. Pope for serving as subjects in exp. V.

MITCHELL, 1967; SNODGRASS et al., 1967; SMITH, 1968), little is known about how to test the validity of any particular application of the subtraction method. The underlying conception of the RT as a sum of durations of a series of stages is now a popular one, but there is remarkably little strong supporting evidence. And there is even less evidence that stage durations are stochactically independent, an assumption often incorporated with the idea of additivity (e.g., MCGILL, 1963; TAYLOR, 1966; HOHLE, 1967).

The early applications of Donders' idea were criticized partly because introspective data suggested that it might be difficult to devise experimental tasks that would add or delete one of the stages between stimulus and response without also altering other stages. In this paper I propose a simple method of testing for additive RT-components that opens up new possibilities for inferring the organization of mental operations from RT data without requiring procedures that add or delete stages. Unlike Donders' method it does not lead to the measurement of stage durations, but like his method it can be used to help establish the existence and properties of stages, and the relations among them. The method is applied to data from two kinds of choice-reaction experiment, a binary-classification ('partial-identification', or many-one) task, and a 'complete-identification' (one-one) task (BUSH et al., 1963). A generalization of the method is used to test the idea that RT components are stochastically independent. And it is shown how these methods also permit localizing the effect of a new experimental factor among a set of stages already established.

2. ASSUMPTIONS ABOUT STAGE DURATIONS IN RECENT STUDIES

2.1. *Three types of assumption*

In recent years three main propositions have been considered in the analysis of RT into components; they are listed in fig. 1. The proposition that is of main interest, and the one that reflects Donders' idea, is that there are successive functional stages between stimulus and response, whose durations are additive components of the RT. Here T_a and T_b are random variables representing the durations of two different stages, and T_w is a wastebasket category representing the total duration of all other events between stimulus and response. The first proposition implies that the mean RT is the sum of the means of the components.

A supplementary assumption sometimes treated as inseparable from that of additivity is that the RT-components are stochastically independ-

278   SAUL STERNBERG

| Proposition of main interest | Strong supplementary assumption | Stronger supplementary assumption |

SUCCESSIVE FUNCTIONAL   RT COMPONENTS T_w, T_a, T_b COMPONENT DISTRIBUTIONS

STAGES BETWEEN S,R   STOCHASTICALLY INDEPENDENT f_w, f_a, f_b SPECIFIED

(i.e. additive RT
components:

$RT = T_w + T_a + T_b$)

Additive component   Additive component   RT-distribution

means: variances and higher   deducible by

$\overline{RT} = \overline{T}_w + \overline{T}_a + \overline{T}_b$.   cumulants $(r = 2,3,\ldots)$:   convolution:

                  $\kappa_r(RT) = \kappa_r(w) + \kappa_r(a) + \kappa_r(b)$. $f_{RT} = f_w * f_a * f_b$

Additive factor   Additive factor effects   Effects of each factor

effects on mean RT.   on variances and higher   limited to parameters

                   cumulants of RT.   of relevant component

                                    distribution.

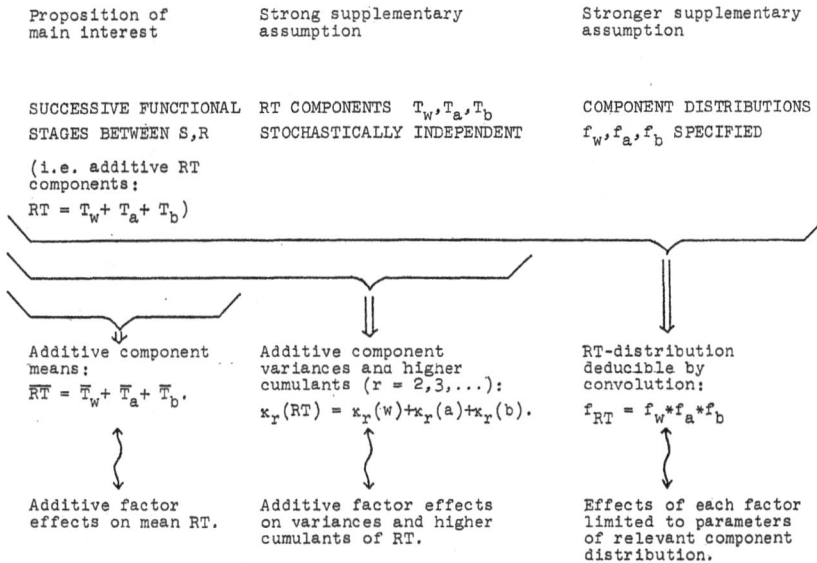

Fig. 1. Three types of assumption in the decomposition of RT, and their implications. Wavy arrows show loose implications (see section 3.1); statements in bottom row apply only to experimental factors that influence no stages in common.

ent. (I will show in section 5.4 why these assumptions should be examined separately and why a definition of stage that involves additivity without independence might be a useful one.) Taken together with the first proposition, the assumption of independence has strong implications: not only are the component variances additive – since the variance of the sum of independent quantities is the sum of their variances – but all the higher cumulants are additive as well. (Cumulants are statistics of a distribution that are closely related to its moments and that are estimated without bias by k-statistics; see KENDALL and STUART, 1958.)

An even stronger supplementary assumption is one that specifies the forms of the components' distributions. (Exponentially-distributed stage durations, for example, have sometimes been assumed.) Given the distributions and the other assumptions, one can deduce the RT distribution itself. (Intermediate cases arise when a feature of the RT distribution is inferred from assumptions in which the forms of components are only partially specified: LUCE and GREEN (1969) provide an example.)

2.2. *Tests of the assumptions*

Almost always, a 'strong' model has been tested, in which the proposition of main interest is combined with both of the supplementary assumptions. This approach is exemplified by the work of CHRISTIE and LUCE (1956), AUDLEY (1960), RESTLE and DAVIS (1962), McGILL (1963), McGILL and GIBBON (1965), and HOHLE (1967). A central notion in such work is that the form of the RT distribution (which depends on the postulated distributions of the components and on their independence, as well as on their additivity) is a key to the underlying process.

According to Hohle, for example, the RT is the sum of an exponentially-distributed 'decision' component and an independent, normally-distributed 'residual' component (representing the summed durations of all other processes). He has successfully fitted the resulting theoretical distribution to RTs from several experiments. To examine the model further he obtains parameter estimates for the theoretical distribution from RTs at two or more levels of an experimental factor. One consequence of Hohle's choice of hypothetical component distributions is that these estimates reveal the extent to which each of the components is responsible for the effect of the factor on RT. If the model is correct, changes in some factors should influence only the decision component, while changes in others should influence only the residual component. But overall findings from a series of studies by HOHLE (1967) and GHOLSON and HOHLE (1968a,b) are not entirely consistent with this expectation.

Unlike Donders' method, in which experimental manipulations are required to add or delete entire stages, Hohle's requires only that the amount of processing required of a stage, and hence its duration, be manipulated. This feature, which extends the range of situations in which analysis of RTs can be performed, also characterizes the new method to be proposed in section 3.

One problem for an approach such as Hohle's, in which a strong model is invoked, is that when the model fails it is of course difficult to decide which of its several assumptions is at fault. A second problem is that rather different sets of components may give rise to RT distributions that have approximately the same form. There are several advantages, therefore, in testing relatively weaker models, or examining assumptions one at a time.

TAYLOR (1966) has tried to test the main proposition together with only the first supplementary assumption. As in the early applications of Donders' idea, he attempted to construct tasks that would add or delete entire stages. An important innovation in Taylor's work is the inclusion of a test of the additivity of stage durations: if one change in task adds stage a and an increment $\overline{T}_a$ in mean RT, and a different change in task adds stage b and an increment $\overline{T}_b$, then the two changes together should add both stages and a combined increment $\overline{T}_{ab} = \overline{T}_a + \overline{T}_b$. Such a test can validate applications of the subtraction method, and protect it from the early criticisms according to which the change in task that adds a particular stage may also alter other stages. Additivity tests also characterize the method to be proposed in section 3. Unfortunately, Taylor's test cannot be said to have succeeded, mainly because his experiment was insufficiently precise.

Whereas Taylor felt that the assumptions of additivity and independence should be tested jointly, additivity has been examined alone in a series of studies on sentence verification (McMAHON, 1963; GOUGH, 1965, 1966). The hypothesis being tested was that negative and passive transformations in stimulus sentences add separate stages to the process of verification; if they do, the transformations should have additive effects on mean RT. This was found by McMahon, but Gough found a systematic tendency for the combined increment, $\overline{T}_{ab}$, to be less than $\overline{T}_a + \overline{T}_b$, a deviation from additivity in the same direction as the trend in Taylor's data.

Experimental operations like these, which might be thought of as deleting entire stages without altering the functions of other stages, are probably very rare; they should be considered special cases. Another example of this kind of special case arises in certain memory-search tasks (e.g., STERNBERG, 1966) where it can be assumed or inferred that the number of elements scanned, and therefore the number of similar stages, is under experimental control. (Some visual-search tasks, as in NEISSER, 1963, are similar.) Here the desired additivity test of the main proposition is accomplished by evaluating the linearity of the function relating mean RT to the number of elements scanned. The slope of this function represents the mean time to scan one item; its zero-intercept represents the combined durations of all events other than scanning. (Whereas Donders might have attempted to measure the zero-intercept directly, by devising an experiment in which no elements are scanned, here one can estimate its value by extrapolation.) In such search tasks, moreover, the independence assumption can be tested separately by examining the relations between each of the cumulants of the RT distribution and the number of elements scanned: if the assumption of independence is justified, these relations are also linear, and the slopes and zero-intercepts of the linear functions can be used as estimates of the cumulants of the components. These estimates in turn can be used to determine the forms of the component distributions (STERNBERG, 1964).

3. SUCCESSIVE STAGES AND ADDITIVE FACTOR-EFFECTS: A NEW METHOD

3.1. *Implications of factor-stage relations*

The method I shall propose seems to apply to a wide variety of RT situations, rather than only to those special cases where experimental manipulations can add entire stages or produce known changes in the number of identical stages. Yet it seems to permit the proposition of main interest to be tested by itself. Suppose that stages *a*, *b*, and *c* shown in fig. 2 are among a series of stages between stimulus and

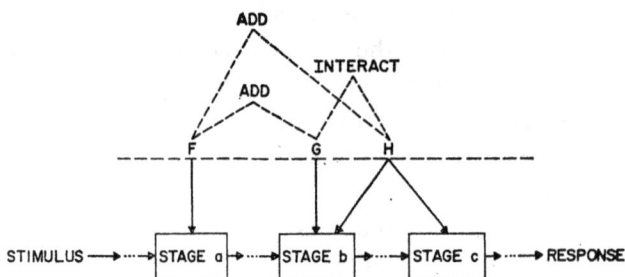

Fig. 2. Example of an arrangement of stages (*a*, *b*, and *c*) and factors (F, G, and H). Below the horizontal line are shown three hypothetical stages between stimulus and response. Horizontal arrows represent inputs and outputs of stages; time proceeds from left to right. Dots indicate the possibility of other stages in a string in which the hypothetical stages are embedded. Arrows are drawn from factors to the stages assumed to be influenced by those factors. Above the line are indicated the relations among effects of the factors on mean RT that are expected from the arrangement.

response. Suppose further that there are three experimental factors, F, G, and H, such that factor F influences only the duration of stage *a*, factor G influences only the duration of stage *b*, and factor H influences stages *b* and *c*, but not *a*. (By a 'factor' here is meant an experimentally manipulated variable, or a set of two or more related treatments called 'levels'; the 'effect' of a factor is the change in the response measure induced by a change in the level of that factor.) What are the most likely relations among the effects of the three factors on mean RT? These relations are shown above the broken line. The general idea is that when factors influence no stages in common, their effects on mean RT will be independent and additive, because stage durations are additive. That is, the effect of one factor will not depend on the levels of the others. Thus, factors F and G should have additive effects on mean RT. On the other hand, when two factors, G and H, influence at least one stage in common (stage *b*) there is no reason to expect their effects on RT to add; the most likely relation is some sort of interaction.

One can imagine exceptions to both of these rules, of course. Factors G and H might just happen to influence stage *b* additively, and their effects on RT would then also be additive, even though they influenced a stage in common. (This notion would gain strength if, for example, *other* factors either interacted with *both* G and H or with *neither*.) Alternatively, if factor F influenced the output of stage *a* as well as its duration, then it might indirectly influence the duration of stage *b*. This could lead to an interaction between the effects of factors F and G even though they did not *directly* influence any stages in common. (An example is given in section 4.4, footnote 4.) But by and large, factors that influence different stages will have additive effects on mean RT, whereas factors that influence stages in common will interact.

3.2. *The additive-factor method and the meaning of 'stage'*

The direction of these inferences is reversed in the 'additive-factor method', in which one searches for pairs of factors, like F and G, that have additive nonzero effects. Whenever such 'additive factors' are discovered, and given no stronger arguments to the contrary, it is reasonable to believe that there exists a corresponding pair of stages, *a* and *b*, between stimulus and response. (Conversely, if one cannot find a pair of additive factors that correspond to a pair of hypothesized stages, this may be taken as evidence against the hypothesis; but see section 3.4 for one exception.) Furthermore, if a third factor, H, is found to interact with G but not with F, this implies that H influences RT at least in part because of its effect on stage *b*, but not because of any effect on stage *a*.

I have deliberately avoided a precise definition of 'stage', which should await further research. The basic idea is that a stage is one of a series of successive processes that operates on an input to produce an output, and contributes an additive component to the RT. The concept of 'additivity' here entails a property of independence for mean stage-durations: the mean duration of a stage depends only on its input and the levels of factors that influence it, and not directly on the mean durations of other stages. The fundamental importance of the relations among factor effects follows from this basic idea. It is not only additivity among factors that is useful, but also the patterns of interaction: the subsets of interacting factors associated with a stage and the ways they interact allow one to infer the operations performed by that stage, and possibly also its location in a series of stages and its internal structure.

Other features that might be incorporated in a formal definition of 'stage' are: (1) Given its input, the output of a stage should be independent of factors influencing its duration. This requirement would preclude indirect factor effects, such as that of factor F on stage *b* mentioned above. (2) The stages in a series should be functionally interesting and qualitatively different and should 'make sense' in terms of other knowledge. (3) A stage should be able to process no more than one 'signal' at a time (as in WELFORD, 1960). (4) Stage durations should be stochastically independent (see section 5.4). It remains to be seen whether the stages defined by additive components have these properties.

3.3. *Additivity in two-factor experiments*

In table 1 the relation between additive RT-components and additive factors is shown in the context of a complete (2×2) two-factor ex-

TABLE 1

Additive RT-components and additive factor-effects in a 2×2 experiment.

factor level	F_0	F_1	G_0	G_1
stage influenced	a	a	b	b
duration of stage	$T_a(0)$	$T_a(1)$	$T_b(0)$	$T_b(1)$

experimental conditions	reaction time
F_0, G_0	$RT(00) = T_w + T_a(0) + T_b(0)$
F_0, G_1	$RT(01) = T_w + T_a(0) + T_b(1)$
F_1, G_0	$RT(10) = T_w + T_a(1) + T_b(0)$
F_1, G_1	$RT(11) = T_w + T_a(1) + T_b(1)$

periment with two levels per factor. Suppose we have found a pair of factors, F and G, that influence different stages, a and b, as in fig. 2, and we study each factor at two levels, labeled zero and one. At the top of the table are given the durations of each stage as a function of the factor influencing that stage. The four pairs of experimental conditions are shown below, with corresponding RTs, T_w again represents the durations of all processes other than stages a and b. Given only the proposition of successive stages, it follows from the equations in table 1 that the means of the four RT distributions should be related by eq. (1), which is an expression of the additivity of factor effects on means:

$$\mu'(00) + \mu'(11) = \mu'(01) + \mu'(10). \tag{1}$$

With the supplementary assumption of the stochastic independence of RT components, a series of similar equations must hold for all the cumulants:

$$\varkappa_r(00) + \varkappa_r(11) = \varkappa_r(01) + \varkappa_r(10), r = 1,2,\ldots \tag{2}$$

For example, our two factors must show the same kind of additivity in their effects on the RT variance ($\varkappa_2$) as on its mean:

$$\sigma^2(00) + \sigma^2(11) = \sigma^2(01) + \sigma^2(10). \tag{3}$$

(The relations shown in eqs. (1)-(3) describe properties of population distributions, of course; because of sampling error – which grows with the order of the cumulant – it is a statistical question whether a set of empirical distributions has these properties.) Finally, if the forms, f_w, f_a, and f_b, of the component distributions are known, then the effects of a factor, say F, on parameters of the resulting RT distribution are limited to those that correspond to changes in parameters of the relevant component, in this instance, f_a. (Hohle's method, described in section 2.2, makes use of this last implication.) These ideas are summarized at the bottom of fig. 1.

Generalization of the above analysis to an experiment with p levels of factor F and q levels of factor G is straightforward (see, e.g., SCHEFFÉ, 1959). If F and G influence different stages, then for the mean RTs from the pq conditions there must exist constants $\overline{T}_w$, $\overline{T}_a(i)$, $i=1,\ldots,p$, and $\overline{T}_b(j)$, $j=1,\ldots,q$ such that

$$\overline{RT}(i,j) = \overline{T}_w + \overline{T}_a(i) + \overline{T}_b(j), i=1,\ldots,p, j=1,\ldots,q. \tag{4}$$

Similar conditions exist for all cumulants if independence is assumed. Equivalently, eq. (1), (2), or (3) is replaced by equating to zero each of $(p-1)(q-1)$ linearly-independent contrasts in the RT means or cumulants. Each of these contrasts represents one of the degrees of freedom associated with deviations from the additive model of eq. (4). Additivity may be evaluated either by examining deviations from an explicitly-fitted additive model (eq. (4)), by evaluating the appropriate contrasts, or by testing the interaction term in an analysis of variance.

Evidence that RT components are stochastically independent adds strength to the proposition that they represent the durations of different stages. But a failure to confirm the assumption of independence does not necessarily weaken this proposition. In section 5.4 I shall show why stage durations might be additive but not independent.

3.4. *Generalization of the method to multiple-factor experiments*

Generalization of the additive-factor method to experiments with more than two factors is not only direct, but has at least two distinct virtues. Let us consider the case of three experimental factors, F, G, and H. If any pair of these factors, such as F and G in fig. 2, influence no stages in common, then their effects should be additive not only when averaged over levels of a third factor, H *(overall interaction* of F and G zero), but also at each level of H (all *simple interactions* of F and G zero). This is true whether factor H interacts with one or both of the other factors (fig. 2) or not (fig. 3i). The fact that simple interactions of F and G are all zero implies that the three-factor interactions of F, G, and H must also be zero, and provides a more demanding test of a theory of successive stages.

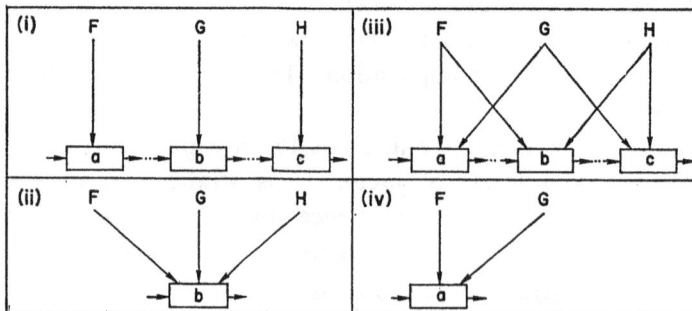

Fig. 3. Some possible arrangements of factors and stages.

In fact, of the various possible relations between three factors and a series of stages, the only ones that are expected to produce a nonzero three-factor interaction are those in which at least one of the stages is influenced by all three factors (fig. 3ii). This underlies the second virtue of multiple-factor experiments, exemplified by the contrast between the arrangements shown in figs. 3ii and 3iii. In terms of the three two-factor interactions the arrangements are equivalent: with neither do we expect any of these interactions to be zero. But for fig. 3iii, unlike 3ii, it can be shown that the three-factor interaction must be zero, even though the factors in each pair influence a stage in common. A three-factor experiment is therefore capable of discriminating between interesting alternative arrangements of stages that would be indistinguishable in a series of two-factor experiments, and is capable of leading to the discovery of successive stages even when no pair of additive factors can be found.

When all the members of a set of factors are found to influence a stage in common, a limitation of the additive-factor method is revealed: without studying additional factors there is no way to determine whether there are also other stages influenced by less than the full set. Thus, for the arrangement in fig. 2, although the data from a three-factor experiment can show that there is a stage *a* influenced by F, but not G or H, it cannot show whether there is a stage *c* influenced by H, but not by G. Similarly, for the arrangement in fig. 3iii, if one examined factors F and G only, one would be able to infer only that there was a stage *a* influenced by both F and G (fig. 3iv), and could not also discover the stage *b* influenced by F but not G. Such a stage *b* could be identified, however, in an experiment where factor H was studied at the same time as F and G (fig. 3iii).

3.5. *On applying the method and interpreting interactions*

Before we turn to experimental data, several comments about applying the method are in order.

(1) Procedures that test (or assume) the idea of stages use RT itself as the basic measure by which to assess additivity, and not any transformation of it. Additivity will in general be destroyed by nonlinear transformation of measurements. One consequence, for example, is that arithmetic means rather than harmonic or geometric means are appropriate. Furthermore, the median is inappropriate for our purpose because it is not, in general, additive. (For example, the median of a

sum of components need not be the sum of the component medians.) If stage durations are assumed to be stochastically independent, then the population minimum and maximum are suitable quantities, even though they are not, in general, linearly related to the mean (see DONDERS, 1868, Note II; TAYLOR, 1965). The difficulty here is in finding appropriate estimating statistics.

Whereas in some other domains, interactions that are removable by transformation can be regarded as arising from observations having been recorded on an inappropriate scale (COX, 1958, p. 105; KRUSKAL, 1965), here even such failures of additivity are of interest, since the basic measurement scale is specified.

(2) Experimental artifacts are more likely to obscure true additivity of factor effects than true interaction. Given the general idea of additive components, therefore, one test of an experimental procedure is the additivity of certain factor pairs that *ought* to influence different stages, such as stimulus intensity and responding limb (HOHLE, 1967, section III.D). For the same reason I would place highest credence in those two-factor interactions that are discovered in experiments in which the effects of a different pair of factors are found to add.

(3) In using the additive-factor method to test hypotheses about stages with specified functions, one cannot avoid also testing subsidiary hypotheses about the relations between the factors studied and the hypothesized stages. Suppose, for example, that we wish to test the following hypothesis, H1: stimulus encoding and response selection are accomplished by different stages, *a* and *b*. This can be tested only jointly with an additional hypothesis, H2: a particular factor, F, influences stage *a* and not *b*, and a particular factor, G, influences stage *b* and not *a*. If F and G are found to be additive, both hypotheses gain in strength. But the falsity of either H1 or H2 could produce a failure of additivity. To conclude from an observed interaction that H1 is false without assessing the validity of H2 (as in RABBITT, 1967) might therefore be an error.

(4) Certain interesting views of human information-processing are antithetical to the idea of stages whose mean durations are independent and additive. One such viewpoint has been expressed by MORAY (1967), TAYLOR et al. (1967), and POSNER and ROSSMAN (1965), for example, who propose a limited information-processing *capacity* that can be allocated to different functions in accordance with task demands. If 'capacity' is interpreted as a rate of processing, this viewpoint leads one

288   SAUL STERNBERG

to expect that in a task where process *a* has to accomplish more, less capacity is made available for process *b*. If more is then also demanded of process *b*, its duration will increase more than if the available capacity had been greater.

In considering the implications of this discussion for patterns of factor interactions, two definitions are useful. Let an 'increase' in factor level be a change in level that increases the mean RT. And let an interaction of factors be 'positive' ('negative') if the effect of combined increases in level is greater (less) than the sum of effects of separate increases. Then even though two factors influenced different members of a pair of capacity-sharing serial processes, their effects on mean RT, rather than being additive, would interact positively. If two such processes were embedded in a series of stages, they would be identified as a single stage by the additive-factor method, and the positive interaction of the corresponding factors might indicate a capacity-sharing relation.

(5) Other forms of interaction are also of considerable interest. Suppose, for example, that two independent processes occur in parallel and that both must be completed before the next stage can begin. Then two factors that influenced them separately would interact negatively, and the processes would be identified as a single stage by the additive-factor method. A further instance of inferences from the form of an interaction – in this case, its linearity – can be found in STERNBERG, 1967.

4. APPLICATION OF THE ADDITIVE-FACTOR METHOD TO MEAN RTS IN A BINARY-CLASSIFICATION TASK

4.1. *The factors in four experiments*

I shall describe the application of these ideas first to four experiments on binary classification of numerals (three of them reported in STERNBERG, 1966 and 1967). [2]

The task in these experiments has the following paradigm: on each

---

[2] These experiments were designed to study the effects of factors on mean RTs. Various design features appropriate for the analysis of higher cumulants were not included, such as the use of well-practised subjects and the possibility of within-subject and within-stimulus comparisons. Where higher cumulants have been examined in these experiments (e.g. STERNBERG, 1964) some tests appeared to support the independence assumption and others did not. These analyses will be described in other reports; in the present paper only the question of additivity will be considered for binary-classification data, and not the issue of stochastic independence.

of a sequence of trials a digit is presented visually as a test stimulus. The ensemble of possible test stimuli consists of the digits from 0 to 9. The subject makes a *positive response* if the test digit is a member of a small memorized set of digits, called the *positive set,* and makes a *negative response* otherwise. By the use of payoffs that weigh accuracy heavily relative to speed, errors are held to 1 or 2 percent.

The factors to be considered here that were varied in the experiments are as follows: (1) *Stimulus quality.* The digit was presented normally ('intact') in some trial blocks, and with a superimposed checkerboard pattern ('degraded') in others. Luminance of the pattern was chosen so that degradation would increase RT without greatly increasing the error rate. (2) *Size of positive set.* In exp. I the positive set was varied from trial to trial and contained from one to six digits. In exps. II, III, and IV the positive set was fixed throughout a series of trials and contained, one, two, or four digits, each subject having a series with each set size. It was the linear increase of mean RT with this factor that was the focus of previous reports of this work. (3) *Response type (positive or negative).* Analyses are based on correct responses only. The level of this factor is therefore determined by which response was required, that is, by whether the test stimulus was a member of the positive set. (4) *Relative frequency of response type.* The relative frequency with which positive and negative responses were required was varied between subjects by manipulation of the proportion of trials on which the test stimulus was contained in the positive set.

Factors 2 and 3 were studied in exps. I and II (STERNBERG, 1966), whose results will be used here only to provide supplementary information concerning the effect of factor 2 and the interaction of factors 2 and 3. Factors 1, 2, and 3 were examined in exp. III with twelve subjects in two sessions (STERNBERG, 1967); data from session 2 only are presented here. Factors 2, 3, and 4 were examined in exp. IV with 36 subjects in one session (unpublished). Although not designed with the additive-factor method in mind, exps. III and IV provide evidence about five of the six possible two-factor interactions among the four factors, and two of the four possible three-factor interactions.

4.2. *Results: additivity among effects of the factors on mean RT*

Evidence concerning the overall two-factor interactions in exps. III and IV is shown in the five panels of fig. 4. In each panel is shown the mean response 'profile' over subjects for levels of one factor at each

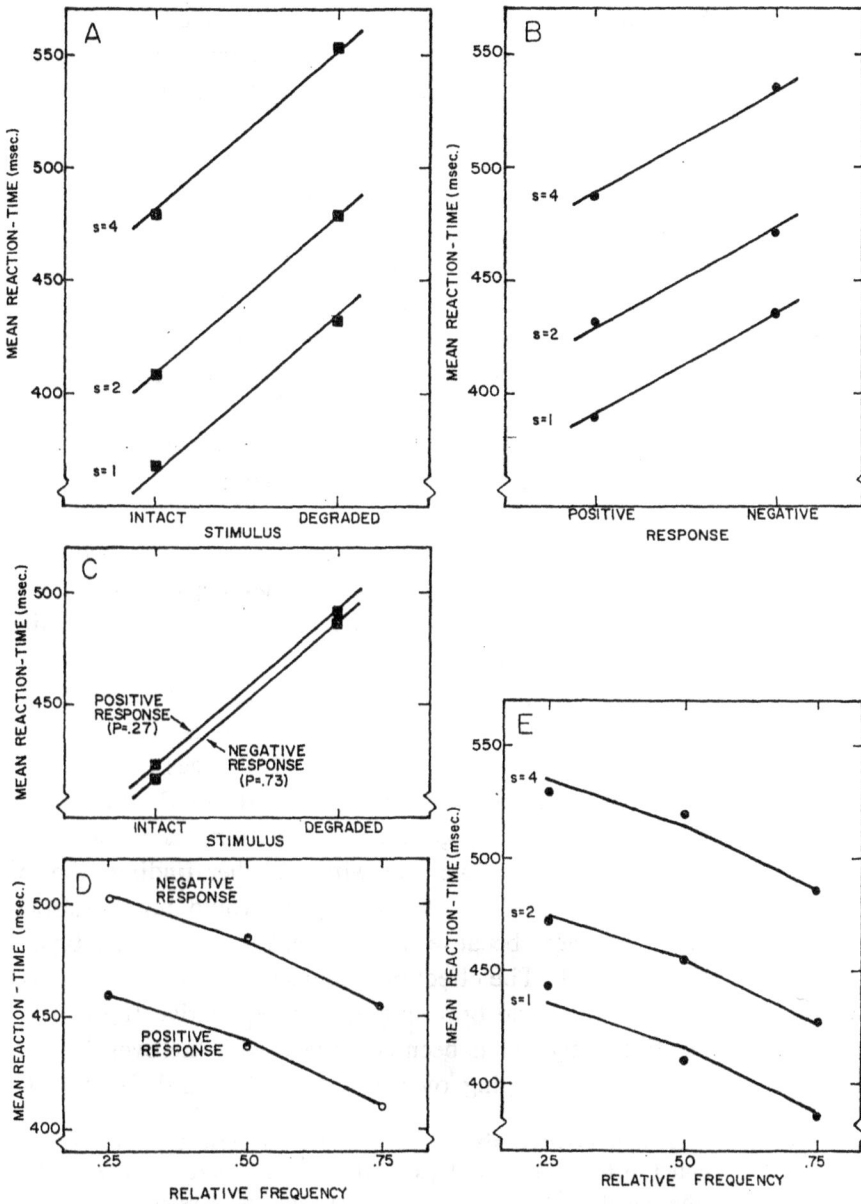

Fig. 4. Observed and best-fitting additive relations between factor effects in exp. III (squares) and exp. IV (circles). A: Effect of stimulus quality for three sizes (*s*) of positive set. RMSD (root mean squared deviation of points from parallel lines) is 1.8 msec, with 2 df. B: Effect of response type for three sizes of positive set. RMSD is 1.7 msec, with 2 df. C: Effect of stimulus quality for two response types. RMSD is 0.5 msec, with 1 df. Relative frequency (P) favored

level of another, averaged over levels of the third. For additive factors these profiles should be parallel; the lines in each panel represent the parallel profiles that best fit the data, in the sense of least squares. (Profiles are parallel if and only if equations such as (1) or (4) in section 3.3 obtain.) Goodness of fit is indicated by the square root of the mean squared deviation (RMSD) of the observed means from the best-fitting profiles, which is a quantity minimized by the fitting procedure. The RMSD should be evaluated in light of the number of degrees of freedom (df) associated with it (see section 3.3), and the size of the effect of that factor whose effect is smallest. (Where results are less clearcut, tests based on an evaluation of sampling error, as in analysis in variance, would be most appropriate.)

In all these cases the data are fitted remarkably well by an additive model. Thus, the increase in mean RT resulting from degradation was about 70 msec, regardless of the size of the positive set (fig. 4A) and regardless of the response type (fig. 4C); after averaging over the three response frequencies in exp. IV, one discovers that negative responses were about 45 msec slower than positive responses for each set size (fig. 4B); [3] as relative frequency of response was varied from 0.25 to 0.75, mean RT was shortened by about 50 msec regardless of response type (fig. 4D); and the decrease in mean RT of a response as its frequency was increased was about the same for all set sizes (fig 4E). An additive model fits worst in this last case, but with an RMSD of 3.9 msec it is satisfactory. As a very good approximation, then, these five pairs of factors are additive. (Note that without other findings the instance of additivity in exp. III shown in fig 4C would not be strong evidence for separate stages because the main effect of response type – about 6 msec – is so small. The effect of response type shown in fig. 4D was hidden in exp. III by the opposing effects of relative frequency.)

Each of these five analyses has been concerned with the overall interaction of two factors (averaging over levels of the third factor). To

---

[3] The additive relation between size of set (*s*) and response type has already been documented in the reports of exps. I, II, and III, where it was described in terms of the equality of slopes of the linear functions relating mean RT to *s* for the two response types.

---

the negative response. D: Effect of relative frequency of response for two response types. RMSD is 1.9 msec with 2 df. Filled, half-filled, and open circles each represent a different group of twelve subjects. E: Effect of relative frequency of response for three sizes of positive set. RMSD is 3.9 msec, with 4 df.

292 SAUL STERNBERG

examine the simple interactions (section 3.4), and thereby assess the three-factor interaction, I fitted three-factor additive models analogous to eq. (4) to the data of exp. III (viewed as a $2 \times 3 \times 3$ experiment) and exp. IV (viewed as a $2 \times 3 \times 3$ experiment). The resulting RMSDs were 4.9 msec with 7 df for exp. III, and 5.8 msec with 12 df for exp. IV, both representing good agreement.

4.3. *Linearity as additivity, and its implications*

Another form of additivity revealed by the data from these experiments is shown in fig. 5. The effect of size of positive set on mean RT

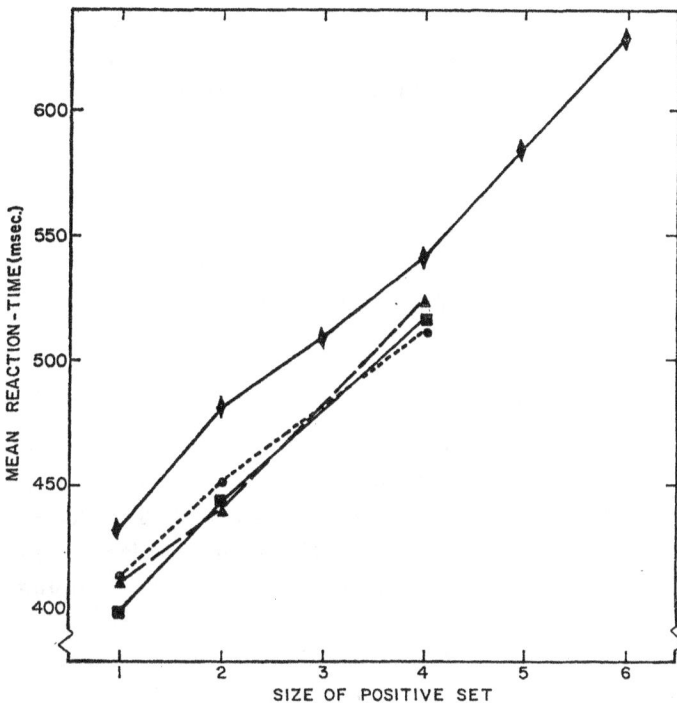

Fig. 5. Effect of size of positive set on mean RT in exp. I (diamonds), exp. II (triangles), exp. III (squares), and exp. IV (circles).

is linear. Another way of saying this is that the addition of an item to the positive set has the same effect, regardless of the size of the set. This kind of additivity suggests that each item in the positive set corresponds to a (sub)stage between stimulus and response, and that the durations of these substages represent additive components with equal means. The slope of the linear function then represents the mean duration of a substage. Various lines of evidence (STERNBERG, 1964, 1966, 1967) suggest that in each substage the test stimulus is compared to one of the items in the memorized positive set. Given this interpretation, the binary-classification experiment is one of the special cases mentioned in section 2.2, where appropriate changes in the subject's task can change the number of stages between stimulus and response. This, of course, was the original aim of Donders. Varying the number of stages is to be contrasted with merely controlling the durations of stages that are always present, as in the additive-factor method. The finding that the effect of size of positive set adds to the effects of other factors suggests that the number of stages can be varied without in this case influencing other stages; it thereby protects this particular application of Donders' idea from one source of criticism.

4.4. *Interpretation: four stages in binary classification*

In summary, then, of the six possible two-factor interactions among the four factors, all but one (stimulus quality with relative frequency of response) have been tested and found to be zero. These findings imply that at least three distinct stages are required to account for the effects of the factors studied. One stage is influenced by size of positive set and a second by response type. Whether one or two more stages are required to account for the influence of stimulus quality and relative frequency of response could be answered by the additive-factor method only in an experiment involving both of these factors. (To distinguish n stages on the basis of experiments involving n factors, using exclusively the additive relations among factor effects, *all* two-factor interactions must be shown to be zero.) The analysis is given added support by the absence of three-factor interactions in the cases examined. The linearity of the effect of size of positive set indicates that the stage associated with this factor includes a series of substages, one for each member of the set.

If we combine these inferences from the additive-factor method with supplementary arguments and plausible conjectures we are led to the more detailed picture shown in fig. 6. The additional features that have been incorporated are four stages rather than three, the functions assigned to these stages, and their order. The reasoning is as follows:

(1) The stage influenced by stimulus quality is most simply interpreted as a preprocessing or encoding stage which prepares a stimulus re-

294   SAUL STERNBERG

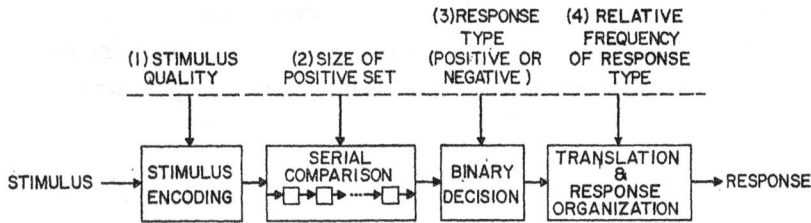

Fig. 6. Processing stages in binary classification. Above the broken line are shown the four factors examined. Below the line is shown the analysis of RT inferred from additive relations between factor pairs 1&2, 1&3, 2&3, 2&4, and 3&4, the linear effect of factor 2, and other considerations described in the text. The quality of the test stimulus influences the duration of an encoding stage in which a stimulus representation is formed. This representation is then used in a serial-comparison stage, whose duration depends linearly on size of positive set; in each of its substages the representation is compared to a memory representation of one member of the set. In the third stage a binary decision is made that depends on whether a match has occurred during the serial-comparison stage that precedes it; its mean duration is greater for negative than for positive decisions. The selection of a response based on the decision is accomplished in the final stage whose duration depends on the relative frequency with which a response of that type is required.

presentation to be used in the serial-comparison process. Otherwise it would be hard to understand how stimulus quality could influence RT without (fig. 4A) also affecting the time per comparison. [4] Any other arrangement is less plausible; this is argued in more detail in STERNBERG, 1967.

(2) The purpose of the serial-comparison stage must be to provide information for response selection. Hence any stage that depends on such information — in particular, the stages influenced by factor 3 (response type) and factor 4 (relative frequency of response type) — must follow the serial-comparison stage. (As an alternative, one might be tempted to describe the response-frequency factor in terms of the cor-

---

[4] Although no interaction was observed between stimulus quality and size of set during the second session in exp. III, an interaction was observed during the first. The form of the interaction was linear: degrading the stimulus increased the slope of the function relating mean RT to set size. This interaction is best viewed as resulting from an *indirect* influence of a factor on a stage, of the kind described in section 3.1. In this instance it is attributed to the influence of stimulus quality on the *output* of the encoding stage as well as on its duration.

related stimulus-frequencies, but the observed effects on RT would then have to be described as resulting from complicated interactions among stimulus frequency, size of set, and response type. Furthermore, relative frequency *per se* of the stimulus need have no effect on RT, as implied by results in STERNBERG, 1966.)

(3) Since factor 1 influences a stage that precedes serial comparison, and factor 4 influences a stage that follows serial comparison, these two factors must influence different stages; for this reason four stages, rather than three, are shown in the RT-analysis of fig. 6.

Included in the above argument is the rationale for all of the decisions about ordering the stages as shown in fig. 6 except the order of the stages influenced by factors 3 and 4. The functions assigned to stages, as indicated by their labels, are plausible, but should be regarded as hypotheses rather than conclusions, particularly for the last two stages. The order shown for the stages influenced by factors 3 and 4 then follows from their hypothesized functions. But confirmation of these hypotheses requires further research.

4.5. *Further comments on the method*

Given the above example, the general comments on applying the additive-factor method that were made in section 3.5 can be supplemented by four others. First, although instances of additivity of factor effects lead to the postulation of separate stages, other considerations must be used to determine the order in which these postulated stages occur. Second, any analysis produced by the method must be tentative. On the one hand, if a new factor is discovered that interacts with none of the others, then one is led to postulate an additional stage. On the other hand, new factors that interact with one or more of the others may lead to the redefinition of the functions of particular stages. Third, analyses produced by the method may be testable by new experiments, in this instance, for example, by one in which the effects of factors 1 and 4 are tested for additivity. And finally, the additive-factor method tells little about the total duration of a stage; in that sense it does not completely fulfill Donders' aims. But, as urged by some of the early investigators (e.g., JASTROW, 1890, p. 30), overall duration of a stage is more difficult to study and of less interest than whether there is such a stage, what influences it, what it accomplishes, and what its relation is to other stages.

296   SAUL STERNBERG

5. APPLICATION OF THE ADDITIVE-FACTOR METHOD TO NUMERAL-
   NAMING AND RELATED TASKS

5.1. *Rationale and procedure for experiment V*

Let us turn now to a more traditional experiment with a one-one stimulus-response mapping, that is, one using a complete-identification task. Unlike the binary-classification experiments, exp. V was explicitly designed to permit tests of the additivity of stage durations and also of their stochastic independence. Thus, I used practised subjects, collected more data per subject, balanced the design so that linear trends in time would not destroy additivity and so that additivity could be evaluated separately for each subject, and took pains to reduce variability in both performance and measurement so that estimates of variances as well as means would be stable.

As shown in fig. 7, three factors were examined, each at two levels. The stimuli were numerals and the responses were spoken digits. The

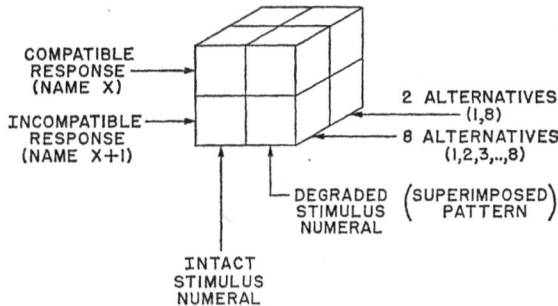

Fig. 7. Design of exp. V. Factors, each studied at two levels, were S-R compatibility, stimulus quality, and number of S-R alternatives.

number of equally-likely stimulus-response alternatives could be two or eight; *stimulus quality* was varied by presenting the numeral either intact, or degraded by a superimposed checkerboard pattern; and *S-R compatibility* was varied by making the correct response either the name of the numeral, or the name of the numeral plus one. (For example, if the numeral '1' was the stimulus, the compatible response was the spoken word 'one'; the less compatible response the spoken word 'two'.) This method of studying the relation between S-R compatibility and the effect of number of alternatives, by rearranging a compatible mapping, has the virtue of leaving stimulus and response ensembles essentially invariant; it was used earlier by ALLUISI et al. (1964) and

BROADBENT and GREGORY (1965). I chose 'adding one' rather than a random assignment as the less compatible mapping so as to minimize errors and effects of practice.

In a subsequent report, I shall present full accounts of the rationale and procedure of the present experiment, with several related experiments. In brief, the choice of stimulus quality and compatibility as factors was based on the popular supposition that they must influence widely separated parts of the processes between stimulus and response in this task. Hence if these processes were organized to any extent as stages, then two different stages should be influenced by these factors, so that their effects on mean RT should be additive. If they were additive, one could go further and test the assumption of stochastic independence of stage durations by assessing the additivity of factor effects on variances and higher cumulants of the RT distribution. (Only the results concerning means and variances will be presented here.)

An incidental reason for varying number of alternatives was that the tests of additivity could be carried out more than once. But the primary reason was that a number of other experiments (e.g., BRAINARD et al., 1962; ALLUISI et al., 1964; BROADBENT and GREGORY, 1965; RABBITT, 1963) had indicated that this factor would interact with at least one of the others. I hoped to confirm this interaction in conditions under which an instance of additivity could also be found. More important, the locus of interaction might show which of the two stages was influenced by number of alternatives. The purpose of exp. V, then, was to identify a pair of stages by additivity, and simultaneously by a failure of additivity, to locate an interesting effect in one or both of them.

Conditions and payoffs were arranged to reduce errors; the average error-rate was about 2 %. There were five subjects, whose previous experience in RT experiments ranged from none to seven years. All were given practice in the task for six sessions before data were taken; the additional six sessions on which analyses are based yielded for each of four conditions 256 observations per subject for the large ensemble and 128 for the small.

5.2. *Results: additivity and interaction among effects of the factors on mean RT*

Mean RTs are shown in fig. 8, together with the pairs of best-fitting parallel lines that represent perfect additivity of the effects of stimulus quality and S-R compatibility. Since the design of exp. V permitted

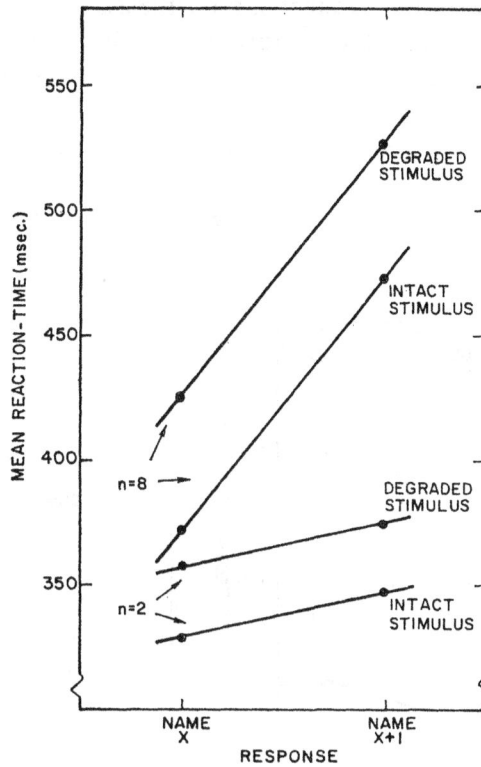

Fig. 8. Mean RTs for the eight conditions in exp. V. On the abscissa are indicated the two levels of compatibility; parameters are number of alternatives (*n*) and stimulus quality. For each value of *n* is also shown the best-fitting pair of parallel lines, which represent perfect additivity of the effects on mean RT of stimulus quality and compatibility. For $n=2$, the mean interaction-contrast is -0.9 msec with an SE of 0.9 msec For $n=8$ the mean interaction-contrast is $+0.4$ msec with an SE of 1.0 msec.

additivity for each number of alternatives to be assessed separately for each subject, two 1-df interaction contrasts, one for each *n*, were formed for each subject. This was done by taking the difference between the left and right sides of eq. (1), and normalizing (dividing by 4) so that its absolute value would equal the RMSD. The magnitude of these contrasts reflects the extent of deviation from additivity, their signs indicate whether the interaction, if any, is positive or negative (defined in section 3.5), and the standard error (SE) of their means can be evaluated by using the 4 df associated with intersubject variation. Analysis of a signed interaction contrast has the virtue of being sensitive to deviations from additivity that are systematic. Nonetheless, the analysis indicates excellent agreement with the additive model. Since these tests revealed additivity at both levels of the third factor (absence of simple interactions) there is, *a fortiori*, no three-factor interaction. In short, the effects of compatibility and stimulus quality on mean RT are perfectly additive.

But both of these factors interact with the third factor, number of alternatives. These interactions are shown more clearly in fig. 9, where

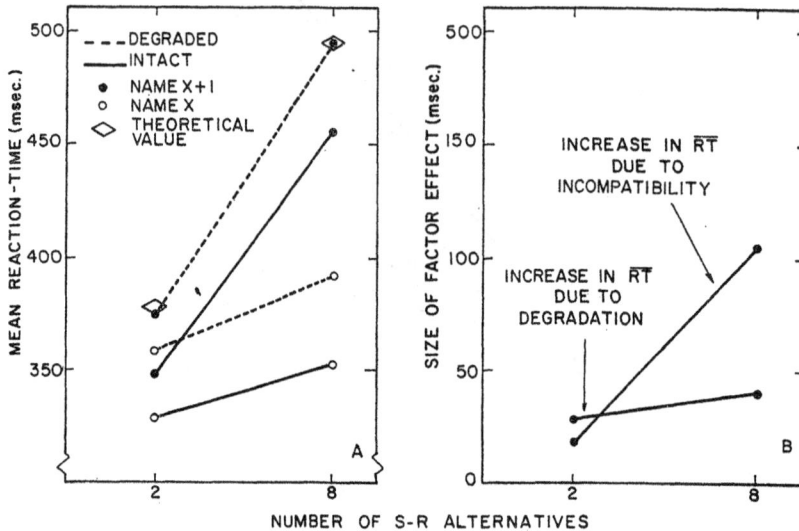

Fig. 9. Interactions between number of alternatives (*n*) and the other factors in exp. V. A: Mean RT to stimuli '1' and '8' as a function of *n* under four conditions. Theoretical values for the topmost points in each set of four are the values expected from the other three points, combined with the assumption that effects of S-R compatibility and stimulus quality are additive for each value of *n*. B: Effects of stimulus quality (averaged over compatibility levels) and of compatibility (averaged over quality levels) as a function of *n*; derived from values in panel A. Lines would be horizontal if these factors did not interact with *n*.

number of alternatives is indicated on the abscissa. Because we are interested in comparisons between levels of this factor without contamination from differences between stimuli or between responses, the data from the *n* = 8 conditions shown in fig. 9 are derived from the subset of trials on which the stimuli presented were the same as in the *n* = 2 conditions. The lowest pair of points in fig. 9A shows the well-known but poorly-understood fact that in the naming of highly discriminable numerals, number of alternatives has very litle effect (see SMITH, 1968); the increase in mean RT from $n = 2$ to $n = 8$ is about 20 msec. The increase is slightly greater when degraded numerals are named, substantially greater with less compatible responses, and greatest with both degraded stimuli and less compatible responses.

Fig. 9B summarizes the interactions of each of the two additive factors with number of alternatives. Number of alternatives interacts weakly with stimulus quality and strongly with S-R compatibility; expressed as a percentage of the main effect, the difference between simple effects was 35 % and 141 % respectively.[5] Such interactions are not new, of course; they have been found in other studies mentioned above, although not with the sets of stimuli and responses used here. But the use I make of these findings is, I think, new; it is shown in fig. 10.

5.3. *Interpretation: stages and factor-stage relations in the complete-identification task*

The relations found among the three factors are summarized above the horizontal line in fig. 10; the inferred analysis of RT into processing stages is shown below. Additivity of the effects of stimulus quality and S-R compatibility implies that the task is accomplished by means of at least two separate stages, designated (1) stimulus encoding (transformation of the visual stimulus into some representation of the numeral or its identity) and (2) translation and response organization. The idea of these independent subprocesses underlay Donders' work, of course, and has been discussed widely since; it is now given strong support by the additive-factor method.

Since number of alternatives interacted with both of the other factors, we must conclude that it influences the operations of both stages. (Note that one cannot justify such a conclusion simply on the grounds that RT is influenced by separate variation of both stimulus and response en-

---

[5] Superficially the interaction between stimulus quality and number of alternatives (n) in exp. V may appear to conflict with the absence of interaction found in exp. III between stimulus quality and size of positive set (s). But this conflict is not a real one, since variation of n in exp. V involved changing the ensemble of possible test stimuli, whereas variation of s in exp. III was accomplished without changing that ensemble. Indeed, this difference between the effects of ensemble size (n) and size of positive set (s) in relation to stimulus quality supports the view that they depend on radically different mechanisms, a view that one is also led to from the fact that, whereas mean RT usually increases logarithmically with n, it increases linearly with s.

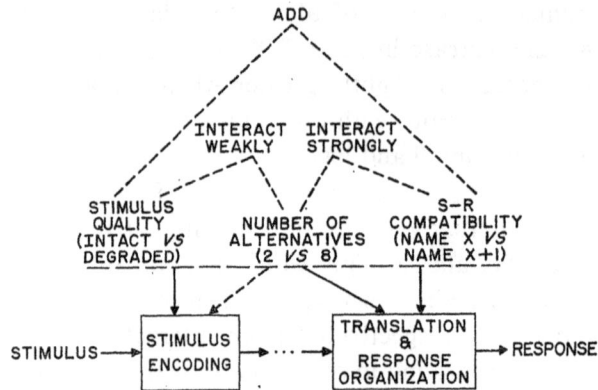

Fig. 10. Relations among factors in exp. V and the inferred stages
of processing.

tropy, as in SCHLESINGER and MELKMAN, 1966; those two effects on
RT could result from the influence of both factors on a single translation stage.) One might want to argue from the relative weakness of the
interaction with discriminability to the relative weakness of the effect
of number of alternatives on the first stage; this is why the arrow
between these two is broken. These conclusions agree with those of
early workers who used Donders' method; in his summary of their
findings, JASTROW (1890, p. 35) concluded that number of alternatives
influences the durations of both 'distinction' and 'choice', and that 'with
an increase in number, the difficulty of choice increases more rapidly
than the difficulty of distinction'.

As discussed in section 4, analyses of this kind are tentative. Future
experiments might show, for example, that the functions assigned to the
second stage in fig. 10 are accomplished by two separate stages, as in
WELFORD, 1960, a 'translation' stage which was influenced by the S-R
mapping, and a 'response organization' stage which was not; it would
then be an open question whether number of alternatives influenced the
response-organization stage as well as the other two.

The present experiment used that variety of S-R compatibility that
depends on the mapping of stimuli in a fixed ensemble onto responses
in a fixed ensemble. A second variety is the compatibility between
entire stimulus and response ensembles, which one might call 'SE-RE
compatibility'. This kind of compatibility is, of course, an interaction
between factors SE and RE. In the light of our ideas about implications
of interaction, a major implication of SE-RE compatibility is the

existence of a nontrivial translation stage (i.e., a stage that is influenced by both SE and RE factors and that is more than merely a 'rewiring') as well as possible stimulus-encoding and response-organizing stages influenced separately by SE and RE. Indeed, the three-factor interaction found by BRAINARD et al. (1962) among SE, RE, and number of alternatives may now be interpreted as indicating the existence of a stage influenced by all three of these factors, just as the present results imply the existence of a stage influenced by both the S-R mapping and number of alternatives.

The existence of an effect of number of alternatives on both of the inferred stages in fig. 10 has at least two substantive implications. First, it suggests that the relative insensitivity of numeral-naming to this factor is a consequence of special properties of both stages. That is, both the encoding of numerals, and their translation into spoken digits, are unusual. Second, the finding conflicts with the attribution of the effect of number of alternatives to a single process, such as the single statistical decision of STONE (1960) or LAMING (1968), the single series of dichotomous choices of HICK (1952), or the single parallel process of LAMING (1966).

5.4. *On additivity of means without stochastic independence*

Let us now turn to the issue of the stochastic independence of stage durations. As I mentioned earlier, the assumption that stage-durations are additive has often been incorporated with the idea that they are independent. We have already seen that such independence has powerful consequences: for factors that influence no stages in common, it implies additivity of factor effects not only on variances, but on all the higher cumulants of the RT distribution. And a good deal of theorizing about RT-distributions is practicable only if stage durations are independent.

It is quite conceivable, however, that in some situations stage durations might be additive but not independent. As one example, consider what would happen in exp. V if a subject were 'prepared' on particular trials for a particular stimulus-response pair. Some of the implications of this idea have been explored in detail by FALMAGNE (1965). Suppose that if the stimulus presented is the one for which the subject is prepared, then both the encoding and translation stages are shorter than they would otherwise be. The result of such preparation would be a positive correlation of the durations of the two stages, rather than independence. But this effect would not alter the additivity of their mean durations.

If one thinks of 'preparation for the stimulus that is to appear' as a factor, one can place this source of correlation in the context of experimental factors and their relations to stages. Preparation can be viewed as a factor that influences both stages (like number of alternatives), but is under the subject's control rather than the experimenter's, and therefore can vary in level from trial to trial. Any such factor that was permitted to vary would induce a correlation of stage durations, whose sign would depend on whether the varying factor influenced the durations of the two stages in the same or opposite directions. So long as the variation of the subject-controlled factor (here, preparation) was not influenced by levels of the experimenter-controlled factors (here, stimulus quality and S-R compatibility) its variation would not disrupt the independence of stage-duration means or the additivity of factors that influenced the two stages separately. (If the level of a subject-controlled factor could be measured from trial to trial, even though it could not be controlled by the experimenter, and if subsets of trials on which the factor assumed the same levels were examined separately, then stage durations would presumably appear independent within those subsets.)

As a second example, in which there is a *negative* correlation between stage durations, suppose that the duration of a stage is shorter if its input is of higher quality. Furthermore, suppose that this input *is* of higher quality if the preceding stage, which produces it, has operated for a longer time. On trials on which the first stage happened to take longer, the second would be shorter, and so on. The result would be a *negative* correlation between stage durations, although, again, factor effects might remain additive.

Should the ultimate definition of 'stage', then, include a requirement of stochastic independence? In the preparation example the correlation could be viewed as a result of poor experimental control or inappropriate analysis. One might decide to retain the requirement of independence, but to conceive of this property as easily camouflaged, revealing itself only in highly refined experiments. But the second example is harder to view in this way; to retain the independence requirement one would have to identify the two processes in that example as a single stage.

The above discussion shows that the assumptions of addtivity and

304   SAUL STERNBERG

independence should be examined separately, because the latter may
not hold, even when the former does. On the other hand, finding
evidence that the durations of a set of hypothesized stages were stochastically independent would contribute to one's belief in the hypothesis,
while a persistent failure to find independence might cast suspicion on
either the existence of stages, or the appropriateness of the experimental
methods used to study them.

5.5. *Further results: effects of the factors on RT variance*

In fig. 11 are shown the average RT-variances for each of the eight
conditions in exp. V. Variances were calculated for each stimulus digit

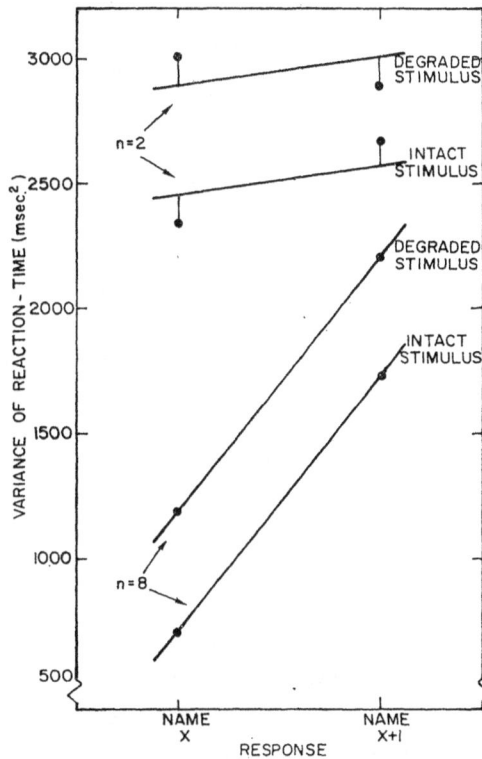

Fig. 11. Average RT-variances for the eight conditions in exp. V. On the
abscissa are indicated the two levels of compatibility; parameters are number
of alternatives (n) and stimulus quality. For each value of n is also shown the
best-fitting pair of parallel lines, which represent perfect additivity of the effects
on the RT variance of stimulus quality and compatibility. For $n=2$ the mean
interaction-contrast is -111 msec^2 with an SE of 45 msec^2. For $n=8$ the mean
interaction-contrast is -7 msec^2 with an SE of 41 msec^2.

in each session and were then averaged over stimuli and sessions. These averages were used to evaluate additivity for each subject separately, and for each number of alternatives, as in the case of mean RTs. Variances shown in the figure, which are averages over subjects, range from about 700 to 3000 msec^2.

For conditions with $n = 8$, shown is the lower part of the figure, the results agree extremely well with the additive model, lending considerable support to the assumption of independence. On the other hand, there is a definite failure of additivity for the conditions with $n = 2$ shown in the upper part of the figure. The two-choice situation seems to provide an instance where RT components are additive but not stochastically independent. In the $n = 2$ conditions subjects reported considerable variation from trial to trial in their preparedness for the stimulus that was presented. In the $n = 8$ conditions they were less aware of preparation for any particular stimulus. At present, trial-to-trial variation in the appropriateness of preparation, as in the theory of FALMAGNE (1965), appears to be the most likely source of dependence in the two-alternative conditions.

We have an instance, then, of violation of the independence assumption for RT components that we associate, on other grounds, with different stages. One implication is that methods of RT-decomposition that require the independence assumption, such as some of those described in section 2.2, may be of limited use.

An incidental finding shown in fig. 11 that is of considerable substantive interest is the marked increase in variance as the number of alternatives is reduced. This change in variance is, of course, in the opposite direction from the change in mean. It was shown by every subject and has since been replicated. For example, in the naming of intact numerals, whereas mean RT decreased by about 20 msec as number of alternatives was changed from eight to two, the variance increased by a factor of more than three. Although a change of variance in this direction may appear only under some experimental conditions, that is *can* occur is relevant to selecting among competing explanations for the well-known effect of number of alternatives on RT.

6. NEW INTERPRETATIONS OF SOME EXISTING
   INSTANCES OF ADDITIVITY

Clearcut instances of additive effects are relatively rare among published results, partly because factorial experiments are not popular, and perhaps also because additivity is easily destroyed by experimental artifacts and inappropriate design. But a few cases of additivity that do exist become provocative when seen from the viewpoint of the additive-factor method, and illustrate its potential to reveal not only stages of processing but also some of their properties.

6.1. *Expectancy and the stimulus-detection process*

In a simple-reaction task RAAB et al. (1961) found the effects of foreperiod and stimulus luminance to be additive. Three values of luminance were varied between sessions; mean RT decreased by 39 msec from lowest to highest. Three values of foreperiod were varied randomly from trial to trial; mean RT decreased by 14 msec from shortest to longest. An additive model fits the 3×3 matrix of means extremely well, giving an RMSD of 0.5 msec with 4 df.

Suppose that luminance influences the duration of a stimulus-detection stage. Then Raab's finding leads to the surprising conclusion that 'expectancy' (THOMAS, 1967) influences a different stage, rather than, for example, governing criteria in a statistical decision performed during the detection stage (McGILL, 1963, section 2.3; FITTS, 1966), or controlling an independent 'anticipation' process that operates in parallel with the detection process (OLLMAN, 1968).

One conjecture prompted by Raab's finding is that expectancy influences response organization rather than stimulus processing. To validate such a conjecture by the additive-factor method one would need to show also that the effect of an experimental factor that was clearly associated with response organization (and not with detection) interacted with factors such as the foreperiod in a simple-reaction task, or the relative response-frequency in a choice-reaction task.

6.2. *Expectancy and the psychological refractory period*

A second example of an additive effect of time uncertainty is found in an experiment on the psychological refractory period by BERNSTEIN et al. (1968, exp. 2). Presence of a warning signal (factor 1) two seconds before the first of two stimuli S_1 and S_2 decreased the means of both RT_1 and RT_2 by about 50 msec. Varying the interval between S_1 and S_2 (factor 2) from 0 to 100 msec changed the mean of RT_1 by about 20 msec and of RT_2 by about 50 msec. The effects of these two factors were approximately additive for both responses. The implication is that the stage influenced by time uncertainty is different from the stage that displays refractoriness; such a conclusion further weakens an expectancy theory of the psychological refractory period (reviewed in SMITH, 1967).

6.3. *Sensory transmission and discrimination*

Donders and his followers believed that there exist separate stages for the transmission of sensory information from the periphery, and for its discrimination. A choice-reaction experiment of HOWELL and DONALDSON (1962) provides an instance of additivity that supports this belief. Under three stimulus-modality conditions (factor 1), one visual, one tactual, and one auditory, each of three responses was correct for one of three stimulus intensities (factor 2). To make the design orthogonal, levels of factor 2 were adjusted by cross-modality matching to be the 'same' in the three modalities. Mean RT decreased by 106 msec from visual (slowest) to auditory (fastest) modality, and by 80 msec from low to high intensity. An additive model fits the 3×3 matrix of means reasonably well, giving an RMSD of 4.5 msec with 4 df. Findings such as these would support the old idea of a transmission stage influenced by modality but not intensity, and a discrimination stage influenced by intensity but not modality.

6.4. *The selective influence of practice*

From the viewpoint of the additive-factor method, experiments occasionally suggest that practice influences some but not all of the stages in a task. In exp. III (section 4.1), for example, subjects had the same conditions in each of two sessions. For intact stimuli, mean RT declined by about 36 msec from session to session. This effect was almost perfectly additive with the effect of size of positive set, s, which increased the mean RT by 110 msec as it was varied from $s = 1$ to $s = 4$. The RMSD in this instance is 1.0 msec with 2 df. The finding of additivity suggests that practice had its effect on stages other than serial comparison.

7. USE OF INDIVIDUAL DIFFERENCES IN INFERENCES ABOUT STAGES

7.1. *'Subjects' as an additive factor*

Individual differences are often thought of as little more than an ubiquitous nuisance. Yet they seem to have the potential of providing at least supplementary information about processing stages. The simplest instance would be one in which an effect of 'subjects' on mean RT combined additively with the effect of some experimental factor, factor

E. That is, the effect of E would be invariant over subjects, despite the existence of individual differences in mean RT. Such additivity (the absence of a treatment-by-subject interaction) could be taken to imply the existence of at least two stages, one influenced by 'subjects' and not factor E, and the other influenced by E and not 'subjects'.

7.2. *'Subjects' as an interacting factor*

Interactions between 'subjects' and experimental factors can also be useful. Suppose that we have found a pair of factors, F and G, whose effects on mean RT, averaged over a set of subjects, are additive. We wish to infer that they influence no stages in common. An additional test of this inference is available if there is reliable variation from subject to subject in the sizes of the effects, that is, if 'subjects' inter-acts with each of the other factors. 'Subjects' would then be thought of as influencing a stage in common with F, and a stage in common with G. But if F and G influence no stages in common with each other, then the three-factor interaction of F, G, and 'subjects' should be zero (section 3.4). In other words, the effects of F and G should be additive for each subject separately and not merely for the group means, even though sizes of the effects vary over subjects. It is for this reason that the two-factor interaction contrasts of sections 5.2 and 5.5 were evaluated separately for each subject and used to obtain the SE of the mean interaction-contrast; if the mean contrast is small, such an SE would also be small only insofar as all subjects show additivity.

7.3. *Stage sensitivity and correlations of factor effects*

Finally, let us consider individual differences in the effects of factors that interact and are therefore thought to influence the same stage. Individual differences in the size of a factor's effect may be described as differences among subjects' 'sensitivity' to that factor. It is plausible that for factors that influence the same stage, sensitivities will be more highly correlated (over subjects) than for factors that influence no stages in common. (A stage can be thought of as associated with an ability or capacity, an increase in the level of any factor that influences that stage as a test of that ability, and the resulting increase in RT as the score on the test.) This idea corresponds to two properties that may be useful additions to the conception (section 3.2) of stage: (1) A stage itself is more or less sensitive, varying from subject to subject in its sensitivity to *all* the factors that influence it,[6] and (2) the sensitivities of different stages are less than perfectly correlated with one another.

If stages had these two properties, the pattern of correlations among factor effects would then supplement the pattern of interactions in providing information about stages and factor-stage relations; moreover, tentative evidence about stages could even be derived from the correlations in a set of one-factor experiments performed with the same group of subjects.

Consider as an example the analysis shown in fig. 10 of performance in exp. V. If sensitivities of the encoding and translation stages varied somewhat independently over subjects, then of the three pairs of factors, that pair whose effects should be most highly correlated are compatibility and number of alternatives (n), and the pair with the lowest correlation should be compatibility and stimulus quality. This was observed, confirming the analysis: product-moment coefficients over the five subjects for pairs of main effects are 0.88 ($p = 0.05$) for compatibility and n, 0.16 for compatibility and stimulus quality, and the intermediate value 0.42 for effects of quality and n. If this kind of finding appeared in larger experiments it would tend to confirm the usefulness of the idea of a stage having a sensitivity that varies over subjects and is uncorrelated from stage to stage.

8. CONCLUDING REMARKS

The additive-factor method cannot distinguish *processes*, but only *processing stages*. This distinction bears on the interpretation, for example, of the interaction of time uncertainty and relative signal-frequency found by BERTELSON and BARZEELE (1965) and correctly felt by them to be important in the understanding of preparation. The interaction does allow one to reject the idea of *separate stages* (i.e., no stage influenced by both factors). But it does not allow one to reject the more general proposition of *separate processes;* a pair of independent processes influenced separately by the factors could conceivably operate

---

[6] Let α and β be parameters each influenced by the level of a different factor, and Θ_i and λ_i be individual-difference parameters that are uncorrelated over subjects. A model for the mean duration of a stage with interacting factor effects and also with the sensitivity property is $\bar{T} = \Theta_i \alpha \beta$; here the effects of both factors depend on the subject's value of Θ_i. Factor interactions could occur without the sensitivity property, however, as in a stage whose duration is $\bar{T} = (\alpha + \Theta_i)(\beta + \lambda_i)$.

310   SAUL STERNBERG

in parallel, for example, and thereby produce the interaction (section 3.5).

A second proviso about the additive-factor method is related to techniques of data analysis. The usual significance tests performed in conjunction with analysis of variance are asymmetric: one is forced to assume that effects are additive (null hypothesis) unless the contrary can be proved. Given the strong implications of additivity, this assymmetry seems particularly inappropriate. To avoid this difficulty one might present findings in terms of mean interaction-contrasts and their SEs, or choose alternative hypotheses that specify interaction contrasts of theoretically-interesting magnitudes, and adjust tests so that errors of types 1 and 2 have equal probabilities with respect to such alternatives.

The idea of a processing stage that I have presented should be thought of as tentative and subject to refinement by future research. Some of the properties one might want to consider incorporating in a definition of 'stage' to make it most useful were discussed in section 3.2. As the additive-factor method is applied in various experimental situations we may want to impose an additional requirement of *stage invariance:* only those stages that emerge from the study of several different situations are of interest. (Thus, it would be desirable if the 'stimulus-encoding' stages inferred in sections 4 and 5 could be shown to have similar properties.)

Most previous attempts to use RT measurements for studying stages of processing between stimulus and response fall into two classes. Donders' subtraction method required task changes that inserted or deleted entire stages. Its range of application was limited by the difficulty of finding operations that did this but also left other stages invariant, and by the absence of tests other than introspection for determining whether the requirement of invariance was met. The second approach involves the application of precise stochastic models – 'strong' models that embody several assumptions simultaneously. This approach is limited because it does not permit the assumption of main interest – that of the existence of additive components – to be examined in isolation from assumptions about the stochastic independence of components and the forms of their distributions.

The additive-factor method is proposed as a third approach to the study of processing stages, one which avoids the limitations of both Donders' method and the strong-model approach. With it one can test the interesting assumptions in isolation, yet do so by means of operations that do not insert or delete hypothesized stages, but merely change their durations. This method had limitations too, however. Although it leads to the decomposition of a set of stages, it cannot decompose the RT itself: the absolute durations of the stages discovered are not determined. And like the other approaches, the method does not give the order of a set of stages it distinguishes. It can, however, establish the existence of processing stages and, by exposing their relations to experimental factors, help in ascertaining their properties. Its power stems from the fundamental significance of additivity, which in turn depends on the existence in RT experiments of a basic measure – that of physical time.

The concept of interaction in multifactor experiments and the associated focus on additive models was originated in the 1920's by R. A. Fischer (SCHEFFÉ, 1959, p. 90). It is perhaps not surprising that Donders and others of his time, working without this theoretical appartus, were not stimulated to perform factorial experiments or examine interactions, and that only recently (e.g., BERTELSON and BARZEELE, 1965; BROADBENT and GREGORY, 1965) has the important role of factor interactions in the study of RT been hinted at.

·REFERENCES

ALLUISI, E. A., G. S. STRAIN and J. B. THURMOND, 1964. Stimulus-response compatibility and the rate of gain of information. Psychon. Sci. **1**, 111—112.

AUDLEY, R. J., 1960. A stochastic model for individual choice behavior. Psychol. Rev. **67**, 1—15.

BERNSTEIN, I. H., R. R. BLAKE and M. H. HUGHES, 1968. Effects of time and event uncertainty upon sequential information processing. Percept. & Psychophys. **3**, 177—184.

BERTELSON, P. and J. BARZEELE, 1965. Interaction of time-uncertainty and relative signal frequency in determining choice reaction time. J. exp. Psychol. **70**, 448—451.

BRAINARD, R. W., T. S. IRBY, P. M. FITTS and E. A. ALLUISI, 1962. Some variables influencing the rate of gain of information. J. exp. Psychol. **63**, 105—110.

BROADBENT, D. R. and M. GREGORY, 1965. On the interaction of S-R compatibility with other variables affecting reaction time. Brit. J. Psychol. **56**, 61—67.

BUSH, R. R., E. GALANTER and R. D. LUCE, 1963. Characterization and classification of choice experiments. In: R. D. Luce, R. R. Bush and E. Galanter (eds.), Handbook of mathematical psychology, vol. 1. New York; Wiley, 77—102.

312 SAUL STERNBERG

CHRISTIE, L. S. and R. D. LUCE, 1956. Decision structure and time relations in simple choice behavior. Bull. math. Biophys. **18**, 89—112.

COX, D. R., 1958. Planning of experiments. New York: Wiley.

DONDERS, F. C., 1868. Over de snelheid van psychische processen. Onderzoekingen gedaan in het Physiologisch Laboratorium der Utrechtsche Hoogeschool, 1868—1869, Tweede reeks, II, 92—120. Transl. by W. G. Koster, this volume, 412—431.

FALMAGNE, J. C., 1965. Stochastic models for choice reaction time with applications to experimental results. J. math. Psychol. **2**, 77—124.

FITTS, P. M., 1966. Cognitive aspects of information processing: III. Set for speed versus accuracy. J. exp. Psychol. **71**, 849—857.

GHOLSON, B. and R. H. HOHLE, 1968a. Verbal reaction times to hues vs. hue names and forms vs. form names. Percept. & Psychophys. **3**, 191—196.

———— and ————, 1968b. Choice reaction times to hues printed in conflicting hue names and nonsense words. J. exp. Psychol. **76**, 413—418.

GOUGH, P. B., 1965. Grammatical transformations and speed of understanding. J. verb. Learn. verb. Behav. **4**, 107—111.

————, 1966. The verification of sentences: the effects of delay of evidence and sentence length. J. verb. Learn. verb. Behav. **5**, 492—496.

HICK, W. E., 1952. On the rate of gain of information. Quart. J. exp. Psychol. **4**, 11—26.

HOHLE, R. H., 1967. Component process latencies in reaction times of children and adults. In: L. P. Lipsett and C. C. Spiker (eds.), Advances in child development and behavior, vol. 3. New York: Academic Press, 225—261.

HOWELL, W. C. and J. E. DONALDSON, 1962. Human choice reaction time within and among sense modalities. Science **135**, 429—430.

JASTROW, J., 1890. The time-relations of mental phenomena. New York: N. D. C. Hodges.

KENDALL, M. G. and A. STUART, 1958. The advanced theory of statistics, vol. 1. London: Griffin.

KRUSKAL, J. B., 1965. Analysis of factorial experiments by estimating monotone transformations of the data. J. roy. statist. Soc. B. **27**, 251—263.

KÜLPE, O., 1895. Outlines of psychology. New York: MacMillan, Secs. 69, 70.

LAMING, D. R. J., 1966. A new interpretation of the relation between choice-reaction time and the number of equiprobable alternatives. Brit. J. math. stat. Psychol. **19**, 139—149.

————, 1968. Information theory of choice-reaction times. London: Academic Press.

LUCE, R. D. and D. M. GREEN, 1969. Detection of auditory signals presented at random times, II. Percept. & Psychophys. In press.

MCGILL, W. J., 1963. Stochastic latency mechanisms. In: R. D. Luce, R. R. Bush and E. Galanter (eds.), Handbook of mathematical psychology, vol. 1. New York: Wiley, 1—120.

———— and J. GIBBON, 1965. The general-gamma distribution and reaction times. J. math. Psychol. **2**, 1—18.

McMahon, L. E., 1963. Grammatical analysis as part of understanding a sentence. Unpublished doctoral dissertation, Harvard University.

Moray, N., 1967. Where is capacity limited? A survey and a model. In: Attention and performance, A. F. Sanders e(d.), Acta Psychol. **27**, 84—92.

Neisser, U., 1963. Decision-time without reaction-time: experiments in visual scanning. Amer. J. Psychol. **76**, 376—385.

Ollman, R. T., 1968. Anticipation in simple-reaction time. Manuscript in preparation.

Posner, M. I. and R. F. Mitchell, 1967. Chronometric analysis of classification. Psychol. Rev. **74**, 392—409.

———— and E. Rossman, 1965. Effect of size and location of informational transforms upon short-term retention. J. exp. Psychol. **70**, 496—505.

Raab, D., E. Fehrer and M. Hershenson, 1961. Visual reaction time and the Broca-Sulzer phenomenon. J. exp. Psychol. **61**, 193—199.

Rabbitt, P. M. A., 1963. Information-load and discriminability. Nature, **197**, 726.

————, 1967. Signal discriminability, S-R compatibility and choice reaction time. Psychon. Sci. **7**, 419—420.

Restle, F. and J. H. Davis, 1962. Success and speed of problem solving by individuals and groups. Psychol. Rev. **69**, 520—536.

Scheffé, H., 1959. The analysis of variance. New York: Wiley.

Schlesinger, I. M. and R. Melkman, 1966. The effect on choice-reaction time of stimulus information varied independently of transmitted information. J. genet. Psychol. **74**, 165—172.

Smith, E. E., 1968. Choice reaction time: an analysis of the major theoretical positions. Psychol. Bull. **69**, 77—110.

Smith, M. C., 1967. Theories of the psychological refractory period. Psychol. Bull. **67**, 202—213.

Snodgrass, J. G., R. D. Luce and E. Galanter, 1967. Some experiments on simple and choice reaction time. J. exp. Psychol. **75**, 1—17.

Sternberg, S., 1964. Estimating the distribution of additive reaction-time components. Paper presented at the meeting of the Psychometric Society, Niagara Falls, Ont., October, 1964.

————, 1966. High-speed scanning in human memory. Science, **153**, 652—654.

————, 1967. Two operations in character recognition: some evidence from reaction-time measurements. Percept. & Psychophys. **2**, 45—53.

Stone, M., 1960. Models for choice-reaction time. Psychometrika, **25**, 251—260.

Taylor, D. H., 1965. Two dimensions for reaction time distributions. Nature, **206**, 219—220.

————, 1966. Latency components in two-choice responding. J. exp. Psychol. **72**, 481—487.

Taylor, M. M., P. H. Lindsay and S. M. Forbes, 1967. Quantification of shared capacity processing in auditory and visual discrimination. In: Attention and performance, A. F. Sanders (ed.), Acta Psychol. **27**, 223—229.

314 SAUL STERNBERG

THOMAS, E. A. C., 1967. Reaction-time studies: the anticipation and interaction of responses. Brit. J. math. stat. Psychol. **20,** 1—29.

WELFORD, A. T., 1960. The measurement of sensory-motor performance: survey and reappraisal of twelve years' progress. Ergonomics, **3,** 189—230.

DISCUSSION

Peacock: You have considered a set of factors and a set of stages; have you also mapped a set of theories for example, for expectancy and single channel, on to the former sets.

Sternberg: I would like to believe that this kind of analysis might be relevant to understanding mechanisms. I have tried to indicate how it might apply in explaining what causes choice RT to increase with the number of S-R alternatives. The fact that there appear to be two separate stages that are influenced by the number of S-R alternatives should have a great influence on the kind of theories one develops.

Nickerson: I am very interested in the reversal of the variances with the number of alternatives. Have you any speculation on it?

Sternberg: Subjects reported qualitative changes in their experience as number of alternatives was changed. In the two-alternative case, subjects reported experiencing preparation, i.e. on some trials the stimulus that appeared was the one they expected, whereas on other trials it was not. They claimed that whereas appropriate preparation speeded their responses, they were slowed down by having been prepared for the wrong stimulus. In the 8-alternative case, on the other hand, they claimed that they did not prepare. They just sat and waited for the stimulus. That could reduce the variance. My feeling is that the variance finding supports very strongly Falmagne's approach to the explanation of the effect of number of alternatives. His kind of theory, in which there are states of preparation and of non-preparation, could lead to either an increase or a decrease in variance with number of alternatives. Most other theories could not. For example, serial dichotomous choices could not easily be made to produce an increase in variance when the number of alternatives is reduced.

Nickerson: Have you found any other situation where this is true?

Sternberg: We are doing a literature search, but in fact variances are not reported in most papers. If any of you has some information on this, that would be extremely useful.

Mowbray: If you mean in a situation where it is not true, I have some. We published in about 1960 a study in which the variances were almost identical for a two-choice and a four-choice alternative in the same situation.

Hyman: I am wondering if independence and additivity could change as a function of practice. I have a notion that they would.

Sternberg: We started with already-trained subjects.

Schouten: Sanders just remarked to me how much Donders would have loved to hear this rejection of the growing scepticism by the end of the last century.

In our own work we grew a little sceptical for very circumstantial reasons. We were doing all sorts of time-study movements relating to the time-study systems in industry. These systems work in terms of allotting a time for separate elementary movements and then hoping that the sum of all these separate times will be equal to the total time. This is a case where it definitely does not hold because the whole thing becomes one gradual movement. I would like to say that your lecture and your ideas seem to me extremely inspiring for further research, just to make out where there is this additivity and where this interaction.

Kornblum: How do you expect the probabilities to work on these stages?

Sternberg: In fact your data provided an interesting case where you reported three factors, two of which interact and the third of which is additive with the others.

Falmagne: The more I hear on the problem of additivity the more I have the impression that we are getting very close to some problem that people have in measurement theory. I should like to have your comments on this.

Sternberg: There is a point here that is related to Mick's paper. It has to do with question whether you should permit yourself to transform the measurement scale from the physical scale in RT experiments. We know that in some cases one can eliminate interactions by transformation of variables. Should that be permitted in reaction time? My contention is that if you are concerned with the idea of serial processes or component stages, then you should not permit it, because what is important is whether you have additivity or not on the scale of physical time and not on any transformed scale.

[19]

Ecological Constraints on Internal Representation: Resonant Kinematics of Perceiving, Imagining, Thinking, and Dreaming

Roger N. Shepard
Stanford University

This article attempts a rapprochement between James Gibson's ecological optics and a conviction that perceiving, imagining, thinking, and dreaming are similarly guided by internalizations of long-enduring constraints in the external world. Phenomena of apparent motion illustrate how alternating presentations of two views of an object in three-dimensional space induce the experience of the simplest rigid twisting motion prescribed by kinematic geometry—provided that times and distances fall within certain lawfully related limits on perceptual integration. Resonance is advanced as a metaphor for how internalized constraints such as those of kinematic geometry operate in perception, imagery, apparent motion, dreaming, hallucination, and creative thinking, and how such constraints can continue to operate despite structural damage to the brain.

Oxford philosopher of science Rom Harré in his book *Great Scientific Experiments: Twenty Experiments That Changed our View of the World* (Harré, 1983) includes James J. Gibson's work on perception along with ex-

This article, which I dedicate to the memory of James J. Gibson, is an expanded version of the Gibson Memorial Lecture, which I gave at Cornell University on October 21, 1983. I thank the members of the Department of Psychology at Cornell for providing me with an opportunity to clarify the relation of my thinking to Gibson's, and the National Science Foundation for supporting both the preparation of this article and most of the research on which it is based (especially through Grants GB-31971X, BNS 75-02806, and BNS 80-05517).

The faults that undoubtedly remain have at least been greatly reduced as a result of the helpful suggestions made by numerous colleagues including Fred Attneave, Maya Bar-Hillel, Lynn Cooper, Joyce Farrell, John Flavell, David Foster, Jennifer Freyd, Randy Gallistel, Frank Keil, Edward Kessler, Carol Krumhansl, Laurence Maloney, Ann O'Leary, Edward Oshins, Herbert Simon, Elizabeth Spelke, Richard Thompson, Brian Wandell, Benjamin White, and, especially, Gerald Balzano, James Cutting, Julian Hochberg, Michael Kubovy, and Ulric Neisser. Each of these last five contributed extraordinarily painstaking, thoughtful, and enlightening comments.

Requests for reprints should be sent to Roger N. Shepard, at Department of Psychology, Uris Hall, Cornell University, Ithaca, New York 14853, 1984–1985.

periments by such giants of the natural sciences as Aristotle, Galileo, Newton, Boyle, Lavoisier, Rutherford, and Pasteur. Counting myself among students of perception who have come to recognize the challenge that Gibson posed to many long-accepted ideas, I have been moved to work out how the essential insight that informs Gibson's ecological approach might be extended into a realm that has been for me of great and continuing interest.

My efforts in this direction have not proceeded without trepidation. Gibson himself is widely considered to have regarded this realm as insignificant or, worse, nonexistent. I refer to the realm of what I have called *internal representation* (Shepard, 1975; Shepard & Chipman, 1970). Even in my title, which begins auspiciously enough with that good word *ecological*, I have risked anathema by moving immediately on to those very words *internal representation*. How can one who finds Gibson's insight into perception to be so congenial persist in exploring the application of this insight to a realm that Gibson himself never countenanced? At least part of the answer must be that even investigators who agree that they are studying perception may be found, on closer examination, to have quite different objectives.

Differing Goals in the Study of Perception

Goal of Understanding a Sensory Organ's Transduction of Incident Energy

Those who call themselves psychophysicists or vision researchers tend to seek laws relating judgments about sensory events to physically measurable properties of proximal stimuli, and those who call themselves sensory psychophysiologists seek, in addition, relations of these kinds of variables to physically measurable activities within the nervous system. The primary goal for both of these classes of researchers seems to be the elucidation of the mechanisms whereby energy impinging on a sensory organ is transduced into neural activity and thence into behavior.

Goal of Understanding an Organism's Perception of its Environment

Helmholtz (1856/1962, chap. 1), while pursuing the goal of understanding sensory transduction of proximal stimulation, also recognized that an organism must interact appropriately with distal objects in its environment. Yet this latter, ecologically oriented objective was not fully articulated as the primary goal of the study of perception until Brunswik (1956) and J. Gibson (1950) stressed that as the organism, objects, and sources of illumination move about in space, the variations in proximal stimulation bear little resemblance to the particular unidimensional variations of retinal size, brightness, wavelength, or duration that psychophysicists and psychophysiologists have typically manipulated in their laboratories.[1]

True, early investigators such as Hering (1878/1964), Mach (1886/1959), and even Helmholtz (1856/1962) suggested that the flux of proximal stimulation does contain some features that are invariantly related to distal objects. For example, although the light energies reaching the eye from two surfaces of different reflectances vary widely with changes in illumination, the ratio of those two energies remains constant. Then Cassirer (1944) explicitly introduced the mathematical concept of invariance over a group of trans-

formations as a characterization of such perceptual constancies. Nevertheless, it remained for Gibson to adopt the radical hypothesis of what he called the *ecological* approach to perception (Gibson, 1961, 1979), namely, the hypothesis that under normal conditions, invariants sufficient to specify all significant objects and events in the organism's environment, including the dispositions and motions of those objects and of the organism itself relative to the continuous ground, can be directly picked up or extracted from the flux of information available in its sensory arrays.

In the case of the modality that most attracted Gibson's attention—vision—the invariants generally are not simple, *first-order* psychophysical variables such as direction, brightness, spatial frequency, wavelength, or duration. Rather, the invariants are what J. Gibson (1966) called the higher order features of the ambient optic array. (See J. Gibson, 1950, 1966, 1979; Hay, 1966; Lee, 1974; Sedgwick, 1980.) Examples include (a) the invariant of radial expansion of a portion of the visual field, *looming*, which specifies the approach of an object from a particular direction, and (b) the projective cross ratios of lower order variables mentioned by J. Gibson (1950, p. 153) and by Johansson, von Hofsten, and Jansson (1980, p. 31) and investigated particularly by Cutting (1982), which specify the structure of a spatial layout regardless of the observer's station point.

For invariants that are significant for a particular organism or species, Gibson coined the term *affordances* (J. Gibson, 1977). Thus, the ground's invariant of level solidity affords walking on for humans, whereas its invariant of friability affords burrowing into for moles and worms. And the same object (e.g., a wool slipper) may primarily afford warmth of foot for a person, gum stimulation for a teething puppy, and nourishment for a larval moth. The invariants of shape so crucial for the person are there in all three cases but are less critical for the dog and wholly irrelevant for the moth.

---

[1] Correspondingly, I have elsewhere argued for a kind of psychophysics that does not restrict itself to the consideration of proximal variables (see Shepard, 1981a, 1981b, 1982a).

Although the goal of identifying the invariants in the optic array that correspond to all such affordances is far from having been attained (Hochberg, 1982; Neisser, 1977), progress has been made in identifying the invariants underlying the perception of individual human gaits (Cutting, Proffitt, & Kozlowski, 1978; Kozlowski & Cutting, 1977) and of age in human and animal faces (Pittenger & Shaw, 1975; Shaw & Pittinger, 1977), and in establishing that the ability to pick up such invariants as rigidity versus nonrigidity emerges early in human infancy (E. Gibson, 1982; E. Gibson, Owsley, & Johnston, 1978; E. Gibson & Spelke, 1983; Spelke, 1982).

According to James Gibson, the notion—widely accepted since Helmholtz—that we must construct our percepts by combining sensory cues was a misguided consequence of elementaristic, ecologically invalid laboratory experiments in which, for example, a physically restrained observer was permitted only a brief, monocular glimpse of the stimulus. In natural settings we enjoy binocularity, free mobility, and persisting illumination. In that case, Gibson claimed, no inference is required because invariants in the shifting optic array uniquely specify the layout of the environment.

Goal of Understanding the Capabilities of an Organism Under Reduced Circumstances (of Incomplete Information, Insufficient Time, or Damaged Brain)

Even those who follow Gibson this far in pursuing the goal of understanding how organisms function in their natural environment may nevertheless disagree about what to include under its heading. For most of those who follow the ecological approach, the goal has been confined to the identification and specification of the invariants that are sufficient for the veridical perception of the local environment under favorable conditions of visibility, mobility, and neural integrity. They have manifested little interest in three other kinds of questions: First (noted, e.g., by Ullman, 1980), they have not pursued questions, raised by students of neurophysiology and artificial intelligence, concerning the mechanisms that enable an individual to extract the appropriate invariants from the information available at its sensory surfaces.

Second, they have neglected questions, raised by students of cognitive science, concerning how we know about (a) objects, relations, and events that are obscured by darkness or by obstructed, monocular, brief, or intermittent access and also (b) those that are beyond the region that is directly affecting us during a given period of time. There often is no information in sensory arrays about events that have occurred in the past, that are occurring in another place, that will occur in the future, or that might occur under altered circumstances, even though such events can be of great importance and can be known to us in our natural environment.

Third, students of ecological optics have ignored questions, raised by experimental cognitive psychologists and by clinical neurologists, concerning what happens when the information available in the sensory arrays—although sufficient to specify the immediate environment—exceeds the processing capabilities of the individual. I argue that there are limits on the intervals of space and time over which we can integrate information available in the sensory arrays and that these limits are themselves lawful in ways that cry out for explanation. Moreover, there are questions of what happens when this processing capability is further reduced as a result of brain damage, which also occurs in our natural environment as a result of injury, disease, or (as I am increasingly reminded) advancing age. Why do brain lesions lead to particular perceptual dysfunctions, and especially, how can the brain often reestablish more or less normal functioning despite such lesions?

In short, although I agree with Gibson that the brain has evolved to extract invariants under favorable conditions, I also presume that it has evolved to serve the organism under less favorable conditions of nighttime, obstructed, and spatially or temporally limited viewing and, even, of structural damage to the brain itself.

Proposed Extension of the Ecological Approach

In striving to accommodate questions from all three classes just mentioned, without abandoning Gibson's essential insight, one seemingly has to come to terms with the relation between the organism's representation of objects that are and those that are not immediately affecting its sensory arrays, that is, with the relation between perception and mental imagery.

Problem of Mental Imagery

I conjecture that Gibson disavowed the term *mental image* because he could not imagine what sort of thing a mental image could be. He readily spoke of *perceiving* an object, because that object is a physical thing. But in his view "the notion of 'mental images' as distinguished from 'material images' seems to be wholly wrong" (J. Gibson, 1974, p. 42). On the one hand, if a mental image is not a physical thing, what on earth is it?

We certainly do not summon up pictures inside our head for they would have to be looked at by a little man in the head. . . .Moreover, the little man would have eyes in *his* head to see with and then a still littler man and so *ad infinitum*. (J. Gibson, 1974, p. 42)

On the other hand, if a mental image is a physical (i.e., neural) process in the brain, we must admit that we know next to nothing about the process. Surely, what determines whether an animal survives is its interaction with its external environment, regardless of which of the possible internal mechanisms for mediating that interaction is realized in that particular animal. However, in neglecting the representation of objects and events that are not physically present, Gibson seems to have given up too much.

I proposed to accommodate mental imagery by saying that (a) imagining, like perceiving, is surely performed by physical processes in the brain but (b) we do not need to know any details of these processes in order to study imagining (any more than Gibson had to have such knowledge in order to study perceiving). What we imagine, as much as what we perceive, are external objects; although in imagining, these objects may be absent or even nonexistent. We can therefore carry out experiments on both perception and imagery by probing individuals with appropriately chosen external stimuli (Podgorny & Shepard, 1978, 1983; Shepard, 1975, 1981b; Shepard & Chipman, 1970; Shepard

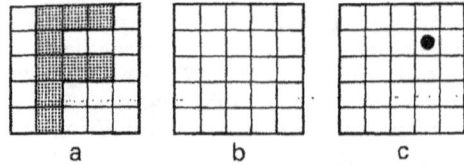

Figure 1. Displays used for the perceptual condition (Part a), the imaginal condition (Part b), and the ensuing test probe (Part c) in one of the experiments by Podgorny and Shepard (1978). (From "The Mental Image" by R. N. Shepard, 1978, *The American Psychologist, 33*, p. 133. Copyright 1982 by the American Psychological Association. Adapted by permission.)

& Cooper, 1982; Shepard & Podgorny, 1978; and, for a brief overview, Shepard, 1978c).

An experiment that Podgorny and I carried out illustrates the point. On each trial, a person looked at a square grid. In the perceptual condition, some squares had been shaded to form a certain object (such as the block letter F in Figure 1, Part a); in the imaginal condition, no squares were shaded but the person was asked to imagine that the same squares had been shaded (Figure 1, Part b). In both conditions, we then flashed a colored probe dot in one of the squares (Figure 1, Part c) and measured the latency of the person's response indicating whether the dot did or did not fall on the (perceived or imagined) object. With experiments of this type, we obtained two major results: First, the reaction times depended on the position of the probe relative to the figural object in a way that implicates orderly constraints in the perceptual mechanism. For example, responses were consistently slower to probes that were closer to boundaries between figural and nonfigural squares. Second, the reaction times exhibited virtually the same pattern in the imagery and the perceptual conditions, suggesting that the object was internally represented in the same way regardless of whether it was physically present or only imagined. (Podgorny & Shepard, 1978, 1983.)

Although I thus speak of internal representations, I agree with J. Gibson (1970, p. 426) as well as with Neisser (1976, p. 57) that one invites unnecessary perplexities by speaking— as imagery researchers sometimes carelessly do—of "seeing," "looking at," "inspecting," or "rotating" one's images or internal representations. Rather than say that one sees or rotates the image of an object (as if the image were itself a physical thing), one can avoid such perplexities by simply saying that one imagines the object and/or its rotation (which *are* potentially physical things). The distinction is, for example—as Michael Kubovy (1983) has well put it—between the acceptable formula *Imagine [Rotation of (Object)]* and the problematic *Rotate [Image of (Object)]*. On occasion, I have spoken of "experiencing" an image or similarly a percept, but only as a kind of shorthand for "undergoing the corresponding (but largely unknown) physical processes in the brain" (cf. Place, 1956; Smart, 1959). Properly speaking, our experience is of the external thing represented by those brain processes, not of the brain processes themselves. At the same time, by acknowledging that perceiving and imagining—as well as remembering, planning, thinking, dreaming, and hallucinating—do correspond to brain processes, we at least open the door to possible connections with evolutionary biology, clinical neurology, and artificial intelligence.

Evolutionary Perspective on Perception and Representation

Whatever we possess in the way of a perceptual and/or representational system must be the product of a long evolutionary history. Our remote ancestors, like many surviving primitive species (ranging from single-celled animals to worms), could not extract *higher order* invariants corresponding to distal objects of the sort that usually concern us now. Instead, they proceeded on the basis of proximal stimuli of a chemical or mechanical nature. Only with the evolution of increasingly powerful mechanisms for the processing of optical, acoustical, and tactual information have we gained access to remote objects and events.

In keeping with the ecological approach, I believe that (initially) the primary function served by this more sophisticated perceptual processing was to partition the information available in these various incoming forms into (a) the invariants uniquely corresponding to distal objects, events, and layouts, and (b) the complementary variables corresponding

to the moment-to-moment changes in the disposition of those objects, events, and layouts, and of the self in relation to them. Such a partitioning is now pervasive: We visually perceive both a persisting object and its current spatial relation to us. We also recognize both the face of a friend and its momentary expression, both what has been written and the format in which it is written, both what has been said and the emotional state of the speaker, and both a particular melody and the pitch height and timbre at which it has been played.

However, this is not the end of the evolutionary story. As Gibson emphasized, higher organisms are not merely observers; they are active explorers and manipulators of their environment. If such exploration and manipulation is not just random trial and error, it must be guided by some internal schema (Hochberg, 1981, 1982; Neisser, 1976) or hypothesis (Krechevsky, 1932). At this point, a new type of function emerges that is related to perceptual and to motoric functions, but is not identical to either. I refer once again to the ability to remember, to anticipate, and to plan objects and events in their absence. The alternative claim (cf. Gibson, 1970), that such functions are entirely separate from perception, is untenable in view of experimental results of the sort reported by Podgorny and Shepard (1978, 1983) and others (as reviewed in Finke, 1980; Finke & Shepard, in press; Shepard & Cooper, 1982; Shepard & Podgorny, 1978). This claim is further weakened by neurophysiological and clinical evidence from brain injuries in which failures in the perception of objects or their (real) motions were accompanied by corresponding failures in the imagination of those objects (Bisiach & Luzzatti, 1978) or by the experience (of the type to be considered) of their *apparent* motions (Zihl, von Cramon, & Mai, 1983).

Endogenous Biological Rhythms as a Model for Internal Representation

Because the circadian behavioral cycle is correlated with the presence or absence of daylight, people long drew the inference that an animal's emergence from and return to its nest or burrow was wholly controlled by this obvious external stimulus. It was little more than 50 years ago, when experimenters first began to maintain animals in artificial laboratory conditions of constant illumination and temperature, that they discovered that the circadian (and even the circannual) rhythm had in fact been internalized (Bünning, 1973). Hamsters, for example, would continue their cycles of alternating activity and sleep indefinitely in the absence of a corresponding environmental periodicity, each animal maintaining a cycle of 24 hours plus or minus no more than a few minutes per day (see Rusak & Zucker, 1975).

Of course, a few minutes of deviation from a 24-hour cycle in each animal would cause it gradually to drift out of phase with other animals in the laboratory and with the true diurnal cycle. Yet, no more than a brief period of increased illumination introduced at the same time each day, or even at the same time just on occasional days, would entrain the endogenous cycles and resynchronize all the animals in the laboratory.

Here is an environmental regularity that has continued with celestial–mechanical precision throughout biological evolution. Even though it is correlated with the waxing and waning of daylight, this periodicity has become internalized so that it continues autonomously in the absence of the correlated stimulus, freeing the animal from a direct dependence on that stimulus. Thus, a diurnal animal while still in the darkness of its burrow can begin to awake and to prepare for active emergence toward the onset of sunrise, and can do so as well on a cloudy as on a sunny day. At the same time, the animal can use what photic cues (weak or strong) are available as to the true onset and offset of daytime to keep its internal cycle in synchronous tuning.

Perception is very much like this. Under favorable conditions of illumination, mobility, and so on, our experience of the environment is so tightly guided by the externally available information that we readily feel the appropriateness of Gibson's term *direct perception* (J. Gibson, 1972; also see Austin, 1962; Michaels & Carello, 1981). At the same time, however, we know that our perceptual experience is mediated by many complex though highly automatic neural processes. Any interruption of these processes by drugs, accident, or disease can alter or disrupt perception. Moreover, these processes embody constraints appropriate only to the world in which we have evolved. Therefore, just as an animal that had evolved on a planet with a very different period of rotation would not synchronize well to our daily cycle, a being that had evolved in a radically different world would not perceive this one in the way that we do—even under favorable conditions. Precisely because our own internal constraints so well match the external constraints in our world, these internalized constraints reveal themselves only when externally available information is degraded or eliminated. Being less tightly controlled from without, activity in the perceptual system is then necessarily guided more by whatever constraints operate within.

Internalized Constraints of Kinematic Geometry

I believe the external constraints that have been most invariant throughout evolution have become most deeply internalized, as in the case of the circadian rhythm. Such constraints may be extremely general and abstract: The world is spatially three dimensional, locally Euclidean, and isotropic except for a gravitationally conferred unique upright direction, and it is temporally one dimensional and isotropic except for a thermodynamically conferred unique forward direction (see Davies, 1977). In it, material bodies are bounded by two-dimensional surfaces and move, relative to each other, in ways that can be approximately characterized, locally and at each moment, by six degrees of freedom (three of translation and three of rotation). Light, until absorbed or deflected by the surface of such bodies, travels between them in straight lines and at a constant, vastly greater velocity. Consequently, the optical information about other bodies available at the sensory surface of each organism is governed by the geometrical laws of perspective projection.

The constraints with which I am primarily concerned are those of *kinematic geometry* (Hunt, 1978, p. 2), which govern the relative motions of rigid objects, or of local parts of nonrigid objects, during brief moments of time. Although there are infinitely many ways in which an object might be moved from any position A to any other position B, in three-dimensional space there is a simplest way of effecting the displacement—a fact that was established between 1763 and 1830 through the efforts of Mozzi, Giorgini, and finally, Chasles (1830; see Ball, 1900, pp. 4, 510; Hunt, 1978, p. 49). For any two positions, A and B, Chasles's theorem states that there is a unique axis in space such that the object can be moved from A to B by a rotation about that axis together with a simultaneous translation along that same axis: a helical twist or "screw displacement" (Ball, 1900; Coxeter, 1961; Greenwood, 1965). Moreover, even for an arbitrary motion between A and B, the motion at any instant in time will approximate a twisting of this kind about a momentarily unique axis (Ball, 1900, p. 10). A twist thus bears the same relation to a rigid body as an ordinary vector bears to a point, the special cases of pure rotation and pure translation being realized as the pitch of the twist becomes zero or infinite, respectively.

I consider also the two-dimensional case of Chasles's theorem: For any two positions, A and B, of a two-dimensional object in the plane, there is always a unique pivot point, P, such that the object can be displaced from A to B by a rigid rotation in the plane about P (Coxeter, 1961). Here, pure translation is realized as the pivot point P recedes to the *point at infinity* in a direction orthogonal to the direction of the translational displacement. As before, an arbitrary motion between A and B will, at any instant *t*, approximate a rigid rotation about a momentarily unique point, P(*t*).[2]

Illustrative Experiments on Apparent Motion

The phenomenon of *apparent motion,* which seems to fall somewhere between perception and imagery, provides perhaps the best illustration of how internalized constraints of kinematic geometry may govern the perceptual/imaginal representation of objects and their transformations. In apparent motion, the alternating presentation of two different views of an object gives rise to the experience of one object smoothly transforming back and forth—provided both that the time between the onset of one view and the onset of the other (called the stimulus onset asynchrony, SOA) is not too short and that the time between the offset of one view and the onset of the other (called the interstimulus interval, ISI) is not too long. That these transformations are experienced as traversing well-defined trajectories is of the greatest significance: In the absence of any external support for such trajectories, the form they take provides an indication of what I call the *internalized constraints.*

Internalized Constraints Revealed in Apparent Motion

In what is perhaps the simplest case of apparent motion, already investigated by Helmholtz's student Exner (1875) and then by the founder of Gestalt psychology, Wertheimer (1912), two laterally separated dots are presented in alternation. For appropriate time intervals, the experience is of a single dot moving back and forth over the straight path between the two positions of presentation. We thus have an intimation that the experienced impletion is an embodiment of general principles of object conservation and least action (Shepard, 1981b). The richness of these internalized principles is revealed in recent experiments in which the two alternately presented stimuli are views of more complex objects differing by more complex transformations—transformations of (in addition to translation) rotation, reflection, expansion or contraction, and various combinations of these. (See Bundesen, Larsen, & Farrell, 1983; Farrell, 1983; Farrell, Larsen, & Bundesen, 1982; Farrell & Shepard, 1981; Foster, 1975; Shepard & Judd, 1976.)

In Figure 2, each of the 12 panels shows a different pair of views of a polygonal object,

---

[2] In three dimensions, the displacement of a point has three degrees of freedom (two for the direction of the corresponding vector and one for its magnitude) and the displacement of a rigid object has six (four for the axis of the twist and the fifth and sixth for its pitch and amplitude). Similarly, in two dimensions, the displacements of a point and of a rigid object have, respectively, two and three degrees of freedom.

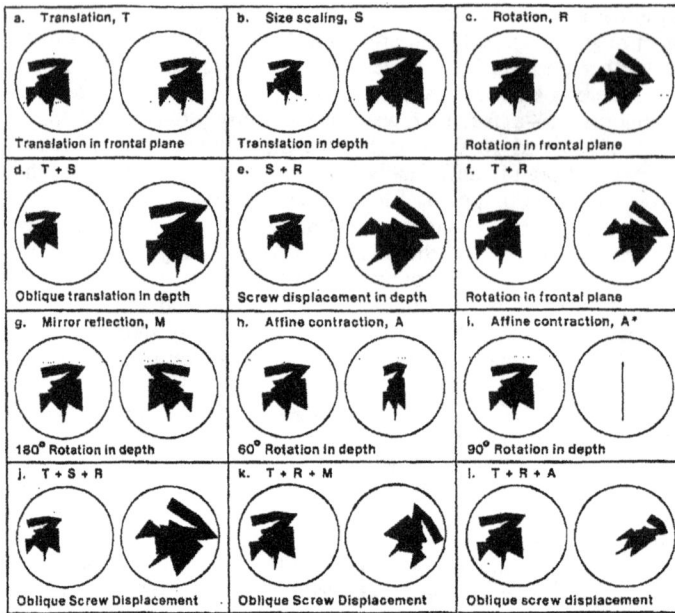

Figure 2. Pairs of two-dimensional shapes that when alternately presented in the indicated positions within the same (circular) field, give rise to rigid apparent motion in space. (For each pair, the transformation that maps one shape into the other has the form indicated above the pair if the transformation is confined to the picture plane, and the form indicated below if it is the simplest rigid transformation in space.)

which might be displayed in alternation within the same two-dimensional field. Thus, Panel a depicts the case in which the polygon alternately appears on the left and the right of a circular field, giving rise to back-and-forth apparent motion. The polygon is one of the forms of the type introduced by Attneave & Arnoult (1956) that Lynn Cooper generated and used to such advantage in her elegant series of experiments on mental rotation (Cooper, 1975, 1976; Cooper & Podgorny, 1976) and that Sherryl Judd and I later adopted for some of our investigations of apparent rotational motion (see Shepard & Cooper, 1982, p. 313).

As indicated at the top of the panels, each pair illustrates a way in which the two views might be related by a transformation in the picture plane: in the top row, shape-preserving transformations of translation (T), size scaling (S), and rotation (R); in the second row, combinations of two of these shape-preserving transformations (T + S, S + R, and T + R);

in the third row, shape-altering affine[3] transformations (A, its degenerate case A*, and its negative extension or mirror reflection M); and in the last row, combinations of three transformations (T + S + R, T + R + M, and T + R + A). When they are thus defined as transformations within the plane of the picture, only in 3 of the 12 pairs are the two views related by a rigid motion of the planar polygon: those in Panels a, c, and f, which are composed only of translations, rotations, or both. In each of the nine remaining pairs, the transformation within the plane is nonrigid because it includes a change in the polygon's size, shape, or in both the size and shape.

Nevertheless, in each of these cases, if the rate of alternation is not too great, the motion tends to be experienced as the rigid transfor-

---

[3] An affine transformation permits differential linear expansion or contraction along different directions but preserves straightness and parallelism of lines.

mation prescribed by Chasles's theorem, as indicated below each pair. Invariance in perceived size and shape is achieved by liberating the transformation and the object from the confines of the picture plane into three-dimensional space. Thus a viewer tends to experience for Panel b an approach and recession rather than an expansion and contraction; for Panel e a unified twisting approach and recession (the helical or screwlike motion) rather than a rotation, expansion, and contraction; and for Panels h and i, respectively, a 60° or 90° rotational oscillation about a vertical axis, rather than a horizontal compression and expansion.[4]

Out of the infinite set of transformational paths through which the one shape could be rigidly moved into congruence with the other, one tends to experience that unique, minimum twisting motion prescribed by kinematic geometry. The axis of the helical motion may however be aligned with the line of sight (as in Panels c, e, f), orthogonal to the line of sight (as in Panels g, h, i), or oblique (as in Panels j, k, l), and the pitch of the twist may be zero, yielding purely circular motion (as in Panels c and f), or it may become infinite, yielding purely translational motion, whether it is one that is confined to the plane (as in Panel a), orthogonal to the plane (as in Panel b), or oblique (as in Panel d).

Abstractness of Internalized Perceptual Constraints

The two-dimensional case of Chasles's theorem provides the simplest illustration of the abstractness of the internalized constraints. From considerations of physical dynamics, one might guess that two planar figures alternately presented in positions that differ arbitrarily (and hence by both a translation and a rotation, as in Panel f of Figure 2) would give rise to an apparent motion in which the center of mass of the apparently moving body traverses the shortest, straight line between its two terminal positions. Because the two views also differ by a rotation, such a motion would have to be accompanied by an additional, apparent rotational transformation, as illustrated for two rectangles in Figure 3, Part a. Instead of such a double transformation, however, Foster (1975) found

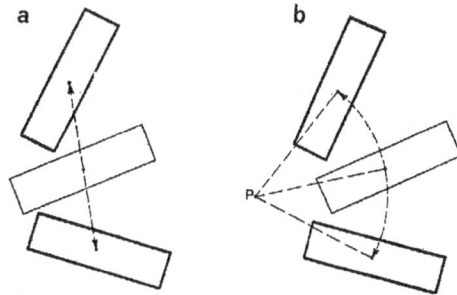

Figure 3. Intermediate positions of a rectangle (drawn in thin lines) between the same two rectangles (drawn in heavy lines), which differ arbitrarily in both position and orientation, along a path consisting of a combined rectilinear translation and a rotation (Part a), and the path (which Foster, 1975, found to be preferred in apparent motion) consisting of a rotation only (Part b). (From *Mental Images and Their Transformations* by R. N. Shepard and L. A. Cooper, 1982, p. 316. Copyright 1982 by The Massachusetts Institute of Technology. Adapted by permission.)

that the motion is generally experienced over a curved path. By having observers adjust the variable intermediate rectangle (indicated in Figure 3 by thinner lines) so that it appeared to fall on the path of motion, he found that (under conducive conditions) the motion tended to be experienced over that unique circular path that rigidly carries the one figure into the other by a single rotation about a fixed point, P, in the plane, as shown in Figure 3, Part b.

It seems that here, as in the case of the moiré pattern of Glass (1969; an example of which is shown in Figure 4, Part b), the visual system picks out the fixed point implied by the two presented positions of a rigid configuration in the plane and, hence, identifies the two configurations with each other by means of a simple rotation. (See Foster, 1975, 1978; Shepard, 1981b; and for a review and theoretical discussion, Shepard & Cooper,

---

[4] In an investigation of apparent motion motivated by similar objectives, Warren (1977) reported that alternation between two-dimensional shapes differing by an affine transformation did not yield rigid apparent motion. However his allegedly affine pair (Panel g) was not affine, and his instructions and resulting subjective reports are open to questions of interpretation, choice of criterion, and effects of perceptual set or expectancy.

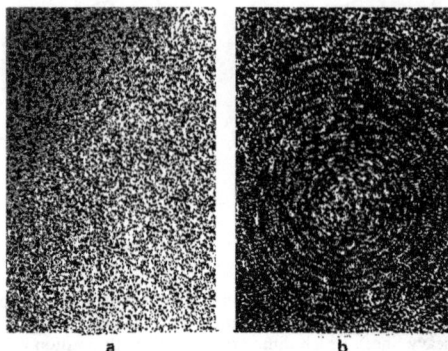

Figure 4. Moiré pattern described by Glass (1969), in which two identical transparencies of a random texture (Part a), when superimposed in an arbitrary misalignment, give rise to the appearance of concentric circles (Part b). (As one transparency is shifted with respect to the other, the center of the concentric circles moves in an orthogonal direction.)

1982.) Incidentally, the visual system also extracts fixed points in the case of nonrigid transformations, as has been demonstrated by Johansson (1950, 1973), Wallach (1965/1976), and most extensively by Cutting and his associates (see Cutting, 1981; Cutting & Proffitt, 1982).

There are good reasons why the automatic operations of the perceptual system should be guided more by general principles of kinematic geometry than by specific principles governing the different probable behaviors of particular objects. Chasles's theorem constrains the motion of each semirigid part of a body, during each moment of time, to a simple, six-degrees-of-freedom twisting motion, including the limiting cases of pure rotations or translations. By contrast, the more protracted motions of particular objects (a falling leaf, floating stick, diving bird, or pouncing cat) have vastly more degrees of freedom that respond quite differently to many unknowable factors (breezes, currents, memories, or intentions). Moreover, relative to a rapidly moving observer, the spatial transformations of even nonrigid, insubstantial, or transient objects (snakes, bushes, waves, clouds, or wisps of smoke) behave like the transformations of rigid objects (Shepard & Cooper, 1982).

It is not surprising then that the automatic perceptual impletion that is revealed in apparent motion does not attempt either the impossible prediction or the arbitrary selection of one natural motion out of the many appropriate to the particular object. Rather, it simply instantiates the continuing existence of the object by means of the unique, simplest rigid motion that will carry the one view into the other, and it does so in a way that is compatible with a movement either of the observer or of the object observed.

Possibly some pervasive principles of physical dynamics (such as a principle of momentum), in addition to the more abstract principles of purely kinematic geometry, have been internalized to the extent that they influence apparent motion (Foster & Gravano, 1982; Freyd, 1983a, 1983c, 1983d, 1983e; Freyd & Finke, 1984; Ramachandran & Anstis, 1983). But there evidently is little or no effect of the particular object presented. The motion we involuntarily experience when a picture of an object is presented first in one place and then in another, whether the picture is of a leaf or of a cat, is neither a fluttering drift nor a pounce; it is, in both cases, the same simplest, rigid displacement. True, we may *imagine* a leaf fluttering down or a cat pouncing, but in doing so we voluntarily undertake a more complex simulation (just as we might in imagining a leaf pouncing or a cat fluttering down). Such mental simulations may be guided by internalizations of more specific principles of physical dynamics and even perhaps of animal behavior.

Pervasive Constraints of Time and Distance

I have taken the sources of the perceptual constraints considered so far to be corresponding constraints in the world, for example, the 24-hour diurnal cycle and principles of kinematic geometry and perhaps of physical dynamics. However, there are other highly orderly perceptual regularities that may not be reflections of constraints that happened to prevail in our world so much as manifestations of constraints that are unavoidable in any system that could exist in this world. Thus, much as the velocity of light limits the speed of communication between distant bodies, the necessarily finite velocity of signal

ECOLOGICAL CONSTRAINTS ON INTERNAL REPRESENTATION 427

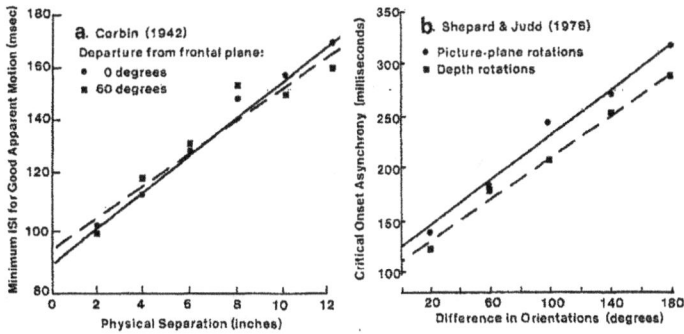

Figure 5. Minimum stimulus-onset asynchronies (critical SOAs) for good apparent motion as a function of extent of transformation in three-dimensional space, as obtained by Corbin (1942) for translational motion (Part a) and by Shepard and Judd (1976) for rotation (Part b). (Note, in both cases, the linearity of the data and the similarity in slope between the data for transformations parallel to the frontal plane and for transformations in depth. Part a is from *Mental Images and Their Transformations* by R. N. Shepard and L. A. Cooper, 1982, p. 306. Copyright 1982 by The Massachusettes Institute of Technology. Adapted by permission. Part b is from "Perceptual Illusion of Rotation of Three-Dimensional Objects" by R. N. Shepard and S. A. Judd, 1976, *Science, 191,* p. 953. Copyright 1976 by the American Association for the Advancement of Science. Adapted by permission.

propagation within a body must limit its processing of information (perhaps with consequences analogous to those of special relativity—cf. Caelli, Hoffman, & Lindman, 1978). Therefore, the possibility of a simple rigid transformation between two alternately presented views is not alone sufficient for the brain to instantiate that transformation as a rigid apparent motion. The extent of the transformation must not be too great in relation to the time available for its neural impletion. Similarly, in connection with the experiment by Foster (1975), the distance to the center of rotation and/or the angle of that rotation must not be too large (cf. Farrell, 1983; Mori, 1982).

In line with these expectations, the minimum SOA that yields apparent motion over a particular path generally increases linearly with the length of that transformational path. In the case of simple translational apparent motion, such a relation was enunciated as the third law of apparent motion by Korte (1915). However, a linear relation of this kind holds for other types of transformations as well, including rotations (Shepard & Judd, 1976), expansions or contractions, and combinations of these with rotations and translations (Bundesen, Larsen, & Farrell, 1983; Farrell, 1983; Farrell et al. 1982). We have

also found such a relation for apparent motion over curved paths externally defined by flashing, very briefly and at low contrast, a particular path during the interstimulus interval (Shepard & Zare, 1983).

These critical times have confirmed that what is being represented (in the absence of real motion) is a transformation of the distal object in three-dimensional space and not a transformation of its projection on the retina (Attneave & Block, 1973; Corbin, 1942; Ogasawara, 1936; Shepard & Judd, 1976). Figure 5, Parts a and b, shows the closeness of the agreement between the critical times for apparent motion in the picture plane and in depth for translational apparent motion (Corbin, 1942) and for rotational apparent motion (Shepard & Judd, 1976).

The phenomena of apparent motion arise in the auditory and in the tactual modalities as well (see, e.g., Kirman, 1983). Moreover, the linear dependence of critical time on transformational distance has been found even when the transformation is not literally spatial. For example, there is a similar increase in critical SOA with increasing separation in pitch between two alternately presented tones (see Jones, 1976; McAdams & Bregman, 1979; Shepard, 1981b, 1982a; van Noorden, 1975).

Phenomenally Distinct Modes of Apparent Motion

.Some pairs of stimuli can be transformed into each other by different transformations of approximately equal extent. For example, if the two alternately presented orientations of an asymmetric object differ by 180°, the rotational apparent motion can be experienced in either direction through equal angles (Farrell & Shepard, 1981; Robins & Shepard, 1977; Shepard & Judd, 1976). An analogous ambiguity occurs in auditory pitch. I have argued (Shepard, 1982a) that Chasles's theorem similarly constrains the motions of rigid auditory objects (e.g., melodies and chords) in pitch space. Because pitch possesses circular components, one can synthesize tones that differ only in their orientations around a chroma circle (Shepard, 1964). As a consequence, when two tones that are diametrically opposite on this circle are sounded in alternation, they are heard as moving (through a tritone interval of pitch) in either of two ways (up-down-up-down- . . . or down-up-down-up- . . .) corresponding to opposite directions of movement around the chroma circle (see Shepard, 1983, and hear the accompanying Sound Demonstration 4).

In both visual and auditory cases, the apparent motion experienced can depend on the rate of switching between stimuli (Farrell & Shepard, 1981; Shepard, 1981b; Shepard & Zare, 1983). For example, we have replicated Brown and Voth's (1937) finding that when dots are cyclically flashed at the four corners of a square, the apparent motion follows the straight paths between successive corners for slow rates of switching but becomes a continuous circular motion at higher rates. Here too, under conducive conditions, a fixed point is evidently extracted, permitting the representation of a single transformation (a continuous rigid rotation about that fixed point) in place of four successive transformations (e.g., linear translations repeating through the cycle: move right, down, left, up, . . .). The conducive conditions in this case presumably require that the time within which three successive dots appear (the minimum number necessary to define the center of the circle) fall within the relevant perceptual integration time.[5]

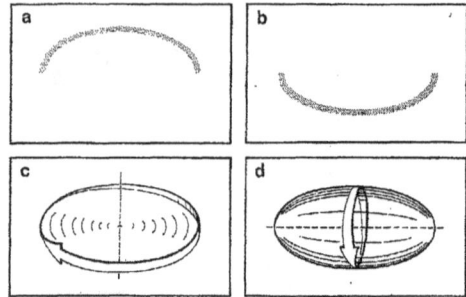

Figure 6. Alternately presented halves of a low-contrast homogeneous elliptical path (Panels a and b), and examples of particular modes of the two principal types of apparent motion experienced: a circular rim spinning about a vertical axis (Panel c) and a "jump rope" whirling about a horizontal axis (Panel d).

Even in the simplest case of the *path-guided* apparent motion studied by Shepard and Zare (1983)—namely, that in which the faint path that is briefly flashed between the two alternately presented dots is the shortest, straight path—the usual report of a reciprocating or back-and-forth motion of a dot is often replaced, at higher rates of alternation, by reports of a rapidly spinning disk viewed edge on or, occasionally, of a horizontal rod rapidly spinning about its own axis. Following up these observations, Susan Zare and I have been systematically investigating a display in which the upper and lower halves of a low-contrast elliptical path are briefly displayed in alternation (Figure 6, Panels a and b). This display gives rise to a variety of alternative percepts.

At high rates of alternation (between SOAs of 50 and 100 ms), observers most often experience a circular rim spinning in a plane tipped back in depth (Figure 6, Panel c), and do so in one of four modes corresponding to whether the plane is experienced as viewed from above or below and whether the spinning motion in that plane is experienced as clock-

---

[5] Similarly, I suggest that a seemingly related phenomenon of apparent motion reported by Ramachandran and Anstis (1982), though interpreted by them in terms of a dynamical principle of *visual momentum,* could just as well be interpreted, in terms of the more abstract principles of kinematic geometry advanced here, as the extraction of a globally simpler, overall rectilinear motion.

wise or counterclockwise. These are variants of path-guided apparent motion (Shepard & Zare, 1983) in that the motion is experienced along the presented curve. At slower rates (beyond SOAs of 100 ms), observers more often experience a "jump rope" whirling around a horizontal axis (Figure 6, Panel d) and do so in one of several modes corresponding to whether the rope goes down in front and up in back, whirls in the opposite direction, or oscillates up and down. These are variants of standard apparent motion in that it is the presented stimulus that is experienced as moving—along a path that is not itself presented. Other percepts may also arise; at relatively fast rates, these include what are described as *jaws* or a *clam shell* vibrating between open and partially closed and, at slower rates, something whirling around the perimeter of a disk that is at the same time wobbling up and down. Occasionally, a second-harmonic variation of the jump rope is described, in which one side of the rope appears to go up while the other goes down and then vice versa (yielding a horizontally oriented figure-eight pattern of oscillation). These various preferred modes of experienced impletion may reflect what are, in each case, the simplest motions in three-dimensional Euclidean space for which the distances of motion are compatible with the time allowed for the internal impletion of such a motion (the SOA).

A Competence–Performance Distinction for Perception

The pairs illustrated in Figure 2 generally induce an experience of a transformation in three-dimensional space because only in this way can the size and shape of the object uniformly be represented as invariant. Likewise, the transformations experienced for the pairs shown in Figure 2, Part f, and in Figure 3 consist of a rotation about a point in the plane exterior to the object, rather than about a point that is interior to the object but that also undergoes a translation, because only in this way is the transformation represented as pivoting around an invariant point. This much is harmonious with Gibson's emphasis on invariance. However, unlike Gibson, I have sought quantitative determinations of

exactly when the ability of the perceptual system to capture an invariant breaks down, as an experimentally controlled display departs more and more from conditions that are conducive for the capture of that invariance.

Gibson did not concern himself with failures to achieve (or to extract) invariance because he confined himself to the most conducive conditions. Instead of investigating apparent motion, he studied real motion. At the other extreme, many vision researchers, who often presented only extremely impoverished and nonconducive stimuli, have tended to undervalue the capacity of the perceptual system to represent invariances of a high order. I suggested (see Shepard, 1982a) that the two approaches might be reconciled by applying to the study of perception, the competence–performance distinction that Chomsky (1965) proposed for the study of language. Information-processing limitations that prevent people from producing or comprehending certain very long sentences do not preclude that people normally produce and comprehend shorter sentences by means of internalized rules of syntax. Similarly, information-processing limitations that prevent people from computing the rigid transformation between two very widely separated views of an object do not preclude that they normally compute such a transformation between less widely separated view by means of internalized principles of kinematic geometry.

Some Relations to Past and Future Studies of the Representation of Motion

There has of course been a considerable history of investigations into the role of rigidity in the perception of motion (e.g., Ames, 1951; Braunstein, 1976; Dunker, 1929/1937; E. Gibson et al., 1978; Johansson, 1950, 1973, 1975; Metzger, 1953; Proffitt & Cutting, 1979; Restle, 1979; Spelke, 1982; Wallach, 1965; Wallach & O'Connell, 1953) and of apparent motion (e.g., Foster, 1972; Hochberg & Brooks, 1974; Kolers, 1972; Kolers & Pomerantz, 1971; Mori, 1982; Navon, 1976; Orlansky, 1940; Squires, 1959; Warren, 1977). The results are generally consonant with the notion that the perceptual system tends to represent a motion as rigid under conducive conditions. However, in the absence of a unified framework for specifying which particular rigid motion is chosen and for characterizing the conducive conditions, specific conclusions have varied from one study of apparent motion to another.

With regard to the selection of a particular motion, I proposed that out of the infinite set of possible rigid motions, an observer tends to experience the simplest helical motion (including its limiting circular or rectilinear motions) prescribed for three-dimensional Euclidean space by kinematic geometry and, specifically, by Chasles's theorem. In case there are alternative motions of this type that are equal or nearly equal in extent (such as 180° rotations in opposite directions), I claim that observers experience only one of these motions on any one trial but that they can be predisposed towards a particular one of these motions by presenting, for example, a corresponding real motion just before the trial. By implication, I also claim that motions that are not of this simplest helical type, whether rigid or nonrigid, will not be experienced unless they are forced on the observer by external conditions. Thus, one can devise a sequence of stationary views that will induce the appearance of, say, a cat pouncing, (rather than rigidly translating), but only if one presents (a) beginning and ending views that are different, (b) other intermediate views (as in stroboscopically or cinematically displayed animation), or (c) the blurred path of motion (as described by Shepard & Zare, 1983).

With regard to the conducive conditions for impletion of a particular apparent motion, I have proposed two primary requirements: (a) The ISI between sequentially presented views must fall within the appropriate period of temporal integration. (b) Corresponding parts of successive views must fall within the appropriate range of spatial integration relative to the SOA available for making the connections, and relative to the prevalence of similar but noncorresponding parts. Only then can the observer identify corresponding parts of the two views and complete the global transformation that rigidly carries those in one view into the corresponding ones in the other view (Attneave, 1974; Farrell & Shepard, 1981; Shepard, 1981b; Ullman,

1979). More specifically, as a generalization of Korte's third law, I have claimed that in the absence of strongly competing alternative transformations, the critical SOA (i.e., the minimum time between stimulus onsets needed to complete this rigid transformation) increases linearly with the extent of the transformation, whether that transformation is rectilinear (Corbin, 1942; Korte, 1915), circular (Shepard & Judd, 1976; Shepard & Zare, 1983), or helical (Shepard, 1981b).

Putting the considerations concerning preference for the simplest transformation that preserves rigid structure together with those concerning the conducive conditions for impletion of such a transformation, I have posited a hierarchy of structural invariance (Shepard, 1981b). At the top of the hierarchy are those transformations that preserve rigid structure but that require greater time for their impletion. As the perceptual system is given less time (by decreasing the SOA), the system will continue to identify the two views and hence to maintain object conservation, but only by accepting weaker criteria for object identity. Shorter paths that short-circuit the helical trajectory will then be traversed, giving rise to increasing degrees of experienced nonrigidity (Farrell & Shepard, 1981). Likewise, if the two alternately presented views are incompatible with a rigid transformation in three-dimensional space, the two views will still be interpreted as a persisting object, but again a nonrigid one.

These considerations provide a basis for reconciling many of the apparent inconsistencies in the literature on rigid apparent motion. Often, experiments that (a) fail to obtain rigid motion between two views of the same object or (b) fail to obtain the simplest motion prescribed by Chasles's theorem have not ensured that the SOA was sufficiently long (when the transformations were large) and/or that the observers were sufficiently primed for that particular motion (when the competing alternatives were strong).

The theory outlined leads to a number of expectations that remain to be empirically tested. The simplest helical motion that displaces an asymmetric object from one position to another is generally unique, except for cases in which there are equivalent alternative paths (e.g., 180° rotations in opposite directions). However, there are always other helical motions that yield the same result, but by means of a larger number of rotations. Moreover, in the case of symmetrical objects there are still more possibilities. Thus, a horizontal rectangle alternately displayed on the left and right could be seen as translating back and forth, rotating through 180° in the picture plane (either above or below), rotating 180° in depth (either in front or in back), and so on.

All such transformations correspond to *geodesic* or locally shortest paths in the curved manifold of distinguishably different positions of the object, that is, to the analogues of straight lines in Euclidean space, great circles on the surface of a sphere, or helices on the surface of a torus (Shepard, 1978a, 1981b). Accordingly, I predict that when alternative geodesic paths are not too widely different in length, observers can be induced (e.g., by a preceding display) to experience transformations over different ones of these alternative paths, with critical SOAs proportional to the length of each path. I further predict that motions cannot be induced in this way along arbitrary paths that are not geodesic, and that the semantic interpretation of the object will in any case have little or no influence on the path of motion or its critical SOA.

Determinants of Internal Representations

The fact that the same alternating visual or auditory display can lead to distinctly different apparent motions reinforces the point, often made on the basis of other ambiguous stimuli (such as the Necker Cube), that perception cannot adequately be described simply as an individual act of picking up an invariant that is present in that particular stimulus. What is perceived is determined as well by much more general and abstract invariants that have instead been picked up genetically over an enormous history of evolutionary internalization. Although some constraints (e.g., of the sorts considered by Chomsky, 1965; Freyd, 1983b; or Keil, 1981) may not have an external origin, I find such an alternative to be less appealing because it would seem to imply that those constraints are arbitrary (cf. Shepard, 1981b, 1982b).[6] Accordingly, I propose a tentative classifica-

tion of the determinants of internal representations into immediate external determinants and three subclasses of internalizations of originally external determinants.

Immediate External Determinants

Here I include all (variant and invariant) information that is available in the optic array and in the corresponding arrays of the other senses of hearing, touch, and so on, within what I have been calling the relevant "period of temporal integration."

Internal Determinants

I classify any determinants that do not fall under immediate external determinants as internal because they are, by this rule of classification, not externally acting on the organism within the given period of temporal integration. However, these determinants are mostly *internalizations* of current or previously prevailing external circumstances—although of increasingly remote origin as specified:

1. Determinants temporarily established by the current context. Here I include both (a) transitory bodily or emotional states (which are, in turn, largely determined by preceding external circumstances, such as presence or absence of food or traumatic events) and (b) mental sets or attentional biases (which are largely established by the external context, including such things as preceding stimuli and instructions given in a psychological experiment). For example, we can predispose an observer toward either of two alternative apparent motions by presenting the corresponding real motion just before (see Shepard, 1981b; Shepard & Cooper, 1982). Analo-

---

[6] I conjecture that the elaborate, special apparatus of syntax has evolved in humans primarily for one purpose: to furnish automatic rules for mapping between complex, multidimensional structures in the representational system and one-dimensional strings of discrete communicative gestures (vocal or manual). I have also argued, however, that these rules, which could not have sprung full fledged from nowhere, may have been built upon already highly evolved rules of spatial representation and transformation (Shepard, 1975, 1981b, 1982b). If so, syntactic rules may be to some extent traceable, after all, to abstract properties of the external world.

gously, a sequence of two tones on opposite sides of the computer-generated chroma circle will be heard as jumping up or jumping down in pitch when immediately preceded by an unambiguously rising or falling sequence, respectively (Shepard, 1983, Sound Demonstration 4).

2. Determinants acquired through past experience by each individual. These are the more enduring but modifiable constraints that have been internalized through learning or *perceptual differentiation* (E. Gibson, 1969; J. Gibson & E. Gibson, 1955). For example, perceptual discrimination is better (a) in the case of adults, between upright than between inverted faces (e.g., Carey, 1981; Hochberg & Galper, 1967; Yin, 1969), and (b) in the case of chess masters, between board positions that might occur in an actual game of chess than between ones arranged at random (e.g., Chase & Simon, 1973; de Groot, 1965).

3. Determinants incorporated into the genetic code during the evolution of the species. These place constraints on each individual that are predetermined at the time of birth. Because the internalization of these constraints has taken place over by far the longest span of time, they presumably tend to reflect the most enduring and ubiquitous invariances in the world. I have conjectured (Shepard, 1981b) that they include those that enable us to perceive a rigid rotation (or, generally, helical motion) on the basis of a two-dimensional projection of a moving three-dimensional structure (Wallach & O'Connell, 1953; also see Braunstein, 1976; Green, 1961; Noll, 1965), and to do so from early infancy (E. Gibson et al., 1978; Spelke, 1982), but leave us unable to perceive rigid motion on the basis of a similar projection of a moving four-dimensional structure (whether that projection is two-dimensional, as in a computer-generated film produced by Bert Green, or three-dimensional, as in a stereoscopic display later devised by Mike Noll).

After some delay, of course, a stimulus that was an immediate external determinant must become a preceding context and hence an internal determinant; that is, beyond a certain temporal integration time, what was a percept must shade off into a memory. Likewise, there may be a continuum between a short-term memory (as in Determinant 1) and a

long-term memory (as in Determinant 2). Moreover, some long-term determinants, although learned (as in Determinant 2), may be acquirable only during a critical period of early development of the individual (Hess, 1959; Lorenz, 1935) and may thereafter remain as unalterable as one that is genetically encoded (as in Determinant 3). Possibly, humans acquire absolute pitch only in this way (Jeffress, 1962). In any case, I assume that determinants of each of the types that I have listed constrain the determinants of all previously listed types. Thus, genetic endowment constrains what can be learned, hence what can be attended to, and thence what will be perceived. If so, the actual extraction of invariants from the externally available information classified under immediate external determinants is made possible by our biologically internalized constraints. Certainly neither an empty black box nor a randomly wired system can be expected to carry out such extractions.

The adaptive significances of all four of the listed types of determinants seem clear. An organism must be perceptually responsive (as under immediate external determinants) to the immediate, locally unfolding events, which (even in a deterministic world) could never be fully deduced or anticipated (see Ford, 1983). In addition, the organism can profit by more or less temporarily and flexibly internalizing (through contextual guidance or through learning) those predictabilities that are likely to prevail in the immediate situation or throughout the current epoch or locale. Finally, there would be an advantage in having the most permanent and certain constraints in its world prewired (as in Determinant 3); then each separate animal need not run the risks of having to learn those constraints de novo through its own trial and possibly fatal error. Such prewired constraints would constitute internalizations of external constraints in the very real sense that a being that had evolved in a very different world would have correspondingly different internalized constraints.

Internal Representation as a Resonance Phenomenon

The closest Gibson came to speaking of internal mechanisms subserving perception was when he likened perception to the physical phenomenon of *resonance* (Gibson, 1966). Despite the reservations that Gibson (p. 271) himself expressed, I believe that the metaphor of resonance, also proposed for cognition by Dunker (1945), alone enables me to make the main points I wish to make about internal representations and their constraints.

Instead of saying that an organism picks up the invariant affordances that are wholly present in the sensory arrays, I propose that as a result of biological evolution and individual learning, the organism is, at any given moment, tuned to resonate to the incoming patterns that correspond to the invariants that are significant for it (Shepard, 1981b). Up to this point I have not departed significantly from what Gibson himself might have said. Moreover, with the notion of selective tuning I can encompass the notion of *affordance* and thus explain how different organisms, with their different needs, pick up different invariances in the world.

However, as I pursue the resonance metaphor further, implications come to light that are at variance with the prevailing ecological approach. Indeed it may have been this potential discord that deterred Gibson from use of the resonance metaphor in his last book (J. Gibson, 1979). However, these further implications seem to be just what is needed to accommodate remembering, imagining, planning, and thinking.

Properties of a Resonant System

The first implication of the metaphor is that a tuned resonator embodies constraints. Resonators respond differently to the same stimuli, depending on their tuning. The second implication is that a resonant system can be excited in different ways. Most efficiently, of course, it is excited by the pattern of energy to which it is tuned. (Indeed, it continues to ring for a while following the cessation of that stimulus, manifesting a kind of short-term memory.) However, it is also excited, though to a lesser degree, by a signal that is slightly different, weaker, or incomplete. Finally, it can also be caused to ring quite autonomously by administering an unstructured impulse from within. An undamped piano string tuned to middle C (262 Hz)

resonates most fully to a continuing acoustic signal of that particular frequency. But it also resonates to some extent to a related acoustic signal that is very brief, is of a slightly different frequency, or stands in some harmonic relation to that frequency. Finally, it similarly responds simply to a single blow of the padded hammer inside the piano. The third implication is that a resonant system may have many different modes of excitation. Thus, different disturbances that induce sympathetic vibrations in that same middle-C string may excite the fundamental and its various harmonics to different relative degrees.

Perhaps the perceptual system has evolved resonant modes that mirror the significant objects and their transformations. When stimulated by a strong natural signal, as under favorable conditions of motion and illumination, the system's resonant coupling with the world would be tight enough to give rise to what Gibson called *direct perception*. However, the coupling is tight only because an appropriate match has evolved between the externally available information and the internalized constraints—just as animals behaviorally resonate to illumination briefly introduced at 24-hour intervals only because they have already internalized the 24-hour period of the earth's rotation.

Even when there is generally an appropriate match, the information available in particular situations may be impoverished, as in a nocturnal, brief, obstructed, schematic, or pictorial view. Necessarily, the system is then less tightly coupled to that information. The resulting resonant response may nevertheless be quite complete, as in the many phenomena of perceptual filling in, subjective contours, amodal completion, and path impletion (in the various phenomena of apparent motion), but it may also be much less stable and, as in the perception of ambiguous stimuli, may exhibit different modes of resonance on different occasions. Finally, in the complete absence of external information, the system can be excited entirely from within. Something internal may "strike the mind," giving rise to the various "ringings" that we call mental images, hallucinations, and dreams.[7]

---

[7] The first occasion on which I myself advanced the idea that imagery and dreams correspond to the sponta-

Of course, the piano is an inadequate model in several respects. The tendency for one perceptual interpretation to dominate its alternatives at any one time implies a mechanism of mutual inhibition that the piano lacks. Also, unlike the different modes of resonance of a piano string, the different modes of resonance in the perceptual system are not related by anything so rigid as inherent frequency ratios. Through evolution, learning, and contextually induced states of attention, the resonances of the perceptual system have been shaped instead to *mesh* with the external world (Shepard, 1981b).

Hierarchical Organization of the Resonant Modes

Even within a piano, a complex acoustic event may simultaneously excite many different modes of resonance; that is, sympathetic vibrations arise to different degrees at certain harmonics in particular (undamped) strings. Similarly, the perceiving of a complex object or event, such as a rotating cube or a laughing face, presumably corresponds to the excitation of many different resonant modes of the perceptual system. Moreover, these modes vary from those that resonate to very specific, sensory features such as the particular length, direction, and motion of an edge of the cube or the particular size, color, and texture of the iris of an eye, to those that resonate to more abstract, conceptual categories such as the presence of rotation (regardless of the object rotating) or of a face (regardless of age, sex, color, hairstyle, expression, orientation, or distance). There is therefore reason to suppose that perceptual processes are in this sense hierarchical, following neurophysiologists (e.g., Gross, Rocha-Miranda, & Bender, 1972; Hubel & Wiesel, 1965; Konor-

ski, 1967; Lettvin, Maturana, McCulloch, & Pitts, 1959), computer scientists (e.g., Marr, 1982; Selfridge, 1959), experimental psychologists (e.g., Bruner, 1957; Neisser, 1967, p. 254; Posner, 1969; Shepard, 1975), and philosophers (e.g., Price, 1946; James, 1890/1950, p. 49; cf. also Kant, 1781/1961, pp. 104–106, on schemata).

An important qualification, however, is that one mode is not assigned to a higher level than are other modes in the hierarchy because its excitation is preceded or caused by excitation of those other modes. Rather, it is assigned to the higher level solely because it resonates to a wider natural class of external objects or events. Thus the mode that represents *face* is considered a high-level mode because it resonates to any face (but to nothing else), and does so regardless of the identity, expression, orientation, or illumination of that face, whereas a low-level mode resonates to detailed local features of lightness, color, texture, orientation, and so on, which are possessed by only a few faces in a few poses, and perhaps by some stimuli that are not faces at all.

As is indicated by phenomena of perceptual completion, excitation of a mode tends to induce sympathetic activity in other modes. When these other modes are "above" or "below" the initially excited mode, we have what information-processing theorists refer to as *bottom-up* and *top-down* processes. However, in accordance with Gibson's radical insight, a high-level mode may resonate to an abstract external invariant directly; its excitation need not depend on excitation of modes that are lower in the hierarchy and that correspond to more elementary features of the external object or event (cf. Runeson, 1977; and the further discussion in Pomerantz & Kubovy, 1981). Neisser (1976, pp. 112–113) characterized the essential relation between different levels of such a hierarchy as one of *nesting* or *embedding* rather than one of causation.[8]

---

neous internal excitation of a perceptual system that has evolved to resonate with natural processes in the external world was a meeting of a student-run Monday Evening Discussion Group at Yale while I was a graduate student there in the early 1950s. The idea has, if nothing else, the virtue of not requiring the assumption that during dreaming, some other part of the brain must, in the manner of a movie projector, play upon the cortex with specifically programmed patterns of excitation—as seemed to be implied by the otherwise admirable neurophysiological account of dreaming offered by Dement (1965).

[8] More accurate than my implied one-dimensional hierarchical scheme, ranging from abstract and conceptual to concrete and sensory, would be a two-dimensional triangular scheme in which the three corners represent (a) abstract concepts (e.g., face, smile, triangle, or rotation), (b) concrete percepts (e.g., John's smiling face or a blue

Externally and Internally Instigated Representational Processes

In Figure 7, I use a vertical rectangle to represent the hierarchy of resonant modes, ranging between those that are most abstract and conceptual, at the top, and those that are most concrete and sensory, at the bottom. Each triangle represents a currently excited mode of the system. I assume that the system preserves no record of the sources of excitation of any mode, which could be primarily from within the system (whether from above or below) or from without. To show how the same system may be differently excited in experiencing sensations and in perceiving, dreaming, hallucinating, imagining, or thinking, I have nevertheless distinguished the active modes in Figure 7 according to whether the primary sources of their excitation were external (triangles pointing up) or internal (triangles pointing down).

Because unstructured stimuli (including direct mechanical, electrical, or chemical irritations of sensory pathways or their cortical projection areas) are not matched to higher level resonances, they produce only the meaningless "lights, colors, forms, buzzes, hums, hisses, and tingles" (see Penfield, 1958, pp. 11–13) that correspond to low-level resonances of the system (as illustrated in Figure 7, Rectangle a). In contrast, perception of meaningful external objects and events arises when resonant activity is induced at all levels of the system (as in Figure 7, Rectangle b).

Even when there is no external input, resonant modes may still become spontaneously excited. Subjective reports, supported by some neurophysiological evidence (e.g., Dement, 1965; Penfield, 1958; West, 1962), suggest that when the system becomes functionally decoupled from sensory input during REM sleep or perhaps in hypnagogic, hypnopompic, or hallucinatory states, even the lowest level resonances may become entrained by higher level activity (as depicted in Figure

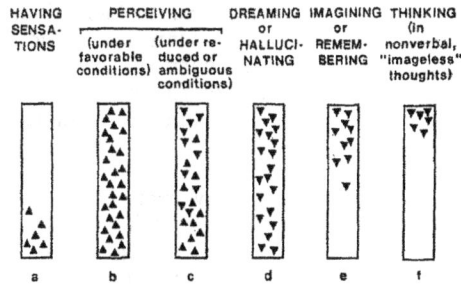

Figure 7. Schematic portrayal of the subsets of excited modes in the perceptual/representational system when it is activated to different extents from without (triangles pointing up) and from within (triangles point down) in sensation, perception, and various types of imagery and thought. (The triangles in the lower and upper extremes of each rectangle correspond to relatively more concrete, sensory modes of resonance and to relatively more abstract, conceptual modes of resonance, respectively.)

7, Rectangle d), giving rise to a full-blown, if illusory, perceptual experience (Shepard, 1978b, 1978c).

Subjective reports concerning waking imagination and memory imagery, as well as objective performance in experiments requiring such imagery, indicate that while these images represent external objects and events (Shepard, 1978c) and obey constraints on their transformations (Shepard & Cooper, 1982), they are fairly abstract or schematic. As shown in Figure 7, Rectangle e, they do not fully engage the lowest, most concrete, and richest sensory levels of the system (cf. also, Finke, 1980; Finke & Shepard, in press). In the extreme case of excitation confined to the highest, conceptual modes (illustrated in Figure 7, Rectangle f), there may be what is called *thinking* or *imageless thought* (Külpe, 1920; Woodworth, 1915).[9]

In *The Interpretation of Dreams*, Freud (1900/1931) similarly contrasted the internal processes of perception, waking memory and

---

equilateral triangle rotating clockwise), and (c) sensations (e.g., flashes, colors, buzzes, or tingles). For simplicity of exposition here (and in Figure 7), I have in effect collapsed such a triangle into a one-dimensional (rectangular) scheme by compressing the "percept" corner toward the opposite side, halfway between concepts and sensations.

---

[9] That thinking is restricted to only the highest portion of the representational hierarchy is an indication not of the unimportance of thought but of the power and generality that it gains through abstraction. I have largely neglected here the special syntactic constraints that underlie verbal productions (whether vocalized or merely thought) and that contribute vastly to the powers of abstract thought. (See, however, Footnote 2 concerning the possible spatial origin of these constraints.)

thought, and dreaming and hallucination. According to Freud, in dreams and hallucinations the normal direction of flow from the perceptual system through memorial and ideational systems (and ultimately to motor actions) is reversed: There is "a retrogression in the psychic apparatus from some complex act of ideation to the raw material of the memory-traces which underlie it" (p. 398) until we have, in the end, "thoughts transformed into images" (p. 400). But in "intentional recollection and other component processes of our normal thinking . . . during the waking state this turning backwards does not reach beyond memory-images; it is incapable of producing the hallucinatory revival of perceptual images" (Freud, 1931, p. 398).

Perceiving under reduced or ambiguous conditions (as at night, in the psychological laboratory, or in looking at pictures) is intermediate between normal perceiving and pure imagining. Although many of the modes are directly excited by the externally available information, other modes, perhaps especially at higher levels, are sympathetically excited by purely internal activities corresponding to set, expectation, and bodily state. The final result tends to be the overall pattern of mutually resonant activity that is most internally consistent throughout all levels of the system.

Thus, although J. Gibson (1970) held that perceiving is an entirely different kind of activity from thinking, imagining, dreaming, or hallucinating, I like to caricature perception as *externally guided hallucination,* and dreaming and hallucination as *internally simulated perception.* Imagery and some forms of thinking could also be described as internally simulated perceptions, but at more abstract levels of simulation.

Resonance as a Spontaneous Emergent in Neural Networks

In proposing resonance as a metaphor, I have intentionally remained noncommittal concerning neural mechanisms. In particular, I am not claiming that resonant activity in the brain is necessarily a periodic oscillation like the vibration of a string, although there is evidence that some responses of the perceptual system do have this character (e.g.,

Bialek, 1983; Freeman, 1975). Certainly, the most concrete interpretation of the metaphor, in terms of conservation and dissipation of energy, would be inappropriate. Independently of sensory input, the brain's metabolism contributes energy to the process of perceptual interpretation and, hence, provides for a kind of amplification not found in a passive resonator. The resonance I speak of is therefore not strictly a resonance to energy; as J. Gibson (1966) implied, it is a resonance to information. Subject to this proviso, however, resonance may arise in the brain in a more literal sense than I have so far claimed.

Such a notion of neural resonance has a variety of precursors going back over 30 years to related ideas of cortical standing waves or *interference patterns* (e.g., Lashley, 1942), *reverberatory circuits* (e.g., Ashby, 1954; Rashevsky, 1948), and especially, reverberatory *cell assemblies* and *phase sequences* (Hebb, 1949). Moreover, the concept of resonance itself has come into recent prominence in connection with biology and communication (Thom, 1972/1975, pp. 134, 145), brain science (Changeux, 1983), and sensory psychophysiology (Ratliff, 1983). In the latter connection, vision researchers have of course long referred to the *tuning curves* of individual receptor mechanisms. Indeed, in receiving the 1983 Pisart Vision Award, Floyd Ratliff went as far as to say that "the neural networks in our visual systems are not only *figuratively* tuned, they are *literally* harmonic systems" (Ratliff, 1983, p. 10).[10]

Moreover, mathematical analyses have indicated that resonance is to be expected as a natural emergent in neural networks. Drawing on the theory of linear systems, Greene (1962a, 1962b) showed that if information is represented by graded signals (e.g., by dendritic potentials and by rates of axonal firing),

---

[10] In connection with the possible harmonic nature of the visual system, I find it amusing that many vision researchers, who (unlike Ratliff) insist on an exclusively nonmetaphorical approach to their subject, nevertheless use the term *octave* to refer to a two-to-one ratio of spatial frequencies. Perhaps they have not noticed that the term does not derive from a physical relation between frequencies but from the fact that the seven-tone diatonic musical scale (which is determined more by cognitive than by physical constraints; see Balzano, 1980; Shepard, 1982a) returns to the tonic with the eighth step.

then even networks composed only of linear elements will possess characteristic resonances, unless "special apparatus is installed to suppress the transients and resonant modes" (Greene, 1962a, p. 257). He concluded that "evolution either suppressed this feature or exploited it. Since its properties resemble those of animal behavior, the latter might be suspected" (Greene, 1962b, p. 395).

Some of the properties that Greene (1962b) derived for nonhomogeneous neural networks are (a) that "resonant modes . . . selected (through natural selection) as the bearers of meaningful information . . . will tend to be stabilized against random disturbances" (p. 409) and (b) that "extremely complex configurations may be represented by a small number of simple intensities," enabling the organism to "switch from one highly integrated behavior pattern to another, without seeming to be required to make adjustments in the multitude of parameters that would be necessary to specify all the individual parts of the patterns" (p. 407). Essentially the same properties have more recently been deduced for hierarchical, nonlinear neural networks by Grossberg (1980), who similarly concluded that "adaptive resonances are the functional units of cognitive-coding" (p. 29).

Greene (1962b), Grossberg (1980), and Anderson, Silverstein, Ritz, and Jones (1977) cited *categorical perception* and the perceptual reversals experienced while viewing ambiguous stimuli as examples of the global switches from one meaningful organization to another that are expected to arise in a resonant network. Of complex resonant systems in general, René Thom said "Usually the system must choose from several possible resonances, and this *competition of resonances* has never been studied mathematically, even though it seems to be of the greatest importance" (Thom, 1972/1975, p. 134). Nevertheless, Greene (1962a), within the context of the particular linear systems investigated by him, derived the reorganizations that occur with increasing speed in the gait of a quadruped as but another manifestation of discontinuous shifts between resonant modes. Shifts of this last type seem suggestively like the discontinuous changes in perceptual organization (e.g., from whirling jump rope to spinning disk) that Zare and I found to occur as the alter-

nation between the apparent motion displays of Figure 6 (Panels a and b) is gradually accelerated.

Apparently then, resonant modes might naturally arise in neural circuits and might contribute to coherence both among internal processes and between those processes and significant environmental constraints. The notion of resonance that I have been advocating differs from the earlier proposals concerning cortical waves and reverberatory circuits in focusing less on the form of the neural activity itself and more on the functional mesh (Shepard, 1981b) that must hold between that activity and the external objects and events that it represents. Admittedly, we have yet to determine exactly how kinematic geometry is embodied in the resonant modes. Nevertheless, if the characteristics of these modes are determined by the connectivity and synaptic transmission coefficients of the neural circuit, there is no obvious reason why evolutionary selection and individual learning could not shape a circuit with the requisite properties.[11]

The most radical departure from the mechanisms usually proposed for perceptual processing is motivated, here, by the desire to encompass dreaming, imagining, and thinking. Even the undamped strings of a piano, in the absence of an acoustic stimulus, begin to vibrate only when struck by their corresponding padded hammers—events that depend on the intervention of an agency external to the piano itself. Has the homunculus of the picture-in-the-head metaphor of perception and imagery (although differently guised as performer rather than perceiver) reared again its ugly head? Not necessarily. The strings of an aeolian harp, for example, are excited not by intentional hammer blows but by random gusts of wind. Yet the ensuing activity is harmonious—provided, of course, that the strings have already been properly tuned.

---

[11] See, for example, Changeux (1983). Note that the isomorphism required between the external constraints and their internal representation need be no more than an abstract or second-order type (see Shepard, 1975) and that related, spatially distributed parallel processes (such as *relaxation* methods) for satisfying constraints have already been shown to be effective for scene analysis in computer vision (e.g., see Rosenfeld, 1982; Waltz, 1975).

Similarly, the natural modes of resonance of a neural network, if they are already tuned to naturally occurring external objects and events tend to ring and hence to represent such objects and events when, in the REM state, under the influence of fever or drugs, or; to some extent, during mere idle meditation, the network is played on by random internal "gusts" of neural or chemical excitation. Of course, to the extent that either abstractly formulated goals or pressing bodily states become ascendent, they tend to entrain the entire ongoing activity into a more directed course.

In his acceptance address, Ratliff (1983) noted that a resonance theory of thinking can in fact be traced back at least to Coleridge, who, in his 1795 poem "The Eolian Harp," after writing (lines 13–17)

"that simplest Lute,
Placed length-ways in the clasping casement,
    hark!
How by the desultory breeze carress'd . . .
It pours forth such sweet upbraiding,"

went on to ask

"And what if all of animated nature
Be but organic Harps diversely fram'd,
That tremble into thought?"

(lines 44–46; see Richards, 1950, pp. 65–67).

*Implications Concerning Robustness
of Brain Function*

I have suggested that what is being represented within the system corresponds to which modes are ringing—without regard to which of the complete, incomplete, and generally redundant sources of influence caused each mode to ring. This proposal is, in this one respect, analogous to Müller's (1842) principle of *specific nerve energies*, which asserted that the consequences of the firing of a neuron depend only on the identity of that neuron and not on the events (whether optical, chemical, mechanical, or neural) that precipitated its firing.

A familiar perceptual phenomenon is illustrative: There are many redundant sources of information as to the (relative) distances of an object in depth, for example, binocular disparity, oculomotor convergence, aerial perspective, retinal size, textural gradients, linear size, height relative to the horizon, interposition, motion parallax, and so on. However, only some of these sources may be available in any given situation. Although we experience an object at a definite distance, we have no awareness of how much each of the sources contributed to this experience. Looking at a landscape painting, we may obtain a sense of three dimensions as a result of the artist's rendering of aerial perspective, linear perspective, gradients of size, and so on, but this impression of depth is considerably muted by counteracting information from binocular disparity, which tells us that we are looking at a flat surface. I have found that if I look at the same painting with one eye, from a distance that precludes resolution of the microstructure of the painted surface, and through a reduction tube (formed, e.g., by rolling up a sheet of paper) so as to hide the surrounding frame, I can obtain an experience that seems as vividly three dimensional as if I were looking with both eyes at the corresponding real scene. Although a single source of information may not support as accurate a judgment of depth as would multiple sources, as long as that single source is in no way contradicted by any other source, it may still yield a compelling experience of depth.

In general, an assemblage of partially redundant resonant subsystems, loosely coupled to each other and capable of autonomous excitation, will be robust against structural damage. Each subsystem will resonate in much the same way whether it is excited by all or by only a few of the redundant inputs from other subsystems to which it is coupled. All that is required is that the residual inputs exhibit a sufficient part of the characteristic pattern to which the given subsystem is tuned. In this way we can understand why persons who have undergone a transection of the million fibers of the corpus callosum connecting the two cerebral hemispheres are indistinguishable from intact individuals, except under testing conditions that have been carefully contrived to prevent contralateral transmission of information through other (for example, auditory, kinesthetic, or somatic) channels (Gazzaniga, 1970; Sperry, 1968). Like the perceiver of objects at different depths, each part of the brain resonates to the same world, not knowing which or how many specific channels of input have been left to cause it thus to ring. To venture a revision of Leibniz (and to risk a further mixing of his metaphors!), the mind is no more a "windowless monad" with a "preestablished harmony" (Leibniz, 1714/1898) than it is an unharmonized monad with a picture window. More nearly is it a community of pretuned monads that come into harmonious action, with each other and with the world outside, through many glasses darkly.

Implications Concerning Creative Thought

To the extent that the natural modes of resonance of the representational system embody the constraints governing transformations in the world, we have a unified basis for treating both how we perceive external objects and events and how—in the absence of such objects and events—we remember or think about them. Such a possibility was already envisioned by Heinrich Hertz, who began his 1894 treatise, *The Principles of Mechanics,* as follows:

The most direct, and in a sense the most important, problem which our conscious knowledge of nature should enable us to solve is the anticipation of future events, so that we may arrange our present affairs in accordance with such anticipations. . . . In endeavouring thus to draw inferences as to the future . . . We form for ourselves images or symbols of external objects; and the form which we give them is such that the necessary consequents of the images in thought are always the images of the necessary consequents in nature of the things pictured. In order that this requirement may be satisfied, there must be a certain conformity between nature and our thought. (Hertz, 1894/1956, p. 1)

In studies that my associates and I carried out on mental transformations (see Cooper & Shepard, 1978; Shepard & Cooper, 1982), we found that the principles that constrain involuntarily experienced real and apparent transformations guide voluntarily imagined transformations as well. The trajectories of imagined translations, rotations, dilations, and combinations of these appear to be exactly the spontaneously occurring trajectories of corresponding rigid apparent motions (Shepard, 1978a). Moreover, the times needed to complete such imagined transformations in-

crease linearly with the extent of those transformations in three-dimensional space just as in the case of apparent motions. Note the similarity between the results of our first study of mental rotation (Shepard & Metzler, 1971), reproduced in Figure 8, and the corresponding results for rotational apparent motion, shown in Figure 5, and between the parallel results obtained for other types of

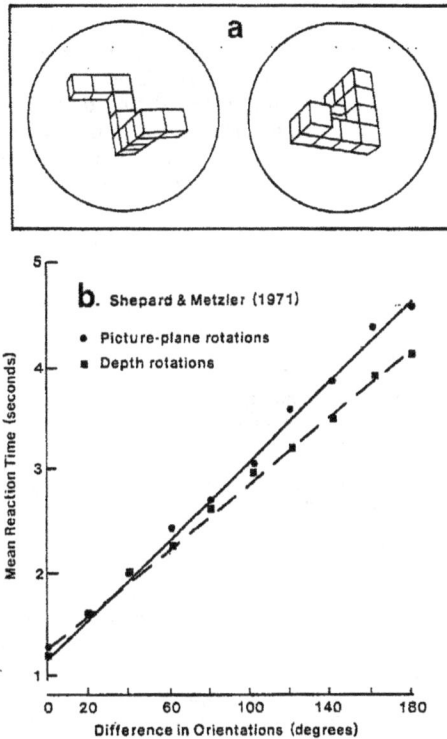

Figure 8. One of Shepard and Metzler's pairs of perspective views of a three-dimensional object (Part a), and the times that people took to imagine such an object rotated from one portrayed orientation into the other to verify that the objects were in fact identical rather than enantiomorphic (mirror reversed) in intrinsic shape (Part b). (The data are plotted as a function of angular difference in portrayed orientations, for differences corresponding simply to a rigid rotation in the picture plane or, as illustrated in Part a, to a rotation in depth. Note the similarity in pattern to the data displayed in Figure 5 for apparent motion of these same objects. From "Mental Rotation of Three-Dimensional Objects" by R. N. Shepard and J. Metzler, 1971, *Science, 171,* p. 702. Copyright 1971 by the American Association for the Advancement of Science. Adapted by permission.)

mental transformations and their corresponding apparent motions, reported by Bundesen, Larsen, and Farrell (1981, 1983).

As I have documented elsewhere (Shepard, 1978b, 1978c), a number of creative thinkers who have most transformed our understanding and control of the world about us have reported that they arrived at their revolutionary ideas through "visualizing . . . effects, consequences, and possibilities" by means of "more or less clear images which can be 'voluntarily' reproduced and combined"—to put together two quotations from Einstein (in Holton, 1972, p. 110, and Hadamard, 1945, p. 142, respectively). Could it not be that the constraints on visualizing that have guided such insights, and whose sources must lie in the world, are like those that we have been investigating in the laboratory?

Epilogue: Two Approaches Reconciled?

For those students of the ecological approach who still reject any talk of internal representation, I cannot refrain from quoting Gibson himself:

The theory of perceptual systems emphasizes the external loops that permit orientation, exploration and adjustment but it also admits the existence of internal loops, more or less contained within the central nervous system. Only in this way could the facts of dreaming be explained. In the waking state, the internal loops are driven or modulated by the external ones but in sleep they may become active spontaneously, the internal component of a perceptual system running free as it were, like a motor without a load. In the case of daydreams and waking fantasies, one can suppose that internal experiencing of a similar sort occurs in parallel with ordinary perceiving, the former being split off from the latter, and the latter being reduced.

There is no doubt but what the brain alone can generate experience of a sort. (J. Gibson, 1970, p. 426)

And, with regard to perceptual ambiguity:

The fact of two alternative percepts from the same drawing is very puzzling. The light to the eye has not changed when a pair of faces is seen instead of a goblet but the percept has.

If such drawings are analyzed as sources of information instead of mere stimulation, however, the puzzle becomes intelligible. The information in the array is equivocal. There are two incompatible kinds of pictorial information in the light to the eye and the percept changes when the beholder shifts from one kind to the other. (J. Gibson, 1971, p. 33)

Finding that I myself resonate to what Gibson is saying in these excerpts, I have to ask: In what respect, finally, do I go beyond Gibson? Gibson emphasized the strong constraint that external reality places on perceiving when that reality is an integral part of the organism–environment "loop." It was, I suppose, his sense of the objective, shared, and binding character of this direct, external constraint that Gibson (1970) insisted that (a) "the act of perceiving is essentially different from the act of imagining" (p. 427), (b) "what the brain alone . . . *cannot* do is to generate *perceptual* experience," and (c) "the dreamer is *trying to look,* as it were. But since there is no feedback . . . the dream wanders on uncontrolled" (p. 426).

I, on the other hand, have been impressed by how extensively internal loops have incorporated external constraints. When Gibson said that in dreaming and imagining, the perceptual system runs "free . . . like a motor without a load" and that the dream "wanders on uncontrolled," he expressed insufficient appreciation of the fact that a dream, however bizarre or regressive in thematic content, is not a random eruption of meaningless lights, colors, hums, hisses, and tingles but a deceptively realistic simulation of meaningful objects and events unfolding in space.

It was apparently through such dream simulations that Jack Nicklaus changed his golf grip and subsequently improved his waking golf game by 10 points; Taffy Pergament, the 1963 national novice figure-skating title winner, originated her new jump, the "Taffy;" a gynecologist discovered how to tie a surgical knot deep in the pelvis with one hand; Elias Howe had the crucial insight necessary for his perfection of the sewing machine; Louis Agassiz found a way to extract a fossil, undamaged, from a slab of stone; James Watt came up with a simpler method of manufacturing lead shot; H. V. Hilprecht realized how to fit certain archaeological fragments together, enabling him subsequently to decipher their cuneiform inscriptions; Friedrich Kekulé solved the outstanding problem of the molecular structure of benzene; Otto Loewi devised the experiment that led to his 1936 Nobel Prize for the discovery of the chemical basis of neural transmission; and (in the related hypnopompic state) I myself conceived of the experimental study of mental rotation. (See Shepard, 1978b; Shepard & Cooper, 1982, chap. 1 & 2, for fuller documentation and sources.) And every waking day, by thought alone, physicists, stereochemists, mechanical engineers, inventors, architects, carpenters, interior decorators, and just plain folks successfully anticipate the consequences of carrying out complex physical manipulations and rearrangements of objects in the three-dimensional world.

"An observer can orient his head and eyes to some component of an optic array. . . . But [not] to an afterimage or a memory image" (J. Gibson, 1970, p. 426). Yet in a dream, one can orient one's (dream) head and eyes to one's (dream) environment or even, in a hallucination, orient one's (real) head and eyes to a hallucinated object in one's (real) environment, and, in both cases, one experiences the appropriate perceptual consequences. See particularly the description of just such a hallucinatory experience by the 19th-century astronomer and chemist Sir John Herschel (1867; quoted in Shepard & Cooper, 1982, p. 5). Apparently, internal loops can mimic the feedback furnished by external loops. Foreshadowing the commutative diagram that I much later proposed (Shepard, 1981b, p. 294), Heinrich Hertz succinctly stated that "the consequents of the images must be the images of the consequents" (Hertz, 1894/1956, p. 2).

Gibson is correct in insisting that an observer cannot literally "*scan*, or *inspect* or *examine*" a subjective image" (J. Gibson, 1970, p. 426; also see J. Gibson, 1979, pp. 256ff.). Nevertheless, following Kubovy's (1983) proposed rewording, we are able to *imagine* scanning a spatially extended object, map, or scene, or to *imagine* approaching it for closer (mental) examination of its parts (as has been extensively demonstrated by Kosslyn, 1980). We are also able to *imagine* inspecting a three-dimensional object in different orientations, as was noted long ago by Helmholtz (1894; as translated in Warren & Warren, 1968, pp. 252–254, and quoted in Shepard & Cooper, 1982, p. 1) and as is now chronometrically investigated in the psychological laboratory (Shepard & Cooper, 1982; Shepard & Metzler, 1971). Moreover, the experimental results for such mental scanning, approaching, and manipulating of imagined objects are all

quite parallel to those for the corresponding scanning, approaching, and manipulating of real objects (Finke & Shepard, in press; Kosslyn, 1980; Shepard & Cooper, 1982).

Our ability to take account of events with which we are not in physical interaction provides the strongest motivation for a concept of internal representation. Two kinds of such events are those that have happened already and those that have happened not yet. In seeking to eliminate the need for the concept of internal representation, Gibson therefore had to depart most radically from prevailing psychological theories in his treatment of temporal notions, particularly, the notion of the present. He came to the conclusions that "resonance to information has nothing to do with the present" (J. Gibson, 1966, p. 276) and that "what we see *now* refers to the *self*, not the environment" (J. Gibson, 1979, p. 254). Gibson held that the enduring invariants in an individual's environment are available to be picked up (over time) by the exploring individual. Thus, as we move about an object, we pick up its layout as seen from many points of view or, equivalently, from no particular point of view (J. Gibson, 1974; also see J. Gibson, 1966, pp. 275 ff.). Such considerations led Gibson to a novel characterization of visualization: "We see formless and timeless invariants when we perform visual thinking" (J. Gibson, 1974, p. 42).

Although I share with Gibson the idea that visualization reflects invariants in the world, I believe that the invariants that are most deeply internalized are those that constrain the possible transformations of all possible objects relative to the observer and not those that characterize a particular object or layout. As theoretical justification, I have argued that the objects that have been important to us over evolutionary history have been informationally complex (requiring vast numbers of degrees of freedom for their characterization) and, furthermore, have changed over the eons. In contrast, the rigid displacements of those objects have been constrained for all time to the same six degrees of freedom (Shepard, 1981b, p. 327). As empirical justification, I have cited the results of the experiments that my associates and I have reported on mental rotation, which clearly indicate that an object, despite having been repeatedly seen in many orientations or from many points of view, is still visualized or imagined in only one of these ways at a time (Cooper, 1975, 1976; Shepard & Metzler, 1971; see especially Metzler & Shepard, 1974, p. 196). If an individual could directly visualize the inherent structure of an object without regard to point of view, then that observer could immediately "see" whether two objects were of the same shape regardless of their respective orientations. Such seeing is not immediate, however; the time to determine such sameness increases markedly with differences in presented orientation (Figure 8).

Although our visualizations of objects and their transformations may be schematic, they are nevertheless concrete in the sense that the objects are represented in a particular orientation and their transformations are represented over a particular path (Shepard & Cooper, 1982). What is internalized at the deepest and most abstract level is not any particular object or transformation (which are arbitrary with respect to orientation and path) but the set of constraints that in three-dimensional Euclidean space govern the possible projections and transformations of an object (Shepard, 1981b). Although we do more fully pick up the structure of an object when we are able to view it in different orientations, we still only visualize that structure fully from one viewpoint at a time; to visualize it in a different orientation requires additional time that increases with the difference in orientation. Moreover, different views can effectively be related to each other only if they fall within an appropriate integration time. An individual can pick up the layout of an environment and then visualize that environment as it would successively appear from the station points that are traversed as the individual walks about blindfolded. But, at any one moment, the representation is always from a particular station point and, in the absence of a further look, decays in about 8 s (Thomson, 1983).

Gibson's focus on the external loop led him to suggest that performance in a tachistoscopic experiment (in which brief exposure is used "to prevent the occurrence of exploratory eye movement" and, hence, to block "completion of . . . [the] external loop") is "a mere laboratory curiosity, unrepresentative of day-to-day activity" (J. Gibson, 1970, pp. 426–427). However, the most direct way to find out whether internal mechanisms, or internal loops, have incorporated external constraints is to block the external loop. Thus, by establishing an ecologically invalid environment in which the diurnal cycle of light and darkness was eliminated, animal behaviorists discovered that animals have internalized the invariant period of the earth's rotation. And by presenting ecologically invalid displays in which the physical motion between two positions of an object is deleted, we are beginning to discover that humans have internalized the invariant principles of kinematic geometry.

References

Ames, A. (1951). Visual perception and the rotating trapezoidal window. *Psychological Monographs, 65*(7, Whole No. 234).

Anderson, J. A., Silverstein, J. W., Ritz, S. A., & Jones, R. S. (1977). Distinctive features, categorical perception, and probability learning: Some applications of a neural model. *Psychological Review, 84*, 413–451.

Ashby, W. R. (1954). *Design for a brain.* New York: Wiley.

Attneave, F. (1974). Apparent movement and the what–where connection. *Psychologia, 17*, 108–120.

Attneave, F., & Arnoult, M. D. (1956). The quantitative study of shape and pattern perception. *Psychological Bulletin, 53*, 452–471.

Attneave, F., & Block, G. (1973). Apparent movement in tridimensional space. *Perception & Psychophysics, 13*, 301–307.

Austin, J. L. (1962). *Sense and sensibilia.* Oxford, England: Oxford University Press.

Ball, R. S. (1900). *A treatise on the theory of screws.* Cambridge, England: Cambridge University Press.

Balzano, G. J. (1980). The group-theoretic description of twelve-fold and microtonal pitch systems. *Computer Music Journal, 4*, 66–84.

Bialek, W. (1983). Thermal noise, quantum noise, and sensory thresholds. *Bulletin of the American Physical Society, 28*, 358.

Bisiach, E., & Luzzatti, C. (1978). Unilateral neglect of representational space. *Cortex, 14*, 129–133.

Braunstein, M. L. (1976). *Depth perception through motion.* New York: Academic Press.

Brown, J. F., & Voth, A. C. (1937). The path of seen movement as a function of the vector field. *American Journal of Psychology, 49*, 543–563.

Bruner, J. S. (1957). On perceptual readiness. *Psychological Review, 64*, 123–152.

Brunswik, E. (1956). *Perception and the representative design of psychological experiments* (2nd ed.). Berkeley: University of California Press.

Bundesen, C., Larsen, A., & Farrell, J. E. (1981). Mental transformations of size and orientation. In A. D.

Baddeley & J. B. Long (Eds.), *Attention and performance IX* (pp. 279–294). Hillsdale, NJ: Erlbaum.

Bundesen, C., Larsen, A., & Farrell, J. E. (1983). Visual apparent movement: Transformations of size and orientation. *Perception, 12,* 549–558.

Bünning, E. (1973). *The physiological clock.* New York: Springer.

Caelli, T., Hoffman, W. C., & Lindman, H. (1978). Subjective Lorentz transformations and the perception of motion. *Journal of the Optical Society of America, 68,* 402–411.

Carey, S. (1981). The development of face recognition. In G. Davies, H. Ellis, & J. Shepherd (Eds.), *Perceiving and remembering faces.* New York: Academic Press.

Cassirer, E. (1944). The concept of group and the theory of perception. *Philosophical and Phenomenological Research 5,* 1–35.

Changeux, J.-P. (1983). *L'homme neuronal* [Neuronal man]. Paris, France: Fayard.

Chase, W. G., & Simon, H. A. (1973). The mind's eye in chess. In W. G. Chase (Ed.), *Visual information processing* (pp. 215–281). New York: Academic Press.

Chasles, M. (1830). Note sur les propriétés générales du système de deux corps semblables entr'eux et placés d'une manière quelconque dans l'espace; et sur le déplacement fini ou infiniment petit d'un corps solide libre [A note on the general properties of a system of two similar bodies arbitrarily positioned in space; and on the finite or infinitely small displacement of an unconstrained solid body]. *Bulletin des Sciences Mathématiques,* Férussac, *14,* 321–326.

Chomsky, N. (1965). *Aspects of the theory of syntax.* Cambridge, MA: M.I.T. Press.

Cooper, L. A. (1975). Mental rotation of random two-dimensional shapes. *Cognitive Psychology, 7,* 20–43.

Cooper, L. A. (1976). Demonstration of a mental analog of an external rotation. *Perception & Psychophysics, 19,* 296–302.

Cooper, L. A., & Podgorny, P. (1976). Mental transformations and visual comparison processes: Effects of complexity and similarity. *Journal of Experimental Psychology: Human Perception and Performance, 2,* 503–514.

Cooper, L. A., & Shepard, R. N. (1978). Transformation on representations of objects in space. In E. C. Carterette & M. P. Friedman (Eds.), *Handbook of perception: Vol. VIII. Perceptual coding* (pp. 105–146). New York: Academic Press.

Corbin, H. H. (1942). The perception of grouping and apparent movement in visual depth. *Archives of Psychology, 38*[Series No. 273], 5–50.

Coxeter, H. S. M. (1961). *Introduction to geometry.* New York: Wiley.

Cutting, J. E. (1981). Six tenets for event perception. *Cognition, 10,* 71–78.

Cutting, J. E. (1982). Cross-ratio: An invariant of layout sometimes perceived, sometimes not. *Bulletin of the Psychonomics Society, 20,* 146 (Abstract).

Cutting, J. E., & Proffitt, D. R. (1982). The minimum principle and the perception of absolute, common, and relative motions. *Cognitive Psychology, 14,* 211–246.

Cutting, J. E., Proffitt, D. R., & Kozlowski, L. T. (1978). A biomechanical invariant for gait perception. *Journal of Experimental Psychology: Human Perception and Performance, 4,* 357–372.

Davies, P. C. W. (1977). *The physics of time asymmetry.* Berkeley: University of California Press.

de Groot, A. (1965). *Thought and choice in chess.* The Hague, Netherlands: Mouton.

Dement, W. C. (1965). An essay on dreams: The role of physiology in understanding their nature. In *New directions in psychology II* (pp. 135–257). New York: Holt, Rinehart & Winston.

Dunker, K. (1937). Induced motion. In W. D. Ellis (Ed.), *A source-book of Gestalt psychology.* London: Routledge & Kegan Paul. (Original work published 1929 in German)

Dunker, K. (1945). On problem-solving. *Psychological Monographs, 58*(5, Whole No. 270).

Exner, S. (1875). Über das Sehen von Bewegungen und die Theorie des zusammengesetzen Auges [On the perception of movements and the theory of the integrative eye]. *Sitzungsberichte Akademie Wissenschaft Wien, 72,* 156–190.

Farrell, J. E. (1983). Visual transformations underlying apparent movement. *Perception & Psychophysics, 33,* 85–92.

Farrell, J. E., Larsen, A., & Bundesen, C. (1982). Velocity constraints on apparent rotational movement. *Perception, 11,* 541–546.

Farrell, J. E., & Shepard, R. N. (1981). Shape, orientation, and apparent rotational motion. *Journal of Experimental Psychology: Human Perception and Performance, 7,* 477–486.

Finke, R. A. (1980). Levels of equivalence in imagery and perception. *Psychological Review, 87,* 113–132.

Finke, R. A., & Shepard, R. N. (in press). Visual functions of mental imagery. In L. Kaufman & J. Thomas (Eds.), *Handbook of perception and human performance.* New York: Wiley.

Ford, J. (1983, April). How random is a coin toss? *Physics Today, 36,* 40–47.

Foster, D. H. (1972). A method for the investigation of those transformations under which the visual recognition of a given object is invariant: I. The theory. *Kybernetik, 11,* 217–222.

Foster, D. H. (1975). Visual apparent motion and some preferred paths in the rotation group SO(3). *Biological Cybernetics, 18,* 81–89.

Foster, D. H. (1978). Visual apparent motion and the calculus of variation. In E. L. J. Leeuwenberg & H. F. J. M. Buffart (Eds.), *Formal theories of visual perception* (pp. 67–82). New York: Wiley.

Foster, D. H., & Gravano, S. (1982). Overshoot of curvature in visual apparent motion. *Perception & Psychophysics, 5,* 411–420.

Freeman, W. J. (1975). *Mass action in the nervous system.* New York: Academic Press.

Freud, S. (1931). *The interpretation of dreams* (A. A. Brill, Trans.). New York: Carlton House. (Original work published 1900 in German)

Freyd, J. J. (1983a). *Dynamic mental representations and apparent accelerated motion.* Unpublished doctoral dissertation, Stanford University.

Freyd, J. J. (1983b). Shareability: The social psychology of epistomology. *Cognitive Science, 7,* 191–210.

Freyd, J. J. (1983c). The mental representation of action. *The Behavioral and Brain Sciences, 6,* 145–146.

Freyd, J. J. (1983d). The mental representation of movement when static stimuli are viewed. *Perception & Psychophysics, 33,* 575–581.

Freyd, J. J. (1983e). Representing the dynamics of a static form. *Memory & Cognition, 4,* 342–346.

Freyd, J. J., & Finke, R. A. (1984). Representational momentum. *Journal of Experimental Psychology: Learning, Memory, and Cognition, 10,* 126–132.

Gazzaniga, M. (1970). *The bisected brain.* New York: Appleton-Century-Crofts.

Gibson, E. J. (1969). *Principles of perceptual learning and development.* New York: Appleton-Century-Crofts.

Gibson, E. J. (1982). The concept of affordances in development: The renascence of functionalism. In W. A. Collins (Ed.), *The concept of development* (pp. 55–81). Hillsdale, NJ: Erlbaum.

Gibson, E. J., Owsley, C. J., & Johnston, J. (1978). Perception of invariants by five-month-old infants: Differentiation of two types of motion. *Developmental Psychology, 14,* 407–415.

Gibson, E. J., & Spelke, E. S. (1983). The development of perception. In J. H. Flavell & E. M. Markman (Eds.), *Handbook of child psychology: Vol. 3. Cognitive development* (pp. 1–76). New York: Wiley.

Gibson, J. J. (1950). *The perception of the visual world.* Boston, MA: Houghton-Mifflin.

Gibson, J. J. (1961). Ecological optics. *Vision Research, 1,* 253–262.

Gibson, J. J. (1966). *The senses considered as perceptual systems.* Boston, MA: Houghton Mifflin.

Gibson, J. J. (1970). On the relation between hallucination and perception. *Leonardo, 3,* 425–427.

Gibson, J. J. (1971). The information available in pictures. *Leonardo, 4,* 27–35.

Gibson, J. J. (1972). Outline of a theory of direct visual perception. In J. R. Royce & W. W. Rozeboom (Eds.), *The psychology of knowing.* New York: Gordon & Breach.

Gibson, J. J. (1974). Visualizing conceived as visual apprehending without any particular point of observation. *Leonardo, 7,* 41–42.

Gibson, J. J. (1977). The theory of affordances. In R. E. Shaw & J. Bransford (Eds.), *Perceiving, acting, and knowing.* Hillsdale, NJ: Erlbaum.

Gibson, J. J. (1979). *The ecological approach to visual perception.* Boston, MA: Houghton Mifflin.

Gibson, J. J., & Gibson, E. J. (1955). Perceptual learning: Differentiation or enrichment? *Psychological Review, 62,* 32–41.

Glass, L. (1969). Moiré effect from random dots. *Nature, 223,* 578–580.

Green, B. F., Jr. (1961). Figure coherence in the kinetic depth effect. *Journal of Experimental Psychology, 62,* 272–282.

Greene, P. H. (1962a). On looking for neural networks and 'cell assemblies' that underlie behavior: I. A mathematical model. *The Bulletin of Mathematical Biophysics, 24,* 247–275.

Greene, P. H. (1962b). On looking for neural networks and 'cell assemblies' that underlie behavior: II. Neural realization of the mathematical model. *The Bulletin of Mathematical Biophysics, 24,* 395–411.

Greenwood, G. D. (1965). *Principles of dynamics.* Englewood Cliffs, NJ: Prentice-Hall.

Gross, C. G., Rocha-Miranda, C. E., & Bender, D. B. (1972). Visual properties of neurons in inferotemporal cortex of the macaque. *Journal of Neurophysiology, 35,* 96–111.

Grossberg, S. (1980). How does the brain build a cognitive code? *Psychological Review, 87,* 1–51.

Hadamard, J. (1945). *The psychology of invention in the mathematical field.* Princeton, NJ: Princeton University Press.

Harré, R. (1983). *Great scientific experiments: Twenty experiments that changed our view of the world.* Oxford, England: Oxford University Press.

Hay, J. (1966). Optical motions and space perception: An extension of Gibson's analysis. *Psychological Review, 73,* 550–565.

Hebb, D. O. (1949). *The organization of behavior.* New York: Wiley.

Helmholtz, H. von. (1894). Uber den Ursprung der richtigen Deutung unserer Sinneseindrucke [On the origin of correct interpretation of our sensory impressions]. *Zeitschrift für Psychologie und Physiologie der Sinnesorgane, 7,* 81–96.

Helmholtz, H. von. (1962). *Treatise on physiological optics* (Vol. 3, p. 495). In J. P. Southall, Ed. & Trans. New York: Dover. (Original work published 1856 in German)

Hering, E. (1964). *Outlines of a theory of the light sense* (L. M. Hurvich & D. Jameson, Trans.). Cambridge, MA: Harvard University Press. (Original work published 1878 in German)

Herschel, Sir J. F. W. (1867). *Familiar lectures on scientific subjects.* London: Strahan.

Hertz, H. (1956). *The principles of mechanics* (D. E. Jones & J. T. Walley, Trans.). New York: Dover. (Original work published 1894 in German)

Hess, E. H. (1959). Imprinting. *Science, 130,* 133–141.

Hochberg, J. (1981). On cognition in perception: Perceptual coupling and unconscious inference. *Cognition, 10,* 127–134.

Hochberg, J. (1982). How big is a stimulus? In J. Beck (Ed.), *Organization and representation in perception* (pp. 191–217). Hillsdale, NJ: Erlbaum.

Hochberg, J., & Brooks, V. (1974). The integration of successive cinematic views of simple scenes. *Bulletin of the Psychonomic Society, 4,* 263.

Hochberg, J., & Galper, R. E. (1967). Recognition of faces: I. An exploratory study. *Psychonomic Science, 9,* 619–620.

Holton, G. (1972). On trying to understand scientific genius. *American Scholar, 41,* 95–110.

Hubel, D. H., & Wiesel, T. N. (1965). Receptive fields and functional architecture in two nonstriate visual areas (18 and 19) of the cat. *Journal of Neurophysiology, 28,* 229–289.

Hunt, K. H. (1978). *Kinematic geometry of mechanisms.* Oxford, England: Oxford University Press.

James, W. (1950). *The principles of psychology* (Vol. 2). New York: Dover. (Original work published 1890)

Jeffress, L. A. (1962). Absolute pitch. *Journal of the Acoustical Society of America, 34,* 1386–1395.

Johansson, G. (1950). *Configuration in event perception.* Uppsala, Sweden: Almqvist & Wiksell.

Johansson, G. (1973). Visual perception of biological motion and a model for its analysis. *Perception & Psychophysics, 14,* 201–211.

Johansson, G. (1975). Visual motion perception. *Scientific American, 232*(6), 76–89.

Johansson, G., von Hofsten, C., & Jansson, G. (1980). Event perception. *Annual Review of Psychology, 31,* 27–63.

Jones, M. R. (1976). Time, our lost dimension: Toward a new theory of perception, attention, and memory. *Psychological Review, 83,* 323–355.

Kant, I. (1961). *Critique of pure reason* (F. M. Müller, Trans.). Garden City, NY: Doubleday. (Original work published 1781 in German)

Keil, F. C. (1981). Constraints on knowledge and cognitive development. *Psychological Review, 88,* 197–227.

Kirman, J. H. (1983). Tactile apparent movement: The effects of shape and type of motion. *Perception & Psychophysics, 34,* 96–102.

Kolers, P. A. (1972). *Aspects of motion perception.* Oxford, England: Pergamon Press.

Kolers, P. A., & Pomerantz, J. R. (1971). Figural change in apparent motion. *Journal of Experimental Psychology, 87,* 99–108.

Konorski, J. (1967). *Integrative activity of the brain.* Chicago, IL: University of Chicago Press.

Korte, A. (1915). Kinematoskopische Untersuchungen [Cinematoscopic investigations]. *Zeitschrift für Psychologie, 72,* 193–296.

Kosslyn, S. M. (1980). *Image and mind.* Cambridge, MA.: Harvard University Press.

Kozlowski, L. T., & Cutting, J. E. (1977). Recognizing the sex of a walker from a dynamic point–light display. *Perception & Psychophysics, 21,* 575–580.

Krechevsky, I. (1932). "Hypotheses" in rats. *Psychological Reveiw, 39,* 516–533.

Kubovy, M. (1983). Mental imagery majestically transforming cognitive psychology [Review of *Mental images and their transformations*]. *Contemporary Psychology, 28,* 661–663.

Külpe, O. (1920). *Vorlesungen über Psychologie* [Lectures on psychology]. Leipzig, E. Germany: Hirzel.

Lashley, K. S. (1942). The problem of cerebral organization in vision. In H. Klüver (Ed.), *Biological Symposia, VII* (pp. 301–322). Lancaster, PA: Jaques Cattell Press.

Lee, D. N. (1974). Visual information during locomotion. In R. B. MacLeod & H. L. Pick (Eds.), *Perception: Essays in honor of James J. Gibson.* Ithaca, NY: Cornell University Press.

Leibniz, G. W. (1898). *Monadology and other philosophical essays* (R. Latta, Trans.). Oxford, England: Oxford University Press. (Original work written 1714, published 1840 in French)

Lettvin, J. Y., Maturana, H. R., McCulloch, W. S., & Pitts, W. H. (1959). What the frog's eye tells the frog's brain. *Proceedings of the Institute of Radio Engineers, 47,* 1940–1951.

Lorenz, K. (1935). Der Kumpan in der Umvelt des Vogels. Der Artgenosse als auslösendes Moment sozialer Verhaltungsweisen [Buddies in the world of birds. Species-mates as releasers of social behavior-patterns]. *Journal of Ornithology, 83,* 137–213.

Mach, E. (1959). *The analysis of sensations* (S. Waterlow, Trans.). New York: Dover. [From the 5th German edition, 1886.]

Marr, D. (1982). *Vision.* San Francisco: Freeman.

McAdams, S., & Bregman, A. (1979). Hearing musical streams. *Computer Music Journal, 3,* 26–43.

Metzger, W. (1953). *Gesetze des Sehens* [Laws of perception]. Frankfurt-am-Main, W. Germany: Waldermar Kramer.

Metzler, J., & Shepard, R. N. (1974). Transformational studies of the internal representation of three-dimensional objects. In R. Solso (Ed.), *Theories of cognitive psychology: The Loyola Symposium* (pp. 147–201). Potomac, MD: Erlbaum.

Michaels, C. F., & Carello, C. (1981). *Direct perception.* Englewood Cliffs, NJ: Prentice-Hall.

Mori, T. (1982). Apparent motion path composed of a serial concatenation of translations and rotations. *Biological Cybernetics, 44,* 31–34.

Müller, J. (1842). *Elements of physiology: Vol. 2* (W. Baly, Trans.). London: Taylor. (Original work published 1838 in German)

Navon, D. (1976). Irrelevance of figural identity for resolving ambiguities in apparent motion. *Journal of Experimental Psychology: Human Perception and Performance, 2,* 130–138.

Neisser, U. (1967). *Cognitive psychology.* New York: Appleton-Century-Crofts.

Neisser, U. (1976). *Cognition and reality.* San Francisco: W. H. Freeman.

Neisser, U. (1977). Gibson's ecological optics: Consequences of a different stimulus description. *Journal for the Theory of Social Behavior, 7,* 17–28.

Noll, A. M. (1965). Computer-generated three-dimensional movies. *Computers & Automation, 14,* 20–23.

Ogasawara, J. (1936). Effect of apparent separation on apparent movement. *Japanese Journal of Psychology, 11,* 109–122.

Orlansky, J. (1940). The effect of similarity and difference in form on apparent visual movement. *Archives of Psychology, 246,* 85.

Penfield, W. (1958). *The excitable cortex in conscious man.* Liverpool, England: Liverpool University Press.

Pittenger, J. B., & Shaw, R. E. (1975). Aging faces as viscal–elastic events: Implications for a theory of nonrigid shape perception. *Journal of Experimental Psychology: Human Perception and Performance, 1,* 374–382.

Place, U. T. (1956). Is consciousness a brain process? *British Journal of Psychology, 47,* 44–50.

Podgorny, P., & Shepard, R. N. (1978). Functional representations common to visual perception and imagination. *Journal of Experimental Psychology: Human Perception and Performance, 4,* 21–35.

Podgorny, P., & Shepard, R. N. (1983). The distribution of visual attention over space. *Journal of Experimental Psychology: Human Perception and Performance, 9,* 380–393.

Pomerantz, J. R., & Kubovy, M. (1981). Perceptual organization: An overview. In M. Kubovy & J. R. Pomerantz (Eds.), *Perceptual organization* (pp. 423–456). Hillsdale, NJ: Erlbaum.

Posner, M. I. (1969). Abstraction and the process of recognition. In G. H. Bower & J. T. Spence (Eds.),

The psychology of learning and motivation (Vol. 3, pp. 44–96). New York: Academic Press.

Price, H. H. (1946). Thinking and representation. *Proceedings of the British Academy, 32,* 83–122.

Proffitt, D. R., & Cutting, J. E. (1979). Perceiving the centroid of configurations on a rolling wheel. *Perception & Psychophysics, 25,* 389–398.

Ramachandran, V. S., & Anstis, S. M. (1983). Extrapolation of motion path in human visual perception. *Vision Research, 23,* 83–85.

Rashevsky, N. (1948). *Mathematical biophysics.* Chicago, IL: University of Chicago Press.

Ratliff, F. (1983, September). [Acceptance speech on receiving the Pisart Vision Award]. Presented at The Light House, The New York Association for the Blind. (Available from F. Ratliff, Rockefeller University, 1230 York Avenue, New York, NY 10021)

Restle, F. (1979). Coding theory of the perception of motion. *Psychological Review, 86,* 1–24.

Richards, I. A. (1950). *The portable Coleridge.* New York: Viking Press.

Robins, C., & Shepard, R. N. (1977). Spatio-temporal probing of apparent rotational movement. *Perception & Psychophysics, 22,* 12–18.

Rosenfeld, A. (1982). Relaxation processes for perceptual disambiguation in computer vision. In J. Beck (Ed.), *Organization and representation in perception* (pp. 145–150). Hillsdale, NJ: Erlbaum.

Runeson, S. (1977). On the possibility of "smart" perceptual mechanisms. *Scandinavian Journal of Psychology, 18,* 172–179.

Rusak, B., & Zucker, I. (1975). Biological rhythms and animal behavior. *Annual Review of Psychology, 26,* 137–171.

Sedgwick, H. (1980). The geometry of spatial layout in pictorial representation. In M. Hagen (Ed.), *The perception of pictures: Vol. 1.* New York: Academic Press.

Selfridge, O. G. (1959). Pandemonium: A paradigm for learning. In D. V. Blake & A. M. Uttley (Eds.), *The mechanisation of thought processes* (pp. 511–529). London: H. M. Stationery Office.

Shaw, R. E., & Pittenger, J. (1977). Perceiving the face of change in changing faces: Implications for a theory of object perception. In R. E. Shaw & J. Bransford (Eds.), *Perceiving, acting, and knowing.* Hillsdale, NJ: Erlbaum.

Shepard, R. N. (1964). Circularity in judgments of relative pitch. *Journal of the Acoustical Society of America, 36,* 2346–2353.

Shepard, R. N. (1975). Form, formation, and transformation of internal representations. In R. Solso (Ed.), *Information processing and cognition: The Loyola Symposium.* Hillsdale, NJ: Erlbaum.

Shepard, R. N. (1978a). The circumplex and related topological manifolds in the study of perception. In S. Shye (Ed.), *Theory construction and data analysis in the behavioral sciences* (pp. 29–80). San Francisco: Jossey-Bass.

Shepard, R. N. (1978b). Externalization of mental images and the act of creation. In B. S. Randhawa & W. E. Coffman (Eds.), *Visual learning, thinking, and communication* (pp. 139–189). New York: Academic Press.

Shepard, R. N. (1978c). The mental image. *The American Psychologist, 33,* 125–137.

Shepard, R. N. (1981a). Psychological relations and psychophysical scales: On the status of "direct" psychophysical measurement. *Journal of Mathematical Psychology, 24,* 21–57.

Shepard, R. N. (1981b). Psychophysical complementarity. In M. Kubovy & J. R. Pomerantz (Eds.), *Perceptual organization* (pp. 279–341). Hillsdale, NJ: Erlbaum.

Shepard, R. N. (1982a). Geometrical approximations to the structure of musical pitch. *Psychological Review, 89,* 305–333.

Shepard, R. N. (1982b). Perceptual and analogical bases of cognition. In J. Mehler, M. Garrett, & E. Walker (Eds.), *Perspectives in mental representation* (pp. 49–67). Hillsdale, NJ: Erlbaum.

Shepard, R. N. (1983). Demonstrations of circular components of pitch. *Journal of the Audio Engineering Society, 31,* 641–649.

Shepard, R. N., & Chipman, S. (1970). Second-order isomorphism of internal representations: Shapes of states. *Cognitive Psychology, 1,* 1–17.

Shepard, R. N., & Cooper, L. A. (1982). *Mental images and their transformations.* Cambridge, MA: MIT Press/Bradford Books.

Shepard, R. N., & Judd, S. A. (1976). Perceptual illusion of rotation of three-dimensional objects. *Science, 191,* 952–954.

Shepard, R. N., & Metzler, J. (1971). Mental rotation of three-dimensional objects. *Science, 171,* 701–703.

Shepard, R. N., & Podgorny, P. (1978). Cognitive processes that resemble perceptual processes. In W. K. Estes (Ed.), *Handbook of learning and cognitive processes, V.* Hillsdale, NJ: Erlbaum.

Shepard, R. N., & Zare, S. (1983). Path-guided apparent motion. *Science, 220,* 632–634.

Smart, J. J. C. (1959). Sensations and brain processes. *Philosophical Review, 68,* 141–156.

Spelke, E. S. (1982). Perceptual knowledge of objects in infancy. In J. Mehler, E. C. T. Walker, & M. Garrett (Eds.), *Perspectives on mental representation.* (pp. 409–430). Hillsdale, NJ: Erlbaum.

Sperry, R. W. (1968). Hemisphere deconnection and unity in conscious awareness. *The American Psychologist, 23,* 723–733.

Squires, P. C. (1959). Topological aspects of apparent visual motion. *Psychologie Forschung, 26,* 1–12.

Thom, R. (1975). Structural stability and morphogenesis (D. H. Fowler, Trans.). Reading, MA: W. A. Benjamin. (Original work published 1972 in French)

Thomson, J. A. (1983). Is continuous visual monitoring necessary in visually guided locomotion? *Journal of Experimental Psychology: Human Perception and Performance, 9,* 427–443.

Ullman, S. (1979). *The interpretation of visual motion.* Cambridge, MA.: MIT Press.

Ullman, S. (1980). Against direct perception. *The Behavioral and Brain Sciences, 3,* 373–415.

van Noorden, L. P. A. S. (1975). *Temporal coherence in the perception of tone sequences.* Unpublished doctoral dissertation, Technishe Hogeschool, Eindhoven, Holland.

Wallach, H. (1965). Visual perception of motion. In G. Kepes (Ed.), *The nature and the art of motion* (pp. 52–59). New York: George Braziller. [Revised in Wallach, H. (1976). *On perception.* New York: Quadrangle/ New York Times.]

Wallach, H., & O'Connell, D. N. (1953). The kinetic depth effect. *Journal of Experimental Psychology, 45,* 205–217.

Waltz, D. (1975). Understanding line drawings of scenes with shadows. In P. H. Winston (Ed.), *The psychology of computer vision* (pp. 19–91). New York: McGraw-Hill.

Warren, R. M., & Warren, R. P. (1968). *Helmholtz on perception: Its physiology and development.* New York: Wiley.

Warren, W. H. (1977). Visual information for object identity in apparent movement. *Perception & Psychophysics, 22,* 264–268.

Wertheimer, M. (1912). Experimentalle Studien uber das Sehen von Bewegung [Experimental studies of motion perception]. *Zeitschrift für Psychologie, 61,* 161–265. [Translated in part in T. Shipley (Ed.). (1961). *Classics in psychology.* New York: Philosophical Library.]

West, L. J. (Ed.): (1962): *Hallucinations.* New York: Grune & Statton.

Woodworth, R. S. (1915). A revision of imageless thought. *Psychological Review, 22,* 1–27.

Yin, R. K. (1969). Looking at upside-down faces. *Journal of Experimental Psychology, 81,* 141–145.

Zihl, J., von Cramon, D., & Mai, N. (1983). Selective disturbance of movement vision after bilateral brain damage. *Brain, 106,* 313–340.

Received December 14, 1983
Revision received March 22, 1984 ∎

Instructions to Authors

Authors should prepare manuscripts according to the *Publication Manual of the American Psychological Association* (3rd ed.). All manuscripts must include an abstract of 75–100 words typed on a separate sheet of paper. Typing instructions (all copy must be double-spaced) and instructions on preparing tables, figures, references, metrics, and abstracts appear in the *Manual*. Also, all manuscripts are subject to editing for sexist language.

APA policy prohibits an author from submitting the same manuscript for concurrent consideration by two or more journals. APA policy also prohibits duplicate publication, that is, publication of a manuscript that has already been published in whole or in substantial part in another journal. Also, authors of manuscripts submitted to APA journals are expected to have available their raw data throughout the editorial review process and for at least 5 years after the date of publication.

Blind reviews are optional, and authors who wish blind reviews must specifically request them when submitting their manuscripts. Each copy of a manuscript to be blind reviewed should include a separate title page with authors' names and affiliations, and these should not appear anywhere else on the manuscript. Footnotes that identify the authors should be typed on a separate page. Authors should make every effort to see that the manuscript itself contains no clues to their identities.

Manuscripts should be submitted in quadruplicate (the original and three photocopies), and all copies should be clear, readable, and on paper of good quality. Authors should keep a copy of the manuscript to guard against loss. Mail manuscripts to the Editor, Martin L. Hoffman, *Psychological Review,* Department of Psychology, University of Michigan, 3433 Mason Hall, Ann Arbor, Michigan 48109, according to the instructions provided above.

[20]

Neural dynamics of perceptual grouping: Textures, boundaries, and emergent segmentations

STEPHEN GROSSBERG and ENNIO MINGOLLA

Boston University, Boston, Massachusetts

A real-time visual processing theory is used to analyze and explain a wide variety of perceptual grouping and segmentation phenomena, including the grouping of textured images, randomly defined images, and images built up from periodic scenic elements. The theory explains how "local" feature processing and "emergent" features work together to segment a scene, how segmentations may arise across image regions that do not contain any luminance differences, how segmentations may override local image properties in favor of global statistical factors, and why segmentations that powerfully influence object recognition may be barely visible or totally invisible. Network interactions within a Boundary Contour (BC) System, a Feature Contour (FC) System, and an Object Recognition (OR) System are used to explain these phenomena. The BC System is defined by a hierarchy of orientationally tuned interactions, which can be divided into two successive subsystems called the OC filter and the CC loop. The OC filter contains two successive stages of oriented receptive fields which are sensitive to different properties of image contrasts. The OC filter generates inputs to the CC loop, which contains successive stages of spatially short-range competitive interactions and spatially long-range cooperative interactions. Feedback between the competitive and cooperative stages synthesizes a global context-sensitive segmentation from among the many possible groupings of local featural elements. The properties of the BC System provide a unified explanation of several ostensibly different Gestalt rules. The BC System also suggests explanations and predictions concerning the architecture of the striate and prestriate visual cortices. The BC System embodies new ideas concerning the foundations of geometry, on-line statistical decision theory, and the resolution of uncertainty in quantum measurement systems. Computer simulations establish the formal competence of the BC System as a perceptual grouping system. The properties of the BC System are compared with probabilistic and artificial intelligence models of segmentation. The total network suggests a new approach to the design of computer vision systems, and promises to provide a universal set of rules for perceptual grouping of scenic edges, textures, and smoothly shaded regions.

1. Introduction: Toward a Universal Set of Rules for Perceptual Grouping

The visual system segments optical input into regions that are separated by perceived contours or boundaries. This rapid, seemingly automatic, early step in visual processing is difficult to characterize, largely because many perceived contours have no obvious correlates in the optical input. A contour in a pattern of luminances is generally defined as a spatial discontinuity in luminance. Although usually sufficient, however, such discontinuities are by no means necessary for sustaining perceived contours. Regions separated by visual contours also oc-

S. Grossberg was supported in part by the Air Force Office of Scientific Research (AFOSR 85-0149) and the Army Research Office (DAAG-29-85-K-0095). E. Mingolla was supported in part by the Air Force Office of Scientific Research (AFOSR 85-0149). We wish to thank Cynthia Suchta for her valuable assistance in the preparation of the manuscript and illustrations.

The authors' mailing address is: Center for Adaptive Systems, Department of Mathematics, Boston University, Boston, MA 02215.

cur in the presence of: statistical differences in textural qualities such as orientation, shape, density, or color (Beck, 1966a, 1966b, 1972, 1982, 1983; Beck, Prazdny, & Rosenfeld, 1983), binocular matching of elements of differing disparities (Julesz, 1960), accretion and deletion of texture elements in moving displays (Kaplan, 1969), and classical "subjective contours" (Kanizsa, 1955). The extent to which the types of perceived contours just named involve the same visual processes as those triggered by luminance contours is not obvious, although the former are certainly as perceptually real and generally as vivid as the latter.

Perceptual contours arising at boundaries of regions with differing statistical distributions of featural qualities have been studied in great detail (Beck, 1966a, 1966b, 1972, 1982, 1983; Beck et al., 1983; Caelli, 1982, 1983; Caelli & Julesz, 1979). Two findings of this research are especially salient. First, the visual system's segmentation of the scenic input occurs rapidly throughout all regions of that input, in a manner often described as "preattentive." That is, subjects generally describe boundaries in a consistent manner when exposure times are short (under 200 msec) and without prior knowledge of the regions in a display at which boundaries are likely to occur. Thus, any theoretical account of boundary extraction for such displays must cxlain how early "data driven" processes rapidly converge on boundaries wherever they occur.

The second finding of the experimental work on textures complicates the implications of the first, however: the textural segmentation process is exquisitely context-sensitive. That is, a given texture element at a given location can be part of a variety of larger groupings, depending on what surrounds it. Indeed, the precise determination even of what acts as an element at a given location can depend on patterns at nearby locations.

One of the greatest sources of difficulty in understanding visual perception and in designing fast object recognition systems is such context sensitivity of perceptual units. Since the work of the Gestaltists (Wertheimer, 1923), it has been widely recognized that local features of a scene, such as edge positions, disparities, lengths, orientations, and contrasts, are perceptually ambiguous, but that combinations of these features can be quickly grouped by a perceiver to generate a clear separation between figures and between figure and ground. Indeed, a figure within a textured scene often seems to "pop out" from the ground (Neisser, 1967). The "emergent" features by which an observer perceptually groups the "local" features within a scene are sensitive to the global structuring of textural elements within the scene.

The fact that these emergent perceptual units, rather than local features, are used to group a scene carries with it the possibility of scientific chaos. If every scene can define its own context-sensitive units, then perhaps object perception can only be described in terms of an unwieldy taxonomy of scenes and their unique perceptual units. One of the great accomplishments of the Gestaltists was to suggest a short list of rules for perceptual grouping that helped to organize many interesting examples. As is often the case in pioneering work, the rules were neither always obeyed nor exhaustive. No justification for the rules was given other than their evident plausibility. More seriously for practical applications, no effective computational algorithms were given to instantiate the rules.

Many workers since the Gestaltists have made important progress in advancing our understanding of perceptual grouping processes. For example, Dev (1975), Julesz (1971), and Sperling (1970) introduced algorithms for using disparity cues to coherently separate figure from ground in random-dot stereograms. Later workers, such as Marr and Poggio (1976), have studied similar algorithms. Caelli (1982, 1983) has emphasized the importance of the conjoint action of orientation and spatial frequency tuning in the filtering operations that preprocess textured images. Caelli and Dodwell (1982), Dodwell (1983), and Hoffman (1970) have recommended the use of Lie group vector fields as a tool for grouping together

orientational cues across perceptual space. Caelli and Julesz (1979) have presented evidence that "first order statistics of textons" are used to group textural elements. The term "textons" designates the features that are to be statistically grouped. This view supports a large body of work by Beck and his colleagues (Beck, 1966a, 1966b, 1972, 1982, 1983; Beck et al., 1983), who have introduced a remarkable collection of ingenious textural displays which they have used to determine some of the factors that control textural grouping properties.

The collective effect of these and other contributions has been to provide a sophisticated experimental literature about textural grouping which has identified the main properties that need to be considered. What has not been achieved is a deep analysis of the design principles and mechanisms that lie behind the properties of perceptual grouping. Expressed in another way, what is missing is the raison d'etre for textural grouping and a computational framework that dynamically explains how textural elements are grouped, in real time, into easily separated figures and ground.

One manifestation of this gap in contemporary understanding can be found in the image-processing models that have been developed by workers in artificial intelligence. In this approach, curves are analyzed using models different from those that are used to analyze textures, and textures are analyzed using models different from the ones used to analyze surfaces (Horn, 1977; Marr & Hildreth, 1980). All of these models are built up using geometrical ideas—such as surface normal, curvature, and Laplacian—that were used to study visual perception during the 19th century (Ratliff, 1965). These geometrical ideas were originally developed to analyze *local* properties of physical processes. By contrast, the visual system's context-sensitive mechanisms routinely synthesize figural percepts that are not reducible to local luminance differences within a scenic image. Such emergent properties are not just the effect of local geometrical transformations.

Our recent work suggests that 19th century geometrical ideas are fundamentally inadequate to characterize the designs that make biological visual systems so efficient (Carpenter & Grossberg, 1981, 1983; Cohen & Grossberg, 1984a, 1984b; Grossberg, 1983a, 1983b, 1984a, 1985; Grossberg & Mingolla, 1985a, 1985b). This claim arises from the discovery of new mechanisms that are not designed to compute local geometrical properties of a scenic image. These mechanisms are defined by parallel and hierarchical interactions within very large networks of interacting neurons. The visual properties that these equations compute emerge from network interactions, rather than from local transformations.

A surprising consequence of our analysis is that the same mechanisms that are needed to achieve a biologically relevant understanding of how scenic edges are internally represented also respond intelligently to textured images, smoothly shaded images, and combinations thereof. These new designs thus promise to provide a *universal* set of rules for the preattentive perceptual grouping processes that feed into depthful form percept and object recognition processes.

The complete development of these designs will require a major scientific effort. The present article takes two steps in that direction. The first goal of the article is to indicate how these new designs render transparent properties of perceptual grouping which previously were effectively manipulated by a small number of scientists, notably Jacob Beck. A primary goal of this article is thus to provide a dynamic explanation of recent textural displays from the Beck school. Beck and his colleageus have gone far in determining which aspects of textures tend to group and under what conditions. Our work sheds light on how such segmentation may be implemented by the visual system. The results of Glass and Switkes (1976) on grouping of statistically defined percepts and of Gergory and Heard (1979) on border locking during the café wall illusion will also be analyzed using the same ideas. The second goal of the article is to report computer simulations that illustrate the theory's formal competence for generating perceptual groupings that strikingly resemble human grouping properties.

Our theory first introduced the distinction between the Boundary Contour System (BC System) and the Feature Contour System (FC System) to deal with paradoxical data concerning brightness, color, and form perception. These two systems extract two different types of contour-sensitive information—called BC signals and FC signals—at an early processing stage. The BC signals are transformed through successive processing stages within the BC System into coherent boundary structures. These boundary structures give rise to topographically organized output signals to the FC System (Figure 1). FC signals are sensitive to luminance and hue differences within a scenic image. These signals activate the same processing stage within the FC System that receives boundary signals from the BC System. The FC signals here initiate the filling-in processes whereby brightnesses and colors spread until they either hit their first boundary contour or are attenuated by their spatial spread.

Although earlier work examined the role of the BC System in the synthesis of individual contours, whether "real" or "illusory," its rules also account for much of the segmentation of textured scenes into grouped regions separated by perceived contours. Accordingly, Sections 2-9 of this paper review the main points of the theory with respect to their implications for perceptual grouping. Sections 10-15 and 17-19 then examine in detail the major issues in grouping research to date and describe our solutions qualitatively. Section 16 presents computer simulations showing how our model synthesizes context-sensitive perceptual groupings. The model is described in more mechanistic detail in Section 20. Mathematical equations of the model are contained in the Appendix.

2. The Role of Illusory Contours

One of the main themes in our discussion is the role of illusory contours in perceptual grouping processes. Our

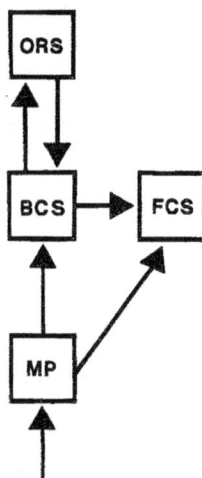

Figure 1. A macrocircuit of processing stages: Monocular preprocessed signals (MP) are sent independently to both the Boundary Contour System (BCS) and the Feature Contour System (FCS). The BCS preattentively generates coherent boundary structures from these MP signals. These structures send outputs to both the FCS and the Object Recognition System (ORS). The ORS, in turn, rapidly sends top-down learned template signals to the BCS. These template signals can modify the preattentively completed boundary structures using learned information. The BCS passes these modifications along to the FCS. The signals from the BCS organize the FCS into perceptual regions wherein filling-in of visible brightnesses and colors can occur. This filling-in process is activated by signals from the MP stage.

results make precise the sense in which percepts of "illusory contours"—or contour percepts that do not correspond to one-dimensional luminance differences in a scenic image—and percepts of "real contours" are both synthesized by the same mechanisms. This discussion clarifies why, despite the visual system's manifestly adaptive design, illusory contours are so abundant in visual percepts. We also suggest how illusory contours that are at best marginally visible can have powerful effects on perceptual grouping and object recognition processes.

Some of the new designs of our theory can be motivated by contrasting the noisy visual signals that reach the retina with the coherence of conscious visual percepts. In humans, for example, light passes through a thicket of retinal veins before it reaches retinal photoreceptors. The percepts of human observers are fortunately not distorted by their retinal veins during normal vision. This is due, in part, to the action of mechanisms that attenuate the perception of images that are stabilized with respect to the retina as the eye jiggles in its orbit with respect to the outside world. Suppressing the percept of the stabilized veins does not, in itself, complete the percept of retinal images that are occluded and segmented by the veins. Boundaries need to be completed and colors and brightnesses filled in to compensate for the image degradation

144   GROSSBERG AND MINGOLLA

that is caused by the retinal veins. A similar discussion follows from a consideration of why human observers do not typically notice their blind spots (Kawabata, 1984).

Observers are not able to distinguish which parts of such a completed percept are derived directly from retinal signals and which parts are due to boundary completion and featural filling-in. The completed and filled-in percepts are called, in the usual jargon, "illusory" figures. These examples suggest that both "real" and "illusory" figures are generated by the same perceptual mechanisms, and suggest why "illusory" figures are so important in perceptual grouping processes. Once this is understood, the need for a perceptual theory that treats "real" and "illusory" percepts on an equal footing also becomes apparent.

A central issue in such a theory concerns whether boundary completion and featural filling-in are the same or distinct processs. One of our theory's primary contributions is to show, by characterizing the different processing rules that they obey, that these processes are different.

At our present stage of understanding, many perceptual phenomena can be used to make this point. We find the following three phenomena to be particularly useful: the Land (1977) color and brightness experiments, the Yarbus (1967) stabilized-image experiments, and the reverse-contrast Kanizsa square (Grossberg & Mingolla, 1985a).

3. Discounting the Illuminant: Color Edges and Featural Filling-In

The visual world is typically viewed under inhomogeneous lighting conditions. The scenic luminances that reach the retina thus confound fluctuating lighting conditions with invariant object colors and lightnesses. Helmholtz (1890/1962) aleady knew that the brain somehow "discounts the illuminant" to generate color and lightness percepts that are more veridical than those in the retinal image. Land (1977) has clarified this process in a series of striking experiments wherein color percepts within a picture constructed from overlapping patches of colored paper are determined under a variety of lighting conditions. These experiments show that color signals corresponding to the interior of each patch are suppressed. The chromatic contrasts across the edges between adjacent patches are used to generate the final percept. It is easy to see how such a scheme "discounts the illuminant." Large differences in illumination can exist within any patch. On the other hand, differences in illumination are small across an edge on such a planar display. Hence, the relative chromatic contrasts across edges, assumed to be registered by black-white, red-green, and blue-yellow double opponent systems, are good estimates of the object reflectances near the edge.

Just as suppressing the percept of stabilized veins is insufficient to generate an adequate percept, so too is discounting the illuminant within each color patch. Without further processing, we could at best perceive a world of colored edges. Featural filling-in is needed to recover estimates of brightness and color within the interior of each

patch. Thus, extraction of color edges and featural filling-in are both necessary for the perception of a color field or a continuously shaded surface.

4. Featural Filling-In Over Stabilized Scenic Edges

Many images can be used to firmly establish that a featural filling-in process exists. The recent thesis of Todorović (1983) provides a nice set of examples that one can construct with modest computer graphics equipment. Vivid classical examples of featural filling-in were discovered by artificially stabilizing certain image contours of a scene (Krauskopf, 1963; Yarbus, 1967). Consider, for example, the image schematized in Figure 2. After the edges of the large circle and the vertical line are stabilized on the retina, the red color (dots) outside the large circle fills in the black and white hemidisks, except within the small red circles whose edges are not stabilized (Yarbus, 1967). The red inside the left circle looks brighter and the red inside the right circle looks darker than the uniform red that envelopes the remainder of the percept.

When the Land (1977) and Yarbus (1967) experiments are considered side by side, one can recognize that the brain extracts two different types of contour information from scenic images. Feature contours, including "color edges," give rise to the signals that generate visible brightness and color percepts at a later processing stage. Feature contours encode this information as a *contour-*

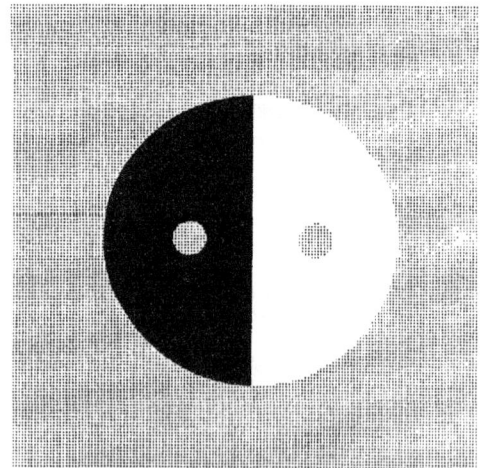

Figure 2. A classical example of featural filling-in: When the edges of the large circle and the vertical line are stabilized on the retina, the red color (dots) outside the large circle envelopes the black and white hemidisks except within the small red circles whose edges are not stabilized (Yarbus, 1967). The red inside the left circle looks brighter and the red inside the right circle looks darker than the enveloping red.

sensitive process in order to discount the illuminant. Boundary contours are extracted in order to define the perceptual boundaries, groupings, or forms within which featural estimates derived from the feature contours can fill in at a later processing stage. In the Yarbus (1967) experiments, once a stabilized scenic edge can no longer generate a boundary contour, featural signals can flow across the locations corresponding to the stabilized scenic edge until they reach the next boundary contour. The phenomenon of neon color spreading also illustrates the dissociation of boundary-contour and feature-contour processing (Ejima, Redies, Takahashi, & Akita, 1984; Redies & Spillmann, 1981; Redies, Spillmann, & Kunz, 1984; van Tuijl, 1975; van Tuijl & de Weert, 1979; van Tuijl & Leeuwenberg, 1979). An explanation of neon color spreading is suggested in Grossberg (1984a) and Grossberg and Mingolla (1985a).

5. Different Rules for Boundary Contours and Feature Contours

Some of the rules that distinguish the BC System from the FC System can be inferred from the percept generated by the reverse-contrast Kanizsa square image in Figure 3 (Cohen & Grossberg, 1984a; Grossberg & Mingolla, 1985a). Prazdny (1983, 1985) and Shapley and Gordon (1985) have also used reverse-contrast images in their discussions of form perception. Consider the vertical boundaries in the perceived Kanizsa square. In this percept, a vertical boundary connects a pair of vertical scenic edges with opposite direction of contrast. In other words, the black Pac-Man figure causes a dark-light vertical edge with respect to the gray background. The white Pac-Man figure causes a light-dark vertical edge with respect to the gray background. The process of boundary completion whereby a boundary contour is synthesized between these inducing stimuli is thus indifferent to direction of contrast. The boundary completion process is, however, sensitive to the orientation and amount of contrast of the inducing stimuli.

The feature contours extracted from a scene are, by contrast, exquisitely sensitive to direction of contrast. Were this not the case, we could never tell the difference between a dark-light and a light-dark percept. We would be blind.

Another difference between BC and FC rules can be inferred from Figures 2 and 3. In Figure 3, a boundary forms *inward* in an *oriented* way between a *pair* of inducing scenic edges. In Figure 2, featural filling-in is due to an *outward* and *unoriented* spreading of featural quality from *individual* FC signals that continues until the spreading signals either hit a boundary contour or are attenuated by their own spatial spread (Figure 4). The remainder of the article develops these and deeper properties of the BC System to explain segmentation data. Certain crucial points may profitably be emphasized now.

Boundaries may emerge corresponding to image regions in which no contrast differences whatsoever exist. The BC System is sensitive to statistical differences in the dis-

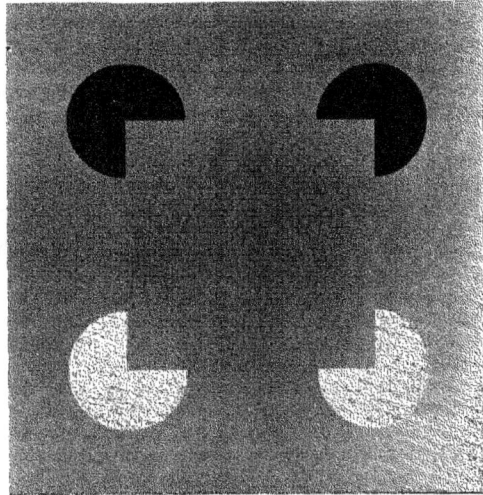

Figure 3. A reverse-contrast Kanizsa square: An illusory square is induced by two black and two white Pac-Man figures on a gray background. Illusory contours can thus join edges with opposite directions of contrast. (This effect may be weakened by the photographic reproduction process.)

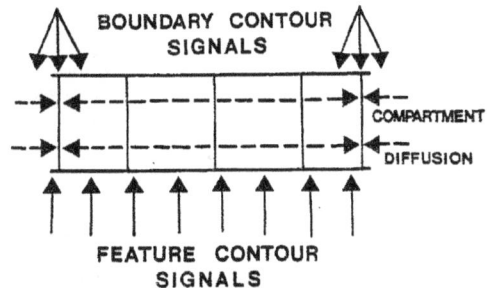

Figure 4. A monocular brightness and color stage domain within the FC System: Monocular feature contour signals activate cell compartments which permit rapid lateral diffusion of activity, or potential, across their compartment boundaries, except at those compartment boundaries which receive boundary contour signals from the BC System. Consequently, the FC signals are smoothed except at boundaries that are completed within the BC System stage.

tribution of scenic elements, not merely to individual image contrasts. In particular, the oriented receptive fields, or masks, that initiate boundary processing are not edge detectors; rather, they are local contrast detectors which can respond to statistical differences in the spatial distribution of image contrasts, including but not restricted to edges. These receptive fields are organized into multiple subsystems, such that the oriented receptive fields within each subsystem are sensitive to oriented contrasts over spatial domains of different sizes. These subsystems can therefore respond differently to spatial frequency information within the scenic image. Since all these oriented receptive fields are also sensitive to amount of contrast, the BC System registers statistical differences in luminance, orientation, and spatial frequency even at its earliest stages of processing.

Later stages of BC System processing are also sensitive to these factors, but in a different way. Their inputs from earlier stages are already sensitive to these factors. They then actively transform these inputs, using competitive-cooperative feedback interactions. The BC System may hereby process statistical differences in luminance, orientation, and spatial frequency within a scenic image in multiple ways.

We wish also to dispel misconceptions that a comparison between the names "Boundary Contour System" and "Feature Contour System" may engender. As indicated above, the BC System does generate perceptual boundaries, but neither the data nor our theory permit the conclusion that these boundaries must coincide with the edges in scenic images. The FC System does lead to visible percepts, such as organized brightness and color differences, and such percepts contain the elements that are often called features.

On the other hand, both the BC System and the FC System contain "feature detectors" which are sensitive to luminance or hue differences within scenic images. Although both systems contain "feature detectors," these detectors are used within the BC System to generate boundaries, not visible "features." In fact, within the BC System, all boundaries are perceptually invisible.

Boundary contours do, however, contribute to visible percepts, but only indirectly. All visible percepts arise within the FC System. Completed boundary contours help to generate visible percepts within the FC System by defining the perceptual regions within which activations due to feature contour signals can fill in.

Our names for these two systems emphasize that conventional usage of the terms "boundary" and "feature" needs modification to explain data about form and color perception. Our usage of these important terms captures the spirit of their conventional meaning, but also refines this meaning, to be consistent within a mechanistic analysis of the interactions leading to form and color percepts.

6. Boundary-Feature Tradeoff: Every Line End Is Illusory

The rules obeyed by the BC System can be fully understood only by considering how they interact with the rules of the FC System. Each contour system is designed to offset insufficiencies of the other. The most paradoxical properties of the BC System can be traced to its role in defining the perceptual domains that restrict featural filling-in. These also turn out to be the properties that are most important in the regulation of perceptual grouping.

The inability of previous perceptual theories to provide a transparent analysis of perceptual grouping can be traced to the fact that they did not clearly distinguish boundary contours from feature contours; hence they could not adequately understand the rules whereby boundary contours generate perceptual groupings to define perceptual domains adequate to contain featural filling-in.

When one frontally assaults the problem of designing boundary contours to contain featural filling-in, one is led to many remarkable conclusions. One conclusion is that the end of *every* line is an "illusory" contour. We now summarize what we mean by this assertion.

An early stage of boundary-contour processing needs to determine the orientations in which scenic edges are pointing. This is accomplished by elongated receptive fields, or orientationally tuned input masks (Hubel & Wiesel, 1977). Elongated receptive fields are, however, insensitive to orientation at the ends of thin lines and at object corners (Grossberg & Mingolla, 1985a). This breakdown is illustrated by the computer simulation summarized in Figure 5a, which depicts the reaction of a lattice of orientationally tuned cells to a thin vertical line. Figure 5a shows that in order to achieve some measure of orientational certainty along scenic edges, the cells sacrifice their ability to determine either position or orientation at the end of a line. In other words, Figure 5a summarizes the effects of an "uncertainty principle" whereby "orientational certainty" along scenic edges implies "positional uncertainty" at line ends and corners. Stated in a vacuum, this breakdown does not seem to be particularly interesting. Stated in the shadow of the featural filling-in process, it has momentous implications. Without further processing that is capable of compensating for this breakdown, the BC System could not generate boundaries corresponding to scenic line ends and corners. Consequently, within the FC System, boundary signals would not exist at positions corresponding to line ends (Figure 6). The FC signals generated by the interior of each line could then initiate spreading of featural quality to perceptual regions beyond the location of the line end. In short, the failure of boundary detection at line ends could enable colors to flow out of every line end! In order to prevent this perceptual catastrophe, orientational tuning, just like discounting the illuminant, must be followed by a hierarchy of compensatory processing stages in order to gain full effectiveness.

To offset this breakdown under normal circumstances, we have hypothesized that outputs from the cells with oriented receptive fields input to two successive stages of competitive interaction (Grossberg, 1984a; Grossberg & Mingolla, 1985a), which are described in greater detail in Section 20 and the Appendix. These stages are designed to compensate for orientational insensitivity at the ends of lines and corners. Figure 5b shows how these competitive interactions generate horizontal BC signals at the end of a vertical line. These "illusory" boundary contours help to prevent the flow of featural contrast from

OUTPUT OF
ORIENTED MASKS

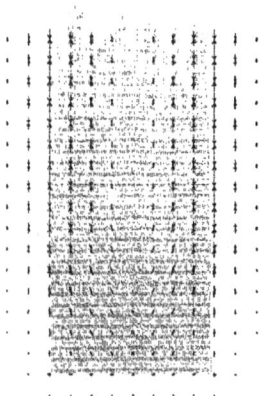

(a)

OUTPUT OF
COMPETITION

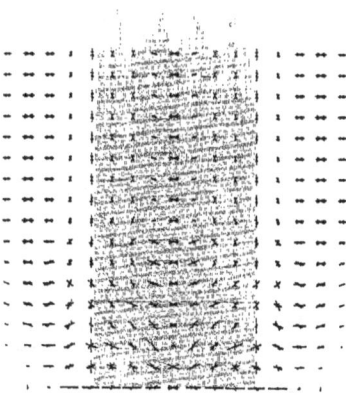

(b)

Figure 5. (a) An orientation field: Lengths and orientations of lines encode the relative sizes of the activations and orientations of the input masks at the corresponding positions. The input pattern, which is a vertical line end as seen by the receptive fields, corresponds to the shaded area. Each mask has total exterior dimension of 16×8 units, with a unit length being the distance between two adjacent lattice positions. (b) Response of the potentials y_{ijk} of the dipole field defined in the Appendix to the orientation field of Figure 5a: End cutting generates horizontal activations at line end locations that receive small and orientationally ambiguous input activations.

FEATURE
CONTOUR
SIGNALS

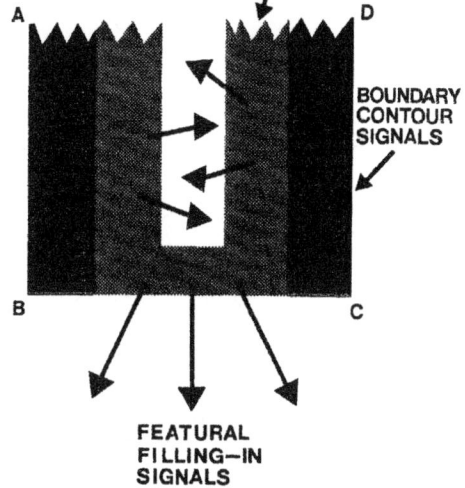

BOUNDARY
CONTOUR
SIGNALS

FEATURAL
FILLING—IN
SIGNALS

Figure 6. Possible spurious flow within the FC System of featural quality from line ends: Labels ABCD outline the positions corresponding to the tip of a vertically oriented thin line. The black areas from A to B and from C to D indicate regions of the FC System which receive signals due to direct image-induced activation of vertically oriented receptive fields within the BC System. The stippled areas indicate regions of the FC System which receive FC signals from the interior of the line image. FC System receptive fields, being small and unoriented, may be excited at line ends, even if the oriented receptive fields of the BC System are not. The arrows indicate that filling-in due to these FC signals can spread outside the putative boundary ABCD of the line end.

the line end. Such horizontal boundary contours induced by a vertical line end are said to be generated by end cutting, or orthogonal induction.

The circle illusion that is perceived by a glance at Figure 7 can now be understood. The BC end cuts at the line ends can cooperate with other end cuts of similar orientation that are approximately aligned across perceptual space, just as boundary contours do to generate the percept of a Kanizsa square in Figure 3. These boundary contours group "illusory" figures for the same reason that they complete figures across retinal veins and blind spots. Within the BC System, both "real" and "illusory" contours are generated by the same dynamical laws.

7. Parallel Induction by Edges Versus Perpendicular Induction by Line Ends

Knowing the directions in which boundary contours will form is obviously essential to understanding perceptual grouping. Why does a boundary form *parallel* to the inducing edges in Figure 3 but *perpendicular* to the line ends in Figure 7? This is clearly a question about spatial scale, since thickening a line until its end becomes an edge will

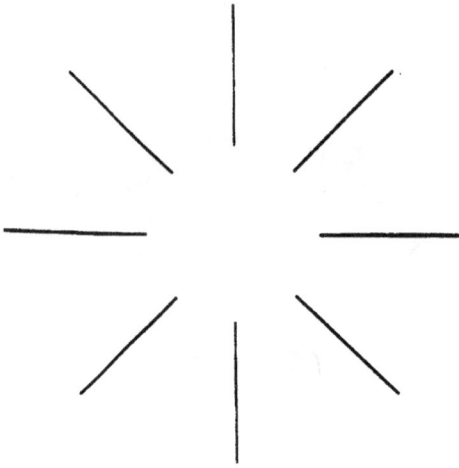

Figure 7. Cooperation among end-cut signals: A bright illusory circle is induced perpendicular to the ends of the radial lines.

8. Boundary Completion via Cooperative-Competitive Feedback Signaling: CC Loops and the Statistics of Grouping

Another mechanism important in determining the directions in which perceptual groupings occur will now be summarized. As in Figure 5b, the outputs of the competitive stages can generate bands of oriented responses. These bands enable cells sensitive to similar orientations at approximately aligned positions to begin cooperating to form the final BC percept. These bands play a useful role, because they increase the probability that spatially separated BC fragments will be aligned well enough to cooperate.

Figure 8 provides visible evidence of the existence of these bands. In Figure 8a, the end cuts that are exactly perpendicular to their inducing line ends can group to form a square boundary. In Figure 8b, the end cuts that are

cause induction to switch from being perpendicular to the line to being parallel to the edge.

An answer to this question can be seen by inspection of Figure 5. In Figure 5a, strong vertical reactions occur in response to the long vertical edge of the line. Figure 5b shows that these vertical reactions remain vertical when they pass through the competitive stages. This is analogous to a parallel induction, since the vertical reactions in Figure 5b will generate a completed vertical boundary contour that is parallel to its corresponding scenic edge. By contrast, the ambiguous reaction at the line end in Figure 5a generates a horizontal end cut in Figure 5b that is perpendicular to the line. If we thicken the line into a bar, it will eventually become wide enough to enable the horizontally oriented receptive fields at the bar end to generate strong reactions, in just the same way as the vertically oriented receptive fields along the side of the line generated strong vertical reactions there. The transition from ambiguous to strong horizontal reactions as the line end is thickened corresponds to the transition between perpendicular and parallel boundary contour induction.

This predicted transition has been discovered in electrophysiological recordings from cells in the monkey visual cortex (von der Heydt, Peterhans, & Baumgartner, 1984). The pattern of cell responding in Figure 5a is similar to the data which von der Heydt et al. recorded in area 17 of the striate cortex, whereas the pattern of cell responding in Figure 5b is similar to the data that von der Heydt et al. recorded in area 18 of the prestriate cortex. See Grossberg (1985) and Grossberg and Mingolla (1985a) for a further discussion of these and other supportive neural data.

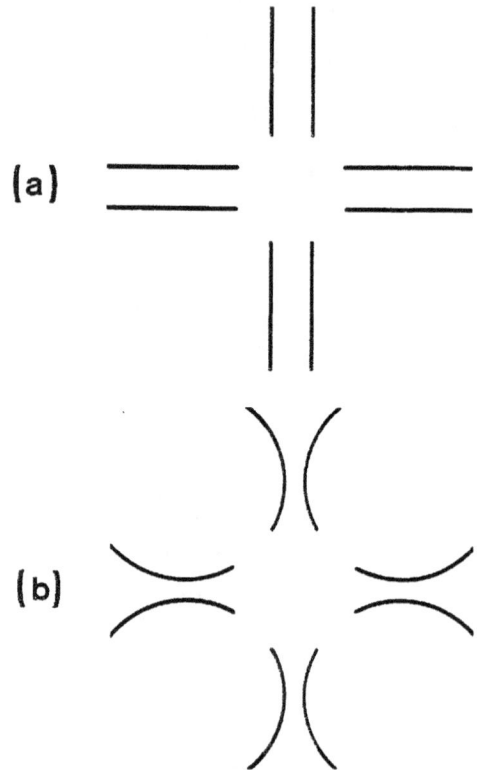

(a)

(b)

Figure 8. Evidence for bands of orientation responses: In (a), an illusory square is generated with sides perpendicular to the inducing lines. In (b), an illusory square is generated by lines with orientations that are not exactly perpendicular to the illusory contour. Redrawn from Kennedy (1979).

exactly perpendicular to the line ends cannot group, but end cuts that are almost perpendicular to the line ends can.

Figure 8 also raises the following issue. If bands of end cuts exist at every line end, then why cannot all of them group to form bands of different orientations, which might sum to create fuzzy boundaries? How is a single sharp global boundary selected from among all of the possible local bands of orientations?

We suggest that this process is accomplished by the type of feedback exchange between competitive and cooperative processes that is depicted in Figure 9. We call such a competitive-cooperative feedback exchange a CC loop. Figure 9a shows that the competitive and cooperative processes occur at different network stages, with the competitive stage generating the end cuts depicted in Figure 5b. Thus, the outcome of the competitive stage serves as a source of inputs to the cooperative stage and receives feedback signals from the cooperative stage.

Each cell in the cooperative process can generate output signals only if it receives a sufficient number and intensity of inputs within *both* of its input-collecting branches. Thus, the cell acts like a type of logical gate,

(a)

(b)

Figure 9. Boundary completion in a cooperative-competitive feedback exchange (CC loop): (a) Local competition occurs between different orientations at each spatial location. A cooperative boundary completion process can be activated by pairs of aligned orientations that survive their local competitions. This cooperative activation initiates the feedback to the competitive stage that is detailed in Figure 9b. (b) The pair of pathways 1 activate positive boundary completion feedback along pathway 2. Then pathways such as 3 activate positive feedback along pathways such as 4. Rapid completion of a sharp boundary between pathways 1 can hereby be generated. See text for details.

or statistical dipole. The inputs to each branch come from cells of the competitive process that have an orientation and position that are similar to the spatial alignment of the cooperative cell's branches. When such a cell is activated, say by the conjoint action of both input pathways labeled 1 in Figure 9b, it sends excitatory feedback signals along the pathways labeled 2. These feedback signals activate cells within the competitive stage which code a similar orientation and spatial position.

The cells at the competitive stage cannot distinguish whether they are activated by bottom-up signals from oriented receptive fields or by top-down signals from the cooperative stage. Either source of activation can cause them to generate bottom-up competitive-to-cooperative signals. Thus, new cells at the cooperative stage may now be activated by the conjoint action of both the input pathways labeled 3 in Figure 9b. These newly activated cooperative cells can then generate feedback signals along the pathway labeled 4.

In this way, a rapid exchange of signals between the competitive and cooperative stages may occur. These signals can propagate inward between pairs of inducing BC inputs, as in the Kanizsa square of Figure 3, and can thereby complete boundaries across regions that receive no bottom-up inputs from oriented receptive fields. The process of boundary completion occurs discontinuously across space by using the gating properties of the cooperative cells (Figure 9b) to successively interpolate boundaries within progressively finer intervals. This type of boundary completion process is capable of generating sharp boundaries, with sharp endpoints, across large spatial domains (Grossberg & Mingolla, 1985a). Unlike a low-spatial-frequency filter, the boundary-completion process does not sacrifice fine spatial resolution to achieve a broad spatial range.

Quite the contrary is true, since the CC loop sharpens, or contrast-enhances, the input patterns it receives from oriented receptive fields. This process of contrast enhancement is due to the fact that the cooperative stage feeds its excitatory signals back into the competitive stage. Thus, the competitive stage does double duty: it helps to complete line ends that oriented receptive fields cannot detect, and it helps to complete boundaries across regions that may receive no inputs whatsoever from oriented receptive fields. In particular, the excitatory signals from the cooperative stage enhance the competitive advantage of cells with the same orientation and position at the competitive stage (Figure 9b). As the competitive-cooperative feedback process unfolds rapidly through time, these local competitive advantages are synthesized into a global boundary grouping which can best reconcile all these local tendencies. In the most extreme version of this contrast-enhancement process, only one orientation at each position can survive the competition. That is, the network makes an orientational choice at each active position. The design of the CC loop is based upon theorems that characterize the factors that enable contrast-enhancement and choices to occur within nonlinear cooperative-competitive feedback networks (Ellias &

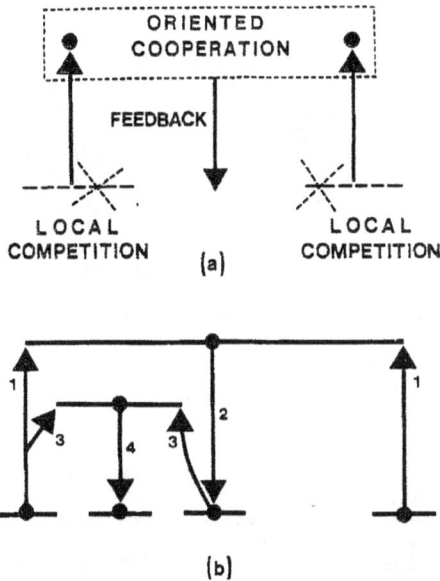

Grossberg, 1975; Grossberg, 1973; Grossberg & Levine, 1975).

As this choice process proceeds, it completes a boundary between some, but not all, of the similarly oriented and spatially aligned cells within the active bands of the competitive process (Figure 8). This interaction embodies a type of real-time statistical decision process whereby the most favorable groupings of cells at the competitive stage struggle to win over other possible groupings by initiating advantageous positive feedback from the cooperative stage. As Figure 8b illustrates, the orientations of the grouping that finally wins is not determined entirely by local factors. This grouping reflects global cooperative interactions that can override the most highly favored local tendencies, in this case the strong perpendicular end cuts.

The experiments of von der Heydt et al. (1984) also reported the existence of area 18 cells that act like logical gates. These experiments therefore suggest that either the second stage of competition, or the cooperative stage, or both, occur within area 18. Thus, although these BC System properties were originally derived from an analysis of perceptual data, they have successfully predicted recent neurophysiological data concerning the organization of mammalian prestriate cortex.

9. Form Perception vs. Object Recognition: Invisible but Potent Boundaries

One final remark needs to be made before turning to a consideration of textured scenes. Boundary contours in themselves are invisible. Boundary contours gain visibility by separating FC signals into two or more domains whose featural contrasts, after filling-in takes place, turn out to be different. (See Cohen & Grossberg, 1984a, and Grossberg, 1985, for a discussion of how these and later stages of processing help to explain monocular and binocular brightness data.) We distinguish this role of boundary contours in generating visible form percepts from the role played by boundary contours in object recognition. We claim that completed BC signals project directly to the object-recognition system (Figure 1). Boundary contours thus need not be visible in order to strongly influence object recognition. An "illusory" BC grouping that is caused by a textured scene can have a much more powerful effect on scene recognition than the poor visibility of the grouping might indicate.

We also claim that the object-recognition system sends learned top-down template, or expectancy, signals back to the BC System (Carpenter & Grossberg, 1985, in press; Grossberg, 1980, 1982, 1984b). Our theory hereby both agrees with and disagrees with the seminal idea of Gregory (1966) that "cognitive contours" are critical in boundary completion and object recognition. Our theory suggests that boundary contours are completed by a rapid, preattentive, automatic process as they activate the bottom-up adaptive filtering operations that activate the object-recognition system. The reaction within the object-recognition system determines which top-down visual templates to the BC System will secondarily complete the BC grouping based upon learned "cognitive" factors. These "doubly completed" boundary contours send signals to the FC System to determine the perceptual domains within which featural filling-in will take place.

We consider the most likely location of the boundary completion process to be area 18 (or V2) of the prestriate cortex (von der Heydt et al., 1984), the most likely location of the final stages of color and form perception to be area V4 of the prestriate cortex (Desimone, Schein, Moran, & Ungerleider, 1985; Zeki, 1983a, 1983b), and the most likely location of some aspects of object recognition to be the inferotemporal cortex (Schwartz, Desimone, Albright, & Gross, 1983). These anatomical interpretations were chosen after a comparison was made between theoretical properties and known neural data (Grossberg & Mingolla, 1985a). They also provide markers for performing neurophysiological experiments to further test the theory's mechanistic predictions.

10. Analysis of the Beck Theory of Textural Segmentation: Invisible Collinear Cooperation

We now begin a dynamical explanation and refinement of the main properties of Beck's important theory of textural segmentation (Beck et al., 1983). One of the central hypotheses of the Beck theory is that "local linking operations form higher-order textural elements" (p. 2). "Textural elements are hypothesized to be formed by proximity, certain kinds of similarity, and good continuation. Others of the Gestalt rules of grouping may play a role in the formation of texture .... There is an encoding of the brightness, color, size, slope, and the location of each textural element and its parts" (p. 31). We will show that the properties of these "textural elements" are remarkably similar to the properties of the completed boundaries that are formed by the BC System. To explain this insight, we will analyze various of the images used by Beck et al. in the light of BC System properties.

Figure 10 provides a simple example of what the Beck school means by a "textural element." Beck et al. (1983) write: "The short vertical lines are linked to form long lines. The length of the long lines is an 'emergent feature' which makes them stand out from the surrounding short lines" (p. 5). The linking per se is explained by our theory in terms of the process whereby similarly oriented and spatially aligned outputs from the second competitive stage can cooperate to complete a collinear intervening boundary contour.

One of the most remarkable aspects of this "emergent feature" is not analyzed by Beck et al. Why do we continue to see a series of short lines if long lines are the emergent features that control perceptual grouping? In our theory, the answer to this question is as follows. Within the BC System, a boundary structure emerges corresponding to the long lines described by Beck et al. This structure includes a long vertical component as well as short horizontal end cuts near the endpoints of the short scenic lines. The output of this BC structure to the FC System

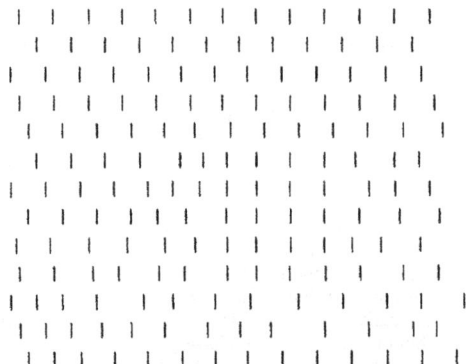

Figure 10. Emergent features: The collinear linking of short line segments into longer segments is an "emergent feature" which sustains textural grouping. Our theory explains how such emergent features can contribute to perceptual grouping even if they are not visible. (Reprinted, by permission, from Beck, Prazdny, & Rosenfeld, 1983.)

prevents featural filling-in of dark and light contrasts from crossing the boundaries corresponding to the short lines. On the other hand, the output from the BC System to the object-recognition system reads out a long-line structure without regard to which subsets of this structure will be perceived as dark or light.

This example points to a possible source of confusion in the Beck model. Beck et al. (1983) claim that "there is an encoding of the brightness, color, size, slope, and the location of each textural element and its parts" (p. 31). Figure 10 illustrates a sense in which this assertion is false. The long BC structure can have a powerful effect on textural segmentation even if it has only a minor effect on the brightness percepts corresponding to the short lines in the image, because an emergent boundary contour can generate a large input to the Object Recognition System (OR System) without generating a large brightness difference. The Beck model does not adequately distinguish between the contrast sensitivity that is needed to activate elongated receptive fields at an early stage of boundary formation and the effects of completed boundaries on featural filling-in. The outcome of featural filling-in, rather than the contrast sensitivity of the BC System's elongated receptive fields, helps to determine a brightness or color percept (Cohen & Grossberg, 1984a; Grossberg & Mingolla, 1985a).

A related source of ambiguity in the Beck model arises from the fact that the strength of an emergent boundary contour does not even depend on image contrasts, let alone brightness percepts, in a simple way. The Beck model does not adequately distinguish between the ability of elongated receptive fields to activate a boundary contour in regions where image contrast differences do exist and the cooperative interactions that complete the boundary contour in regions where image-contrast differences may or

may not exist. The cooperative interaction may, for example, alter boundary contours at positions that lie *within* the receptive fields of the initiating orientation-sensitive cells, as in Figure 8b. The final percept, even at positions that directly receive image contrasts, may be strongly influenced by cooperative interactions that reach these positions by spanning positions that do not directly receive image contrasts. This property is particularly important in situations in which a spatial distribution of statistically determined image contrasts, such as dot or letter densities, form the image that excites the orientation-sensitive cells.

11. The Primacy of Slope

Figure 11 illustrates this type of interaction between bottom-up direct activation of orientationally tuned cells and top-down cooperative interaction of such cells. Beck and his colleagues have constructed many images of this type to demonstrate that orientation or "slope is the most important of the variables associated with shape for producing textural segmentation.... A tilted T is judged to be more similar to an upright T than is an L. When these figures are repeated to form textures ... the texture made up of Ls is more similar to the texture made up of upright Ts than to the texture made up of tilted Ts" (Beck et al., 1983, p. 7). In our theory, this fact follows from several properties acting together: the elongated receptive fields in the BC System are orientationally tuned. This property provides the basis for the system's sensitivity to slope. As collinear boundary completion takes place due to cooperative-competitive feedback (Figure 9), it can group together approximately collinear boundary contours that arise from contrast differences due to the different letters. Collinear components of *different* letters are grouped just as the BC System groups image contrasts due to a *single* scenic edge that excites the retina on opposite sides of a retinal vein. The number and density of inducing elements of similar slope can influence the strength of the final set of boundary contours pointing in the same direction. Both Ls and Ts generate many horizontal and vertical boundary inductions, whereas tilted Ts generate diagonal boundary inductions.

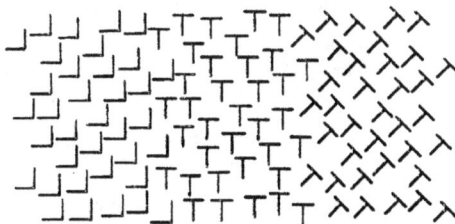

Figure 11. The primacy of slope: In this classic figure, textural segmentation between the tilted and upright Ts is far stronger than between the upright Ts and Ls. The figure illustrates that grouping of disconnected segments of similar slope is a powerful basis for textural segmentation. (Reprinted, by permission, from Beck, Prazdny, & Rosenfeld, 1983.)

The main paradoxical issue underlying the percept of Figure 11 concerns how the visual system overrides the perceptually vivid individual letters. Once one understands mechanistically the difference between boundary completion and visibility, and the role of boundary completion in forming even individual edge segments without regard to their ultimate visibility, this paradox is resolved.

12. Statistical Properties of Oriented Receptive Fields: OC Filters

Variations on Figure 11 can also be understood by refining the above argument. In Beck (1966a), it is shown that Xs in a background of Ts produce weaker textural segmentation than a tilted T in a background of upright Ts, even though both images contain the same orientations. We agree with Beck et al. (1983) that "what is important is not the orientation of lines per se but whether the change in orientation causes feature detectors to be differentially stimulated" (p. 9). An X and a T have a centrally symmetric shape that weakens the activation of elongated receptive fields. A similar observation was made by Schatz (1977), who showed that changing the slope of a single line from vertical to diagonal led to stronger textural segmentation than changing the slope of three parallel lines from vertical to diagonal.

Both of these examples are compatible with the fact that orientationally tuned cells measure the statistical distribution of contrasts within their receptive fields. They do not respond only to a template of an edge, bar, or other definite image. They are sensitive to the relative contrast of light and dark on either side of their axis of preferred orientation (Appendix, Equation A1). Each receptive field at the first stage of boundary contour processing is divided into two halves along an oriented axis. Each half of the receptive field sums the image-induced inputs it receives. The integrated activation from one of the half-fields inhibits the integrated activation from the other half-field. A net output signal is generated by the cell if the net activation is sufficiently positive. This output signal grows with the size of the net activation. Thus, each such oriented cell is sensitive to amount of contrast (size of the net activation) and to direction of contrast (only one half-field inhibits the other half-field), in addition to being sensitive to factors such as orientation, position, and spatial frequency.

A pair of such oriented cells corresponding to the same position and orientation, but opposite directions of contrast, send converging excitatory pathways to cells defining the next stage in the network. These latter cells are therefore sensitive to factors such as orientation, position, spatial frequency, and amount of contrast, but they are insensitive to direction of contrast.

Together, the two successive stages of oriented cells define a filter that is sensitive to properties concerned with orientation and contrast. We therefore call this filter an OC filter. The OC filter inputs to the CC loop. The BC System network is a composite of OC filter and CC loop. The output cells of the OC filter, being insensitive to direction of contrast, are the ones that respond to the relative contrast of light and dark on either side of their axis of preferred orientation.

Both the Xs studied by Beck (1966a) and the multiple parallel lines studied by Schatz (1977) reduce this relative contrast. These images therefore weaken the relative and absolute sizes of the input to any particular orientation. Thus, even the "front end" of the BC System begins to regroup the spatial arrangement of contrast differences that is found within the scenic image.

13. Competition between Perpendicular Subjective Contours

A hallmark of the Beck approach has been the use of carefully chosen but simple figural elements in arrays whose spatial parameters can be easily manipulated. Arrays built up from U shapes have provided a particularly rich source of information about textural grouping. In the bottom half of Figure 12, for example, the line ends of the Us and of the inverted Us line up in a horizontal direction. Their perpendicular end cuts can therefore cooperate, just as in Figures 7 and 8, to form long horizontal boundary contours. These long boundary contours enable the bottom half of the figure to be preattentively distinguished from the top half. Beck et al. (1983) note that segmentation of this image is controlled by "subjective contours" (p. 2). They do not use this phrase to analyze their other displays, possibly because the "subjective" boundary contours in other displays are not as visible.

The uncertainty within Beck et al. (1983) concerning the relationship between "linking operations" and "subjective contours" is illustrated by their analysis of Figure 13. In Figure 13a, vertical and diagonal lines alternate. In Figure 13b, horizontal and diagonal lines alternate. The middle third of Figure 13a is preattentively segmented better than the middle third of Figure 13b. Beck et al. (1983) explain this effect by saying that "the linking of the lines into chains also occurred more strongly

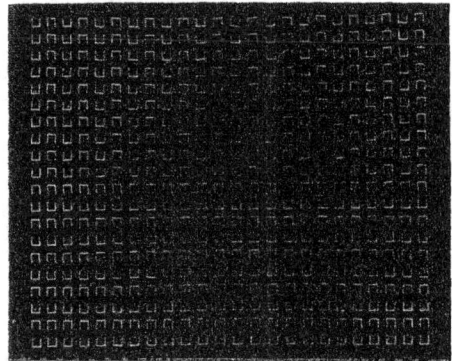

Figure 12. Textural grouping supported by subjective contours: Cooperation among end cuts generates horizontal subjective contours in the bottom half of this figure. (Reprinted, by permission, from Beck, Prazdny, & Rosenfeld, 1983.)

(a)

(b)

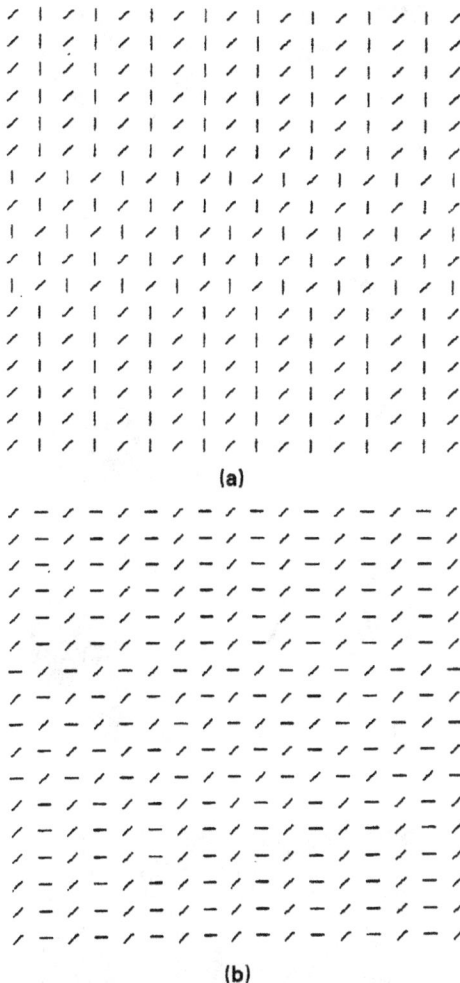

Figure 13. Effects of distance, perpendicular orientations, and collinearity on perceptual grouping: In both (a) and (b), vertical and horizontal subjective boundaries are generated. The text explains how the groupings in (a) better segregate the middle third of the figure. (Reprinted, by permission, from Beck, Prazdny, & Rosenfeld, 1983.)

when the lines were collinear than when they were parallel, i.e., the linking of horizontal lines to form vertical columns'' (p. 21). "The horizontal lines tend to link in the direction in which they point. The linking into long horizontal lines competes with the linking of the lines into vertical columns and interferes with textural segmentation'' (p. 22).

Our theory supports the spirit of this analysis. Both the direct outputs from horizontally oriented receptive fields and the vertical end cuts induced by competitive processing at horizontal line ends can feed into the collinear boundary completion process. The boundary completion process, in turn, feeds its signals back to a competitive stage where perpendicular orientations compete (Figure 9). Hence, direct horizontal activations and indirect vertical end cuts can compete at positions that receive both influences due to cooperative feedback.

Beck et al. (1983) do not, however, comment upon an important difference between Figures 13a and 13b that is noticed when one realizes that linking operations may generate both visible and invisible subjective contours. We claim that, in Figure 13b, the end cuts of horizontal and diagonal line ends can cooperate to form long vertical boundary contours that run from the top to the bottom of the figure. As in Figure 8b, global cooperative factors can override local orientational preferences to choose end cuts that are not perpendicular to their inducing line ends. We suggest that this happens with respect to the diagonal line ends in Figure 13b due to the cooperative influence of the vertical end cuts that are generated by collinear horizontal line ends. The long vertical boundary contours that are hereby generated interfere with textural segmentation by passing through the entire figure.

This observation, by itself, is not enough to explain the better segmentation of Figure 13a. Due to the horizontal alignment of vertical and diagonal line ends in Figure 13a, horizontal boundary contours could cross this entire figure. In Figure 13a, however, vertical lines within the top and bottom thirds of the picture are contiguous to other vertical lines. In Figure 13b, diagonal lines are juxtaposed between every pair of horizontal lines. Thus, in Figure 13a, a strong tendency exists to form vertical boundary contours in the top and bottom thirds of the picture due both to the distance dependence of collinear cooperation and to the absence of competing intervening orientations. These strong vertical boundary contours can successfully compete with the tendency to form horizontal boundary contours that cross the figure. In Figure 13b, the tendencies to form vertical and horizontal boundary contours are more uniformly distributed across the figure. Thus, the disadvantage of Figure 13b may not just be due to the "linking into long horizontal lines [which] competes with the linking of the lines into vertical columns,'' as Beck et al. (1983, p. 22) suggest. We suggest that, even in Figure 13a, strong competition from horizontal linkages occurs throughout the figure. These horizontal linkages do not prevent preattentive grouping, because strong vertical linkages exist at the top and bottom thirds of the figure and these vertical groupings cannot bridge the middle third of the figure. In Figure 13b, by contrast, the competing horizontal linkages in the top and bottom third of the figure are weaker than they are in Figure 13a. Despite this, the relative strengths of emerging groupings corresponding to different parts of a scene, rather than the strengths of oriented activations at individual scenic

154   GROSSBERG AND MINGOLLA

positions, determine how well a region of the scene can
be segmented.

14. Multiple Distance-Dependent Boundary Contour Interactions: Explaining Gestalt Rules

Figure 14 illustrates how changing the spatial separation of figural elements without changing their relative
positions can alter interaction strengths at different stages
of the BC System; different rearrangements of the same
scenic elements can differentially probe the hierarchical
organization of boundary processing. This type of insight
leads us to suggest how different Gestalt rules are realized by a unified system of BC System interactions.

In the top half of Figure 14a, horizontal boundary contours that cross the entire figure are generated by horizontal end cuts at the tips of the inverted Us. These long
boundary contours help to segregate the top half of the
figure from its bottom, just as they do in Figure 12. This
figure thus reaffirms that collinear cooperative interactions can span a broad spatial range. Some horizontal BC
formation may also be caused by cooperation between the
bottoms of the Us. We consider this process to be weaker
in Figure 14a for the same reason that it is weaker in
Figure 12: the vertical sides of the Us weaken it via competition between perpendicular orientations. Beck et al.
(1983, p. 23), by contrast, assert that "the bottom lines
of the U's link on the basis of colinearity (a special case
of good continuation)," and say nothing about the
horizontal boundary contours induced by the horizontal
end cuts.

In Figure 14b, the U and inverted-U images are placed
more closely together without otherwise changing their
relative spatial arrangement. End cuts at the tips of the
inverted Us again induce horizontal boundary contours
across the top half of the figure. New types of grouping
are also induced by this change in the density of the Us.
The nature of these new groupings can most easily be understood by considering the bottom of Figure 14b. At a
suitable viewing distance, one can now see diagonal
groupings that run at 45° and 135° angles through the
bases of the Us and inverted Us. We claim that these diagonal groupings are initiated when the density gets sufficiently high to enable diagonally oriented receptive fields
to record relatively large image contrasts. In other words,
at a low density of scenic elements, orientationally tuned
receptive fields can be stimulated only by one U or inverted U at a time. At a sufficiently high density of scenic
elements, each receptive field can be stimulated by parts
of different scenic elements that fall within that receptive
field. Once the diagonal receptive fields get activated, they
can trigger diagonally oriented boundary completions. A
similar possibility holds in the top half of Figure 14b.
Horizontally and vertically tuned receptive fields can begin to be excited by more than one U or inverted U. Thus,
the transition from Figure 14a to Figure 14b preserves
long-range horizontal cooperation based on competitive
end cuts and other collinear horizontal interactions, and
enables the earlier stage of oriented receptive fields to create new scenic groupings, notably in diagonal directions.

(a)

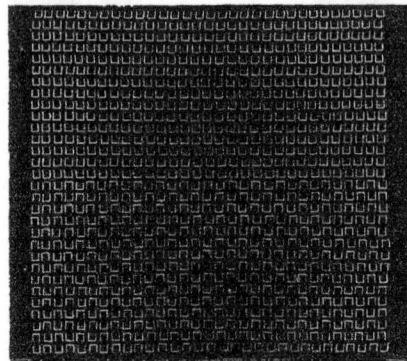

(b)

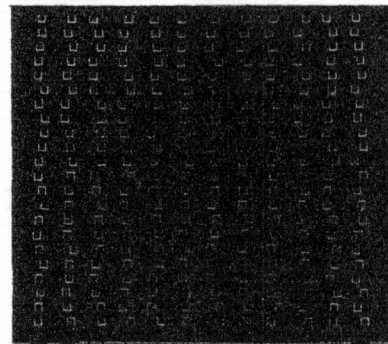

(c)

Figure 14. The importance of spatial scale: These three figures
probe the subtle effects on textural grouping of varying spatial scale.
For example, the diagonal grouping at the bottom of (b) is initiated
by differential activation of diagonally oriented masks, despite the
absence of any diagonal edges in the image. See the text for extended
discussion. (Reprinted, by permission, from Beck, Prazdny, &
Rosenfeld, 1983.)

Beck et al. (1983) analyze Figures 14a and 14b using Gestalt terminology. They say that segmentation in Figure 14a is due to "linking based on the colinearity of the base lines of the Us" (p. 24). Segmentation in Figure 14b is attributed to "linking based on closure and good continuation" (p. 25). We suggest that both segmentations are due to the same BC System interactions, but that the scale change in Figure 14b enables oriented receptive fields and cooperative interactions to respond to new local groupings of image components.

In Figure 14c, the relative positions of Us and inverted Us are again preserved, but they are arranged to be closer together in the vertical than in the horizontal direction. These new columnar relationships prevent the image from segmenting into top and bottom halves. Beck et al. (1983) write that "strong vertical linking based on proximity interferes with textural segmentation" (p. 28). We agree with this emphasis on proximity, but prefer a description which emphasizes that the vertical linking process uses the same textural segmentation mechanisms as are needed to explain all of their displays. We attribute the strong vertical linking to the interaction of five effects within the BC System. The higher relative density of vertically arranged Us and inverted Us provides a relatively strong activation of vertically oriented receptive fields. The higher density and stronger activation of vertically oriented receptive fields generates larger inputs to the vertically oriented long-range cooperative process, which enhances the vertical advantage by generating strong top-down positive feedback. The smaller relative density of horizontally arranged Us and inverted Us provides a relatively weak activation of horizontally oriented receptive fields. The lower density and smaller activation of these horizontally oriented receptive fields generates a smaller input to the horizontally oriented cooperative process. The horizontally oriented cooperation consequently cannot offset the strength of the vertically oriented cooperation. Although the horizontal end cuts can be generated by individual line ends, the reduction in density of these line ends in the horizontal direction reduces the total input to the corresponding horizontally oriented cooperative cells. All of these factors favor the ultimate dominance of vertically oriented long-range BC structures.

Beck et al. (1983) analyze the different figures in Figure 14 using different combinations of classical Gestalt rules. We analyze these figures by showing how they differentially stimulate the same set of BC System rules. This type of mechanistic synthesis leads to the suggestion that the BC System embodies a universal set of rules for textural grouping.

15. Image Contrasts and Neon Color Spreading

Beck et al. (1983) used regular arrays of black and gray squares on a white background and of white and gray squares on a black background with the same incisiveness as they used U displays. All of the corresponding perceptual groupings can be qualitatively explained in terms of the contrast sensitivity of BC System responses

to these images. The most difficult new property of these percepts can be seen by looking at Figure 15. Diagonal gray bands can be seen joining the gray squares in the middle third of the figure. We interpret this effect to be a type of neon color spreading (van Tuijl, 1975). This interpretation is supported by the percept that obtains when the gray squares are replaced by red squares of similar contrast, as we have done using our computer graphics system. Then diagonal red bands can be seen joining the red squares in the middle of the figure. Neither these red diagonal bands nor, by extension, the gray bands seen upon inspection of Figure 15, can be interpreted as being merely a classical contrast effect due to the black squares.

The percept of these diagonal bands can be explained using the same type of analysis that Grossberg (1984a) and Grossberg and Mingolla (1985a) have used to explain the neon color spreading that is induced by a black Ehrenstein figure surrounding a red cross (Figure 16; Redies & Spillmann, 1981) and the complementary color induction and spreading that is induced when parts of an image grating are achromatic and complementary parts are colored (van Tuijl, 1975). These explanations indicate how segmentation within the BC System can sometimes induce visible contrasts at locations where no luminance contrasts exist in the scenic image.

Neon spreading phenomena occur only when some scenic elements have greater relative contrasts with respect to the background than do the complementary scenic elements (van Tuijl & de Weert, 1979). This prerequisite is satisfied by Figure 15. The black squares are much more contrastive relative to the white ground than are the gray squares. Thus, the black-to-white contrasts can ex-

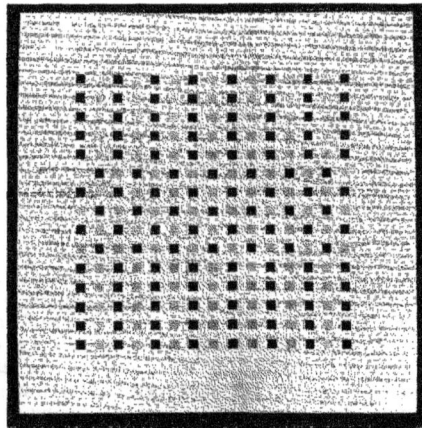

Figure 15. Textural segmentation and neon color spreading: The middle third of this figure is easily segmented from the rest. Diagonal flow of gray featural quality between the gray squares of the middle segment is an example of neon color spreading. See also Figures 16 and 17. (Reprinted from Beck, Prazdny, & Rosenfeld, 1983. We are grateful to Jacob Beck for providing the original of this figure.)

156   GROSSBERG AND MINGOLLA

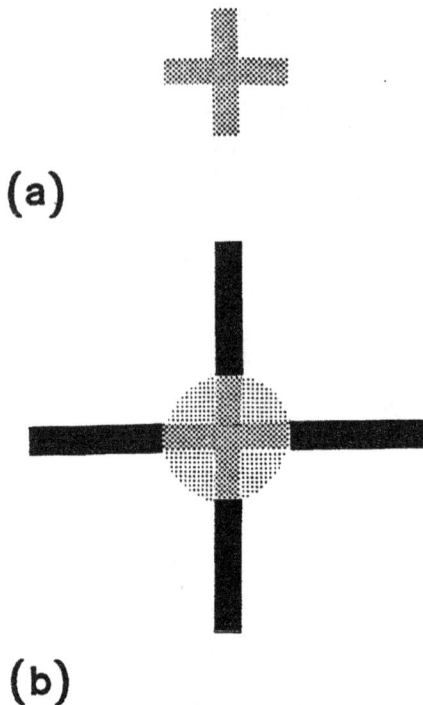

(a)

(b)

Figure 16. Neon color spreading: (a) A red cross in isolation appears unremarkable. (b) When the cross is surrounded by an Ehrenstein figure, the red color can flow out of the cross until it hits the illusory contour induced by the Ehrenstein figure.

cite oriented receptive fields within the BC System much more than can the gray-to-white contrasts. As in our other explanations of neon color spreading, we trace the initiation of this neon effect to two properties of the BC System: the contrast-sensitivity of the oriented receptive fields and the lateral inhibition within the first competitive stage among like-oriented cells at nearby positions (Section 20 and Appendix). Due to contrast sensitivity, each light-gray square activates oriented receptive fields less than does each black square. The activated orientations are, by and large, vertical and horizontal, at least on a sufficiently small spatial scale. At the first competitive stage, each strongly activated vertically tuned cell inhibits nearby weakly activated vertically tuned cells, and each strongly activated horizontally tuned cell inhibits nearby weakly activated horizontally tuned cells (Figure 17).

In all, each light-gray square's boundary contours receive strong inhibition both from the vertical and the horizontal direction. This conjoint vertical and horizontal inhibition generates a gap within the boundary contours at each corner of *every* light-gray square and a net

tendency to generate a diagonal boundary contour via disinhibition at the second competitive stage. These diagonal boundary contours can then link up via collinear cooperation to further weaken the vertical and horizontal boundary contours as they build completed diagonal boundary contours between the light-gray squares. This lattice of diagonal boundary contours enables gray featural quality to flow out of the squares and fill in the positions bounded by the lattice within the FC System. In the top and bottom thirds of Figure 15, on the other hand, only the horizontal boundary contours of the gray squares are significantly inhibited. Such inhibitions tend to be compensated at the cooperative stage by collinear horizontal boundary completion. Thus, the integrity of the horizontal boundary contours near such a gray square's corner tends to be preserved.

It is worth emphasizing a similarity and a difference between the percepts in Figures 14b and 15. In both percepts, diagonal boundary contours help to segment the images. However, in Figure 14b, the diagonals are activated directly at the stage of the oriented receptive fields, whereas in Figure 15, the diagonals are activated indirectly via disinhibition at the second competitive stage. We suggest that similar global factors may partially determine the Hermann grid illusion. Spillmann (1985) has reviewed evidence that suggests a role for central factors in generating this illusion, notably the work of Preyer (1897/1898) and Prandtl (1927) showing that when a white

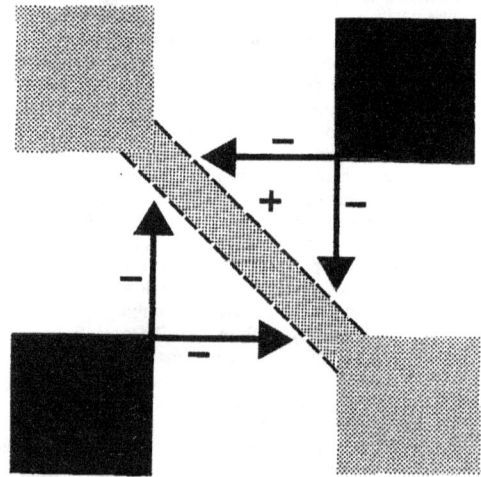

Figure 17. Boundary contour disinhibition and neon color spreading: This figure illustrates how the neon spreading evident in Figure 16 can occur. If gray squares are much lighter than black squares and the squares are sufficiently close, the net effect of strong inhibitory boundary signals from the black squares to the weakly activated gray square boundaries leads to disinhibition of diagonal boundary contours. Cooperation between these diagonal boundaries enables diagonal featural flow to occur between the gray squares.

grid is presented on a colored background, the illusory spots have the same color as the surrounding squares. Wolfe (1984) has presented additional evidence that global factors contribute to this illusion.

Although we expect our theory to be progressively refined as it achieves a greater behavioral and neural explanatory range, we believe that the types of explanation suggested above will continue to integrate the several classical Gestaltist laws into a unified neo-Gestaltist mechanistic understanding. In this new framework, instead of invoking different Gestalt laws to explain different percepts, one analyses how different images probe the same laws in context-sensitive ways.

16. Computer Simulations of Perceptual Grouping

In this section, we summarize computer simulations that illustrate the BC System's ability to generate perceptual groupings akin to those in the Beck et al. displays. In the light of these results, we then analyze data of Glass and Switkes (1976) about random-dot percepts and of Gregory and Heard (1979) about border locking during the café wall illusion before defining rigorously the model neuron interactions that define the BC System.

Numerical parameters were held fixed for all of the simulations; only the input patterns were varied. As the input patterns were moved about, the BC System sensed relationships among the inducing elements and generated emergent boundary groupings among them. In all of the simulations, we defined the input patterns to be the output patterns of the oriented receptive fields, as in Figure 18a, since our primary objective was to study the CC loop, or cooperative-competitive feedback exchange. This step reduced the computer time needed to generate the simulations. If the BC System is ever realized in parallel hardware, rather than by simulation on a traditional computer, it will run in real time. In Figures 18-25, we have displayed network activities after the CC loop converges to an equilibrium state. These simulations used only a single cooperative bandwidth. They thus illustrate how well the BC System can segment images using a single "spatial frequency" scale. Multiple scales are, however, needed to generate three-dimensional form percepts (Grossberg, 1983b, 1985; Grossberg & Mingolla, 1985b).

Figure 18a depicts an array of four vertically oriented input clusters. We call each cluster a Line because it represents a caricature of an orientation field's response to a vertical line (Figure 5a). In Figures 18b, 18c, and 18d, we display the equilibrium activities of the cells at three successive CC loop stages: the first competitive stage, the second competitive stage, and the cooperative stage. The length of an oriented line at each position is proportional to the equilibrium activity of a cell whose receptive field is centered at that position with the prescribed orientation. We will focus upon the activity pattern within the y field, or second competitive stage,

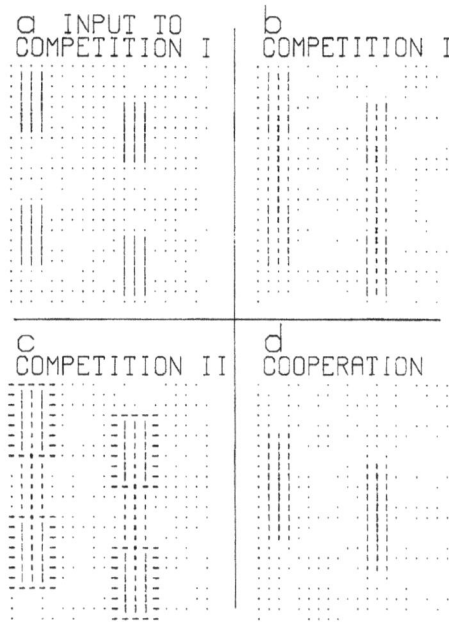

Figure 18. Computer simulation of processes underlying textural grouping: The length of each line segment in this figure and Figures 19-25 is proportional to the activation of a network node responsive to one of 12 possible orientations. The dots indicate the positions of inactive cells. In Figures 18-25, part (a) displays the results of input masks which sense the amount of contrast at a given orientation of visual input, as in Figure 5a. Parts (b)-(d) show equilibrium activities of oriented cells at the competitive and cooperative layers. A comparison of (a) and (c) indicates the major groupings sensed by the network. Here only the vertical alignment of the two left and two right Lines is registered. See text for detailed discussion.

of each simulation (Figure 18c). This is the final competitive stage that inputs to the cooperative stage (Section 8). The w-field (first competitive stage) and z-field (cooperative stage) activity patterns are also displayed to enable the reader to achieve a better intuition after considering the definitions of these fields in Section 20 and the Appendix.

The input pattern in Figure 18a possesses a manifest vertical symmetry: Pairs of vertical Lines are collinear in the vertical direction, whereas they are spatially out-of-phase in the horizontal direction. The BC System senses this vertical symmetry, and generates emergent vertical lines in Figure 18c, in addition to horizontal end cuts at the ends of each Line, as suggested by Figure 10.

In Figure 19a, the input pattern shown in Figure 18a has been altered, so that the first column of vertical Lines is moved downward relative to the second column of vertical Lines. Figure 19c shows that the BC System begins to sense the horizontal symmetry within the input configuration. In addition to the emergent vertical grouping and horizontal end cuts like those of Figure 18c, an approximately horizontal grouping has appeared.

In Figure 20, the input Lines are moved so that pairs of Lines are collinear in the vertical direction and their Line ends are lined up in the horizontal direction. Now both vertical and horizontal groupings are generated in Figure 20c, as in Figure 13.

In Figure 21a, the input Lines are shifted so that they become noncollinear in a vertical direction, but pairs of their Line ends remain aligned. The vertical symmetry of Figure 20a is hereby broken. Thus, in Figure 21c, the BC System groups the horizontal Line ends, but not the vertical Lines.

Figure 22 depicts a more demanding phenomenon: the emergence of diagonal groupings where no diagonals whatsoever exist in the input pattern. Figure 22a is generated by bringing the two horizontal rows of vertical Lines closer together until their ends lie within the spatial bandwidth of the cooperative interaction. Figure 22c shows that the BC System senses diagonal groupings of the Lines, as in Figure 14b. It is remarkable that these di-

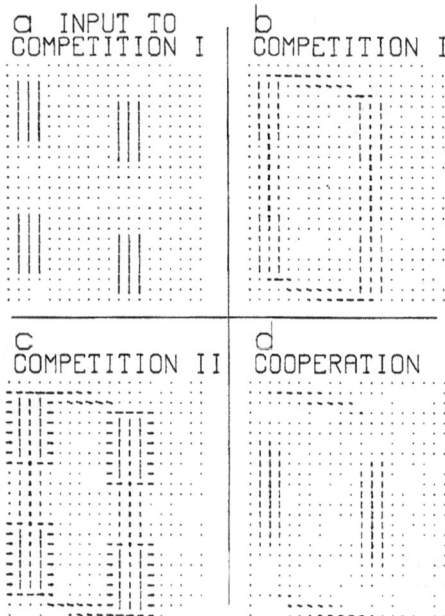

Figure 20. Coexistence of vertical and horizontal grouping: Here both horizontal and vertical groupings are completed at all Line ends.

agonal groupings emerge both on a microscopic scale and a macroscopic scale. Thus, diagonally oriented receptive fields are activated in the emergent boundaries, and these activations, as a whole, group into diagonal bands.

In Figure 23c, another shift of the inputs induces internal diagonal bands while enabling the exterior grouping into horizontal and diagonal boundaries to persist.

In Figure 24a, one of the vertical Lines is removed. The BC System now senses the remaining horizontal and diagonal symmetries (Figure 24c). In Figure 25a, the lower Line is moved further away from the upper pair of lines until the cooperation can no longer support the diagonal groupings. The diagonal groupings break apart, leaving the remaining horizontal groupings intact (Figure 25c).

17. On-Line Statistical Decision Theory and Stochastic Relaxation

These figures illustrate the fact that the BC System behaves like an on-line statistical decision theory in response to its input patterns. The BC System can sense only those groupings of perceptual elements which possess enough "statistical inertia" to drive its cooperative-competitive feedback exchanges toward a nonzero stable equilibrium configuration. The emergent patterns in Figures 18-25 are thus as important for what they do *not* show as they are for what they do show. All possible groupings of the

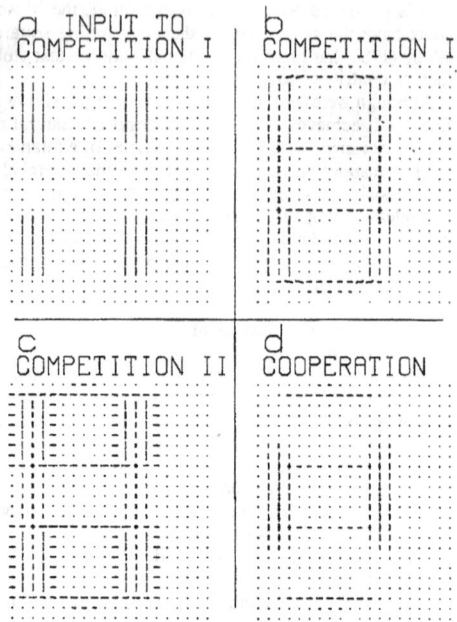

Figure 19. The emergence of nearly horizontal grouping: The only difference between the input for this figure and that of Figure 18 is that the left column of Lines has been moved downward by one lattice location. The vertical grouping of Figure 18 is preserved as the horizontal grouping emerges. The horizontal groupings are due to cooperation between end cuts at the Line ends.

oriented input elements could, in principle, have been generated, since all possible groupings of the cooperative-competitive interaction were capable of receiving inputs.

In order to compare and contrast BC System properties with other approaches, one can interpret the distribution of oriented activities at each input position as being analogous to a local probability distribution, and the final BC System pattern as being the global decision that the system reaches and stores based upon all of its local data. The figures show that the BC System regards many of the possible groupings of these local data as spurious, and suppresses them as being functional noise. Some popular approaches to boundary segmentation and noise suppression do adopt a frankly probabilistic framework. For example, in a stochastic relaxation approach based upon statistical physics, Geman and Geman (1984) slowly decrease a formal temperature parameter that drives their system towards a minimal-energy configuration with boundary-enhancing properties. Zucker (1985) has also suggested a minimization algorithm to determine the best segmentation.

Such algorithms provide one way, indeed a classical way, to realize coherent properties within a many-body system. These algorithms define open-loop procedures in which external agents manipulate the parameters leading to coherence. In the BC System, by contrast, the only "ex-

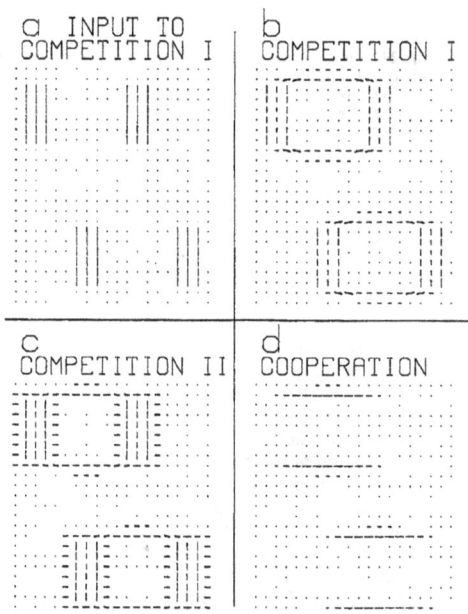

Figure 22. The emergence of diagonal groupings: The Boundary Contour System (BCS) is capable of generating groupings along orientations which have no activity in the oriented mask responses. Individual diagonally oriented cells are activated within the diagonally oriented groupings.

ternal parameters" are the input patterns themselves. Each input pattern defines a different set of boundary conditions for the BC System, and this difference, in itself, generates different segmentations. The BC System does not need extra external parameters, because it contains a closed-loop process—the CC loop—which regulates its own convergence to a symmetric and coherent configuration via its real-time competitive-cooperative feedback exchanges.

The BC System differs in other major ways from alternative models. Geman and Geman (1984), for example, build into the probability distributions of their algorithm information about the images to be processed. The dynamics of the BC System clarify the relevance of probabilistic concepts to the segmentation process. In particular, the distributions of oriented activities at each input position (Figure 5) play the role of local probability distributions. On the other hand, within the BC System, these distributions emerge as part of a real-time reaction to input patterns, rather than according to predetermined constraints on probabilities. The BC System does not incorporate hypotheses about which images will be processed into its probability distributions. Such

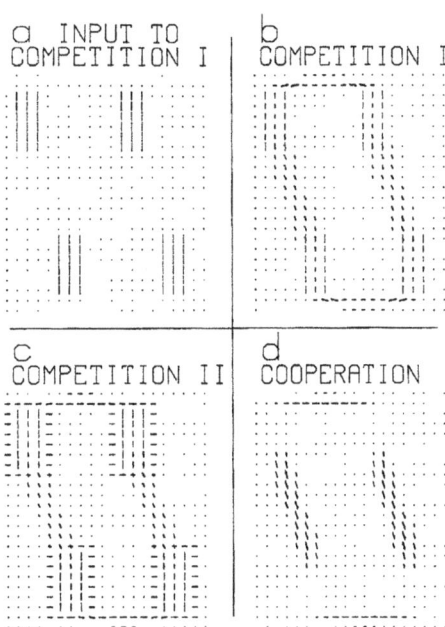

Figure 21. Horizontal grouping by end cuts: A horizontal shift of the lower two Lines in Figure 20 breaks the vertical groupings but preserves the horizontal groupings.

knowledge is not needed to achieve rapid preattentive segmentation.

The OR System does encode information about which images are familiar (Figure 1). Feedback interactions between the BC System and the OR System can rapidly supplement a preattentive segmentation using the templates read out from the OR System in response to BC System signals. Within our theory, however, these templates are not built into the OR System. Rather, we suggest how they are learned, in real time, as the OR System self-organizes its recognition code in response to the preattentively completed output patterns from the BC System (Carpenter & Grossberg, 1985, in press; Grossberg, 1980, 1984b).

Thus, the present theory sharply distinguishes between the processes of preattentive segmentation and of learned object recognition. By explicating the intimate interaction between the BC System and the OR System, the present theory also clarifies why these distinct processes are often treated as a single process. In particular, the degree to which top-down learned templates can deform a preattentively completed BC System activity pattern will depend upon the particular images being processed and the past experiences of the OR System. Thus, by carefully selecting visual images, one can always argue that one or the other process is rate-limiting. Furthermore, both

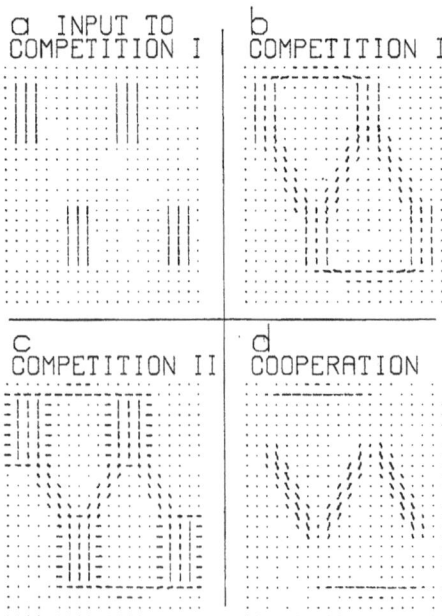

Figure 23. Multiple diagonal groupings: A new diagonal grouping emerges as a result of the shifting of input Lines. As in Figure 20, grouping in one orientation does not preclude grouping in an (almost) perpendicular orientation at the same Line end.

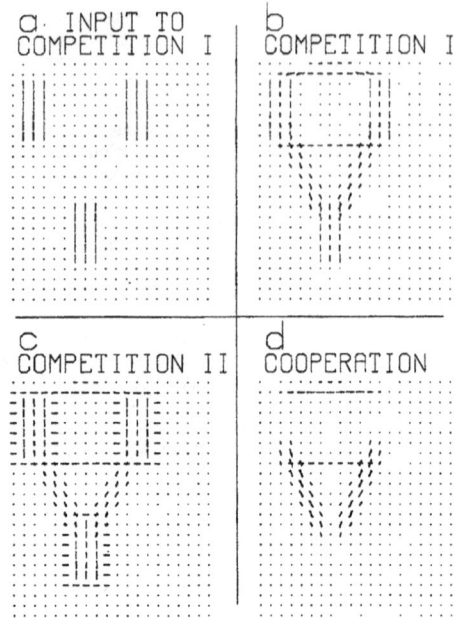

Figure 24. Global restructuring due to removal of local features: The inputs of this figure and those of Figure 23 are identical, except that the lower right Line has been removed. A comparison of Figure 24b and Figure 23b shows that, although gross aspects of the shared grouping are similar, removal of one Line can affect groupings among other Lines.

the preattentive BC System interactions and the top-down learned OR System interactions are processes of *completion* which enhance the *coherence* of BC System output patterns. They can thus easily be mistaken for one another.

18. Correlations That Cannot Be Perceived: Simple Cells, Complex Cells, and Cooperation

Glass and Switkes (1976) described a series of striking displays which they partially explained using the properties of cortical simple cells. Here we suggest a more complete explanation of their results using properties of the BC System. In their basic display (Figure 26), when "a random pattern of dots is superimposed on itself and rotated slightly ... a circular pattern is immediately perceived.... If the same pattern is superimposed on a negative of itself in which the background is a halftone gray and is rotated as before ..., it is impossible to perceive the circular Moiré. In this case spiral petal-like patterns can be seen" (p. 67).

The circular pattern in Figure 26 is not "perceived" in an obvious sense. All that an observer can "see" are black dots on white paper. We suggest that the percept

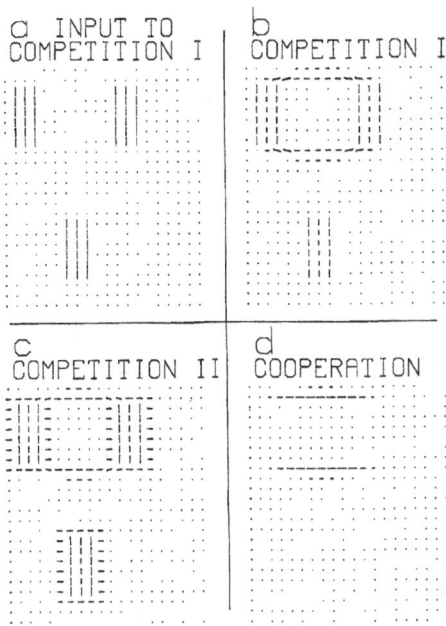

Figure 25. Distance-dependence of grouping: Relative to the inputs of Figure 24, the bottom Line has moved outside of the cooperative bandwidth that supported diagonal grouping. Although the diagonal grouping vanishes, the horizontal grouping at the bottom of the top Lines persists.

Figure 26. A Glass pattern: The emergent circular pattern is "recognized," although it is not "seen," as a pattern of differing contrasts. The text suggests how this can happen. (Reprinted, by permission, from Glass & Switkes, 1975.)

of circular structure is *recognized* by the OR System, whereas the FC System, wherein percepts of brightness and color are *seen*, generates the filled-in contrast differences that distinguish the black dots from the white background (Figure 1). A similar issue is raised by Figure 10, in which short vertical lines are seen even though emergent long vertical lines influence perceptual grouping. Thus, in the Glass and Switkes (1976) displays, no less than in the Beck et al. (1983) displays, one must sharply distinguish the recognition of perceptual groupings from the percepts that are seen. These recognition events always have properties of "coherence," whether or not they can support visible contrast differences. It then remains to explain why inverting the contrast of one of the images can alter what is recognized as well as what is seen.

We agree with part of the Glass and Switkes (1976) explanation. Consider a pair of black dots in Figure 26 that arises by rotating one image with respect to the other. Let the orientation of the pair with respect to the horizontal be $\theta°$. Since the dots are close to one another, they can activate receptive fields that have an orientation approximately equal to $\theta°$. This is due to the fact that an oriented receptive field is not an edge detector per se, but, rather, is sensitive to relative contrast differences across its medial axis. Only one of the two types of receptive fields at each position and orientation will be strongly activated, depending on the direction of contrast in the image. Each receptive field is sensitive to direction of contrast, even though pairs of these fields corresponding to like positions and orientations pool their activities at the next processing stage to generate an output that is insensitive to direction of contrast. We identify cells whose receptive fields are sensitive to direction of contrast with simple cells and the cells at the next stage which are insensitive to direction of contrast with complex cells of the striate cortex (DeValois, Albrecht, & Thorell, 1982; Gouras & Krüger, 1979; Heggelund, 1981; Hubel & Wiesel, 1962, 1968; Schiller, Finlay, & Volman, 1976; Tanaka, Lee, & Creutzfeldt, 1983). Glass and Switkes (1976) did not proceed beyond this fact.

We suggest, in addition, that long-range cooperation within the BC System also plays a crucial role in grouping Glass images. To see how cooperation is engaged, consider two or more pairs of black dots that satisfy the following conditions: Each pair arises by rotating one image with respect to the other. The orientation of all pairs with respect to the horizontal is approximately $\theta°$. All pairs are approximately collinear and do not lie too far apart. Such combinations of dots can more strongly activate the corresponding cooperative cells than can random combinations of dots. Each cooperative cell sends positive feedback to cells at the competitive stages with the same position and orientation. The competing cells that receive the largest cooperative signals gain an advantage over cells with different orientations. After competition among all possible cooperative groupings takes place, the favored groupings win and generate the large circular boundary contour structure that is recognized but not seen. Small circular boundaries are also generated around each

162   GROSSBERG AND MINGOLLA

dot and support the visible percept of dots on a white background within the FC System. Thus, the orientation $\theta°$ of a pair of rotated black dots engages the BC System in two fundamentally different ways. First, it preferentially activates some oriented receptive fields above others. Second, it preferentially activates some cooperative cells above others due to combinations of inputs from preferentially activated receptive fields. As in the displays of Beck et al. (1983), the Glass images probe multiple levels of the BC System.

The other Glass images probe different levels of the BC System, notably the way in which simple cells activate complex cells which, in turn, activate the competitive layers. These images are constructed by reversing the contrast of one of the two images before they are superimposed. Then an observer sees black and white dots on a gray background. The recognition of circular macrostructure is, however, replaced by recognition of a more amorphous spiral petal-like pattern. Glass and Switkes (1976) noted that their "hypothesized neural mechanism does not appear to explain the observation of spiral-like patterns" (p. 71). To explain this recognition, we first note that the black dots on the gray background generate light-dark contrasts. Hence, the simple cells which responded to pairs of rotated black dots in Figure 26 are now stimulated by only one dot in each pair. Two or more *randomly* distributed black dots may be close enough to stimulate individual simple cells, but the orientations of the cells favored by stimulation by two or more random dots will be different from those of the cells stimulated by two or more rotated black dots in Figure 26. In addition, simple cells that are sensitive to the opposite direction of contrast can respond to the white dots on the gray background. These cells will be spatially rotated with respect to the cells that respond to the black dots. Moreover, since the black-to-gray contrast is greater than the white-to-gray contrast, the cells that respond to the black dots will fire more vigorously than the cells that respond to the white dots. Thus, although both classes of simple cells feed into the corresponding complex cells, the complex cells that respond to the black dots will be more vigorously activated than the complex cells that respond to the white dots. The cooperative stage will favor the most active combinations of complex cells whose orientations are approximately collinear and which are not too far apart. Due to the differences in spatial position and orientation of the most favored competitive cells, a boundary grouping different from that in Figure 26 is generated. A similar analysis can be given to the Glass and Switkes displays that use complementary colors.

In summary, the Glass and Switkes (1976) data emphasize three main points: Although simple cells sensitive to the same orientation and opposite direction of contrast feed into complex cells that are insensitive to direction of contrast, reversing the direction of contrast of some inputs can alter the positions and the orientations of the complex cells that are most vigorously activated. Although many possible groupings of cells can initially activate the cooperative stage, only the most favored groupings can

survive the cooperative-competitive feedback exchange, as in Figures 18-25. Although all emergent boundary contours can influence the OR System, not all of these boundary countours can support visible filled-in contrast differences within the FC System. Prazdny (1984) has presented an extensive set of Glass-type displays, which have led him to conclude that "the mechanisms responsible for our perception of Glass patterns are also responsible for the detection of extended contours" (p. 476). Our theory provides a quantitative implementation of this assertion.

19. Border Locking: The Café Wall Illusion

A remarkable percept which is rendered plausible by BC System properties is the café wall illusion (Gregory & Heard, 1979). This illusion is important because it clarifies the conditions under which the spatial alignment of collinear image contours with different contrasts is normally maintained. The illusion is illustrated in Figure 27.

The illusion occurs only if the luminance of the "mortar" within the horizontal strips lies between, or is not far outside, the luminances of the dark and light tiles, as in Figure 27. The illusion occurs, for example, in the limiting case of the Münsterberg figure, in which black and white tiles are separated by a black mortar. Gregory and Heard (1979) have also reported that the tile boundaries appear to "creep across the mortar during luminance changes" (p. 368). Using a computer graphics system, we have generated a dynamic display in which the mortar luminance changes continuously through time. The perceived transitions from parallel tiles to wedge-shaped tiles and back are dramatic, if not stunning, using such a dynamic display.

Some of the BC System mechanisms that help to clarify this illusion can be inferred from Figure 28. This figure depicts a computer simulation of an orientation field that was generated in response to alternating black and white tiles surrounding a black strip of mortar. Figure 29 schematizes the main properties of Figure 28. The hatched areas in Figure 29a depict the regions in which the greatest activations of oriented receptive fields occur. Due to the

Figure 27. The café wall illusion: Although only horizontal and vertical luminance contours exist in this image, strong diagonal groupings are perceived. (Reprinted, by permission, from Gregory & Heard, 1979).

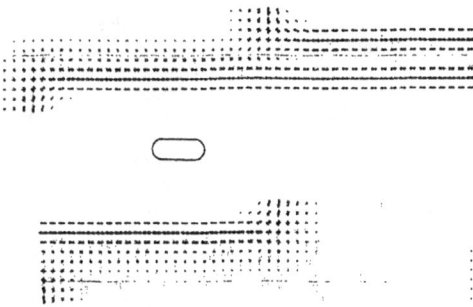

Figure 28. Simulation of the responses of a field of oriented masks to the luminance pattern near the mortar of the café wall illusion: The right of the bottom row joins to the left of the top row. The relative size of the masks used to generate the figure is indicated by the oblong shape in the center.

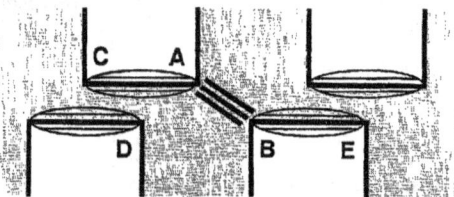

(a)

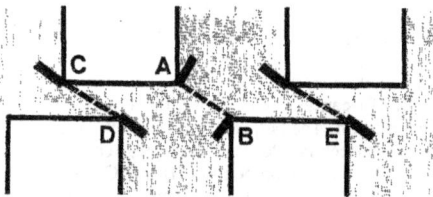

(b)

Figure 29. A schematic depiction of the simulation in Figure 28: (a) shows the region of strong horizontal activity and indicates a possible diagonal grouping between positions A and B. (b) suggests that cooperation may occur in response to direct activations of oriented masks at positions C and D, as well as in response to end cuts at positions A and B. See text for additional discussion.

approximately horizontal orientations of the activated receptive fields in Figure 29a, diagonal cooperative groupings between positions such as A and B can be initiated, as in Figures 22-24. Figure 28 thus indicates that a macroscopic spatial asymmetry in the activation of oriented receptive fields can contribute to the shifting of borders which leads to the wedge-shaped percepts.

Figure 29b schematizes the fact that the microstructure of the orientation field is also skewed in Figure 28. Diagonal orientations tend to point into the black regions at the corners of the white tiles. Diagonal end cuts induced near positions A and B (Section 6) can thus cooperate between A and B in approximately the same direction as the macrostructure between A and C can cooperate with the macrostructure between B and E (Figure 29a). Diagonal activations near positions C and D can cooperate with each other in a direction almost parallel to the cooperation between A and B. These microscopic and macroscopic cooperative effects can help to make the boundaries at the top of the mortar seem to tilt diagonally downward.

Several finer points are clarified by the combination of these macroscale and microscale properties. By themselves, the microscale properties do not provide a sufficient explanation of why, for example, an end cut at position D cannot cooperate with direct diagonal activations at A. The macroscale interactions tilt the balance in favor of cooperation between A and B. In the Münsterberg figure, the black mortar under a white tile may seem to glow, whereas the black mortar under a black tile does not. Using a dark-gray mortar, the gray mortar under a white tile may seem brighter, whereas the gray mortar under a black tile may better preserve its gray appearance. McCourt (1983) has also called attention to the relevance of brightness induction in explaining the café wall illusion. A partial explanation of these brightness percepts can be inferred from Figure 29. End cuts and diagonal groupings near position A may partially inhibit the parallel boundary between A and C. Brightness can then flow from the white tile downward, as during neon color spreading (Figure 16). The more vigorous boundary activations above positions such as D and E (Figure 29a) may better contain local featural contrasts within a tighter web of boundary contours. This property also helps to explain the observation of Gregory and Heard (1979) that the white tiles seem to be pulled more into the black at such positions as A than at such positions as C.

Our analysis of the café wall illusion, although not based on a complete computer simulation, suggests that the same three factors which play an important role in generating the Glass and Switkes (1976) data also play an important role in generating the Gregory and Heard (1979) data. In addition, perpendicular end cuts and multiple spatial scales seem to play a role in generating the Gregory and Heard (1979) data, with different combinations of scales acting between such positions as A-B than between such positions as C-D. This last property may explain why opposite sides A and C of an apparently wedge-shaped tile sometimes seem to lie at different depths from an observer (Grossberg, 1983b).

20. Boundary Contour System Stages: Predictions About Cortical Architectures

This section outlines in greater detail the network interactions that we have used to characterize the BC System. Several of these interactions suggest anatomical and physiological predictions about the visual cortex. These predictions refine our earlier predictions that the data of von der Heydt et al. (1984) have since supported (Grossberg & Mingolla, 1985a).

Figure 30 summarizes the proposed BC System interactions. The process whereby boundary contours are built up is initiated by the activation of oriented masks, or elongated receptive fields, at each position of perceptual space

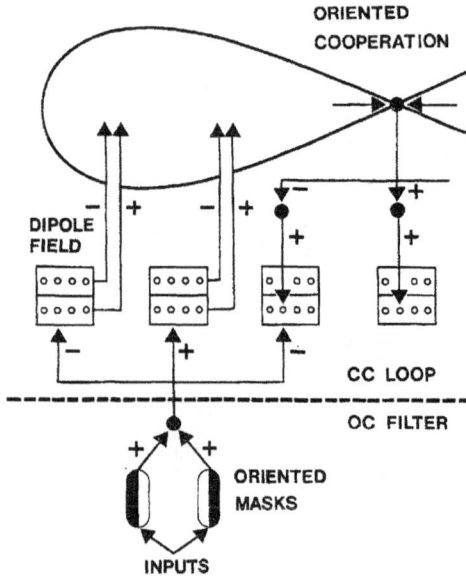

Figure 30. Circuit diagram of the BC System: Inputs activate oriented masks which cooperate at each position and orientation before feeding into an on-center–off-surround interaction. This interaction excites like-orientations at the same position and inhibits like-orientations at nearby positions. The affected cells are on-cells within a dipole field. On-cells at a fixed position compete among orientations. On-cells also inhibit off-cells which represent the same position and orientation. Off-cells at each position, in turn, compete among orientations. Both on-cells and off-cells are tonically active. Net excitation (inhibition) of an on-cell (off-cell) excites (inhibits) a cooperative receptive field corresponding to the same position and orientation. Sufficiently strong net positive activation of both receptive fields of a cooperative cell enables it to generate feedback via an on-center–off-surround interaction among like-oriented cells. Dipole on-cells which receive the most favorable combination of bottom-up signals and top-down signals generate the emergent perceptual grouping.

(Hubel & Wiesel, 1977). An oriented mask is a cell, or cell population, that is selectively responsive to oriented scenic-contrast differences. In particular, each mask is sensitive to scenic edges that activate a prescribed small region of the retina, and whose orientations lie within a prescribed band of orientations with respect to the retina. A family of such oriented masks lies at every network position, such that each mask is sensitive to a different band of edge orientations within its prescribed small region of the scene.

A. Position, orientation, amount of contrast, and direction of contrast. The first stage of oriented masks is sensitive to the position, orientation, amount of contrast, and direction of contrast at an edge of a visual scene. Thus, two subsets of masks exist corresponding to each position and orientation. One subset responds only to light-dark contrasts, and the other subset responds to dark-light contrasts. Such oriented masks do not, however, respond only to scenic edges. They can also respond to any image that generates a sufficiently large net contrast with the correct position, orientation, and direction of contrast within their receptive fields, as in Figures 14b and 26. We identify these cells with the simple cells of striate cortex (DeValois et al., 1982; Hubel & Wiesel, 1962, 1968; Schiller et al., 1976).

Pairs of oriented masks that are sensitive to similar positions and orientations but to opposite directions of contrast excite the next BC System stage. The output from this stage is thus sensitive to position, orientation, and amount of contrast, but is insensitive to direction of contrast. A vertical boundary contour can thus be activated by either a close-to-vertical light-dark edge or a close-to-vertical dark-light edge at a fixed scenic position, as in Figure 3. The activities of these cells define the orientation field in Figure 5a. We identify the cells at this stage with the complex cells of striate cortex (DeValois et al., 1982; Gouras & Krüger, 1979; Heggelund, 1981; Hubel & Wiesel, 1962, 1968; Schiller et al., 1976; Tanaka et al., 1983). Spitzer and Hochstein (1985) have independently developed an essentially identical model of complex cell receptive fields to explain parametric properties of their cortical data.

B. On-center–off-surround interaction within each orientation. The outputs from these cells activate the first of two successive stages of short-range competition, which are denoted by Competition (I) and Competition (II) in Figures 18-25. At the first competitive stage, a mask of fixed orientation excites the like-oriented cells at its position and inhibits the like-oriented cells at nearby positions. Thus an on-center–off-surround interaction between like-oriented cells occurs around each perceptual location. This interaction predicts that a stage subsequent to striate complex cells organizes cells sensitive to like orientations at different positions so that they can engage in the required on-center–off-surround interaction.

C. Push-pull competition between orientations at each position. The inputs to the second competitive stage are the outputs from the first competitive stage. At the second competitive stage, competition occurs between different orientations at each position. Thus, a stage of competition between like orientations at different, but nearby, positions (Competition I) is followed by a stage of competition between different orientations at the same position (Competition II). This second competitive stage is tonically active. Thus, inhibition of a vertical orientation excites the horizontal orientation at the same position via disinhibition of its tonic activity.

The combined action of the two competitive stages generates the perpendicular end cuts in Figure 5b that we have used to explain the percepts in Figures 7, 8, 12, and 13. Conjoint inhibition of vertical and horizontal orientations by the first competitive stage leading to disinhibition of diagonal orientations at the second competitive stage (Figure 17) was also used to explain the diagonal groupings in Figure 15. A similar interaction was used to help explain the neon color-spreading phenomenon described in Figure 16 (Grossberg & Mingolla, 1985a). Thus, the interactions of the first and second competitive stages help to explain a wide variety of seemingly unrelated perceptual groupings, color percepts, and illusory figures.

D. Dipole field: Spatial impenetrability. The process described in this section refines the BC System model that was used in Grossberg and Mingolla (1985a). This process incorporates a principle of cortical design that has been used to carry out related functional tasks in Grossberg (1980, 1983a). The functional role played by this process in the BC System can be understood by considering Figure 18c.

At the second competitive stage of this figure, horizontal end cuts border the vertical responses to the inducing input Lines. What prevents the end cuts at both sides of each line from cooperating? If these end cuts could cooperate, then each Line could activate one of a cooperative cell's pair of receptive fields (Figure 9). As a result, horizontal boundary contours could be generated throughout the region between pairs of vertical Lines in Figure 18d, even though these Lines are spatially out-of-phase. The problem can thus be summarized as follows: Given the need for a long-range cooperative process to complete boundaries over retinal veins, the blind spot, and so forth, what prevents this cooperative process from leaping over intervening images and grouping together inappropriate combinations of inputs? In situations wherein no image-induced obstructions prevent such grouping, it can in fact occur, as in Figures 7 and 8. If, however, cooperative grouping could penetrate all perceived objects, then many spurious groupings would occur across every Line. The perceptual space would be transparent with respect to the cooperative process.

To prevent this catastrophe, we propose a postulate of *spatial impenetrability*. This postulate suggests that mechanisms exist which prevent the cooperative process from grouping across all intervening percepts. Figure 18c discloses the primary computational properties that such a process must realize. It must *not* prevent like-oriented

responses from cooperating in a spatially aligned position, because that is the primary functional role of cooperation. It need only prevent like-oriented responses (such as the horizontal end cuts in Figure 18a) from cooperating across a region of *perpendicularly* oriented responses (such as the vertical responses to the vertical Lines in Figure 18c). We therefore hypothesize that the vertical responses to the Lines generate inhibitory inputs to horizontally oriented receptive fields of the cooperative process (Figure 31). The *net* input due to both horizontal end cuts and vertical lines at the horizontally oriented cooperative cells is thus very small or negative. As a result, neither receptive field of a horizontally oriented cooperative cell between the vertical Lines can be supraliminally excited. That is why the cooperative responses in Figure 18d ignore the horizontal end cuts.

It remains to say how both excitatory and inhibitory inputs are generated from the second competitive stage to the cooperative stage. We hypothesize that the second competitive stage is a dipole field (Grossberg, 1980, 1983a) and that inputs from the first competitive stage activate the on-cells of this dipole field. Suppose, for example, that an input excites vertically oriented on-cells, which inhibit horizontally oriented on-cells at the same position, as we have proposed in Section 20C. We assume, in addition, that inhibition of the horizontal on-cells excites the horizontal off-cells via disinhibition. The excited vertically oriented on-cells send excitatory inputs to the receptive fields of vertically oriented cooperative cells, whereas the excited horizontally oriented off-cells send

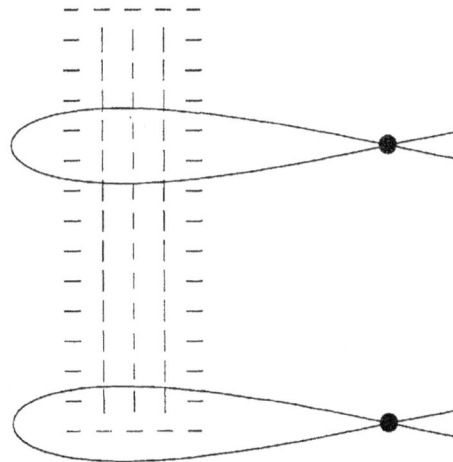

Figure 31. A mechanism to implement the postulate of spatial impenetability: The left receptive fields of two horizontally tuned cooperative cells are crossed by a thin vertical Line. Although horizontal end-cut signals can excite the upper receptive field, these are cancelled by the greater number of inhibitory inputs due to the vertical Line inputs. Within the lower receptive field, the excitatory inputs due to end cuts prevail.

inhibitory inputs to the receptive fields of horizontally oriented cooperative cells (Figure 30).

Two new cortical predictions are implied by this dipole-field hypothesis: Both the on-cell subfield and the off-cell subfield of the dipole field are tonically active, thereby enabling their cells to be activated due to disinhibition. Excitation of on-cells generates excitatory inputs to like-oriented cooperative receptive fields, whereas excitation of off-cells generates inhibitory inputs to like-oriented cooperative receptive fields. The tonic activity of the on-cell subfield helps to generate perpendicular end cuts, thereby preventing color flow from line ends. The tonic activity of the off-cell subfield helps to inhibit like-oriented cooperative cells, thereby augmenting spatial impenetrability.

E. Long-range oriented cooperation between like-oriented pairs of input groupings. The outputs from the dipole field input to a spatially long-range cooperative process. We call this process the boundary completion process. Outputs due to like-oriented dipole-field cells that are approximately aligned across perceptual space can cooperate via this process to synthesize an intervening boundary, as in Figures 18-25. A cooperative cell can be activated only if it receives a sufficiently positive net input at both of its orientationally tuned receptive fields (Figure 9).

Two types of parameters must be specified to characterize these receptive fields: macroscale parameters, which determine the gross shape of each receptive field,

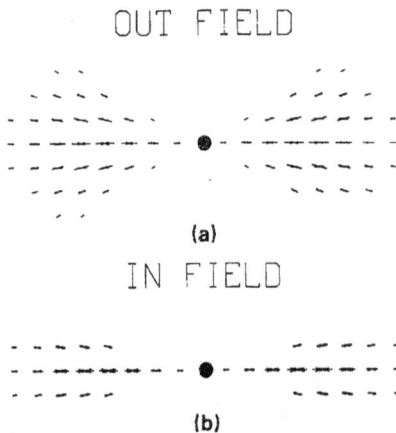

Figure 32. Cooperative in-field and out-field: Line lengths are proportional to the strengths of signals from a horizontally tuned competitive cell to cooperative cells of various orientations at nearby positions. Thus, in (a) strong signals are sent to horizontal cooperative cells 5 units to the left or the right of the competitive cell (center circle), but signal strength drops off with distance and change of orientation. (b) shows the dual perspective of weights assigned to incoming signals by the receptive field of a horizontal cooperative cell. (Note that only excitatory signal strengths are indicated in this figure.) The parameters used to generate these fields are identical to those used in Figures 18-25.

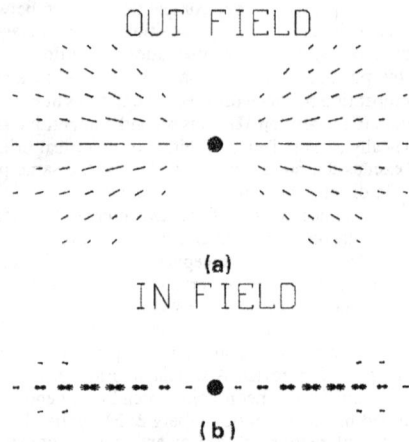

Figure 33. Extreme cooperative in-field and out-field: This figure employs more extreme parameter choices than were used in the simulations of Figure 18-25. Greater orientational uncertainty at one location of the in-field corresponds to greater positional uncertainty in the out-field, thereby illustrating the duality between in-field and out-field.

and microscale parameters, which determine how effectively a dipole-field input of prescribed orientation can excite or inhibit a cooperative receptive field. Figure 32 describes a computer simulation of the cooperative receptive field that we used to generate Figures 18-25. The cooperative out-field, or projection field, in Figure 32a describes the interaction strengths, or path weights, from a single horizontally oriented dipole-field on-cell to all cells within the cooperative stage. The length of each line is proportional to the size of the interaction strength to on-cells with the depicted positions and orientations. The cooperative in-field, or receptive field, in Figure 32b describes the path weights from all dipole-field on-cells with the depicted positions and preferred orientations to a single cooperative cell with a horizontally oriented receptive field. The length of each line is thus proportional to the sensitivity of the receptive field to inputs received from cells coding the depicted positions and orientations. The cell in Figure 32b is most sensitive to horizontally oriented inputs that fall along a horizontal axis passing through the cell. Close-to-horizontal orientations and close-to-horizontal positions can also help to excite the cell, but they are less effective. Figures 32a and 32b describe the same information, but from different perspectives of a single dipole-field on-cell source (Figure 32a) and a single cooperative cell sink (Figure 32b).

Figure 33 depicts a cooperative out-field (Figure 33a) and in-field (Figure 33b) due to a different choice of numerical parameters. In Figure 33a, a single dipole-field on-cell can spray inputs over a spatially broad region, but the orientations that it can excite are narrowly tuned at each position. From the perspective of a cooperative cell's receptive fields, the out-field in Figure 33a generates an in-field that is spatially narrow, but the orientations that can excite it are broadly tuned. Figures 32 and 33 illustrate a duality between in-fields and out-fields that is made rigorous by the equations in the Appendix.

F. On-center–off-surround feedback within each orientation. This process refines the BC System that was described in Grossberg and Mingolla (1985a). In Section 8, we suggested that excitatory feedback from the cooperative stage to the second competitive stage—more precisely to the on-cells of the dipole field—can help to eliminate fuzzy bands of boundaries by providing some orientations with a competitive advantage over other orientations. It is also necessary to provide some positions with a competitive advantage over other positions, so that only the favored orientations *and* positions will group to form a unique global boundary. Topographically organized excitatory feedback from a cooperative cell to a competitive cell is insufficient. Then the spatial fuzziness of the cooperative process (Figure 32) favors the same orientation at multiple noncollinear positions. Sharp orientational tuning but fuzzy spatial tuning of the resultant boundaries can then occur.

We suggest that the cooperative-to-competitive feedback process realizes a postulate of *spatial sharpening* in the following way. An active cooperative cell can excite like-oriented on-cells at the same position (Figure 30). An active cooperative cell can also inhibit like-oriented on-cells at nearby positions. Then both orientations *and* positions that are favored by cooperative groupings gain a competitive advantage within the on-cells of the dipole field.

Figures 18-25 show that the emergent groupings tend to be no thicker than the inducing input Lines due to this mechanism. Figure 30 shows that both the bottom-up inputs and the top-down inputs to the dipole field are organized as on-center–off-surround interactions among like orientations. The net top-down input is, however, always nonnegative due to the fact that excitatory interneurons are interpolated between the on-center–off-surround interaction and the dipole field. If this on-center–off-surround interaction were allowed to directly input to the dipole field, then a single Line could generate a spatially expanding lattice of mutually perpendicular secondary, tertiary, and higher order end cuts via the cooperative-competitive feedback loop. This completes our description of BC System interactions.

21. Concluding Remarks: Universality of the Boundary Contour System

The BC System and FC System interactions of our theory have suggested quantitative explanations and predictions for a large perceptual and neural data base, including data about perceptual grouping of textures and borders, illusory figures, monocular and binocular brightness percepts, monocular and binocular rivalry, the Land retinex demonstrations, neon color spreading and related filling-in phenomena, complementary color induction, fading of stabilized images, multiple scale interactions, shape-from-shading, metacontrast, hyperacuity, and various other global interactions between depth, lightness, length, and form properties (Cohen & Grossberg, 1984a; Grossberg, 1980, 1983a, 1984a, 1985; Grossberg & Mingolla, 1985a).

This expanded explanatory and predictive range is due, we believe, to the introduction and quantitative analysis of several fundamental new principles and mechanisms to the perceptual literature, notably the principle of boundary-feature tradeoff and the mechanisms governing BC System and FC System interactions.

The present article has refined the mechanisms of the BC System by using this system to quantitatively simulate emergent perceptual grouping properties that are found in the data of such workers as Beck et al. (1983), Glass and Switkes (1976), and Gregory and Heard (1979). We have hereby been led to articulate and instantiate the postulates of spatial impenetrability and of spatial sharpening, and to thereby make some new predictions about prestriate cortical interactions. These results have also shown that several apparently different Gestalt rules can be analyzed using the context-sensitive reactions of a single BC System. Taken together, these results suggest that a *universal* set of rules for perceptual grouping of scenic edges, textures, and smoothly shaded regions is well on the way to being characterized.

REFERENCES

Beck, J. (1966a). Effect of orientation and of shape similarity on perceptual grouping. *Perception & Psychophysics, 1,* 300-302.

Beck, J. (1966b). Perceptual grouping produced by changes in orientation and shape. *Science, 154,* 538-540.

Beck, J. (1972). Similarity grouping and peripheral discriminability under uncertainty. *American Journal of Psychology, 85,* 1-19.

Beck, J. (1982). Textural segmentation. In J. Beck (Ed.), *Organization and representation in perception.* Hillsdale, NJ: Erlbaum.

Beck, J. (1983). Textural segmentation, second-order statistics, and textural elements. *Biological Cybernetics, 48,* 125-130.

Beck, J., Prazdný, K., & Rosenfeld, A. (1983). A theory of textural segmentation. In J. Beck, B. Hope, & A. Rosenfeld (Eds.), *Human and machine vision.* New York: Academic Press.

Caelli, T. (1982). On discriminating visual textures and images. *Perception & Psychophysics, 31,* 149-159.

Caelli, T. (1983). Energy processing and coding factors in texture discrimination and image processing. *Perception & Psychophysics, 34,* 349-355.

Caelli, T., & Dodwell, P. C. (1982). The discrimination of structure in vectorgraphs: Local and global effects. *Perception & Psychophysics, 32,* 314-326.

Caelli, T., & Julesz, B. (1979). Psychophysical evidence for global feature processing in visual texture discrimination. *Journal of the Optical Society of America, 69,* 675-677.

Carpenter, G. A., & Grossberg, S. (1981). Adaptation and transmitter gating in vertebrate photoreceptors. *Journal of Theoretical Neurobiology, 1,* 1-42.

Carpenter, G. A., & Grossberg, S. (1983). Dynamic models of neural systems: Propagated signals, photoreceptor transduction, and circadian rhythms. In J. P. E. Hodgson (Ed.), *Oscillations in mathematical biology.* New York: Springer-Verlag.

Carpenter, G. A., & Grossberg, S. (1985). Neural dynamics of category learning and recognition: Attention, memory consolidation, and amnesia. In J. Davis, W. Newburgh, & E. Wegman (Eds.), *Brain structure, learning, and memory.* Washington, DC: AAAS Symposium Series.

Carpenter, G. A., & Grossberg, S. (in press). Neural dynamics of category learning and recognition: Structural invariants, evoked potentials, and reinforcement. In M. Commons, R. Herrnstein, & S. Kosslyn (Eds.), *Pattern recognition and concepts in animals, people, and machines.* Hillsdale, NJ: Erlbaum.

COHEN, M. A., & GROSSBERG, S. (1984a). Neural dynamics of brightness perception: Features, boundaries, diffusion, and resonance. *Perception & Psychophysics, 36,* 428-456.

COHEN, M. A., & GROSSBERG, S. (1984b). Some global properties of binocular resonances: Disparity matching, filling-in, and figure-ground synthesis. In P. Dodwell & T. Caelli (Eds.), *Figural synthesis.* Hillsdale, NJ: Erlbaum.

DESIMONE, R., SCHEIN, S. J., MORAN, J., & UNGERLEIDER, L. G. (1985). Contour, color, and shape analysis beyond the striate cortex. *Vision Research, 25,* 441-452.

DEV, P. (1975). Perception of depth surfaces in random-dot stereograms: A neural model. *International Journal of Man-Machine Studies, 7,* 511-528.

DEVALOIS, R. L., ALBRECHT, D. G., & THORELL, L. G. (1982). Spatial frequency selectivity of cells in macaque visual cortex. *Vision Research, 22,* 545-559.

DODWELL, P. C. (1983). The Lie transformation group model of visual perception. *Perception & Psychophysics, 34,* 1-16.

EJIMA, Y., REDIES, C., TAKAHASHI, S., & AKITA, M. (1984). The neon color effect in the Ehrenstein pattern: Dependence on wavelength and illuminance. *Vision Research, 24,* 1719-1726.

ELLIAS, S., & GROSSBERG, S. (1975). Pattern formation, contrast control, and oscillations in the short term memory of shunting on-center off-surround networks. *Biological Cybernetics, 20,* 69-98.

GEMAN, S., & GEMAN, D. (1984). Stochastic relaxation, Gibbs distribution, and the Bayesian restoration of images. *IEEE Patent Analysis & Machine Intelligence, 6,* 721-741.

GLASS, L., & SWITKES, E. (1976). Pattern recognition in humans: Correlations which cannot be perceived. *Perception, 5,* 67-72.

GOURAS, P., & KRÜGER, J. (1979). Responses of cells in foveal visual cortex of the monkey to pure color contrast. *Journal of Neurophysiology, 42,* 850-860.

GREGORY, R. L. (1966). *Eye and brain.* New York: McGraw-Hill.

GREGORY, R. L., & HEARD, P. (1979). Border locking and the café wall illusion. *Perception, 8,* 365-380.

GROSSBERG, S. (1973). Contour enhancement, short-term memory, and constancies in reverberating neural networks. *Studies in Applied Mathematics, 52,* 217-257.

GROSSBERG, S. (1980). How does a brain build a cognitive code? *Psychological Review, 87,* 1-51.

GROSSBERG, S. (1982). *Studies of mind and brain: Neural principles of learning, perception, development, cognition, and motor control.* Boston: Reidel Press.

GROSSBERG, S. (1983a). Neural substrates of binocular form perception: Filtering, matching, diffusion, and resonance. In E. Basar, H. Flohr, H. Haken, & A. J. Mandell (Eds.), *Synergetics of the brain.* New York: Springer.

GROSSBERG, S. (1983b). The quantized geometry of visual space: The coherent computation of depth, form, and lightness. *Behavioral & Brain Sciences, 6,* 625-692.

GROSSBERG, S. (1984a). Outline of a theory of brightness, color, and form perception. In E. Degreef & J. van Buggenhaut (Eds.), *Trends in mathematical psychology.* Amsterdam: North-Holland.

GROSSBERG, S. (1984b). Some psychophysiological and pharmacological correlates of a developmental, cognitive, and motivational theory. In R. Karrer, J. Cohen, & P. Tueting (Eds.), *Brain and information: Event related potentials.* New York: New York Academy of Sciences.

GROSSBERG, S. (1985). *Cortical dynamics of depth, brightness, color, and form perception: A predictive synthesis.* Manuscript submitted for publication.

GROSSBERG, S., & LEVINE, D. (1975). Some developmental and attentional biases in the contrast enhancement and short term memory of recurrent neural networks. *Journal of Theoretical Biology, 53,* 341-380.

GROSSBERG, S., & MINGOLLA, E. (1985a). Neural dynamics of form perception: Boundary completion, illusory figures, and neon color spreading. *Psychological Review, 92,* 173-211.

GROSSBERG, S., & MINGOLLA, E. (1985b). *Neural dynamics of surface perception: Boundary webs, illuminants, and shape-from-shading.* Manuscript in preparation.

HEGGELUND, P. (1981). Receptive field organisation of complex cells in cat striate cortex. *Experimental Brain Research, 42,* 99-107.

HELMHOLTZ, H. L. F. VON. (1962). *Treatise on physiological optics* (J. P. C. Southall, Trans.). New York: Dover. (Original work published 1890)

HOFFMAN, W. C. (1970). Higher visual perception as prolongation of the basic Lie transformation group. *Mathematical Biosciences, 6,* 437-471.

HORN, B. K. P. (1977). Understanding image intensities. *Artificial Intelligence, 8,* 201-231.

HUBEL, D. H., & WIESEL, T. N. (1962). Receptive fields, binocular interaction and functional architecture in the cat's visual cortex. *Journal of Physiology, 160,* 106-154.

HUBEL, D. H., & WIESEL, T. N. (1968). Receptive fields and functional architecture of monkey striate cortex. *Journal of Physiology, 195,* 215-243.

HUBEL, D. H., & WIESEL, T. N. (1977). Functional architecture of macaque monkey visual cortex. *Proceedings of the Royal Society of London (B), 198,* 1-59.

JULESZ, B. (1960). Binocular depth perception of computer-generated patterns. *Bell System Technical Journal, 39,* 1125-1162.

JULESZ, B. (1971). *Foundations of cyclopean perception.* Chicago: University of Chicago Press.

KANISZA, G. (1955). Margini quasi-percettivi in campi con stimolazione omogenea. *Revista di psicologia, 49,* 7-30.

KAPLAN, G. A. (1969). Kinetic disruption of optical texture: The perception of depth at an edge. *Perception & Psychophysics, 6,* 193-198.

KAWABATA, N. (1984). Perception at the blind spot and similarity grouping. *Perception & Psychophysics, 36,* 151-158.

KENNEDY, J. M. (1979). Subjective contours, contrast, and assimilation. In C. F. Nodine & D. F. Fisher (Eds.), *Perception and pictorial representation* (pp. 167-195). New York: Praeger.

KRAUSKOPF, J. (1963). Effect of retinal image stabilization on the appearance of heterochromatic targets. *Journal of the Optical Society of America, 53,* 741-744.

LAND, E. H. (1977). The retinex theory of color vision. *Scientific American, 237,* 108-128.

MARR, D., & HILDRETH, E. (1980). Theory of edge detection. *Proceedings of the Royal Society of London (B), 207,* 187-217.

MARR, D., & POGGIO, T. (1976). Cooperative computation of stereo disparity. *Science, 194,* 283-287.

McCOURT, M. E. (1983). Brightness induction and the café wall illusion. *Perception, 12,* 131-142.

NEISSER, U. (1967). *Cognitive psychology.* New York: Appleton-Century-Crofts.

PRANDTL, A. (1927). Über gleichsinnige Induktion und die Lichtverteilung in gitterartigen Mustern. *Zeitschrift für Sinnesphysiologie, 58,* 263-307.

PRAZDNY, K. (1983). Illusory contours are not caused by simultaneous brightness contrast. *Perception & Psychophysics, 34,* 403-404.

PRAZDNY, K. (1984). On the perception of Glass patterns. *Perception, 13,* 469-478.

PRAZDNY, K. (1985). On the nature of inducing forms generating perception of illusory contours. *Perception & Psychophysics, 37,* 237-242.

PREYER, W. (1897/1898). On certain optical phenomena: Letter to Professor E. C. Sanford. *American Journal of Psychology, 9,* 42-44.

RATLIFF, F. (1965). *Mach bands: Quantitative studies on neural networks in the retina.* New York: Holden-Day.

REDIES, C., & SPILLMANN, L. (1981). The neon color effect in the Ehrenstein illusion. *Perception, 10,* 667-681.

REDIES, C., SPILLMANN, L., & KUNZ, K. (1984). Colored neon flanks and line gap enhancement. *Vision Research, 24,* 1301-1309.

SCHATZ, B. R. (1977). The computation of immediate texture discrimination. *MIT AI Memo 426.*

SCHILLER, P. H., FINLAY, B. L., & VOLMAN, S. F. (1976). Quantitative studies of single-cell properties in monkey striate cortex, 1: Spatiotemporal organization of receptive fields. *Journal of Neurophysiology, 39,* 1288-1319.

Schwartz, E. L., Desimone, R., Albright, T., & Gross, C. G. (1983). Shape recognition and inferior temporal neurons. *Proceedings of the National Academy of Sciences*, **80**, 5776-5778.

Shapley, R., & Gordon, J. (1985). Nonlinearity in the perception of form. *Perception & Psychophysics*, **37**, 84-88.

Sperling, G. (1970). Binocular vision: A physical and a neural theory. *American Journal of Psychology*, **83**, 461-534.

Spillmann, L. (1985). *Illusory brightness and contour perception: Current status and unresolved problems.* Manuscript submitted for publication.

Spitzer, H., & Hochstein, S. (1985). A complex-cell receptive field model. *Journal of Neurophysiology*, **53**, 1266-1286.

Tanaka, M., Lee, B. B., & Creutzfeldt, O. D. (1983). Spectral tuning and contour representation in area 17 of the awake monkey. In J. D. Mollon & L. T. Sharpe (Eds.), *Colour vision*. New York: Academic Press.

Todorović, D. (1983). *Brightness perception and the Craik-O'Brien-Cornsweet effect.* Unpublished MA thesis, University of Connecticut.

van Tuijl, H. F. J. M. (1975). A new visual illusion: Neonlike color spreading and complementary color induction between subjective contours. *Acta Psychologica*, **39**, 441-445.

van Tuijl, H. F. J. M., & de Weert, C. M. M. (1979). Sensory conditions for the occurrence of the neon spreading illusion. *Perception*, **8**, 211-215.

van Tuijl, H. F. J. M., & Leeuwenberg, E. L. J. (1979). Neon color spreading and structural information measures. *Perception & Psychophysics*, **25**, 269-284.

von der Heydt, R., Peterhans, E., & Baumgartner, G. (1984). Illusory contours and cortical neuron responses. *Science*, **224**, 1260-1262.

Wertheimer, M. (1923). Untersuchungen zur Lehre von der Gestalt, II. *Psychologische Forschung*, **4**, 301-350.

Wolfe, J. M. (1984). Global factors in the Hermann grid illusion. *Perception*, **13**, 33-40.

Yarbus, A. L. (1967). *Eye movements and vision*. New York: Plenum Press.

Zeki, S. (1983a). Colour coding in the cerebral cortex: The reaction of cells in monkey visual cortex to wavelengths and colours. *Neuroscience*, **9**, 741-765.

Zeki, S. (1983b). Colour coding in the cerebral cortex: The responses of wavelength-selective and colour coded cells in monkey visual cortex to changes in wavelength composition. *Neuroscience*, **9**, 767-791.

Zucker, S. W. (1985). *Early orientation selection: Tangent fields and the dimensionality of their support* (Technical Report 85-13-R) Montreal: McGill University.

APPENDIX

Boundary Contour System Equations

The network we used to define the Boundary Contour System (BC System) is defined in stages below. This network further develops the BC System that was described in Grossberg and Mingolla (1985a).

A. Oriented Masks

To define a mask, or oriented receptive field, centered at position (i,j) with orientation k, divide the elongated receptive field of the mask into a left-half L_{ijk} and a right-half R_{ijk}. Let all the masks sample a field of preprocessed inputs. If S_{pq} equals the preprocessed input to position (p,q) of this field, then the output J_{ijk} from the mask at position (i,j) with orientation k is

$$J_{ijk} = \frac{[U_{ijk} - \alpha V_{ijk}]^+ + [V_{ijk} - \alpha U_{ijk}]^+}{1 + \beta(U_{ijk} + V_{ijk})} . \quad (A1)$$

where

$$U_{ijk} = \sum_{(p,q) \in L_{ijk}} S_{pq}, \quad (A2)$$

$$V_{ijk} = \sum_{(p,q) \in R_{ijk}} S_{pq}, \quad (A3)$$

and the notation $[p]^+ = \max(p,0)$. The sum of the two terms in the numerator of Equation A1 says that J_{ijk} is sensitive to the orientation and amount of contrast, but not to the direction of contrast, received by L_{ijk} and R_{ijk}. The denominator term in Equation A1 enables J_{ijk} to compute a ratio scale in the limit where $\beta(U_{ijk} + V_{ijk})$ is much greater than 1. In all of our simulations, we have chosen $\beta = 0$.

B. On-Center-Off-Surround Interaction Within Each Orientation (Competition I)

Inputs J_{ijk} with a fixed orientation k activate potentials w_{ijk} at the first competitive stage via on-center-off-surround interactions: each J_{ijk} excites w_{ijk} and inhibits w_{pqk} if $|p-i|^2 + |q-j|^2$ is sufficiently small. All the potentials w_{ijk} are also excited by the same tonic input I, which supports disinhibitory activations at the next competitive stage. Thus,

$$\frac{d}{dt} w_{ijk} = -w_{ijk} + I + f(J_{ijk}) - w_{ijk} \sum_{(p,q)} f(J_{pqk}) A_{pqij}, \quad (A4)$$

where A_{pqij} is the inhibitory interaction strength between positions (p,q) and (i,j) and $f(J_{ijk})$ is the input signal generated by J_{ijk}. In our runs, we chose

$$f(J_{ijk}) = BJ_{ijk}. \quad (A5)$$

Sections C and D together define the on-cell subfield of the dipole field described in Section 20.

C. Push-Pull Opponent Processes Between Orientation at Each Position

Perpendicular potentials w_{ijk} and w_{ijK} elicit output signals that compete at their target potentials x_{ijk} and x_{ijK}, respectively. For simplicity, we assume that these output signals equal the potentials w_{ijk} and w_{ijK}, which are always nonnegative. We also assume that x_{ijk} and x_{ijK} respond quickly and linearly to these signals. Thus,

$$x_{ijk} = w_{ijk} - w_{ijK} \quad (A6)$$

and

$$x_{ijK} = w_{ijK} - w_{ijk}. \quad (A7)$$

D. Normalization at Each Position

We also assume that, as part of this push-pull opponent process, the outputs y_{ijk} of the second competitive stage become normalized. Several ways exist for achieving this property (Grossberg, 1983b). We have used the following approach.

The potentials x_{ijk} interact when they become positive. Thus, we let the output $O_{ijk} = O(x_{ijk})$ from x_{ijk} equal

$$O_{ijk} = C[w_{ijk} - w_{ijK}]^+, \quad (A8)$$

170   GROSSBERG AND MINGOLLA

where C is a positive constant and $[p]^+ = \max(p, 0)$. All these outputs at each position interact via a shunting on-center-off-surround network whose potentials y_{ijk} satisfy

$$\frac{d}{dt} y_{ijk} = -Dy_{ijk} + (E - y_{ijk})O_{ijk} - y_{ijk} \sum_{m \neq k} O_{ijm}. \quad (A9)$$

Each potential y_{ijk} equilibrates rapidly to its input. Setting

$$\frac{d}{dt} y_{ijk} = 0$$

in Equation A9 implies that

$$y_{ijk} = \frac{EO_{ijk}}{D + O_{ij}}, \quad (A10)$$

where

$$O_{ij} = \sum_{m=1}^{n} O_{ijm}. \quad (A11)$$

Thus, if D is small compared with O_{ij}, then $\sum_{m=1}^{n} y_{ijm} \cong E$.

E. Opponent Inputs to the Cooperative Stage

The next process refines the BCS model used in Grossberg and Mingolla (1985a). It helps to realize the postulate of spatial impenetrability that was described in Section 20. The w_{ijk}, x_{ijk}, and y_{ijk} potentials are all assumed to be part of the on-cell subfield of a dipole field. If y_{ijk} is excited, an excitatory signal $f(y_{ijk})$ is generated at the cooperative stage. When potential y_{ijk} is excited, the potential y_{ijK} corresponding to the perpendicular orientation is inhibited. Both of these potentials form part of the on-cell subfield of a dipole field. Inhibition of an on-cell potential y_{ijk} disinhibits the corresponding off-cell potential $\bar{y}_{ijK}$, which sends an inhibitory signal $-f(\bar{y}_{ijK})$ to the cooperative level. The signals $f(y_{ijk})$ and $-f(\bar{y}_{ijk})$ thus occur together. In order to instantiate these properties, we made the simplest hypothesis, namely that

$$\bar{y}_{ijK} = y_{ijk}. \quad (A12)$$

F. Oriented Cooperation: Statistical Gates

The cooperative potential z_{ijk} can be supraliminally activated only if both of its cooperative input branches receive enough net positive excitation from similarly aligned competitive potentials (Figure 9). Thus,

$$\frac{d}{dt} z_{ijk} = -z_{ijk} + g\left(\sum_{(p,q,r)} [f(y_{pqr}) - f(\bar{y}_{pqr})] F_{pqij}^{(r,k)} \right)$$

$$+ g\left(\sum_{(p,q,r)} [f(y_{pqr}) - f(\bar{y}_{pqr})] G_{pqij}^{(r,k)} \right). \quad (A13)$$

In Equation A13, $g(s)$ is a signal function that becomes positive only when s is positive, and has a finite maximum value. A slower-than-linear function,

$$g(s) = \frac{H[s]^+}{K + [s]^+}, \quad (A14)$$

was used in our simulations. A sum of two sufficiently positive $g(s)$ terms in Equation A13 is needed to activate z_{ijk} above the firing threshold of its output signal $h(z_{ijk})$. A threshold-linear signal function,

$$h(z) = L[z - M]^+, \quad (A15)$$

was used. Each sum, such as

$$\sum_{(p,q,r)} f(y_{pqr}) F_{pqij}^{(r,k)} \quad (A16)$$

and

$$\sum_{(p,q,r)} f(y_{pqr}) G_{pqij}^{(r,k)}, \quad (A17)$$

is a spatial cross-correlation that adds up inputs from a strip with orientation (approximately equal to) k, which lies to one side or the other of position (i,j), as in Figures 32 and 33. The orientations r that contribute to the spatial kernels $F_{pqij}^{(r,k)}$ and $G_{pqij}^{(r,k)}$ also approximately equal k. The kernels $F_{pqij}^{(r,k)}$ and $G_{pqij}^{(r,k)}$ are defined by

$$F_{pqij}^{(r,k)} = \left[\exp[-2(N_{pqij}P^{-1} - 1)^2] \right.$$
$$\left. \times \left[|\cos(Q_{pqij} - r)| \right]^R [\cos(Q_{pqij} - k)]^T \right]^+ \quad (A18)$$

and

$$G_{pqij}^{(r,k)} = \left[-\exp[-2(N_{pqij}P^{-1} - 1)^2] \right.$$
$$\left. \times \left[|\cos(Q_{pqij} - r)| \right]^R [\cos(Q_{pqij} - k)]^T \right]^+, \quad (A19)$$

where

$$N_{pqij} = \sqrt{(p - i)^2 + (q - j)^2}, \quad (A20)$$

$$Q_{pqij} = \arctan\left(\frac{q - j}{p - i} \right), \quad (A21)$$

and P, R, and T are positive constants. In particular, R and T are odd integers. Kernels F and G differ only by a minus sign under the $[\cdots]^+$ sign. This minus sign determines the polarity of the kernel, namely, whether it collects inputs for z_{ijk} from one side or the other of position (i,j). Term

$$\exp\left[-2\left(\frac{N_{pqij}}{P} - 1 \right)^2 \right]$$

determines the optimal distance P from (i,j) at which each kernel collects its inputs. The kernel decays in a Gaussian fashion as a function of N_{pqij}/P, where N_{pqij} in Equation A20 is the distance between (p,q) and (i,j). The cosine terms in Equations A18 and A19 determine the orientational tuning of the kernels. By Equation A21, Q_{pqij} is the direction of position (p,q) with respect to the position of the cooperative cell (i,j) in Equation A13. Term $|\cos(Q_{pqij} - r)|$ in Equations A18 and A19 computes how parallel Q_{pqij} is to the receptive field orientation r at position (p,q). By Equation A21, term $|\cos(Q_{pqij} - r)|$ is maximal when the orientation r equals the orientation of (p,q) with respect to (i,j). The absolute value sign around this term prevents it from becoming negative. Term $\cos(Q_{pqij} - k)$ in Equations A18 and A19 computes how parallel Q_{pqij} is to the orientation k of the receptive field of the cooperative cell (i,j) in Equation A13. By

Equation A21, term $\cos(Q_{pqij}-k)$ is maximal when the orientation k equals the orientation of (p,q) with respect to (i,j). Positions (p,q) such that $\cos(Q_{pqij}-k) < 0$ do not input to z_{ijk} via kernel F because the $[\cdots]^+$ of a negative number equals zero. On the other hand, such positions (p,q) may input to z_{ijk} via kernel G due to the extra minus sign in the definition of kernel G. The extra minus sign in Equation A19 flips the preferred axis of orientation of kernel $G_{pqij}^{(r,k)}$ with respect to the kernel $F_{pqij}^{(r,k)}$ in order to define the two input-collecting branches of each cooperative cell, as in Figures 9 and 30. The product terms $[\,|\cos(Q_{pqji}-r)\,|\,]^R[\cos(Q_{pqij}-k)]^T$ in Equations A18 and A19 thus determine larger path weights from dipole field on-cells whose positions and orientations are nearly parallel to the preferred orientation k of the cooperative cell (i,j), and larger path weights from dipole-field off-cells whose positions and orientations are nearly perpendicular to the preferred orientation k of the cooperative cell (i,j). The powers R and T determine the sharpness of orientational tuning: Higher powers enforce sharper tuning.

G. On-Center-Off-Surround Feedback Within Each Orientation

The next process refines the BC System model used in Grossberg and Mingolla (1985). It helps to realize the postulate of spatial sharpening that was described in Section 20. We assume that each z_{ijk} activates a shunting on-center-off-surround interaction within each orientation k. The target potentials v_{ijk} therefore obey an equation of the form

$$\frac{d}{dt} v_{ijk} = -v_{ijk} + h(z_{ijk}) - v_{ijk} \sum_{(p,q)} h(z_{pqk}) W_{pqij}. \qquad (A22)$$

The bottom-up transformation $J_{ijk} \to w_{ijk}$ in Equation A4 is thus similar to the top-down transformation $z_{ijk} \to v_{ijk}$ in Equation A22. Functionally, the $z_{ijk} \to v_{ijk}$ transformation enables the most favored cooperations to enhance their preferred positions and orientation as they suppress nearby positions with the same orientation. The signals v_{ijk} take effect by inputting to the w_{ijk} opponent process. Equation A4 is thus changed to

$$\frac{d}{dt} w_{ijk} = -w_{ijk} + I + f(J_{ijk}) + v_{ijk} - w_{ijk} \sum_{(p,q)} f(J_{pqk}) A_{pqij}. \qquad (A23)$$

At equilibrium, the computational logic of the BC System is determined, up to parameter choices, by the equations

$$J_{ijk} = \frac{[U_{ijk} - \alpha V_{ijk}]^+ + [V_{ijk} - \alpha U_{ijk}]^+}{1 + \beta(U_{ijk} + V_{ijk})}, \qquad (A1)$$

$$w_{ijk} = \frac{I + BJ_{ijk} + v_{ijk}}{1 + B\Sigma_{(p,q)} J_{pqk} A_{pqij}}, \qquad (A24)$$

$$O_{ijk} = C[w_{ijk} - w_{ijk}]^+, \qquad (A8)$$

$$y_{ijk} = \frac{EO_{ijk}}{D + O_{ij}}, \qquad (A10)$$

$$z_{ijk} = g\left(\sum_{(p,q,r)} [f(y_{pqr}) - f(y_{pqR})] F_{pqij}^{(r,k)} \right)$$
$$+ g\left(\sum_{(p,q,r)} [f(y_{pqr}) - f(y_{pqR})] G_{pqij}^{(r,k)} \right), \qquad (A25)$$

and

$$v_{ijk} = \frac{h(z_{ijk})}{1 + \Sigma_{(p,q)} h(z_{pqk}) W_{pqij}}. \qquad (A26)$$

Wherever possible, simple spatial kernels were used. For example, the kernels W_{pqij} in Equation A22 and A_{pqij} in Equation A23 were both chosen to be constant within a circular receptive field:

$$A_{pqij} = \begin{cases} A & \text{if } (p-i)^2 + (q-j)^2 \leq A_0 \\ 0 & \text{otherwise} \end{cases} \qquad (A27)$$

and

$$W_{pqij} = \begin{cases} W & \text{if } (p-i)^2 + (q-j)^2 \leq W_0 \\ 0 & \text{otherwise.} \end{cases} \qquad (A28)$$

(Manuscript received April 4, 1985;
revision accepted for publication August 9, 1985.)

[21]

The Negative Priming Effect: Inhibitory Priming by Ignored Objects

Steven P. Tipper

*Department of Experimental Psychology,
South Parks Road, Oxford, U.K.*

A priming paradigm was employed to investigate the processing of an ignored object during selection of an attended object. Two issues were investigated: the level of internal representation achieved for the ignored object, and the subsequent fate of this representation. In Experiment 1 a prime display containing two superimposed objects was briefly presented. One second later a probe display was presented containing an object to be named. If the ignored object in the prime display was the same as the subsequent probe, naming latencies were impaired. This effect is termed negative priming. It suggests that internal representations of the ignored object may become associated with inhibition during selection. Thus, selection of a subsequent probe object requiring these inhibited representations is delayed. Experiment 2 replicated the negative priming effect with a shorter inter-stimulus interval. Experiment 3 examined the priming effects of both the ignored and the selected objects. The effect of both identity repetition and a categorical relationship between prime and probe stimuli were investigated. The data showed that for a stimulus selected from the prime display, naming of the same object in the probe display was facilitated. When the same stimulus was ignored in the prime display, however, naming of it in the probe display was again impaired (negative

Requests for reprints should be sent to S. P. Tipper, Department of Psychology, Mount Allison University, Sackville, New Brunswick, Canada, EOA 3CO.

This work has benefited from discussions with Alan Allport, Donald Broadbent, Gordon Baylis and Nik Chmiel; it was supported by an S.E.R.C. studentship and MRC project grant (48313910N).

The experiments were conducted as part of work towards the author's doctoral dissertation,[1] reported to the Meeting of the Experimental Psychology Society, Amsterdam, July 1984, and briefly described in Allport, Tipper and Chmiel (in press) as Experiment 3 and part of Experiment 5.

[1]S. P. Tipper (1984), "Negative priming and visual selective attention". University of Oxford, D.Phil.

priming). That negative priming was also demonstrated with categorically related objects suggests that ignored objects achieve categorical levels of representation, and that the inhibition may be at this level.

GENERAL INTRODUCTION

Biological organisms are bombarded by sensory information. A basic issue is how organisms select particular objects for action and successfully ignore other competing objects. One approach to the study of selection mechanisms is to examine the processing of the objects that are ignored. Two central questions are at issue: What level of representation does the ignored object achieve, and what is the subsequent fate of this representation? The main two opposing positions concerning the level of internal representation achieved by the ignored object can be termed precategorical and postcategorical selection. The precategorical view maintains that the initial parallel analysis of a visual scene achieves internal representations of only the physical features of objects, for example, the colour of an object, its location in space, etc. (Broadbent, 1971; Kahneman and Treisman, 1984). Representations of what an object "means" to an organism are only achieved when the object is selected for further processing. The contrary position of postcategorical selection maintains that the initial parallel analysis of a visual scene achieves at least categorical levels of internal representation, as well as lower physical features (Deutsch and Deutsch, 1963; Allport, 1977, 1980; Van der Heijden, 1981).

The second question is this: During and after selection of the target, what happens to the representations of ignored objects, whether these representations are at low level (physical) or higher (categorical) levels? Again, there are two opposing views. The first can be termed passive decay. This position is held by both pre- and postcategorical theorists. For example, Broadbent (1970) represents the precategorical view. He suggests that information is initially received into a buffer store of low-level physical representations. Some of this information may then proceed to further processing mechanisms. The information that fails to pass this stage of serial processing before the time limit on the buffer store expires will be lost. Van der Heijden (1981) holds a postcategorical view of the initial processing of a display prior to selection. However, like Broadbent, he feels that distractors decay when not selected. Indeed, he goes further and suggests that distractor decay is one of the mechanisms of selection. He says: "Attention functions by maintaining the count level of the correct logogen until the count level of the other [irrelevant distractors] logogens are sufficiently decreased" (p. 188).

The alternative view can be termed distractor inhibition. That is, the internal representations of competing distractor representations are associated with inhibition during target selection. Keele and Neill (1978) write: "... when it [the control process of attention] selects some information, other conflicting information can be inhibited" (p. 42). In this view the mechanisms of selection involve target facilitation/maintenance *and* distractor inhibition. Such a dual mechanism may explain the remarkable efficiency of selection.

To examine whether decay or inhibition occurs, it is necessary to observe the fate of the representation of the ignored object subsequent to the initial encounter with the object. Previous methods have looked for the effect of an ignored distractor on the processing of a simultaneous target, for example, Stroop (1935). Such an approach can show that ignored objects achieve particular levels of internal representation, but cannot tell us whether these representations then passively decay or are actively inhibited. One way to study the fate of a representation over time is to use a priming paradigm. A display containing a prime object is presented, then, after a delay, a probe display is presented for rapid naming. Previous research has shown that when the prime is attended to and is the same as, or semantically related to, a subsequent probe, the response to the probe is facilitated (Warren and Morton, 1982; Carr, McCauley, Sperber and Parmelee, 1982; Meyer and Schvaneveldt, 1975).

The research reported here, however, looks at the priming effects of ignored objects. If an ignored object influences the subsequent processing of the same, or a semantically related object presented as a probe, it may be possible to infer the type of internal representation achieved in the processing of an ignored object and what happens to this representation. For example, if the selection process functions by inhibiting the internal representations of the ignored object, then we might predict that the processing of a probe related to the ignored object may be subsequently impaired or delayed.

Some previous research using a priming paradigm has indeed suggested that ignored distractors are associated with inhibition. Dalrymple-Alford and Budayr (1966), Neill (1977) and Tipper[2] have demonstrated that in a Stroop colour-word ink-naming task, if the word ignored on trial N is the same as the ink name response to be output on trial $N+1$, then naming latencies are longer. This suggests that inhibition of the response to the distracting word on trial N carries over and impairs naming of the ink on trial $N+1$. Greenwald (1972) produced analogous results employing a task where subjects named visual digits

---

[2]S. P. Tipper (1984). "Negative priming and visual selective attention". University of Oxford, D.Phil.

whilst ignoring auditory distractors. The data showed that when an auditory distractor was re-presented as a visual target, naming latencies were impaired. (See also Harvey, 1980.)

The experiments described below employ a similar priming paradigm. Subjects are presented with two competing objects and are told by means of a physical cue which one to select and which to ignore. Both objects are presented above threshold, thus they are both potentially available to control overt response. These objects will be referred to according to the directions given to subjects, i.e. as the "selected" and "ignored" objects.

Throughout the experiments, selection is by colour. For example, a red selected object may be superimposed over a green ignored object. Previous research has suggested that subjects are able to select successfully targets superimposed on the same spatial location as distractors, when using colour as the selection cue (Rock and Gutman, 1981; Irwin, 1979, 1981). Neisser and his colleagues (Bahrick, Walker and Neisser, 1981; Neisser and Becklen, 1975) have also demonstrated selection of targets from spatially superimposed distractors when using kinetic information as the selection cue.

In the current paradigm, subjects were presented initially with a pair of superimposed objects: the prime display. They were always told to identify one, specified by colour, and to ignore the other. A second display containing a pair of objects was then presented: the probe display. Subjects were requested to name the selected probe (specified by colour) as fast as possible. The main experimental manipulation was whether or not the ignored prime was the same as or related to the subsequent selected probe.

EXPERIMENT 1

This experiment examined the effect of ignored primes on the naming of identical selected probes. The latency to name the selected probe was used to examine the processing of the ignored prime. Subjects' abilities to recall and to recognize the ignored stimuli were also examined. Hence both indirect (priming) and direct (recall/recognition) measures of the processing of ignored stimuli were available.

Method

Subjects

Twenty-four female subjects from the Oxford subject panel were each paid £1.25 to take part in the experiment. They were aged between 18 and 45. All were right-handed and had normal colour vision and normal or corrected-to-normal acuity in both eyes.

Apparatus and Materials

A six-field tachistoscope having 2 three-field power units (Electronic Developments Ltd) was used for stimulus presentation. A hand-held microswitch was used by subjects for starting each trial. A voice key and a millisecond timer (Behavioural Research and Development Electronics Ltd) were used to measure oral naming latencies.

Simple line drawings of objects were used to construct the stimuli. All drawings had previously been shown to have better than 90% naming agreement, using other similar subjects (G. Ratcliffe, M.R.C. Neuropsychological Unit, Oxford, personal communication). Examples can be found in Figure 1. The drawings were traced onto white paper (with Platignum nylon-tip pens), centralized, and glued onto $6 \times 4''$ cards. Red was used as the colour for the selected drawing that was superimposed over a green ignored drawing. [In other experiments[3] selected and ignored colours were reversed, ensuring that the effects obtained were not due to the particular pertinence of one colour.] Red and green were chosen for compatibility with Rock and Gutman (1981), Goldstein and Fink (1981) who used similar superimposed figures, and Irwin (1979, 1981) who used superimposed words.

The colour and contrast of the selected drawing was enhanced slightly by drawing over its contours twice, while the ignored drawing was traced over once. This was done to facilitate selection of the selected object and reduce possible intrusions of the ignored. Humphreys (1981) has pointed out that the contrast of a stimulus influences processing speed as reflected by reaction times. (In his data black stimuli with greater contrast had shorter reaction times than red stimuli.)

The drawings ranged in size from 6° vertical visual angle and 6° horizontal to 8° vertical and 10° horizontal. Figure 1 demonstrates examples of typical prime and probe displays used. The prime display contained two superimposed figures: a selected (red) figure and an ignored (green) figure. In all cases the selected prime was unrelated to the following selected probe and to the ignored prime. This ignored prime was either identical to the following selected probe (ignored repetition) or unrelated to it (control). The ignored drawings in the ignored repetition and control conditions were approximately matched for size and physical complexity. The selected drawings in the control and ignored repetition conditions were the same.

The probe drawings were prepared in a similar way. They were red and were superimposed over random green lines. The requirement of selecting the probe from distracting contours was to make it more sensitive to priming effects. Meyer, Schvaneveldt and Ruddy,[4] Becker and Killion (1977), Sperber, McCauley, Ragain and Weil (1979) have shown that the processing of degraded probe words or drawings is facilitated more than the processing of undegraded probes, by a semantically related prime. A second reason for requiring selection of the

---

[3]See S. P. Tipper (1984). "Negative priming and visual selective attention". University of Oxford, D.Phil.

[4]D. Meyer, R. W. Schvaneveldt and M. G. Ruddy (1972). Activation of lexical memory. Paper presented at the meeting of the Psychonomic Society, St Louis.

PRIMES

| CONTROL:
EXPERIMENT 1 | IGNORED REPITITION:
EXPERIMENT 1 & 2 | CONTROL:
EXPERIMENT 2 |

PROBE

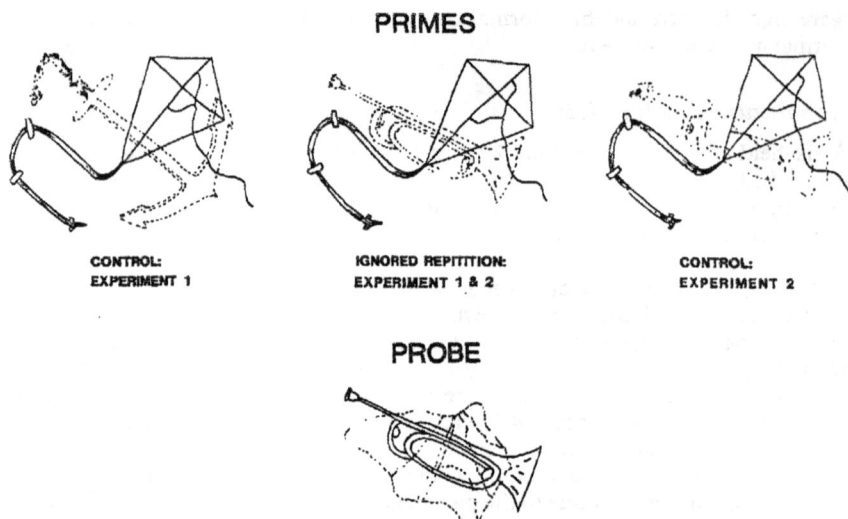

Figure 1.   Prime and Probe displays used in Experiments 1 and 2. The lines depicted as solid were Red (selected); the lines depicted as broken were Green (ignored).

probe was to make processing of prime and probe displays as similar as possible. That is, they both require selection from superimposed green distractors. A constant selection strategy should allow subjects to become adjusted to this somewhat unusual selection task quickly, and thus allow efficient selection.

Five pairs of superimposed drawings were used in the initial procedure for setting stimulus onset asynchrony (SOA) between priming stimulus and a pattern mask. Nine superimposed priming pairs, plus nine probes, were used in the priming practice session; 24 priming pairs plus 24 probes were used in the experimental trials (i.e. 12 RTs in each priming condition). Each drawing was only presented once. Using different stimuli on every trial put a severe constraint on the number of trials available for SOA setting and RT data.

Stimuli for a recognition memory test were also prepared. Five drawings were randomly chosen from the selected primes, five were chosen from the ignored primes of the control condition, and five were previously unseen drawings. These were drawn in random order onto a large ($11\frac{1}{2} \times 24''$) sheet of paper and numbered.

Two black fixation crosses and two red and green picture fragment pattern masks were used. The pattern masks were picture fragments drawn with the same pens used to prepare the experimental stimuli.

Design

A within-subjects design was used in which the independent variable was the nature of the distractor prime, either identical or unrelated to the following selected probe. The dependent variable was the latency to name the selected probe drawing.

Each subject received half ignored repetition and half control trials. The stimuli were counterbalanced such that one-half occurred in ignored repetition trials for subjects 1 to 10 and in control trials for subjects 11 to 20, and vice versa.

Procedure

Subjects were informed that the experiment was concerned with recognition memory for line drawings. They were shown an example of the stimuli they would see throughout the experiment. Subjects were told to select the red drawing and ignore the green drawing. It was emphasized that the green drawing was irrelevant and only there to make the task harder, so the more it was ignored, the better they would perform.

There were four parts to the experimental procedure: Part 1 established the appropriate masking SOA for each subject. These durations were approximate minimum viewing times required to identify the selected drawing explicitly in the absence of any other interfering or intervening task. Evidence for explicit identification was the subjects' ability to name the drawing. Brief exposure durations and pattern masking were employed to reduce the possibility of switching attention to the ignored object after selection of the attended object.

When subjects pressed the microswitch, a fixation cross appeared for 900 msec, followed by the selected and ignored drawings superimposed; both were presented monoptically to the left eye. This was followed by a pattern mask to the right eye for 100 msec. All presentation fields in the tachistoscope were adjusted to be of equal luminance.

Stimulus–mask SOA began at 10 msec and was increased using the method of ascending limits, by 5 msec steps. The same stimulus drawing was repeatedly presented, until subjects correctly identified it. Five msec was then added to the longest SOA required for the five stimuli presented. This was then used as the presentation SOA for the prime for that subject. A further 5 msec was added for presentation SOA for the probe. Mean SOA for the prime was 35 msec (range 20–45 msec) and 40 msec for the probe.

Part 2 consisted of the experimental trials. When subjects pressed the microswitch they saw a series of events as follows:

1. a fixation cross presented to their left eye for 900 msec;
2. a red line drawing superimposed on a green drawing to their left eye;
3. a pattern mask presented for 100 msec to their right eye;
4. a fixation cross presented to their right eye for 900 msec;
5. a second red drawing superimposed on a green fragmented picture, presented to their right eye;
6. Finally, a pattern mask presented for 100 msec to their left eye.

Subjects were not informed about the pattern masks. No subject complained about, or questioned them in pilot studies, and some subjects appeared not to notice them. Subjects were, however, informed that the stimuli alternated between eyes. This presentation of the prime to the left eye and the probe to the right ensured that the priming effects were not due to peripheral (retinal) factors.

Subjects were then given instructions concerning the stimulus sequence. They were told that they should correctly identify the first red (prime) drawing, as they would have to recall it shortly afterwards and recognize it in a later recognition test. However, it was stressed that they should not name the drawing when it was presented. When the second (probe) stimulus appeared, subjects were requested to name the red drawing as fast as possible. They were then asked to recall the selected prime. The recall and recognition of the selected prime were used to ensure that subjects attended to the red drawing.

The intertrial interval was approximately 15 to 20 sec, during which subjects noted down their own reaction times, thus receiving feedback on naming latency performance; these were verified by the experimenter.

Part 3 comprised a test for subjects' awareness of the ignored distractor drawing and was adapted from the procedures used by Rock and Gutman (1981). On the last trial only, there was no probe drawing to be named. It was replaced by a white card. As this blank white card was presented, subjects were asked the surprise question of what the previous green drawing had been. Thus they were asked to recall any information that may have been available for conscious scrutiny at about the time when the probe would have been presented.

Part 4 was a recognition test, also adapted from the procedures used by Rock and Gutman (1981). A sheet containing attended, ignored and new drawings was presented to subjects; they were instructed to call out the numbers of any drawings they recognized from the experiment, independent of whether it had been red or green, or whether it had been named.

Results

1. *Direct Reports of Distractor Drawings*

In the single catch trial at the end of the experiment, subjects were asked to report the identity of the distractor drawing. (The same stimulus was used for all subjects.) Four subjects were able to report the distractor. These subjects were replaced (preserving the counterbalancing of materials) until there were 10 in each item assignment group. It was suspected that the replaced subjects may have been poor selectors (as reported by Goldstein and Fink, 1981). The fact that these four subjects failed to report the selected prime correctly on 36% and 29% of trials in the control and ignored repetition conditions, as opposed to 14% and 13.6% for the remaining 20 subjects, was further evidence for this interpretation. These four subjects reported the ignored prime on 6.8% and 2.3% of trials in the control and ignored repetition conditions, while the remaining 20 subjects reported 2.3% and 3% in the control and ignored repetition conditions.

In the recognition test at the end of the experiment, subjects gave confident recognition judgements for 73% of the attended target drawings. For ignored drawings, 12% received confident recognition judgements. Finally, for new control drawings, subjects confidently recognized 8%. Statistical analysis of the confident recognition raw data in a one-way within-subjects ANOVA was significant [$F(2,38) = 105.65$, $p < 0.001$]. Further analysis using the Newman–Keuls test showed a significant difference between positive recognition of selected stimuli versus both ignored and new stimuli, but there was no significant difference between the false positive rate to the new drawings and recognition of the ignored objects.

2. *Indirect Measures: Reaction Time to Name Probe Drawings*

When subjects failed to name correctly the selected probe, 5.5% and 5.8% of RTs were lost in the control and ignored repetition conditions, respectively. Also, trials in which subjects failed to recall the selected prime (termed "misses" from now on) were dropped from RT analysis.

The average RT to name the selected probe drawing in the ignored repetition condition was 797 msec. For the control it was 749 msec. These data were analysed in a one-way within-subjects ANOVA. This contrast was significant [$F(1,19) = 17.39$, $p < 0.01$]. Analysis within materials did not reach significance [$F(1,23) = 2.31$].

A further post hoc analysis was carried out to compare probe naming RT as a function of whether subjects could recall the selected prime after naming the selected probe. Successful report of the selected prime may reflect successful selection, while failure to report anything from the priming display may reflect a failure of target selection. Fourteen subjects failed to report at least one attended prime drawing in both the prime and control conditions. When the subject reported the selected prime, there was *inhibitory* priming by the ignored prime of 51 msec; when the subjects failed to report the prime target, there was *facilitative* priming by the ignored prime of 52 msec. This contrast between inhibitory and facilitatory priming was significant [$F(1,13) = 5.17$, $p < 0.05$].

Discussion

As in previous work by Rock and Gutman (1981) and Goldstein and Fink (1981), the majority of subjects could effectively select (for later report and recognition) between two superimposed stimuli using colour as the selection cue. For the ignored prime, however, there was little ability to recall the stimulus shortly after presentation (only 16% of subjects could do so), and recognition was no better than chance.

The RT data from this experiment indicate that the time taken to name a selected object is increased when that object is identical to one previously ignored. This effect is opposite to the usual priming effects produced by repetition primes (whether attended or subliminal), where facilitation of the probe processing is found. An appropriate term for this (opposite) priming effect is thus "negative priming" (Marcel, 1980, p. 453). In this experiment, "negative priming" only occurred when subjects reported the selected prime. When they failed to report the selected prime (misses), facilitative priming was produced. This suggests that "negative priming" only occurs when selection is successful.

EXPERIMENT 2

This experiment was designed in order to confirm and extend the effect of negative priming found in Experiment 1.

One difference from the first experiment concerned the ignored prime in the control condition. These were changed from meaningful drawings that were unrelated to the probe, to structural parts of the ignored repetition prime broken down into meaningless contours (see Figure 1). The rationale for this change was to explore the possible level or levels at which the inferred inhibition takes place. Thus, inhibition may occur at a low-level (structural) representation of the ignored object. If this is correct, then the similar structure between ignored repetition prime and control objects may reduce the effect.

Two further changes were introduced: first, the inter-stimulus interval (ISI) between prime and probe was reduced from 1,000 to 300 msec to examine whether the negative priming effect was influenced by the time between prime and probe displays. Second, monoptic rather than dichoptic masking was employed to examine whether presenting a pattern mask to the same eye as the prime display influenced the priming effects.

Method

This was as in Experiment 1, except for the following details. There were 22 subjects.

Stimuli were taken from the same source as those used in Experiment 1, but the ignored prime in the control condition was produced by arranging the structural information in the ignored object in such a way that the object was no longer recognizable. The contours of this stimulus crossed the contours of the selected prime in approximately the same place as those of the ignored repetition prime (see Figure 1). There were now 17 trials in each priming condition.

The timing of events on a trial was as follows: A fixation cross was presented for 600 msec (as against 900 msec in Experiment 1), the prime display (duration was adjusted for each subject) and a pattern mask (presented for 100 msec) were presented to the subject's left eye; followed by a fixation cross (presented for 200 msec), the probe display (duration adjusted for each subject) and a pattern mask (presented for 100 msec) presented to the subject's right eye.

Mean SOA was 74 msec for the prime (range 50 to 100 msec) and 79 msec for the probe. The recognition test was not used, as there were no meaningful ignored primes in the control condition.

Results

In the catch trial at the end of the experiment, two subjects were able to recall the ignored drawing, and were thus replaced (to yield 10 subjects in each item assignment group). As in Experiment 1, it was suspected that these two subjects were poor selectors, or that their SOAs were not correctly adjusted. Like the four rejected subjects in Experiment 1, they were poorer at reporting the selected prime (24% and 21% failures in control and ignored repetition conditions, as opposed to 9% and 11.2% for the 20 subjects unable to report the ignored drawing). They also reported 6% of ignored primes in the ignored repetition condition, as opposed to 1.5% for the other subjects.

RT Data

Subjects failed to name the selected probe correctly on 9.4% and 6.2% of trials in the control and ignored repetition conditions, respectively. All errors were dropped from the main RT data analysis. The overall average RT for naming the selected probe was 909 msec in the ignored repetition and 865 msec for the control condition. These data were analysed in a one-way within-subjects ANOVA. The difference was significant [$F(1,19)=7.31$, $p<0.05$]. Analysis within materials did not reach significance [$F(1,33)=2.58$].

As in Experiment 1, RT to name selected probes was given further post hoc analysis in terms of hits and misses in selected prime report. Nine subjects were available for this analysis, showing misses in both ignored repetition and control conditions. The hits showed an overall cost of -43.45 msec, the misses showed a benefit of $+101.22$ msec. This pattern of costs (inhibition) and benefits (facilitation) in the hit and miss trials parallels that found in Experiment 1, though this was non-significant [$F(1,8)=2.63$] due to the small number of subjects and RTs in each cell.

Discussion

This experiment has replicated the negative priming obtained in Experiment 1 with a different kind of ignored prime in the control condition, shorter ISI and monoptic masking. However, RTs in this experiment are approximately 100 msec longer than those in Experiment 1, perhaps because of the reduced ISI between prime and probe displays. The fact that the effect has been obtained when the ignored prime of the ignored repetition and control conditions contain the same features suggests inhibition is not at the level of local features.

Furthermore, as in Experiment 1, there is some indication that negative priming is produced only when subjects can successfully report the selected prime; and that failure to report the selected prime leads to facilitative priming.

Finally, in both experiments analysis within materials did not reach significance. This is probably due to the large variance in the materials caused by their complexity. Examples of such complexity are: (1) familiarity of the object, (2) saliency of characteristic features, (3) typicality, (4) physical complexity (cf. Snodgrass and Vanderwart, 1980); in addition, these may interact when two drawings are superimposed. Further work is necessary for an understanding of the above factors in terms of object recognition and priming effects. However, a method of reducing such variance is to use a smaller set of materials, as used by Sperber et al. (1979) and Carr et al. (1982), and this approach is adopted in the next experiment.

EXPERIMENT 3

Experiments 1 and 2 have tentatively demonstrated the phenomenon of negative priming by ignored primes on identical selected probes. The data, however, provide little information concerning the level of processing that the distractors may have achieved, or the levels of representation where the hypothesized mechanism of inhibition may take place. Thus, perceptual analysis and inhibition may have been confined to structural levels, as would be suggested by the precategorical selection view of attention. Alternatively, analysis and inhibition may be at some higher, more abstract level of representation. To resolve this issue, the priming effects of ignored primes that are categorically related to (but have few structural features in common with) subsequent selected probes were investigated.

A further aim of this experiment was to confirm the contrast between selected and ignored primes. As discussed, substantial amounts of research have confirmed that primes that subjects attend to facilitate responses to subsequent related probes. This may also occur with stimuli pattern masked to prevent identification (Marcel, 1983). The data in Experiments 1 and 2 have suggested a reversal of this facilitatory priming to one of negative priming when objects are ignored. In this experiment, therefore, the effects of both selected and ignored primes on subsequent selection were examined.

Method

Subjects

Eleven subjects from the long-term Oxford Subject Panel were paid £1.25 to take part in this experiment. All had normal or corrected-to-normal acuity and normal colour vision and were right-handed.

Apparatus and Materials

The apparatus was the same as described in the previous experiments.

Ten drawings were used in this experiment. They were adjusted to be approximately equal in size with the aid of a reducing photocopier. Visual angles ranged between 4.7° and 6.4°. They were drawn with Bic Biros. The related pairs were: Cat–Dog, Chair–Table, Hammer–Spanner, Trumpet–Guitar, Hand––Foot.

As in previous work, the selected prime (red) was superimposed over the ignored prime (green), and similarly for the selected and ignored probes. This was to make selection of the target harder, as discussed. The superimposed drawings of a given display were always in different semantic categories.

Design

A within-subjects design was used such that each subject contributed naming RTs to each of five experimental conditions. The only relationships between prime and probe displays were as follows (see Figure 2 for examples). Except as mentioned, other components of the displays were unrelated.

1. *Attended Repetition:* The selected prime object was identical to the selected probe.

2. *Attended Semantic:* The selected prime was semantically related to the selected probe (Cat–Dog).

3. *Neutral Control:* The selected and ignored primes were both unrelated to the subsequent selected probe.

4. *Ignored Semantic:* The ignored prime was semantically related to the selected probe.

5. *Ignored Repetition:* The ignored prime was identical to the subsequent selected probe.

There were 20 trials in each condition. Stimulus presentation was randomized for each subject. Filler trials were implemented after subjects made an error in an effort to reduce the variability produced by longer RTs after errors (Rabbitt, 1966).

Procedure

Subjects were initially shown a series of 5 cards, each containing 2 drawings. The drawings were in their associate pairs on each card (e.g. Cat–Dog). Although it was not explicitly stated that the drawings were related, it was hoped that such paired presentations might increase the associative strength between the stimuli within the experimental context. The rationale for this procedure comes from McKoon and Ratcliffe (1979), who obtained contextual facilitation using newly learned experimenter-defined associates.

The SOA setting procedure was basically as described in Experiment 2.

584   S. P. Tipper

PRIMES

| ATTENDED REPETITION | ATTENDED SEMANTIC | CONTROL | IGNORED SEMANTIC | IGNORED REPETITION |

PROBE

Mean Naming Latencies

| 615 msec | 677 msec | 695 msec | 726 msec | 746 msec |

Errors
Failures to recall the selected prime

| 1% | 4% | 1.5% | 2.5% | 1.5% |

Report of the ignored prime

| 0% | 0% | 0.5% | 1.5% | 0% |

Failures to name the probe

| 1.5% | 1.5% | 1.5% | 0.5% | 1.5% |

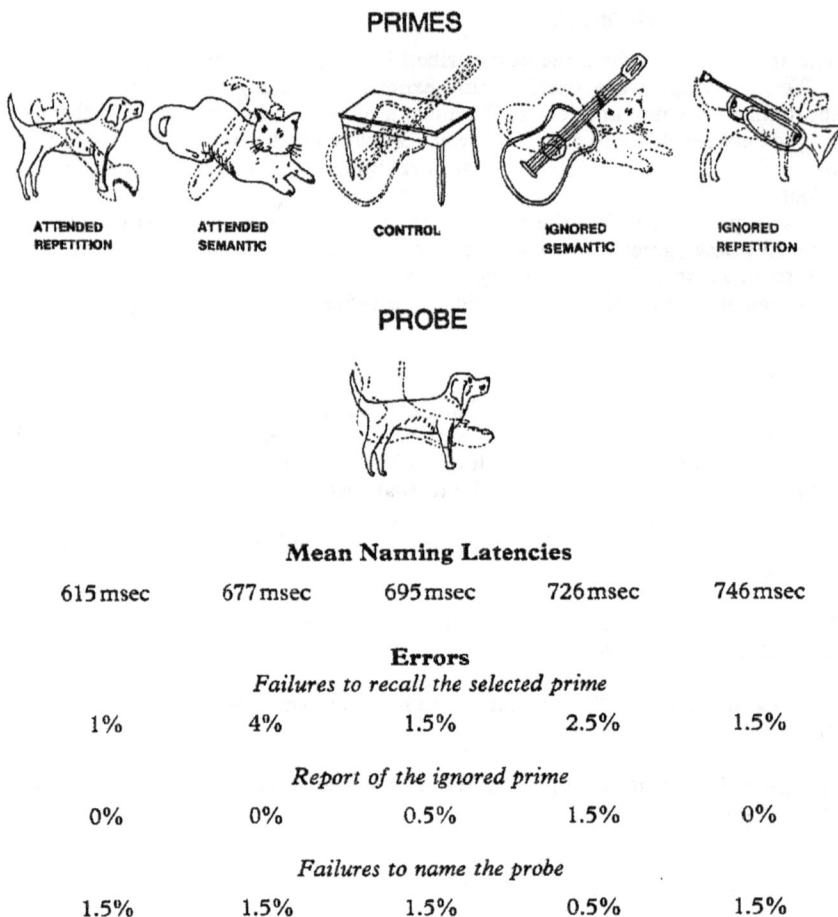

Figure 2.   Examples of the Prime and Probe displays, and the corresponding mean probe naming latencies and errors, for the five conditions in Experiment 3. The lines depicted as solid were Red (selected); the lines depicted as broken were Green (ignored).

Subjects had to report the red drawing as soon as possible; 5 msec were added to the longest presentation time, and this became the presentation SOA of the prime; a further 5 msec were added for probe SOA. Means were 112 (range 70 to 140 msec) and 117 msec, respectively.

As previously described, after pressing the microswitch subjects saw the following sequence: (1) a fixation cross (600 msec), (2) the prime display, from which subjects should identify but not name aloud the red drawing, (3) a pattern mask (100 msec). These displays were all presented to the left eye. (4) A second fixation cross was then presented for 1,100 msec, (5) a second red drawing, which they were to name as fast as possible into the voice key, and, finally, (6) a second pattern mask was presented (100 msec). These three displays were presented to the right eye. Subjects were then requested to report what the first red drawing had been. The ISI between prime and probe was 1,200 msec (100 msec pattern mask, 1,100 msec fixation cross).

Subjects were informed that the first eight trials were practice. A further six trials in the experiment were also practice, although subjects were not informed of this. Probe naming reaction times were collected from 100 trials (20 in each of the 5 conditions, thus each probe object was named twice in each condition). Subjects were informed that trials only counted when they were able to recall the selected prime.

At the end of the RT data collection a catch trial was included. No probe drawing was presented, and subjects were asked the question of what the previous ignored (green) drawing had been.

Results

Only one subject was able to recall the ignored drawing in the catch trial at the end of the experiment. As in Experiments 1 and 2, this subject was replaced, to yield 10 subjects included in the data analysis. (This catch trial cannot be considered exactly equivalent to those used in Experiments 1 and 2. In Experiments 1 and 2 a different stimulus array was presented on every trial. Thus correct report of the ignored object could not be explained by a probabilistic guessing strategy. in this experiment, on the other hand, a small stimulus set of 10 drawings was used. After identifying the selected object, the ignored must be one of the nine possible drawings remaining. Therefore the expected frequency of correct guessing of the ignored object is 11% of trials.)

Each of the subjects contributed to a mean RT for each of the five conditions. The mean RTs and errors are shown in Figure 2.

The RT data were analysed in a one-way within-subject ANOVA, which was significant [$F(4,36) = 21.18$, $p < 0.001$]. Analysis within materials (the 10 possible probe objects) was also highly significant [$F(4,36) = 14.41$, $p < 0.01$]. Further post hoc analysis of the RT data was carried out using the Newman–Keuls test. The main contrasts of interest showed that attended repetition was significantly faster than control and attended semantic (which were not significantly different). Ignored repetition and ignored semantic were significantly slower than control, and there was no significant difference between them.

Discussion

The central concern of this experiment was to test for negative priming effects with semantically related stimuli. This effect was obtained: naming of the probe was 31 msec longer when the selected probe was semantically related to the ignored prime (compared to the control condition). This implies that ignored objects may receive analysis to a categorical level and provides support for a postcategorical inhibition model.

A further possibility is that this effect reflects a process of "spreading inhibition" in semantic memory networks, analogous to that of spreading activation (Meyer and Schvaneveldt, 1975, Collins and Loftus, 1975). When an internal representation is activated this can lead to a spread of activation to related concepts in semantic memory space (Osgood, Suci and Tannenbaum, 1955) or hierarchical networks (Collins and Loftus, 1975). However, if a stimulus has been ignored during selection of a simultaneous target, the internal representation (of the ignored object) is associated with inhibition, which may spread to related concepts. Other theorists have proposed the possibility of spreading inhibition between related concepts in semantic memory, for example Roediger and Neely (1982).

This experiment has also confirmed the contrast between selected and ignored primes previously hypothesized. When primes received attentional processing, they facilitated processing of identical probes; when the same primes were ignored, processing of subsequent probes was delayed (negative priming). A similar contrast is seen when stimuli are semantically related, though the facilitative effect of the attended semantic prime did not reach significance, perhaps because of possible subject strategies (cf. Neely, 1977).

Finally, the replication of negative priming in this experiment is highly significant in both subjects and materials analyses, suggesting that the failure to produce significant materials effects in Experiments 1 and 2 was indeed due to the large variability among complex drawings.

GENERAL DISCUSSION

In summary, these experiments have raised the following points. Subjects appear to be able to select between briefly presented, spatially superimposed objects, using colour as a selection cue. Prior to selection, both objects were potentially available. The subjects generally could not recognize the ignored objects in subsequent recognition tests, though they could recognize selected objects. They also appeared to be generally unable to report the ignored object in a surprise catch trial, as in previous work that has examined report of unattended material (Rock and Gutman, 1981; Martin, 1978; FitzGerald[5]).

It has been pointed out (A. Treisman, personal communication) that

---

[5]P. FitzGerald (1984). "Memory for attended and unattended stimuli". University of Oxford, D.Phil.

it is difficult to decide whether subjects were never aware of the identity of the ignored prime; or were briefly aware, but that target selection included the suppression of the ignored objects from conscious awareness. The phenomenological experiences of subjects subsequent to prime presentation would be the same in both cases. It is difficult to test between these alternatives. Obviously, the surprise element in the catch trial may disrupt any available representations of the "ignored" object. Alternatively, constantly requiring subjects to attempt to report the ignored objects would probably have changed their selection strategies.

The priming effects of these ignored drawings have revealed that reaction time to name a probe are increased if it has the same identity or is categorically related to a previously ignored object. The following theoretical points can be suggested from this negative priming effect. Following the interpretation offered by Tipper,[6] the initial analysis of these kinds of displays takes place in parallel prior to selection. If the objects are well learned and meaningful to the subject, they appear to achieve categorical internal representations that are beyond the level of specific physical features.

During target selection, the initial representations produced of ignored and selected objects are both further processed, but in different ways. Representations of selected objects appear to receive further processing to enable naming of the object, recall some seconds later, and recognition some minutes later. The resulting internal representations facilitate selection of subsequent probes requiring identical or similar representations. Representations of the ignored object also appear to receive further processing, as opposed to passive decay. In this case, the internal representations produced are such that selection of subsequent objects requiring those representations is delayed. It may be suggested that this delay reflects inhibition associated with the internal representations of ignored objects during selection.

The hypothesized relationship between selective attention and inhibition was highlighted in Experiments 1 and 2, where negative priming by ignored objects appeared to depend on successful selection of the target. Similarly, Tipper[7] demonstrated that when the prime display SOA was long enough for successful selection, negative priming was produced by ignored objects. However, when the same prime displays were pattern masked such that subjects were above chance in reporting whether objects had been presented but were unable to identify either selected or ignored drawings, facilitative priming was produced both for selected and for ignored drawings.

[6,7]S. P. Tipper (1984). "Negative priming and visual selective attention". University of Oxford, D. Phil.

However, an alternative interpretation for negative priming has been suggested by Allport, Tipper and Chmiel (in press) (see also Lowe, in press). In this model no mechanisms of inhibition are required to account for negative priming. Rather, the cost is due to an object being encoded as both green and ignored in the prime display, and subsequently as red and selected in the probe display. This dual representation of the same object requires further processing to resolve the ambiguity, reflected in the longer RTs. However, further work (Tipper and Cranston, this issue) has produced results that can only be accounted for by the inhibition model.

A final point that should be made is that negative priming effects are not confined to the selection of superimposed objects. Tipper[8] used the same stimulus set as that of Experiment 3. In this case, however, the selected object was always green and presented to fixation; the (red) ignored object was presented in a different location, i.e. its nearest edge was 2.4° to the right or left of fixation. Negative priming was again demonstrated. Similarly, further recent work by the author has demonstrated negative priming with letter displays where the ignored objects were presented 0.76° to the right and left of the fixated target.

GENERAL CONCLUSION

In conclusion, the priming paradigm employed in these experiments has demonstrated the phenomenon of negative priming. Negative priming may be a reflection of inhibition as one of the mechanisms of selective attention. Thus, the objects that impinge on an organism's senses, if meaningful and well learned, may achieve at least categorical levels of internal representation in the initial parallel analysis of a scene. Subsequently the unwanted competing representations of the distractor objects may be de-coupled from the overt response mechanisms by a process of inhibition. Further work is required to specify at what level(s) inhibition takes place—whether at perceptual or response stages.

REFERENCES

Allport, D. A. (1977). On knowing the meaning of words we are unable to report: The effects of visual masking. In Dornic, S. (Ed.), *Attention and performance* VI. Hillsdale, N.J.: Lawrence Erlbaum Associates.

Allport, D. A., Tipper, S. P. and Chmiel, N. C. (In press). Perceptual integration and post-categorical filtering. In M. Posner and O.S. Marin

---

[8]S. P. Tipper (1984). "Negative priming and visual selective attention". University of Oxford, D.Phil.

(Eds.), *Attention and performance* XI. Hillsdale, N.J.: Lawrence Erlbaum Associates.

Bahrick, L. E., Walker, A. S. and Neisser, U. (1981). Selective looking by infants. *Cognitive Psychology*, **13**, 377–390.

Becker, L. A. and Killion, T. H. (1977). Interaction of visual and cognitive effects in word recognition. *Journal of Experimental Psychology: Human Perception and Performance*, **3**, 389–401.

Broadbent, D. E. (1970). Stimulus set and response set. In D. I. Mortofsky (Ed.), *Attention: Contemporary theories and analysis*. N.Y.: Appleton-Century-Crofts.

Broadbent, D. E. (1971). *Decision and stress*. London: Academic Press.

Carr, T. N., McCauley, C., Sperber, R. D. and Parmelee, C. M. (1982). Words, pictures and priming: On semantic activation, conscious identification, and automaticity. *Journal of Experimental Psychology: Human Perception and Performance*, **8**, 757–777.

Collins, A. M. and Loftus, E. (1975). A spreading activation theory of semantic processing. *Psychological Review*, **82**, 407–428.

Dalrymple-Alford, E. C. and Budayr, B. (1966). Examination of some aspects of the Stroop colour-word test. *Perceptual and Motor Skills*, **23**, 1211–1214.

Deutsch, J. A. and Deutsch, D. (1963). Attention: Some theoretical considerations. *Psychological Review*, **70**, 80–90.

Goldstein, E. B. and Fink, S. I. (1981). Selective attention in vision: Recognition memory for superimposed line drawings. *Journal of Experimental Psychology: Human Perception and Performance*, **7**, 954–967.

Greenwald, A. G. (1972). Evidence for both perceptual filtering and response suppression for rejected messages in selective attention. *Journal of Experimental Psychology*, **94**, 58–67.

Harvey, N. (1980). Non-informative effects of stimuli functioning as cues. *The Quarterly Journal of Experimental Psychology*, **32**, 413–425.

Humphreys, G. W. (1981). Flexibility of attention between stimulus dimensions. *Perception and Psychophysics*, **30**, 281–302.

Irwin, J. (1979). A method for testing selective attention in vision. *Perception and Motor Skills*, **48**, 899–902.

Irwin, J. (1981). Processing interaction in semantic analysis of attended and unattended visual inputs: A directional effect. *Journal of General Psychology*, **CIV–CV**, 870–893.

Kahneman, D. and Treisman, A. M. (1984). Changing views of attention and automaticity. In R. Parasuraman, R. Davies and J. Beatty (Eds.), *Varieties of attention*. New York: Academic Press.

Keele, S. W. and Neill, W. T. (1978). Mechanisms of attention. In E. C. Carterette and P. Friedman (Eds.), *Handbook of perception*, Vol. 8. New York: Academic Press.

Lowe, D. G. (In press). Further investigations of inhibitory mechanisms in attention. *Memory and Cognition*.

Marcel, A. J. (1980). Conscious and pre-conscious recognition of polysemous wards. In R. Nickerson (Ed.), *Attention and performance* VIII. Hillsdale, N.J.: Lawrence Erlbaum Associates.

Marcel, A. J. (1983). Conscious and unconscious perception: Experiments on visual masking and word recognition. *Cognitive Psychology*, **15**, 187–237.

Martin, M. (1978). Retention of attended and unattended auditorily and visually presented materials. *Quarterly Journal of Experimental Psychology*, **30**, 187–200.

McKoon, G. and Ratcliffe, R. (1979). Priming in episodic and semantic memory. *Journal of Verbal Learning and Verbal Behaviour*, **18**, 463–471.

Meyer, D. E. and Schvaneveldt, R. W. (1975). Meaning, memory structure and mental processes. In L. Cofer, *The structure of human memory*. San Francisco: W. H. Freeman and Co.

Neely, J. H. (1977). Semantic priming and retrieval from lexical memory. *Journal of Experimental Psychology: General*, **106**, 226–254.

Neill, W. T. (1977). Inhibition and facilitation processes in selective attention. *Journal of Experimental Psychology: Human Perception and Performance*, **3**, 444–450.

Neisser, U. and Becklen, P. (1975). Selective looking: Attending to visually specified events. *Cognitive Psychology*, **7**, 480–494.

Osgood, C. E., Suck, G. J. and Tannenbaum, P. H. (1957). *The measurement of meaning*. Urbana, Ill.: University of Illinois Press.

Rabbitt, P. M. A. (1966). Errors and error correction in choice RT tasks. *Journal of Experimental Psychology*, **71**, 264–272.

Rock, I. and Gutman, D. (1981). Effect of inattention on form perception. *Journal of Experimental Psychology: Human Perception and Performance*, **7**, 275–285.

Roediger, H. L. and Neely, J. H. (1982). Retrieval blocks in episodic and semantic memory. *Canadian Journal of Psychology*, **36**, 213–242.

Snodgrass, J. G. and Vanderwart, M. (1980). A standardized set of 260 pictures: Norms for name agreement, image agreement, familiarity, and visual complexity. *Journal of Experimental Psychology: Human Learning and Memory*, **6**, 174–215.

Sperber, R. D., McCauley, C., Ragain, R. D. and Weil, C. M. (1979). Semantic priming effects on picture and word processing. *Memory and Cognition*, **7**, 339–345.

Stroop, J. R. (1935). Studies of interference in serial verbal reactions. *Journal of Experimental Psychology*, **18**, 643–662.

Van der Heijden, A. H. C. (1981). *Short term visual information forgetting*. London: Routledge and Kegan Paul.

Warren, R. E. and Morton, J. (1982). The effect of priming on picture recognition. *British Journal of Psychology*, **73**, 117–129.

Manuscript received 23 October 1984

Name Index

Abrams, R.A. 330
Adelson, E.H. 318
Ahissar, M. 74
Akita, M. 441
Alahzen xi
Albert, M.K. 343, 344
Albert, M.L. 40
Albrecht, D.G. 457
Albright, T.D. 261, 446
al-Haytham, Ibn 346
Allport, D.A. 470, 486
Alpern, M. 85, 87, 106
Anderson, J.R. 169, 174
Angell, J.R. 314
Anstis, S.M. 86
Aoki, P. 331
Argyle, L. 347
Arias, C. 319
Arnell, K.A. 333
Aronchick, D. 314
Arthur, B. 107
Asada, H. 214
Aschersleben, G. 314
Ashcraft, M.H. 162
Ashmead, D.H. 319
Assal, G. 327
Attneave, F. xiv, 215, 342, 347
Audley, R.J. 368
Averbach, E. 85, 88, 89, 109, 111

Bachoud-Lévi, A.-C. 343
Badler, N. 190
Bahrick, L.E. 472
Baillargeon, Renée xiii, 145–50
Bajcsy, R. 190
Baker, F.H. 95
Balantyne, P. 314
Ball, K. 44
Ballard, D. 190, 214
Balzsano, G.J. 155
Banks, B.S. 333
Banks, W. 260, 277
Barlow, H.B. 88

Barrow, H.G. 214
Bartlett, F.C. 219, 223
Bartram, D. 220, 237, 238
Basri, R. 359
Bassok, M. 169
Bateman, A. 262
Battaglia, F. 86
Battersby, W.S. 104
Baumgart, B. 190
Baylis, G.C. 247, 307, 343, 344, 346, 347, 350, 357
Beck, J. 217, 437, 438, 446, 447, 448, 449, 450, 451, 457, 463
Becker, B.B. 86
Becker, L.A. 473
Becklen, P. 472
Bedworth, N. 95, 101, 102
Behrmann, M. 250
Beiring, E. 233
Bellmann, A. 327
Bender, D.B. 88
Benevento, L.A. 89, 90, 98, 102
Beranek, L.L. 312
Bergen, J.R. 318
Berlin, B. 154, 155, 162, 163, 172, 173
Berlucchi, G. 110
Bertamini, Marco xiv–xv, 341–62
Bertelson, P. 314
Besl, P.J. 215, 229
Biederman, I. xiii–xiv, 39, 85, 109, 110, 211–43, 249, 346
Binford, T. 190, 196, 213, 214, 215, 216
Birdsall, R.G. 44
Blaha, J. 46
Blake, R. 91, 102
Blakemore, C. 91, 97
Blanch, N. 319
Blauert, J. 311
Blickle, T. 216, 221, 229, 233, 234
Bodis-Wollner, I. 91
Bower, G.H. 169
Boyes-Braem, P. 153, 212
Boynton, R. 89, 104

Bozzi, P. 349, 351, 353, 357
Bradshaw, J.L. 247, 248, 260
Brady, J.M. 190, 214, 221
Brainard, R.W. 391
Breedlove, D.E. 154
Bregman, A.S. 312, 317, 329
Brehaut 305
Breinlinger, K. 145
Breitmeyer, B.G. xiii, 59, 83–118
Bridgeman, B. 87
Broadbent, D.E. 470
Brooks, B. 98, 106
Brooks, R.A. 190, 213
Brown, C.H. 154, 163, 169, 190, 214
Brown, J.S. 303
Brown, R. 155
Bruce, C. 261
Bruce, V. 248, 261
Bruno, N. 359
Budayr, B. 471
Bullock, M. 174
Bülthoff, H. xiv
Burchard, S. 85
Burchfiel, J.L. 108
Burkell, J. 266
Bush, R.R. 366

Caelli, T. 437, 438
Caesar, Julius 174
Cale, E.M. 346, 359
Campbell, F.W. 91
Carey, S. 248, 249, 260
Carpenter, G.A. 438, 446, 456
Carpenter, P. 91
Carr, T.N. 471
Casati 341, 343, 344, 345, 347
Cavanagh, P. 77
Cave, K.R. xiii
Cavedon, A. 349
Cervetto, L. 95
Chakravarty, I. 216
Checkosky, S.F. 216, 219
Chitty, A.J. 261
Chmiel, N.C. 486
Chouvet, G. 108
Christie, L.S. 368
Chun, M.M. 333
Cisek, P. 326
Clapper, J. 217, 225
Clark, E. 172, 173

Clarke, S. 327
Clayton, R. 39
Cleland, B.G. 59, 90, 93
Clifton, R.K. 314
Clowes, M. 190
Clymer, A. 109
Cohen, M.A. 438, 446, 447
Cohen, Y. 61, 64
Cohn-Vossen 207
Collins, A.M. 173, 484
Collins, J.F. 107
Collins, W.E. 303
Coltheart, M. 87, 88, 89, 107, 111, 280
Connell, J.H. 214
Coriell, A.S. 85, 88, 89, 109, 111
Corneil, B. 314
Cornsweet, T. 91, 97
Corteen, R.S. 6
Cottrell, G.W. 261
Cowey, A. 261
Craft, W.D. 358
Crawford, B.H. 104
Crisafi, M.A. 172
Critchley, M. 39
Croucher, Camilla J. xiv–xv, 341–62
Cruse, D.A. 155, 171
Crutzfeldt, O.D. 89, 90, 95, 98, 101, 102, 457
Culling, J.F. 330
Curet, C.A. 319
Cutting, J.E. 6

Dalrymple-Alford, E.C. 471
Darwin, C.J. 330
Davidson, Brian J. xiii, 43–57
Davidson, M.L. 97
Davis, J.H. 368
de Gelder, B. 343
De Valois, K.K. 4
De Valois, R.L. 4, 457, 460
de Weert, C.M.M. 441
Dember, W.N. 87
Denis, M. 171
Desimone, R. 247, 261, 446
Deutsch, D. 470
Deutsch, J.A. 470
Dev, P. 438
DeVos, J. 146
DeYoe, E.A. 126
Diamond, R. 248, 249, 260
DiLollo, V. 74, 280

Do Carmo, M. 190
Dodson, D. 203
Domini, F. 359
Donaldson, J.E. 396
Donders, F.C. 365, 366, 368, 369, 382, 384, 389, 390, 400
Dorris, M. 314
Dougherty, J.W.D. 156
Dow, B.M. 93, 94, 97, 98, 106, 108, 111
Drain, Maxwell 247–63
Dreher 93, 95
Driver, J. 305, 307, 343, 344, 346, 347, 350, 357
Dubin, M.W. 90, 93
Duffy, F.H. 108
Duncan, J. 51, 76, 307
Dunn, J. 273
Dziurawiec, S. 247

Eason, R.G. 44
Efron, R. 6, 89
Egeth, H. 60, 217, 222
Ehrenfels, C. von 322
Ejima, Y. 441
Ellis, A.J. 328
Ellis, H.D. 247
Empedocles xi
Engle, F.L. 45, 54, 55
Enroth-Cugell, C. 107
Eriksen, C.W.W. 38, 46, 64, 66, 69, 86, 89, 104, 107, 110, 111, 307
Erman, L.D. 304
Estes, W.K. 20, 25

Falmagne, J.C. 391
Farah, Martha J. xiv, 247–63
Farrell, R.D. 304
Fehrer, E. 85, 106, 109, 110
Felder, R.C. 107
Fildes, B.N. 217
Fink, S.I. 473, 476, 477
Finlay, B.L. 457
Fiorentini, A. 89, 90, 91, 95, 96, 97, 102
Fischer, R.A. 400
Fisk, A.D. 60
Fitts, P.M. 395
Fitzhugh, R. 89
Fleming, M. 261
Florack, L.M.J. 345
Fodor, J. 190, 200
Forster, P.M. 7

Fox, R. 91, 102
Franzel, xiii
Friedenberg, J. 347
Fukuda, Y. 93, 94, 106, 113

Ganz, L. xiii, 59, 83–118
Gardner, G.T. 20, 25, 39, 46
Garner, W.R. 4, 162, 213, 216, 217, 218
Gelade, Garry xii, 3–42, 60, 221
Gelman. R. 174
Geman, D. 455
Geman, S. 455
Gentner, D. 174
Gerhardstein, P.C. 343
Gholson, B. 368
Gibbs, Brian J. xiv, 265–309
Gibson, B.S. 344, 346, 347, 350, 351, 359
Gibson, E.J. 19
Gibson, J.J. 318, 405
Ginsburg, A.P. 91, 248, 260
Glass, A.L. 39, 169, 249, 283, 439, 453, 457, 459, 463
Gleitman, H. 26
Gluck, A. 212, 238
Glucksberg, S. 273, 283, 301
Goldberg, M.E. 44
Goldring, J. 314
Goldstein, E.B. 473, 476, 477
Golomb, B.A. 261
Goodale, Melvyn A. xiii, xiv, 123–28, 334
Goodman, N. 200
Gough, P.B. 369
Gouras, P. 457, 460
Govier, E. 7
Graham 91
Gray, W. 153, 212
Green, D.M. 44, 367
Green, J. 6
Green, M. 270
Greenspoon, T.S. 86, 104
Greenwald, A.G. 471
Gregory, R.L. 200, 458, 459, 463
Grice, H.P. 162
Grindley, C.G. 46
Gross, C.D. 88, 261, 446
Grossberg, Stephen xv, 437–67
Growney, R.L. 85, 87, 106, 108
Guillemin, V. 183
Gummerman. K. 85
Gutman, D. 472, 473, 476, 477, 484

Guzman, A. 190, 213, 230

Haber, R.N. 85, 87, 88, 89, 109, 111, 112
Halper, F. 39
Hammond, P. 90
Hampton, J.A. 154, 162
Handel, S. 317, 329
Harmon, L.D. 91, 248, 260
Harre, Rom 405
Harter, R. 44
Harvey, N. 472
Hasher, L. 60
Haver, B. 260
He, Z.J. 358
Heard, P. 453, 458, 459, 463
Hebb, D.O. 91, 102
Hecaen, H. 40
Hecht, S. 43
Heggelund, P. 457, 460
Heldmeyer, K.H. 169
Helmholtz, H. 200
Hemenway, Kathleen xiii, 153–77, 213
Henderson 303
Henik, A. 39, 307
Hespos, S.J. 147
Hess, R. 98
Heywood, C.A. 261
Hick, W.E. 391
Hilbert, D. 207
Hildreth, E. 438
Hillyard, S.A. 44
Hilz, R. 92
Hinton, G.E. 306
Hochstein, S. 74, 460
Hockey, R. 277
Hoffman, D.D. 169, 171, 179–210, 213, 218,
    248, 249, 343, 346, 347
Hoffman, J.E. 38, 46, 86, 93, 94, 95, 106, 110
Hoffman, W.C. xiv, 438
Hohle, R.H. 366, 368
Holst, E. von 108
Homa, D. 260
Hood, D.C. 91
Horn, B.K.P. 438
Horowitz, Todd S. xiii, 73–79
Howell, E.R. 91
Howell, W.C. 396
Hubel, D.H. 88, 89, 90, 95, 98, 457, 460
Huffman, D. 190
Hughes, H. 314

Hukin, R.W. 330
Hume, G. 344, 360
Humphreys, G.W. 76, 221, 262
Hunn, E. 156

Ikeda, H. 93, 94, 96, 97, 106, 107, 108, 110
Ilan, C. 354
Inhelder, B. 173
Irwin, D. 302, 303
Irwin, J. 472, 473
Ittleson, W.H. 215
Iwama, K. 94

Jacobs, D.W. 359
Jacobson, K. 145
Jain, R.C. 215, 229
James, William 73
Jastrow, J. 365, 390
Jay, M.F. 314
Jeannerod, M. 108
Jenison, R. 314
Joekes, S. 319
Johansson, G. 318
Johnson, M.H. 247, 253, 262
Johnson-Laird, P.N. 162, 173
Johnston, D.L. 69, 70
Johnston, J.C. 70, 153, 212
Jolicoeur, P. 212, 236, 238, 333
Jonides, John xiii, 26, 59–72
Ju, G. 217, 225, 228, 233
Judson, H.F. 173
Juletz, B. 31, 32, 88, 91, 92, 102, 135, 437, 438
Jung, R. 98, 106

Kahneman, Daniel xiv, 39, 60, 71, 84, 87, 92,
    111, 265–309, 470
Kanade, T. 216, 261
Kanizsa, Gaetano xiii, 131–35, 222, 342
Kanwisher, N.G. 307, 359
Kay, P. 154
Keck, M.J. 107
Keele, S.W. 471
Keesey, U.T. 92, 96, 113
Kellman, Philip xiii, 137–43
Kendale, M.G. 367
Kenney, F.A. 86
Kewley-Port, D. 107
Kiger, J.I. 283
Killion, T.H. 473
King, M.E. 86, 216, 221

Kinsbourne, M. 84, 86, 104, 107
Kirsner, K. 273, 283, 301, 302
Klatsky, G.C. 221
Klein, K.L. 247
Knoll, R.K. 280
Koenderink, J. xiv, 188, 192, 206, 207, 344, 345, 346, 358
Koffka, K. 343, 360
Kolers, P.A. 84, 85, 95, 106, 107, 270, 281
Konishi, M. 101
Koriat, A. 273, 283, 301
Kosslyn, S.M. 169, 212, 239
Kourtzi, Z. 359
Krajicek 277
Krauskopf, J. 440
Kreuz, R.J. 273
Krüger, J. 457, 460
Krumhansl, C.L. 60
Kubovy, Michael xiv, 311–40
Kuffler, S.W. 89
Kuhnt, U. 89, 102
Kulikowski, J.J. 92, 96, 113
Külpe, O. 365

LaBerge, D. 8, 19, 44, 111
Lamarre, Y. 95
Lambert, A. 61, 277
Laming, D.R.J. 391
Lamy, D. 354
Land, E.H. 440
Langer, P. 283
Lappin, J.S. 44, 48, 358
Law, M.B. 330
Lawrence, D.H. 6
Lawrence, D.T. 261
Lawson, R.B. 85
Lazar, R. 8
Lee, J.R. 91
Leeuwenberg, E.L.J. 441
Lefton. L.A. 84, 86
Lennie, P. 59
Leonard, C.M. 247
Levi, I. 200
Levick, W.R. 59, 90, 93
Levine, D. 446
Levinson, E. 107
Levinson, K.L. 247
Lewis, D. 344
Lewis, J.L. 6
Lewis, S. 344

Libermann, A. 190
Lipschutz, M. 203
Lisberger 127
Liu, Z. 359
Lloyd, M. 237
Lockhead, G.R. 3
Loftus, E. 484
Logan, G.D. 60
Logothetis, Nikos K. xiii, 119–21
Love, R. 85
Lowe, D.G. 215, 222, 486
Luce, R.D. 367, 368
Luo, Y. 145, 146, 147

MacKay, D.G. 6, 108
Mackworth, A. 190
Macomber, J. 145
Maffei, L. 89, 90, 91, 95, 96, 97, 102
Makin, L. 313
Malt, B.C. 157, 159, 162, 165
Marcel, A.J. 477, 480
Marr, D. xiii, 190, 192, 196, 213, 222, 239, 249, 346, 438
Marslen-Wilson, W. 211
Martin, M. 484
Mathews, M.L. 248
Matin, E. 108, 109
Matin, L. 109
Matsunami, K. 101
Mayzner, M.S. 85, 89
McCauley, C. 471, 473
McClelland, J.C. 253, 262
McClelland, J.L. 283, 304, 306
McConkie, G.W. 302
McFadden. D. 85
McGill, W.J. 366, 368, 395
McKoon, G. 481
McMahon, L.E. 369
Medin, D.L. 171
Melchner, M.J. 45
Melkman, R. 169
Mermelstein, R. 260
Mertens, J.J. 46
Merton, P. 108
Mervis, C.B. 153, 154, 155, 163, 167, 172, 212
Metzler, J. 237
Meuli, R.A. 327
Meyer, D.E. , 68, 216, 471, 473, 484
Mezzgnotte, R.J. 221
Michaels, C.F. 86, 88, 98, 107

Miller, G.A. 91, 162, 173, 212, 217, 222, 283
Miller, J. 352
Milner, A. David xiii, xiv, 123–28, 334
Mingolla, Ennio xv, 437–67
Mishkin, M. 124
Mistlin, A.J. 261
Mitchell, R.F. 366
Mittelstadt, H. 108
Mohindra, N. 61
Mohler, C.W. 44
Mollon, J. 313
Monahan, J.S. 3
Mondor, T.A. 333, 334
Monge, G. 313
Moran, J. 446
Moray, N. 56
Morton, H. 108
Morton, J. 247, 471
Mosca, F. 359
Moscovitch, M. 250
Moulden, B.P. 86
Movshon 127
Mowrer, O.H. 46
Moyano, H.F. 319
Mozer, M.C. 307
Muckenhoupt, M. 333
Müller, H.J. 61
Munoz, D. 314
Murphy, G.L. 155
Murphy, T.D. 64

Nadal, L. 145
Nakayama, K. 298, 358
Naveh-Benjamin, M. 60
Neely, J.H. 484
Neely, R.B. 304
Negishi, K. 98
Neill, W.T. 471
Neisser, U. 3, 8, 26, 73, 87, 88, 215, 365, 472
Nelson, M. 314
Nelson, R. 349
Nicod 200
Nielsen, G.D. 248
Nishihara, H.K. xiii, 190, 213, 222, 239, 346
Nissen, M.J. 45
Norman, D.A. 54, 174
Norman, J. 92, 273, 301, 346, 347
Novick, R. 8

O'Rourke, J. 190

Oesterreich, R.E. 104
Ogden, W.C. 45
Ohno, T. 101
Oldfield, R.C. 227
Ollman, R.T. 395
Orjesson, E.B. 318
Osgood, C.E. 484
Osman, A.M. 68
Ostrovsky, Y. 77
Ozog, G. 87

Pachella, R. 217, 222
Pallela, T.D. 107
Palmer, J. 60
Palmer, L.A. 106
Palmer, S.E. 169, 215, 241, 249, 341, 342, 343,
    344, 345, 347, 349, 359, 360
Pantle, A.J. 92, 107
Parmelee, C.M. 471
Paterson, S. 145, 147
Peachey, C. 331
Peirce, C. 200
Penrose, L.S. 216
Penrose, R. 216
Pentland, A. 261
Perkins, D.N. 216
Perrett, D.I. 261
Peterson, M.A. 343
Phillips, J. 280, 346
Piaget, J. 173
Pierce, L. 64, 66
Pinker, Steven xiv
Pirenne, M.H. 43
Pittenger, J.B. 319
Plato xi
Poggio, G.B. 95, 192, 438
Pollack, A. 183
Pollatsek, A. 302, 303
Pollen, D.A. 91
Pomerantz, J.R. 219
Pöppel, E. 90
Posner, M.I. xiii, 37, 43–57, 60, 61, 64, 365
Poston, T. 203
Potter, M.C. 333
Pragnanz, J. 222
Prandtl, A. 452
Pratt, J. 330
Prazdny, K. 217, 437, 441
Preyer, W. 452
Prinzmetal, W. 260

Purcell, D.G. 85, 86, 87, 88, 106, 107
Pylyshyn, Z. 200, 305

Quigley, S. 331
Quillian, M.R. 173

Raab, D. 85, 106, 109, 110
Rabbitt, P.M.A. 8, 61
Rafal, R.D. 64
Ragain, R.D. 473
Rapcsak, S.Z. 343
Ratcliffe, R. 481
Ratliff, F. 438
Rauschecker, J.P. 326
Raven, P.H. 154
Rayner, K. 302, 303
Reddy, D.R. 304
Redies, C. 441, 451
Reed, S.K. 249
Reeves, N. 331
Regan, J.E. 60
Reicher, B.M. 248
Remington, R. 64, 66
Restle, F. 368
Rho, S. 273
Rhodes, G. 248, 260
Richards, W.A. xiv, 169, 179–210, 213, 218, 249, 346
Riddoch, M.J. 262
Rifkin, A.J. 172
Riggs, L. 108, 109
Rizzolatti, G. 110
Robson, J.G. 91, 107
Roch-Miranda, C.E. 88
Rock, I. 39, 200, 214, 344, 359, 360, 472, 473, 476, 477, 484
Rolls, E.T. 247
Ronner, S.F. 91
Rosch, E. 153, 154, 155, 156, 157, 159, 160, 162, 163, 166, 167, 171, 172, 212
Rosenfeld. A. 217, 437
Rosenquist, A.C. 106
Rosner, B.S. 85, 95, 106
Ross, H.E. 346
Rosser, R. 145
Rubin, Edgar 342, 343, 360
Ruddy, C.R. 473
Rumelhart, D.E. 283, 306
Rumiati, R.I. 262

Saito, H.-I. 93, 113
Samuels, J. 44
Sanders, M. 283
Sanderson, K.J. 59, 93
San-severino, E.R. 95
Schall, Jeffrey D. xiii, 119–21
Scharf, B. 86, 322, 331
Schatz, B.R. 448
Scheerer, E. 84, 87, 89, 98, 111
Scheffé, H. 373, 400
Schein, S.J. 446
Schick, A. 108
Schiller, P. 85, 86, 104, 109, 110, 457, 460
Schlaer, S. 43
Schlesinger, I.M. 390
Schneider, G.E. 110
Schneider, W. 8, 25, 26, 60
Schober, H.A.W. 92
Schultz, D.W. 69
Schvaneveldt, R.W. 471, 473, 484
Schwartz, T. 260
Seidenberg, M.S. 283
Sejnowski, T.J. 261
Sekuler, R. 44, 107, 298
Sengco, J.A. 250
Sergen, J. 260
Shaw, M.L. 46, 52, 56, 68
Shaw, P. 46, 52, 56
Shepard, R.N. xv, 4, 237, 269, 405–35
Sherman, S.M. 93
Shiffrin, R.M. 8, 25, 26, 46, 60
Shih, S. 330
Shimojo, S. 298, 358
Shipley, Thomas F. xiii, 137–43
Shipley, W.C. 86
Shuntich, R. 86, 87, 88, 89, 107
Siegfried, J.B. 104
Silverman, G.K. 298
Singer, W. 90, 95, 101, 102
Sinha, P. 77
Smith, E.E. 155, 159, 162, 165, 171, 252, 366
Smith, J.E.K. 68
Smith, M.C. 85, 86, 104, 109, 110
Smith, S.W. 46
Snodgrass, J.D. 366
Snyder, C.R.R. xiii, 43–57, 60
Sololov, E.N. 44
Soroka, B. 190
Sparks, D.L. 314
Sparrow, J.M.B. 88

Spelke, E.S. 145, 148
Spencer, E. 61
Spencer, T.J. 86, 87, 88, 89, 107, 109, 111
Sperber, R.D. 471, 473
Sperling, G. 45, 88, 104, 109, 111, 112, 438
Spillman, L. 441, 451, 452
Spitzer, H. 460
Sprague, J.M. 110
Squire, R. 6
St. James, J.D. 64, 66
Stacy, E.W. 39
Standen, P. 273
Standing, L. 112
Starr, Ringo 341
Steck, J.A. 327
Sternberg, Saul xv, 247, 280, 365–404
Stevens, A.L. 174
Stewart, A.L. 85, 86, 87, 88, 106, 107
Stigler, R. 84
Stoffregen, T.A. 319
Stone, J. 93, 94, 95, 106
Stone, M. 391
Storm, R.W. 305
Stromeyer, C.F. 102
Strong 306
Stroop, J.R. 471
Stuart, A. 367
Sturr, G.F. 104
Suci, G.J. 484
Sugihara, K. 230
Sugitani, M. 94
Sukale-Wolf, S.U. 85, 109
Summerfield, Q. 330
Sutherland, N.S. 190
Swets, J.A. 44
Switkes, E. 439, 453, 456, 457, 458, 459, 463
Sykes, M. 4
Szoc, R. 87

Takahashi, S. 441
Tanaka, James N. 247–63, 457, 460
Tangney, J. 216
Tannenbaum, P.H. 484
Tarr, Michael xiv
Taylor, D.H. 365, 366, 368
Taylor, J.H. 91
Teitelbaum, R.C. 221
Tenenbaum, J.M. 214, 215
ter Haar Romeny, B.M. 345
Ternus, J. 270

Terrio, N.A. 333, 334
Thompson, D'Arcy 184
Thorell, L.G. 457
Tinker, M.A. 109
Tipper, Steven P. xv, 469–88
Tobin, E.A. 97
Todd, J.T. 59
Todorovic, D. 440
Tokashiki, S. 101
Tolhurst, D.J. 92, 96, 113
Townsend, V. 46
Toyama, K. 101
Treisman, Anne M. xii, xiv, 3–42, 60, 71, 73, 75,
    221, 265–309, 470, 484
Tresselt, M.E. 89
Trevarthen, C.B. 110
Triggs, T.J. 217
Tsal, Y. 354
Turgeon, M. 326
Turk, M. 261
Turock, D.L. 280
Turvey, M.T. 86, 87, 88, 89, 98, 104, 107, 111,
    112
Tversky, Barbara xiii, 153–77, 213, 239

Ullman, S. 269, 270, 284, 304
Ulrich, R. 352
Ungerleider, L.G. 124
Ungerleider, L.G. 446
Uttal, W.R. 44, 48, 87, 89

Valentine, T. 247
Van der Heijden, A.H.C. 470
van Doorn, A. 188, 192, 206, 207
Van Essen, D.C. 126
Van Gelder, P. 59
van Tuijl, H.F.J.M. 441, 451
Van Valkenburg, David xiv, 311–40
Varzi 341, 343, 344, 345, 347
Verhoeff, F.H. 86
Virsuk, V. 217
Volman. S.F. 108, 109, 457
von der Heydt, R. 446, 460
Von Voorhis, S. 44

Walker, A.S. 472
Walker, J. 155
Wall, S. 60
Wallace, G. 247, 248, 260, 262
Waltz, D. 190

Wanatabe, S. 101
Wang, S. 145, 146, 147, 149
Warren, R.E. 269, 471
Warrington, E.K. 84, 86, 103, 107
Waters, G.S. 283
Watkins, A.J. 313
Weber, C. 86
Weil, C.M. 473
Weiskrantz, L. 88
Weisstein, N. 84, 85, 86, 87, 88, 89, 95, 98, 102, 106, 107, 109, 111
Welford, A.T. 373, 390
Wepman, B. 85
Werner, H. 85, 98
Wertheimer, M. 86
Wheeler, D.D. 248
White, C.T. 44
Whitehead, A. 306
Whitlock. D. 216, 219
Whitney, H. 206
Wiesel, T.N. 88, 89, 90, 95, 98, 457, 460
Wightman, F.L. 314
Wilcox, T. 145

Wilson, Kevin D. 247–63
Wingfield, A. 227
Winocur, G. 250
Winston, P.A. 214
Witkin, A.P. 215
Witkowski, J.J. 163
Wolfe, Jeremy M. xiii, 73–79, 453
Wolford, G. 20, 21, 25
Wood, B. 6
Wright, M.J. 93, 94, 96, 97, 106, 108, 110
Wurtz, R.H. 44
Wynn, V.T. 326

Yantis, Steven xiii, 59–72
Yarbus, A.L. 440
Yin, R. 200
Yuille, A. 190, 261
Yund, E.W. 6

Zacks, R.T. 60, 303
Zeki, S.M. 3, 88, 110, 446
Zola, D. 302
Zucker, S.W. 455

For Product Safety Concerns and Information please contact our EU
representative GPSR@taylorandfrancis.com
Taylor & Francis Verlag GmbH, Kaufingerstraße 24, 80331 München, Germany